Regionalism and Multilateralism after the Uruguay Round

Convergence, Divergence and Interaction

Series *European Policy*
No.12

EUROPEAN INTERUNIVERSITY PRESS - EIP
Brussels
1997

Paul DEMARET — Jean-François BELLIS

Gonzalo GARCÍA JIMÉNEZ

Regionalism and Multilateralism after the Uruguay Round

Convergence, Divergence and Interaction

Institut d'Études Juridiques Européennes (IEJE)

University of Liège

Institut d'Études Juridiques Européennes "Fernand Dehousse" - IEJE
3 boulevard du Rectorat - Bât. B33/bte 9
B - Liège (Belgium)
Tel.: +32 (0)2 366 31 56
Fax: +32 (0)2 366 31 55
Email: ieje@ulg.ac.be
IEJE homepage: <http://www.ulg.ac.be/ieje>

ISBN 90-5201-706-9
D/1997/5678/08

FOREWORD

The present volume reproduces the reports and comments, often revised and updated, which were presented at the Conference on "Regionalism and Multilateralism after the Uruguay Round: Convergence, Divergence and Interaction" held in Liège in October 1996. In addition, it contains several contributions written in the wake and as a result of the conference. This conference was organized by the *Institut d'Études Juridiques Européennes* (IEJE) Fernand Dehousse of the University of Liège in the framework of *"Pôle d'Attraction Interuniversitaire"* No.36 (European Integration Law) granted by the Belgian Prime Minister's office to the University of Liège and the University of Ghent (1990-1996), now joined by the University of Brussels (1997-2001). The Institut is pleased to acknowledge the generous financial support it received from the European Commission (DG I and General Secretariat), the Belgian National Foundation for Scientific Research and the Belgian French Community.

Special thanks are due to Mr. Xavier Denoël, Research Fellow at the *Institut d'Études Juridiques Européennes*, who, after the conference, acted as a most efficient and diligent *agent de liaison* between the publisher and the numerous contributors. He played an invaluable role in the production of this volume. The IEJE Fernand Dehousse wishes him good luck now that he is leaving the Institut to embark on a new career.

Paul DEMARET, Jean-François BELLIS
& Gonzalo GARCÍA JIMÉNEZ
September 1997

7

List of Abbreviations

AB	Appellate Body
ACP	African, Caribbean and Pacific Countries
AD	Anti-Dumping
AEM	ASEAN Economic Ministers
AER	**American Economic Review**
AFTA	ASEAN Free Trade Area
AIJV	ASEAN Industrial Joint Ventures
ALADI	See "LAIA"
ANZCERTA	Australia-New Zealand Closer Economic Relations Trade Agreement (also referred to as "CER")
APEC	Asian-Pacific Economic Cooperation
ASEAN	Association of South-East Asian Nations
ASEM	Asia-Europe Meeting
BISD	**GATT Basic Instruments and Selected Documents**
BIT	Bilateral Investment Treaties
C/E	Central/Eastern Countries
CACM	Central American Common Market
CAP	Common Agricultural Policy (of the EC)
Caricom	Caribbean Community
CCC	Customs Cooperation Council
CCT	Common Customs Tariff
CEECs	Central and Eastern European Countries
CEFTA	Central European Free Trade Agreement
CEN	*Comité Européen de Normalisation*
CEPAL	*Comisión Económica Para America Latina*
CEPT	Common Effective Preferential Tariff

9

CER	See "ANZCERTA"
CFSP	Common Foreign and Security Policy
CMEA	Council for Mutual Economic Aid
CMLR	**Common Market Law Report**
CMLRev	**Common Market Law Review**
CTE	Committee on Trade and Environment
CTH	Change in Tariff Heading
CU	Customs Union
CUSFTA	Canada-United States Free Trade Agreement
CVDs	Countervailing Duties
DS	Dispute Settlement
DSB	Dispute Settlement Body
DSU	Dispute Settlement Understanding
EC	European Community
ECJ	EC Court of Justice
ECLAC	Economic Commission for Latin America and the Carribean
ECLR	**European Competition Law Report**
ECR	**European Court of Justice Reports**
ECSC	European Coal and Steel Community
EEA	European Economic Area
EFTA	European Free Trade Association
ELR	**European Law Review**
EMU	Economic and Monetary Union
EPA	Environmental Protection Agency
ESA	EFTA Surveillance Authority
EU	European Union
FAO	Food and Agriculture Organization
FDI	Foreign Direct Investment
FTAA	Free Trade Area of the Americas
FTAs	Free Trade Agreements
GATS	General Agreement on Trade in Services
GATT	General Agreement on Tariffs and Trade
GDP	Gross Domestic Product

GPA	Government Procurement Agreement
GSP	General System of Preferences
IDA	International Dairy Arrangement
IEC	International Electrotechnical Commission
IGC	Intergovernmental Conference
IIC	**International Review of Industrial Property and Copyright Law**
ILM	**International Legal Materials**
ILO	International Labour Office
IMF	International Monetary Fund
IPRs	Intellectual Property Rights
ISO	International Standard Organization
JWT	**Journal of World Trade**
LA	Latin America
LAFTA	Latin American Free Trade Association
LAIA	Latin American Integration Association
MAI	Multilateral Agreement on Investment
MCs	Mediterranean Countries
MEAs	Multilateral Environmental Agreements
MEE	Measures having an Equivalent Effect
Mercosur	Southern Common Market *(Mercado Común del Sur)*
MFA	Multi-Fibre Arrangement
MFN	Most-Favored-Nation
MNMCs	Mediterranean Non-Member Countries
MRAs	Mutual Recognition Agreements
MTNs	Multilateral Trade Negotiations
MTS	Multilateral Trading System
NAAEC	North American Agreement on Environmental Cooperation
NAALC	North American Agreement on Labour Cooperation
NACEC	North American Commission on Environmental Cooperation
NAFTA	North American Free Trade Area/Agreement
NAO	National Administrative Office
NAPE	National Agency for the Protection of the Environment

NGO	Non-Governmental Organization
NT	National Treatment
NTBs	Non-Tariff Barriers
NTM	New Transatlantic Marketplace
ODA	ESA/EFTA Court (Norwegian abbreviation)
OECD	Organization for Economic Cooperation and Development
OJ	**Official Journal**
PHARE	Poland and Hungary Assistance with Restructuring the Economy
PTA	Preferential Tariff Concessions
QRs	Quantitative Restrictions
RAs	Regional Agreements
RBPs	Restrictive Business Practices
RIAs	Regional Integration Agreements
SAFTA	South American Free Trade Area
SEA	Single European Act
SPS	Sanitary and Phytosanitary
TABD	Transatlantic Business Dialogue
TAFTA	Transatlantic Free Trade Area
TBT	Technical Barrier to Trade
TNC	Trade Negotiations Committee
TREMs	Trade-Related Environmental Measures
TRIMs	Trade-Related Investment Measures
TRIPs	Trade-Related Aspects of Intellectual Property Rights
UNCITRAL	UN Commission on International Trade Law
UNCTAD	United Nations Commission on Trade and Development
UNEP	United Nations Environmental Program
UR	Uruguay Round
VCLT	Vienna Convention on the Law of Treaties
WHO	World Health Organization
WIPO	World Intellectual Property Organization
WP	Working Party
WTO	World Trade Organization

Table of Contents

III. REGIONALISM AND MULTILATERAL TRADE RULES:
AN INTERACTIVE RELATIONSHIP

BY WAY OF CONCLUSION

INTRODUCTION

by Paul DEMARET & Jean-François BELLIS

For many years, regional trade agreements were mainly seen as exceptions to be tolerated within the GATT framework. Economic regionalism was also first and foremost a Western European phenomenon. Admittedly, many other regional trade agreements were set up, notably in Latin America. However, on the world scale, they carried less weight than the EEC and its preferential agreements. They were also less successful. Things have now changed.

The completion of the Uruguay Round, which has made the multilateral trade system more relevant than before and should increase its effectiveness, coincided with the development of a worldwide trend towards increased regionalism. This trend is illustrated by the conclusion of NAFTA, the emergence of Mercosur and the signing of many new free trade agreements in Latin America, the new steps taken by the members of ASEAN to free trade between themselves, the deepening of the Australia-New Zealand Closer Economic Relations Trade Agreement, and the launching of APEC. Not only does regionalism expand free trade geographically, it also tends to extend its substantive coverage beyond trade in goods to include services, investment and intellectual property rights. This is true whether the regional agreement is in the form of a customs union or a free trade area, as exemplified by NAFTA. While this new trend has caused some observers to evoke the prospect of a world economy increasingly divided among rival "trade blocs", recent studies by the OECD and the WTO suggest that regional trade agreements may complement rather than threaten the multilateral trade system. The purpose of this book is to take a closer look at the complex relationship between regional trade agreements and multilateral trade rules in the wake of the Uruguay Round.

The first part of the book is devoted to a presentation of the major regional trade agreements in Europe, (with the exclusion of the EC Internal Market), the Americas and the Asia Pacific area. This first part also covers an emerging new form of regionalism, namely inter-regionalism, as witnessed by the agreement between Mercosur and the European Union, and concludes with a paper discussing the institutional shape which the trade relations between North America and the European Community might take in the future.

The survey of regional agreements does not include a presentation of the Australia-New Zealand Closer Economic Relations Trade Agreement. However, this regional agreement is the subject of specific developments in three papers found in the second part of the book[1].

The EC system of integration is not described in the first part. On the other hand, several contributions deal with the regional agreements which the European Union[2] has concluded, or is about to conclude, with its

---

[1] See *infra* P. SAUVÉ, *"Regional versus Multilateral Approaches to Services and Investment Liberalization: Anything to Worry About ?"* (where the main features of the ANZCERTA are presented); J.F. BELLIS, *"The Treatment of Dumping, Subsidies and Anticompetition Practices in Regional Trade Agreements"*; D. PALMETER, *"Rules of Origin in Regional Trade Agreements"*.

[2] "European Union" is a concept which was introduced by the Maastricht Treaty to supplement, but not to replace, the European (Economic) Community. Since then, when referring to the European integration system, one is confronted with the question as to which term should be used: European Union or European Community. As this question arises throughout the book, a few words of clarification may seem appropriate here, particularly for the non-European reader. It is a fact that today the words "European Union" tend to be used as if they were more or less synonymous with "European Community". However, strictly speaking, the concept of European Union is both broader and less precise than the concept of European Community. According to the Maastricht Treaty, the European Union consists of three pillars. The first pillar comprises the three original European Treaties: the Treaty establishing the European Community (formally called the European Economic Community), the Coal and Steel Treaty and the Euratom Treaty. The first pillar rests on what has come to be known as the Community method, with its reliance on supranational mechanisms. European economic integration is essentially based on the Treaty establishing the European Community (EC Treaty). The second and third pillars deal respectively with the foreign and security policy of the Union and with Justice and Home Affairs. They rely mainly on intergovernmental cooperation between the Member States of the Union.

Depending on the context in which the term European Union is used, it may thus cover the European Community (EC Treaty) or the Member States, when the latter are acting as members of the Union within the framework of the second or third pillar, or even the European Community and the Member States, when they act together, the former on the basis of the EC Treaty, the latter on the basis of the second or third pillar. From a strictly legal point of view, when dealing with matters relating to European economic integration which fall within the scope of the EC Treaty, the term "European Community" ought to be preferred. However, the choice of the term "European Union" may seem appropriate in all those cases where the European Community and the Member States appear together on the international stage.

European neighbours or with Southern Mediterranean countries[3]. The following reasons explain this choice. First, the main substantive and institutional features of the European Community are well known and should thus be familiar to the reader. Second, the level of legal and economic integration reached by the European Community sets it apart somewhat from other existing regional trade agreements. The Community may rely on supranational institutions (the European Commission, the European Court of Justice and the European Parliament) and supranational mechanisms (qualified majority voting for the adoption of legislation relating to the Internal Market or for the adoption of trade measures). It has succeeded in establishing an internal market and a common external trade policy, at least with respect to goods and cross-border services[4]. As a result, it tends to behave and is normally treated as a single entity in the

---

Precisely, when international agreements have to be concluded whose subject-matter falls in part outside the exclusive competence of the European Community, the Member States are either entitled or indeed obliged to appear alongside the Community in order for the agreements to be concluded. In practice — and in accordance with the present case law of the European Court of Justice — international agreements which extend beyond trade in goods or cross-border trade in services and cover, for instance, investment and the movement of persons are concluded by the European Community and the Member States. The Uruguay Round agreements were concluded according to this so-called mixed procedure. The same procedure was used for the conclusion of the agreement establishing the European Economic Area (with EFTA countries), for the conclusion of the Europe Agreements with Central and Eastern European countries and also for the conclusion of the cooperation agreement with Mercosur *(see infra)*. As a result, these regional agreements could enter into force in full only after having been ratified by the European Community and the fifteen Member States. However, provisions covering matters pertaining to the exclusive competence of the European Community could enter into force upon the ratification of the agreements by the Community alone, pending the ratification by the fifteen Member States.

In sum, for the purpose of this book, the term "European Community" is the most appropriate when referring to the EC domestic system, but the use of the term "European Union" may be justified when referring to regional agreements concluded by the EC and its Members States. When referring to the foreign relations of the European entity, and not to its external economic relations, only the term "European Union" should be used.

This somewhat lengthy terminological explanation actually reflects the complex legal and political nature of the European integration system in the 1990s. In the course of this volume, each contributor has been left free to use the terms "European Union" and "European Community" as he or she has seen fit.

[3] These agreements are the subject of the papers reproduced in Part I-A of this volume. With respect to the preferential relations between the European Community and South Mediterranean countries, see also the paper of E. LANNON, *"The Compatibility of the Euro-Mediterranean Regional Integration with the Multilateral Rules"*, reproduced in Part III, at the end of the volume.

[4] Today, the European Community is exclusively competent with respect to trade in goods and trade in services (excluding commercial presence and movement of persons). With respect to investment, movement of natural persons or intellectual property rights it normally has to share competence with the Member States, see *Opinion 1/94* (Uruguay Round), (1994) **ECR**, I-5267 and *Opinion 2/92* (OECD), (1995) **ECR**, I-521. The draft Treaty of Amsterdam (June 1997) provides that subject to

multilateral trade framework[5]. Third, the issue under discussion today at the WTO level is not whether the EC Treaty conforms with Article XXIV of GATT or Article V of GATS[6], but rather whether the regional agreements which the European Community (and its Member States) have negotiated or are negotiating with third countries do or will conform with these provisions.

What precedes does not, of course, imply that the EC experience in regional economic integration is of no interest or may not provide valuable lessons for other regional agreements or for the multilateral trade system itself. Even where the EC experience cannot be transposed, it may nevertheless be used as a sort of yardstick to measure the degree of trade liberalization achieved, or able to be achieved, in the context of other regional agreements or in the context of the multilateral system. Indeed, many papers found in the second part of the book explicitly refer in one way or another to the EC system.

In this second part, the issue of regionalism/multilateralism is approached from a different angle. A series of specialized reports present a comparative analysis of the treatment of selected issues under the world's major regional trade arrangements and their relation with existing or

---

the Council's unanimous approval, Article 113 (the EC Treaty commercial policy provision) could be extended to international negotiations and agreements on services and intellectual property rights insofar as they would not already be covered by Article 113. This is not a straightforward extension of the scope of Article 113 and of the trade policy concept. First, it is on a case-by-case basis that the Council would decide to give a Community character to agreements (such as the GATS or the TRIPs agreement, for instance) which presently, according to the ECJ, fall partly outside the Community competence and thus require the participation of the Member States. Second, whereas decisions regarding commercial matters understood in the narrow sense are taken by qualified majority voting, here each Member State could block a Council decision. Third, since the Community would in any event not become exclusively competent with regard to trade in services involving a commercial presence or movement of personnel or with regard to intellectual property rights, Member States could insist on concluding the agreements together within the Community following the mixed procedure. Finally, it appears that the Member States have not yet accepted the idea that the case-by-case enlargement of the commercial policy provision should also apply to international agreements covering specifically foreign direct investment, such as the Multilateral Agreement on Investment which is being negotiated in the OECD framework.

[5] Assuming that when the European Community **and** its Member States are parties to a multilateral trade agreement (such as the GATS or the TRIPs agreement), they speak with one voice.

[6] Even though the question still arises when a new country joins the European Community and has to apply the EC common customs tariff and other EC commercial policy measures. In that respect, the situation is similar when a third country, without joining the EC, forms a customs union with the EC. This is the case of Turkey.

emerging multilateral rules: rules of origin[7], dumping, subsidies and anticompetitive practices; government procurement; services and investment; intellectual property rights; social protection and the social clause; environmental standards; national treatment, mutual recognition and legislative harmonization; and technical standards. For these issues, an attempt is made to determine whether some of the solutions found at the regional level could be applied at the multilateral level or, conversely, whether the solutions reached at the multilateral level did have an influence at the regional level. In view of the special nature of trade in agricultural products and in addition to the fact that regional experiences could not realistically be seen as possible models for the multilateral system, the choice was made not to deal specifically with this subject, despite its economic and political importance[8].

The third and final part of the book discusses the extent to which multilateral rules acted as a constraint on regional trade arrangements under the GATT of 1947 and, more particularly, whether the constraint might increase under the new WTO system. The issue is examined first from a general perspective[9] and second from a regional perspective. Here the focus is on the European Community and its preferential agreements. Special attention is given to the questions raised by the network of free trade agreements which the European Union has signed or is about to sign with those Southern Mediterranean countries which are not prospective candidates to join the European Union. In view of its importance in relation to the topics covered by this book, and especially the compatibility of new regional agreements (or the enlargement of existing ones) with Article XXIV of GATT and Article V of GATS, the final part opens with a presentation of the new WTO Dispute Settlement Mechanism. The degree of constraint exerted by multilateral rules depends not only on

---

[7] Rules of origin are specifically addressed in the contributions of D. PALMETER and E. NAVARRO VARONA. In addition, the question of cumulation of origin, which is of great economic significance in the context of free trade areas, is treated in detail in A. TOVIAS' paper *"The EU and Mediterranean countries"* reproduced in Part I-A. Concerning rules of origin in the context of trade liberalization between ASEAN members, see J. PELKMANS' paper, *"ASEAN and APEC: A Triumph of the 'Asian Way'?"*, reproduced in Part I-B.

[8] For a recent and concise presentation of the possible effects of the Uruguay Round Agreement on Agricultural Products on the Common Agricultural Policy (CAP) of the European Community in the years to come, see K.J. THOMSON, *"The CAP and the WTO after the Uruguay Round Agreement on Agriculture"*, in: **European Foreign Affairs Review**, No.1, 1996, pp.169-183.

[9] See the paper of S. DEVOS and the comments of W.J. DAVEY. The issue is also briefly discussed in the paper of P. SAUVÉ and the comments of K. FALKENBERG reproduced in Part II of the book.

the effectiveness of the WTO Dispute Settlement Mechanism, but also on the effects which the domestic laws of the WTO Members will attach to these rules. This is why two short papers address the question from the standpoint of EC and US law, with the European Community and the United States being today not only the main players on both a regional as well as a multilateral level.

The book concludes with an analysis of the reciprocal influence between regional and multilateral trade rules as perceived from different viewpoints.

In addition to the references or bibliographies accompanying each individual contribution, the reader will find a general bibliography at the end of the volume.

A last word concerning the presentation of the book. Initially, each topic was supposed to be dealt with in a main report, followed by short comments. However, in many instances, comments became papers in their own right, whereas additional papers were produced after the conference. This explains why the intended structure could not be adhered to throughout the volume and only emerges occasionally.

PART I

THE WORLDWIDE TREND
TOWARDS INCREASED REGIONALISM

The first part of the book is devoted to a comparative analysis of the major regional trade agreements in Europe (excluding the EC domestic market system), the Americas and the Asia Pacific area.

This chapter also covers an emerging new form of regionalism, namely inter-regionalism, the most spectacular example of which could be the Transatlantic Free Trade Area (TAFTA) currently under discussion.

PART I

THE WORLDWIDE TREND
TOWARDS ENLARGED REGIONALISM

European Economic Area and Switzerland-European Union Bilateral Agreements in Comparative Perspective: What Lessons?

René SCHWOK & Christophe BONTE

Associate Professor, European Graduate Institute and Political Science Department, University of Geneva;

Research Assistant, European Graduate Institute, University of Geneva

INTRODUCTION

Our main objective is to compare the European Economic Area (EEA) with the bilateral agreements between Switzerland and the European Union (CH-EU) in order to assess what lessons can be applied to the Central and Eastern European Countries (CEECs), as well as to Turkey, Cyprus, and Malta, the three Mediterranean Countries (MCs) who have applied for EU membership.

The first part of this article aims at putting the origin and development of both the EEA and the CH-EU agreements in historical perspective in order to better understand their specificities, their assets and their weaknesses. Indeed, it would be sterile to study these treaties without understanding the geo-strategic, political, economic and social circumstances which shaped their main elements. Particular attention will be devoted to the CH-EU agreements as they constitute a new, original and often more ignored exercise than the EEA.

The second part is the core of this study. It compares in a systematic way the institutional and legal aspects of both the EEA and the CH-EU agreements in order to point out their analogies and differences. One should note that such a comparison has never been officially done by either the European Commission or by the Swiss bureaucracy, which seems to be uneasy with its political implications.

An epistemological remark is necessary: on the one hand, all legal aspects of the EEA are known, published and have been studied by numerous scientific books and articles (see bibliography). On the other hand, the CH-EU agreements have not yet been initialled (September 1997) and will perhaps never be signed and ratified. This has caused us some difficulties as we could work only on so-called "information sheets", unofficial reports and press articles. We have tried to compensate for this weakness by having private meetings with high level civil servants and diplomats from the European Union, the EFTA Surveillance Authority (ESA) and Switzerland. It is nevertheless obvious that such a method is not sufficient from a scientific point of view, and that it will be necessary to wait for the final outcome of the negotiations in order to reach a definitive judgement of the CH-EU agreements. Confronted with so much uncertainty, we should have used the conditional form more often. For stylistic reasons, however, and in order to publish a more readable text, we have used the indicative.

The objective of the third part is to assess what lessons the CEECs and MCs can learn from both the EEA and the CH-EU agreements. We are, of course, fully aware that there are numerous differences between, on the one hand, the CEECs/MCs, and, on the other hand, the EFTA countries. We are, nevertheless, convinced that a few CEECs and MCs will not join the EU in the coming years, and that they, therefore, have to find intermediary solutions in order to be integrated in the EU system. From this perspective, it is interesting to assess to what extent the European Union has not made a conceptual break by accepting to negotiate the enlargement of its Single Market to an individual country (Switzerland), and no longer with a bloc as in the case of the EEA.

HISTORICAL CONTEXT

This article aims to analyze the positive and negative elements of both the European Economic Area (EEA) and Switzerland-European Union (CH-EU) agreements in order to learn lessons for the Central and Eastern European Countries (CEECs) and the Mediterranean Countries

(MCs). Such a study cannot be done, however, through a solely legal-institutionalist approach. It is also necessary to put those two agreements in an historical perspective in order to fully take into consideration the political specificity of each actor and the contexts of the different negotiations.

First, it is important to remember that both the EEA and the CH-EU agreements are products of the history of the European Free Trade Association (EFTA), which was founded in 1960 by seven Western European countries (Austria, Denmark, Portugal, Norway, Sweden, Switzerland, and the UK). Its two main achievements included: (1) the removal of tariffs and quotas on industrial goods; (2) the building of bridges with the European Community (EC). The subsequent accession of the United Kingdom, Denmark, Norway and Ireland to the EC in the early 1970s had a profound effect on the remaining EFTA members who signed agreements in 1972 to remove tariffs and quotas on industrial goods (Pedersen, 1994).

Origins and Evolution of the EEA

In Luxembourg in April 1984, a new boost to EC-EFTA cooperation was given by the first meeting at a ministerial level between the then eighteen countries of the EC and EFTA. Also for the first time the expression "European Economic Space" was used. It was then only a general framework for **bilateral** and **sectoral** agreements between the EC and each individual EFTA country. A year later, in 1985, the Internal Market programme posed an even greater challenge to the EFTA countries. In order to deter new membership applications at a time when the Community was attempting to deepen rather than widen, the Commission proposed that the EFTA countries join the EC Member States in a new European Economic Area (EEA). This would give the EFTA countries most of the benefits of the Internal Market, without actually giving them full EC membership (Schwok, 1991). Long and difficult negotiations led to the May 1992 Porto Agreement.

EEA has been EFTA's swan song, leading this association in the direction of both growth and deliquescence. On the one hand, EFTA became much more important, structured, bureaucratic and expansive with the constitution of the EFTA pillar of the EEA. The EEA/EFTA countries got a Court of Justice, a Surveillance Authority (ESA), participation in numerous EU committees and an obligation to finance the EU structural funds. On the other hand, EFTA has been undermined by the 1992 Swiss negative referendum on EEA, as well as by the departures of

Austria, Finland, and Sweden who joined the EU in January 1995. There are now only four remaining countries in EFTA: Norway, Iceland, Liechtenstein and Switzerland. The three first countries (4.4 million people) belong to the EEA/EFTA pillar, while Switzerland (7 million people) is active only in the tiny Geneva-based EFTA Secretariat.

The EEA system might have perhaps worked a few more years if the end of Cold War had not accelerated the pace of European integration. As long as the East-West conflict continued, the possibility of EC membership for the neutral states was almost frozen. The events of 1989, however, upset the *status quo*. Deepening the EC through the Maastricht Treaty was one of the answers to the crumbling of the Soviet Union, the partial American withdrawal, the German unification, and the liberation of Central and Eastern Europe. This had a profound impact on the most important EFTA countries by strengthening the domestic pro-EU lobbies (Pedersen, 1994: 82-105).

To sum up, the combination of (1) the institutional weakness of the EEA, (2) the end of the Cold War, and (3) the growing appeal of the EU led most EFTA states to join the organization founded by Jean Monnet and Robert Schuman.

Origins of the CH-EU Agreements

The proposed EEA disappointed Switzerland in three important respects: it was based solely on EC law; it created a kind of mini-supranational organization within the EFTA pillar of the EEA; and it did not allow *de facto* any country to opt out of future EC directives pertaining to the EEA *(infra)*.

Dissatisfied with the EEA offer, in June 1992, Bern applied for full EC membership. Apart from a desire to overcome the proposed EEA's drawbacks by acquiring full EC decision-making capabilities, Switzerland was motivated by three main objectives: to adapt to the changing post-Cold War international environment; to meet the challenge of deeper integration inherent in the recently-negotiated Maastricht Treaty; and to keep pace with the other EFTA countries wanting to join the EC *(Conseil fédéral, 1992)*.

The issue soon became moot, however, contrary to the advise of a large majority of economic, political, and trade union leaders, 50.3% of the electorate (and approximately three-quarters of the cantons) rejected EEA membership in December 1992.

To compensate for this setback, the Swiss Government began to negotiate a series of bilateral agreements covering most aspects of the EEA agenda (Kahil, 1995). Not surprisingly, the most contentious questions concerned sensitive domestic political issues: the free movement of people, and truck transit through the Alps.

Apart from specific events and developments that have affected Switzerland-EU relations in recent years, there are a number of underlying factors that negatively influence Swiss attitudes toward European integration. These are Swiss nationalism, neutrality, economic particularism, and the weakness of the central government (Schwok, 1994(a)).

This is the context in which Switzerland is now negotiating bilateral agreements with the EU. The position of Bern is paradoxical: the Swiss government is, on the one hand, committed to full EU membership and is keeping some nostalgia for the EEA (a treaty tailored-made for Switzerland) and, on the other hand, is negotiating from a very restricted position (in regards to the free movement of persons, free movement of capital, and transportation) in order to appease the large domestic Euro-sceptical mood.

The EU negotiation's position is also rather paradoxical. On the one hand, the Fifteen are ready to grant to Switzerland rather privileged treatment, but, at the same time, they do not want to grant it all the EEA advantages (especially in relation to Technical Barriers to Trade (TBT)) and demand that Switzerland accept EEA principles, such as the free movement of persons. This explains why the CH-EU negotiations have been so long and difficult.

1. LEGAL ASPECTS

1.1. LEGAL BASIS

The **EEA AGREEMENT** comes under Article 238 EC which rules Association Agreements concluded by the EC with third countries (or international organizations). In Community jargon the EEA is a so-called *mixed agreement*, i.e. a treaty which covers areas under Community external competencies and national competencies (Blanchet, 1994: 19-20), with the Community and the fifteen Member States as Contracting Parties (Article 2(c) EEA).

Formally, it is an agreement under public international law. However, due to its close relationship to the Community legal system, as well as its dynamic character *(infra 2.3)*, it is of a unique character (Norberg, 1993: 73; 81; 93; 202). Indeed, through the conclusion of the EEA Agreement the Contracting Parties have created a new legal order, EEA law, which is parallel to EC law (for more discussion, see Jacot-Guillarmod, 1991).

All the **CH-EU BILATERAL AGREEMENTS** are mixed agreements based on Article 228 EC. Note that the CH-EU agreements related to the common trade policy are also based on Article 113 EC and that the air transport agreement is based on Article 84 EC (Friedländer, 1996: 6).

1.2. RATIFICATION PROCESS

Ratification of the EEA had to be given by the EU and EEA/EFTA national parliaments in accordance with their respective constitutional requirements as stated in Article 129 EEA (Norberg, 1993: 306-307), as well as by the

The EU has imposed the notion of *appropriate parallelism* that is a kind of political, although not legal, linkage. This means that the seven treaties will have to enter into force at the same time. In other words, the Fifteen will not

32

European Parliament *(assent procedure)*.

ratify the seven agreements as long as Switzerland has not ratified all of them (Kahil, 1995: 29-30).

In the fields of road transportation, the free movement of persons and theoretically, public procurement, the European Parliament (EP) will be involved through the *assent procedure*. In the other sectors, it seems so far that the EP will only be consulted. Note that the ratification by each of the fifteen national parliaments will be required in the two sensitive fields that are road transportation and the free movement of persons; this procedure could easily last from two to five more years although the agreements could *ad interim* enter into force.

At the Swiss domestic level, the EEA Agreement is based on Article 89 §5 of the Federal Constitution which demands the organization of a referendum requiring the majority of both the citizens and the cantons, as joining the EEA has been considered for legal and domestic political reasons as similar to joining a supranational organization (Blanchet, 1994: 247-248).

In Switzerland the CH-EU agreements will be based on Article 89 §3 of the Constitution which does not compel the organization of a referendum but allows a facultative referendum if 50,000 citizens want one. Note that in this case of facultative referendum, only the popular majority is needed, i.e. it is easier for the government to win the consultation.

1.3. DENOUNCEMENT / CANCELLATION

Each Contracting Party can denounce the agreement in writing on a twelve months notification basis as stated in Article 127 EEA (Norberg, 1993: 304-305).

There is no legal linkage between the seven agreements. Each of them will have its own rules of denouncement, even though these rules will probably be identical.

33

(It should be noted that the Preamble to the EEA Agreement states that the conclusion of the agreement does not prejudge in any way the possibility of an EFTA state acceding to the EU).

One logical consequence of the EC notion of *appropriate parallelism* is the following: if one agreement was denounced by one of the Contracting Parties, the other side could act the same way by denouncing another of the seven agreements.

1.4. REVISION / WIDENING

The EEA Agreement can be revised or widened. Article 118 EEA contains what has been referred to as the *evolutionary clause* of the agreement. It lays down the procedure to be applied when a Contracting Party considers that the material scope of the agreement should be extended to fields not covered by the relations thereby established (Norberg, 1993: 293-294).

Every modification of its core text needs to be ratified by each Contracting Party in accordance with their own procedures. The simplified revision procedure according to which the EEA Joint Committee can carry out modifications by consensus is only applicable to modifications of technical detail in annexes and protocols; this procedure seems to have been the most often used up to now (EFTA and EFTA Surveillance Authority, *Reports '95*).

According to the notion of *parallelism of forms*, each agreement should include a provision for its revision. The Contracting Party that would like to alter or add something to one agreement will have to address to the Joint Committee in charge of it. This complex procedure means the possibility of a facultative referendum for each important revision.

Note that a simplified procedure of revision would be possible on the least important points (i.e. adaptation to technical progress or lists of products).

2. INSTITUTIONAL ASPECTS

2.1. INSTITUTIONS

The EEA is based on a two-pillar structure: the EC on the one hand, and the EFTA on the other hand. It is important to point out that the EEA/EFTA states have to **speak with one voice** (Article 93 EEA) within the institutions that administer the EEA (i.e. the EEA Council and the EEA Joint Committee). To that effect, those countries have set up an EFTA Standing Committee which is an interstate organ made up of representatives from Iceland, Norway and Liechtenstein (with only observers from Switzerland). The function of the EFTA Standing Committee is to elaborate by consensus common positions of the EEA/EFTA states on issues related to the EEA (Norberg, 1993: 107-126).

The EEA has set up its own distinct common institutions in which decisions are taken only by consensus: the EEA Council, the EEA Joint Committee, the EEA Joint Parliamentary Committee and the EEA Consultative Committee (Articles 89-96 EEA). It should be noted that there is no transfer of legislative powers from any Contracting Party to any institution of the EEA (Norberg, 1993: 74).

In addition to providing for the establishment of specific EEA institutions, the agreement also obliged the EFTA states to set up, by a separate agreement, two new

Each sectoral agreement will have its Joint Committee (CH-EU), like the ones set up by the Free Trade Agreements (FTA) of 1972 (Kahil, 1995: 59). Some of those Joint Committees will have to be newly established whereas others already function, such as in the fields of research and road transport.

Note the following exception: only the European Commission is competent for the rules of competition in air transport and Switzerland will have to accept the European Commission decisions in that field (SDES, 1996: 45-46). Switzerland will possibly have to set up an independent surveillance authority in the fields of air transport and public procurement.

If Switzerland does not comply with EC rules in the six other agreements, the EU could eventually take safeguard provisions or other forms of counter-measures.

The CH-EU agreements will be based on the principle of trust and fairness between the Contracting Parties (so they will depend, to a large extent, upon civil servants).

institutions, an EFTA Surveillance Authority (ESA) and an EFTA Court (Article 108 EEA) in order to provide for a system of surveillance and judicial control on the EFTA side corresponding to that existing on the EC side, i.e. the Commission and the ECJ. In doing so, they have thus created a mini-supranational organization.

The main task of the ESA is to ensure that EEA rules are properly enacted and applied by the EFTA States, especially the rules of competition. With regard to its surveillance function, ESA has been given powers corresponding to those of the European Commission. The Authority can thus investigate possible infringements either on its own initiative or on the basis of complaints. It can also refer to the EFTA Court (Norberg, 1993: 209-272).

Note that, initially, the EC and the EFTA states wanted to set up an EEA Court composed by EFTA, as well as EC Court of Justice judges. The EC Court of Justice opposed, however, the creation of an EEA Court on the basis that the EEA/EFTA states would not have been committed to its rulings (Opinion 1/91, December 14, 1991, ECR I-6079). So, in the absence of an EEA judicial body, EC and EFTA negotiators elaborated the new following jurisdictional mechanism:

As the EC does not usually admit any kind of arbitration on the settlement of disputes, one cannot expect that such a mechanism would be applied in the CH-EU agreements despite Swiss wishes to build an exceptional legal mechanism based on the model of the CH-EU Agreement concerning Direct Insurance other than Life Insurance (OJ L 205, 27.07.1991, p.2). A diplomatic solution will, therefore, certainly prevail.

1. **The EC Court of Justice** is now exclusively competent in interpreting the *acquis communautaire*; through Article 6 EEA and Article 3 ESA/EFTA Court the Contracting Parties take over all the EEA relevant case law of the ECJ given prior to the date of signature of this agreement (Norberg, 1993: 104-105 and Norberg in Stuyck, 1994: 16-19). There is also a need to consider the case law of the ECJ delivered after the signature of the EEA. On the EC side this will be ensured through the ECJ. On the EFTA side Article 3(2) of the ESA/EFTA Court Agreements obliges the EFTA Court and the ESA to pay due account to the principles laid down by the relevant rulings of the ECJ given after the signature of the EEA Agreement and which concern the interpretation of the EEA Agreement or of such rules of Community law which are identical in substance to the EEA Agreement (Treumer, 1994; see also Mr. Myhre's interesting comment on that book on the decisions of the ECJ prior and after the date of signature of the agreement).

Furthermore, an EFTA state institution may solicit the European Court of Justice on the interpretation of a provision of the agreement (Article 107 and Protocol 34 EEA).

2. **The EFTA Court**, set up by the EEA/EFTA states, is competent for sanctions concerning the surveillance procedure regarding the EEA/EFTA states, calls against decisions taken by the European Surveillance Authority in the field of competition policy, and settles disputes between two or more EEA/EFTA states (Article 108 EEA). The EFTA Court has already delivered decisions (Blanchet, 1996).

3. **A procedure of conciliation** (Article 105 EEA) will apply in case of divergence of jurisprudence between the two institutions (Norberg in Stuyck, 1994: 29-32); a *procedure of arbitration* (Protocol 33 EEA) is also envisaged at a last recourse in case of political deadlock (Norberg, 1993: 113; 284).

2.2. INVOLVEMENT IN THE SHAPING PROCESS

The EEA Agreement aims at solving the dilemma of, on the one hand, keeping the sovereignty of the EFTA states, and, on the other hand, respecting the EC autonomy of decision, as well as maintaining the homogeneity of the EEA Agreement.

When adopting a new EC legislation the EEA/EFTA states are involved in the following different ways (Article 97 and following EEA):

Phase 1: EFTA experts are consulted on the same basis as EU

The EC is reluctant to give Switzerland the right to benefit from the advantages granted to the EEA/EFTA states in the shaping process.

Swiss experts will neither have any formal right to be consulted nor will they have the possibility to express their opinions. They will only have the opportunity to be informed by the European Commission according to its own goodwill and to submit their comments.

Regarding the Swiss participation in different committees, a unique

38

experts in the preparatory phase of any new Community legislative act relevant to the EEA (note that banking and financial issues are excluded from the first phase).

Phase 2: a copy of the Commission's proposal is transmitted at the same time to the EU Council of Ministers and to the EEA/EFTA states; a preliminary exchange of views takes place within the EEA Joint Committee if one of the Contracting Parties requests it (general principle of *droit d'évocation individuel* stated in Article 5 EEA). Note that there is no corresponding article in the EC Treaty (Norberg, 1993: 103-104).

Phase 3: the EEA/EFTA states get the right to be fully informed and consulted within the EEA Joint Committee regarding any new EC legislative act at the same time the EU Council of Ministers and the European Parliament are examining it.

Phase 4: at the time of the final decision, the EU Council of Ministers has the final say (in agreement with the Parliament if required). The EEA/EFTA states cannot make use of any co-decision right (Norberg, 1993: 133-141).

access will be granted in the technological cooperation and research committees (as is already the case for Israel in the same field). But it goes without saying that Switzerland could not be a projects' leader (SDES, 1996: 7-9).

2.3. Involvement in the Decision-Making Process

After a decision has been adopted by the EU Council of Ministers (with the approval of the EP, as required) it is implemented in the

Switzerland will retain the possibility of not adopting new EC legislation, but at the risk of countermeasures or safeguard provisions

EEA through the EEA Joint Committee as soon as possible in order to permit an almost simultaneous application in the EC and the EEA/EFTA states (Blanchet, 1994: 33-34). Meanwhile, the EEA/EFTA states can use their right of veto, although only on a collective basis. In order to do so, they will have to first enter into negotiations within the EEA Joint Committee to find a mutually acceptable solution (for more details, see Norberg, 1993: 143). If, in the six following months, there is no agreement, the part of the legislative act that has been rejected will be considered provisionally suspended for each EEA/EFTA state — Article 102 EEA (Norberg, 1993: 141-148).

The important point is that the veto of one EFTA state is considered as a *collective opting out*. This then opens all EFTA states to possible counter-measures or safeguard provisions, i.e. unilateral suspension of one part of the EEA Agreement. Note that the EC can make use of counter-measures that are also available in fields other than those in which one or some EEA/EFTA states have made use of veto right — see Articles 112-114 EEA (*infra*).

To keep its homogeneity, the EEA Agreement is designed to be dynamic and is amended on a quasi-automatic and continuous basis to ensure that relevant and acceptable Community legislation in corresponding areas is extended to the EEA/EFTA states. Article 102 which could be undertaken by the Community in order to preserve the general balance of the CH-EU agreements. The most effective counter-measure would be the denouncement (or temporary suspension) by the EC of another agreement which binds it to Switzerland.

Furthermore, the CH-EU agreements will not be amended on a quasi-automatic and continuous basis as in the EEA (no such dynamic aspect as the Community *opting in* exists). And even if every modification of an agreement will *a priori* bring about a new round of negotiations, it should not be forgotten that adoption of continuing law in a bilateral agreement will carry out new legal and political questions. The alternative to an adaptation of the *droit évolutif* by decisional mechanism would consist in denouncing the former agreement and concluding a new one. This will be difficult. There would be a serious problem with individual rights acquired during the existence of the first agreement (Kahil, 1995: 31-32).

EEA states that the EEA Joint Committee shall take as soon as possible a decision on any new Community legislation within the framework of the agreement for making such amendment part of the EEA Agreement (Norberg, 1993: 142-143 and Norberg in Stuyck, 1994: 19-21).

3. CONTENTS

3.1. LEGAL BASIS

All relevant Community rules of primary and secondary EC law regarding the four freedoms and other Internal Market fields have been integrated into the agreement. The primary law rules have been integrated in the main agreement and the secondary legislation in the annexes to the agreement (Norberg in Stuyck, 1994: 15).

Specifically the EEA is based on the extension of the Community legislation on the removal of technical barriers to the four freedoms of movement (relevant *acquis communautaire*).

The CH-EU sectoral agreements are partial agreements, so they do not take over the whole relevant *acquis communautaire*.

Seven issues (which will then make seven agreements) are now under discussion between Switzerland and the EU. Five were accepted by the EC: road and air transport, research, public procurement and Technical Barriers to Trade (TBT). The EC asked to add two more issues: agriculture and the free movement of persons (Kahil, 1995: 7). In addition, Switzerland would like to negotiate in the second round on five other issues: training, passive textile improvement, processed agricultural products, audiovisual services (participation in the MEDIA Community Programme) and cooperation in the field of statistics *(Bureau de l'intégration, 1996)*.

3.2. FOUR FREEDOMS OF MOVEMENT

The EEA is based only on the removal of technical barriers on the four freedoms of movement as well as on the so-called horizontal and flanking measures. It means in other words that it **does not include**:

1. **Tariff barriers**: the EEA is not an agreement on the removal of tariff barriers and quantitative restrictions. Remember that those *first generation* barriers were already abolished by the 1972 Free Trade Agreements between each individual EFTA state and the EC. Note however that customs and border formalities are simplified and that a common rule establishes the origin of all goods traded in the EEA (as each Member State retains its own external tariff).

2. The **common external trade policy**: the EEA Agreement forms a fundamentally improved free trade area, and not a customs union with a common external tariff. The autonomy in external economic policy matters is warranted.

3. The **fiscal harmonization** (VAT and excise duties).

4. The **common agricultural policy**: EEA/EFTA countries are not concerned by the CAP although there is increased free trade in agricultural products, especially from some EC Member States, by way of bilateral agreements (Norberg, 1993: 74). Indeed,

The CH-EU agreements cover only partly the four freedoms of movement *(Bureau de l'intégration, 1996)*:

Free movement of goods: the EU has accepted the principle of an agreement on Technical Barriers to Trade (TBT). So far, Brussels has, however, differentiated between the so-called *harmonized* and *non-harmonized* fields. In regard to the *harmonized* sectors, the Commission is ready to grant Switzerland the same kind of agreement as the EEA.

Regarding the *non-harmonized* sectors, the EU is not keen on extending the principle of *Cassis de Dijon* to Switzerland (SDES, 1996; see also the interesting discussion about the extension of the *Cassis de Dijon* case law to EC external trade in Prof. Demaret's report in this book). The EC position is based on the argument that in the CH-EU agreements, there will not be any jurisdictional mechanism (such as the EFTA Court) to monitor the Swiss non-harmonized norms.

This would result in a serious difference with the EEA, for in this treaty the EFTA countries also got an agreement on the non-harmonized fields. In the negotiations, Bern is trying to reverse Brussels' attitude in order to get the same privileges as the EEA/ EFTA states *(Bureau de l'inté-*

Iceland, Norway, Austria, Finland and Sweden concluded — at that time — in parallel to the EEA Agreement, bilateral agreements with the EC granting removal of tariffs and other concessions in the field of agriculture (Blanchet, 1994: 18). A general evolutive clause is also included in the EEA Agreement (Article 19 EEA).

5. The **common fisheries policy**: the EEA Agreement contains, nevertheless, a partial liberalization of trade in fish and the conclusion of bilateral agreements between some of the EFTA states and the Community (Norberg, 1993: 365-368).

6. The **common economic and monetary policy**: no participation in the EMU.

7. The **political union**: no participation to the Common Foreign and Security Policy (CFSP), except for a related political dialogue on a common defence policy in the long run and on cooperation in the fields of Justice and Home Affairs.

gration, 1996: 29-30).

Note that a new law entered into force on July 1st, 1996, that prescribes that *all* new Swiss technical norms have to be *systematically* harmonized with those of its main trade partners. This is a euphemism for adapting to new EC technical legislative acts partners *(Bureau de l'intégration*, 1996: 30).

The CH-EU Agreement in the field of *public procurement* allows the extension of GATT provisions to municipalities as well as to entities operating in the fields of water, energy, transport and telecommunication. Note that provisions on public procurement are less integrated in GATT than in the EEA. (SDES, 1996).

Free movement of services: most services are not included in this first round of the negotiations with the exception of air and road transport. Note that the initial Swiss proposals of 1993 were much more ambitious as they covered all services.

Free movement of persons: the EU has demanded its inclusion in the first round of the negotiations despite strong Swiss reluctance. This is, so far, the main obstacle in the way of both the conclusion and the ratification of the agreements.

Free movement of capital: Switzerland was not interested in entering into negotiations on this freedom and the EU has so far agreed to leave this issue aside.

3.3. COMPETITION RULES

The Community competition rules in the field of the four freedoms of movement are transposed into the EEA Agreement. Part IV of the EEA Agreement contains the rules on competition (antitrust and state aids), on procurement and on intellectual, industrial, and commercial property. The EEA competition rules play an important role in the integration of the economies of the Contracting Parties into one unified market.

Note that the Contracting Parties were able in Article 26 EEA to include in the EEA Agreement the principle of prohibition of the application of anti-dumping measures (with the exemption of the fisheries sector) to EEA originating products between them (for more discussion, see Mr. Bellis' report in this book). Indeed, it is not logical to apply anti-dumping measures where common competition rules exist, since the latter rules, in principle, encourage price competition between undertakings (Norberg, 1993: 499-500; 389-392).

In the field of competition, surveillance of the implementation of common rules across the area is carried out by the Commission on the one hand and by the EFTA Surveillance Authority on the other *(supra)*.

The Community competition rules are only taken over in the field of air transport *(supra)*.

3.4. FLANKING AND HORIZONTAL POLICIES

In addition to the establishment of the four freedoms, the Contracting Parties cooperate in a wide range of other areas.

Part V of the Agreement (see also Annexes XVIII-XXII) contains provisions which are horizontally relevant to the four freedoms and must facilitate their achievement. The EEA/EFTA states thus take over the EC secondary legislation in the fields of social policy, consumer protection, environmental protection, statistics, and company law. Note that the horizontal areas concern binding Community acts, which is not the case for the so-called *flanking policies*.

Part VI (see also Protocol 31) of the agreement concerns cooperation outside the four freedoms, known as *flanking policies*. This part essentially aims at enabling the EFTA states to participate in EC programmes and other common actions in a number of areas indirectly related to the four freedoms: research and development, information services, education, training and youth, small and medium-sized enterprises, tourism, audiovisual sector and civil protection (Norberg, 1993: 609-670 and Blanchet, 1994: 17-18); Note that EEA/EFTA states are not obligated to adapt their own legislation to the Community legislation in those fields where there is no real harmonization, but

The question of the Swiss participation in the flanking and horizontal policies by way of the bilateral agreements remains open. It is not impossible, but the risk exists that each time the EC believes that its interests are not preserved, it will refuse to negotiate in new fields; this is the case for the participation in Community programmes in the fields of statistics and audiovisual — MEDIA Programme *(Bureau de l'intégration*, 1996: 10-11).

only broadened and strengthened co-operation between the Contracting Parties to the EEA Agreement *(Bureau de l'intégration, 1992: 4.0F)*.

3.5. FINANCIAL MECHANISM

As part of the Agreement on the EEA, the EEA/EFTA states established a Financial Mechanism (Part VIII and Protocol 38 EEA) intended for the development and adjustment of certain economically disadvantaged states or regions of the EEA (namely Greece, Southern and Northern Ireland, Portugal and ten regions of Spain). This Financial Mechanism, restricted to projects carried out by public authorities and public and private firms, has provided, for the year 1995, interest rebates for a total volume of loans of ECU 1,500 million and grants amounting to ECU 500 million. Priority is given to the environment (including urban development), transport (including transport infrastructure), and education and training projects. The European Investment Bank (EIB) administers the mechanism (EFTA, 1996: 28-30 and Norberg, 1993: 673-676).

Until now the EC has not claimed any Swiss contribution to an eventual financial mechanism.

3.6. SAFEGUARD MEASURES

The EEA Agreement includes a general safeguard provision in order to preserve vital interests of EEA states. In case of serious difficulties in economic, social or environmental issues, in a particular area or region, a Contracting

Safeguard measures are one of the most sensitive parts of the CH-EU agreements. Bern emphasizes that it will not begin negotiating on this aspect as long as present negotiations in the most sensitive fields (road transport and free movement

Party has the option of invoking this clause in order to avoid negative consequences of Community legislation. As those measures derogate to the EEA Agreement, they are restricted in their sphere of implementation and in time. They can be initiated unilaterally by an EEA/EFTA state or by the European Commission on behalf of the Fifteen (Article 112 EEA).

Furthermore, proportionate rebalancing measures from other states are possible as stated in Article 114 EEA (Norberg, 1993: 113; 287-290 and Blanchet, 1994: 38-39).

Note that no corresponding provisions are included in the EC Treaty, but similar provisions are normal in trade agreements, one example being Article 27 in most of the FTAs between the EFTA countries and the EC.

of persons) remain unfinalized. Counter-measures will probably be negotiated on the basis of Articles 111 and 112 EEA.

3.7. Transitional Periods

Transitional periods should consist of time-limits allotted to EEA/EFTA states for implementing new Community legislation into their internal legal order (Blanchet, 1994: 65-68).

If Switzerland joins the EEA, it would have the benefit of maximum transitory periods of five years in the fields of the free movement of persons and measures related to the Lex Friedrich, i.e. acquisition of real estate by foreigners *(Bureau de l'intégration*, 1992: 0.8F).

Knowing under which conditions Switzerland could benefit from transitional periods is a strategic element of present negotiations about which nothing can be said for the moment.

WHAT LESSONS FOR THE CEECS AND THE MCS?

Our thesis is that the CEECs and MCs can learn from both the EEA and the CH-EU agreements. Those two treaties prove that it is possible to profit from most advantages of the Internal Market without being a member of the European Union. Moreover, they show that the Fifteen are also ready to let nonmember countries take part in technological, academic, environmental, and other programmes of cooperation. Note finally, that both the EEA and the CH-EU agreements cover fields much larger and go to levels of integration much deeper than North American Free Trade Agreement or Mercosur or the Customs Union between the EU and Turkey.

To what extent are the CEECs and MCs interested in the EEA and the CH-EU agreements? The official answer is: not at all. The three Mediterranean Countries, as well as all of the CEECs, except for the countries of former-Yugoslavia and Albania, have formally applied for EU membership and do not want to take into consideration any other alternative, except, recently, Malta. The EU has also officially declared its readiness to later accept any European country (with the exceptions of Turkey and non-Baltic countries of the former Soviet Union).

The timing for widening the Union is, however, far from being clear. Germany is pressing less as it costs too much, NATO enlargement is taking the priority and there is no imminent danger at its Eastern borders. As pointed out by Mr. Jacques Santer, who used to be a strong proponent of EU enlargement, "only one or two CEECs are likely to gain membership by 2003." (*Financial Times*, December 2, 1996).

So it seems that only Poland, Hungary, the Czech Republic and possibly Slovenia have a serious chance to join the EU in the next years. For the others, (at least a dozen countries!), chances of rapid membership are very slim. As a consequence, it is imperative to envisage for those countries intermediary solutions in order to remove non-tariff barriers.

The case of Malta is particularly relevant: the Mediterranean island is indeed groping for a new relationship with the EU as its government has frozen Malta's long-standing application to join the EU. The so-called "Swiss option" is now officially the aim of the Labour government, as Malta wishes to get most of the advantages of the Internal Market without being a EU Member (*Financial Times*, January 10, 1997).

Another very interesting example is Turkey, as this country is committed through its 1996 Customs Union to negotiate bilaterally the removal of non-tariff barriers, free movement of capital, as well as of services with the EU (interview with Ambassador Lake, EU representative in Ankara, January 7, 1997).

To this list of countries, one can add a few others, which do not have the vocation to join but are nevertheless interested in being much more closely integrated into the EU (Israel, Moldova, Ukraine, Russia, Belarus, Morocco, Tunisia, Algeria). For those states also, the EEA, as well as the CH-EU agreements bear some relevance.

Lessons from the EEA

Positive Elements

1. **Participation in most of the advantages of the Internal Market without being an EU member:** this point seems obvious nowadays but it was far from being the case in the 1980s. Many members of the Commission, as well as experts of the Union considered such a perspective to be a kind of anathema. Even today, most CEEC and MC leaders still have conceptual difficulties admitting that one can take part in the most important elements of the Internal Market without being a member of the Union.

2. **Opportunity of influence:** the Commission is legally committed to consult experts from the EEA/EFTA states at a very early stage of the elaboration of new EU legislation. Moreover, this system of input in the Commission's proposals and at other levels of the EC seems to be functioning in a satisfactory way (*European Voice*, 1-7-8.96, *Tribune de Genève*, 22.8.96). The two main snags are the followings: (a) the relatively small EFTA countries do not always have a sufficient number of trained experts able to exert influence in all of the committees; (b) some EU bureaucrats have not yet adopted the reflex of systematically inviting the EFTA countries. Those problems would nevertheless not hurt the CEECs and the MCs which are usually much more important and powerful.

3. **Vertical evolution:** one of the main benefits of the EEA is that it can evolve in a *quasi* automatic way. In other words, each time the EU adopts new legislation relevant to the EEA, the countries of the EFTA pillar adopt it, within the EEA Joint Committee, without proceeding to any negotiation. To be sure, they have the right to negotiate, and, indeed, the Norwegians have applied their right often in oil matters. Moreover, they have the right to opt out collectively from any new legislation but they do not do it, mainly because they simply do not need to. Such a system

is very practical, especially for the EU, as part of its legal order is adopted by nonmembers without any real intervention.

4. **Potential horizontal evolution:** the EEA Agreement covers of course only the elements which are explicitly mentioned *(relevant acquis communautaire)*. Any extension to fields such as agriculture, fiscal matters, or removal of the physical barriers to the free movement of persons necessitates an extra international agreement. One has nevertheless observed that EEA/EFTA states get much more privileged treatment than any country in the world. They benefit from regular political dialogue (Norway and Iceland are also members of NATO), they are close to the European Monetary System (EMS), they are the first informed about the evolution of the 1996 Intergovernmental Conference (IGC 96) and they have been offered a statute of association to the Schengen Agreement which is a quasi-membership. To be sure, this agreement is extra-Community and the goodwill towards Norway and Iceland comes largely from their belonging to the Nordic Council, but it nevertheless constitutes another sign of the general benevolence of the EU and its Member States *vis-à-vis* the EEA/EFTA states.

5. **Heavy structure runs smoothly:** the EEA system is heavy and costly. It necessitates a Court of Justice (concerning the performing of the EFTA Court see Blanchet, 1996), an institution similar to the Commission (ESA), mixed committees, links between parliamentarians, financial contributions to the EU structural funds among other kinds of links. Many experts doubted that such a system could work after the departures of Austria, Sweden, and Finland. Nevertheless, one has to admit that this system is functioning with relative flexibility (see, for instance, Mr. Myhre's comment in that book on the Norwegian case), it is adaptable and its costs are easily borne by the EEA/EFTA states.

6. **Does not preclude membership:** as it has been shown by the examples of Austria, Sweden and Finland, EEA membership is not an obstacle on the road to any future full EU membership. Furthermore, it can even contribute to better preparation for countries belonging to the EEA/EFTA pillar which have already adapted their legislation to the most important aspects of the Internal Market and have acquired the working habits of the EU.

Negative Elements

1. **No participation in the decision-making process:** EEA/EFTA states do not actually take part in the decision itself which is the sole domain

of the EU. In all the negotiations surrounding EEA, the Community has always categorically refused to grant to nonmembers any right of co-decision. Note that this has been at the origins of numerous controversies, as Jacques Delors, in his January 1989 proposals, used the expression "common decision-making" (*EFTA Bulletin*, April-June 1989: 6).

2. *De facto* **adaptation to the new EU legislative acts:** since the EEA Treaty entered into force in January 1994, EEA/EFTA states have taken over **all** the new EU legislative acts which are relevant. Norway has for instance adopted EU directives on energy (liberalization of the markets) and food (food additives) which did not fit the Norwegian standards at the time (*Tribune de Genève*, 28.8.96). They could have rejected some of them but it was, firstly, not in their interest and, moreover, the procedure is too complicated and heavy. As a matter of fact, if an EEA/EFTA state cannot adopt one new EU legislative act, the other EEA/EFTA states can then not adopt on an individual basis either. Moreover, they take the risk that the Community will adopt counter-measures in another field. This explains why one can speak of a quasi-automatic adaptation to the evolution of EU legislation.

3. **Based on EU law:** the whole Treaty is based on EU law. EEA/EFTA states have to adapt to it, as well as its interpretations by the EC Court of Justice. Symbolically, the tiny Court of Justice of the EFTA pillar which was based in Geneva, showing the independence of EFTA, was moved to Luxembourg on September 1st, 1996.

4. **Supranationality:** the EEA creates two supranational organs: (a) the EFTA Surveillance Authority, which controls the rules of competition in the same way as the Commission; and, (b) the EEA/EFTA Court of Justice. One should also mention that the EU Court of Justice bears, in most, cases the final competence. Finally, to implement the concept of homogeneity throughout the whole area, there is again this notion of collective *opting out*. One can easily imagine the difficulties if the EFTA pillar of EEA would have to integrate CEECs or MCs that cannot adapt to the evolution of the relevant EU *acquis*.

Lessons from the CH-EU Agreements

Positive Elements

1. **It fits the specific needs of a non-EU country in the phase of** *negotiation*: compared to EEA, the main advantage of the CH-EU bilateral agreements is that it allows a third country to negotiate independently.

For instance, Switzerland is not forced to harmonize its position with its EFTA partners before negotiating with the Union. On the other hand, for Brussels, it would have been preferable to negotiate with a bloc of countries which have previously harmonized their positions and, thus, not to grant any preferential treatment to one single state. For the CEECs and MCs, this observation is particularly important because if they had to harmonize their positions before dealing with the Community, it is clear that difficulties would rise in the case of a "Balkanic" pillar with Croatia and Serbia or a "Central European" pillar with the Czech Republic and Slovakia or a "Mediterranean" pillar with Southern Cyprus and Turkey.

2. **It fits the specific needs of a non-EU country in the phase of** *administration*: after the agreements have entered into force, the third country has a much larger freedom and margin to manoeuvre than in the EEA as it is not dependent upon the collective opting out mechanism. Adopting any new EU legislative act relevant to the agreements remains an individual act which is not linked to the possible changes of mood of the pillar's partners. Moreover, there is no risk to be penalized by EU counter-measures which would have been decided following the "wrong" behaviour of another pillar's country. The responsibility is individual and would certainly better fit the needs of the CEECs and the MCs than in the EEA system.

3. **Flexibility of content:** bilateral agreements of the CH-EU type allows the non EU-country to refuse to negotiate in some sectors. Switzerland was for instance not interested in dealing with the free movement of capital, whereas it had to negotiate both the principle and the content within the EEA framework. Note, however, that this notion of flexibility is double edged as it also allows the EU to refuse to negotiate in some sectors. One has only to remember that, in 1993, Bern proposed sixteen areas for talks and that Brussels has accepted only seven in the first round of negotiations. For the CEECs and MCs, such flexibility is particularly interesting as the EU would have a tendency to be less tough with them than with Switzerland (a rich and quite "rebellious" country).

4. **No automatism:** bilateral agreements of the CH-EU type do not force one non-EU country to take over in a quasi-automatic way the new legislative acts relevant to the agreements (except in the field of air transport). In each case, the non-EU country would keep the capacity to judge, without appeal, if it will adopt the acts. One should, nevertheless, avoid being too idealistic, as the Union has imposed the principle of *appropriate parallelism* (which is very close to the concept of *keeping homogeneity* in the EEA). Concretely, it seems (this point has to be confirmed),

that the European Union will retain the right to sustain any bilateral agreement with Switzerland if it estimates that Bern is not observing the principle of *appropriate parallelism.*

5. **No supranationality:** in the CH-EU agreements, there is nothing similar to the ESA, no Court of Justice and no *collective* opting out. This is an advantage for countries which cherish notions such as sovereignty and independence. CEEC and MC leaders will have less difficulty with public opinion (which often is nationalistic) to join a bilateral agreement rather than something like EEA.

6. **Not based on EU law:** except in the field of air transport, CH-EU agreements are based on international law. Moreover, they only have a political jurisdictional mechanism (mixed committees) and no EU-based jurisdictional mechanism (EU Court of Justice, EEA/EFTA Court of Justice). This allows a non-EU country to claim that it keeps its sovereignty better than countries in the EEA. Practically speaking, however, the difference is rather small. If one non-EU country does not adopt new relevant Community legislation, there will no longer be the so-called *parallelism of forms* and the EU will be entitled to take safeguard measures.

7. **Does not preclude membership:** bilateral agreements such as those existing between Switzerland and the EU do not constitute any obstacle to the road to full EU membership. As a matter of fact, Switzerland has not withdrawn its membership application (although it has been *de facto* frozen like in Malta). Note that the Swiss position would, nevertheless, be more credible on the issue of permanent exception (for instance on the free establishment of persons) if Bern had withdrawn its application to full membership. One can indeed not ask for any permanent derogation if one aims to be a full member (i.e. without derogation) of the EU. This point should also be clear for the CEECs and MCs.

Negative Elements

1. **Appropriate parallelism:** first, the Union has forced Switzerland to negotiate in some sectors that Bern did not want to tackle (free establishment of persons) and has refused to extend the principle of *Cassis of Dijon* in the so-called non-harmonized sectors. Moreover, Brussels has demanded, and attained that the seven agreements will enter into force all together. In other words, Switzerland cannot expect that six agreements will apply if the seventh (for instance on persons) did not get the ratification's approval of the population. CEECs and MCs should,

therefore, not expect any *à la carte* treatment although they could expect more favourable conditions from the EU due to their economic backwardness, their political importance and their more positive attitude towards integration than Switzerland.

2. **No automatism:** there is no automatic retaking of the new EU legislative acts in the CH-EU agreements. We have already noticed that this can be an advantage for a non-EU country in terms of sovereignty. But this could become a negative element if the Union does not want to acknowledge the compatibility of the non-EU country with its own. Remember that in the EEA, the EFTA countries have obtained a guarantee that as long as they adopt the new EU legislation, it will be automatically recognized as compatible by Brussels. For the CEECs and MCs, this could be a snag, although one should nevertheless not exaggerate the probability that the EU would not recognize the compatibility of their legislation.

3. **Complex for the EU:** it is obvious that for Brussels, the multiplication of bilateral agreements of the CH-EU type represents a much more complicated and potentially more conflictual exercise than to deal with pillars formed around blocs of countries which have previously harmonized their positions and accept to administer jointly the agreements. Now, with the CEECs and MCs, it is probable that the Union will negotiate bilateral agreements in parallel and that their shape and content would be globally similar (as it is already the case in the European agreements).

4. **No transitivity:** contrary to the EEA, there is no transitivity. It means that one non-EU country will also have to conclude with the other non-EU countries' agreements modelled on the one negotiated with the Union. For instance, Switzerland will have to sign an agreement with Norway and Iceland (maybe not with Liechtenstein as it is already well integrated into the Swiss economy) in the fields which are relevant to its own agreements with the EU. CEECs and MCs will be confronted with the same kind of challenges. This means concretely that if Hungary and Rumania concluded agreements of the CH-EU type, those two countries would have to extend them to their own bilateral relations. For instance, Rumania would have to accept the principle that Hungarians are free to establish themselves in Transylvania.

Differences between the EFTAs and the CEECs/MCs

We are, of course, fully aware that the differences are numerous between, on the one hand, the EFTAs, and, on the other hand, the CEECs and MCs. Let us mention at least six fundamental differences in a list which could be much longer:

1. **Historical context:** as it has already been mentioned in the introduction, the history of the EFTA countries with the European Union bears the stigmas of the years 1950-80 and has been conditioned by events which will not be the same in the future. It is also important to note that most CEECs and MCs want to join the EU for political and strategic motives. Those factors are far less relevant for the current EFTA states.

2. **Economy:** economic standards are very different. EFTA states have the highest GDPs in Europe, modern infrastructures, a well established capitalist tradition, an habit to open their market to foreign competition, etc., which are not found at this level among most of the CEECs and MCs.

3. **Accustomed to collaborating with the European Union:** one of the advantages of the EFTA countries is that they are accustomed to dealing with the EU. Their relations date back to the beginning of the 1960s and have endured until today (it is true also for some MCs). More fundamentally, EFTAs are very close to the working and reasoning patterns of the EU bureaucrats. They do not have any difficulty dealing with them.

4. **Legal order:** EFTA countries have the same kind of law as the EU countries. The development of their legal order has been parallel during the last fifty years. This explains, for instance, why Austria, Sweden and Finland did not have to undertake any fundamental legal upheavals in order to join either the EEA or the EU.

5. **Bureaucratic development:** one of the least studied but most important points has to do with the compatibility between bureaucracies (public and private). As a matter of fact, the EU Internal Market and the EEA can work well only if the national bureaucracies trust each other. In order to agree on minimal criteria and to accept the principle of mutual recognition of norms, standards, tests, certifications and diplomas, as well as the opening of public procurement, this confidence is a *sine qua non* condition. It is possible that this element could be a problem in the future when the EU will have to recognize the compatibility of some CEECs and MCs norms on security, safety and environment.

6. **Euro-sympathy:** one of the differences between the EFTA, on the one hand, and the CEECs and MCs, on the other hand, has to do with the will to get closer to the EU. One could observe that Iceland, as well as Norway and Switzerland do fit all the criteria to join the EU but that the

principal, and almost unique obstacle comes from their population's Euro-reluctance. In the cases of the CEECs and MCs, opinion polls such as the Eurobarometer, show that the people are very supportive of EU membership (although more qualitative analyses would show much greater diversity, i.e. the Islamic fundamentalists in Turkey).

CONCLUSION

The main point of this article is to show that the Union has taken a new step in the direction of variable geometry by accepting **bilateral** and sectoral negotiations on non-tariff barriers with one non-EU country. This means that the CEECs and the MCs are now entitled to ask to get the same kind of deal. This would allow some of them to partly join the EU Internal Market and to participate in part of its horizontal dimension without full membership. By the way, such a dimension is already anticipated in the European agreements and has been applied to Israel in regard to technological cooperation.

Perhaps the best solution for countries not joining the EU is to combine the best aspects of the EEA with those of the CH-EU agreements. From the EEA, they should try to get those advantages such as: influence at the level of the shaping, quasi-automaticity when adopting the relevant Community *acquis*, strong homogeneity with the Internal Market, and transitivity. From the CH-EU agreements, they could find positive elements such as legal flexibility, formal independence, and some margin of manoeuvre during the phases of both negotiation and administration.

It is nevertheless obvious that our observations have to be taken with circumspection. We are fully aware that the EEA is far from being a model as it has suffered from the disaffection from the most important EFTA states and that the CH-EU agreements might never be concluded or ratified. Moreover, we do not doubt that the historical, economic, political, social, legal and bureaucratic contexts are very different between, on the one hand, the EFTA countries, and, on the other hand, the CEECs and MCs. History will not be repeated the same way. Neither the EEA nor the CH-EU agreements constitute proper models but only **experiences** (positive and negative) from which some lessons could be learned by the EU, as well as by the CEECs and the MCs.

BIBLIOGRAPHY

BALDWIN, Richard, *Towards an Integrated Europe*, CEPR, London, 1994.

BALDWIN, Richard, *The Economic Logic of EFTA Countries Joining the EEA and the EC,* **Occasional Paper** No.41, European Free Trade Association, Geneva, 1992.

BLANCHET, Thérèse & WESTMAN-CLÉMENT, Maria, *"La Cour AELE - Un premier bilan"* (2ème partie), in : **Revue du Marché commun et de l'Union européenne**, No.399, 1996, pp.438-446.

BLANCHET, Thérèse, PIIPPONENE, Risto & WESTMAN-CLÉMENT, Maria, **The Agreement on the European Economic Area (EEA): A Guide to the Free Movement of Goods and Competition Rules**, Clarendon Press, Oxford, 1994.

BOULOUIS, J., *"Les Avis de la Cour de Justice des Communautés sur la compatibilité avec le Traité CEE du projet d'accord créant l'Espace Economique Européen"*, in : **Revue trimestrielle de droit européen**, 1992, pp.457-463.

BUREAU DE L'INTÉGRATION, *Suisse-Union européenne. Négociations bilatérales sectorielles*, Fact sheets, Bureau de l'intégration DFAE/DFEP, Berne, 1996.

CONSEIL FÉDÉRAL, *Rapport intermédiaire du Conseil fédéral sur la politique d'intégration européenne de la Suisse*, Feuille fédérale, Volume III, No.191, Berne, 29 March 1995.

CONSEIL FÉDÉRAL, *Message du Conseil fédéral sur le programme consécutif au rejet de l'accord sur l'Espace économique européen*, Berne, 24 February 1993.

CONSEIL FÉDÉRAL, *Accord sur l'Espace économique européen et accords conclus en relation avec l'accord sur l'EEE*, Feuille fédérale, Volume IV, No.33, Berne, 1992a.

CONSEIL FÉDÉRAL, *Rapport sur la question d'une adhésion de la Suisse à la Communauté européenne*, Berne, 18 May 1992(b).

CREMONA, M., *"The Dynamic and Homogeneous EEA: Byzantine Structures and Variable Geometry"*, in: **European Law Review**, 1994, pp.508-526.

DUTHEIL DE LA ROCHERE, Jacqueline, *"L'EEE sous le regard des juges de la Cour de Justice des Communautés européennes"*, in : **Revue du Marché commun et de l'Union européenne**, No.360, Éditions Techniques et Économiques, Paris, 1992, pp.603-612.

EFTA, *1995 EFTA. Thirty-Fifth Annual Report*, Brussels, 1996.

EFTA COURT, *Report of the EFTA Court, 1 January 1994-30 June 1995*, 1995.

EFTA SURVEILLANCE AUTHORITY, *Annual Report '95*, EFTA, Brussels, 1996.

EFTA AGREEMENT ON A SURVEILLANCE AUTHORITY AND AN EFTA COURT, *Commercial Laws of Europe*, Vol.15, Part 10, The European Law Centre at Sweet and Maxwell, London, 1992.

FELDER, Daniel, *"Structure institutionnelle et procédure décisionnelle de l'EEE (Articles 89-114 AEEE)"*, in : JACOT-GUILLARMOD, Olivier (ed.), **Accord EEE : commentaires et réflexions**, Schulthess Polygraphischer Verlag, Zürich, 1992.

FRISCH, Jürgen-Gert & MEYER, Anne-Catherine, *"Le Traité sur l'Espace Économique Européen : cadre juridique d'une Europe du deuxième cercle"*, in : **Revue du Marché commun et de l'Union européenne**, No.360, Éditions Techniques et Économiques, Paris, 1992, pp.596-602.

FRIEDLÄNDER, Ralph, *"Integrationspolitische Wege der Schweiz im Vergleich"*, in: **Europa 2'96**, 1996, pp.4-7.

HJELM-WALLEN, Lena, *"Au sein de l'EEE nous n'avions pas d'influence !"*, in: **Europa 2'96**, 1996, p.8.

JACOT-GUILLARMOD, Olivier (ed.), **Accord EEE : commentaires et réflexions**, Schulthess Polygraphischer Verlag, Zürich, 1992.

JACOT-GUILLARMOD, Olivier, *"Droit international et Droit communautaire dans le futur Traité instituant l'EEE"*, in : **Aussenwirtschaft**, Heft III/IV, Verlag Rüegger, Zürich, 1991, pp.85-108.

KAHIL, Bettina, *Suisse-Europe : mesurer le possible, viser à l'essentiel : aspects politiques et juridiques des négociations bilatérales*, Centre Patronal, Lausanne, 1995.

KELLENBERGER, Jakob, *"Switzerland in the New European Architecture"*, in: **Aussenwirtschaft**, Heft III/IV, Verlag Rüegger, Zürich, 1991, pp.67-84.

KLAU, Thomas, *"EEA Emerges from the Doldrums"*, in: **European Voice**, 1-7 August 1996, pp.12-13.

LIPENS DE CERF, Paul & ARACHTINGI, Thierry, *"Présentation générale de l'Accord sur l'Espace Économique Européen"*, in : **Revue des Affaires européennes**, No.4, LGDJ, 1992, pp.23-42.

MARESCEAU, Marc & MONTAGUTI, Elisabetta, *"The Relations between the European Union and Central and Eastern Europe: A Legal Appraisal"*, in: **Common Market Law Review**, 1995, pp.1327-1367.

NELL, Philippe G., *"Liechtenstein Strategy for joining the European Economic Area while Remaining Part of the Swiss Monetary Union"*, in: **Aussenwirtschaft**, Heft I, Verlag Rüegger, Zürich, 1996, pp.101-124.

NELL, Philippe G., *"Rules of Origin: Problems and Solutions to the Swiss Non-Participation in the European Economic Area"*, in: **Journal of World Trade**, Volume XXVIII, No.6, 1994.

NORBERG, Sven, HOKBORG, K., JOHANSSON, M., ELIASSON, D. & DEDICHEN, L., **EEA Law: A Commentary on the EEA Agreement**, Kluwer and Taxation Publishers and CE Fritzes AB, Stockholm, 1993.

NORBERG, Sven, *"The Agreement on a European Economic Area"*, in: **Common Market Law Review**, No.29, 1992(a), pp.1171-1198.

NORBERG, Sven, *"The European Economic Area: The Legal Answers to a Dynamic and Homogeneous EEA"*, in: **European Business Law Review** No.3(7), 1992(b), pp.195-200.

PEDERSEN, Thomas, **European Union and the EFTA Countries. Enlargement and Integration**, Pinter, London, 1994.

PERSSON, Jan, *"Norway and the EEA"*, in: EMS Emil (ed.), **Thirty-five Years of Free Trade in Europe. Messages for the Future**, European Free Trade Association, Geneva, 1995, pp.64-67.

SCHWOK, René, *"Switzerland: The European Union's Self-appointed Pariah"*, in: REDMOND John (ed.), **Prospective Europeans: New**

Members for the European Union, Harvester Wheatsheaf, New York/ London, 1994, pp.19-39.

SCHWOK, René, *"The European Free Trade Association: Revival or Collapse?"*, in: REDMOND John (ed.), **The External Relations of the European Community. The International Response to 1992**, Macmillan Press, London, 1992, pp.55-76.

SOCIÉTÉ POUR LE DÉVELOPPEMENT DE L'ÉCONOMIE SUISSE (SDES), *Négociations bilatérales Suisse-Union européenne. État des lieux. Information Suisse-Europe*, Société pour le développement de l'économie suisse, Genève, 1996.

SOCIÉTÉ POUR LE DÉVELOPPEMENT DE L'ÉCONOMIE SUISSE (SDES), *Non à l'EEE : des conséquences qui se font toujours plus sentir. Information Suisse-Europe, # 10,* Société pour le développement de l'économie suisse, Genève, 1996.

STUYCK, J. & LOOIJESTIJN-CLEARIE, A. (eds), **The European Economic Area EC-EFTA. Institutional Aspects and Financial Services**, Kluwer Law and Taxation Publishers, Deventer/Boston, 1994.

SVERDRUP, Ulf, *"Governing Institutional Adaptation — Europeanisation of Norwegian Administration"*, paper presented at the Second Pan-European Conference in International Relations, Fondation Nationale des Sciences Politiques, Paris, 13-16 September 1995.

TREUMER, Steen, *"The EFTA Court"*, in: **EIPASCOPE**, No.2, European Institute of Public Administration, 1994, pp.2-4.

WIJKMAN, Per M., *"The Winding Voyage to and beyond the EEA"*, in: EMS Emil (ed.), **Thirty-five Years of Free Trade in Europe. Messages for the Future**, European Free Trade Association, Geneva, 1995, pp.171-190.

ZILLER, Jacques & BROUANT Jean-Philippe, *"L'EEE : une Europe à dix-sept"*, in : **Problèmes politiques et sociaux** No.728, La Documentation française, 1994.

COMMENTS

JONAS W. MYHRE

Supreme Court Advocate,
HJÖRT Law Office DA, Brussels/Oslo

A. The EEA-Agreement — A Status Report

The EEA Agreement was concluded in May 1992 and came into force on January 1st, 1994 with the following EFTA countries participating: Austria, Finland, Iceland, Norway and Sweden. As of January 1st, 1995 only Iceland and Norway remained. In May 1995 Liechtenstein also joined as Party to the EEA Agreement.

This means that presently there is a two pillars system with the EU and 15 Member States representing a total population of approximately 380 million on one side and three countries with a total of approximately 4.5 million representing the EFTA pillar. The imbalance is striking. In spite of that, the EEA Agreement is functioning. Norwegian enterprises have gained access to the EU's Internal Market. The possibility of using anti-dumping measures against Norwegian entities has been abolished, with the possible exception of e.g. the fisheries sector, and Norwegian entities can compete in the European Market as far as public procurement is concerned. The EFTA Surveillance Authority has been performing according to Community law in full cooperation with the Commission. The EFTA Court has already delivered decisions showing that the EFTA Court is fully in line with the Court of Justice's interpretations[1].

---

[1] EFTA Court Case E-1/94 *Ravintoloitsijain Liiton Kustannus OY Restamark* on interpretation of Art. 11 EEA Agreement — Import monopoly of alcoholic beverages, and Case E-2/1994 *Scottish Salmon Growers Association Ltd.* — annulment of ESA's decision to refuse to act on a complaint of State Aid to Norwegian salmon industry.

B. The Fundamental Premise

1. Factual Starting Point

The subject of the study of the comparison is a treaty which is in effect — the EEA Agreement — and seven bilateral treaties between the EU and Switzerland which are under negotiation. The same approach is taken here as in the paper by Schwok and Bonte, that the seven bilateral agreements will indeed be ratified and come into effect, although the assertion that the bilateral agreements will never be concluded is noted[2].

2. Legal Starting Point

The legal point of departure is that the study confirms the basic legal concept that access to the whole or specific sectors of the Internal Market of the European Community is dependent upon acceptance of Community law, *acquis communautaire* and a system of enforcement to secure implementation of the *acquis*.

C. Main Features

1. The Balance between National Sovereignty and Supranational Authority

- The EEA Agreement confers no rights or obligations directly on individuals. Such rights and obligations are dependent upon a parliamentary authorized national incorporation procedure[3].
- The EEA Agreement can be seen as offering a balance between national sovereignty and supranational authority. The Agreement does not directly confer any authority over Norwegian individuals to Community institutions.
- On the other hand, Norway has had to accept some supranational authority in the way of enforcement. To this end the EFTA states were obliged to establish an independent surveillance authority, the EFTA Surveillance Authority and an EFTA Court[4].
- It would seem that the overriding interest on part of Switzerland is in maintaining Switzerland's "self-determination" and taking into consideration Switzerland's comprehensive use of

---

[2] See the Schwok and Bonte's contribution.

[3] See EEA Agreement Arts 7, 103 and 129.

[4] See EEA Art.108 and the Agreement of November 27, 1992 on the setting up of a surveillance authority and an EFTA Court (ODA Agreement).

referendums. Under these circumstances one should not be aston-
ished that negotiations between Switzerland and the EU are difficult and, so far, have not succeeded.

- It is of some interest, however, that in the field of air transport,
  Switzerland will have to accept the European Commission's decisions as binding[5].

2. Involvement in the Decision Shaping Process

It is a remarkable feature of the EEA Agreement that even if the EFTA
states do not relinquish their sovereignty as far as the legislative process
is concerned, the EFTA states have a right to be heard and give advice to
the Commission in the same way as the Commission seeks advice from
experts of the EC Member States when elaborating proposals[6]. There is
a further right of exchange of views within the EEA Joint Committee on
Commission proposals[7]. As duly noted in the paper, there is no corresponding benefit granted to Switzerland under the bilateral agreements[8].

3. The Dynamic Aspect

- Article 102 of the EEA Agreement states that the EEA Joint Committee shall take a decision on any new Community legislation
  within the framework of the agreement for making such amendment part of the EEA Agreement.
- The nonexistence of such a dynamic aspect in the CH-EU agreements[9], would seem to constitute a major obstacle to the smooth
  running of the agreement over a period of time.

4. On the Four Freedoms of Movement

- The real test of the possible free movement of goods is whether
  such free movement is available also to non-harmonized sectors.
  It such be noted that such access is not granted to Switzerland
  according to the CH-EU agreements[10]. Here the nonexistence of
  sufficient surveillance is, not surprisingly, used as an argument
  on part of the EU.

---

[5] See the Schwok and Bonte's contribution.
[6] See EEA Agreement Art.99.
[7] See EEA Agreement Art.102.
[8] See the Schwok and Bonte's contribution.
[9] See the Schwok and Bonte's contribution.
[10] See the Schwok and Bonte's contribution.

- This comment can be interpreted as indirectly confirming that in the harmonized fields, Switzerland will adhere to the EU harmonized rules.

- The fact that most services are not included in the CH-EU agreements, including the free movement of capital and, thus far, the free movement of persons should be noted. The latter has so far been stated as the main obstacle towards a conclusion and ratification of the agreements[11].

D. Lessons to be Learned

1. Positive Elements

- The overriding positive element is that the EEA Agreement has secured access for its signatories to the main part of the Community's Internal Market, with agricultural and fish products being the main exceptions.

2. Negative Elements

- The EEA Agreement has created a somewhat paradoxical situation for Norway because it has not accepted relinquishing its national sovereignty as far as the legislative process is concerned. Norway has consequently required formal decisions by the Norwegian Parliament and/or administrative bodies of EU legislative decisions. These decisions will, however, in the majority of the cases be mere rubber-stamping of EU legislation in which Norway is not allowed to take part, except some input to the Commission's proposal, as previously mentioned.

- With specific reference to interpretations by the Court of Justice, it should be noted that the EEA Agreement explicitly draws up the distinction between the decisions of the Court of Justice prior to and after the date of signature of the agreement[12]. Only decisions prior to signature of the agreement, that is to say prior to Máy 2, 1992, are directly binding for *inter alia* the EFTA Court, EFTA Surveillance Authority (ESA) and the Norwegian authorities in their implementation and interpretation of the EEA Agreement. Decisions after such date are not specifically dealt with in

---

[11] See the Schwok and Bonte's contribution. See also *European Voice* 26.09.-02.10.1996 *("Toughest nuts" still to crack in EU-Swiss talks")*.

[12] See EEA Agreement Art.6.

the EEA Agreement. However, the ODA[13] Agreement (Art.3 No.2) states that later judgements are to be sufficiently taken into consideration. Based on performance until now, the overriding principle of creating and maintaining a homogeneous area with uniform interpretation and application of the agreement and secondary legislation, has prevailed. This would seem to indicate that decisions by the Court of Justice *de facto* will be adhered to. This is, however, not necessarily a negative point. The interesting situation is whether it will be the other way around, that is to say that the Court of Justice will put the same emphasis on judgements or opinions delivered by the EFTA Court. Such a test may be given in the not too far future.

Conclusion

This exercise, as performed, shows the interesting feature that different countries may approach the EU and still obtain solutions which are defined as in accordance with that third country's best interests.

The possibility that ten years from now there will be three countries with specific and separate arrangements with EU: Switzerland, Norway and Albania should not be excluded.

For the CEECs and MCs, the assertion that the EEA Agreement or the CH-EU agreements offer a better solution than the European agreements which for instance the CEECs have concluded is not convincing[14]. The EEA Agreement may be considered too cumbersome, actually taking on the *aquis communautaire*, without getting any real say in the decision making process. The CH-EU agreements may be considered to be too limited in scope and too complicated to practice over a period of years.

It should be concluded that there is no easy access to the Community's Internal Market.

---

[13] "ODA" is the Norwegian abbreviation of the ESA/EFTA Court Agreement of May 2, 1992, establishing the EFTA Surveillance Authority (ESA) and the EFTA Court.

[14] See e.g. Agreement between EU and Slovakia of 31.12.1994 - **OJ** L-359/94.

THE EUROPEAN UNION AND CENTRAL AND EASTERN EUROPE

Marc MARESCEAU[*]

Director, Europees Instituut, University of Ghent

1. Introduction

It is a difficult exercise to summarize the complex legal relationships which have been established between the European Community/European Union and the Central and Eastern European countries[1]. Prior to the dissolution of the COMECON the situation was relatively simple. Political and legal obstacles prevented the establishment of an agreed framework of trade relations between the European Community and COMECON or individual COMECON countries. Except for the bilateral EC-Romania trade agreement of 1980 and a number of bilateral trade "arrangements" on imports of a limited number of specific "sensitive" goods originating in some COMECON countries, trade relations were to a large extent determined by the Community through autonomous commercial policy regulations. In this respect the basic regulations on imports of goods originating in state-trading countries were the leading points of reference. The main characteristic of this import regime was

---

[*] This text is an adapted and updated version of a contribution previously edited by KONSTADINIDIS, *The Legal Regulation of the European Community's External Relations after the Completion of the Internal Market*, Dartmouth, Aldershot, 1996. The author would like to express his thanks to the editor for the permission to reproduce large parts of this text.

[1] In this contribution the expression "Central and Eastern Europe" or "Central and Eastern European countries" refers to the geographical area which belonged to the former European COMECON countries. Neither the countries which belonged to former Yugoslavia — except Slovenia — nor Albania are incorporated in this paper.

the application of a strict quota system ("QRs") reinforced by the active use of Article 115 EEC Treaty derogations. Imports into the Community were furthermore largely affected by an active anti-dumping policy *vis-à-vis* goods originating in state-trading countries[2].

After the coming to power of Gorbachev, the atmosphere of the relationships between the European Community on the one hand and the COMECON and its members on the other gradually began to change. One of the last acts of COMECON as an international organization before being dissolved was the signing of the "Joint Declaration" with the European Community on mutual recognition (June 1988)[3] and in September 1988 the European Community signed the first **Agreement on Trade and Commercial and Economic Cooperation** with (socialist) Hungary. This agreement provided, *inter alia,* for a gradual elimination of QRs which, despite the slow pace of elimination, was a considerable conceptual modification of the Community's previous approach towards state-trading countries.

The fundamental political and economic changes which occurred in Poland and other former COMECON countries meant that the EC-Hungary Agreement could be used as a ready-made model for the establishment of bilateral relations with other countries in Central and Eastern Europe. By October 1990 the Community had established a whole network of bilateral trade and economic cooperation agreements with all the European countries which had formerly belonged to COMECON, including the USSR. Nevertheless, irrespective of how interesting and even revolutionary these agreements might have looked under the old East-West conflictual relationships, with the profound political and economic changes taking shape in Central and Eastern Europe, they were virtually outdated before they even entered into force. The Community became aware of this anomaly and tried to develop a policy whereby some of the most urgent needs for reform in the Central and Eastern European countries could be satisfied. This unilateral Community policy towards the countries concerned, which became known

---

[2] For an analysis of EC-COMECON trade relations, see MASLEN J., *"The European Community's Relations with the State-trading Countries 1981-1983"*, in: **Yearbook of European Law**, 1983, pp.323-346 and by the same author for the years 1984-1986, **Yearbook of European Law**, 1986, pp.335-356; MARESCEAU M., *"A General Survey of the Current Legal Framework of Trade Relations Between the European Community and Eastern Europe"*, in: MARESCEAU M., (ed.), **The Political and Legal Framework of Trade Relations Between the European Community and Eastern Europe**, Martinus Nijhoff, Dordrecht/Boston/London, 1989, p.320.

[3] **OJ** 1988 L 157, p.35.

under the acronym "PHARE", resulted, *inter alia,* in the abolition of the specific QRs in the field of trade and the suspension of the nonspecific ones[4].

However, all these measures could not prevent the growth of much higher expectations in the countries of Central and Eastern Europe, some of whose political leaders expressed the hope for their countries even to become members of the Community. It was against this new background that the Commission published its Communication of August 27, 1990 on the conclusion of **Association Agreements** — called **Europe Agreements** — with countries from Central and Eastern Europe. Association Agreements were seen by the Community as a workable legal framework to develop a new political climate in Europe, to help create the appropriate conditions for trade and investment, to stimulate the transition to a market economy and to develop financial stability and human and cultural cooperation[5].

The first Europe Agreements were signed with Hungary, Poland and the Czech and Slovak Federal Republic on December 16, 1991. However, due to the split of the Czech and Slovak Federal Republic, the agreement of December 16, 1991 had to be renegotiated. New separate Europe Agreements with the Czech Republic on the one hand and with the Slovak Republic on the other were signed on October 4, 1993. Europe Agreements were signed with Romania on February 1st, 1993 and with Bulgaria on March 8, 1993. With the Baltic States similar agreements were also agreed upon on June 15, 1995[6]. The circle of the Europe Agreements was closed on June 10, 1996 with the signature of the agreement with Slovenia[7].

Europe Agreements are based on Article 238 of the EC Treaty and since they cover areas going beyond the Community's competences, they are of a mixed nature. Mixed agreements need ratification by the Member States of the Community. However, in order not to postpone the implementation of the trade chapter of the Europe Agreements, separate

---

[4] See LEQUESNE C., *"Commerce et aide économique : les instruments d'une politique"*, in : DE LA SERRE F., LEQUESNE C. & RUPNIK J., (eds), **L 'Union européenne. Ouverture à l'Est ?**, PUF, Paris, 1994, pp.50-63.

[5] On this evolution, see in particular DE LA SERRE F., *"A la recherche d'une Ostpolitik"*, in : **L'Union européenne : ouverture à l'Est ?**, *op.cit.,* note 4, pp.11-41.

[6] For text: COM (1995) 207 final.

[7] For text: COM (1995) 341 final. The signature of this agreement had been delayed because Italy was dissatisfied with the treatment of Italian minorities and Italian property in Slovenia after the Second World War.

Interim Agreements on trade and trade-related matters were signed parallel or almost parallel to the signature of the Europe Agreements. These Interim Agreements entered into force on March 1st, 1992 as far as Hungary, Poland and the Czech and Slovak Federal Republic were concerned[8]. The dissolution of the Czech and Slovak Federal Republic did not interrupt the application of the Interim Agreement signed on December 16, 1991 with that country. The Interim Agreement with Romania[9] entered into force on May 1st, 1993, while the one with Bulgaria suffered delays due to divergence of views in the Council concerning the common commercial policy instruments, but finally entered into force on January 1st, 1994[10]. The Europe Agreements with Poland and Hungary entered into force on February 1st, 1994[11], while those with the Czech Republic[12], the Slovak Republic[13], Bulgaria[14] and Romania[15] entered into force on February 1st, 1995. They have now replaced all the Interim Agreements with these countries. For the Baltic States the situation is slightly different. At the moment of writing the Europe Agreements with those countries have not yet entered into force. Since the EC had already signed on July 19, 1994 free trade agreements with the Baltic States[16] — replacing the Trade, Commercial and Economic Cooperation Agreements of 1992[17] — the conclusion of Interim Agreements with these countries became superfluous. As regards Slovenia an Interim Agreement signed on November 11, 1996 governs trade and trade-related matters and entered into force on January 1st, 1997[18].

One of the main differences between the first round of Europe Agreements and those signed later is that in the latter reference is made in the Preamble to the need to respect not only the rule of law and human rights, but also "the rights of persons belonging to minorities". Moreover, the agreements signed after the first round contain in their text a provision

---

[8] The text of these Interim Agreements was published in **OJ** 1992 L 114, L 115 and L 116 respectively.

[9] For text see: **OJ** 1993 L 81.

[10] For text see: **OJ** 1993 L 323.

[11] For text see: **OJ** 1993 L 348 (Poland); **OJ** 1993 L 347 (Hungary).

[12] For text see: **OJ** 1994 L 360.

[13] For text see: **OJ** 1994 L 359.

[14] For text see: **OJ** 1994 L 358.

[15] For text see: **OJ** 1994 L 357.

[16] For FTA with Estonia see: **OJ** 1994 L 373; Latvia, **OJ** 1994 L 374; Lithuania, **OJ** 1994 L 375.

[17] For text see: **OJ** 1992 L 403.

[18] For text see: **OJ** 1996 L 344.

according to which "respect for the democratic principles and human rights established by the Helsinki Final Act and the Charter of Paris for a New Europe, as well as the principles of a market economy, inspire the domestic and external policies of the Parties and constitute essential elements of the present association." (Article 6 in all agreements). In addition, all the Europe Agreements allow that "in cases of special urgency" the application of the agreements may be suspended unilaterally without prior consultation[19]. The Czech government, in particular, was not very happy with this modification as compared to the version of the first round of Europe Agreements[20]. Finally, a compromise was reached specifying the use of the "suspension clause". In a joint declaration to the agreement with the Czech Republic and with the Slovak Republic, it was stated that the term "cases of special urgency" included in Article 117 of their respective agreements with the European Communities meant a material breach of the agreement by one of the Parties. It was further specified that such a breach might consist, *inter alia,* of a violation of essential elements of the agreement, namely Article 6. In a unilateral declaration the Community explained the reasons for including an explicit reference to respect for human rights. In a declaration the Community stated that this reference was needed as a result of the Council Declaration of May 11, 1992 which foresaw such a reference in all cooperation and association agreements between the Community and its partners in CSCE.

The European Communities have also signed bilateral agreements with states which belonged to the former USSR, besides the Europe Agreements signed with the Baltic States. In 1994 the European Communities signed **Partnership and Cooperation Agreements** with Russia[21], Ukraine[22], Moldova[23] and in 1995 with Belarus[24]. Although at first sight, this category of agreements may in some respect appear similar to Europe Agreements, they are not intended to have the same ultimate

---

[19] See Europe Agreements with the Czech Republic (Article 117), the Slovak Republic (Article 117), Romania (Article 119), Bulgaria (Article 118), Estonia (Article 122), Latvia (Article 123), Lithuania (Article 124) and Slovenia (Article 123).

[20] See NYSSEN L., *"L'Ostpolitik de l'Union européenne à la lueur de l'Accord d'association avec la République tchèque"*, in : **Revue d'études comparatives Est-Ouest**, 1996, pp.24-25.

[21] For text see: COM (94) 257 final.

[22] See COM (94) 226 final.

[23] For text see: COM (94) 477 final.

[24] For text see: COM (95) 44 final.

political goal as is implied in the Europe Agreements and they do not refer to "accession". There are fundamental differences in other areas as well. For example, in the field of trade liberalization, the situation is substantially different from the Europe Agreements. Thus, the Partnership and Cooperation Agreements with Russia, Ukraine, Moldova and Belarùs only establish the prospect for a future free trade area but the achievement of this goal is made dependent upon a new evaluation of the situation in 1998. Other partnership agreements, such as those signed with the non-European former USSR Republics which have become independent states, are not examined here[25]. Nevertheless it must be noted that these agreements do not incorporate a free trade objective at all.

2. Europe Agreements as an Instrument for Accession

It is not the appropriate place here to enter into a detailed analysis of the accession issue but it cannot be denied that there is a special and intricate relationship between accession and trade liberalization in the Europe Agreements. Therefore, some fundamental steps with regard to accession of associated countries from Central and Eastern Europe will be briefly examined[26].

a) Accession: from a Unilateral to a Joint Objective

From the spirit and wording of the Commission's Communication of August 27, 1990 on association with Central and Eastern Europe[27], it is clear that Europe Agreements were seen as an alternative to accession. It was only in the course of the negotiations with Hungary, Poland and Czechoslovakia when some of these countries threatened to suspend the talks that the Community agreed to make an explicit reference to accession. But the legal significance of this reference remained limited: it was merely in the Preamble of these agreements that the Contracting Parties declared that the final objective of the associated country was to become a member of the Community and that, in the view of the Parties, association would help to achieve this goal. In other words, "accession" was seen and recognized by the Community as an ultimate goal of the associated country; nevertheless, in the Community's view, this objective was not necessarily the first aim of the Europe Agreements.

---

[25] For a comparison with Euro-Mediterranean Association Agreements, see the contribution by E. Lannon in this volume.

[26] For a more detailed analysis see the various contributions in: MARESCEAU (ed.), **Enlarging the European Union. Relations between the EU and Central and Eastern Europe**, Longman, London, 1997.

[27] COM (90) 398 final.

On the issue of "accession", however, the Community's approach towards the countries from Central and Eastern Europe, with whom Europe Agreements have been concluded, has fundamentally changed since the signing of the Europe Agreements, at least in its political formulation. At the Copenhagen Summit of June 21-22, 1993, the European Council unilaterally agreed "that the associated countries in Central and Eastern Europe that so desire shall become members of the European Union."[28] This means that accession became a mutual political goal of the Contracting Parties to the Europe Agreements. But accession will be possible only when a number of political, economic and legal conditions are satisfied and "will take place as soon as an associated country is able to assume the obligations of the membership satisfying the economic and political conditions required." This implies, according to the European Council, political stability, the guarantee of democracy, rule of law, human rights, respect for and protection of minorities, market economy and the capacity to cope with competitive pressure and market forces within the Union. Membership presupposes "the candidate's ability to take on the obligations of membership including adherence to the aims of political, economic and monetary union." On the other hand, for the Union it implies the necessary "capacity to absorb new members, while maintaining the momentum of European integration." The 1996 Intergovernmental Conference leading to the Treaty of Amsterdam *inter alia* has the difficult task of settling these institutional questions, after which the enlargement calendar will be reassessed and negotiations started.

It should be noted that "conclusions" of the European Council of Copenhagen or better "conclusions" of the Presidency as accepted by the European Council cannot on their own modify acts by the Council (of Ministers) or agreements concluded by the Community with third countries. Article D of the Treaty on European Union stipulates that "the European Council shall provide the Union with the necessary impetus for its development and shall define the general political guidelines thereof", while the European Council, as such, has no legislative capacity[29]. In other words, the political options of the European Council have to be implemented through legislative acts of the **European Communities**. This has been done, for example, with the Copenhagen Conclusions referring to trade liberalization (through acts of the Council and

---

[28] For text see: **Bull. EC**, 6-1993, point 1.13.

[29] On the status of the decisions of the European Council, see in general, WERTS J., **The European Council**, North Holland Elsevier, Amsterdam/London, 1992, pp.123-124.

Commission, see below, section 3). The Copenhagen Conclusions regarding "accession" have not led to a formal amendment of the preamble of the agreements or to the signing of an additional protocol between the European Communities and the associated countries; therefore they basically have a political significance.

Be that as it may, the Copenhagen Conclusions, further confirmed at subsequent European summits, are and remain important signals of change of EC policy regarding Central and Eastern Europe. This policy has in the past (too) often been one of "wait and see" so that the agreements which the Community prepared for these countries did not reflect adequately the expectations of the countries concerned: as discussed in the previous section, the trade and economic cooperation agreements signed between 1988 and 1990 were virtually outdated before they entered into force and the same almost happen to occur with the Europe Agreements. These agreements, even before being ratified, already needed a fundamental political reorientation and also an upgrading in the field of trade liberalization (see below, section 3).

The same may also hold true for the Partnership and Cooperation Agreements with Russia and other countries of the former USSR which have not generated great enthusiasm, but rather, and that is worse, frustration in some of the partner countries. Russia, in particular, seems or seemed to have doubts whether these agreements constitute a genuine and solid basis for "partnership" and "cooperation"[30]. Of course, there are many reasons which at least to some extent explain and justify the Community's present attitude to the former USSR and particularly Russia, but it is also an undeniable fact that the Community has at times demonstrated a lack of vision and coherence in its policy towards Central and Eastern Europe as a whole. Closely linked with this question is that of the actual definition of the concept "Central and Eastern Europe". The geopolitical implications of the now clear and distinct treatment of "Europe Agreements" as compared to "Partnership Agreements" within "Central and Eastern Europe" do not necessarily help to create the momentum for a stable and secure Europe on the eve of the 21st century. However, in the short term, this policy may prove to be the only workable one.

---

[30] See for example SHEMIATENKOV V., *"The Relations between Russia and the EU"*, to be published in: **Revue des Affaires européennes**, 1997. For a more positive approach, see BORKO Y., *"The New Intra-European Relations and Russia"*, in: **Enlarging the European Union. Relations between the EU and Central and Eastern Europe**, cited note 25, pp.376-390.

b) The Pre-accession Strategies:
Structured Relations and Approximation of Laws

As implemented and refined through the conclusions of the various European summits, Europe Agreements provide for a basis for "structured relations" between the institutions of the Union and the associated countries. These "structured relations" are to a certain extent a special form of "political dialogue" and they intend to create a "pre-accession atmosphere", whereby the associated countries are progressively involved in the activities of the European Union covering areas of common interest. Of course, it is expected that through these joint meetings working relationships between the Contracting Parties will be established and that the associated countries become gradually more familiar with the work of the European Union. The General Affairs Council Report to the Essen Summit[31] defined a programme of meetings which included, *inter alia,* an annual meeting on the margin of a European Council of the Heads of State and Government, semiannual meetings for ministers of Foreign Affairs of the European Union and ministers of the associated countries, and a variety of other meetings for ministers with common responsibilities. Other presidencies have largely organized similar programmes. Also joint meetings at other levels such as parliaments, experts, etc. were planned and have taken or are taking place. The objective of these different forms of structured dialogue is clear: it intends to develop with the partner practical experience in European Union affairs. However, these meetings, as such, have no legislative capacity except, of course, possible joint meetings organized within the proper institutional frameworks such as the Association Councils as set up through the Association Agreements[32]. These councils, like any association council, have the power to take decisions in the cases provided for in the respective agreements. Such decisions are binding on the Parties.

Another perhaps more important aspect of the pre-accession strategy lies in the legal preparation of the associated countries to be integrated in the Community's Internal Market. This implies for the associated countries the need to implement a vast and complex programme of approximation of laws, norms and standards. At the Cannes Summit of June 1995 the Commission presented a white paper on the approximation strategies

---

[31] See **Agence Europe**, December 14, 1994.

[32] The Association Committee may then have the same decision-making capacity as the Association Council, depending on how its competences have been formulated by the Association Council.

to be followed[33]. It may be true that this aspect of the "learning process" is neither the most pleasant nor the most stimulating one. Indeed the expression "approximation of laws" in the Europe Agreements is often nothing but a euphemistic formulation of a stringent requirement for the associated countries to adapt their laws and practices to those of the Community[34] and not *vice versa*. One of the main problems that the associated countries are faced with here is perhaps not even so much the degree of complexity of Community law itself, but the fact that, at the moment, still only a limited number of people in the associated countries are really familiar with the specificities of the Community legal system. There are important areas where approximation is needed including, in particular, competition rules and state aid, intellectual property and transport legislation. But they are by no means exhaustive: other areas such as customs law, company law, banking law, environment protection law, consumer protection law, etc. also need to be approximated. It should be noted that the approximation effort necessarily implies the establishment of control mechanisms ensuring compatibility of new domestic legislation in the associated countries with that of the Community and appropriate interministerial coordination units.

3. Legal Framework of Trade

The Europe Agreements aim at gradually establishing a free trade zone. This objective applies to all goods except agricultural goods. However, it should be noted that neither a customs union nor an internal market is created with the associated countries.

Trade liberalization is asymmetric, in the sense that the elimination of trade barriers on the part of the Community should be achieved more rapidly than on the part of the associated countries. The principle of free movement of goods is worked out in detail in the agreements and varies according to the category of goods covered. There is a chapter on

---

[33] For an analysis, see GAUDISSART M.-A. & SINNAEVE A, *"The Role of the White Paper in the Preparation of the Eastern Enlargement"*, in: **Enlarging the European Union. Relations between the EU and Central and Eastern Europe**, cited at note 26, pp.41-72.

[34] For an example in the field of competition law, see Article 6 of the Draft Decision of the EC-Hungary Association Council, Proposal for a Council and Commission Decision on the positions to be taken by the Community in the Association Council EC-Hungary with regard to the adoption of the necessary rules for the implementation of Article 62 of the Europe Agreement, COM (94) 639 final. This provision stipulates that the competition authorities in Hungary "shall ensure that the principles contained in the Block Exemptions Regulations in force in the EC shall be applied integrally."

"industrial goods" which also provides for special protocols for "textile products" and "products covered by the Treaty establishing the European Coal and Steel Community (ECSC)". The pace of liberalization of trade in industrial products is more rapid than for "sensitive" goods such as steel and textiles.

As a result of the implementation of the Copenhagen European Council conclusions, the pace of liberalization has been accelerated[35], while as a result of the Essen European Council there has been alignment in the field of trade liberalization of imports from Romania and Bulgaria with that of imports from the Visegrad countries[36].

a) The Principles of Trade Liberalization as Implemented by the Community

All the Europe Agreements provide for an immediate elimination by the Community of quantitative restrictions on industrial products, while tariffs had to be eliminated by January 1st, 1995 for imports from all the associated countries[37].

Trade liberalization in textile products covers tariff concessions and the gradual elimination of the quota system. As a result of the Copenhagen Summit conclusions, as implemented by various measures of the Council and the alignment measures of December 22, 1994, elimination of tariffs was set for the end of 1996, while textile quotas have to be eliminated by the end of 1997[38].

ECSC products are also covered by a specific protocol. Quotas for steel were removed when the Interim Agreements entered into force but tariff quotas remained applicable for a certain time on certain steel

---

[35] For a provisional application to Poland, Hungary, Czech Republic and Slovak Republic, see Council Decisions of July 19, 1993, **OJ** 1993 L 195/42; see also amendments introduced by Council Regulations of August 5, 1993, **OJ** 1993 L 200/1. For definitive application to all countries with whom Europe Agreements have been signed: Council and Commission Decisions of December 20, 1993 on the conclusion of Additional Protocols, **OJ** 1994 L 25/1 et seq.

[36] Implemented by Council Decision of December 22, 1994, **OJ** 1994 L 366/21.

[37] As far as imports from the Baltic States is concerned they were abolished when the Free Trade Agreement entered into force (see Art.4 of the three FTAs). For imports from Slovenia the principle is elimination from the date of entry of the Interim Agreement (January 1st, 1997), except for the products mentioned in Annex II for which the ultimate deadline is January 1st, 2000 (Art.4, §2, Interim Agreement).

[38] For Lithuania and Latvia negotiations are pending with a view of establishing a similar liberalization; for Estonia trade is already liberalized. For quantitative arrangements regarding exports of textile products originating in Slovenia, see Art.3, Protocol 1 on textile and clothing products, **OJ** 1996, L 344/39.

products originating in the Czech and Slovak Republics. They have now been removed[39]. However, the trend of trade flows for certain steel products continues to be sensitive and is closely followed by the Community through the application of a double-checking system[40]. Trade in coal products is also liberalized, but for certain specific coal products (lignite), quotas were applied by some Member States for a limited period of time.

As far as trade in agricultural goods is concerned quantitative restrictions are abolished and levies are reduced for many products but all trade barriers are not yet abolished. The basic idea is that the remaining barriers are further reduced through concessions "on a harmonious and reciprocal basis". The Europe Agreements also stipulate that it is the task of the Association Council to examine, on a product-by-product basis, whether further concessions can be granted. In doing so, the Association Council must take "account of the volume of trade in agricultural products between them, of their particular sensitivity, the rules of the common agricultural policy of the Community and the rules of agricultural policy of the [associated country] and of the consequences of the multilateral trade negotiations under the General Agreement on Tariffs and Trade." Moreover, the Europe Agreements provide that "given the particular sensitivity of the agricultural markets", imports of agricultural products which are subject to concessions but cause serious disturbance on the markets of the importing Party may be subject to immediate consultations between the Parties to find an appropriate solution. This consultation procedure does not prevent the Party concerned to take the measure it deems necessary.

It is not the proper place to make here an economic evaluation of the implementation of the provisions on trade in the agreements. It may suffice to mention that trade liberalization as organized in the Europe Agreements and accelerated as a result of the Copenhagen Summit is substantial and impressive; it has even been said that it is "without precedent in the EU"[41]. However, it must also be observed that the reality is somewhat

---

[39] There is also free trade in ECSC products with the Baltic States and with Slovenia.

[40] For steel originating in the Czech Republic, see Decision 2/96 of the Association Council of April 4, 1996, **OJ** 1996 L 133, renewed on December 20, 1996, **OJ** 1997, L 4. A similar mechanism is applicable for certain steel imports from the Slovak Republic, Bulgaria and Romania.

[41] *"Trade Liberalization with Central and Eastern Europe. An Assessment of the Interim Europe Agreements with Respect to Industrial Products"*, in: **European Economy**, July 1994, Supplement A.

more mixed[42]. Indeed, notwithstanding the asymmetry of commitments in the agreements, trade expansion in the first place seems to have been beneficial for EU exports and has even caused a considerable trade surplus for the EC[43]. It is, *inter alia,* this consideration which led to an acceleration of the trade liberalization measures at the Copenhagen Summit.

A last question to be mentioned in the field of trade concerns the use of commercial defence instruments. Europe Agreements, as opposed to the European Economic Area Agreement, do not preclude the taking of further anti-dumping and/or safeguard measures. Although since the entry into force of the Interim Agreements only a few anti-dumping measures have been taken by the Community, some of them have caused serious concern in the associated countries. On the Community side it is thought that the gradual incorporation of EC competition law and EC state aid policies into the legislation of associated countries will progressively reduce the need for the Community to apply commercial defence instruments. Awaiting this development, it is the Commission's policy to offer information to any associated country before the initiation of commercial defence proceedings and "to give, on a case-by-case basis, where appropriate, a clear preference to price undertakings rather than duties in order to conclude anti-dumping cases where injury is found."[44]

b) The Issue of Specific Protection for the Associated Countries

Besides the asymmetric structure of trade liberalization, Europe Agreements also allow associated countries to take "exceptional measures" for the protection of "infant industries" or "certain sectors undergoing restructuring or facing serious difficulties, producing important

---

[42] See for example INOTAI A., *"Central and Eastern Europe"*, in: RANDALL HENNING C., HOCHREITER E. & HUFBAUER Clyde J., (eds), **Reviving the European Union**, Institute for International Economics, Washington DC, 1994, pp.153-157; European Bank for Reconstruction and Development, *Economic Transition in Eastern Europe and the Former Soviet Union,* Transition Report, October 1994, pp.116-119.

[43] See **Agence Europe**, November 21-22, 1994, with statistical annex.

[44] Report from the Council to the Essen European Council on a strategy to prepare for the accession of the associated CEEC, **Agence Europe**, December 14, 1994. It must be noted that this willingness to inform the other Party is not something "new". It results already from the wording and spirit of the provisions on commercial defence contained in the Europe Agreements. For a comprehensive and recent analysis of the EC anti-dumping practice, see MONTAGUTI E, *"The Europe Agreements' Anti-Dumping Provisions in the EC-CEECs Relations"*, in: **Enlarging the European Union. Relations between the EU and Central and Eastern Europe**, cited note 26, pp.160-178.

social problems."[45] The measures taken under this clause must be transparent and must take the form of an increase in customs duties up to a maximum of 25 percent *ad valorem*. The total value of imports of the products subject to these measures may not exceed 15 percent of the total imports of industrial products from the Community. Moreover, in imposing such measures, the associated country "shall maintain an element of preference for products originating in the Community." Such measures cannot be taken for products for which all trade barriers have been eliminated for more than three years. The measures shall be applied for a maximum period of five years. The associated country must inform the Association Council of the measures it intends to take; if the measures are taken, the associated country should provide the Association Council with a schedule for the elimination of the customs duties introduced under this provision of the agreement. It should be noted that the Europe Agreements do not require an authorization from the Association Council before taking such measures. This means, at least from a strict legal point of view, that the associated countries are entitled to invoke unilaterally the provision of the agreement. Of course, these measures must remain "exceptional" and cannot be applied as an instrument of general economic policy. A frequent use of the "exceptional measures" clause would probably constitute a misleading signal to the Community that these countries cannot cope with one of the main objectives of the agreement, namely that of free trade.

Since the entry into force of the Interim Agreements, there have been a number of applications or attempts to make use of this provision. Hungary was one of the first associated countries to consider invoking the "exceptional measures" clause. A notorious case in this respect was the possible use of this clause to protect its infant car industry (Suzuki), but at the beginning of 1993 the Hungarian government presented an impressive list of other goods which were also thought to come under this provision of the agreement[46]. The Community's reaction was, as can be expected, not very enthusiastic. However, in the end, in late 1994, a limited number of tariff increases based on Article 28 were withheld in principle by the Hungarian government (including certain plant protective agents, certain glass products and printing paper)[47]. The very sensitive

---

[45] The provision is identical in all the Europe Agreements; see e.g. Article 28 in the Agreement EC-Hungary.

[46] A list of seventeen products was presented including several chemical products, glass, paper and tiles.

[47] The taking of the measures was discussed at the second EC-Hungary Association Council meeting. The concrete implementation of these measures proved to be

issue of taking infant industry protection for Japanese cars has not materialized[48]. Poland has also invoked this provision for a number of products in the telecommunications sector. While the impact of these measures remained rather limited those introduced in the oil sector in 1996 are of a more substantial importance[49]. On the whole there is the feeling that the Community is not very eager to allow the associated countries to make use of the "exceptional measures" clause. Therefore, before imposing higher tariffs, the associated country should not only make an evaluation of the potential short term benefits of the measure, but also examine the possible negative effect on its global relations with the Community. The fact that the Europe Agreements have also this highly political connotation gives a particular weight to the position of the European Community on a potential use of the "exceptional measures" provision. This was clearly demonstrated by the stainless steel casks case for which the Czech Republic invoked the infant protection provision of the Europe Agreement but where the European Community managed to dissuade the Czech authorities from taking the measure, particularly by insisting that if such measures were taken they had to contain "an element of preference for products originating in the Community."

Finally, also the possible use of trade protectionist measures for balance of payment purposes is not well received by the European Community. This became clear when in 1997 the Czech and Slovak authorities relied on Article 65 of their respective Europe Agreements to take protectionist measures in order to remedy the balance of payments. The European Commission for its part has not ruled out to have recourse to the dispute settlement procedure of the Europe Agreements.

---

complicated *inter alia* because of their effect on existing free trade agreements concluded by Hungary.

[48] No doubt, the reason for this is basically political.

[49] There is currently under discussion with Commission the intention of Poland to use Article 28 of the EA regarding certain steel imports.

The Proliferation of the European Union Rules on Free Trade in Central and Eastern Europe: Towards a Pan-European Integrated Market*

Stanislaw SOLTYSINSKI

Professor of Law, A. Mickiewicz University, Poznan;
Partner in S. Soltysinski, A. Kawecki & A. Szlezak,
Legal Advisors, Warsaw

1. The EEC Model and its "Mutants"

The Treaty of Rome and the Maastricht Agreement constitute the most advanced forms of free trade agreements within the meaning of Art.XXIV of GATT. The EEC/EU model of free trade agreement was subsequently "transplanted" into the consecutive versions of the association agreements signed between the European Communities and their Member States on the one side and several Southern European countries on the other side[1]. The association agreements made between the EU and several post-socialist countries in Central and Eastern European Countries (CEECs) are closely patterned after the EU free trade rules aimed at establishing a fully integrated European market. They include regulation of all important aspects of establishing and functioning of an advance form of an enlarged Single European Market (e.g. freedom of movement of goods, freedom of establishment and providing services,

---

* This contribution is an outline of the panel presentation.
[1] The EEC entered into several free trade agreements with Mediterranean countries (e.g. with Portugal, Spain, Greece, Cyprus, Malta and Israel).

freedom of movement of capital, competition rules, safeguards, etc.). The European Common Market model incorporated in the Treaty of Rome and further developed in the Maastricht Treaty has been transplanted not only in the Europe Agreements but also in the European Free Trade Association (EFTA), European Economic Area (EEA) and, recently, in the bilateral free trade agreements between EFTA countries and CEECs, as well as in the multilateral agreement established by several CEECs (Central European Free Trade Agreement, hereinafter "CEFTA"). Some solutions developed in the Treaty of Rome have been adopted by a multilateral agreement signed by Russia and a few former Soviet republics (Kazakhstan, Belorussia and Kirgizia).

2. The Comparison between the EU Single Market Concept and other European Free Trade Agreements

The impact of the Treaty of Rome on EFTA, EEA and the association agreements between the EEC and market economies of Southern Europe has been subject to many in-depth studies. I will limit my observation to European free trade agreements which include the participation of CEECs.

a) The Europe Agreements

The Europe Agreements established by the EU and CEECs[2] most closely resemble the European Community's model. Leaving apart the institutional arrangements, they differ from their archetype in several important respects also in the realm of free trade aspects. The "deviations" include, *inter alia*:

i)   "managed" trade in the field of agricultural goods and fisheries based upon orderly and reciprocal concessions;

ii)   no freedom of movement of people;

iii)   freedom of movement of employees in connection with provision of services is limited only to "key-personnel";

iv)   restrictions of the free trade principle in certain sensitive areas (steel, coal, textiles, maritime transportation services, etc.);

---

[2]   So far, such association agreements have been established with Poland, the Czech Republic, Hungary, Slovakia, Romania, Bulgaria and Slovenia. Less comprehensive free trade agreements were signed between the EU and the Baltic States (1995) and Albania (1995). See generally M. MARESCEAU & E. E. MONTAGUTI, *"The Relations between the EU and CEEC: A Legal Appraisal"*, in: **Common Market Law Review** No.32, 1995, at 1327 et seq.

v) the European Union's pace of reduction of tariff and non-tariff barriers is faster than that of the association countries;

vi) parties to the Europe Agreements are free to apply anti-dumping, antisubsidy, antitrust and market disruption measures on their own, pursuant to each side's substantive laws but subject to mutually agreed legal standards set forth in the Europe Agreements;

vii) the association countries are allowed to apply unilateral safeguards to protect industries undergoing restructuring or suffering from serious difficulties, as well as to protect their infant industries[3];

viii) there are doubts whether the principles of freedom of parallel imports and international exhaustion of intellectual property rights apply to trade between the EU and the association countries[4].

Is it debatable whether the Europe Agreements are based on the concept of asymmetry of rights and obligations in favour of the association countries when in the long run all deviations from the principle of free trade protect "sensitive industries" in the EU and limit exports of CEECs in areas where the labour cheap economies enjoy actual or potential comparative advantage (e.g. agricultural products, fisheries, steel, labour intensive products)? Apart from that the Europe Agreements drastically restrict the ability CEECs firms to benefit from the principle of providing services by restricting their ability to use cheap labour. Likewise, the benefits of the EU intellectual property owners resulting from the strengthening of their rights in the CEECs are not balanced by extension of the principle of freedom of parallel imports and international exhaustion to the association countries.

b) The Agreements between EFTA and CEECs

Agreements between CEECs economies and the EFTA countries are also typical free trade agreements. They are closely patterned after the Europe Agreements. Some of their provisions constitute verbatim

---

[3] These safeguards are subject to several constraints and have limited duration. In practice, they must be negotiated and approved by the EU, as demonstrated in the case of Poland's application of Art.28 of Poland-EU Association Agreement measures to protect its oil and steel sectors.

[4] See generally S. SOLTYSINSKI, *"International Exhaustion of Intellectual Property Rights under the TRIPS, the EC Law and the Europe Agreements"*, **GRUR**, 1996, at 316 et seq.

repetitions of the Europe Agreements. The main differences between the two types of free trade agreements can be summarized as follows:

   i) the EFTA/CEECs free trade treaties regulate exclusively economic cooperation, except for some provisions dealing with harmonization of rules of origin, tax regulations and protection of intellectual property;

   ii) the Central and Eastern European signatory states are not required to adopt EFTA legal standards.

c) CEFTA

The EFTA/CEECs free trade agreements have been copied by the founding members of the CEFTA. The agreement entered into force in 1994. After a slow start, the latter free trade agreement has become a key instrument of cooperation between the former satellites of the Soviet Union in Central Europe. The four founding Member States have been joined by Slovenia in 1997. Romania, Bulgaria, Croatia and the Baltic states are potential members of the new free trade area.

Except for rules relating to agricultural policies, which are based on the principle of "managed" reciprocal concessions, the remaining CEFTA arrangements mirror the Europe Agreements and bilateral free trade agreements with EFTA. In some areas, CEFTA contains a few new rules having no equivalents in the former agreements, such as the obligation to notify the other parties about draft technical regulations and draft amendments pertaining to matters affecting free trade (Art.10), the obligation to refrain from introducing any new sanitary and phytosanitary measures that have the effect of unduly obstructing trade (Art.15)[5] and a broadly defined general safeguard clause in addition to those safeguards which exist in the Europe Agreement (Art.14).

CEFTA has become an important free trade agreement for the CEECs. In 1995 imports from the CEFTA countries into Poland increased by almost 100 percent while exports grew by 60 percent. Despite the adoption of the managed trade principle in the field of agricultural products in the Europe Agreements, the signatory states succeeded in eliminating or lowering tariffs for a number of goods in this area. Furthermore, the

---

[5] This obligation was introduced in an effort to limit the abuse of such measures as a non-tariff barrier but CEFTA also contains a rule patterned after Art.36 of the Single European Act which permits application of non-tariff measures justified on grounds of public morality, public policy or public security, the protection of health, animals or plants, etc.

CEFTA countries have achieved a consensus, in principle, that all tariffs for agricultural products should be removed by the end of 1998.

Conclusions

(i)   The free trade rules incorporated in the Single European Act have been successfully transplanted into a growing number of bilateral and multilateral free trade agreements, thus contributing to a gradual unification of the basic rules of economic cooperation among almost all countries of the European continent[6].

(ii)   The free trade rules with EEC origin and their interpretation by the Community institutions often function as precedents in the process of application and construction of the other European free trade agreements.

(iii) Coexistence of several free trade agreements in Europe raises a number of legal problems. For instance: some provisions of the Europe Agreements provide that while applying safeguard measures, an association country shall grant preference to EU exports[7]. Is compliance with such a requirement consistent with the nondiscrimination and the Most-Favoured Nation (MFN) obligations under the CEFTA? Likewise, Article 36 of the CEFTA provides that the latter agreement "shall not prevent the maintenance or establishment of customs unions, free trade areas or arrangements for frontier trade to the extent that these do not negatively affect the trade regime and, in particular, the provisions concerning rules of origin provided by this agreement." While the Europe Agreements contain more provisions requiring preferential treatment of the Community goods, services and firms, the CEFTA and other European free trade agreements have also adopted similar rules[8]. Let us assume that an association country granted a tariff preference to EU imports while applying safeguard measures to protect its infant industry under Art.28 of the Europe Agreement. Does it constitute a violation of the "twin" Art.28 of the CEFTA embodying the same requirement or Art.XXIV of GATT? Is the answer different if the increased tariff rates established by a given CEEC for EU imports are 10 percent, for CEFTA

---

[6] One should also mention the rise of bilateral free trade agreements in CEEC evidenced by the Poland-Lithuania Free Trade Agreement which entered into force on January 1st, 1997.

[7] See, for instance, Art.28 of Poland-EU Europe Agreement.

[8] For instance, Art.28 of CEFTA and Art.22.3 of EFTA-Poland Agreement.

imports 9 percent and for the remaining GATT countries 8 percent? Please note that in the latter case the required element of preference is assured but EU exporters are offered an extra preference *vis-à-vis* the EFTA and CEFTA competitors. Should we accept the proposition that all free trade partners of a country protecting its infant industry by increased customs duties are equal, but some of them, namely, the more powerful ones, are more equal? I think the answer should be in the negative. The famous Orwellian rationale that the most powerful *camerades* are "more equal" should not be tolerated in the emerging European free trade market. Therefore, imports from all free trade countries should be subject to the same tariffs and the requirement of preferential treatment should not lead to discrimination between various free trade partners.

Subregional Cooperation in Central and Eastern Europe, the Visegrád Declaration and the Central European Free Trade Agreement

Péter BALÁZS

Ambassador;
Professor, Budapest School of Economics

The Visegrád Declaration

After the collapse of the Council of Mutual Economic Aid (CMEA or Comecon) new perspectives of integration opened for the Central and East European Countries (CEECs). The main tool of integrating the CEECs with the world economy is the extension of the European Union, on the one hand, and a deep transformation of its external relations involving the CEECs not joining the EU, on the other. At the same time new groupings consisting partly or entirely of CEECs have taken form, too.

One of the first initiatives of this kind was the "Visegrád Declaration". Three countries leading the political and economic transformation process, namely Hungary, Poland and Czechoslovakia, signed a short political declaration on February 15, 1991. The solemn act took place in the ruins of the Visegrád castle in northern Hungary. At the same spot the kings of medieval Hungary, Poland and the Czech Kingdom met in 1355 and concluded a treaty on assuring and using jointly the trade route leading from North to South across the three countries.

The Visegrád Declaration of 1991 set as an objective a closer political and economic cooperation between the three participating countries. As to the political importance of the Declaration, one should highlight that at the moment of its signature the CMEA still existed, at least legally, and the Soviet Army was present in the country of the meeting of the three Heads of State, i.e. in Hungary. In 1991 Visegrád was the symbol of the regaining of national sovereignty by the rapidly transforming member states of the ex-Soviet empire.

As a matter of fact, western countries started the parallel development and the similar characteristics of the transformation process in the three above-mentioned transforming states even earlier than the political leaders of the same countries themselves. Strong economic support of the two front runners, Poland and Hungary, was decided on at the G7 Summit meeting in Paris on July 14, 1989. The PHARE Programme, launched by the European Communities on January 1st, 1990, commemorated the names of these two countries (PHARE : Poland and Hungary Assistance with Restructuring the Economy). The first signs of treating Czechoslovakia together with the above two states could be observed at the CSCE Economic Conference in March and April 1990 in Bonn. In June 1990 the EFTA signed a Joint Declaration with the same three countries foreseeing also the conclusion of free trade agreements. One year later, shortly after the signature of the Visegrád Declaration the OECD signed also a programme with these countries under the name of Partners In Transition (PIT).

The Central European Free Trade Agreement

The main result of the Visegrád Declaration was the conclusion of the first subregional preferential trade agreement between Central and East European Countries. The Central European Free Trade Agreement (CEFTA) was signed in Cracow, Poland on December 21, 1992 by Hungary, Poland, the Czech Republic and Slovakia.

The main objective of the CEFTA is to gradually establish free trade during a transitional period ending on January 1st, 2001. The scope of the agreement is larger than that of the Europe Agreements concluded on December 16, 1991 between the same states, on the one hand, and the EC, on the other. The CEFTA covers, in accordance with the provisions of Article XXIV of GATT, "substantially all trade", whereas the Europe Agreements are limited to the trade of industrial goods (Chapters 25 to 97 of the Harmonized Commodity Description and Coding System), i.e. excluding agriculture from the preferential treatment.

In the CEFTA, basic duties were those applied on February 29, 1992 (the same as in the Europe Agreements of these countries). Provisions on the abolition of customs duties are contained in three bilateral protocols attached to the agreement (the Czech Republic and Slovakia constituted one single customs territory).

The provisions and the structure of the CEFTA reflect the generally accepted content of agreements of this kind concluded under the aegis of GATT. At the same time, they show great similarity to the Europe Agreements (e.g. on state aid, protection of industrial property, rules of origin, etc.). A striking resemblance is the special clause of "structural adjustment", i.e. the protection of infant or restructuring industries (Article 28 of CEFTA) which is a correct copy of the famous "infant industry clause" of the Europe Agreements. The harmony of the "building blocks" of a future all European preferential zone is, without any doubt, a positive development. However, the time table foreseen by the CEFTA to reaching gradually free trade seem to be rather cautious. Neither the rather unimportant market share nor any imminent danger of mutual market disturbances would have supported this cautious approach. Two main reasons can be identified behind the trade policy of the Contracting Parties. On the one hand, the Europe Agreements, of vital importance for the CEECs in question, were signed earlier but they were still under ratification at the moment of concluding the CEFTA negotiations. For obvious reasons, the CEECs concerned did not want to question the provisions of the Europe Agreements by subscribing to other dispositions and wordings in a parallel agreement. On the other hand, they could not read the future as to the further development of economic transition with a special regard to the eventual need of protecting one or another sector of their industry or agriculture. The signatories of the CEFTA, still inspired by the obvious contradiction between the limited market share and the lengthy transitional period, added a Joint Declaration to the CEFTA on the day of its signature on speeding up the implementation of measures foreseen by the agreement. They decided to initiate immediately negotiations under the auspices of the Joint Committee in order to discuss the reduction of the transitional period to five years and to abolish all tariff and non-tariff barriers including both industrial and agricultural products.

Motivations and Forms of Subregional Cooperation

The Visegrád Declaration, and more particularly the Cracow Declaration of October 6, 1991, contained some far reaching objectives, too. The joint development of infrastructure in order to include the "V4" countries into the mainstreams of European transport, telecommunication and energy networks was a realistic goal. At the same time neither the national economies of the participating states nor the level of their economic cooperation were ripe for a "monetary union" or the "free movement of labour". After a short period of enthusiastic subregional integration, governments of the individual Visegrád states took a divergent political movement as to their integration objectives and methods. They made parallel efforts in order to prove their "first place" in the transition process and to be "the first member" of the EU in the region. This erroneous "zero sum game" approach characterized the behaviour of the CEFTA states in the first three-four years of the implementation of the agreement. The only excuse for such a policy is the important difference between the market shares of the EU and the CEFTA countries, the first being about ten times higher than the latter in the overall foreign trade figures of the "V4". For this reason, the Visegrád cooperation did not create any permanent executive body. Its meetings have been organized in turn by the host country. After the conclusion of the CEFTA the Visegrád cooperation did not deepen, but external pressure has grown for its enlargement. Slovenia has joined the agreement and by the end of 1996 the CEFTA had started negotiations with Romania.

In the Central and East European region there is an obvious need for a closer subregional cooperation. Opening markets, disrupted infrastructure networks, serious environment protection problems, and social and ethnic tensions could better be dealt with in such a framework. Subregional integration is not in contradiction to a larger, all European structure based on the European Union. On the contrary, good relations between immediate neighbours are the stepping stones towards larger dimensions of integration. The EU regards the good neighbourliness of the candidate countries as an important precondition of the accession.

The collapse of the Soviet empire (Warsaw Pact and CMEA), on the one hand, and the slow and inadequate reactions of the EU to the sweeping transformation process in its direct neighbourhood, on the other hand, created a political and institutional vacuum in Central and Eastern Europe. This vacuum gave birth, among others, to a multiplication of various subregional initiatives. New structures are taking shape in three geographical areas: Central and Eastern Europe, the Baltic Sea region and the Black Sea region. In Central and Eastern Europe the Pentagonal (transformed into Hexagonal) and later on the rapidly growing number of the participating countries of the Central European Initiative (involving also the CEFTA states) is partly overlapping with the idea of a new South European Cooperation Initiative (SECI). All this reflects the uncertainties of the subregional dimension of integration in the transforming countries.

The main characteristics of the subregional initiatives and organizations in the Central and East European region are the following :

-   all or most participating countries are Central and East European states, in some structures EU members and other countries directly neighbouring with the CEECs are also involved;
-   objectives and financial means of most organizations are not clarified;
-   the number of participating countries in most initiatives shows a growing tendency;
-   an abundance of partly overlapping organizations is to be observed.

Consequently one and the same country can be a member of two, three or even more structures in its own region, most of them without clear objectives and organizational background. This confused situation will most probably tend towards clarification and simplification after the next enlargement of the EU, more particularly if the EU will be in a position to decide about the unavoidable differentiation among the candidate countries. Such a political decision would necessarily involve the definition of a long term external border of the European Union and a new kind of treatment of its immediate eastern and southern neighbourhood, too.

The European Union and Mediterranean Countries*

Alfred TOVIAS

*Deputy Director, Helmuth Kohl Institute
for European Studies;
Associate Professor, Department of International
Relations, Hebrew University, Jerusalem*

1. The Euro-Mediterranean Partnership

Because of the poor record of Maghreb and Mashrek countries combined with the demographic trends and the economic imbalances between the southern and northern shores of the Mediterranean, the European Commission, pushed along by its southern European members who were highly concerned by all this, decided to launch a new initiative in late 1994, known as the Euro-Mediterranean Partnership.

The main economic elements of the partnership are: 1) the creation of a Euro-Mediterranean Free Trade Area to be completed by about 2010; and, 2) a substantial increase of the financial assistance given by the EU, drawn on the Community's own budgetary resources for the period 1995-99[1].

To start with the second item, in practice and in relation to the Mediterranean policies of the past, the system of bilateral financial and

---

* Research contained in this paper has been supported by the Leonard Davis Institute for International Relations of the Hebrew University.

[1] The EC's Council of Ministers has approved a global amount of 4.7 bn ECU for the period 1995-99, while the CEECs have been allocated for the same period 6.7 bn ECU. The Commission expects that the EIB will also increase its own lending efforts to Mediterranean countries, by allocating about 5 billion ECU in the same period.

technical protocols (the last series of which ended in October 1996) is being abrogated and is being replaced by a new Regulation called MEDA dealing with all the Mediterranean Non-Member Countries (MNMCs in what follows) under a unified framework which deals with all cooperation activities on a multi-annual basis[2].

In the field of trade, the establishment of a Euro-Mediterranean Free Trade Area by 2010 implies in relation to the prevailing setting (which has basically been in place since the mid-1970's when the first Global Mediterranean Policy of the EC took shape) an obligation of those MNMCs which have not done so already, (as, for example, Israel has), to give tariff — and quota — free access to industrial products originating both in the EC and probably partial free trade in agricultural products as well. So, quite ironically, those MNMCs which refused to offer reverse preferences to the EC in the 1970's (Maghreb and Mashrek countries), arguing at the time that this would revive colonial times, are being asked to reciprocate by engaging in what is in practice an across-the-board tariff dismantling on manufactured products exported by the EU[3]. Since by 2010 the Union will include most CEECs, the opening includes the latter as well. A second element is that the MNMCs (including Israel) are encouraged to eliminate duties on goods originating in other MNMCs. Moreover, the Commission expects that the MNMCs will adopt the EU competition and origin rules progressively.

Therefore, what the new programme really means is that the adjustment effort is to be made mainly by the Arab MNMCs themselves. Some public officials in the Commission have declared that the idea this time is "to shake up the MNMCs" and that the European role is to be a catalyst, a facilitator (and this includes pushing the MNMCs to deal with each other). In order to shake up the Arab MNMCs' manufacturing sectors, the EC wants to encourage specializations, mergers, company reorganizations, quality improvements, the renewal of equipment, the upgrading of management, privatization, etc.[4].

The question is whether the EC itself is willing to give the example and "shake itself" also a little. The prospects are disappointing. On the EU's side, the Commission asked in its initial proposal of October 1994 for a supplementary effort from the Member States in the agricultural

---

[2] This has the advantage for individual MNMCs that they will be able to participate in bids not directly related to projects conceived for their benefit.

[3] Other MNMCs like Israel, Turkey, Malta and Cyprus have been offering increasingly larger reverse preferences to the EC in varying degrees since the early 1970s.

[4] See RHEIN (1996(a) and 1996(b)).

domain but, later on, the Declaration of Barcelona of November 1995 did not contemplate free trade in agricultural goods at all. In fact, the only reciprocal concessions made by the EU in the domain of trade are: first, in terms of eliminating remaining restrictions on textile and clothing imports, but at a time when the EU has agreed to phase out all the MFA bilateral arrangements with other developing countries by 2005, in accordance with what was agreed in the Uruguay Round of Multilateral Trade Negotiations; second, in terms of studying the possibility of cumulating value in different MNMCs for the purpose of defining the origin of products benefiting from duty-free treatment in the EU. However, the latter was initially on the condition of the prior conclusion of free trade agreements between those MNMCs which wish to benefit from cumulation, which would be implemented in stages. On the basis of different reliable sources, it seems that cumulation will take time to be put into place. In any case, cumulation, if applied, would help to flesh out one of the avowed aims of the Euro-Mediterranean Partnership, namely the promotion of regional integration and industrial cooperation among the MNMCs, particularly in the Middle East (see below for a detailed analysis of the concept). Regarding non-tariff barriers in trade between the EC and the MNMCs, the Commission stated in 1994 that it was prepared to engage in constant dialogue with the MNMCs on a wide range of trade- and investment-related matters such as indirect taxation, standards and customs procedures, but future membership in the European Economic Area or even in European standard institutions has never been mentioned.

In sum, the main supplementary effort to be made by the EU itself is financial, something favored by southern European members over other more daring solutions. The idea underlying the new EU policies is to use finance to help the MNMCs to adjust to the new free trade conditions contemplated in the Euro-Mediterranean Partnership. The financial effort to be made by the EU between 1995 and 1999 seems impressive when compared to the one made in the past. Amounts allocated to MEDA are more than double the aggregated sums allocated under the Fourth Financial Protocols, linked to the bilateral agreements signed by the EC with the MNMCs in the 1970's and covering the period 1992-96. But this point of reference is inadequate. Compared to parallel development aid allocated to the MNMCs by Member States, the financial component of the partnership represents no more than 20-30% of the former and, focusing only on Egypt, an amount of even $1 bn a year set aside for adjustment assistance to be distributed among all the MNMCs does not seem too impressive when compared to bilateral US aid to Egypt which is more than $2 bn per year since 1979. In fact, during the period 1978-92, according to Bensidoun & Chevallier (1996), the US represented 41% of all aid given to Mediterranean countries while the share of the EU (including bilateral aid by the Member States) only represented 24%. And also according to both authors, the aid per capita allocated by the EU to the CEECs will remain three times as high as that allocated to the MNMCs.

2. Focusing on Trade instead of Aid: What is Wrong with the New Initiative?

The underlying assumption of any EU initiative to cope with the economic situation in its southern periphery is that it can make a difference and have some real impact. But through which channels and with which policy instruments? There are basically two approaches: use trade policy or aid policy. It is easy to show that the amounts of aid needed to extract Maghreb and Mashrek countries from their current predicament are both staggering and unavailable. On the other hand, the EU can make a real difference by adopting appropriate trade policies. Why? First because all the MNMCs are open economies (see table 1)[5] and second because all are extremely trade-dependent on the EU (with the possible exception of Jordan).

Table 1:

Degree of Openness of the MNMCs' Economies, 1993

	Exports/GDP ratio	Imports/GDP ratio
Algeria	23.0%	23.4%
Morocco	22.0%	27.8%
Tunisia	39.7%	44.0%
Turkey (*)	20.8%	23.7%
Israel	31.3%	40.0%
Jordan	38.0%	81.4%
Syria (**)	24.2%	33.5%

(*) 1992
(**) 1991

---

[5] Trade represents more than 40% of GDP.

Table 2 points to the fact that the MNMCs have a tremendous overall deficit in their trade with the EU[6], but that there is a large surplus in mining products and almost an equilibrium in agricultural products and "other manufactured products", something reflecting the MNMCs' comparative advantage in these sectors. Table 2 points as well to the fact that Euro-Mediterranean trade amounts to $100 bn, about 50% of the MNMCs' trade but only 7% of extra-EU trade. On the other hand, given the demographic trends in the Maghreb and the Mashrek, there is an urgent need to create jobs (otherwise unwanted people there will flow to the northern shores of the Mediterranean or become alienated at home, causing trouble for the local regimes). This much is clear to everybody, including policy-makers in the EU.

Table 2:
EC Imports and Exports with the MNMCs
by Product Group (1994); Trade Balance

	Imports (Bn ECU)	Exports (Bn ECU)
TB		
All products	42.7	55.0
Primary products	19.7	9.0
Agricultural prod.	4.4	5.7
Mining products	15.2	3.0
Non agr. raw mat.	0.1	0.4
Manufactured products	21.7	44.5
Machinery	3.3	13.7
Transport equipment	1.9	7.4
Chemicals	2.1	6.4
Other manufactured pr.	14.4	16.8
Other products	1.2	1.5

TB = Trade Balance

---

[6] The MNMCs as a region have the largest deficit of all the geographical regions with which the EU trades. For some regions, the EU is itself in large deficit (Japan, South Eastern Asia).

In terms of policy, it seems obvious that the best contribution of the EU to promote job-creation is to import more from the MNMCs. What? Goods regarding which the MNMCs have a comparative advantage of course. In turn, this will induce a reduction in the trade deficit of the MNMCs and thus in their external debt as well.

3. The EU's Contribution to Job-creation in the MNMCs

The development of a job-creating economic strategy would require certain adjustments on the part of the European countries, notably the northern Mediterranean States such as France, Italy, Spain and Portugal, ultimately leading to some alternative patterns of division of labor in the entire Mediterranean zone. For example, the agricultural sector in the southern Mediterranean countries is highly labor-intensive. Therefore, the expansion and modernization of the agricultural sector — including agro-industries — should be given priority. The full realization of the agricultural potential of these countries, however, would require easier access to EU markets which will not be possible without some changes in the EU's Common Agricultural Policy. The petrochemical industry is another sector that has good potential for expansion and job-creation, although their production is essentially capital- rather than labor-intensive. But here, too, part of the burden of adjustment would fall on the EU.

The expansion of trade between the EU and the southern Mediterranean region is vitally important for the economic and industrial development of the Mediterranean countries. The Free Trade Agreement (FTA) initiative focuses almost exclusively on tariffs. However, for the expansion of trade to be beneficial for the latter, it is important that the EU's trade liberalization measures include non-tariff barriers as well, since these are the main impediments to the exports from the southern Mediterranean countries to the EU.

In the author's view, the EU should give highest priority to the following areas and issues in the framework of the Euro-Mediterranean Partnership:

a) Help the southern Mediterranean countries to devise and implement a job-intensive economic development programme with particular attention to the agricultural sector.

b) Substantially enlarge the tariff quotas applied on fruit, vegetables, flowers and other southern Mediterranean agricultural produce in the context of the renewed trade agreements that have been signed (with Tunisia and Israel) or that will be signed shortly (with Egypt,

Morocco and Jordan) and which are now part of the partnership. The concept, introduced after the accession of Spain and Portugal, of allowing duty-free entry for quantities reflecting only "traditional exports" by nonmember Mediterranean countries should be rejected; seasons in which concessions are applied should be substantially enlarged as well.

c) Liberalize the Common Agricultural Policy in the area of fruits and vegetables.

d) Reduce trade barriers applied to petrochemical products.

e) Adopt rules of origin that are as transparent and liberal as possible, so that not only large exporters benefit from the free trade agreements but so do the small and medium-sized enterprises that are typical of firms in the Mediterranean area.

f) Adopt a system of cumulation of rules of origin as liberal as possible in order to promote industrial cooperation among the southern Mediterranean countries and ensure that Turkey is included in this scheme (see below the definition and characteristics of cumulation).

g) Work for the creation of a Euro-Mediterranean Economic Area in the field of goods, by concluding mutual recognition agreements with each country in as many areas as possible, starting with those relating to technical barriers to trade (such as certification, testing, norms and standards)[7].

h) Provide the southern Mediterranean countries with technical advice and funds in their endeavour to raise standards to new and higher harmonized levels introduced in the Single Market in several domains (such as fertilizers).

i) Encourage any move made by the southern Mediterranean to diminish its increased dependence on EU suppliers, which will be one of the negative outcomes of the partnership. This means that regional integration should not only be fostered among these countries, but also with other regions and continents.

j) Encourage EU Member States to "untie" their existing bilateral aid programmes to allow the recipient country to finance the purchase of the equipment of their choice.

---

[7] This implies the gradual harmonization of legal systems with EU law. The aim is to promote inward Foreign Direct Investment (FDI), facilitate exports and enhance competition in domestic markets. This is what is being done with the CEECs now.

k) EU Member States should approve the concession of business
traveller visas for nationals of Arab MNMCs. A smooth functioning of the FTAs is inconceivable if the MNMCs' entrepreneurs
have to get travel visas every time they visit their EU counterparts or participate in a business fair in Europe.

4. Cumulation of Origin Rules
as a Way to Promote Trade among the MNMCs

At the present time, when psychological, political and other obstacles
still undermine the prospects of any form of Arab-Israeli economic integration, the proposal made by the EU Commission to modify the provisions concerning the rules of origin, included in existing bilateral agreements between the EC and individual countries so as to achieve an
improved access to European markets, is highly significant and welcome.
The modification would redefine area products as those "sufficiently
transformed" in the territory covering the EC and all countries in the
region[8]. In the political economist jargon this provision is known as "cumulation of origin", although it should rather be called "cumulation of
value added for the purpose of defining origin". The EC, in fact, has
accepted in principle such a request as part of its own intention to
multilateralize its network of bilateral agreements within the framework
of the Euro-Mediterranean Partnership. Actually, the EU considered cumulation for the first time when discussing the main elements of the new
Euro-Mediterranean Partnership in 1994-95. We find in the Presidency
Conclusions of the Cannes European Council of June 25-26, 1995 the
following:

> ... the ongoing negotiations between the Union and nonmember
> Mediterranean countries will be concluded as soon as possible
> and, in parallel, similar free trade agreements should be negoti-
> ated between the Mediterranean countries themselves. As a sec-
> ond stage, the Mediterranean countries could be encouraged to
> negotiate free trade agreements with the non-Mediterranean Eu-
> ropean countries associated with the Union. In order to facilitate
> trade, the partners would propose to:
> - progress by stages towards cumulation of origin among all the
>   parties, in accordance with conditions comparable to those envis-
>   aged by the Union *vis-à-vis* the CEECs;

---

[8] Rules of origin allow for free trade only in the area of products originating or deemed
to be originating (i.e. "sufficiently transformed") within the territories of the sides
to the FTA Agreement.

- adopt broadly similar rules of origin via the development of customs cooperation among all partners;
- improve certification procedures to facilitate mutual recognition of certificates of conformity and, in the longer term, harmonization of standards;
- adopt the highest possible standards of protection for intellectual property (TRIPs);
- adopt similar competition rules.

However, later on the EC set two preconditions to such cumulation: 1) that FTAs be concluded between the Community and the relevant MNMC in the context of the Euro-Mediterranean Partnership; and, 2) that bilateral FTAs be first concluded between those MNMCs which want to benefit from diagonal cumulation[9]. Press reports indicate that the Community is ready to waive, on an exceptional basis, the second condition with regard to cumulation between Israel and Jordan[10].

The economic logic underlying the preconditions set by the EC to diagonal cumulation is not fully clear. The rationale behind the first condition is evident: to avoid a free riding situation in which a Party which refuses to exchange trade concessions with the Community (through a FTA) will enjoy similar preferential treatment through the cumulation arrangements with other Middle Eastern parties. The reasoning behind the second prerequisite to diagonal cumulation — establishing FTAs between the MNMCs — is less clear. Viewing this requirement from the standpoint of enhancing cooperation among the MNMCs, it seems pretty odd. Cumulation of origin is generally considered as an initial measure to stimulate economic cooperation among countries which for political reasons were not trading among themselves. If successful, cumulation might be followed by the conclusion of a bilateral FTA, which implies the conclusion of a comprehensive bilateral agreement. The latter might be politically difficult to achieve in the short run among former antagonists, where a large part of the public is somewhat hostile to any legal

---

[9] KOREN, O., *"Israel demands from the European Union the Status of East European States regarding Cumulation of Origin"*, in: **Globes**, Jan. 15-16, 1997 [Hebrew]; KOREN, O., *"The European Union requires Trade Agreement between Israel and the Palestinians as a Condition to the Recognition of Cumulation of Origin"*, in: **Globes**, Feb. 18-19, 1997 [Hebrew]; KOREN, O., *"The European Union will recognize Cumulation of Origin between Jordan and Israel"*, in: **Globes**, Feb. 12-13, 1997 [Hebrew].

[10] KOREN, O., *"The European Union will recognize Cumulation of Origin between Jordan and Israel"*, in: **Globes**, Feb. 12-13, 1997 [Hebrew].

act conferring privileges to the former enemy going beyond the sheer normalization of trade relations (i.e. beyond most-favored-nation treatment).

This is why at the present time, when psychological and other obstacles still undermine the prospects of any form of Arab-Israeli economic integration, it may be useful to begin by joining forces to achieve an improved access to the most important third country market, namely the European Single Market. The establishment of cumulation rules in the bilateral agreements, signed by the MNMCs with a key third Party such as the EU, is likely to stimulate commercial cooperation among the former enemies in the Middle East, something which should increase the sustainability of peace, since vested interests in the latter is a function of the amount of commercial intercourse among the former belligerents. This is well understood by those MNMC leaders who do not want to be encumbered by complaints or pressure from local private actors (firms, individuals, NGOs) should they want to reverse the process of *rapprochement* between former political and military rivals.

Also, limiting the cumulation to those countries that will conclude Free Trade Agreements (FTAs) among themselves, would in practice mean that the poorest economies, which most need help, would be excluded from this privilege.

Therefore, posing the establishment of FTAs as a precondition to cumulation puts the various stages of developing cooperation in reverse logical sequence and is like "harnessing the carriage before the horses".

In fact, diagonal cumulation should be one of the initial steps in achieving the European Commission's long-term objective of creating a Euro-Mediterranean Free Trade Area by 2010. The Commission calls this MEFTA, the "Mediterranean Free Trade Area", which should closely follow the pattern set by EFTA in 1959 and by CEFTA, the FTA established among Central and Eastern European Countries, in 1993. In the end, by 2010, the EU envisages the creation of a huge Euro-Mediterranean Free Trade Area of 600 to 800 million people and about forty countries. About 60% of their total trade would be within the region. We tend to agree with this long-term perspective, which will shape the international order in the XXIst century. For the moment, however, "normalization" of trade relations among many MNMCs, which until recently were openly discouraging trade among themselves for political reasons, cannot yet be understood as implying the establishment of common free trade areas.

In fact, the reason behind the above-mentioned precondition to cumulation imposed by the Commission may lie in the economic reality within the Community. The enhanced economic integration within the EC would expose the Community producers to harsher competition and the almost natural tendency is not to easily accept the additional exposure to foreign competition deriving from the application of cumulation of origin. An aggravating factor here is that the prime candidate sectors for cooperation among the MNMCs are textiles and food processing. These sectors are particularly sensitive for the Community and the latter will not be easily persuaded to accord trade concessions in such spheres.

5. Diagonal Cumulation: Definition and Implications

To be sure, legally speaking, all the new Association Agreements signed or to be signed shortly in the context of the Euro-Mediterranean Partnership already allow for what is called bilateral cumulation, meaning, for example, that Israel can use EU-originating materials in goods produced for the EU market, in which case the usual test of "sufficient transformation of non-originating materials" to declare the commodity as originating in Israel is not necessary, provided that processing in Israel is more than symbolic. For instance, referring to textiles, the rule is that in order to get duty-free access to the EU, at least spinning and weaving must take place in Israel if cotton is being imported from a non-EU country. However, if the cotton is bought by the Israeli firm from Greece, than weaving in Israel is not necessary in order to get the duty exemption in the EU. But what the Commission has submitted to the Member States as a proposal to be adopted in the context of the partnership is what is called "diagonal cumulation". It would allow Israel (in the preceding example) to buy cotton from the MNMCs which also have an agreement with the EC (say Egypt) and sell the yarn either in the EU or in other MNMCs even without proof of sufficient transformation. It should be noted that in both bilateral and diagonal cumulation, the cumulation provisions apply only to "originating materials". The Commission is **not** suggesting full cumulation, which is the form applied in the European Economic Area. Full cumulation would provide for the cumulation of processing as well, i.e. firms could process goods where they want, either in the EU or in several MNMCs. Products would be labelled simply as "Euro-Mediterranean" and no longer "Israeli" when entering the EU under the duty-free regime.

Admitting cumulation, even of the diagonal type, would be important for many MNMCs, particularly in the Eastern Mediterranean, because it would improve the MNMCs' market access into the EU, it would increase trade among them with all the positive political consequences such regional trade would bring and it would enlarge sourcing possibilities for materials and products. Several economies in the Eastern Mediterranean, such as Turkey, Israel and Egypt are sufficiently diversified to make capital of the offer of the EC. Given the proximity of Palestinians, Jordanians, Lebanese and Syrians to Israel, one can imagine an immense development of intra-industry trade among countries in this area simply based on diagonal cumulation. A symptom of the potential of this option is that Palestinians, who have benefited from *de facto* cumulation since 1975 at the time Israel signed a FTA with the EC, are very lukewarm, acknowledging that it will mainly benefit Jordan and Egypt. They would also like that, in the multilateral agreement of cumulation, a minimum amount of value added in the combined area of the Eastern Mediterranean be obtained in its less developed countries. One of the paradoxes of the present situation is that whereas until 1994 the Palestinians benefited from cumulation, thanks to the "benign neglect" policy adopted by the EC, this is no longer the case now that a regime of autonomy is in place under the *"Paris Protocol on Economic Relations between the Government of the State of Israel and the PLO Representing the Palestinian People"*. It is therefore in the interest of the Palestinians (and of Israel of course) to re-establish the informal arrangement prevalent before 1994 even if the right of cumulation must be shared with other Israeli neighbours. Both Palestinians and Israelis are asking the EU to apply cumulation independently of the recent conclusion of an association agreement between the EU and the Palestinian Authority (PA).

Full cumulation was provided for in the 1976 cooperation agreements between the EC and the three Maghreb countries[11], but in practice not much was made out of it because local firms there found it difficult to establish themselves in a fellow Maghreb country. This might change in the future with the development of the production base of Morocco and Tunisia, but even so, it would be extremely useful also for Maghreb countries to have cumulation extended to non-Maghreb MNMCs, as the Commission seems prepared to allow in the context of the Euro-Mediterranean Partnership. Of course, the precondition for cumulation is to have the same system of origin rules in all the Association Agreements.

Identical rules of origin to all MNMCs were offered by the Commission in early 1996, and are being studied now. It is obvious that it will be

---

[11] See, e.g. Article 1(2) to Protocol 2 of the 1978 Agreement between Morocco and the EC, **OJ** L 264/38 (27.9.1978).

the "hub" which will impose its system on the "spokes", although the MNMCs might try to fight to get rules of origin tailored to their needs. There are precedents. In the case of the European Economic Area, the Commission took into account the particular needs of non-EC Scandinavian countries, very dependent on the export of fish products to the EU.

It is clear that in addition to widening the region's access to the European market, the implementation of cumulation would promote trade in intermediate goods and services between any two MNMCs, thereby making use of potential complementarities between them. We have shown in a previous article the vast potential of collaboration in the textile and clothing sectors between Egypt and Israel[12], and one can also think in terms of large regional intra-industry trade[13] flows in the chemical and agro-food sectors. In the long run, the more countries that are included in the scheme (including some in Eastern Europe), the higher the potential for promoting regional and sub-regional economic cooperation and maybe eventually integration. The EU may attribute a special significance to such a process as a catalyst for firms in the region to work together and think regional rather than national.

6. The Issues of Fiscal Revenue and Trade Diversion

The two issues are linked. Many tariffs in MNMCs are there for fiscal, not protective reasons. Examples are duties on cars, machinery and household equipment, which are not locally produced at all. It is precisely the elimination of fiscal tariffs on EU- or other MNMC-originating imports which is the more problematic item of the partnership from a welfare point of view for a given MNMC: not only is there a loss of fiscal revenue which requires it either to cut down on expenditure or to replace duties by other suitable taxes, but more importantly, only trade diversion, not trade creation, can be the outcome. Insofar as EU- and MNMC-originating imports are bought at higher prices than the imports being replaced, there is a welfare loss, since there is a deterioration in the terms of trade, which translates in an increase in foreign currency outlays. This is further aggravated if, as a result of the duty elimination,

---

[12] Cf. TOVIAS & WOLPERT Silver (1989). According to recent press reports, Israeli textile industries are already thinking along these lines. Polgat Industries is in negotiations to establish a sewing factory in Egypt and Delta is planning to gradually move its labor-intensive operations to Egypt and Jordan. One of its subsidiaries is already producing $2 Mo. a month. See **Jerusalem Post**, October 24, 1996.

[13] Intra-industry trade refers to cross-border trade in intermediate products, inputs and semi-manufactured goods.

the volume of imports expands[14]. To prevent this from happening it would have been better to exclude from the FTA regime goods which are taxed at the border only for fiscal reasons or else include them but replace the duty by an equivalent VAT. In fact, the FTA idea should be confined to sectors for which there is an overlap between the EU's and the MNMCs' production structures or among the MNMCs themselves so that trade creation can be maximized and trade diversion against outsiders minimized. At present there are overlaps in at least the following sectors:

1) agricultural products,
2) processed food,
3) chemical products,
4) construction materials,
5) leather, wood and textile manufactured and
   semi-manufactured products,
6) tourism services,
7) construction services.

7. A Comparison of the Relationship of the EU with its Two Peripheries

It is well known that Commissioner Marin, in charge of EC relations with MNMCs, launched its partnership project in order to "re-establish balance" in the EC's external relations. By this he referred to the fact that by 1994, when the Project was launched, not only had the EC signed the so-called "Europe Agreements" with CEECs as from 1991, but also that at the 1993 EU Summit in Copenhagen, it had been decided that a further enlargement of the EU to include CEECs was among one of the EU's future goals. Under pressure from the Mediterranean members of the EU (and particularly Spain, France and Italy), Mr. Marin, a Spaniard himself, convinced the Commission that from the security and economic perspective of the EU, the Union's southern periphery deserved as much attention as its eastern periphery.

This is why a comparison between the contractual relations between the EU and its two peripheries is warranted. Without entering into much detail, it appears that the Europe Agreements by themselves represent a relationship of a slightly deeper nature than the one embodied in the bilateral FTAs signed or to be signed with the MNMCs in the context of

---

[14] It also remains to be seen how the US will react to any move perceived as endangering their exports to MNMCs (e.g. of agricultural temperate products or of machinery and equipment).

the partnership. For instance the Europe Agreements include political conditionality clauses requiring CEECs to buttress democracy, transparency and the rule of law. Both types of agreement have as a final goal industrial free trade and asymmetry in transition periods is a rule. However, the latter are shorter in the case of the Europe Agreements (10 years instead of 12 years for the EU-MNMC agreements). Regarding technical harmonization, the Europe Agreements contemplate the approximation of the laws of the CEECs to the EU *acquis* over time, while the Euro-Mediterranean agreements have rather an open-ended approximation objective. Cumulation of rules of origin among CEECs is also contemplated (and is in place since 1995). Regarding safeguards and anti-dumping duties, they can be imposed by the EU only after consultation with the CEECs. There is no such limitation in the case of the Euro-Mediterranean agreements. Regarding services, right of establishment, intellectual property rights and the free movement of capital, again the CEECs are supposed to adjust to the *acquis communautaire* over time. In the case of the MNMCs, there are no substantial provisions regarding these items.

Beyond a strict comparison of the two types of agreements, it is fairly obvious that cultural and political cooperation is already much more developed between the EU and the CEECs than between the former and the MNMCs. For instance, the CEECs are integrated into the ERASMUS and Jean Monnet Chairs Programmes. On the other hand, the "Structured Dialogue" which the EU maintains with CEECs gives the latter access to the EU Council. This goes much beyond the "political dialogue" included in the new Euro-Mediterranean bilateral agreements.

In fact, if we compare more globally the deal offered by the EU to the CEECs with the one offered to the MNMCs, the latter seems much less advantageous than the former. In the case of the CEECs, they are offered membership in the future, entry into the Internal Market and substantial aid (such as PHARE) in exchange for reform and adjustment. The MNMCs are asked to do the latter in exchange for MEDA to cope with the adjustment, but are not even offered the integration into the Internal Market for goods and services, let alone manpower.

Conclusion

If the goal of creating a zone of shared prosperity expressed in the EU initiative on the Euro-Mediterranean Partnership is to have any real meaning or substance, it is not sufficient to encourage the Southern Mediterranean countries to proceed with economic reform and trade liberalization by asking them to eliminate tariffs and Quantitative Restrictions (QRs) on EU originating exports. The EU should also join in the endeavour and work for the extension of the Internal Market of goods and services to the MNMCs. If that is not possible, at least it should improve the terms of market access in the Euro-Mediterranean bilateral agreements, by offering a system of cumulation of origin rules which would promote regional economic cooperation among the MNMCs, something the Commission says is one of the partnership's objectives. In fact, this author has the impression that the EU wants to have FTAs with the MNMCs to equilibrate its relations with the CEECs, compensate for the increasing US influence in the Eastern Mediterranean and increase its exports to the MNMCs (and not its imports from there). It is a EU, rather than a Southern European approach, that is called for. Northern European countries seem to be uninterested by the issue. They are wrong. Why? Because there is an Internal Market since 1993, leading to a border-free Europe. Illegal immigrants heading North looking for work will not stop at the frontiers of Spain, France or Italy. They will be able to proceed until Sweden. And in the short run, the elimination of tariffs in the MNMCs and the ensuing adjustment pressures will increase, not reduce, emigration from the Mediterranean to the North. The answer will have to come from those in Europe who will realize sooner or later that only by importing more agricultural and labor-intensive goods from the MNMCs can the flow from MNMCs be stopped by peaceful means.

Bibliography

ALIBONI, R., *"The Mediterranean Dimension"*, in: WALLACE, W., (ed.), **The Dynamics of European Integration**, Pinter for the Royal Institute of International Affairs, London, 1992.

"Barcelona Declaration Adopted at the Euro-Mediterranean Conference", Final Version, Barcelona, November 28, 1995.

BENSIDOUN, I. & CHEVALLIER, A., **Europe-Méditerranée : Le pari de l'ouverture**, Collection CEPII, Economica, Paris, 1996.

CAMBRA OFICIAL DE COMERC, Industria i Navegacio de Barcelona, *"The Euro-Mediterranean Economy"*, November 1995.

COMMISSION OF THE EUROPEAN COMMUNITIES, *"The European Community and the Mediterranean"*, Office for Official Publications of the European Communities, Luxemburg, 1985.

COMMISSION OF THE EUROPEAN COMMUNITIES, *"Redirecting the Community's Mediterranean Policy. Proposals for the Period 1992-96"*, Communication from the Commission to the Council, SEC(90)812 final, 1990.

COMMISSION OF THE EUROPEAN COMMUNITIES, *"Strengthening the Mediterranean Policy of the European Union: Establishing a Euro-Mediterranean Partnership"*, Communication from the Commission to the Council and to the European Parliament, Brussels, COM(94)427 final, 1994.

EUROPEAN COMMISSION, Spokesman's Service, *"The Commission proposes the Establishment of a Euro-Mediterranean Partnership"*, Brussels, October 19, 1994, P/94/56.

FEATHERSTONE, K., *"The Mediterranean Challenge: Cohesion and External Preferences"*, in: LODGE, J., (ed.), **The European Community and the Challenge of the Future**, St.Martin's Press, New York, 1989.

FORUM CIVIL EUROMED, *"Hacia un nuevo escenario de asociacion euromediterranea"*, Institut Catala de la Mediterranea, Barcelona, 1996.

GRENON, M. & BATISSE, M., **Futures for the Mediterranean Basin: The Blue Plan**, Oxford University Press, Oxford, 1989.

GRILLI, E., **The European Communities and Developing Countries**, Cambridge University Press, Cambridge, 1993.

HOEKMAN, B., *"The WTO, the EU and the Arab World: Trade Policy Priorities and Pitfalls"*, **Discussion Paper Series**, No.1226, CEPR, August 1995.

HOEKMAN, B. & DJANKOV, S., *"Catching up with Eastern Europe? The European Union's Mediterranean Free Trade Initiative"*, **Discussion Paper Series**, No.1300, CEPR, November 1995.

KHADER, B., **Europa y el Mediterraneo**, Barcelona, 1995, Icaria.2.

LUDLOW, P. (ed.), **Europe and the Mediterranean**, Brassey's (for CEPS), London, 1994.

POMFRET, R., **Mediterranean Policy of the European Community**, Macmillan (for the Trade Policy Research Centre), London, 1986.

RHEIN, E., *"The New Euro-Mediterranean Partnership"*, Paper presented at the Transatlantic Workshop on Regionalism, Ebenhausen, July 4-6, 1996(a), (unpublished).

RHEIN, E., *"Europe and the Mediterranean: A Newly Emerging Geopolitical Area"*, in: **European Foreign Affairs Review** No.1, 1996.

SILBER J. & ZILBERFARB B., **The Trade Potential between Israel and the Arab Countries**, 1995 (unpublished paper).

STEVENS, C., *"The Impact of Europe 1992 on the Maghreb and Sub-Saharan Africa"*, in: **Journal of Common Market Studies**, Vol.29, No.2, December 1990, pp.217-41.

TOVIAS A. & WOLPERT Silver H., *"Cooperation between the Textiles and Clothing Industries of Egypt and Israel"*, in: BEN SHAHAR, H. *et al.*, **Economic Cooperation and Middle East Peace**, Weidenfeld and Nicolson, London, 1989, pp.203-24.

TOVIAS, A., *"The EC's Contribution to Peace and Prosperity in the Mediterranean and the Middle East: Some Proposals"*, in: **Jerusalem Journal of International Relations**, Vol.14, No.2, March 1992, pp.123-32.

TOVIAS, A., *"The Mediterranean Economy"*, (Chapter I), in: LUDLOW P. (ed.), **Europe and the Mediterranean**, Brassey's (for CEPS), London, 1994, pp.1-44.

TOVIAS, A., *"The EU's Mediterranean Policies under Pressure"*, in: **Mediterranean Politics**, Vol.2, 1996, pp.9-25.

TOVIAS, A., *"Options for Mashrek-Israeli Regionalism in the Context of The Euro-Mediterranean Partnership"*, **CEPS Paper** No.67, Center for European Policy Studies, Brussels, 1997.

VANDEWALLE D., *"The Middle East Peace Process and Regional Economic Cooperation"*, in: **Survival**, Vol.36, No.4, Winter 1994, pp.21-34.

VERLMUST, E., WAER P. & BOURGEOIS, J. (eds), **Rules of Origin in International Trade**, The University of Michigan Press, Ann Arbor, 1994.

YESILADA, B., *"The EC's Mediterranean Policy"*, in: HURWITZ, L. & LEQUESNE, C. (eds), **The State of the European Community**, Lynne Rienner, Boulder, 1991, pp.359-72.

ZAIMIS N. & CHANCE C., **EC Rules of Origin**, Chancery Law Publishing, London, 1992.

THE TURKISH MODEL OF ASSOCIATION: CUSTOMS UNION BEFORE ACCESSION

Halûk A. KABAALIOGLU

Director, EC Institute,
University of Marmara, Istanbul

Introduction

The paper presented by Alfred Tovias argues that it is not sufficient to encourage the Mediterranean countries to proceed with economic reform and trade liberalization by asking them to eliminate tariffs and quantitative restrictions on exports originating from the EU. According to Tovias, the EU must also join in the endeavour. Tovias certainly draws our attention to an important problem.

Whereas the Central and Eastern European countries are offered membership and entry into the Internal Market in exchange for reform and adjustment, Mediterranean countries are asked to do the same in exchange for money to cope with the adjustment, but are not offered the possibility of integrating their goods and services into the Internal Market. The author of the paper believes that the EU approach is wrong. To demonstrate the unequal approach described by Tovias, a special focus on Turkey's association with Europe is in order.

Among the Mediterranean countries discussed in Tovias' paper, Turkey occupies a unique position. Indeed, in 1996 Turkey has completed the customs union process with the European Community in accordance with her Association Agreement. Thus, integration of Turkey into the Internal Market is almost complete and Turkey has a most intimate relationship with the European Union. The completion of the customs union constitutes a final phase of Turkish association before accession to the

Community in accordance with the agreement. However, at the time of writing, Turkey has not yet appeared on the list of candidate countries whose accession is being considered in the forthcoming accession negotiations. Indeed, the attitude of the European Union towards Turkey — a NATO country for the last forty-five years, defending Western Europe against the Warsaw Pact — puzzles many Europeans in Turkey when countries like Bulgaria and Romania are mentioned as candidates but Turkey is omitted.

All the Member States and the institutions of the European Union face a historical decision with very serious consequences: will Turkey be denied membership on the grounds of her religious credentials thus making Europe a Christian club or will she be admitted to allay the fears (albeit with long transitional periods in areas like free movement of workers) of some Member States in accordance with the Association Agreement of 1963 where full membership was promised?

With the election results of December 1995, whereby the right of center vote was divided almost equally between three political parties but making an Islamist Party the leading political force with a slight 21%, the country's political process enters into a sensitive period in the same year that Turkey completes a customs union with the European Community. Needless to say, the success of the customs union depends on support being provided by the Community. Unfortunately, the EC has not fulfilled her obligations towards Turkey and Turkey remains the only country in the world to have had no financial cooperation with the EC since 1980. Thus, in the Turkish case, the EU expects integration without fulfilling her obligations to Turkey, like the blockage of the Financial Protocols. In order to avoid this, Member States could join forces outside the Community framework to support the customs union process.

Furthermore, the European Union's decision to open negotiations with the Greek Cypriot Administration for accession before a settlement on the island, six months after the completion of the Intergovernmental Conference, totally disregards the Treaties of Guarantee and the Constitution of the island where both the Greek and Turkish communities were established as equal partners in a functional federation.

A. The Association Agreement: From 1963 to the Establishment of the Customs Union

On January 1st, 1996, the customs union between the European Community and Turkey came into effect, thereby creating the closest possible economic and political relationship between the EU and any nonmember country.

Turkey's relations with the Community date back almost to its foundation. In fact, in 1957 before the entry into force of the Treaty of Rome, the Government Program of the late Prime Minister Adnan Menderes underlined the importance of the establishment of "the common market" and "economic initiatives in Europe" declaring that "Turkish Government wanted to participate in these organizations actively."[1] It is interesting to note that this important policy statement was made in the Turkish Parliament on November 11, 1957, seven months after the signing of the Treaty establishing the European Economic Community, some two months prior to its entry into force.

As early as July 31, 1959, Turkey requested an Association Agreement. This request from the Government of Turkey represented a political choice, to be associated with the building of Europe. This application was in line with Turkey's traditional European vocation and looked forward to eventual Turkish membership of the Community. The Community for its part accepted this choice with pleasure as two more European countries, Greece and Turkey, wanted to join this new venture towards European integration[2].

The welcome granted to the Turkish application for an association could be observed in the speed with which the Brussels institutions opened negotiations with the two applicant countries: the Turkish request was transmitted on July 31, and the negotiations with the Turkish delegation started on September 28, 1959.

1. The Agreement of 1963

An Agreement establishing an Association between the European Economic Community and Turkey[3] was signed in Ankara on September 12, 1963. The President of the Council, Mr. Joseph Luns, stated in his speech that this agreement was not a "result" but only a beginning. According to Mr. Walter Hallstein, the first President of the European

---

[1] *Türkiye Cumhuriyeti Hükümet Programlary*, Ak YAYINLARY, Ystanbul, 1967.

[2] SARAÇOLU, T., **Türkiye Avrupa Ekonomik Topluluu Ortaklyy-Anlamalar**, Ystanbul, 1992, p.9.

[3] **OJ** 217, 29.12.1964. English version appeared in **OJ** C 113, 24.12.1973; Collection of the Agreements concluded by the European Communities, vol.3, Bilateral Agreements, Brussels, 1978, p.541.

117

Commission, "with this agreement Turkey has tied her destiny and future to the European Communities."[4]

The establishment of a customs union between Turkey and the EC was agreed in 1963 and constituted the third phase of the Association Agreement. Therefore, it may be useful to analyze the general framework of this agreement and the Additional Protocol which was signed in 1970 before going into the details of the Decision of the Association Council[5] concerning the customs union.

The Association Agreement has been characterized as "an association prior to accession" as well as "an association for the purposes of development"[6]. According to the agreement "Association shall comprise: a) a preparatory stage; b) a transitional stage; c) a final stage." (Art.2 §3).

At the present time the association is in its "final stage" which was foreseen in 1963 as the last phase before actual accession. Indeed Article 5 stipulates that "the final stage shall be based on the customs union and shall entail closer coordination of the economic policies of the Contracting Parties."

A Commission publication entitled *"Turkey-EEC Relations 1963-1967"* which was published both in English and Turkish[7], defined the association as "a permanent, general and institutionalized bond for cooperation representing a participation by the third country in the objectives of the Communities." According to the same book "this association formula is totally different from other association agreements the Community has entered into. In the case of Turkey, as for Greece, the association formula of Article 238 was used as a form of pre-accession. Article 28 of Turkey's Association Agreement provides that the Contracting Parties will examine the possibility of Turkey's accession to the Community. Or to put it differently, association is considered as a preliminary to an eventual accession."

---

[4] Avrupa Topluluu YAYINLARY, **Türkiye-AET Ylikileri**, Ankara, 1977, p.235.

[5] The Association Council is the highest organ of the Turkey-EC Association which will be analyzed below.

[6] *Turkey-EEC Relations 1963-1977*, Ankara, 1977, "produced under the auspices of the EC Commission Office in Ankara" according to Gian Paolo PAPA, Head of the EC Office in Ankara as stated in his "Introduction" of the book. Indeed, the Association has been defined as a "permanent, general and institutionalized bond for cooperation representing a participation by the third country in the objectives of the Communities." (p.3).

[7] *Ibid.*

Article 28 which was referred to above indeed provides that "the Contracting Parties shall examine the possibility of the accession of Turkey to the Community." The possibility of accession will be examined "as soon as the operation of this agreement has advanced far enough to justify envisaging full acceptance by Turkey of the obligations arising out of the Treaty establishing the Community."

There is no automatic transition from the status of association to membership even if the Association Agreement expressly provides for accession. However, it was an express intention of the Contracting Parties to use the Association Agreement as a stepping stone to accession[8].

2. Preparatory and Transitional Stages

With the entry into force of the Association Agreement in December 1964, after being ratified by the parliaments of all of the Member States and that of Turkey, the preparatory stage commenced. During this period, the Community introduced some trade advantages for Turkish exports to the European Community together with a Financial Protocol "desiring to promote the accelerated development of the Turkish economy in furtherance of the objectives of the agreement of Association."[9]

During the preparatory stage, Turkey did not assume any obligation towards the EC. It was a phase during which Turkey was to strengthen her economy with the assistance of the Community, in order to carry out the obligations that she would assume in the following stages.

The passage to the transitional stage was not automatic. According to Article 1 of the Provisional Protocol: "four years after the entry into force of this agreement, the Council of Association shall consider whether, taking into account the economic situation of Turkey, it is able to lay down, in the form of an Additional Protocol, the provisions relating to the conditions, detailed rules and timetables for implementing the transitional stage."[10] At the earliest possible date as provided in the agreement, namely December 9, 1968, the Council of Association decided to start negotiations for the passage to the transitional stage.

---

[8] LASOK, D., *"Turkey and the European Community: Report on the Relations between the Republic of Turkey and the European Community arising from the Ankara Agreement and the Application for Membership"*, in: **Marmara Journal of European Studies**, vol.2:1, 1992, p.14.

[9] **OJ** 217, 29.12.1964.

[10] No similar provision is included for the passage from transitional stage to final stage.

In taking the important decision of concluding the preparatory stage and entering the transitional stage, the Council of Association stated that it had considered not only progress achieved in the Turkish economy following the entry into force of the agreement but also "projections about the future, whether these would permit Turkey to sustain the burden she would face in the Transitional Stage." The operation of the Ankara Agreement during the first four years of the preparatory phase was considered "a success" both from the point of view of the operation of the commercial and financial provisions, and from the point of view of the mutual cooperation and understanding shown by both sides. It was also felt that the passage to the transitional stage would provide the Turkish economy with a new framework which would stimulate economic activity during this period.

Following the decision in December 1968 to start the negotiations for the transitional stage, extensive discussions took place in the Council meetings and in Turkish public opinion and among the industrialists of the country. On November 23, 1970, the "Additional Protocol"[11] was signed and annexed to the Agreement Establishing an Association Between the European Community and Turkey. On the same day, the Second Financial Protocol was also signed.

The Additional Protocol of 1970 was intended to regulate the conditions, detailed rules and timetables for implementing the transitional stage. Thus, in accordance with the principles set out in the Association Agreement, the Additional Protocol fixed the timetable for the establishment of a customs union and of closer economic cooperation between Turkey and the EC over a transitional period of twenty-two years prior to the final period which should witness the accession of Turkey with the status of a full member. The Additional Protocol fully entered into force on January 1st, 1973 after being ratified by the Parliaments of the Member States and Turkey.

3. Why a Customs Union?

In setting the objective of a customs union, both Turkey and the Community were much influenced by the success of the customs union then being realized between the six original members of the Community. Both Turkey and the Community looked for similar benefits from the

---

[11] Additional Protocol and Financial Protocol, signed on November 23, 1970, annexed to the Agreement Establishing an Association Between the European Economic Community and Turkey — Council Regulation No.2760/72 of December 19, 1972, **OJ** L 293, 29.12.1972. English version appears in **OJ** C 113, 24.12.1973.

establishment of a customs union between themselves. In fact, if the final aim was to be Turkey's accession, then it was natural that the foundation of this link was going to be the acceptance of all the basic freedoms of movement. Free movement of goods was going to be established by the customs union. The Additional Protocol also contained a number of detailed provisions for the implementation of the free movement of workers, services and capital in accordance with the Association Agreement.

The Association Agreement clearly outlined that **"in order to attain the objectives set out [in the agreement] a customs union shall be progressively established."** What were the objectives referred to in the agreement? The answer to this question can be found in Article 2: "The aim of this agreement is to promote the continuous and balanced strengthening of trade and economic relations between the Parties, while taking full account of the need to ensure an accelerated development of the Turkish economy and to improve the level of employment and living conditions of the Turkish people."

The drafters of these agreements realized that the liberalization of trade would entail sometimes painful adaptations. In order to counterbalance the negative effects of such adaptations, financial protocols were devised together with the introduction of provisions concerning free movement of workers, services and capital.

The discussions of the last few months have given the impression that establishment of a customs union had been agreed in 1995. In fact, this was not the case. Whilst the commitment to establish a customs union was provided in the Association Agreement, its programme, timetables and rules were established in the Additional Protocol. Thus it was all agreed in 1963 and 1970. Some even argued that Turkey's implementation of this programme and adoption of the Common Customs Tariff would be sufficient for the completion of the second stage, as the timetable for the completion of the customs union was determined in the Additional Protocol of 1970.

4. How was the Customs Union to be Realized?

Whilst the commitment to establish a customs union was provided in the Association Agreement, it was the Additional Protocol of 1970 which specified the programme for bringing it into being. The 1970 Protocol contained timetables for removing barriers on trade between the partners and the timetables whereby Turkey would adopt the EC's Common Customs Tariff on its trade with third countries.

Movement towards a customs union by the EC started even before the entry into force of the Additional Protocol which required ratification by the parliaments of the Member States and Turkey. An Interim Agreement was signed on July 27, 1971 which allowed the commercial provisions of the Additional Protocol to be implemented in advance, on September 1st, 1971. Indeed, the tariff provisions of the Additional Protocol, which will be analyzed below, began to be applied as of September 1st, 1971 for the implementation of the customs union.

Article 9 of the Additional Protocol provided that, on the entry into force of this protocol, the Community would abolish customs duties and charges having equivalent effect on Turkish industrial exports to the EC[12].

In addition to the removal of customs duties, all quantitative restrictions on industrial imports into the Community from Turkey were to be abolished by Article 24: "The Community shall on the entry into force of this protocol, abolish all quantitative restrictions on imports from Turkey. Thus liberalization shall be consolidated in respect of Turkey." The consolidation of this liberalization meant that the Community undertook not to reintroduce any of these restrictions[13].

The abolition of all tariff restrictions on Turkish industrial exports to the Community took effect immediately when the Interim Agreement entered into force on September 1st, 1971. With this move, the Community moved almost all the way to achieving a customs union for industrial products in one step at the beginning of the second stage, namely the transitional period.

5. Turkey's Implementation of the Customs Union

To establish a customs union both Turkey and the EC had to eliminate tariffs and quantitative restrictions on their trade with one another and adopt a common tariff on imports from third countries. The Additional Protocol provided that both Turkey and the EC should refrain from introducing new import duties on their trade with each other.

The Additional Protocol provided a timetable for Turkey to abolish the existing Turkish tariffs on industrial imports from the EC. Articles 10 and 11 established two different lists of goods. For industrial sectors in which Turkey was more competitive, tariffs were to be eliminated over

---

[12] Annexes 1 and 2 allowed four exceptions: some petroleum products, cotton yarn, machine-made carpets of wool, woven fabrics of cotton.

[13] The sole exception to this consolidation was in Article 2 of Annex 2 covering silkworms, cottons and raw silk.

a period of twelve years. For other goods, the tariff reductions were to be spread over twenty-two years.

Charges having equivalent effect to customs duties were also to be reduced according to similar timetables. Within twenty-two years, Turkey was to abolish progressively all quantitative restrictions and measures having equivalent effect on imports from the Community (Art.25).

Adoption by Turkey of the Common Customs Tariff (CCT) of the EC was provided in Articles 17 and 18 which laid down the timetables by which Turkey was to move towards the CCT of the Community. This alignment was to be completed within twelve and twenty-two years for goods appearing in respective lists.

The goal of the Association Agreement is a customs union, both for industrial and agricultural trade. According to Article 11, "The Association shall likewise extend to agriculture and trade in agricultural products" taking into account the Common Agricultural Policy (CAP) of the Community. It was realized that to implement a customs union for agricultural products without first aligning the pricing policies of the EC would cause distortion in agricultural trade. Hence, in the Additional Protocol, Turkey committed herself to adapt her agricultural policy to the CAP during the transitional period to prepare the way for the free movement of agricultural products (Art.34).

6. Final Stage in the Pre-accession Period: Customs Union

Decision No.1/95 of the Association Council on March 6, 1995 — which refers to the final aim of the agreement being "the accession of Turkey to the Community" (Art.28) as provided in the preamble: "determined to establish ever closer bonds between Turkish people and the peoples brought together in the EEC" —, noted the following in its preamble: "Considering that the objectives set out by the Ankara Agreement and in particular by its Article 28, which established the Association between Turkey and the Community, maintain their significance at this time of great political and economic transformation on the European scene; ...", further, "considering that the customs union represents an important qualitative step, in political and economic terms, within the Association relations between the Parties."

The Association Council decided that the third and final phase of the Association which is based on a customs union was to commence as of January 1st, 1996 in accordance with the Association Agreement and the Additional Protocol. Since this was an Association Council Decision for the implementation of the Association Agreement (1963) and Additional Protocol (1970), both of which were duly ratified by the parliaments of all the Member States and entered into force, thereby being "an integral part of the Community legal system", it was believed that the assent procedure of the European Parliament was not required as this was not a new international agreement but simply an implementation measure of an Association Agreement already in force. In any case the Association Council Decision 1/95 of March 6, 1995 received the assent of the European Parliament with an overwhelming majority when it was decided that the Association Council Decision should be submitted under the assent procedure.

The Association Council Decision 1/95 "lays down the rules for implementing the final phase of the customs union" which was foreseen in the Ankara Agreement.

B. The Content of Decision 1/95 establishing the EEC-Turkey Customs Union

1. Free Circulation of Goods

The first and second subparagraphs of Article 3 of the Council Decision 1/95 is actually taken from Article 2 §1 and 2 of the Additional Protocol of 1970 which was based on Article 10 §1 of the Treaty of Rome. This must be considered only normal as "the Community" is "based upon a customs union" (Art.9 of the Treaty of Rome). Thereby, the third stage of the Turkish Association which is also "based upon a customs union" adopted the same provisions.

Accordingly the customs union shall apply to the following goods:

-   goods produced in the Community or Turkey (including those wholly or partially obtained or produced from products coming from third countries which are in free circulation in the Community or in Turkey);
-   goods coming from third countries and in free circulation in the Community or in Turkey.

Since a customs union has been formed, Article 10 §1 of the Treaty of Rome, which was implanted in Article 2 §1 of the Additional Protocol, is also reproduced in Article 3 §2 of the Association Council Decision: "Products from third countries shall be considered to be in free circulation in the Community or in Turkey if the import formalities have been

124

complied with and any customs duties or charges having equivalent effect which are payable have been levied in the Community or in Turkey, and if they have not benefited from a total or partial reimbursement of such duties or charges."

The "customs territory" of the customs union comprises the customs territory of the EC and the customs territory of Turkey (Art.3 §3).

Article 4 on the "Elimination of customs duties and charges having equivalent effect" provides that "import or export customs duties and charges having equivalent effect shall be wholly abolished between the Community and Turkey on the date of entry into force of this Decision (1.1.1996)."

Some other articles in the Decision are simply the repetitions of the corresponding ones in the Additional Protocol which were copied from the Treaty of Rome. Article 12 of the Treaty of Rome which was transplanted into Article 7 of the Additional Protocol of 1970 was again repeated in the Association Council Decision Article 4: "The Community and Turkey shall refrain from introducing any new customs duties on imports or exports or any charges having equivalent effect from that date."

Article 30 of the Treaty of Rome entitled *"Elimination of Quantitative Restrictions Between Member States"* is Article 21 of the Additional Protocol and Article 5 of the Council Decision: *"Quantitative restrictions on imports and other measures having equivalent effect shall be prohibited between the Contracting Parties".*

Article 7 of the Council Decision is another verbatim adoption of a Treaty of Rome provision, that is to say Article 36 on derogations on the grounds of "public morality, public policy or public security; the protection of health and life of humans, animals or plants; the protection of national treasures possessing artistic, historic or archaeological value..." which was already adopted in Article 29 of the Additional Protocol in 1970 and was simply repeated in the Decision. Turkey also undertook to incorporate into its internal legal order the Community instruments relating to the removal of technical barriers to trade within five years from the date of entry into force of this decision (Art.8).

2. Commercial Policy and Common Customs Tariff

In 1995, *Turkey's Official Journal (Resmi Gazete)* published thousands of pages of Turkish legislation based on EC texts. Among others, Turkey adopted the following Community regulations on commercial policy:

- Council Regulation (EC) No.518/94 on common rules for imports;
- Council Regulation (EC) No.519/94 on common rules for imports from certain third countries;
- Council Regulation (EC) No.520/94 establishing a Community procedure for administering quantitative quotas (implementing provisions: Commission Regulation (EC) No.738/94);
- Council Regulations (EEC) No.2423/88, (EC) No.521/94 and (EC) No.522/94 on protection against dumped or subsidised imports;
- Council Regulations (EEC) No.2641/84 and (EC) No.522/94 on the New Commercial Policy instrument;
- Council Regulation (EEC) No.2603/68 establishing common rules for exports;
- Council Decision 93/112/EEC on officially supported export credits;
- Council Regulation (EEC) No.636/82 and Commission Regulation (EEC) No.1828/83 on outward processing arrangements for textiles and clothing;
- Council Regulation (EEC) No.3030/93 as last amended by Commission Regulation (EC) No.195/94 on textile imports under common rules;
- Council Regulation (EC) No.517/94 on textile imports under autonomous arrangements;
- Council Regulation (EEC) No.3951/92 as last amended by Council Regulation (EC) No.217/94 on textile imports from Taiwan.

Furthermore, Turkey aligned her customs tariff with the Common Customs Tariff in relation to countries which are not members of the Community (Art.13).

Adopting the Common Customs Tariff and all the relevant customs legislation is not sufficient for the completion of the customs union[14]. The commercial policy of Turkey will also have to be harmonized with the common commercial policy of the Community. This involves both the autonomous regimes and preferential agreements with third countries. In order to harmonize Turkish commercial policy with that of the EC,

---

[14] Although Turkey has adopted the Common Customs Tariff of the Community as of January 1st, 1996, for a limited number of products (like motor gasoline, petroleum ether, gas oils, diesel, fuel oil, trunks, suitcases, bags, sacks, kraft paper, footwear, porcelain, china, midibus, minibus, motor vehicles, motor cars, lorries) she has retained customs duties higher than the CCT until January 1st, 2001 in respect of third countries. Decision 2/95, March 6, 1996.

Turkey will negotiate agreements on "a mutually advantageous basis" with the countries concerned. Since this will naturally take some time, Article 16 of Decision 1/95 stipulates that Turkey will align itself "progressively with the preferential customs regime of the Community" within five years as from January 1st, 1996.

The autonomous regimes referred to above cover the General System of Preferences (GSP), the regime for goods originating in the Occupied Territories, Ceuta or Melilla, Republics of Bosnia-Herzegovina, Croatia and Slovenia and Macedonia.

The preferential agreements include the Europe Agreements with Bulgaria, Hungary, Poland, Romania, Slovakia and the Czech Republic, Free Trade Agreements with Switzerland, Liechtenstein, Estonia, Latvia, Lithuania and the Faroe Islands, Agreements with Egypt, Jordan, Lebanon, Syria, Algeria, Morocco, Tunisia and Israel and an Association Agreement with Malta. Since the Greek Cypriot Administration in Southern Cyprus is not recognized by Turkey, as the said regime is unconstitutional under the 1960 Constitution and Treaties of Guarantee which brought independence to Cyprus, there will not be an agreement with the said entity until a settlement is reached on the island[15].

Since January 1st, 1996 (Art.12 §2), Turkey has applied substantially the same commercial policy as the Community in the textile sector (including the agreement or arrangements on trade in textiles and clothing).

Turkey and the Community made arrangements in order to prevent the circumvention of the Japan-EC Motor Vehicles Agreement relating to trade in motor vehicles mentioned in the annex of the agreement on safeguards attached to the agreement setting up the World Trade Organization.

3. Customs Provisions

As the customs union meant not only the elimination of customs duties, quantitative restrictions and measures having equivalent effect but also the alignment of the Turkish Customs Tariffs to the Common Customs Tariff of the Community, it was only natural that Turkey had to

---

[15] The EU decision to open negotiations with the Greek Cypriot Administration six months after the completion of the Intergovernmental Conference was an unfortunate move which encouraged the Greek Cypriot side to leave the inter-communal talks. The international treaties forming the Republic and the Constitution of 1960 prevent such a membership.

adopt legislation in line with the Community Customs Code in the following fields:

- origin of goods;
- customs value for goods;
- introduction of goods into the territory of the customs union;
- customs declaration;
- release for free circulation;
- suspensive arrangements and
  customs procedures with economic impact;
- movement of goods;
- customs debt;
- right of appeal. (Art.26)

The Turkish customs legislation already in force, mainly the Customs Law *(Gümrük Kanunu)* of 1970 (No.1615) and all the regulations and bylaws adopted thereunder, were, to a great extent, based on the same international customs agreements and further amended over the years in conformity with the EC requirements. Therefore, the legislation in force was very similar to the Community Customs Code. Although a new law was drafted with over 250 articles, which was to cover all the subjects already regulated in various different texts in one Code in a systematic order, due to the heavy parliamentary schedule it has not been adopted so far. For this reason, a series of regulations, decrees and bylaws were published in order to complete the existing legislation. The customs legislation will, of course, be clarified with the adoption of the Draft Law.

In addition to the above-mentioned fields and Community Customs Code (based on Council Regulation (EEC) No.2913/92 of October 12, 1992) and the Commission Regulation laying down the implementing provisions (No.2454 of July 2, 1993), Turkey has adopted a series of texts to implement the following Community legislation:

- Council Regulation (EEC) No.3842/86 laying down measures to prohibit the release for free circulation of counterfeit goods and Commission Regulation laying down the implementing measures;
- Council Regulation (EEC) No.9189/83 setting up a Community system of reliefs from customs duties and a number of Commission Regulations laying down the implementing measures;
- Council Regulation (EEC) No.616/78 on proof of origin for certain textile products and on conditions for the acceptance of such proof.

As provided in Article 29 of the Decision 1/95, mutual assistance on customs matters between administrative authorities of the Contracting Parties will be governed by a fifteen article text which is annexed to the Decision (Annex No.7). Needless to say, mutual assistance and cooperation of the administrative authorities both in Turkey and in the Community will be extremely important for the successful implementation of the customs union. Indeed, the Parties shall assist each other "... in ensuring that customs legislation is correctly applied, in particular by the prevention, detection and investigation of operations in breach of that legislation" (Art.2 §1 of the Annex 7 on Mutual Assistance). "At the request of the applicant authority, the requested authority shall [...] take all necessary measures in order to deliver all documents, notify all decisions to an addressee residing or established in its territory." (Art.5).

Although close cooperation and mutual assistance between administrative authorities in customs matters is an extremely important element, the Contracting Parties may refuse to give assistance where to do so would:

- be likely to prejudice the sovereignty of Turkey or a Member State of the Community which has been asked for assistance; or
- be likely to prejudice public policy, security or other essential interests; or
- involve currency or tax regulations other than regulations concerning customs duties; or
- violate an industrial, commercial or professional secret (Art.9).

Whenever the Common Customs Tariff is changed, Turkey shall adjust its customs tariff to these changes. Below, the institutional framework of the association and the procedure for consultation and decision-making will be analyzed in detail. Suffice it to say that Turkey will be informed about the following decisions in sufficient time in order to make the necessary amendments:

- decisions taken by the Community to amend the Common Customs Tariff, and
- to suspend or reintroduce duties and any decision concerning tariff quotas or ceilings.

4. Agriculture

The Association Agreement provided that "the Association shall likewise extend to agriculture and trade in agricultural products, in accordance with special rules which shall take into account the Common Agricultural Policy of the Community." Furthermore, "agricultural products" meant the products listed in Annex II of the Treaty of Rome (Art.11).

The Additional Protocol stipulated that, twenty-two years after its entry into force (1995), agricultural products should be able to move freely between Turkey and the EC once the Council of Association had ascertained that Turkey had adapted to the Common Agricultural Policy (Art.34 §1). However, the Council may alter the date by which such free movement should be achieved.

Given the differences in the agricultural policies of both sides, the Parties did not see fit to embark on the free movement of agricultural products. **Thus, the customs union covers only industrial products**.

Decision 1/95 affirmed "the Parties' common objective to move towards the free movement of agricultural products" but noted that "an additional period is required" to establish the conditions necessary to achieve this free movement (Art.24). Thus, Turkey and the Community shall progressively improve the preferential arrangements which they grant each other for their trade in agricultural products. The Council of Association Decision 1/95 contained a requirement to negotiate reciprocal concessions that are mutually advantageous.

5. Processed Agricultural Products

The customs union covers "products other than agricultural products" (Art.2). Therefore, agricultural products are excluded and only industrial goods may benefit from the customs union.

What about processed agricultural products? They are not completely industrial products but contain an important "agricultural component".

Although customs duties and measures having equivalent effect have been abolished, Turkey and the EC may apply "agricultural components" established in accordance with the Decision 1/95.

How can we determine the so-called "agricultural component"? According to Article 19, agricultural components may be obtained by "adding together the quantities of basic agricultural products considered to have been used for the manufacture of the goods in question", multiplied by the "basic amount" corresponding to each of these basic agricultural products. Annex No.5 lists the "basic amounts" for basic agricultural products (ecu/100 kg) applicable to imports originating from third countries: common wheat (7.44), durum wheat (6.39), rye (2.33), barley (2.95), maize (2.91), white sugar (36.68), skimmed milk powder (140.9), whole milk powder (142.31), molasses (15.14), butter (172.17), rice (25.41), isoglucose (23.51).

The Community shall apply to Turkey the same specific duties that represent the "agricultural component" applicable to third countries. Turkey, too, shall apply the "agricultural component" to imports from the Community. There are a number of annexes to the Decision 1/95 explaining the procedure concerning processed agricultural goods.

6. Competition Law:
The Adaptation of Turkish Law to the EC Model

With the 1963 Association Agreement, Turkey and the EC recognized that the Treaty of Rome provisions on competition, taxation and the approximation of laws "must be made applicable in their relations within the Association." (Art.15).

According to the Additional Protocol of 1970, the provisions of the Treaty of Rome on competition (Articles 85, 86, 90, 92) were going to be applied. In order to do so, the Council of Association was to adopt the conditions and rules for the application of the competition principles laid down in those articles by 1979. But such a decision was not taken.

Decision 1/95 provided the "competition rules for the customs union" in Articles 32-38.

Article 32 of the Decision 1/95 is a verbatim copy of Article 85 of the Treaty of Rome. The only difference is in the first sentence where it is stated that: "the following shall be prohibited as incompatible with the proper functioning of the customs union..."; in the original text (Art.85) this reads "the following shall be prohibited as incompatible with the common market..."

Similarly, Article 33 of the Decision 1/95 is a copy of Article 86 of the Treaty of Rome where the phrase "common market" is replaced by "customs union".

Article 34 of the decision corresponds to Article 92 of the treaty where it is provided that "any aid granted by EC Member States or Turkey through state resources" is incompatible with the proper functioning of the customs union.

Since these provisions are copied from the relevant articles of the treaty, Article 35 of the Decision 1/95 provided that "any practices contrary to Articles 32, 33, and 34 shall be assessed on the basis of criteria arising from the application of the rules of Articles 85, 86 and 92 of the Treaty establishing the European Community and its secondary legislation."

There is another duty imposed on the Association Council. By 1998, the Council shall adopt by decision the necessary rules for the implementation of these articles concerning competition (Art.37). Until these rules are adopted, the authorities of both sides shall rule on the "admissibility" of agreements, decisions and concerted practices and on the abuse of the dominant position in accordance with Articles 32 and 33.

If the Community or Turkey considers that a particular practice is incompatible with the competition rules but is not adequately dealt with under the implementing rules (which will be adopted by the Association Council) it may take "appropriate measures" after consulting the Customs Union Joint Committee (Art.36).

As explained above, the Association Council Decision included articles on competition which are the same as treaty provisions on this subject. Furthermore it required implementing measures to be made by a decision of the Council in line with the EC measures. Each Party was authorized to take unilateral action after consulting the Joint Committee. This was not enough and it was provided that Turkey should have a Competition Law (Art.37 §2(a)). Thus, before the entry into force of the customs union, Turkey should adopt a law which would prohibit behaviours of undertakings under the conditions laid down in Articles 85 and 86 of the treaty. Turkey will also ensure that the principles contained in block exemption regulations in force in the Community and its case law shall be applied in Turkey. *"The Law on the Protection of Competition"* was adopted by the Turkish Parliament on December 7, 1994 (No.4054) and appeared in the *Official Journal* (RG) on December 13, 1994 (No.22140). This law is also based on Articles 85, 86 and the relevant Community legislation.

According to Article 37 §1, "With a view to achieving the economic integration sought by the customs union, Turkey shall ensure that its legislation in the field of competition rules is made compatible with that of the EC, and is applied effectively." As explained above, such legislation had been adopted some months before the March 6, 1995 Decision (1/95). It was also required that before 1996 Turkey must "establish a competition authority which shall apply these rules and principles effectively."

The Decision 1/95 imposes a lot of requirements on Turkey which, it may be argued, fall outside the basic customs union structure. As the customs union arrangement is considered only a transitional or temporary measure which should lead to full membership, the requirement of a national law at this stage may be understandable. However, we would like to note that requiring Turkey to have a national competition law is rather excessive as Italy — being a full member, not just having a customs union — did not have a national competition law until 1990. If a Member State had no national competition law for more than thirty years, then was not it too much to ask of Turkey to have national legislation on competition when it was only completing a customs union, not being a Member State? Furthermore, all the Member States' national legislation on competition varied greatly both in structure and in detail. Besides, if an agreement having a prohibiting effect on the Community were to be discovered, even if the agreement was made outside the EC (by foreigners who exercise no activities in the Community) it has long been held that the Commission would have extraterritorial competence. Therefore, even if there were no national legislation, Community competition laws could be applied. In any case, these provisions were included in Decision 1/95.

Turkey passed a Law on Competition in December 1994 which is also based on the competition articles of the Treaty of Rome. However, the Competition Board *(Rekabet Kurulu)* which will be administering this law has not as yet been formed, as the appointment of members by various ministries and institutions has been delayed. At the time of writing, it has been reported that the candidates nominated from relevant ministries and organizations have been presented to the Council of Ministers and the formation of the Board should be completed in the near future. With the entry into force of the Competition Law, the fees paid by companies for their registration is already being accumulated and the Board will have an important sum of money at its disposal once it starts to work.

7. Anti-dumping and other Trade Defence Instruments

In a customs union, allegations of dumping is inconceivable. It was expected that with the completion of the customs union the Community allegations for dumping would be eliminated. Decision 1/95 has four articles in a special section entitled *"Trade Defence Instruments"*.

The application of "trade defence instruments" will be subject to a review by the Association Council. When the Council determines that Turkey has implemented competition provisions, controls on state aids and other parts of the *acquis communautaire* which are related to the Internal Market and ensured their effective enforcement, the Council of Association may decide to suspend the application of these instruments (Art.44). The aim is to provide a guarantee against unfair competition comparable to that existing inside the Internal Market.

The Additional Protocol of 1970, in its Article 47, envisaged a very active role for the Council of Association in dumping cases. Indeed, during the transitional period, the Council of Association was to address "recommendations" to the Party with whom such practices (dumping) originate for the purpose of putting an end to them, if it finds that dumping is actually being practiced. Therefore, any allegations of dumping must be made to the Association Council by one of the Contracting Parties. If the Council establishes that there is dumping, it will address recommendations to the Parties involved.

When the Council issues recommendations concerning the dumping practices, but the practice continues, then the injured Party may take "suitable protective measures" after notifying the Council of Association.

If the interests of the injured Party call for immediate action, then it may introduce "interim measures of protection", i.e. provisional anti-dumping duties, after informing the Council. These "interim" measures may remain in force for up to three months. The Council may, at any time, decide that such protective measures shall be suspended pending the issue of the Council recommendations.

The only provision in the Treaty of Rome which specifically deals with the anti-dumping procedure is Article 91. This article is limited in its scope and time. It could be applied by the Member States only during the transitional period before the customs union was complete. This was appropriate since dumping procedures are not possible in a unified market in which there are no customs and quantitative barriers. In the case of Turkey, as all the customs duties and quantitative restrictions are removed, there should be no dumping allegations.

During the transitional period, the Community did not implement the Article 47 procedure in cases of dumping allegations whereby the matter was to be discussed in the Council of Association and recommendations were to be made. Instead of using this method, the Commission started investigations and without the involvement of the Council of

Association imposed anti-dumping duties during the transitional period, totally disregarding Article 47 of the Additional Protocol. Now, Decision 1/95, which marks the establishment of a customs union, refers back to Article 47 of the Association Agreement and stipulates that "the modalities of implementation of anti-dumping measures" explained in Article 47 (which was applicable only during the transitional period) "remain in force" when the customs union is achieved. This is of course contradictory and we expect that the Association Council will in one of its future meetings suspend the application of these instruments.

It is also contradictory for the following reasons: whereas Decision 1/95 "concerning the rules for implementing the final phase of the customs union" refers to Article 47 of the Additional Protocol which clearly had a limited period of application ("during the period of twenty-two years", 1973-1995) but now, as far as the modalities of implementation of anti-dumping measures set out in Article 47 of the Additional Protocol are concerned, has been declared to "remain in force", the same decision stipulates that "the consultation and decision-making procedures" (provided in Section II of Chapter V) shall not apply to trade defence measures taken by either Party[16].

The aim of Article 47 of the Additional Protocol was of course to settle the disputes concerning dumping allegations within the Council of Association through consultations; this was totally disregarded by the Community authorities during the very period for which it was specifically designed. Now, after the completion of the customs union where allegations of dumping should not be entertained, Decision 1/95 Article 46 not only declares that "modalities of implementation of anti-dumping measures of Article 47" remain in force but goes one step further and excludes the "consultation and decision-making procedures" referred to in Section II of Chapter V of Decision 1/95.

---

[16] Probably the Community felt the need to make a statement in order to avoid this contradiction. Indeed, in a declaration by the Community, it was stated that "the Commission, without prejudice to the position of the Council, in the exercise of its responsibilities for anti-dumping and safeguard measures, will offer information to Turkey before the initiation of proceedings." According to this statement attached to the Decision 1/95, "appropriate modalities of application of Article 47 will be set out jointly before the entry into force of this Decision", i.e. 1.1.1996, but we have no information which would indicate that such modalities were set up. In fact, the Community has been so generous (?) by declaring the following: "Furthermore, the Community will give, on a case by case basis, where appropriate, a clear preference to price undertakings rather than duties in order to conclude anti-dumping cases where injury is found." We believe that in a customs union the application of anti-dumping provisions is totally unjustified and it should be abandoned.

Through a series of laws, regulations and decrees for adapting the Turkish legal system to the European Community, Turkey has already aligned her rules on state aids, incentives, competition and the like and therefore, in principle, it should be expected that the Council take a decision for the suspension of provisions on trade defence instruments. However, safeguard clauses will remain in force.

8. Taxation

The Treaty of Rome aims to prevent the Member States from applying protectionist measures indirectly by discriminatory taxation after the elimination of customs duties and quantitative restrictions has made it impossible to resort to these protective devices. Indeed, Article 95 prohibits the imposition of higher economic charges upon goods from other Member States than are imposed, directly or indirectly, upon similar domestic products.

In line with the Association Agreement, Article 16 (which recognizes that, among others, taxation provisions contained in the Treaty of Rome must be made applicable in the relations between Turkey and the EC), the Additional Protocol in its Article 44 took the relevant provisions of the Treaty of Rome (Art.95) with a slight change whereby the words "No Member State shall impose..." were changed to "Neither Contracting Party shall impose..."

Decision 1/95 of the Association Council repeats these provisions on indirect taxation (Art.52). In terms of direct taxation the following principles are stipulated: no provision of the Decision 1/95 shall have the effect of extending the fiscal advantages granted by either Party in any international agreement or arrangement by which it is bound. Both Turkey and the EC will be able to take any measure aimed at preventing the avoidance or evasion of taxes. Furthermore, both Turkey and the EC could apply the relevant provisions of their tax legislation to taxpayers whose position as regards place or residence is not identical.

9. Government Procurement

As a number of important "founding columns" of the association (like free movement of services, labor) have not yet been implemented, the public procurement market has been left outside the scope of the Decision 1/95 of March 6, 1996. Only implementing the provisions of customs union (free movement of goods) but totally disregarding the other main foundation columns of the association (the remaining basic freedoms) leaves the present situation as a limping animal. It is clear that if the association was to be regarded as a horse, only one leg of this horse is healthy and operational, whereas the remaining legs are paralysed. The legs are there — provisions of the Association Agreement and Additional Protocol, which are considered as "an integral part of the European Law" and in certain cases may have direct effect — but they require decisions of the Council of Association to function. The decisions to be taken by the Council may be likened to special injections to be made to the horse in order to end the paralysis.

"As soon as possible", the Association Council will set a date for the "initiation of negotiations aiming at the mutual opening of the Contracting Parties' respective government procurement markets." (Art.48).

10. Intellectual, Industrial and Commercial Property Rights

In its efforts to prepare the country for full membership, Turkey has made extensive changes in its legislation. In order to complete the customs union, which has been the main core of the final phase of the association before accession, the Turkish Parliament (The Grand National Assembly or TBMM), the Council of Ministers, almost all the Ministries and public institutions passed many laws, regulations, decrees, bylaws and other types of legislative and administrative acts bringing Turkish legislation in line with that of the Community *acquis communautaire*. Another area of regulation where voluminous legislation was adopted and international conventions, protocols and agreements ratified by the Parliament, is intellectual, industrial and commercial property rights.

The only reference to this area of law may be deducted from Article 16 of the Association Agreement, whereby both Turkey and the Community recognized that principles laid down in the provisions on competition, taxation and the **approximation of laws** contained in Title I of Part III of the Treaty of Rome "must be made applicable in their relations within the Association."

Title I of Part III contains "Common Rules" in three different chapters: 1) rules on competition (rules applying to undertakings, dumping, and aids granted by states); 2) tax provisions; and, 3) approximation of laws. Here, Article 100 of the Treaty provided "the approximation of such provisions [...] as directly effect the establishment or functioning of the common market."

In a similar provision to above-mentioned Article 100, the Additional Protocol in its Article 48 authorized the Council of Association "to recommend the Contracting Parties to take measures to approximate the laws, [...] in respect of fields which are not covered by this Protocol, but have a direct bearing on the functioning of the Association..."

Article 33 of the Association Council Decision 1/95 was allocated to this subject where both the Community and Turkey confirmed the importance they attached "to ensuring adequate and effective protection and enforcement of intellectual, industrial and commercial property rights." According to this opinion, the customs union could function properly only if "equivalent levels of effective protection of intellectual property rights" were provided in both constituent parts of the customs union. Accordingly, the Parties undertook to meet the obligations set out in Annex 8 of the Decision 1/95 (Art.33 §2). Naturally, although reference was made to both of the Parties, it was Turkey that was going to implement all these provisions as the Community and Member States had already adopted these texts. However, many countries, which may be referred to as Turkey's competitors in international markets, consistently refused adopting such legislation or conventions, which would further hamper the competitivity of Turkish industry.

Again, it was Turkey that undertook to change the legal system in this area in an overwhelmingly extensive manner, in order to complete the process of the customs union. Annex 8 *"On Protection of Intellectual, Industrial and Commercial Policy"* which Turkey had to join, consisting of four full pages, nine articles but also listing many international conventions and agreements (all of which contain extensive provisions), in addition to extensive national laws to be adopted, shows the dimension of the undertaking that Turkey has entered into.

Under Article 1 of the Annex 8 on protection of intellectual, industrial and commercial property[17], Turkey undertook to implement the Trade-Related Aspects of Intellectual Property Rights (TRIPs) Agreement no later than three years after the entry into force of Decision 1/95. Both sides confirm the importance they attach to the obligations arising from

---

[17] Article 9 of Annex 8 gives a very wide definition of "intellectual, industrial and commercial property". Accordingly, these include copyright (copyright in computer programmes) and neighboring rights, patents, industrial designs, geographical indications including appellations of origin, trade marks and service marks, topographies of integrated circuits as well as protection against unfair competition as referred to in Article 10bis of the Paris Convention for the Protection of Industrial Property and protection of undisclosed information on "know-how". After listing all the above, Article 9 §2 goes on to say that "this decision does not imply exhaustion of intellectual, industrial and commercial property rights applied in trade relations between the two Parties under this decision", that is Turkey and the EC.

the Agreement on TRIPs concluded in the Uruguay Round of Multilateral Trade Negotiations.

Turkey also undertook "to continue to improve the effective protection of intellectual, industrial and commercial property rights in order to secure a level of protection equivalent to that existing in the EC." In order to ensure that these rights are respected, Turkey had to "take appropriate measures". Before January 1st, 1996 Turkey was required to take a number of measures, pass laws and accede to international conventions on intellectual, industrial and commercial property rights.

Article 3 of the annex listed the following conventions which Turkey was to join:

- Paris Act (1971) of the Bern Convention for the protection of literary and artistic works;
- Rome Convention (1961) for the protection of performers, producers of phonograms and broadcasting organizations;
- Stockholm Act (1967) of the Paris Convention for the protection of industrial property (as amended in 1979);
- Nice Agreement concerning the internal classification of goods and services for the purposes of registration marks (Geneva Act, 1977 as amended in 1979); and,
- Patent Cooperation Treaty (PCT, 1970, as amended in 1979 and modified in 1984).

Turkish Parliament passed laws for the ratification of these conventions. For the first two conventions mentioned above see the *Turkish Official Journal (Resmi Gazete)*, (July 12, 1995, No.22341). The third convention and Stockholm Act was ratified on February 1st, 1995. The Nice Agreement concerning the international classification of goods and services for the purposes of the registration of marks was also adopted by the Turkish Parliament (see *Official Journal-Resmi Gazete*, August 13, 1995, No.22373). The Law for accession to the Patent Cooperation Treaty has appeared in the *Official Journal-Resmi Gazete* on July 12, 1995, (No.22341).

A long list of Community legislation was given in Article 4, whereby Turkey was to adopt domestic legislation in these areas. Thus, Turkey has adopted domestic legislation in these areas which is equivalent to the legislation adopted in the EC or its Member States.

Turkey has also undertaken to pass legislation in line with the four Council Directives related to copyright and neighboring rights:

- the terms of protection in line with Council Directive 93/98/EEC (OJ L 290 of 24.11.93);
- protection of neighboring rights in line with Council Directive 92/100/EEC (OJ L 346 of 27.11.92);
- rental and lending rights in line with Council Directive 92/100/EEC (OJ L 346 of 27.11.92);
- the protection of computer programmes as literary works in line with Council Directive 91/250/EEC (OJ L 122 of 17.05.91).

In accordance with this undertaking, the Parliament of Turkey passed a law for a series of amendments to the Law for the Protection of Intellectual and Artistic Rights of 1951 whereby the legislation in force was extensively reformed. This new law (No.4110) was published in the *Turkish Official Journal-Resmi Gazete* on June 12, 1995, (No.22311) well ahead of the January 1st, 1996 deadline when the Decision 1/95 was to enter into force.

It was also clear that Turkey had to modernize its patent legislation and its implementing decrees. Ankara was requested to pass patent legislation which would provide rules on compulsory licensing meeting at least the TRIPs standards, patentability of all inventions (other than pharmaceutical products and processes for human and animal health but including agro-chemical products and processes) and a patent term of twenty years from the filing date.

A Government Decree on the Protection of Patent Rights, which has the force of law, was published in the *Official Journal (Resmi Gazete)* on June 27, 1995 (No.22326), in accordance with the Association Council Decision. The new law which substantially changes the previous Patent Law of 1879 through modern provisions contains 14 chapters and a total of 176 articles. Subsequently, a regulation was published which carried detailed provisions for the implementation of the Patent Rights Decree (*OJ-Resmi Gazete*, November 5, 1995, No.22454).

Another important piece of legislation in this area is the Decree-Law No.554 concerning the establishment of a Turkish Patent Institute, published in the *OJ-Resmi Gazete* on June 24, 1995, (No.21970). This institute will consider the applications, registrations and appeals concerning patents, trade marks, geographical indications on industrial designs and many other related matters.

Another Decree-Law for the Protection of Industrial Designs was published in *OJ-Resmi Gazete* on June 27, 1995, (No.22326) and a regulation for the implementation of this decree appeared in the *Official Journal* on November 5, 1995, (No.22454).

Turkey also accepted to adopt domestic legislation in the trade and service marks area in line with Council Directive 89/104/EEC (OJ L40 of 11.02.89), industrial designs legislation, including the protection of designs in textile products, taking into account a Proposal for a Council Directive on Community Designs; the protection of geographical indications, including appellations of origin in line with EC legislation and legislation on border enforcement against intellectual property right infringements including trademark, copyright and neighboring rights and design rights in line with Council Regulation (EEC) 3842/86 (OJ L 357 of 18.12.86).

In line with these Community regulations and directives, Turkey prepared a new Law on the Protection of Trade Marks replacing the 1965 Law on Trade Marks, with a decree having the effect of a law adopted by the Council of Ministers on 24.6.1995 and published in the *Official Journal-Resmi Gazete* on June 27, 1995, (No.22326, pp.87-113) with 11 chapters and 87 articles.

On June 24, 1995, the Council of Ministers adopted another decree which has the force of law entitled *"... Decree on the Protection of Geographical Indications"* which appeared in the *Official Journal-Resmi Gazete* (No.22326). Regulations for the implementation of this decree-law was published on November 5, 1995, (OJ-RG No.22454) and November 7, 1995, (OJ-RG No.22456).

We do not intend to cover all the legislation adopted in Turkey during the whole of 1994 and 1995 (before the entry into force of the customs union) which would require a very extensive study as the *Turkish Official Journal* appeared many times in thick volume format, sometimes carrying several hundreds of pages with texts adopting Community legislation.

Article 6 of the Annex 8 of the Council Decision 1/95 requires that Turkey accedes to a number of conventions on intellectual, industrial and commercial property. Although a list of such conventions is provided, there is a stipulation to the effect that Turkey will accede to these conventions, "provided that the EC or all its Member States are Parties to them":

- Protocol to the Madrid Agreement concerning the international registration of marks (1989);

- Budapest Treaty on the international recognition of the deposit of microorganisms for the purposes of patent procedure (1977 and amended in 1980); and,

- International Convention for the protection of new varieties of plants (UPOV, Geneva, 1991 Act).

Decision 1/95 of the Association Council is so comprehensive that with the completion of the customs union and the implementation of the legislation, Turkey has already adopted a very important part of the *acquis communautaire*. In fact, as pointed out above, draft texts in terms of Commission proposals to the Council are cited before their adoption by the Community institutions and requirements are underlined for Turkey to adopt domestic legislation in order to reach alignment with draft EC regulations. For example, a proposal for a Council Directive on the legal protection of database (OJ C 156 of 23.06.92) is cited together with another proposal for a Council Regulation (EEC) on Community plant variety rights (OJ C 113 of 23.04.93). In some cases where there is no Community legislation, reference is made to Member States' legislation. For example, Turkey shall adopt domestic legislation for the "protection of know-how information and trade secrets legislation in line with Member States' legislation." In this area Turkish legislators will examine the laws of Member States and prepare a text which should cover the main principles of Member States' laws.

In the copyright and neighboring rights applicable to works transmitted by cable or satellite, Turkey has to adopt legislation in line with Council Directive 93/83/EEC (OJ L 248 of 6.10.93) and on the protection of topographies of semiconductors in line with Council Directive 87/54/EEC (OJ L 24 of 27.01.87).

"Comitology" under the Association Council shows an inclination to widen. The Joint Customs Union Committee (which was established by Decision 1/95) shall monitor the implementation and application of the Intellectual Property Rights (IPRs) provisions of this decision and perform other tasks which the Association Council may assign to it. This Joint Customs Union Committee "shall make recommendations to the Association Council which may include the establishment of a Sub-Committee on IPRs."

C. *Institutions of the Association*

1. The Council of Association

The Ankara Agreement provides a machinery for the decision-making process and a procedure for the resolution of disputes. The main decision-making institution of the Association is the **Council of Association**.

Recent judgments of the Court of Justice of the EC underlined the importance of this institution. Indeed, according to the Court, the decisions of the Association Council under the Association Agreement between Turkey and the EC constitute "an integral part of the Community legal system." In the *Sevince* Case[18], the European Court of Justice held that **"acts (decisions) adopted by the Association Council can be directly effective in the Community if they comply with the same requirements as apply to the Association Agreement."**

The Council of Association consists of members of the governments of the Member States and members of the Council and of the Commission of the Community on one side and of members of the Turkish Government on the other (Art.23). However, to redress the balance of numbers, it was agreed that the decisions must be taken unanimously. This rule reflects the bilateral and equal character of the Association.

A Commission publication on Turkey-EC Association published in 1977[19] sheds some light on the institutional structure: "In studying the **general nature of Association**, we indicated that this **included**, *inter alia*, **the extension** — albeit partial — **of the institutional methods applicable within the Community to the relationship between it and the associated country."** The whole thrust of the Treaty of Rome was precisely to break with the traditional character of a multilateral treaty for the performance of the multilateral treaties usually suffers from a lack of executive or judicial machinery[20]: "In order to attain the objectives of this agreement, the Council of Association shall have the power to take decisions in the cases provided for therein." Both Turkey and the Community shall take the measures necessary to implement the decisions taken. In addition to the decisions, which are binding on the part of the Parties, "the Council of Association may also make appropriate recommendations."

---

[18] *Sevince v. Staatssecretaris von Justitie*, Case c. 192/89, **CMLR** No.57, 1992.

[19] See footnote 6.

[20] Article 145 of the EC Treaty, at the time, reads as follows: "To ensure that the objectives set out in this Treaty are attained, the Council shall, in accordance with the provisions of this Treaty: [...] have power to take decisions."

Article 22 §1 of the Ankara Agreement empowers the Council of Association to take decisions "in order to attain the objectives of this agreement [...] in the cases provided for therein", i.e. the agreement. Therefore, one may assume that the Council of Association may take decisions only in the cases provided for in the agreement. Thus, both the Association Agreement and the Additional Protocol contain many articles which impose a duty on the Council to take necessary measures for the implementation of the agreement covering a range of areas from customs arrangements to agriculture. (These include measures concerning the free movement of agricultural products, social questions like the free movement of workers, social policies, the freedom of establishment, the free movement of services, the extension of the Community transport policy to Turkey, the alignment of economic policies, etc.).

However, the powers of the Council of Association is not limited only to those issues which are specifically mentioned in the agreement or the protocol. In the course of the implementation of the Association arrangement, the "attainment of an objective of this agreement" may call for a "joint action by the Contracting Parties" but the requisite powers were not granted in the Association Agreement. Even in such cases where the agreement does not authorize the Association Council to take joint action, but the attainment of an objective of the Association requires such a measure, then the Council of Association, according to Article 22 §3 "shall adopt appropriate decisions." It is clear that the Contracting Parties in adopting this provision were specifically "guided by" Article 235 of the Treaty of Rome which authorizes the Council to take the "appropriate measures" according to the Community decision-making procedure, even if "the Treaty has not provided the necessary powers", "if action by the Community should prove necessary to attain, in the course of the operation of the Common Market, one of the objectives of the Community."

It must be emphasized that the Council of Association constitutes a body for negotiation and for the implementation of the principal decisions to be taken for the development of the Association. There are many provisions of the Association Agreement and the Additional Protocol which await the decisions of the Council for their implementation.

Its character as an effective decision-making body has been accentuated by the practice, for which the Turkish partner has exerted particular pressure, of not letting "the Council meets for nothing" or in the words of a Foreign Minister of Turkey who served in the 60s and 70s, of not letting the Council meets only "to make declarations of goodwill, promises of a general nature, and minor adaptations which only serve to maintain appearances."[21]

The Council of Association is the place where agreement between the Community and its associate, Turkey, is arrived at. "Therefore each meeting of the Council must lead to the strengthening of EC-Turkey relations in conformity with the objectives of the Association", according to the Commission publication referred to above.

Unfortunately, there have been periods during which the Council could not meet. It is highly regrettable that one Member State should, from time to time, be able to paralyze the functioning of the Association's institutions, raising objections on matters which have nothing to do with the Association relationship.

2. The Committee of Association

According to Article 24 §3 of the Agreement, "the Council of Association may decide to set up committees to assist in the performance of its tasks, and in particular a committee to ensure the continuing cooperation necessary for the proper functioning of the agreement." In order to ensure the necessary cooperation between sessions of the Council, an Association Committee was established by a Decision of the Council of Association (Decision 3/64).

The Association Committee assists the Council in the fulfillment of its tasks: prepares for its proceedings and examines all the questions which are referred to it for this purpose. Based in Brussels, the Committee meets at ministerial level "at least once every six months unless there is a decision to the contrary."

Moreover, the Council of Association can decide on the creation of any other committee able to assist it in its tasks. As the Council is authorized to set up committees especially "to ensure the continuing cooperation necessary for the proper functioning of the agreement", Decision 1/95 of March 6, 1995 established an **EC-Turkey Customs Union Joint Committee** which "shall carry out an exchange of views and information, formulate recommendations to the Association Council and deliver opinions with a view to ensuring the proper functioning of the customs union" (Art.52). This Joint Committee shall meet at least once a month. However, it may be called for a special meeting should the need arise.

---

[21] *Turkey-EEC Relations, op. cit.*, p.31.

The institutional structure and the committees established under the Association Council need an in-depth study. Participation of Turkish experts "in the work of a number of technical committees which assist the European Commission in the exercise of its executive powers in areas of direct relevance to the functioning of the customs union" (Art.60) is also an important matter which must be analysed.

3. Consultation and Decision Procedures

The "institutional void", referred to by Gilsdorf[22], "creates, indeed, enormous problems for a fully comprehensive association agreement, because the third country would be bound to apply Community policies and legislation without taking part in the decision-making as such." Furthermore, the question of legal control and protection of individuals "would raise great difficulties because it is hardly conceivable that the associated country would submit to the jurisdiction of the EC Court." In order to guarantee the uniformity of interpretation and application of the established rules between the associated partners, Gilsdorf proposes full membership "even at the price of a long transitional period".

The present situation has been heavily criticized by leading political parties in Turkey, which argue that Turkey is bound to apply Community policies and legislation without taking part in the decision-making institutions. The only argument put forward in reply to these critics has been the "temporary" nature of the present arrangements and a promise to the effect that the final phase of the association will lead to accession to the Union which should be the natural conclusion of this process.

It is clear that Turkey is not only establishing a customs union with the European Community but is also adopting many of the common policies enforced by the Member States. Indeed, this situation may be qualified as "taking all the obligations" and "responsibilities" of a Member State without enjoying the benefits of membership, the most important of which is being able to take part in the institutions that make all the important decisions.

The Decision of the Association Council of March 6, 1996 (No.1/95) contains seven long articles concerning "consultation and decision procedures". In areas of direct relevance to the operation of the customs union, Turkish legislation "shall be harmonized as far as possible with

---

[22] GILSDORF, P., *Legal Aspects in Relation to the Turkish Application for Accession to the EC*, Revised version of a lecture given at the Seminar in Istanbul, May 14-16, 1987, organized by the TOBB Union of Turkish Chambers of Commerce.

Community legislation" (Art.54). "Areas of direct relevance to the operation of the customs union" has been defined in a very wide and comprehensive manner, including the following:

- commercial policy and agreements with third countries comprising a commercial dimension for industrial products;
- legislation on the abolition of technical barriers to trade in industrial products;
- competition;
- industrial and intellectual property law;
- customs legislation.

Wherever new legislation is drafted by the European Commission in any of these areas which "have direct relevance to the operation of the customs union", the Commission shall "informally consult Turkish experts", together with experts from the Member States of the EC (Art.55).

It remains to be seen how effective an "informal consultation" will be during the months to come. After formal consultations with the Member States' experts and "informal consultations" with Turkish experts, the Commission will transmit its proposal to the Council of the European Community where all the Member States are represented from working groups to COREPER and the Council of Ministers. As Turkey is not a member, the Commission "shall send copies thereof to Turkey", presumably for information purposes. However, before the actual decision of the Council of Ministers, the Community and Turkey may consult each other, upon mutual request, within the Customs Union Joint Committee (Art.55). The drafters of this provision must not be satisfied with the consultation procedure described above as they added this following paragraph to the article concerned: the European Community and Turkey "shall cooperate **in good faith** during the information and consultation phase with a view to facilitating, at the end of the process, the decision most appropriate for the proper functioning of the customs union."

When the Community adopts legislation in those areas which have "direct relevance to the functioning of the customs union", Turkey will be immediately informed within the Customs Union Joint Committee, "to allow Turkey to adopt corresponding legislation which will ensure the proper functioning of the customs union." (Art.56).

Where there may be problems for Turkey in adopting the corresponding legislation, the Customs Union Joint Committee "shall make every effort to find a mutually acceptable solution" in order to maintain a properly functioning customs union (Art.56 §2).

Another contradictory provision is in Article 57 of the Decision 1/95 concerning the implementation of the customs union. The said provision mentions two opposing principles adopted in the decision: on the one hand it talks about the "principle of harmonization" which provides that Turkish legislation shall be harmonized as far as possible with Community legislation; on the other hand the same article mentions "Turkey's right [...] to amend legislation in areas of direct relevance to the functioning of the customs union." While Turkey has a right to amend legislation concerning the customs union — presumably the legislation adopted by the Community will be amended by Turkey before it is implemented or introduced into Turkish internal law — such a right to differ from the Community legislation depends on the approval of the Customs Union Joint Committee. This Committee has to conclude that "the amended legislation does not effect the proper functioning of the customs union."

It is clear that an effective customs union needs complete harmonization of customs legislation which requires the participation of all the members of the customs union to take part in actual decision-making institutions. However a member of a customs union which is not a Member State of the EC is not represented in the institutions (Council, Commission, Parliament, Court of Justice and others). Therefore its chance of influencing the decisions is minimal. Since that country is not a full member, **there is no direct effect or direct application of these texts in the country involved**. Therefore, the legislation adopted by the Community has to be adopted by Turkey in order to introduce these texts into Turkish internal law. On the one hand, the decision recognizes "Turkey's right [...] to amend legislation in areas of direct relevance to the functioning of the customs union", on the other hand it limits this right to the effect that such "amended legislation does not effect the proper functioning of the customs union."

If, on the other hand, Turkey is contemplating new legislation in an area "of direct relevance to the functioning of the customs union", the Turkish Government shall "informally" seek the views of the Commission on the proposed legislation in question.

Furthermore, the wording of Article 55 §2 is not in conformity with the regular diplomatic terminology: Turkey "shall informally seek the views of the Commission on the proposed legislation in question so that the Turkish legislator may take his decision in full knowledge of the consequences for the functioning of the customs union."

Once the proposed legislation has reached a sufficiently advanced stage of drafting, consultations will be held within the Customs Union Joint Committee. If such legislation is likely to disrupt the proper functioning of the customs union, the Customs Union Joint Committee shall try to find a mutually acceptable solution.

If discrepancies between Community and Turkish legislation cause or threaten to cause impairment of the free movement of goods or deflections of trade, the affected Party may take necessary protection measures and notify the Customs Union Joint Committee. Priority should be given to measures which least disturb the functioning of the customs union. The Customs Union Joint Committee may decide whether to amend or abolish these measures.

For the judicial procedure for the settlement of disputes between Parties, the Council of Association Decision 1/95 provided an arbitration method which will be discussed below. At this juncture it is sufficient to note that the "protection measures" taken by the affected Party against such discrepancies in customs union legislation are included within the limited competence of the arbitration tribunal.

4. The Settlement of Disputes

Whereas the legal disputes between Member States and Community institutions may be referred to the Court of Justice of the European Community, there is no provision in the Association Agreement whereby the Court would have automatic jurisdiction.

Should a dispute arise between Turkey and the EC relating to the application or interpretation of the Association Agreement (Additional Protocol or the Decisions of the Association Council), the Contracting Parties may bring the case to the Council of Association for a settlement (Art.25). Complaints by private Parties or other organizations are implicitly excluded. Only Turkey, the Community and Member States of the Community may bring their complaints to the Council. Naturally, individuals or legal entities may bring their case to their respective governments of the Member State or of Turkey. It is interesting to note that a third State may not bring an action to the Association Council.

The Council may resolve the dispute by a decision which shall be binding on the part of the Parties concerned since each Party is required to take the measures necessary to comply with such decisions (Art.25 §3).

In cases where the Association Council cannot resolve the dispute (due to the fact that the decisions can be taken unanimously where both Turkey and the Community have one vote each) the Council may decide to submit the dispute to the Court of Justice of the EC or to any other existing court or tribunal. Naturally, the decision to submit a case to the European Court can only be taken unanimously. Therefore, when one of the Contracting Parties (the Community or Turkey) does not wish to bring the dispute to the Luxembourg Court or to any other judicial authority, the conflict will remain unresolved. This is another facet of the "institutional void" or deficiency in the Association which is so comprehensive and complex that a judicial mechanism will be required for an efficient interpretation and implementation of the customs union. It may be argued that the customs union is not in itself an end to this relationship and is introduced only as a pre-accession period which should lead to full membership in due course; therefore the present anomaly is only temporary.

The agreement provides another possibility for the settlement of disputes where the Council of Association cannot resolve the problem. Article 25 §4 empowers the Council of Association to determine the detailed rules for "arbitration" or for "any other judicial procedure" to which the Contracting Parties may resort during the transitional and final stages of the Association. This is a special mechanism, as the associated country cannot be involved with the European Court before accession.

The Council of Association in its Decision 1/95 (Customs Union) provided a special arbitration procedure with a very limited jurisdiction in terms of the types of conflicts which may be referred to for arbitration (Art.61). Arbitration is only open in the following matters:

1) If discrepancies between Community and Turkish legislation or differences in their implementation in an area of direct relevance to the functioning of the customs union cause or threaten to cause impairment of the free movement of goods or deflections of trade and the affected Party considers that "immediate action" is required, it may itself take the necessary "protection measures". The measures taken by one of the Contracting Parties may be challenged by the other in the Arbitration Panel.

2) Safeguard measures taken in accordance with the agreement may also be brought to the Arbitration Panel[23].

---

[23] Article 60 of the Additional Protocol provides that "if serious disturbances" occur in a sector of the Turkish economy (or of the Community), or prejudice the external

3) Rebalancing measures taken by either Party may also be referred to arbitration[24].

Where the disputes relate only to one of the three above-mentioned cases, a Contracting Party may bring the dispute to arbitration within six months of the date on which this procedure was initiated. Therefore, each Party must bring an action to the Arbitration Panel within six months.

The Arbitration Tribunal consists of three arbitrators. The two Parties to the dispute shall each appoint one arbitrator within thirty days. In such a procedure both Turkey and the Community will appoint one arbitrator each. The two arbitrators so designated shall nominate by joint agreement the third arbitrator who is referred to as the "umpire". The umpire may not be a national of either Turkey or the Community (or a Member State).

If arbitrators appointed by both Parties cannot agree within two months of their appointment, the umpire shall be chosen by them from a list of seven persons established by the Association Council.

The Arbitration Tribunal shall sit in Brussels and take its decisions by majority.

D. Financial Cooperation and Free Movement of Workers: The Non Implemented Provisions

Whereas the establishment of a customs union between Turkey and the European Community has been achieved, the necessary support mechanism in terms of financial cooperation is still in limbo.

In fact, Turkey has not received any financial support from the Community since 1980 when the Fourth Financial Protocol was adopted between the two Parties. From the beginning, the Association Agreement was regarded as "an association for the purposes of **development**" and "an association prior to **accession**". The Preamble of the Ankara Agreement underlined this fact with the following statements:

---

stability or adversely effect the economic situation in a region of Turkey (or the Community), Contracting Parties may take the "necessary protective measures". (Art.60 §1 for Turkey, Art.61 §2 for the Community).

[24] According to Article 64 of the Decision 1/95, "if a safeguard or protection measure taken by a Contracting Party creates an imbalance between the rights and obligations under the — customs union — decision", the other Contracting Party may take "rebalancing measures in respect of that Party".

- Determined to establish ever closer bonds between the Turkish people and the peoples brought together in the European Economic Community;
- Resolved to ensure a continuous improvement in living conditions in Turkey, [...] through accelerated economic progress and the harmonious expansion of trade, and **to reduce the disparity between the Turkish economy and the economies of the Member States of the Community**;
- Mindful both of the special problems presented by the **development of the Turkish economy** and of **the need to grant economic aid to Turkey during a given period**;
- Recognizing that **the support given by the European Economic Community to the efforts of the Turkish people to improve their standard of living will facilitate the accession of Turkey** to the Community at a later date;

[...] have decided to conclude an agreement establishing an Association... (OJ No.217, 29.12.1964).

In order to attain the objectives of the Association Agreement, Financial Protocols were made. The First Financial Protocol (1964) was for an amount of ECU 175 million for the financing of investment projects. Although this may seem to be a negligible amount today, at the time it played an important role. It should be noted that in 1964, Turkey's annual export figure was around 400 million dollars. Similarly, Second and Third Financial Protocols were signed and implemented until 1980 when the Fourth Financial Protocol was agreed. The total amount of Community funds to be allocated to Turkey within the framework of the Fourth Financial Protocol was ECU 600 million for a period of five years. Again, this figure may not impress the reader today but if we recall that in 1980 the yearly exports of Turkey were around the two billion dollar level, it is clear that the Fourth Financial Protocol provided a considerable amount of funds to Turkey. However, this Protocol has never been implemented and since 1980 Turkey has not benefited from any EC fund or credit. It must be added that after the Fourth Financial Protocol which was for a period of five years, Fifth and Sixth Financial Protocols should have been in progress covering the period up to 1996.

Indeed, whereas Turkey was reducing its customs walls towards Community products, the required Community support for the industrial restructuring in Turkey never materialized. Indeed, for a period of fifteen years, the Community failed to fulfill its obligations towards Turkey.

Another important provision of the Association Agreement and Additional Protocol was the implementation of the free movement of workers in accordance with Articles 48, 49 and 50 of the Treaty of Rome. Indeed, the free movement of workers was to be achieved gradually between 1976 and 1986. The logic behind this arrangement was the following: whilst Turkey was opening up its markets to Community industrial products over a twenty-two years period, she was going to have some structural problems. Some industries were going to encounter difficulties and thus the process would result in unemployment. However, the loss of these jobs resulting from Community competition could be compensated by providing jobs for Turkish workers in Member States. Unfortunately, the provision for the free movement of workers was not implemented[25] and the balance of rights and obligations of the two Contracting Parties in the Association Agreement was further disturbed to Turkey's loss. Not only were the financial protocols neglected, but also the free movement of workers could not be implemented. In spite of these negative influences Turkey continued to open up its markets to Community industrial products and by 1996 a customs union had been established.

Although the Commission in its opinion on Turkey's Request for Accession underlined "the importance of financial support to Turkey" in 1989 by stating that "Financial Cooperation should be revitalized by releasing the resources of the Fourth Financial Protocol" and adding that "the Community should further reflect on the possibility of unilaterally granting loans [...] for the financing of infrastructure projects of interest to both Turkey and the Community", no progress was made.

A close observer of Turkey-EC relations, in a lengthy analysis of the balance of rights and obligations of the two Parties, after underlining the importance of the release of the Fourth Financial Protocol, pointed out that there was a need to make "an offer to a direct follow-up by a new Financial Protocol or another measure which would contribute to the **compensation for the negative economic consequences caused by the denial of freedom of movement**" for workers[26].

E. Regional and Economic Effects of the Customs Union

Economists tell us that the liberalization of factor movements may entail the gravitation of productive factors from slow-growth areas to

---

[25] See the Judgment of the European Court of Justice in the *Demirel* Case, (1987) **ECR** 3719.

[26] KRAMER, *op. cit.*, p.532.

fast-growth areas, and this may in the short term cause economic imbalances and inequality which would naturally be unacceptable to Member States. Accordingly, the creation of a customs union profoundly affects the labor and capital markets in the countries concerned, and the integration of production factor markets affects the production of goods and thus trade.

As far as the standard neoclassical economic theory is concerned, it is of no real consequence why regional disparities emerge, since there are mechanisms in an economy which will ensure that they will prove to be only a temporary phenomenon. Tomkins & Twomey argue that "cumulative causation theories" provide "a strong theoretical rationale for widening regional prosperity. The basis of these theories lies in the recognition of the fact that because of the impact of differing levels of productivity or the existence of internal and external economies of scale, it is perfectly feasible that economic benefits begin to accumulate in particular regions of an economy and become self-perpetuating. In such circumstances, market forces may actually come to reinforce this development and contribute to unbalanced regional growth."[27]

It is clear that once the process of economic integration is in progress, it is likely that already existing problems of regional disparities will intensify. The productivity differentials will continue to exist and they will favor the technologically advanced firms of developed areas within the economic union.

Another important factor to be taken into consideration is this: economic integration may encourage the concentration of new industry and relocation of existing industry in certain areas of the union which give superior infrastructure, lower transport costs and availability of skilled labor. Thus, with the enlargement of the market and enhanced competition, the most efficient enterprises will expand by the integration process, while the less efficient will be driven out of the market. Consequently, the economic activity at the periphery of the economic union will be affected negatively and disproportionately from the effects of integration as the enterprises at the periphery are on the whole less efficient, with lower productivity than those at the developed center. Hitiris submits that "in addition to these problems, there is always the possibility that common policies undertaken for the realization of integration objectives, may have profound and sometimes unforeseen regional

---

[27] TOMKINS, J. & TWOMEY, J., *Regional Policy, European Economic Integration*, in: McDONALD & DEARDEN (eds), London, 1992, p.100.

effects."[28] Therefore, it is clear that as a consequence of these reasons, the rates of growth in the developed centres will be higher than those in the less developed regions of the union.

On the one hand, the economic theories point out the advantages of primary forms of integration, namely of the goods markets and production markets, and argue that all partners may profit from the establishment of a customs union. Furthermore, the economic theories also underline that "the profit of integrated product markets is enhanced if the internal movement of the production factors, that is to say movement of labor and capital is liberalized. To let markets function properly, a certain level of positive integration is needed."

Economists and politicians act upon the following assumption: competitive markets (efficiency) generate considerable inequality. Government and other institutions are then required to reduce this inequality by redistribution, even if it means some loss of efficiency[29].

The European Community was created as a common market. The objective was to step up efficiency and stimulate economic growth by integrating the markets of goods and economic factors (Turkey-EC Association Agreement also provided the integration of the markets of goods and productive factors). That the ensuing structural changes in the EC implied some unacceptable consequences for certain sectors of the society was expected (like relocation of economic activities, changing composition of sectoral activity). The most vulnerable groups were concentrated in particular regions of the customs union. In short, regional problems are the disparities in the levels of income in rates of economic growth of output and employment, and in general in the levels of economic inequality between the geographic regions. **Free competition does not tend to equalize factor returns across regions and therefore regional differences in economic development remain an important problem.** Thus, market forces cannot be relied upon to produce the necessary degrees of inter-regional balance in economic growth. Hence, areas that were considered relatively prosperous before integration may turn into the backward regions of the union. Therefore, **the costs and benefits of integration must be properly shared between the member countries and the regions of the economic union as a whole.** To this end, the EC developed a number of instruments and policies which

---

[28] HITIRIS, T., **European Community Economics**, (2nd ed.), Harvester, 1991, p.233.

[29] According to Okun there is a trade-off between efficiency and equality. OKUN, A., **Equality and Efficiency: The Big Trade-Off**, Brookings, Washington, 1975.

should be extended to Turkey being part of the same customs union. Indeed, the Community recognized that the problem of regional disparities between the richest and the poorest areas threatened to disrupt the convergence of economic performance inside the EC and to delay the progress towards integration. Various Community funds and common policies had been designed to function with regional problems among their objectives. These funds finance regional projects for the modernization of industry, investment for job creation, and training and retraining schemes in problem areas[30].

The Community decided that assistance will be provided where the GDP is below the national average or where there is dependence on agriculture or on a declining industry. Community regional funds are used in areas where there is a high rate of unemployment or net migration. Cases where Community policies, in particular free trade, had an adverse effect on Community funds will enter the picture.

"Completion of the Single Internal Market", according to a Commission paper, "renders inevitable that resources both of people and materials, and capital and investment, flow into areas of greatest economic advantage." Increasing openness of product and factor markets will generate gains, but it is not certain that they will be distributed equally among the regions of the Community. Therefore, it was admitted that the integration process may have adverse sectoral and regional effects on the problem regions. As a result, the Single European Act provided important increases in the funds allocated for regional development with particular emphasis on concentrating resources in the regions with per capita GDP of less than 75 percent of the Community average. These funds were ERDF, ESF, Guidance Section of EAGGF, etc.

Thus, all of Portugal, Ireland and Greece, parts of Spain, Italy and Eastern Germany, and the French overseas departments are listed as "first priority areas" because of their structural backwardness. This entitles them to funding of up to 75 percent from Community funds which were doubled by 1992, increasing their share of the overall Community budget from 18 to 28 percent. Indeed, in February 1988, a decision was taken

---

[30] For a detailed analysis of Community regional policies and related questions see, MOLLE, W., **The Economics of European Integration - Theory, Practice, Policy**, Dartmouth, 1990; McDONALD, F. & DEARDEN, S. (eds), **European Economic Integration**, Longman, 1990; EL-AGRAA, A.M., **The Economics of the European Community**, (4th ed.), Harvester Wheatsheaf, 1994; NIELSEN, J., HEINRICH, H. & HANSEN, J., **An Economic Analysis of the EC**, McGraw Hill, 1992; ARTIS, M.J. & LEE, N., **The Economics of the EU**, Oxford, 1994; HITIRIS, T., *op. cit.*, 1991.

for the doubling in real terms of the resources of the three funds in the next five years.

The link established between the Internal Market and the doubling of resources[31] through Structural Funds also meant an implicit recognition of the danger that the weaker regions of the Community could end up as net losers from further market integration.

For the five years period 1989-1993, a total of 60.3 billion ECU (in 1989 prices) was committed for spending through the three Structural Funds.

It may be of interest to students of Turkey-EC relations that by 1992, annual transfers through Structural Funds represented 3.5, 2.9, and 2.3 of GDP for Portugal, Greece and Ireland[32].

It should also be noted that the Commission called for a further substantial increase in the overall resources of the Structural Funds, which should raise expenditure to approximately 33.5 percent of the EC budget in 1997, compared to 27 percent in 1992.

On this matter, **the Agreement on the European Economic Area (EEA)** constitutes an important model as we recall that one of the demands of the less developed EC Member States in the EEA negotiations was that European Free Trade Association (EFTA) should assist in the development and structural adjustment of the poorest Community regions. (This was partly achieved through improved market access for certain agricultural products particularly important to the economies of these countries. Parallel to the EEA Agreement, a number of EFTA countries concluded bilateral agreements with the EC granting tariff and other concessions in the field of agriculture). The main solution was, however, a system of financial assistance provided by EFTA states. The financial mechanism was based on two different elements: grants and interest subsidies provided in connection with loans granted by the European Investment Bank. Among projects submitted by undertakings, special consideration was to be given to small and medium-sized enterprises. It was an interesting model as these EFTA countries were not becoming part of the customs union but were going to benefit from the free trade

---

[31] DE WITTE, B., *"The Reform of the European Regional Development Fund"*, in: **Common Market Law Review**, No.23, 1986, pp.419-440; LOWE, P., *"The Reform of the Community's Structural Funds"*, in: **Common Market Law Review**, No.25, 1988, pp.503-521.

[32] TSOUKALIS, L., **The New European Economy**, Oxford University Press, Oxford, 1993, p.245.

agreement. The less developed Member States of the EC requested these grants as a price for the opening of their markets to EFTA countries (Arts 115-117 and Protocol 38)[33].

With the customs union, Turkey completely opened its markets to a much larger group of countries than the small EFTA states. The EU constitutes an economic power at least twenty times larger than the relevant EFTA countries at the time.

The Commission Opinion on Turkey's application for membership observed the following: "Progressive completion of the customs union will give the Community the opportunity to associate Turkey more closely within the operation of the Single Market, while taking into account the constraints imposed by the economic disparities between Turkey and the Community. This requires a strengthening of the machinery for agreeing concerted economic and social policies between the Turkish Government and the Community institutions."[34]

Conclusion
The Customs Union must progress
Continuously towards further Integration

As pointed out elsewhere in this paper, the establishment of a customs union between Turkey and the European Community was not in itself the final target of the Treaty. All of the four basic freedoms of movement of the Treaty of Rome were included in the Association Agreement. It was not only the establishment of a customs union (where both sides eliminate tariffs between themselves and establish a common tariff schedule on goods from outside countries) but the completion of a real common market, thereby removing all barriers to factor movements between Turkey and the EC, that was provided. So far, only one of the free movements has been achieved with the customs union. The Association Council is expected to start the implementation of other provisions of the agreement where both Turkey and the EC agree to be guided by the principles of the Treaty of Rome "for the purpose of abolishing restrictions on freedom of establishment between them" (Art.13) and "for the purpose of abolishing restrictions on freedom to provide services" between Turkey and the EC. In fact, Article 41 §2 of the Additional Protocol

---

[33] BLANCHET, T., PIIPPONEN, B.R. & WESTMAN-CLEMENT, M., **The Agreement on the European Economic Area (EEA), A Guide to the Free Movement of Goods and Competition Rules** No.198, Oxford, 1994, pp.18-19.

[34] SEC (89) 2290 Final, December 18, 1989, p.9

(1970) directs the Association Council to take necessary decisions to this effect: "The Council of Association shall, in accordance with [...] the Agreement of Association, determine the timetable and rules for the progressive abolition [...] of restrictions on freedom for establishment and on freedom to provide services."

Although the provision for the achievement of free movement of workers as provided in the agreement and the protocol could not be implemented because of unemployment and various social problems existing in some of the Member States, the suggestion put forward by Kramer[35] for a "measure which would contribute to the compensation for the negative economic consequences caused by the denial of freedom of movement" for workers should also be taken into account in future Association Council meetings in order to re-establish the equilibrium between the Community and Turkey.

"One argument for progressive integration" according to William Molle "...springs from **political** rather than economic theory."[36] Molle explains why progressive integration is based on political theory in the following statement: "It is based principally on an analysis of the factors underlying the dynamics of integration, the outcome of which is that under the conditions prevailing in Western Europe, a free trade area and a customs union are unstable forms of cooperation, which can function only if progressing continuously towards further integration. When the progress stagnates, forces opposed to the union's "rules of the game" may gain weight and combine with others to become a serious threat to the freedoms achieved. **Disintegration could then be prevented only by further integration."**

Therefore, in line with the areas referred to above, the Association Council should take the required decisions for the implementation of the principles already agreed on. Indeed, Article 6 of the Association Agreement directs the Association Council in the following terms: "To ensure the implementation of **the progressive development of the Association**, the Contracting Parties shall meet in a Council of Association which shall act within the powers conferred upon it by this agreement."

Furthermore, according to Article 7, "the Contracting Parties shall take all appropriate measures, whether general or particular, to ensure the fulfillment of the obligations arising from this agreement." Both the

---

[35] KRAMER, *op. cit.*
[36] MOLLE, W., *op. cit.*, p.30.

159

Community and Turkey "shall refrain from any measures liable to jeopardize the attainment of the objectives of the agreement." This "solidarity principle" is enshrined in Article 7 of the Association Agreement, which, in identical terms to Article 5 of the EC Treaty, imposes a double duty upon the Parties, i.e. to take appropriate measures to ensure the fulfillment of the obligations arising from the agreement and to refrain from taking any measures liable to jeopardize the attainment of the objectives of the agreement.

In this context, it must be stressed that the Association Agreement in Article 4 underlined the importance of **"mutual and balanced obligations"** of the Contracting Parties: "... the Contracting Parties shall, on the basis of mutual and balanced obligations: [...] align the economic policies of Turkey and the Community more closely in order to ensure the proper functioning of the Association and the progress of the joint measures which this requires."

Without the full implementation of financial cooperation provisions which would be needed for a successful implementation of a customs union between the Community and Turkey (in line with similar support systems available to Member States which were devised to correct the regional imbalances) and without the full implementation of the other free movement factors (free movement of services, right of establishment, free movement of workers or a compensation system for the negative economic consequences caused by the denial of freedom of movement), it cannot be said that the present state of affairs is based on **mutual and balanced obligations**.

The Association Council must take appropriate measures "in order to ensure the proper functioning of the Association and the progress of the joint measures which this requires", on the basis of mutual and balanced obligations.

Some Lessons from the Mercosur Initial Experience

Félix PEÑA

Executive Director, Europa-Argentina Club;
Member of the Board,
Argentinian Council of Foreign Affairs;
Former Mercosur Negotiator

1. Economic Integration Methodologies: The Mercosur Case

The Mercosur experience allows us to draw some lessons concerning economic integration methodologies applied by geographically contiguous like-minded countries willing to work together, sharing efforts in developing a friendly regional environment for democracy, economic modernization and global competitiveness.

Multinational economic integration between Latin American countries has a poor record in history. At least in the former Hispanic colonies, in most cases, relative economic and political irrelevance has been the concrete result of several economic integration processes, after an initial period of great expectations. Within the region, the logic of fragmentation has been stronger than the logic of integration since their independence of the last century.

Economic integration methodologies consist of formal and informal criteria, understandings (mostly implicit), rules of the game, institutions and proceedings that allow sovereign countries to work together sharing, to a certain degree, policies, markets and resources within the framework of common visions and goals. They include, but they go beyond, different techniques of market integration — i.e. free trade area, customs union, common market, quality or comprehensive free trade area.

Methodologies are normally shaped at the founding moment of each concrete process, influenced mainly by the individual economic and political realities of each of the partners and by their relationship throughout history. After the founding moment, the main challenge of these methodologies is their capacity to adapt to highly dynamic domestic and international realities, preserving the vitality of the original vision and of the logic of integration among partners. They are also strongly influenced by the level of economic interdependence — measured mainly by reciprocal trade and investment and by the pattern of distribution of economic and political power among the partners.

This paper will analyze the Mercosur's recent experience concerning their methodology of economic integration and also draw some preliminary lessons from this experience that could be of interest to other similar cases.

Mercosur is a concrete case of sovereign nations working together in order to achieve common visions and goals within a collective discipline framework and preserving a significant degree of independence as regards their own domestic economic and foreign policies.

The analysis has in mind two crucial questions relating to voluntary economic integration processes between sovereign nations. The first is related to factors that explain the founding moment of an integration process: why do countries decide to work together, permanently sharing policies, markets and resources? The second regards the main characteristics of the methodologies that could eventually lead to their relative success: what are the main elements of any economic integration methodology that allow partners to preserve their common project in the long term?

2. The Mercosur Experience

First Argentina and Brazil, and later Uruguay and Paraguay, have walked a major part of the long path towards integrating their economies within a broader common market. A new stage began in January 1995 with the formal establishment of the customs union foreseen in the Asunción Treaty (1991). This is a new stage which could last many years until it eventually reaches a level similar to the one currently arrived at by the European Union.

The strategic objective of this political and economic process between nations of South America has been to create a common regional space in order to strengthen their own domestic efforts towards democracy consolidation, productivity transformation and competitive insertion in the global economy.

It was imagined, since its beginning, as a regional answer to the challenges faced by its member countries — as well as most other countries in the world — at the end of this century in trying to preserve their national identity and democratic values within the realities of international globalization.

Therefore, it cannot be conceived solely from an economic point of view. On the contrary, although it is a process with economic foundations and contents, it also has a clear political nature and consequences. Its most profound rationality can be grasped simply by considering the historic tension between the logic of fragmentation and the logic of integration between autonomous units of power in the international system.

This does not mean that integration does not respond to economic rationality criteria. What it does mean is that economic integration rationality becomes viable only as a result of strong political and cultural factors (i.e. democratic values).

Economic integration became possible once Argentina and Brazil, the two main partners, overcame the hypothesis of conflict in their reciprocal relationship, a legacy of the Hispanic-Portuguese historic rivalry both in Europe and in their former colonial territories.

Since the beginning of the 1980s, both countries have prioritized the hypothesis of cooperation in their mutual relationship. The present situation in 1996 is the accumulative result of almost fifteen years of predominance of the logic of integration within the region.

From the very start, political motivation has been strong. The idea of working together in order to create a broad common space for democratic and economic modernization between the two great nations of South America was realized by the governments of Alfonsin and Sarney (Iguazú Declaration (1985) and Integration and Cooperation Program between Argentina and Brazil (PICAB, 1986)) and of Menem and Collor de Melo (and continued by Itamar Franco and Fernando Henrique Cardoso), which, starting with the Act of Buenos Aires (1990) and the Economic Complementation Agreement (ACE 14, 1990), gave rise to the creation of Mercosur (1991), with the participation of Paraguay and Uruguay.

Mercosur implies the idea of a common perception of the challenges and opportunities that arise from the insertion of both countries in the international arena. It is from a common strategic vision with respect to the challenges of globalization that a shared work space between members was created. Such common vision does not mean identical external policies, as this did not even happen in the case of the European Communities.

Two broader initiatives of regional range, (the Latin American Free Trade Association, LAFTA, in 1960, and the Latin American Integration Association, LAIA, in 1980) have contributed to preparing the field in order to advance with economic integration within the region. Nevertheless, they had a limited impact as a result of the large number of heterogeneous countries and the dimension of the geographic area covered, the predominance of protectionism — import substitution period — and the lack of a common strategic vision that could give them enough motivation and political energy.

In any case, both LAFTA and LAIA have permitted the accumulation of governmental and business experience in the field of economic integration, as well as the development of reciprocal payment mechanisms and customs cooperation, of great practical value for the start of Mercosur. The main paradox is that this has indicated not the paths that lead to integration but on the contrary those that help to preserve fragmentation between national economies. Among other lessons to be drawn from the LAFTA-LAIA period, the most important one is the need to reduce the number of member countries at the beginning of the integration process in order to strengthen the advantages of physical proximity, resulting in more homogeneity and complementarity of economic interests, and to facilitate the flow of governmental and political communication.

But it is important to remember that Mercosur, as with the other preferential trade agreements signed between South American nations and with Mexico, was developed under the legal framework of the Treaty of Montevideo of 1980 which established the LAIA, which itself is under the habilitation clause of GATT, negotiated in the Tokyo Round. This is a crucial aspect to the understanding of the current relationship and negotiations between Mercosur and other LAIA members, as well as its initial relationship with GATT.

The turning point in the bilateral relationship between Argentina and Brazil was the trilateral agreement of 1979 (signed with Paraguay) on the exploitation of the shared hydro resources. This agreement permitted conflictual territorial issues with geopolitical implications to be cleared away from the path towards a spirit of cooperation between both countries.

Since then, the spirit of integration has been strengthened as a result of the return of democratic institutions and values to the four countries, the support of public opinion and the strong political will of the presidents and other high officials. The personal involvement of the political leaders has been a crucial positive factor.

From political will comes the sense of strategic direction, which is one that prevails notwithstanding the changing of persons or the difficulties that may arise. This was proved in the first big crisis in Mercosur in June 1995. A presidential meeting in Sao Paulo permitted Presidents Fernando Henrique Cardoso and Carlos Menem to put the conflict within the broader political context of a strategic alliance between both countries, leaving the path open to a quick solution of the controversy.

Between 1981 and 1983, the new spirit that characterizes the bilateral relationship between Argentina and Brazil began to manifest itself in an embryonic form, with the creation of a bilateral working group that met every three months formed by high level officials of both Foreign Relations and Economic Ministries. This group was particularly active in the 1982-1983 period and, after various meetings, progress towards the identification of the obstacles to trade expansion and the relationship between both countries was made, as well as the analysis of potential economic cooperation. This group constitutes a precedent in the methodology applied in the following stage, especially in what was later called the Common Market Group. Also during these years, important business meetings opened the path to subsequent cooperation actions, such as the one held in Sao Paulo in September 1982.

But, notwithstanding the progress made between 1981 and 1983, the true stimulus to bilateral integration was given in 1984 with the return of democratic institutions to Argentina and Brazil.

Given the methodologies applied since then, two stages can be distinguished. Both can be characterized by their strong doses of heterodoxy and pragmatism. In both cases, rather than the predominance of theoretical concepts and previous models, there is a political and strategic vision and a strong practical imagination. In both stages, the focus is on generating greater economic interdependence between the partners, starting from a high relative economic marginality. The common characteristics of both stages are the incremental character of the methodology applied (successive steps in order to create a greater economic interdependence) and the permanent participation of the respective presidents in order to distinguish the common interests originating in the perception of external challenges of those domestic interests and factors that, left to their own dynamics, would have inclined the relationship towards a field of fragmentation and conflict. In the case of Argentina, the interest and personal conviction of Presidents Alfonsín and Menem had a determining effect both in the launching of the initial idea of bilateral integration, as well as in the decision to create Mercosur.

The first stage is that of the Argentina-Brazil bilateral integration and cooperation program (PICAB), in which a sectoral approach was used in order to obtain an intrasectoral specialization and a trade balance. The sectors in which greatest progress was made were the automobile, capital goods and food sectors. Also, important progress was made in other fields of cooperation, such as technology, nuclear development and aeronautics.

The second stage is the Argentina-Brazil bilateral economic complementation agreement (ACE 14) and Mercosur, both of which come under the framework of LAIA, which establishes a gradual and automatic trade liberalization program and a common external tariff (only in Mercosur, not in ACE 14) at the end of a four year transition period. Both instruments are first steps towards a long-term common market. In this stage, the sectoral focus is formally preserved, regulated by Decision 3/91 concerning sectoral agreements, but only one is signed in the steel sector. A distinctive characteristic of this stage, then, is the acceleration of the rhythm and the global coverage of the trade liberalization program that covers all the goods included in the tariff schedule.

The transition from one stage to the other can partly be explained by the perception of the exhaustion of the methodology of partial sectoral progress, by the introduction of new policies of economic openness of the main members and by the chain effect of the "Enterprise for the Americas" Initiative proposed by President Bush in 1990 and the launching of the NAFTA negotiations.

The sum of these three factors explains the political decision of taking a step forward which meant sending a clear and irreversible sign to the markets (the idea of unrestricted market access for all kind of goods in a short period of time — four years) about the willingness to create a customs union (the term of four years was linked to the duration of presidential mandates both in Argentina and Brazil, as well as to the term of the four year Brazilian tariff reduction program that was supposed to end in 1994). This customs union was conceived as being open to economic competition through relatively low tariffs and, in the long-term, to hemispheric integration (the idea of negotiating together a framework agreement on trade and investment consultations between the four members of Mercosur and the United States, which was signed in 1991 and is known as the "4+1").

3. Ten Years Later: The Results

The results achieved in these ten years of economic integration in South America are very significant. Different factors have influenced these results: the economic integration measures, the cumulative effect of geographic proximity and the economic openness of Argentina and Brazil.

These are the main results:

a) Reciprocal trade between Argentina and Brazil increased eight-fold between 1985 and 1995 and intra-Mercosur trade tripled in the 1990-1995 period.

b) In the case of Argentina, the exchange with Mercosur countries represents 32% of its global trade, while at the beginning of 1985 it only represented 11%. Brazil's exchange has gone from 4% to 14% in the same period.

c) Internal trade tariffs have been eliminated, except for a reduced number of products that were included in lists for the final adaptation to the trade liberalization program, which by 1999 (in the case of Argentina and Brazil) will be gradually reduced to zero. The automobile and sugar sectors still maintain a special regime. Most of the non-trade barriers have been eliminated as well (according to the Asunción Treaty, they should have been completely eliminated by now).

d) A flexible customs union has been established with a common external tariff already applicable to a substantial number of the products listed in the nomenclature and a limited number of products included in the exceptions lists, but with a convergence programmed towards the CET in a four year term. Special convergence regimes have been created for capital goods and for computers and telecommunications goods.

e) A growing number of companies are investing and organizing themselves in order to compete in the broader market, assuming . the irreversibility of the economic integration. This is evident in sectors with multinational enterprises with productive facilities in various Mercosur countries. In the automobile sector, in 1995, investment of 13 billion dollars were announced. This can also be seen in a large number of small and medium-sized enterprises which have established strategic alliances (even with foreign partners) in order to produce in the Mercosur area.

f) Credibility on the accomplishment of Mercosur's objectives has grown both among the members as well as on an international level even though there is a history of failures. This increasing credibility is a result of the success of the Real Plan in Brazil, the approval in Ouro Preto of the common external tariff, the privatization and economic deregulation processes both in Argentina and Brazil, and the confirmation of the political will to continue after the recent elections in Brazil, Uruguay and Argentina, and after the automobile crisis of June 1995.

During the transition period, the economic context was not always favorable to the development of Mercosur. The main difficulties arose from the macroeconomic instability of Brazil's economy during the long months between 1992 and 1994, creating doubts among its members (especially Argentina) about the viability of the Mercosur trade liberalization program as well as about the realism of the idea of a customs union in a context of strong economic and monetary instability. Indeed, from this originated the second source of difficulties: the strong doubts in some Argentine sectors as to the possibility of advancing with Mercosur according to the terms agreed in the Asunción Treaty. Instead, some sectors proposed the idea of integrating into NAFTA or of signing a bilateral free trade agreement with the United States.

The launching of the Real Plan in June 1994, as well as the impossibility (at least momentarily) of individually joining NAFTA (even before the Mexican crisis of December 1994), contributed to the re-establishment of a greater sense of credibility among the Mercosur partners regarding the possibility of accomplishing the objectives of the Asunción Treaty.

New difficulties arose from the economic difficulties of the first semester of 1995 as a result of the effects of the Mexican crisis on Argentina's economy and on Brazil's trade balance.

Nevertheless, during these first five years of Mercosur, neither partner lost the affinity created by the existence of common objectives and shared values. The integration pact prevailed because both members considered themselves "like-minded countries" both politically and economically. The fact that Brazil surmounted the crisis produced by the resignation of president Collor de Melo, and that it firmly maintained the market opening figures of 1990 during the 1992-1994 period, were crucial factors in the achievement of the transition period overcoming the macroeconomic difficulties.

As had been the case with PICAB, a key factor in its success was the personal interest shown by the presidents. Their presence in the half yearly summits introduced a political content into an otherwise too technically and economically oriented process. On the other hand, the relationship between the Ministers for Foreign Relations and Economy was also very smooth, frequent and direct, characteristics that were even stronger at the level of high officials and negotiators.

The methodology applied in order to integrate the markets during the transition period was heterodox and very practical. It presented a very dominant characteristic, namely the formal introduction of only one non-negotiable element: the trade liberalization program. Its automatic system put a stop to the pressures from the protectionists' interests who, as in the LAFTA-LAIA period, tried to solve their adjustment problems by postponing the liberalization calendar. The original idea is linked to the concept introduced in the Convertibility Plan of Argentina (1991): to remove from the negotiating table the key factors of failure from past experiences of economic integration (tariff negotiation) and of economic stabilization (exchange parity) in the Argentinian case.

But, within this rigid trade liberalization program, the members have shown a level of pragmatism by maintaining a certain amount of flexibility in order to overcome different negative effects produced by the economic asymmetries (i.e. Brazil's attitude towards the statistical tariff introduced in 1992 by Argentina and Argentina's attitude not to pressurize Brazil during the latter's economic crisis of 1992-1994). In each case, the political interest of not affecting the other country's efforts to overcome those difficulties that were considered to be surpassable prevailed. As one negotiator said: "Brazil's economic stability is in the common interest of Mercosur." This factor helps to understand the pragmatism with which the negotiation was handled in the 1993-1994 period.

Another factor that helped to speed up the markets' liberalization was the need to secure the regional supply of products sensitive to internal inflationary pressures. This can be seen in Argentina, especially in 1991, and in Brazil in the second half of 1994 and first half of 1995.

The incremental character, the presence of only one rigid factor and the flexibility in the application of all the remaining elements were largely possible due to Mercosur's institutional mechanisms, inspired by those of the PICAB period. These have allowed a great proximity between the decisions taken in Mercosur and the concrete requirements of the economic realities of its members.

The fact that the Common Market Group was formed by high level officials of both the External Relations and Economics Ministries (under the instructions of the Economics Minister) also contributed to the pragmatism and realism that prevailed in the transition period.

In conclusion, in this period there was a strong sense of strategic direction, promoted at the highest political level, supported in the fact that the same basic economic approaches were shared, and facilitated by a great flexibility. The idea was to advance towards a determined direction without forcing the margins of manoeuvre permitted by the dynamic internal realities.

The three key components of the Mercosur formula in its transition period were firmness in the direction, audacity in the objectives, accelerated rhythm and instrumental prudence. The two most relevant results are, without hesitation, the spectacular growth in the level of economic interdependence and the gradual development of an embryo of economic and trade collective disciplines, based on increasing mutual confidence and a dynamic consensus.

4. Lessons from the Experiences of Mercosur

From the experience obtained from the methodology applied in the building of Mercosur, which is still incomplete, we can draw some conclusions:

A) A first conclusion is that some of its features are common to almost all of the efforts of integration and free trade areas that are developing in the hemisphere.

These features are:

a) The countries' understanding of the need to develop a new regional friendly environment with their neighboring countries, with economic integration as the catalyst of a new reality. The objectives of this new reality are the creation of an external environment that will favor the internal consolidation of democracy, a productive transformation through the incorporation of technological progress and greater social cohesion, and a competitive insertion into the world economy.

b) The importance of fixing a long-term objective and of approaching it with an incremental process that combines, with mutual benefits, few substantive elements of rigidity with others of great operative flexibility.

c) The need to emphasize the automatic mechanism of trade liberalization and the extended deregulation of international economic transactions. This will help to limit the governmental discretion for unilateral actions and will promote a larger role for the economic agents.

d) A low external tariff, eventually a common one for all the countries, and a drastic elimination of non-tariff barriers, in search of stimulating global competitiveness.

e) A collective macroeconomic discipline based on the control of the respective macroeconomic equilibriums and oriented towards the creation of systemic competitive conditions.

f) The cautious application of a collective trade discipline in such a way that it does not affect legal security but contemplates the occasional short-term situations of member countries that could jeopardize their domestic efforts regarding both economic and political stabilization.

g) The negotiation of basic rules of the game, protected by efficient arbitral jurisdictional mechanisms (permanent or *ad hoc*), especially for cases of unilateral action taken by governments against what has been agreed, in order to stimulate investment within the new market.

h) The institutionalization of flexibility by escape clauses that will allow a predictable resolution of eventual problems.

i) To benefit from the increased bargaining capacity produced by the new economic space in order to have a greater influence in the negotiations on both the WTO and hemispheric level.

j) The insertion of each economic integration process into a broader international strategy of flexible and dynamic multiple alliances of each country and their respective firms.

B) A second conclusion refers to some factors that in the Mercosur case help to explain the progress made and the methodology that was applied to achieve it. But they are not necessarily useful when placed in another context or in a larger scale, or when used as a model in other countries. These factors are:

a) A limited number of members with geographical continuity. Mercosur has shown the advantages of advancing first among countries that are geographically close with common political and economic interests and values.

b) The importance given to the appearance of a gradual trade and macroeconomic collective discipline among its members. This might have been one of the most important effects of Mercosur, observable in at least three aspects: in the international trade rules of the game (zero tariffs and a flexible external common tariff); in international trade negotiations, especially since the introduction in 1995 of the flexible customs union; and, finally, in economic stabilization policies, as reflected during the smooth consultations made during the most critical moments of the financial crisis of the first four months of 1995.

c) The massive market opening and deregulation of the most important economies of the area. Argentina and Brazil have considerably opened their economies to world trade and are implementing, or have already done so, the privatization of their public enterprises and services.

d) The automaticity of the trade liberalization program. The fact that this idea was incorporated into the treaty, with very rigid modifying conditions, was crucial for explaining how, at the end of the period of transition, with some limited exceptions, the zero tariff objective had been reached.

e) The strength in preserving the original strategic direction established for the integration process. Two factors contributed to this: first, the direct participation of the presidents in the periodic Mercosur Council meetings, which helped maintain the political momentum necessary to overcome critical situations in the evolution of the established plan; second, although there has been discontinuity at government levels, the most important economic policies referring to the opening of international trade have not been changed.

f) Instrumental flexibility. With the only exception of the trade liberalization program, the Asunción Treaty gives great flexibility to confront the dynamic situations of its members. An example of this is that the treaty never determined precisely what the common external tariff would mean, nor how macroeconomic coordination was to be reached. Even the objective of reaching a common market was defined only by the general elements that would characterize it, leaving the definition of the specific instruments, and the moment to achieve them, open to discretion. It was never said that the common market would be configured with all the elements of Article 1 of the treaty by December 31, 1994.

g) The understanding of the occasional difficulties of the members. Never was a member pressured into taking decisions that could aggravate a serious domestic economic difficulty it might have had. On the contrary, the prevailing idea was that the best way to advance with Mercosur was that each country, especially those with larger economies, should overcome their serious economic difficulties, even adopting measures that could be seen as arguable from a legal point of view in the framework of the Asunción Treaty.

h) The simplicity of the institutional structure and the direct participation of senior government officials. The characteristics of the Common Market Group and its eleven sub-working groups were of crucial importance for this. They allowed direct contact and the development of a informal spirit between the senior government officials of the areas involved in the integration strategy (Foreign Affairs, Economy, Trade, Industry, Central Banks) and hundreds of technical public officials. This gave the Mercosur agenda a great affinity with the crucial problems of each national government. It also helped the continuous process of consulting the political wings of each national government.

i) The external challenges raised by the competition between the big economic blocs. Since it began in 1990, Mercosur has been influenced by the perception that Argentina and Brazil had opportunities and challenges resulting from the initiatives from the United States (Enterprise for the Americas Initiative, National Export Strategy), NAFTA, APEC, and from the European Union (its expansion towards Eastern Europe, the proposal of an inter-regional alliance). In Brazil's case (the most important market of the area), this meant an encouragement to deepen an economic alliance with Argentina and to promote initiatives that will preserve a position for its industrial exports in very dynamic South American markets. In Argentina's case, it reinforced the idea of an economic space of privileged access while remaining open to alliances with other economic blocs.

j) The preservation of a mutual relatively beneficial situation for each member (win-win situation), as a way of sustaining the associative bond and the spirit of team work.

k) The absence of serious conflicts in the bilateral relations, especially between Argentina and Brazil. The occasional differences concerning foreign affairs problems have been no greater, in any case, to what we could observe in the same period of time between the members of the European Union. It has been recognized that an economic integration process does not necessarily require agreements in all the policies referring to the foreign affairs of each of the members.

l) The response from the business sector and the gradual development of an extended network of strategic business alliances. Almost all of the multinational corporations that operate in the region have been influenced by the existence of Mercosur. They are either rationalizing their production and their commercialization systems, or they are investing significant amounts with the new market in mind. Similarly, there are hundreds of cases of small and medium-sized enterprises in the industrial and service sectors that have organized themselves in order to compete in Mercosur, developing in many cases strategic alliances with other firms from their own countries or from another member of Mercosur.

m) A positive attitude from public opinion and from the political forces concerning the idea of the economic integration of the countries of South America.

C) A third conclusion refers to the methodology of expansion of the common economic space that Mercosur implies. The idea has been to create gradually, through negotiations and incremental approaches, larger economic spaces that will favor the global competitiveness efforts of the firms operating in Mercosur, subsequently stimulating productive investment and technological modernization. In this perspective, the initiative (originally proposed by Brazil) of a South American Free Trade Area was introduced and is now being carried out through negotiations of free trade agreements between Mercosur and the other South American members of LAIA, the first agreement having been concluded in 1996 with Chile. Also, there are the beginnings of a path towards an inter-regional transatlantic economic and political alliance of Mercosur with the European Union (the 1995 Madrid framework agreement). We must also include a future negotiation between Mercosur and NAFTA, originating from the experience acquired in the actual "4+1" with the United States and its gradual expansion to the other members of NAFTA. This type of approach would enable the central strategic idea, incorporated in the Action Plan resulting from the Miami Summit (1994), and confirmed by the Denver and Cartagena Trade Ministerial meetings, namely that hemispheric integration be based on the convergence of regional integration and free trade schemes already existing in the area, to be carried out.

THE ANDEAN COMMUNITY CASE[*]

Alan FAIRLIE REINOSO

Professor, Economics Department;
Member, Institute of European Studies,
Catholic University of Peru

In order to comment on the paper of Dr. Félix Peña: *"Building Economic Integration Areas in Latin America: Some Lessons from the Mercosur Initial Experience"*, we have made a comparative analysis with the integration process of the Andean countries.

As in Dr. Peña's paper, our analysis includes some antecedents, the experience of the integration process and a balance of its achievements. We also discuss some aspects which define the intrabloc dynamics in the Andean Community and a note about the relationship with Mercosur.

In the last section of his paper, Dr. Peña points out some lessons from the Mercosur experience. In our last section we present a contrast between these aspects and those of the Andean Community case.

In general, we agree with the outstanding aspects Dr. Peña found in Mercosur and in the need of an approach based not only on economics but also on the use of political, cultural and international variables. Certainly, the Mercosur results are impressive, most of all because of the short time in which they were obtained. Dr. Peña's opinion is that some doses of heterodoxy and pragmatism permitted the advance in

---

[*] This paper takes some aspects developed in a document about the relationship between the European Union and the Andean Community that the author submitted to the *Irela Yearbook*, Madrid.

consecutive steps and have generated an important degree of economic interdependence between the associated countries.

Certainly, similar opening politics in the region have contributed to greater intraregional trade, with different results within the blocs or among regional blocs because of the present asymmetries.

We will now present a version of the facts in the Andean Community case in order to make a comparison in the last section of this paper with the lessons Dr. Peña deduced from the Mercosur experience.

I. THE ANDEAN COMMUNITY

A. A Short Historic Review

The Andean Group is one of the most advanced integrationist projects of the developing countries. It searches to promote the balanced and harmonious development of its member countries and to encourage the process of regional integration.

The five Andean countries together have a territorial expanse of 4,710,000 km^2 with a population of about 98 million inhabitants. 78 percent of these live in urban zones and the labor force is made up of 35 million people.

The Andean Group was created on May 26th, 1969 with the subscription to the Andean Subregional Integration Agreement (Cartagena Agreement) by the plenipotentiaries of Bolivia, Colombia, Chile, Ecuador and Peru, and it took up its functions on October 16, of the same year.

This agreement was accomplished in order to encourage the integration of Latin America, which started in 1969 with the Montevideo Agreement (ALALC). This agreement intended to create a free trade zone throughout the whole continent, but the project was not viable because of the different Latin American economies.

In 1973 Venezuela joined the Cartagena Agreement and in 1976 Chile left it.

The doctrine since the creation of the Cartagena Agreement is based on the need of integration in order to achieve development. The agreements obtained by the members have been made in outstanding areas of the international economic process.

The Andean Group had the original projects of improving the position of its members within the international economic context and of reducing the different levels of development that exist among the member countries.

From a system based on the classic model of import substituting industrialization, with high tariffs and external investment restrictions, the Andean Group changed to an open integration model with common norms in accordance with international standards.

B. Strategies of Development and Integration

The integration process in Latin America has gone through multiple phases. Depending on the development strategy and the hegemony politics, this process changed from multilateralism to bilateralism and from the substitution of regional imports to a free trade zone, which became the new integration model, and since Viner & Balassa, was considered the first step towards integration.

In fact, the Andean Group accepted the substitution of regional imports as an agglutinating strategy. It sought to overcome some trade schemes, trying to introduce some instruments of sectoral management and creating redistributive mechanisms that corrected the asymmetries and permitted the growth of the relatively less developed countries. It was also intended to maintain common policies with regard to third countries, using such mechanisms as the common external tariff. There was progress made with the creation of financial institutions (CAF, FLAR) which had a very important role in the crisis context, and a number of supranational juridical organisms were set up. The conceptual scheme was to create a customs union following the Viner & Balassa concept.

Since structuralism, the integration process has been seen as an instrument that would enable imports to substitute industrialization on a regional level. This strategy, with the export of manufactured goods, should contribute to the solution of the external limit which is a structural problem in our economies and a very great restriction to their development.

It is true that there were mistakes and limitations, but this is no reason to destroy the agreement. There are two factors that are not usually mentioned, and that in my opinion are very important. The first is the fact that at the beginning there were no mechanisms for participation of the economic agents, particularly of the Andean businessmen. This would have permitted the project to develop further than the vicissitudes of politics. The institutions and strategies launched by the states were not adopted by the economic agents. The second factor is that the development strategy that would have articulated the integration process was not ready on time. Not much care was taken to enforce non-traditional exports, particularly of manufactured goods, where the Andean group could have given a regional scope as the basis of the conquest of world markets. Although not the specific objective, the role of these intraregional exports during the eighties should not been disdained. These are two pending tasks that must be reviewed.

At present the liberalization policies and strategies are being discussed in most of the Latin American countries. In the most extreme version, the integration agreements are of no importance because a unilateral opening has been established which would permit integration with the rest of the world without any kind of discrimination.

These policies are not new and were applied in the region during the eighties in order to establish a system of relative prices which permits the liberation of foreign exchange destined for the external debt service. This debt has operated as an important restriction to the normal functioning of our economies.

The adjustment policies, the recession and the context of crisis also affected the intrasubregional trade flow in different ways depending on the group we consider. An analysis of the institutional context and the kind of mechanisms that articulate the different groups is important.

We consider it essential to discuss the Latin American integration problems from an integral perspective. In this task the three above-mentioned elements — the development strategy that articulates integration, the macroeconomic policies and their coordination, and the institutional mechanisms — are some of the elements that should be considered.

While in the eighties the opening process was associated with smaller intraregional trade, during the nineties the opposite has occurred and the intraregional flow has grown substantially. On the other hand, extreme opening policies, like those practised in Peru, carried this country to its virtual retirement from the Integration Agreement in 1992 which complicated the consolidation process.

Another subject of discussion is the one referring to the type of exports that are promoted and the development strategy in progress. Some critics think that the indiscriminate opening has encouraged primary or limited added value exports, while the requirement is to increase the export of manufactured goods and services which are dynamic sectors of world trade.

In other words, the discussion is about whether or not there is compatibility between some extreme opening economies and the integration agreements (Andean Community for example). These agreements may be used to reach a strategy to export manufactured goods, create greater intraindustrial trade, improve competitiveness (by scale economies and "learning") and subsequently export to extraregional markets.

C. Advances towards the Customs Union in the Opening Context

The process of adaptation to the changes which occurred in the international, Latin American and Andean reality took place in consecutive agreements between the members of the Andean Group, which were designed on the basis of a series of meetings of the representatives of the five member countries.

In December 1989, the Galapagos Meeting took place in which the Presidents of Bolivia, Ecuador, Colombia, Peru and Venezuela prepared the so-called Strategic Design of the Andean Group in order to consolidate the Andean economic space and to improve the international articulation of the Andean Group and its contribution to the unity of Latin America.

In November 1990, during the La Paz Meeting, there was an acceleration of the steps designed to achieve the integration process.

On September 5, 1995, the VII Presidential Congress was accomplished in Quito with the subscription to the Act of Quito, which contained the presidential directions for the institutional reforms of the Andean Pact and the New Agenda of the Andean Integration or Strategic Design. There was a ratification of the creation of an Andean Common Market objective[1].

In accordance with the open model of integration, the Andean Group reaffirmed the need for change to adapt itself to the international economic opening. It established a free trade zone; and as the most important and recent policy, the Andean Group adopted the Common External

---

[1] Quito Declaration.

Tariff[2] (AEC, by the 370 Decision of the Agreement of Cartagena Commission). This constitutes an important step for the customs union, and has the purpose of avoiding some distortions, unifying protections, perfecting the customs union and easing the operation of the wide market. For possible revisions to the AEC, the Andean Group has adopted a Council of Tariff Coordination formed by important representatives from the member countries.

The AEC has four levels: 5, 10, 15 and 20 percent, in accordance with the elaboration level of the products. Both the inputs and raw materials have a tariff of 5 percent, the semi-elaborated products one of 10 and 15 percent and the final goods for consumption are in the 20 percent level. For a group of farming products, the AEC could be automatically reduced or increased on the basis of the procedures in the Prices Fringe[3] of the Andean System.

They also promulgated the removal of obstacles to foreign direct investment[4], the Common Tariff Nomenclature (NANDINA), based on the Harmonized Designing and Codification of Merchandise System that most of the countries in the world have adopted, and the Norms about Customs Valuation[5] that subscribes to the GATT Agreement about valuation.

The transportation services were liberated[6] and community norms were applied to eliminate the technical[7] and sanitary[8] obstacles. These norms harmonize the member countries' sanitary legislation in general, and the medicine, food packaging and cosmetics legislation in particular.

The subsidies to the intrasubregional exports[9] were eliminated in order to avoid distortions in the wide economic space. Now there are norms to correct, *ex post*, the competition distortions, which derive from dumping and subsidies; exports and free trade restrictions, and the norms regarding the origins of merchandise which are valid in the Andean Group are being reviewed.

---

[2] Since February 6, 1995, the Andean Group has applied a Common External Tariff for merchandise coming from third countries.

[3] Decision 371.

[4] Decision 291 and Decision 292.

[5] Decision 379.

[6] Decisions 257, 288, 289, 297, 314, 320 and 327.

[7] Decision 376.

[8] Functioning since 1992.

[9] Decisions 324 and 330.

Since January 1994, the Andean Group has a Common Regime on Industrial Property which regulates the conferring of trade marks and patents and, for the first time, protects industrial secrets and origin denominations.

1. The Financial Institutions

Andean businessmen can take advantage of the financial institutions created by the Andean Group to promote trade development and to finance investment projects in the subregion.

a) The Andean Corporation of Promotion (CAF) was legally constituted in February 1968 and operates as a development, investment and external trade bank; it also works like an economic-financial promotion agency. It can obtain resources from third countries and has been successful over the past few years.

b) In 1976, the Andean Reserve Fund was created with the participation of the five member countries; because of its success, this subsequently became known as the Latin-American Reserve Fund (FLAR) in March 1991.

   This financial institution supports the payment balance of countries of the Andean Group through credits or warrants of loans.

c) The Reciprocal Payments and Credits Agreement (CPCR). This was created in 1965, inside ALADI. It promotes trade among Latin American countries.

2. Other Institutions

a) The Council of the Cartagena Agreement (JUNAC). This is the technical organ of the agreement. It has propositional and performing functions. With the Trujillo Protocol it will become the General Secretary's Office of the Andean Community.

b) The Andrés Bello Agreement. This was established in 1970 and is the organism that preserves the cultural Andean identity within the context of the cultural heritage of Latin America.

c) The Hipólito Unánue Agreement. This was created in 1971 and is the organism responsible for improving health in the Andean area.

d) The Simón Rodríguez Agreement. This was created in 1976 with the aim of designing strategies to improve the living and working conditions in the member countries.

e) The Court of Justice. This was established in 1979 in Cartagena and is the jurisdictional organism of the Cartagena Agreement.

f) The Andean Parliament. This was created in 1979 and is the deliberating organism of the System. It is composed of representatives of the national congresses.

g) The Business Consultative Council and the Labor Consultative Council. These are the consultative institutions of the System and they are composed of representatives of both the business and labor sectors of each one of the member countries.

D. The Andean Community

1. Changes in Relation to the Previous Scheme

On May 9-10, 1996, during the VII Presidential Council in Trujillo, Peru, the Act of Trujillo and the Modifying Protocol of the Andean Subregional Integration Agreement (Cartagena Agreement) were signed and important institutional changes were introduced.

The Andean Community, which will substitute the present Andean Group, will be composed of Bolivia, Colombia, Ecuador, Peru and Venezuela and of the organisms and institutions of the Andean System of Integration.

On May 17, 1983, the Permanent Coordination System (as a part of the Andean Integration Organism) and a Technical Coordination Committee were constituted with the representation of the Cartagena Agreement Council, the CAF, the FLAR and the agreements. But this coordination mechanism was of no relevance because of a deficiency in the determination of its direction and because it only took into account the existence of one technical instance. In this way, the chancelleries became the principal elements in the stimulation of the governments' integration policies.

In agreement with the Trujillo Protocol, the Andean System of Integration will be composed of the following organisms and institutions:

a) The Andean Presidential Council. Maximum organism of the Andean Integration System, created in May 1990. This is composed of the presidents of the member countries and it emits directives about the different spheres of the Andean Subregional Integration Agreement.

b) The Andean Council of External Relationship Ministers. This was established in 1979 and is composed of the External Relationship Ministers of the member countries. It is the organism which formulates, executes and evaluates the general policies of the process of the Andean Subregional Integration Agreement.

c) The Commission of the Andean Community. This is composed of a plenipotentiary representative of each one of the member countries and an Alternate Member. It is the organism that formulates, executes and evaluates the general policies of the process of the Andean Subregional Integration Agreement in trade and investment matters.

d) The General Secretary's Office of the Andean Community. This will be the executive organism of the Andean Community. It will be directed by a General Secretary and it will express itself through resolutions.

e) The organisms created in the past are also considered: the Andrés Bello Agreement, the Hipólito Unánue Agreement, the Simón Rodríguez Agreement, the Court of Justice, the Andean Parliament, the Business Consultative Council and the Labor Consultative Council, and the Andean Corporation of Promotion (CAF) and the Latin American Reserve Fund.

The Trujillo Protocol introduces important changes and modifications to the Cartagena Agreement. There has been considerable improvement because not only does it take into account the technical organisms, the role of the plenipotentiary representatives in the formulation of obligatory devices for the member countries, but now the chancelleries can stimulate the integration agreements.

The Commission of the Andean Community should be able to formulate, execute and evaluate the subregional integration policy, but these are tasks that require the coordination of the Andean Chancellery. The General Secretary's Office of the Andean Community can incite all these measures and it could coordinate this with the organism that had been performing that task in the past.

Apparently there is emphasis on the fact that the integration process should not stop at trade relations but should also include technological, financial and cultural aspects as well. The challenge is to define instruments and institutions that can stimulate, in an integral way, the process of regional integration.

Having completed the total liberalization of reciprocal trade and, with the operation of the Andean Free Trade Zone (ZALC), having activated the Common External Tariff (AEC), all the essential instruments necessary to configurate the customs union and to advance towards a common market are there.

The Modifying Protocol modernizes and adapts the institutional aspect of the Andean Group to modern times, allowing a renewed stimulus to the Andean Integration Agreement.

2. Intrasubregional Trade

In the seventies, the Andean countries exported an average of 12,274 million dollars a year, a number that has grown in the nineties by around 160% (32,000 million dollars a year in average). Imports have followed a growing tendency too, rising from an average of 9,464 million dollars a year in the seventies to 27,668 million dollars per year in the nineties.

The trade balance showed surpluses throughout almost all the 1969-1994 period (except 1977, 1978 and 1988). The tendency of this balance has been decreasing since 1990, with an increase in 1994 and coming to deficit in 1995[10]. Between 1969-1995 the trade interchange grew constantly (Table 1).

This tendency can be observed during the nineties in particular, where the Andean countries exported a value 22% superior to the 1990 value, and the imports grew by 111% in relation to the 1990 value.

In respect to intrasubregional trade, during the nineties the rate of Colombian and Bolivian exports to the Andean Group have been growing. For Colombia, the Andean Group represented 5% of its exports in 1990 and 13% in 1994; and in Bolivia, the rate changed from 6% to 18% over the same period. In the case of Peru this rate was constant (8%).

When analyzing the trade balance different variations appear. In Peru, in the first half of the eighties, there were surpluses that at the end of the decade became deficits. But these *desequilibriums* tripled themselves in the 1990-1994 period, coming to 330 million dollars in the last year.

In Colombia, this situation is similar (1993 and 1994). The rest of the associate countries present favorable balances in general in their trade

---

[10] The 1995 figures are preliminary.

balance with the Andean Group (especially Venezuela and Bolivia). Bolivia and Ecuador are the countries which obtained the greatest historical advantages from the Integration Agreement because they are considered to be relatively less developed countries (Table 2).

To get a precise idea about the interchange, we have reviewed the data, eliminating the fuel transaction (Table 3). In Peru, the deficits in the latter part of the eighties became surpluses and the deficits in the nineties were reduced to a fifth and third of their value. In the Bolivian case there are no major differences from the previous situation and the surpluses continue throughout the whole period. Colombia shows a significant decrease in its deficit during the last two years of analysis, but it does not show variations at the beginning of the nineties.

Ecuador drastically changed its situation from surplus to a general deficit, showing its dependence on petroleum. This also happened in Venezuela during the period between 1991 to 1992, and its positive balance is almost the same for the rest of the period.

In general, the fuel trade explains most of the Peruvian deficit with the Andean Group but it does not affect the Bolivian and Venezuelan surpluses. This last country demonstrated the importance of the integration agreement for its strategy of export diversification. It also shows the Ecuadorian dependence on fuel, in spite of twenty-five years of special treatment.

II. THE ANDEAN COMMUNITY AND MERCOSUR

A. *Intrabloc Dynamic*

As we have previously shown, there has been a great dynamism in the last years which is not free from risk. These risks have been shown by different authors, especially Irela, and they refer to the approach of the Andean Members to other forms of integration. In the next few lines we will compare these risks with recent events so as to make a hypothesis about some of the tendencies in the relationship with the regional and extraregional blocs.

1) The importance of Mercosur countries to Bolivia is unquestionable. They are its principal associates in trade. There is an objective basis that explains the search and achievement of a "4+1" agreement[11] to make a

---

[11] The "4+1" Agreement refers to a group of countries (for example the Mercosur) that negotiate an agreement with an individual country.

free trade zone, leaving the way free for its complete incorporation. To make this happen, Bolivia should quit the Andean Community. This hypothesis seems to be very distant because of at least two principal factors.

If Bolivia has any traditional and/or manufacturing exports, these are traded in the Andean area, mainly with Peru, its principal associate in the agreement. Bolivia and Ecuador have always had special treatment because they are considered as being relatively less developed countries. They would hardly obtain this advantage in Mercosur.

The other item does not only refer to economic aspects. Bolivia is a law locked country since it lost its seaports to Chile during the Pacific War. A great volume of Bolivian production is exported through this country, but it has special concessions in the Southern Cone of Peru (Ilo seaport). There are projects for frontier integration that will offer Bolivia considerable possibilities for gaining access to the Pacific Ocean, thereby improving its trade relations with the exterior. In short, without pretending to ignore the convenience of the Bolivian nearness to Mercosur, it is also true that Bolivia keeps a strategic interest in the Andean zone which will be affected to some degree by its eventual exit from the Andean Group.

2) Another risk concerns the constitution of the Group of the Three by Venezuela, Colombia and Mexico (which could include Ecuador). They could consolidate a region with Central American and Caribbean countries. This is also objectively true. There is an obvious projection and influence from these countries (especially Mexico) over the smaller countries.

On the other hand, there is extraordinary complementarity between Colombia and Venezuela in an extensive range of products and sectors. They are the principal Andean associates and this has permitted the consolidation of an important dynamism. The other great interest of these countries was the projection of the North American market in NAFTA, through their link with Mexico.

These advantages are not so evident in the short-term mainly because the United States have clearly announced that they will not incorporate new members and they are not very well disposed to giving great concessions to countries that are excluded from the agreement. Moreover, as we know, NAFTA will have a period of consolidation of approximately ten years. This is a similar period to the one proposed to create the hemispheric free trade zone. It is not obvious that they will get better conditions (Colombia and Venezuela) through the Group of the Three, instead of getting these conditions from the Andean Community and the negotiation of a free trade zone with Mercosur, making the South American Free Trade Area.

It is also true that Venezuela has been in intensive negotiations with Mercosur, (especially Brazil), in order to obtain a similar agreement to that of Bolivia. This shows the great interest of Venezuela in having links with Southern Latin America, and could be more or less negative for the Andean Community depending on how the negotiations evolve. Something that demonstrates this phenomenon is that the consolidation of the Group of the Three to the north is not excluded.

3) If the factors that act against the strengthening of the Andean Community were to develop, the Peruvian situation would be very delicate; it would be isolated or otherwise it would join Mercosur. In fact, the virtual Peruvian retirement from the Andean Group in 1992 was a hard knock to the integration process, not only because of the economic aspect but also because of the interruption of the democratic order (which was later re-established), which debilitated the relationship with Europe.

There are some sectors in Peru that have shown the suitability of an articulation with Mercosur. These are business sectors and others for geopolitical reasons (we must remember that there was a warlike conflict between Ecuador and Peru in 1995).

We have previously shown how regional trade has grown rapidly during the nineties. However, in the Peruvian case, the trade deficits have been increasing both with its Andean associates and Mercosur. An explanation of this phenomenon is the radical experiment of liberalization (the most extreme in the region) that was established in the nineties and that supported the convenience of a flat tariff. Peru moved away from the integration process, arguing that in other countries subsidies and other distortions were being applied because of lesser progress in terms of reform.

Peru has a privileged location in the Southern Hemisphere and along with Chile, they constitute the countries that make up the bi-oceanic corridor and give the countries of Mercosur (mainly Brazil) access to the Asia-Pacific region. It is convenient for Peru to strengthen this position from the Andean Community, tightening links with Mercosur.

Agglutinating Factors

4) Certainly the most important aspect is the consolidation of the Andean Community. There has been a renewed political stimulus, which is organically shaped with the direction of the chancellors in the process, and a greater capacity in the decisions.

Three of the national congresses have ratified the agreement and it is thought that the rest of them will do so before the end of 1996. Also, the Council of the Cartagena Agreement is working on the transition norms which will permit the Andean Community to begin its function from the first quarter of next year. For instance, March 1997 will see the next meeting of the Andean presidents that will give a decisive stimulus to the process.

With this institutional mechanism, the free trade zone and the still imperfect customs union that exist (because of some exceptions to the differentiated tariff scale system) will be given a new lease of life. Considering these aspects and the present normative, this integration process will advance beyond that of Mercosur. Certainly in this case, the size of its principal members, in population and economy, makes the real difference.

5) On the other hand, there are doubts regarding the political desire of Peru to stimulate the integration process. In fact, the birth of the Andean Community took place in the Peruvian city of Trujillo. Moreover, the Industry and Integration Minister announced (with confirmation from the President) the subscription of a **flexible** tariff system between 5 and 15 percent. These are not the exact levels agreed by the other member countries (except Bolivia) but it took the discussion onto a different level.

There are still some conflicts within the Government which are reflected in different positions, and although most economic and social agents agree on the need to consolidate the process, the Peruvian position will shortly be defined, and this fact will not necessarily stimulate the integration process[12].

---

[12] In fact, in April 1997, the new Industry Minister announced that Peru will not continue as a member of the Andean Community. This is not yet formalized and, in the recent Andean Presidential Meeting, one of the points of discussion was to continue the negotiations with Peru in order to define the methodology to follow according to whether the issue of permanence in the Andean Community is ratified or not. In any case, the situation is very complicated. We are preparing another paper about its consequences.

B. A Note about the Relationship with Mercosur

In my opinion, there is consensus regarding the Brazilian proposition to constitute a free trade zone in South America which, as we remember, was proposed two months after the approval of NAFTA. This means the articulation of the Andean Community and Mercosur. Chile, which is the remaining country, has a "4+1" agreement with Mercosur, and they are creating the conditions necessary for its virtual incorporation into Mercosur. Also, Chile has signed bilateral agreements with most of the Andean Countries.

The discussion is about how to produce the links between the two regional blocs in South America. In previous lines we have introduced some ideas from Andean countries which have advanced to more or less of a degree. Nevertheless, we have to mention that Mercosur (especially Brazil) has been propitiating individual negotiations with the Andean Community members while it was understood that the region must negotiate together as a whole with the other regional (NAFTA) and extraregional (European Union, Asia-Pacific) blocs.

This fact has introduced the possibility of a virtual absorption of the Andean countries by Mercosur. Nevertheless, the dynamism of the consolidation of the Andean Community does not seem to value this hypothesis. Moreover, on September 16-17, 1996, the Andean countries' chancellors and the Industry and Integration Ministers met in Lima. In this important meeting, it was decided that they will negotiate as a bloc for a free trade zone with Mercosur in a term of ten years. The negotiations will be planned in these countries' next meetings which will take place in Fortaleza, Brazil, where a normative agreement will be subscript.

Bolivia will also participate in this process but will respect its advances in bilateral performance. Nevertheless, the so-called Historic Patrimony[13] will be negotiated because the agreements in the ALADI context will finish on December 31st, 1996. As for the meetings on October 17-18, it was decided that the Mercosur countries should be invited to a technical negotiation meeting about the General Agreement, with the participation of the chancellors.

There is a principal aspect which characterizes intraregional trade. It has been demonstrated that for all the Latin American countries, those

---

[13] The Historic Patrimony refers to a set of agreements that were in force until a new agreement took over from them.

exports with the greater added value are designated to regional countries. We can see this in documents of CEPAL, the Cartagena Agreement, etc.

This aspect is reflected in sectors where there is significant intraindustrial trade among the regional countries and there is documented support both for the Mercosur and the Andean Community. In such a way the integration process creates economies of scale and learning conditions that subsequently allow the conquest of market niches and other extraregional markets. From this point of view, everyone wins even if there are asymmetric problems that must be taken into account.

Consequently, the component of intraindustrial trade among the Andean countries is more significant than that with Mercosur, which is another favorable argument for the consolidation of the Andean Community in order to establish, as a bloc, a free trade zone with Mercosur.

With the consolidation of the subregional blocs, we will have better possibilities of negotiating with the European Union and NAFTA.

III. LESSONS FROM MERCOSUR AND THE ANDEAN EXPERIENCE

For Dr. Peña, the firmness in the direction, audacity in the objectives, accelerated rhythm and instrumental prudence have been the three keys to the successful Mercosur formula.

If our version about what happened into the Andean Community is plausible, these factors would not be found systematically.

Dr. Peña extracts three conclusions:

1) First, some common characteristics in the different hemispheric integration efforts. The need for a new regional environment with the neighboring countries, the consolidation of democracy, the search for a competitive insertion in the world community and social cohesion, are also central aspects of the Andean Community.

This is also true for the emphasis on the opening policies, macroeconomic discipline and stability, and the institutionalization of flexibility (the preferential treatment of Ecuador and Bolivia, the tolerance with Peru and the present Venezuelan macroeconomic crisis). Obviously the Andean countries do not have the international weight of Mercosur, but this could be achieved with the consolidation of a free trade zone in South America.

2) Second, some factors that are not always models in other countries are pointed out. In my opinion, the Andean Community has had in the past years a new strategic direction, instrumental flexibility, deregulation and opening in different markets, and has understood, with some occasional difficulties, its members.

There are in fact some important differences. The institutional structure of the Andean integration process is not as simple as the one Dr. Peña showed for Mercosur. There are frontier conflicts (Peru-Ecuador) that fortunately are in negotiation and although there are enterprises that export almost exclusively to the Andean market, the strategic alliances and the impressive Mercosur dynamism have not been consolidated.

3) A fundamental factor is the coincidence in promoting integration among the South American countries. There are eventual discrepancies either within the blocs or between the blocs concerning its methods and instruments but, in general, we can be moderately optimistic that they are respected.

This could promote the implementation of an integral and differential strategy with other blocs such as NAFTA, the Asian countries, and Europe which has, without a doubt, a very important role.

TABLE N° 1

ANDEAN GROUP: MERCHANDISE TRADE AND TRADE BALANCE
(Million of US$)

AÑOS	EXPORTS	IMPORTS	TRADE BALANCE	TRADE INTERCHANGE
1969	4,911	3,710	1,201	8,621
1970	5,380	4,100	1,280	9,480
1971	5,035	4,254	781	9,289
1972	5,324	4,588	736	9,912
1973	7,660	5,529	2,131	13,189
1974	15,912	9,001	6,911	24,913
1975	13,259	11,744	1,515	25,003
1976	14,301	12,244	2,057	26,545
1977	15,785	16,946	-1,161	32,731
1978	16,283	18,770	-2,487	35,053
1979	23,801	18,463	5,338	42,264
1980	30,215	22,711	7,504	52,926
1981	29,026	25,616	3,410	54,642
1982	25,469	25,150	319	50,619
1983	23,197	15,927	7,270	39,124
1984	25,534	16,657	8,877	42,191
1985	24,565	16,718	7,847	41,283
1986	18,957	17,362	1,595	36,319
1987	20,538	20,165	373	40,703
1988	20,420	22,911	-2,491	43,331
1989	25,264	17,339	7,925	42,603
1990	31,407	18,057	13,350	49,464
1991	29,495	22,695	6,800	52,190
1992	28,351	26,861	1,490	55,212
1993	29,739	29,411	328	59,150
1994	34,370	30,704	3,666	65,074
1995	38,258	38,279	-21	76,537

Source: JUNAC - Departamento de Informática

TABLE N° 2

TRADE INTO THE ANDEAN GROUP

(Million dollars)

TRADE BALANCE

Country	1980	1981	1982	1983	1984	1985	1986	1987	1988	1989	1990	1991	1992	1993	1994
BOLIVIA	12.48	10.83	14.9	2.06	-12.12	-10.69	6.87	15.36	9.8	28.33	30.1	49.06	59.56	42.52	92.05
COLOMBIA	9	-151.01	-150.12	-438.46	-386.08	-215.48	32.61	177.11	29.85	-74.1	-100.83	302.59	366.65	-158.99	-432.01
ECUADOR	8.04	31.5	40.9	62.79	-20.34	-8.52	-48.2	-184.65	99	90.1	6.86	-29.99	5.52	112.13	-108.71
PERU	200.3	101.71	129.64	43.99	111.95	164.51	-20.72	-85.14	-113.81	-44.69	-126.56	-276.82	-298.16	-253.11	-335.64
VENEZUELA	-0.72	-2.67	-102.66	158.09	134.57	53.67	3.72	15.23	-54.88	133.21	259.13	50.62	48.23	472.26	931.05
TOTAL	229.1	-9.64	-67.34	-171.53	-172.02	-16.51	-25.72	-62.09	-30.04	132.85	68.7	95.86	181.8	214.81	146.74

TRADE INTERCHANGE (X + M)

Country	1980	1981	1982	1983	1984	1985	1986	1987	1988	1989	1990	1991	1992	1993	1994
BOLIVIA	72.7	78.19	53.56	45.56	43.38	44.39	41.63	46.06	45.2	71.65	89.8	115.58	139.54	197.42	297.89
COLOMBIA	766.76	1064.35	1055.92	802.2	723.26	651.42	530.07	632.85	686.25	692.78	846.33	1234.23	1662.11	2436.25	2651.65
ECUADOR	286.46	246.72	276.1	201.19	133.16	156.04	134.06	434.77	255.28	275.88	370.18	437.01	350.78	477.49	880.05
PERU	415.96	383.51	348.28	181.87	261.65	335.09	312.28	399.18	490.99	437.05	554.6	815.68	837.38	791.29	955.94
VENEZUELA	606.72	712.25	700.34	445.85	509.47	424.09	318.18	414.91	496.28	466.99	728.23	906.92	1283.45	1618.38	1921.71
TOTAL	2148.6	2485.02	2434.2	1676.67	1670.92	1611.03	1336.22	1927.77	1974	1944.35	2589.14	3529.42	4273.26	5520.83	6707.24

Source: JUNAC

195

TABLE N° 3

INTRASUBREGIONAL TRADE BALANCE, WITHOUT FUEL

(Million dollars)

	1980	1981	1982	1983	1984	1985	1986	1987	1988	1989	1990	1991	1992	1993	1994
BOLIVIA															
Colombia	2.25	2.34	3.83	1.43	2.59	2.47	0.63	2.19	1.78	1.37	-0.39	23.97	14.77	20.91	36.98
Ecuador	0.82	-0.09	0.28	-0.24	-0.1423	-0.09	-0.33	-0.38	-0.4	-0.16	-0.77	-0.33	2.51	5.14	11.93
Perú	0.79	3.99	6.71	-3.72	-15.46	-12.52	7.37	12.26	5.41	28.47	30.86	26.06	34.86	22.23	57.08
Venezuela	4.27	4.64	4.16	-0.25	0.82	-0.459	-0.779	-0.74	-0.68	-1.29	0.49	-0.47	7.71	-0.42	-4.21
GRAN	8.12	10.88	14.97	-2.79	-12.11	-10.6	6.9	13.34	6.12	28.39	30.2	49.23	59.86	47.88	101.78
MUNDO	127.88	-255.52	-45.17	-175.27	-94.62	-390.61	-363.61	-450.83	-207.26	-12.59	-3.15	-375.28	-460.28	-476.48	-206.43
COLOMBIA															
Bolivia	-5.19	-3.56	-5.89	-2.5	-4.2	-4.39	-2.87	-1.95	-2.41	-2.91	-1	-17.26	-38.68	-31.6	-25.49
Ecuador	9.26	-11.47	-38.3	-5.54	-12.7	7.43	11.9	27.42	-5.56	20.52	29.04	87.22	95.88	37.82	60.84
Perú	13.24	21.12	-31.52	-33.88	-60.04	-35.84	0.93	44.04	-17.16	-57.77	-23.43	41.7	65.27	76.81	133.73
Venezuela	231.85	253.88	269.33	23.93	-17.58	55.81	34.56	102.38	89.53	20.01	-44.24	172.14	209.75	-119.88	-453.68
GRAN	249.16	259.99	193.61	-17.99	-94.53	23.04	44.54	171.89	64.4	-20.14	-39.62	283.79	332.22	-36.86	-284.63
MUNDO	-255.86	-1552.51	-1938.29	-1682.23	-1025.07	-548.655	933.94	-465.768	-789.81	-440.95	-447.282	1100.59	-509.47	-3688.06	-4379.22
ECUADOR															
Bolivia	0.05	-0.4	-0.68	-0.24	0.079	-0.005	-0.06	0.061	0.12	0.21	0.19	-0.13	0.475	1.412	2.06
Colombia	40.85	20.89	39.26	-1.4	-8.31	-9.71	-15.8	-7.67	3.66	-11.64	-25.41	-62.53	-39.78	47.81	-56.8
Perú	-33.94	-19.05	-18.79	-18.63	-18.99	-23.56	-25.81	-4.93	-9.64	-18.23	-12.11	-11.39	0.16	2.11	1.66
Venezuela	25.05	38.75	39.24	-6.71	-1.18	1.53	-5.7	-231.71	-16.91	-10.97	-87.55	-34.37	-27.11	-33.46	-136.12
GRAN	32	40.17	59.017	-26.97	-28.4	-31.73	-47.39	-244.26	-22.8	-40.6	-124.87	-108.43	-66.27	17.87	-189.21
MUNDO	-1117.8	809.52	-1464.64	-873.22	-715.096	-761.4	-562.26	-928.13	-481.891	-626.91	-522.21	-607.91	-688.93	-715.83	-1039.95

PERU															
Bolivia	52.71	8.15	-0.81	-4.41	14.08	2.2	-8.01	-18.05	-1.28	-4.34	-10.03	-29.95	6.23	16.51	-10.6
Colombia	13.95	-6.33	15.99	16.71	45.72	26.4	-22.38	-41.71	13.744	39.29	8.56	-51.79	-93.36	-105.59	-156.92
Ecuador	76.11	4.01	10.14	17.2	20.41	25.63	5.42	2.32	9.91	21.82	6.21	-4.31	7.63	4.46	9.58
Venezuela	32.04	21.78	35.4	12.54	26.94	21.99	4.51	13.52	32.28	19.48	11.73	32.33	43.23	-14.48	-41.58
GRAN	174.82	27.6	60.71	42.03	107.14	76.24	-20.38	-43.91	54.66	76.25	16.48	-53.73	-36.28	-99.11	-199.52
MUNDO	122.07	-1828.93	-1143.332	-138.63	150.45	634.43	-270.38	-940.05	8.27	1315.34	655.12	157.32	-28.32	-743.49	-1109.14
VENEZUELA															
Bolivia	-3.088	-4.97	-5.32	-0.6952	-1.6809	0.234	0.18	0.363	-1.49	-1.18	-2.61	-3.28	0.07	-0.13	0.82
Colombia	-151.21	-180.22	-233.49	-81.17	-64.48	-58.3	20.93	12.34	-26.2	131.4	200	-40.85	-28.06	385.49	656.56
Ecuador	-31.28	-46.08	-51.82	-1.86	-1.28	-0.58	1.17	-1.33	8.16	18.3	19.89	30.3	24.81	32.18	121.48
Perú	-41.93	-44.7	-44.88	-27.111	-30.4	-38.38	-31.24	-28.22	-59.51	-29.83	-32.34	-40.46	-43.07	-14.47	1.94
GRAN	-227.52	-275.92	-335.51	-110.79	-97.76	-97.02	-8.97	-16.86	-79.031	118.71	184.96	-54.31	-46.25	403.08	780.79
MUNDO	-1054.26	-12312.44	-12419.12	-5840.62	-6649.71	-6711.23	-6926	-8083.86	-10701.45	-4412.41	-3458.01	-7999.95	-10176.76	-7873.02	-4202.94
ANDEAN GROUP															
Bolivia	44.49	-0.71	-12.71	2.19	8.35	-1.95	-10.76	-19.58	-5.05	-8.21	-13.45	-50.62	-31.89	-13.74	-33.24
Colombia	-94.15	-163.32	-174.43	-64.42	-24.49	-39.12	-16.62	-34.85	-7	160.43	182.77	-131.23	-146.45	348.62	479.82
Ecuador	54.91	-53.63	-79.7	9.55	6.34	32.38	18.27	28.03	12.12	60.48	54.39	112.89	130.83	79.6	203.8
Perú	-61.85	-38.63	-88.49	-33.33	-124.88	-110.28	-48.74	23.15	-80.89	-77.31	-37.01	15.9	57.21	86.68	194.41
Venezuela	293.22	319.03	348.12	29.51	9	78.89	32.57	-116.57	104.2	27.24	-119.56	169.62	233.57	-168.24	-635.6
GRAN	236.59	62.72	-7.18	-116.48	-125.66	-40.06	-25.3	-119.8	23.36	162.61	67.12	116.56	243.25	332.87	208.2
MUNDO	-1217.98	-16797.41	-17010.54	-8709.98	-8334.03	-7777.45	-7188.3	-10868.62	-12172.13	-4177.53	-3775.54	-7725.24	-11863.76	-13532.88	-10937.68

Source: JUNAC - Sistema Subregional de Información Estadística. Decisión 115

ASEAN AND APEC
A TRIUMPH OF THE "ASIAN WAY"?

Jacques PELKMANS

Senior Research Fellow,
Centre for European Policy Studies, Brussels;
Former Research Director,
European Institute for Asian Studies, Brussels

The contrasts between economic regionalism in Europe and in East Asia are striking. In terms of the methods employed, the American and East Asian ways of going regional also exhibit radical differences. The present paper will attempt to explain these contrasts and differences. The reader is warned, however, that a proper understanding requires a prior acceptance on the part of the reader about the avoidance of "legalistic" approaches in the two groupings at issue. Europeans and (North) Americans tend to be sceptical about such avoidance. For lawyers, given their training, mindset and professional interests, the "Asian way" may be met with disbelief.

The paper will first deal with Association of South-East Asian Nations (ASEAN). Section 1 will provide the general characteristics of ASEAN, including the absence of a treaty. Section 2 will explain the main features of the ASEAN Free Trade Area (AFTA) followed by some reflections on ASEAN's future course in Section 3. Section 4 will describe Asian-Pacific Economic Cooperation (APEC)'s emergence, followed by a closer analysis of its avowed principles and methods, having been articulated in the Osaka Action Plan of November 1995 and the run-up to the Subic APEC summit of November 25, 1996. Section 6 concludes.

1. The ASEAN: Aims and Substance

ASEAN (the Association of South-East Asian Nations) has emerged as a response to internal and external threats or threat perceptions. Being a cold war phenomenon *par excellence*, the "end of the cold war" might have pushed the association into oblivion. However, ASEAN has deepened and enlarged, and shows inclinations of widening its scope as well. It is appropriate to continue to consider ASEAN as primarily aimed at security, stability and fundamental foreign policy interests, even though in much of the following, trade, investment and economic cooperation issues would seem to be central. Although ASEAN has very little in common with the EU, the ultimate rational of peace and security in the region is similar.

ASEAN is a highly informal association by European (or American) standards. The 1967 Bangkok Declaration is a purely political document with little more than vague intentions about economic cooperation, covering up the genuine purpose of political consultation and cooperation. Yet, it is this declaration which signifies the birth of ASEAN. Even more difficult to interpret is the ZOPFAN Declaration of 1971 (Zone of Peace, Freedom and Neutrality) in Kuala Lumpur, which enunciates a kind of nonalignment in the cold war (or "equidistance"), even though several ASEAN members had explicit security links with the US. The only treaty that ASEAN has ever adopted is the Treaty of Amity and Cooperation which stipulates the renunciation of the use of force against one another and contains consultative mechanisms for the peaceful settlement of disputes. Legally, it is not bound to ASEAN; on the other hand, ASEAN had made it a policy that a prior condition for ASEAN membership is the adherence to this (vague and short) treaty.

ASEAN has been slow in developing economic cooperation. For decades its economic substance consisted of typical project cooperation (which, in international diplomacy, goes under the curious label "economic cooperation") as well as almost entirely symbolic preferential tariff concessions, the so-called PTA. Both tracks of ASEAN were basically an excuse to gradually build up a network of contacts between the respective economic or sectoral ministries. A special learning process took place over two decades (!) with respect to the promotion of (ASEAN-wide) scale of selected industrial activities. Starting from the notion of joint investment planning, the products of which would eventually obtain a much greater preferential status than the PTA, these attempts ended with the much more market-driven ASEAN Industrial Joint Ventures (AIJV), very few of which have actually been implemented.

National development policies and similarity of initial production structures in a protectionist environment (for the "big three" founding member states Indonesia, Philippines and Thailand) prevented these experiences from having any economic impact on ASEAN's markets. What remained and intensified was the networking, as the solid, yet "invisible" and intangible dividend of a pursuit of regional stability through numerous routine contacts at all levels. The economic growth and development miracle, observable in the ASEAN countries, has arisen despite ASEAN's economic cooperation, not because of it. Economic cooperation, without substance and loaded with rhetoric, was a critical investment in stability. Only in this stability sense did ASEAN matter.

After the "end of the cold war" and with the peace in Cambodia, the peace dividend was reaped. Suddenly, the costs of the ASEAN "flying circus" was acutely felt. Moreover, APEC was born and the new enthusiasm of ASEAN for GATT and its Uruguay Round threatened to expose the irrelevance of intra-ASEAN economic cooperation and trade liberalization. ASEAN responded in two ways: it restructured and gave its minuscule Secretariat more status and a greater role; it also agreed to build an ASEAN Free Trade Area (AFTA). Neither of these decisions were adopted in treaty form. Rather, "agreements" were employed for this purpose, signed by the Heads of States and Government in the ASEAN Singapore Summit of January 1992. The fifth ASEAN summit in December 1995 in Bangkok enounced an enlargement strategy, such that ASEAN would eventually comprise all of South-East Asia (that is, Myanmar, Laos and Cambodia were "invited"; Vietnam became a member in June 1996). The summit also hinted at various forms of widening of scope. Since 1993 the ASEAN Regional Forum has assumed some prominence. Organized by ASEAN, this is actually an Asia/Pacific Forum for security consultations. It has catapulted ASEAN into "high politics" as never before, again without formalization and with virtually no resources spent.

2. The ASEAN Free Trade Area

The ASEAN Free Trade Area is not a traditional free trade area like EFTA. This is apparent from the objectives, the unique tariff reduction scheme, the avoidance of a treaty and continuous negotiation over time on other aspects such as non-tariff barriers and dispute settlement, as if they are after thoughts addressed one by one. It is a conventional free trade area in that — assuming proper implementation — intra-AFTA tariffs fall to zero (but see the caveat below) and, arguably, for "substantially all the trade" (cf. Art.24, GATT). Let us take a closer look at all these aspects.

a) The Economic Fundamentals

The economies of ASEAN are open to very open (see for instance, Fukasaku (1996) for empirical evidence). Yet, they trade little with each other. Intra-ASEAN trade in goods would seem to hover around 20% of total foreign trade by ASEAN countries, but this includes relatively large transshipment and entrepot traffic through Singapore. Without the latter intra-ASEAN trade is probably some 9%-10% of ASEAN trade[1]. The reasons behind this low intra-share are crucial to understanding AFTA and its significance.

Empirical economic studies based on the so-called gravity model have shown that trade is a positive function of "economic size" (product of population and GNP per-capita) and a negative one of economic distance (e.g. door-to-door transport and handling costs). The economic size of ASEAN countries was tiny until recently, and is still small today. ASEAN countries' physical distance to one another is short relative to almost any other trading link for them but this is not so for "economic distance". Cost-increasing factors in intra-ASEAN trade include serious infrastructural weaknesses in harbours, roads, distribution centres, etc. rendering transport relatively costly, besides a range of problems in customs handling (from pre-shipment inspection to delays in clearing) and underdeveloped transport and logistics services. The dominance of Singapore's transit facilities is built on eminent quality of precisely the services underdeveloped elsewhere, as well as on the so-called (cost) economies of scope arising from hub-and-spoke maritime transport systems. Until recently even passenger air transport within ASEAN was dominated by a hub-and-spokes effect, but rapid economic growth has caused "thin" routes to become profitable and many "secondary" routes now enjoy frequent direct flights. In the long run, and assuming economic growth to continue, the relative significance of Singapore's maritime service for intra-ASEAN will decline as "economic distances" will "shorten" (i.e. lower costs) in the region. The strong growth performance will also enhance "economic" size, which should be expected to lead to sustained long-run growth of intra-ASEAN trade.

---

[1] Compare intra-EFTA trade in the late 1980s being around 12%-15% (but EFTA was then far smaller and more dispersed than ASEAN), intra-NAFTA trade being around 35% and intra-EU trade being around 60% of their respective total trade values.

But for the 1980s and early 1990s one can identify another fundamental reason for the (relatively) lacklustre performance of intra-ASEAN trade. In the 1980s all ASEAN countries except Singapore were developing countries with fairly similar production structures and a significant (sometimes high) share of the working population in agriculture and fisheries. This implied that there was little prospect for intra-industry trade in the region (which presumes scale and product differentiation) and — given similar relative scarcities of factors of production — for inter-industry trade. Hence, ASEAN countries' openness was developed *vis-à-vis* the TRIAD markets: Japan (later East Asia), the US and the EU. Hence, their increasingly strong backing of the WTO and the Uruguay Round. Hence, emphasis on repeated unilateral tariff reductions on an MFN-basis by the ASEAN big three (Indonesia, Philippines, Thailand), recently joined by a fourth big but underdeveloped member, Vietnam. Given the still medium-high tariffs of the big-three, a free trade area could therefore lead to considerable trade diversion. That would imply a burden on the overall economy and a possible source of friction with major trading partners, the markets of which are far more important to ASEAN than intra-regional trade.

Against this background some characteristics of AFTA become more intelligible. The ultimate **objective** of AFTA is to increase ASEAN's competitive edge as a production base geared for the world market. The reasoning behind this overall aim comprises both political and economic arguments. Economically, intra-ASEAN tariff reduction is expected to augment competitive exposure of domestic industries, both via actual and potential import competition as well as via enhanced efforts to penetrate neighbouring markets. In the big three, and in Malaysia even at an earlier stage, the sustained high growth performance and buoyant exports have increased the confidence of policy makers to open up markets. It is widely recognized that the increased exposure to import and export competition is a suitable element in long-run reform strategies, including privatization and deregulation, to underpin a continuation of rapid economic development. A second economic argument is an extension of the idea, long around in ASEAN, to exploit the entire ASEAN economy, and not insular national markets only, for industrial supply and manufacturing networks based on economies of scale. AFTA, with its eventual intra-ASEAN free trade and automatic market access (be it with certificates of origin), should be a superior alternative to the AIJVs and other "managed" or negotiated solutions. In this sense, it is held that AFTA increases the attractiveness for multinationals to invest in ASEAN.

The political argument for AFTA is hidden in the economic reasoning and rarely made explicit. In the big three, protectionism has weakened, but has by no means disappeared. AFTA can be seen as an appealing regional project, with a rather limited impact on sensitive sectors and — initially — with several years of grace period and a total of fifteen years of adjustment. As a controlled pilot project for liberalization, initiated by the political leaders of the region, the problem of domestic political feasibility was overcome. Thus, in the strategic thinking about long-term development, AFTA was an ideal precursor. It has indeed been used by the governments and opinion-shapers in the domestic debates about economic and trade policy reform in general. Once initial fears were laid to rest, confidence of policy makers increased and the ambition of AFTA was raised.

As a consequence of all this, one should note that AFTA's success is not measured by an eventual absolute and relative increase in intra-ASEAN trade. Interestingly, though, the practical impact of AFTA may well be that entrepreneurs begin to pay attention to the opportunities for intra-ASEAN ventures and exports, a new phenomenon. To Europeans to present this as a novelty for ASEAN may seem odd. But one should not forget that ASEAN countries do not know each other well, for historical and developmental reasons, their cultural affinities notwithstanding. Also, intense information, travel and transport flows are a recent phenomenon within the region. Besides, two "big" ASEAN countries are archipelagos and the other ones are only now in the process of building adequate road and rail networks. Thus, the 1994 intra-ASEAN exports of products falling under AFTA increased by a whopping 51.7%, followed by another 21% in 1995. Since there was hardly any tariff reduction implemented yet, this sharp increase is likely to be explained by a strong business response to the AFTA campaign.

b) Technical Properties of AFTA

The **tariff reduction scheme** has special characteristics: it blends a sectoral with a horizontal approach, it is cooperative, it includes complex forms of reciprocity (tied to quota removal as well) and is based on liberal rules of origin.

Tariff reduction follows the so-called Common Effective Preferential Tariff (CEPT) scheme, an extension of an older Indonesian proposal to accelerate the PTA selectively. Hence, the sectoral bias in this CEPT scheme. The basic idea was to realize a reduction to 0%-5% by 2008 for non-agricultural products, starting in 1993. For this purpose a

204

CEPT Agreement was concluded during the Singapore Summit of January 1992. Since that date, there has been considerable regulatory "drift", mostly in the direction of faster reduction and greater product scope. Because ASEAN does not have an official journal or gazette, it is often hard to come by the proper information. In Chiang Mai, in September 1994, the Economic Ministers decided to shorten the CEPT programme to 10 years, i.e. being completed by January 1st, 2003. Unfortunately, the author has not yet received the new tariff reduction schedules — the tables are still based on the 1993 decision on CEPT.

CEPTs are pursued via (a) a fast track programme, split into a 10-year period for tariffs above 20% and a 7-year programme for tariffs of 20% and lower; (b) a normal track programme, split into a 15-year period for tariffs above 20% (in turn, divided into a period up to 2001, for reduction to 20%; and the remainder of up to seven years) and a 10-year period for tariffs of 20% and lower; (c) a horizontal approach after 2001 (for the initially high normal-track tariffs, the only ones "left" i.e. 15% in 2003, 10% in 2005 and 0%-5% in 2007); (d) a decentralized approach varying from member state to member state. There are three types of exclusions: (unprocessed) agricultural products, although AFTA has begun to incorporate some of them recently; general (e.g. weapons, etc.) and temporary (to be reviewed in 2001). However, it should be noted that those dates have now been brought forward to (at the latest) 2003, and 2006 for Vietnam.

Table 1 provides an idea of the CEPT scheme based on the number of tariff lines. Though indicative, it is good to realize that ASEAN countries have divergent tariff classifications and the relevant tariff lines for business may vary from the 6-digits level to the 10-digits level. As a result Malaysia has almost twice as many tariff lines as the Philippines. In other words, the data in Table 1 is very rough indeed. This also has implications for unweighed tariff rates of ASEAN countries. In sensitive products, tariff schedules tend to be extremely disaggregated, with the sensitive product varieties receiving high tariffs at, say, the 9-digits level and many other varieties low tariffs: the unweighed average is then low, but the afforded protection to incumbents high. Thus, the 118 Thai products under temporary exclusion are defined at the 10-digit level and are probably very sensitive; similarly, the Philippines 714 items contain a big block of textiles & clothing lines where the classification is excessively detailed. Note that the fast track of 15 products, to be found in the CEPT Agreement has meanwhile been widened to cover mechanical appliances and mineral products.

Table 1
Summary of CEPT Product Lists (late 1993)

No	Country	HS Digit Level	INCLUSION				EXCLUSION				
			Fast Track	Normal Track	Sub-Total	%	Temporary Exception	General Exception Products	Unprocessed Agricultural Products	Sub-Total	Total
(a)	(b)	(c)	(d)	(e)	(f)	(g)	(h)	(i)	(j)	(k)	(l)
1	Brunei Darussalam	9	2,420	3,659	6,079	92.89	208	201	56	465	6,544
		6	1,975	2,604	4,579	.	.	.	.	.	.
2	Indonesia	9	2,816	4,539	7,355	78.39	1,654	50	324	2,028	9,383
		6	1,445	2,734	4,179	80.07	834	30	176	1,040	5,219
3	Malaysia	9	3,166	5,611	8,777	87.39	627	98*	541	1,266	10,043
		6	1,725	2,419	4,144	85.50	273	98*	332	703	4,847
4	Philippines	9	1,033	3,418	4,451	79.61	714	28	398	1,140	5,591
		6	974	3,079	4,053	.	.	.	.	.	.
5	Singapore	9	2,205	3,517	5,722	97.95	Nil	120	Nil	120	5,842
		6	1,896	3,078	4,974	100.00	Nil	-	Nil	-	4,974
6	Thailand	Tariff Line	3,509	5,254	8,763	94.00	118**	26*	415	559	9,322
		6	1,736	2,777	4,513	91.56	-	26*	390	416	4,929

* Products
** at HS-10 digit level

Source: ASEAN Secretariat.

Figure 1 provides a sectoral picture of the tariff reduction as foreseen late 1993, for agriculture (processed), electronics, machinery, and textiles and clothing. The biggest single manufacturing product in world trade — cars — is carefully kept out of AFTA, because Thailand, Indonesia, the Philippines and Malaysia all have interventionist development programmes for the car sector behind high protection.

Figure 1
CEPT Reductions in Selected Sectors

CEPT REDUCTION FOR AGRICULTURE

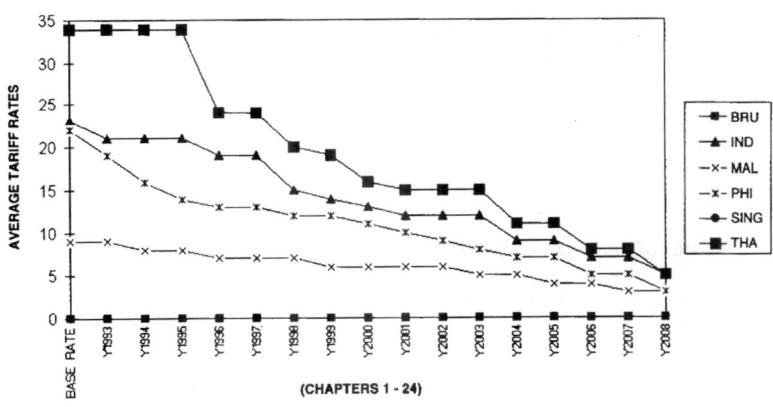

(CHAPTERS 1 - 24)

CEPT REDUCTION FOR ELECTRONICS

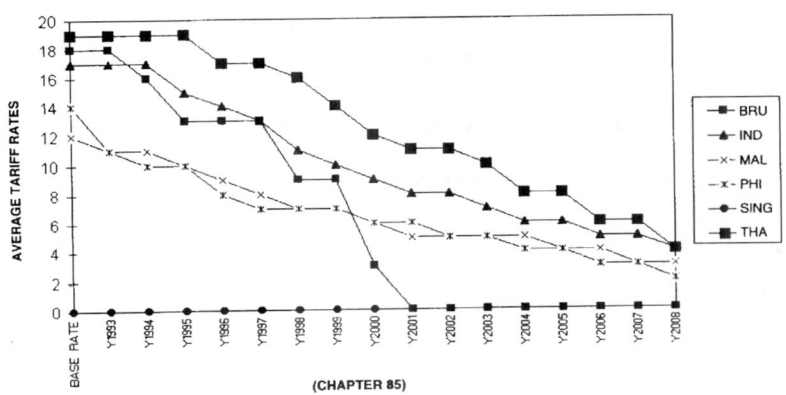

(CHAPTER 85)

CEPT REDUCTION FOR TEXTILE

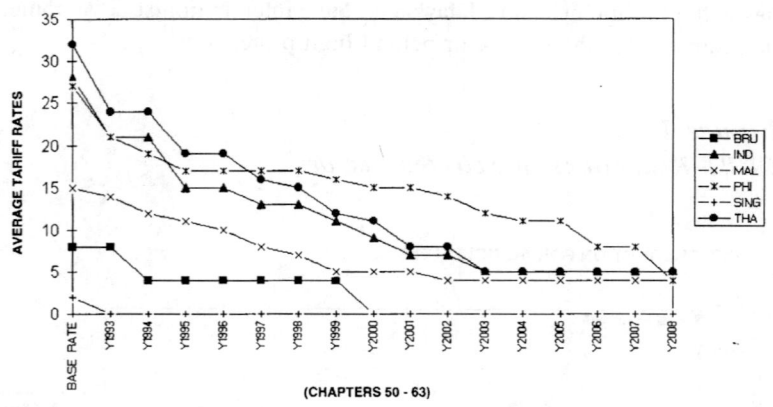

(CHAPTERS 50 - 63)

CEPT REDUCTION FOR MACHINERY

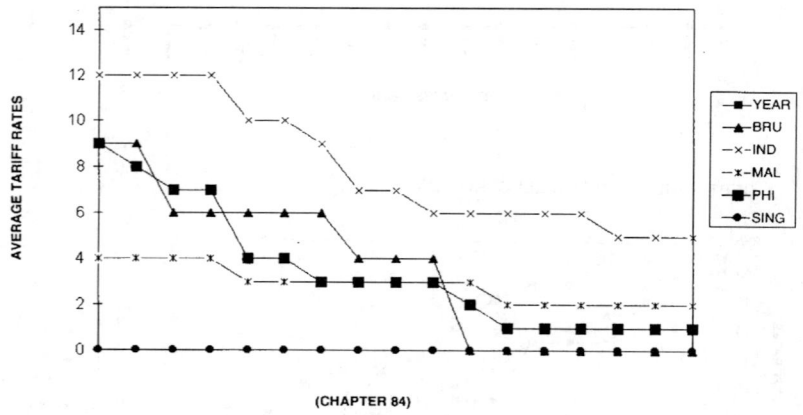

(CHAPTER 84)

208

There have been continuous pressures to adapt the CEPT scheme, by widening the scope (e.g. some unprocessed agricultural products), accelerating the speed (now to 2003) and encouraging smaller temporary exclusion lists.

The CEPT scheme is **cooperative**. The term refers to the great aversion against centralization or "supranational" provisions in ASEAN. The "ASEAN way" emphasizes peer pressure, confidence building (by the highest political leaders, whose commitment has almost force of law) and avoidance of confrontation or public disputes. The cooperative nature implied that national "offers" were only made **after** the Singapore Summit, and were subsequently improved under peer pressure and a kind of "beauty-contest" iterative process. In a climate of very high economic growth for all ASEAN countries (the Philippines has now joined the high growth league, with an expected 1996 growth rate of over 6%), the effective outcome for business would seem to be very much the same as with EU-type common legislation. Moreover, AFTA is notified in the GATT, and this gives it a compulsory character (note however, that ASEAN has not notified it under Art.24, but under the Enabling Clause, which does not accord well with ASEAN's avowed support of WTO and its critical stance *vis-à-vis* other countries' regionalism). The cooperative nature of CEPT has also helped the Philippine government to argue that AFTA, because of CEPT, is merely a radical extension of the PTA, so that no formal ratification was required (thereby getting round the Senate, comprising many individuals with huge vested interests in protectionism). Other ASEAN countries did not face a similar ratification issue.

Over time the "cooperative" nature of AFTA has no doubt reduced. The CEPT Agreement of January 1992 has been followed by Interpretative Notes[2] and a stagewise programme to harmonize tariff classification. AFTA is based on the Harmonized System, but only up to six digits inclusive. The genuine tariff lines are more often than not at 8, 9 or 10 digits, and definitions differ at these levels. In addition, Operational Certification Procedures for the rules of origin[3] and a common specimen form for the Certificate of Origin[4] have been adopted. In meetings of the AFTA Council, a ministerial body (including the Secretary General of ASEAN) and the ASEAN Economic Ministers, to which the AFTA Council reports, efforts have been undertaken to reduce the complexity

---

[2] Published in **AFTA Reader**, Vol.1, ASEAN Secretariat, Jakarta, November 1993, pp.40 ff.

[3] *Ibid.*, pp.57 ff.

[4] *Ibid.*, p.69

arising from the cooperative nature of AFTA. Thus, although starting dates for national tariff reduction differed at first, as a result of domestic pressures, later the ASEAN Economic Ministers (AEM) converged the starting dates to January 1st, 1994. This led to a retroactive (!) tariff reduction by Malaysia in July 1994. The AFTA Council of Chiang Mai (Sept. 21, 1994) decided not to wait 8 years before reviewing the temporary exclusion list, but to transfer one-fifth every year to the CEPT list between 1995 and 2000. Work on customs procedures and customs valuation is ongoing.

AFTA comprises complex forms of **reciprocity** during the transition period. Since this period has been shortened, this aspect is no longer of great importance. It is indicative, however, of the delicacy of the initial negotiations. The point was that, with no general, horizontal tariff cutting obligations for a considerable period, at least two problems would arise: tariffs peaks and unsynchronized market access. Tariff peaks create a reciprocity problem because cutting of tariff peaks may take a long while before effective access becomes possible. That is the main reason why the reduction process is split into above-20% tariffs and 20%-and-below tariffs. Lack of synchronization may be sensitive if decentralization would go so far as to permit very late, deep tariff cuts whilst others would "frontload" their cuts in the same product[5]. The AFTA solution is to apply the "concessions" (i.e. the preferential CEPT tariff will apply to intra-AFTA imports) only for tariffs at or below 20%, whereas for those above 20% concessions are contingent on the export country's application of a CEPT preferential tariff. In the presence of decentralized reduction schemes, this conditionality creates a major information problem for business. To overcome this hurdle, ASEAN countries are committed to produce CEPT Concessions Exchange Manuals. Where concessions are enjoyed, quota removal (for AFTA countries) is obligatory, although the CEPT Agreement does not give a deadline; presumably, the removal is expected to be immediate upon enjoyment of the concessions. The author does not avail of information with respect to (WTO-based) tariffication of quotas of ASEAN countries. The real problem would appear to be import licensing in Indonesia and Malaysia, and to a (much) smaller extent, Thailand and the Philippines. There are also some problems with import bans and state-trading and/or distribution monopolies[6]. It is an

---

[5] Both tariff peaks and synchronization played a role in the EEC Treaty approach to tariff cutting, although the solutions were different from those of ASEAN (see PELKMANS, 1997, ch.2)

[6] See e.g. European Commission, *"Creating a New Dynamic in EU-ASEAN Relations"*, COM (96) 314, July 3, 1996, Annex 6.

interesting question whether or not all these restrictive practices would fall under "quotas" in the AFTA sense. The CEPT Agreement also speaks of "other non-tariff barriers", but the obligation to eliminate them is not specified in any way and merely imposes a period of no more than five years after the enjoyment of concessions. Work on removing Non-Tariff Barriers (NTBs) has meanwhile begun with customs surcharges. Again, the economic meaning of this work is unclear as yet, especially since import surcharges on bound tariffs in WTO are to be abolished at the latest by 2005. ASEAN countries have drastically increased the number of bound tariffs as a result of the Uruguay Round, but the shares are still far from 100% (e.g. Philippines: 37%; Malaysia: 65%; Singapore: 70%; Thailand: 68%).

The **rules of origin** are liberal by almost any standard. Both the national and cumulative origin requirement is 40%; cumulation is granted to all ASEAN countries, without requiring "substantial process transformation". Obviously, this protects Singapore's transit function and minimizes any restrictive effect on non-ASEAN multinationals wishing to invest in ASEAN but relying heavily on non ASEAN-origin inputs. The "net" cumulative regional content may turn out to be much lower than 40% and still the eligibility for ASEAN-origin may be valid[7]. This liberal system is bound to induce trade deflection via Singapore or Brunei (which have low or zero tariffs) as well as ingenious forms of transfer pricing in multinationals to boost value-added via inflated "local" profits. A strong offsetting factor is the existing practice of granting multinationals tariff-free imports (via export processing zones, tariff drawbacks, etc.) as long as certain (high) export targets are met.

c) Avoiding Legalistic Commitments

The **flexible legal framework** is another non-traditional property of AFTA. First of all, AFTA has no treaty, just like ASEAN lacks a treaty basis. This may be baffling for lawyers and trade negotiators, used to hammering out details, implementation provisions and a compliance machinery for free trade areas. Of course, one may wish to query whether "agreements" are "treaties" in the meaning of the Vienna Convention on Treaties but this is besides the point. The "ASEAN way" of approaching the problem is fundamentally different from the treaty route. Prior to

---

[7] This may be puzzling. If product x has a value of 100, of which 40% is local content in ASEAN country A, it may be exported to B at a CEPT rate, where — say — only 5% local content is added for a total value-added in B of 100. Upon export to ASEAN country C it is considered to have 45% ASEAN content even though "net" cumulative content is 22.5% of 200. Example adapted from ARIFF, 1995, p.59.

deeper commitments, one seeks confidence building at the highest political level, which is then, step by step, transformed into "deepening". The ASEAN *acquis* so obtained is not viewed as assigned to a "higher" level of government (as in the EU) or as overriding sovereignty (which is jealously guarded in ASEAN countries with their short histories of self reliance). The EU notion of "pooling" sovereignty is also alien to ASEAN.

Second, and a corollary of the first point, there is a permanent regulatory drift. In the description of AFTA (see section 2.b.) this has been noted more than once. Problems which are barely touched upon in the CEPT Agreement or in other documents of the Singapore Summit[8], will be addressed later. Besides the question of tariff harmonization (where AFTA will eventually move to an 8-digit HS system), rules of origin, operational certification procedures, "interpretative notes", shorter tariff reduction procedures, greater strictness with respect to the temporary exclusions, the inclusion of agriculture and the institutional structure, several other areas of policy activity have meanwhile begun to be addressed.

This new work involves both deepening and widening, and includes customs valuation (expected to follow the GATT Code), a Framework Agreement on Services, a Framework Agreement on Intellectual Property Cooperation and a start on the removal of technical barriers by the ASEAN Committee on Certification, Standards and Quality. In August 1996 a draft Protocol on Dispute Settlement Mechanism was proposed. This protocol is a telling step beyond "consultations" and "amicable settlement" between Parties in Article 8 of the CEPT Agreement, topped up by political or bureaucratic review if necessary.

The Framework Agreement on Services, signed during the Bangkok Summit of December 1995, appears to be an attempt to stay ahead of the new WTO commitments in the GATS. Besides the aim of enhancing cooperation in services amongst Member States with a view to increase competitiveness, Article 1(c) speaks of the aim to realize a "free trade area in services". Multiple velocities in cooperation or liberalization are allowed and arrangements are possible between as few as two Member States. Cooperation will be sectoral, and based on action plans, programmes and understandings. Liberalization has no calendar or deadline,

---

[8] The Singapore Declaration of 1992, and the Framework Agreement on Enhancing ASEAN Economic Cooperation, published as annexes to SINGH, 1993, pp.19 ff., for example. The many shortcomings of, and open questions raised by, the initial AFTA (CEPT) Agreement, are extensively discussed in PELKMANS, 1992.

not even for the standstill provision (Art.III(b)). Specific commitments will be sectorally negotiated and "directed towards achieving commitments beyond" those entered to in GATS. Such (extra) commitments will be extended preferentially to one another "on an MFN basis". Whether this means an extension to all ASEAN countries, including those not entering specific negotiations, is not clear from the text — probably it refers to reciprocity for the negotiating Parties. The MFN clause presumably means conditional MFN in the region only. Mutual recognition is permitted but in no way compulsory. Since there is no free-movement obligation (like the EC has) this will be merely on an *ad hoc* basis. In line with the multiple-velocities provision, new members of ASEAN need not swallow the *acquis* for services but can negotiate. On the face of it the agreement offers a weak and hardly committing framework. Applied to an area where deregulation and (GATS) liberalization have only just begun, the framework makes sense in the typical ASEAN fashion of facilitation, with initially the greatest possible discretion. It is now possible to argue that WTO is not ahead of ASEAN, although, in substance, the point cuts no ice. However, it is likely that further regulatory reforms in services sectors in ASEAN countries will increase the willingness to go for specific commitments on a preferential basis in a few years from now.

The Framework Agreement on Intellectual Property Cooperation exhibits analogies to the Services Framework. Besides the encouragement of cooperation, both for public regulation and enforcement, and at the private level, the framework essentially removes possible inhibitions to explore common institutions and regulations. In highly circumspect language, it is said that studies will be made about the feasibility of an ASEAN Patent Office, an ASEAN Trademark Office, an ASEAN data base on intellectual property registration, a regional training institute and — for the private sector — an ASEAN Intellectual Property Association. A weak "consultation" mechanism (rather than a genuine dispute settlement mechanism) is modelled on that of the original CEPT Agreement. It is explicitly foreseen that funding of these activities will, as a rule, be national, which may act as an obstacle to dynamic implementation. Finally, the framework refers explicitly to the WTO TRIPs Agreement and international standards and practices in the field.

The draft Protocol on Dispute Settlement Mechanism expands and refines, procedurally, Article 9 of the Framework Agreement on Enhancing ASEAN Economic Cooperation (see footnote 8) which is comparable to Article 8. of the CEPT Agreement. These weak, consultative provisions have no deadlines, are silent on compensations or retaliation ("suspension of concessions") and contain no details about the review procedures other than a reference to the AFTA Council or the AEM. In contrast, and clearly inspired by the WTO Dispute Settlement Mechanism, the ASEAN Draft Protocol explicitly provides for all these procedural details and guarantees. The encouragement to settle disputes amicably is now followed by an encouragement to accept mediation (an important tradition in Asia). Failing all these consultations within sixty days, the Senior Economic Officials Meeting will establish a panel, and, after receiving the panel's report, will make a ruling, without the Parties to the dispute. An appeal is possible to the AEM; this is final and binding. Noncompliance may lead to compensation via bilateral talks or to retaliation ("suspend the application... of concessions"), the latter only upon approval of the AEM.

Stricter dispute settlement procedures were sensitive in ASEAN — they were viewed as too confrontational or "legalistic". To go beyond this and establish even a weak kind of judicial review would be still less acceptable. However, the Uruguay Round has improved the WTO Dispute Settlement, signed by ASEAN countries (Vietnam is not yet a WTO Member, however). Thus, the curious situation arose that far-reaching AFTA commitments were not subject to effective dispute settlement procedures, whereas weaker multilateral commitments were. Early 1995 this led to an embarrassing complaint to WTO by Singapore about a sudden sharp increase of Malaysian tariffs on petrochemicals products so as to protect a huge Taiwanese/Malaysian joint venture in Malaysia. Since Singapore's supply to Malaysia nosedived the dispute was mainly regional and would have been a natural candidate for AFTA procedures. Initial consultations failed and Singapore felt that the urgency of the matter required fast and adequate access-to-justice. The irony of this case is not only that it was the very first one under the new WTO (precisely from a region taking pride in avoiding "legalistic" and confrontational settlement) but even more that AFTA had no adequate mediation or panel procedures and that the matter could have dragged on for a long period. It is likely that this uncharacteristically public dispute gave the necessary push for the draft protocol.

3. Prospects for ASEAN

It is widely held that ASEAN is doing well and enjoys bright prospects. Before uncritically accepting this view it is crucial to be clear about what one means precisely. If the statement refers to the ASEAN region — South East Asia — and its individual countries, then it would be hard to disagree, be it with a few caveats. ASEAN countries, with China, are now the growth miracles of the world; social and economic indicators of development have improved rapidly; internal stability and regional security face no major threat (if China continues to be cooperative in the ASEAN Regional Forum); relations with the largest so-called "dialogue partners" of ASEAN are good (US) to very good (EU; Japan) and ASEAN is a wanted partner for many other countries. Frictions about human rights and democracy have probably reduced in intensity — although this is difficult to measure — because Thailand and the Philippines have improved their records considerably and Indonesia is wavering but with much greater openness (and a human rights committee in its parliament).

The question for this paper is however whether this is congruent with, or at least positively reflecting upon, the Association itself and AFTA. A satisfactory analysis of this question is beyond the confines of the present paper, but a few considerations on ASEAN can be offered. In addition, a review of the Bangkok ASEAN Summit would seem to be useful as well.

As noted, the overriding objective of ASEAN remains external security, peace and stability in the region. And when looking at AFTA, one should not forget that ASEAN countries are first of all interested in the TRIAD markets. AFTA is a means for the higher goal of stability and in this light its imperfections hardly matter. In trade terms AFTA is secondary to multilateral improvements of (TRIAD) market access, hence "legalistic" perfections of AFTA (going against local traditions anyway) are hardly felt to be an issue.

For ASEAN the main security issue is China. It is keen to keep the US hub-and-spoke security ties with East Asia if only for this reason. One prominent reason behind ASEAN's great stride to involve the EU more with East Asia through Asia-Europe Meeting (ASEM) is the actual or potential contribution the EU can provide in the "constructive engagement" of China in world affairs, both political and economic, if possible also in security terms. The rising influence of Japan is welcomed as long as the preponderance remains clearly "civil". A painful political problem is Myanmar (Burma) because it is, one the one hand, no threat whatsoever to the region's stability, but, on the other hand, a contentious issue for the EU and the US as dialogue partners, yet a potential member of ASEAN. With the very small countries Laos and Cambodia lining up for membership, Myanmar would be the odd-man-out in South-East Asia. The Bangkok ASEAN Summit has unequivocally declared that Myanmar should eventually come in. Hopes are put on change in Myanmar induced by economic openness and interdependence with ASEAN and others, in sharp contrast with the adversarial approaches of the US and EU.

One could argue that membership of the three Indo-China countries and Myanmar would reintroduce the extreme differentiations in levels of development (including large scale poverty) that economic growth in ASEAN-6 had so successfully reduced. Moreover, Vietnam is still politically communist and it is not *a priori* clear that the well-known Vietnamese pragmatism would extend to an annihilation of the Party and its power position. In the long run, an argument in favour of membership of these four poor countries is that it would reduce the natural dominance of Indonesia, which is bound to be expressed more strongly over the years. ASEAN as a form of regionalism will therefore remain foreign-policy-driven for the foreseeable future and important structural issues will have to be addressed, both internally and externally.

With respect to economic cooperation and trade the Bangkok Summit expressed determination and confidence. On AFTA, Vietnam is admitted with a calendar stretching to 2006 (the new calendar for the other AFTAns now being 2003). The summiteers made an attempt to further accelerate AFTA from 2003 to 2000 but this proved too daring. The commitment is unclear since "Member countries will maximize the number of items with tariffs reduced to 0%-5% by the year 2000 as well as expand the number of products with tariffs reduced to 0% by the same year."

On the Services Framework Agreement, there was specificity for the first time. A first round of negotiations on specific commitments on market access, national treatment and additional commitments is scheduled from January 1st, 1996 up to late 1998. Sectors specifically mentioned include financial services, maritime transport, telecoms, air transport, tourism, construction and business services. The summit also calls for an ambitious series of action plans for:

- an ASEAN Investment Region,
- an ASEAN Plan on Infrastructure Development,
- the existing ASEAN Plan in Transport and Communication (interconnectivity and harmonization), said to consider an "open-sky policy" (which would be very significant progress),
- on Energy Cooperation,
- on Development of Small & Medium-Sized Enterprises.

A curious label is chosen for all these proposals, the Agenda for Greater Economic Integration. Knowing how much of a taboo the word "integration" was in ASEAN until recently, one is left wondering what the meaning of this wording is. Furthermore, ASEAN reaffirms a large number of instances of "functional cooperation", from human resources to the fight against drugs.

The ASEAN rhetoric often covers up rather modest activities. The actual impact and effectiveness of this project cooperation is extremely hard to come by. Some observers have noted somewhat cynically that the South-East Asian Games do more to spread the notion of ASEAN and what the summiteers call the "sense of community" than all the project cooperation at present scale could ever achieve. It is thus no exaggeration to say that ASEAN as an association benefits a great deal from the economic miracles of individual countries, whilst, at the same time, those miracles can be attributed to the climate of stability and co-operation that ASEAN has brought. One could even go further and assert, with some justification, that regulatory competition between Member States, competition in attracting foreign direct investment and the very strong "beauty contest" effect on following the examples of earlier growth miracles through reform and liberalization has engendered successful development in the region. If this is true ASEAN cooperation hardly matters. To the extent this is true, APEC would appear to be a more appropriate grouping to promote these processes since ASEAN's export markets (except the EU) are represented in APEC, and so are all the examples ASEAN countries might wish to follow.

4. What is APEC?

It is not so easy to answer the query what APEC is. Is it an "international organization" in the traditional sense, or, is it merely a network for dialogue and (project) cooperation? Since there is no treaty or underlying "agreement", is APEC driven by annual summits, by the more frequent ministerials, or, as is often asserted, by business and markets? How "regional" is APEC? Can one maintain that the collection of countries bordering the immense Pacific ocean — North and South, East (i.e. the America's) and West (i.e. East Asia plus Australasia and Oceania) — is a "region"? Should the "C" of APEC be considered as a Community — as was often suggested in 1993, even by President Clinton — or as Co-operation (the official name) or perhaps as a Caucus?

Few of these questions can be answered unequivocally[9]. Informality

---

[9] In the following, the confines of this paper will limit the number of aspects which can be treated. More of such questions are raised in PELKMANS & SHINKAI,

and very loose institutional structures characterize APEC. Its beginning in 1989 amounted to no more than an informal dialogue. The motives behind the acceptance of the Australian idea were mixed. Paramount among them was the fear for a Fortress Europe, in particular that the EU could wreck the Uruguay Round by failing to deliver in agriculture with major ramifications for the main markets of Australia and much of East Asia. Equally strong was the desire to underpin the market-led economic integration taking place within East Asia, and with Australia, as well as North America. All founding countries were eager to promote measures or avoid conflicts that would help sustain these growth markets and their access to them. Initially, APEC was low-key, and concentrated on project cooperation and trade facilitation. Areas of attention included energy, human resources, industrial science and technology, telecoms, tourism, trade and investment data and transport. Later, an informal group on regional trade liberalization was established. The first major success of APEC was not on substance but on membership. In 1991 the three Chinas (P.R. of China, Taiwan, Hong Kong) were admitted at the same time. This was acceptable to Beijing because Hong Kong and Taiwan can be considered as separate "customs territories", without implying any recognition of sovereignty[10]. This is in keeping with the WTO. Indeed, Taiwan might be admitted to the WTO with China, but the former as a "customs territory".

An important basic document, reflecting the preponderance of the "Asian way" in APEC, is once again a declaration, that of Seoul of 1991. Besides a strong recognition of the "important contribution of the private sector to the dynamism of APEC economies" and a call for more active business participation (the effect of which would be to sustain informality) the four objectives of APEC were defined as follows:

- to sustain the growth and development of the region for the common good of its people and, in this way, to contribute to the growth and development of the world economy;

- to enhance the positive gains, both for the region and the world economy, resulting from increasing economic interdependence, by encouraging the flow of goods, services, capital and technology (note: not persons JP);

1996. The reader is also referred to other forthcoming papers e.g. MORRISON, 1996 and JANOW, 1996.

[10] This is precisely the reason why ASEM (the Bangkok Summit of March 1-2, 1996) cannot include Taiwan, according to the P.R. of China. ASEM is not only about trade and facilitation, it also includes foreign policy. Customs territories have no foreign policy.

- to develop and strengthen the open multilateral trading system in the interest of Asia-Pacific and all other economies;
- to reduce barriers to trade in goods and services among participants in a manner consistent with GATT principles, where applicable, and without detriment to other economies[11].

Broadly, these objectives could serve as a modernized version of the goals of the OECD. The only possible difference is development cooperation, a subject increasingly pressed by Japan in APEC.

Indeed, one could argue that APEC initially seemed to be heading towards an OECD, (East) Asian style[12]. APEC's extreme decentralization and initial lack of a central Secretariat forced it into seminars, projects and own-initiative studies by member states seeking to be in the driving seat for a particular topic. An OECD-type APEC Economic Outlook was initiated and rapid progress was made with linking data sets and with statistics, again something the OECD has been doing successfully for decades. The OECD analogy is particularly striking if one compares like with like: the OECD of the 1960s with APEC in its early days. The then OECD regarded itself as the driving force of GATT in a manner now called "open regionalism" by APEC. It went ahead in functional cooperation, weak and uncommitting codes and other "facilitation", and stimulated the technical work of the Kennedy and later GATT Rounds. The motives were also quite similar, as was the economic environment. In the 1960s the EC (and EFTA to a lesser degree) was a fast grower and attracted a great deal of foreign investment. Sustaining growth through facilitation and otherwise found strong support. Moreover, not unlike in East-Asia nowadays, tariff and non-tariff barriers were still significant. In analogy to today's strong market links between East Asia and North America, the transatlantic economic axis in the 1960s was absolutely critical to Europe. Also, the Atlantic security links, on a separate "track" from purely economic work at the OECD, have an imperfect analogy across the Pacific in the US hub-and-spoke security ties with a number of East Asian countries and Australia/New Zealand, also on a separate track from the pure economic work in APEC. Of course, there are differences too. One is China. Another one is the end of the cold war, which had decisively shaped the OEEC as the forerunner of the OECD, and the

---

[11] Quoted from APEC Secretariat, *"Asia-Pacific Economic Cooperation"*, Singapore, 1996.

[12] In a sharp and blunt article, former World Bank top official Helen Hughes seems to suggest this too; HUGHES H., *"Why APEC?"*, in: **ASEAN Economic Bulletin**, 1991. However, since she dismisses the OECD as a model, she does not elaborate.

OECD as the bulwark (yet, no Fortress) of the advanced market economies of the free world.

A third difference is harder to assess: in the early 1990s GATT had already achieved significant results, in the 1960s much of this still had to be accomplished. But for East-Asian countries other than (OECD member) Japan, their perceptions probably differed little from OECD perceptions in the 1960s. China is not a WTO Member, neither is Taiwan. The other ones were, or had recently become, GATT Contracting Parties and their protection levels were high. Until as late as the mid-1980s they were sceptical about GATT and strongly vocal about United Nations Commission on Trade and Development (UNCTAD) (except, of course, Hong Kong and Singapore). Following the sharp appreciation of the yen in 1985 and the surge of Japanese foreign direct investment in the region, it proved possible to have very high growth rates of trade among East Asian countries. Moreover, China opened up and repeated unilateral trade liberalization packages were introduced by many countries. In this climate, the East Asian stakes in GATT rose quickly and nervousness about "results" emerged concomitantly. For all the roughness and acrimony of US trade diplomacy in the (APEC) "region", all countries were conscious of the fact that relatively easy access to the US market had been a crucial factor contributing to their export successes. The EU's EC-1992 deepening and brinkmanship in the Uruguay Round with respect to agriculture caused this nervosity to be transposed into the search for a louder voice — Mahathir's 1990 Proposal for an East Asian Economic Grouping — or, better still, an alternative with enough "critical mass" to get around Europe's obstinacy.

But 1993 altered the nature of APEC. Or did it? Swung by US recognition of the great potential of East Asia, and its dynamics[13], President Clinton decided to kill two birds with one stone. APEC could be used more aggressively, but still cooperatively, to improve market access to East Asia — thereby also overcoming the fear about NAFTA's possible trade diversion — while, at the same time, impressing Europe to be more forthcoming in Geneva. The US, helped by Australia/New Zealand and Canada came to dominate APEC, both in style and substance. Its style changed towards upgrading the institutional structure, including an annual summit and a Secretariat. The emphasis in substance shifted towards trade and investment liberalization[14]. The November 1993 Summit in

---

[13] Note that, in 1992 and 1993, East Asian growth remained around 7% despite flat economies in North America, Europe and Japan.

[14] Strongly encouraged by a report of an Eminent Persons Group chaired by (US) Fred Bergsten. Cf. **A Vision for APEC**, Singapore, October 1993.

Seattle and Blake Island was clearly aimed to force APEC into a higher gear by having Asian political leaders commit themselves visibly — an important prerequisite for progress in Asia — while, at the same time, showing "Brussels" that it risked to be marginalized.

After the EU and the US solved the agricultural issue in the Uruguay Round, however, the US preponderance produced much weaker echoes in APEC. The second and third reports of the APEC Eminent Persons Group no longer mentioned APEC as "Community". APEC began to be split into a school aiming at "open regionalism" but with explicit reciprocity provisions (targeted against possible "free riding" of the EU) and a much looser interpretation of "open regionalism" as "concerted unilateral liberalization". At the moment there is little prospect that the former view will prevail. The "Asian way" will govern APEC, both in style and in substance. The echoes of 1993 and the fact that annual summits have become a tradition might cause a somewhat confusing picture. This is mainly due to intra-APEC interest configuration (see section 5) but changing perceptions about Europe do play a role as well. East Asia has now recognized that the EC-1992 programme, if anything, increased market access and helped the GATT negotiations in e.g. services. It is also enthusiastic about the EU's New Asia Strategy[15] and ASEM, which is enjoying a forceful follow-up. Not least, the EU's less acrimonious style (compared to the US) of bilateral trade diplomacy with Japan, Korea, China and ASEAN countries, and the rapidly intensifying Euro-Asian trade links[16] have impressed East Asian policy makers.

APEC's summits have continued to waver about liberalization. The Jakarta/Bogor Declaration of Common Resolve (Nov. 1994) established very distant deadlines for free trade and investment "in the region": 2010 for the developed economies (which are also OECD members, except Hong Kong and Singapore) and 2020 for the developing countries. This brilliant formula caused both schools to claim that their respective approaches were approved.

The Osaka Action Agenda (Nov. 1995) established nine principles of liberalization and facilitation and no less than fifteen areas of "action" with more concrete objectives for policy work. In addition, upon strong East Asian insistence, another thirteen "action" agendas were adopted in the field of "economic and technical cooperation", partly to be interpreted

---

[15] See COM (94) 314, July 13, 1994, and PELKMANS & BALAOING, 1996.

[16] See PELKMANS & FUKASAKU, (1995) for an analysis of secular trade flows between the EU and Asia.

as a modern version of development assistance. Also, the business sector became more involved. After two reports (1994 and 1995) of the Pacific Business Forum, an APEC Business Advisory Council was established in Osaka. It has now become common practice for business to participate routinely in meetings of civil servants about "facilitation", a trend also emerging in the Transatlantic Partnership.

The APEC Summit in Subic (near Manila) on November 25, 1996 has blessed (because formal approval is not wanted; neither is there a legal basis for it) the unilateral action plans of the Osaka Action Agenda. The Filipino chair has to ensure that those plans and announced commitments accord with the principles and with the details of the Osaka Agenda. Peer pressure in the ministerial meetings and in committees will have to do the rest. Implementation would start on January 1st, 1997. A highly tentative impression of the APEC countries' action plans is that they are diverse, though usually modest. However, they will be revolving over the years[17].

---

[17] See DE DIOS, (1996); and, YAMAZAWA, (1996), for early assessments.

5. APEC: Principles, Substance and Interests

The Osaka Action Agenda starts with nine principles to be applied to the entire APEC liberalization and facilitation process. Table 2 provides a concise summary.

Table 2
Nine APEC Principles since Osaka

	principles	key words
1.	comprehensiveness	addressing all impediments to achieving the long-run goal of free and open trade and investment
2.	WTO consistency	(see also 4.)
3.	comparability	"endeavour to ensure the overall comparability of.. liberalisation"
4.	non-discrimination	- "apply or endeavour to apply the principle" - "outcome... will be the actual reduction of barriers ... also between APEC economies and non-APEC economies"

5.	transparency	- " of... laws, regulations and administrative procedures" - "create... predictable .. environment"
6.	standstill	"endeavour to refrain"
7.	simultaneous start, continuous process and dif-ferentiated time-tables	"begin.. without delay"
8.	flexibility	(given diversity)
9.	cooperation	economic and technical

For a European observer, or for the WTO for that matter, there is much to compliment and little to disagree with. It is almost too good to be true. Upon closer reading and a little reflection, however, many question marks appear. A few examples. The principles of transparency would be admirable progress in Asia. But a serious effort in this direction would have to be guided by a set of performance criteria for the public administration, for access to information, etc. which — in different degrees — would amount to a transformation of traditions, of bureaucratic power configuration, of regulatory techniques and of the scope for corruption and for *quid-pro-quo* networking. APEC countries cannot be expected to agree on such criteria or measuring rods, even if APEC members would be willing to be explicit about them in the first place. So, in actual practice, what does the principle mean for business?

Several principles are weakly formulated. Comparability, nondiscrimination and standstill are merely based on "endeavours". The principle of flexibility is entirely justified in the light of the enormous diversity of APEC as to size, level of development, culture, economic order, etc. Yet, it is undeniable that it is an open invitation for foot-dragging or free riding. Finally, Table 2 has to be assessed against the backdrop of a very long process (to 2010, respectively 2020), even though principle No.7 is an attempt to keep the momentum.

The rest of the Osaka Action Agenda is about actions in specific areas of liberalization and facilitation, as well as in economic and technical cooperation. The agenda is truly impressive. Several areas in the liberalization/facilitation track are divided in objective(s), guidelines and "collective actions" with fairly specific projects or activities. Economic and technical cooperation often uses a subdivision with "common policy concepts" and "joint activities/dialogue". Table 3 merely lists the areas of action in the Agenda.

Table 3
Specific Actions Foreseen in Osaka Agenda

liberalisation/facilitation	econ/techn. cooperation
1. tariffs	1. human resources development
2. non-tariff measures	2. industrial S & T
3. services (telecoms, transport , energy. tourism)	3. SMEs
4. investment	4. economic infrastructure
5. standards & conformance (incl. world standards, mutual recognition, technical infrastructure, transparency)	5. energy
6. customs procedures (incl. Kyoto Convention and a host of detail)	6. transport
7. intellectual property rights	7. telecoms and information
8. competition policy	8. tourism
9. government procurement	9. trade/investment data
10. deregulation	10. trade promotion
11. rules of origin	11. marine resource conservation
12. dispute mediation	12. fisheries
13. mobility of business people	13. agricultural technology
14. implementation Ur. Round	
15. information & analysis	

It is too early to begin to assess the substance in Table 3. The APEC countries' action plans have been tabled in mid-1996 and the Philippines as the APEC chair was charged with the painstaking exercise of verifying whether the plans abide by the principles and specifications of the Osaka Agenda. What is clear, however, is that a lot of the activities, if not void of substance and if implemented, will have the effect of facilitating **all** business and **all** competition, not just that of APEC origin. Thus, even if no progress were possible on the tariff or non-tariff front, APEC should have positive externalities, which can be enjoyed by those eager to do business with East Asia (and, where relevant, other parts of APEC). However, exploiting these opportunities and facilitation requires an Asian business strategy with close involvement, local presence or local partners. With respect to market access measures at the border, the agenda for customs procedures (a notorious problem in Asia) is commendable. However, the tariff issue, as well as non-tariff barriers (where the specifications are rather prudent, except for abolition of export subsidies and "unjustifiable" export prohibitions) remains of overriding importance, given the fairly high tariffs in several Asian countries, and the surcharges still applied. In some countries where tariffs have come down, other barriers or anti-competitive practices restrict imports selectively. Expectations cannot be set high in these cases.

Against the backdrop of this bird's eye view of the Osaka Agenda it is interesting to ask two questions. One is about the meaning of the slogan "open regionalism". The other question is about the interest configuration in APEC. Both questions help to judge whether and how APEC can be or become associated with "regionalism".

Open regionalism means that regional economic intercourse is to be promoted if and only if it is consistent with GATT/WTO and not to the detriment of other economies[18].

This is the positive connotation, which is worth inspecting a little closer. The concept of "open regionalism", however, and the ways its advocates explain it, carry a negative connotation, too. They suggest that other ("non-open") regionalisms are closed or inward-looking. It is then a small step to illustrate this idea with the EU, as it represents by far the most important, and arguably, the most successful example of "other" regionalism. For example, Elek (1992) notes:

---

[18] This subsection draws heavily from PELKMANS & FUKASAKU, 1995, pp.161-163.

For the first time, a powerful regional group of economies has come together to promote global economic interests, rather than to defend their own narrower markets by forming a trading bloc. APEC's concept of open regionalism is radically different from the discriminatory nature of the EC. *(Ibid., p.74)*

The EC's experience of almost four decades indicates that what counts in the long run are actual effects on market access (in goods and services), market penetration and the scope and degree of preferentialism. On all these points, there is no doubt that the EU has opened up its markets steadily and lowered its degree of preferentialism. In agriculture (and to some extent, in coal) it has not done so, to the detriment of agro-exporters (see Pelkmans & Carzaniga, 1996).

One may distinguish three categories of activities for APEC, and in principle, also for other groupings:

- **Nondiscriminatory confidence-building measures**, such as enhanced exchange of macroeconomic information, increased transparency of trade policies, trade and investment facilitation, consultation, voluntary codes, studies, networking, etc.; the OECD does this, so could APEC.

- **Voluntary, but preferably common liberalization decisions about national trade measures and regulatory provisions**; if such national measures are nondiscriminatory, they are neither fully multilateral (although APEC could assume credible leadership in WTO, to be sure), nor plurilateral (because this would require reciprocity), not (by definition) bilateral or regional. If anything, it would be **concerted unilateral liberalization**. The Bogor Summit Declaration in November 1994 may refer to this ambitious idea. In terms of the habitual incentives for trade negotiations between and among countries, concerted unilateralism is unique. But if traditional political economy is a guide, it would not be realistic to expect co-ordinated unilateralism to succeed beyond marginal measures, because of the "free riding" problem under voluntarism and the nonbinding nature of policy commitments.

- **Common reciprocal market opening**; this is another term for "regionalism" such as free trade areas and customs union. This category is inconsistent with "open regionalism" as defined by its advocates. However, as demonstrated by the way AFTA seems to be developing, such regionalism may still be rather "outward-looking" (e.g. a FTA with a 40 percent cumulative rule of origin).

It is also possible to minimize trade diversion. What is **not** possible, however, is to practize regionalism in the sense that it does not amount to trade discrimination[19].

In short, "open regionalism" may consist of either or both of the first two categories, but not the third one. The first category would be not too far from a Pacific OECD whereas the second, if substantial, might suffer from severe political economy disincentives. The Osaka Agenda — in principles No.2 and No.4 — has opted for the rejection of reciprocity, and hence the rejection of an APEC free trade area idea.

This leads us to the final question about the interest configuration driving, conditioning or impeding the course of APEC. Behind APEC, especially now that the Uruguay Round has been completed, looms the issue of an East Asian free trade area. As Panagariya (1994) shows, however, this is most unlikely. First, Japan, Korea and China are still too strong rivals to begin imagine this; unlike the Europe of the 1950s and 1960s these three countries are not under cold war pressure. Second, the distribution of gains from such a form of regionalism would be uneven and dynamically uncertain, given sharp differences in the level of development (and initial protection). Third, AFTA is a pointer on how difficult it would be, precisely because in the East Asia case intra-trade is far more important than intra-AFTA trade, and the link with foreign direct investment is very strong.

However, the real problem is the US. Its position is internally inconsistent but that is a fact of Asia-Pacific life. Although the US insists on reciprocity in APEC, it almost certainly would not wish to join a free trade area with East Asia. Among the many reasons, a deep distrust about the lack of a level-playing field in Japan, Korea and China and the sensitivity of the NAFTA jobs debate are prominent. At the same time, the US is firmly opposed to even the slightest beginning of an economic caucus in East Asia, as is evident from its staunch opposition to the East Asia Economic Caucus[20]. And yet it proceeded with NAFTA, giving rise to fears of trade diversion in East Asia, especially for cars and textiles and clothing.

---

[19] For the interested reader, the pretence and contradictions of "open regionalism" have led to a debate in APEC, whether or not the term is an "oxymoron". See e.g. SMITH (1996).

[20] The irony is that EAEC has, for the first time, coordinated positions **in the framework of ASEM**, in a ministerial meeting in Chiang Rai, before the Bangkok Summit.

So, APEC can be interpreted as a kind of "economic security" without much (or any) binding on the part of the main partners. It leaves lots of room to continue with major issues on the agenda which are not dealt with in APEC (see e.g. Smith, 1996). One is US bilateralism which may have become less problematic since WTO but is still sharpest precisely with respect to East Asia (especially, Japan and China). Perhaps the most important issue is the WTO membership of China. APEC has not contributed here at all, except if one were to maintain that it encourages the kinds of reforms which would be helpful for its accession. However, the elusive language of APEC is hardly of any help.

There is also the enlargement of APEC, temporarily stopped until 1997. Yet, ASEAN member Vietnam is hard to keep out, and who will be next? APEC has also failed to push for a major initiative in the run-up of the WTO ministerial in Singapore. Many APEC countries are faced with considerable resistance against the mere implementation of Marrakesh. Where one to go into further detail, in terms of instruments used and sectors affected, APEC initiatives are unlikely to overcome free riding easily.

The conclusion is that open regionalism is the current policy of APEC, partly because reciprocity is resisted or the consequences (e.g. in Europe) are feared, but partly as well because the "hard" liberalization measures (tariffs, non-tariff barriers) are unlikely to be found in significant packages for years to come, with the exception of China and, maybe, Vietnam.

6. Conclusions

ASEAN and APEC are not comparable with regionalism as customarily defined in Europe nor are they fully comparable with each other. The present paper has attempted to provide an insight into the unique properties of both instances of cooperation, as well as a good deal of their technical substance. The reader may be helped by Appendix 1, provided by the discussant Dr. Fukasaku, juxtaposing some of the major characteristics.

ASEAN is first of all a low-cost, high-gains security and foreign policy association which uses essentially economic, bureaucratic and political means to achieve its goals. In terms of trade and investment its preponderant interests lay **outside** the region. For this reason alone, AFTA might be called an outward free trade area.

Whether APEC is an instance of regionalism is questionable. Its current agenda gives the impression of a modernized OECD, Asian style, against the backdrop of the level and structure of protection and the differences in the levels of development of the APEC members. Attempts, initially led by the US and inspired by three reports of the APEC Eminent Persons Group, to pursue ambitious intra-APEC trade liberalization on the basis of reciprocity have come to nothing. The school of "open-regionalism" has prevailed. This can be explained both by "the Asian way" of economic cooperation, and by a complex interest configuration which would make an APEC free trade area politically infeasible for the foreseeable future. The ingenious solution was to move the dates to the unforeseeable future — 2020 for the developing countries — and to call it "free trade in the region". This elusive expression leaves open all the options.

Neither AFTA nor APEC exhibit any major problem of incompatibility of WTO. A minor disappointment is ASEAN's notification of AFTA under the Enabling Clause. Deepening and widening of AFTA is almost entirely inspired and promoted by achievements in the WTO. APEC's avowed aims to promote multilateralism and, thus far, its agenda express the principle of open regionalism.

References

ARIFF M., *"The Prospects for an ASEAN Free Trade Area"*, in: **The World Economy**, (special issue on Global Trade Policy), Vol.18, 1995.

DE DIOS E., *"The APEC Dividend: Assessing the Results of Concerted Unilateral Liberalisation"*, paper for the conference "APEC and Europe", European Institute for Asian Studies, Brussels, Oct. 11, 1996 (conference volume forthcoming).

ELEK A., *"Trade Policy Options for the Asia Pacific Region in the 1990s. The Potential of Open Regionalism"*, in: **American Economic Review**, Vol.82, No.2, May 1992.

FUKASAKU K., *"Macroeconomic Framework for Sustaining ASEAN's Outward-oriented Growth"*, paper for the ASEAN Round Table, ISEAS & OECD Development Centre, Singapore, Sept. 16/17, 1996 (conference volume forthcoming).

JANOW M., *"Assessing APEC's Role in Economic Integration in the Asia-Pacific Region"*, Columbia University, New York, August 1996, (unpublished paper).

MORRISON Ch., *"Regime Building in Asia Pacific and the Dangers of Regulatory Rift in US-European Relations"*, paper for the workshop "Towards Rival Regionalism?", Stiftung Wissenschaft und Politik, Ebenhausen, July 4-6, 1996, (conference volume forthcoming).

PANAGARIYA A., *"East Asia and the New Regionalism in World Trade"*, in: **The World Economy**, Vol.17, No.6, November 1994.

PELKMANS J., *"Institutional Requirements of ASEAN, with Special Reference to AFTA"*, in: IMADA P. & NAYA S. (eds), **AFTA, the Way Ahead**, ISEAS, Singapore, 1992.

PELKMANS J., **European Integration, Methods and Economic Analysis**, Longman/Addison Wesley, London, 1997 (forthcoming).

PELKMANS J. & BALAOING A., *"EU's New Asia Policies, Twinning European and Multilateral Interests"*, revised paper for the workshop "Towards Rival Regionalism?", Stiftung Wissenschaft und Politik, Ebenhausen, July 4-6,1996; (conference volume forthcoming).

PELKMANS J. & CARZANIGA A., *"The Trade Policy Review of the EU"*, in: **The World Economy**, (special issue on Global Trade Policy), Vol.19, 1996.

PELKMANS J. & FUKASAKU K., *"Evolving Trade Links between Europe and Asia: Towards "Open Continentalism"?"*, in: FUKASAKU K., **Regional Cooperation and Integration in Asia**, OECD, Paris, 1995.

PELKMANS J. & SHINKAI H., *"APEC and its Meaning for Europe"*, paper. for the conference "APEC and Europe", European Institute for Asian Studies, Brussels, Oct. 11, 1996 (conference volume forthcoming).

SINGH B., *"The Fourth ASEAN Summit. A New Milestone in Political Will"*, in: LEE L.T. & WEHRHOERNER A. (eds), **ASEAN and the EC in the 1990s**, SIIA & FES, Singapore, 1993.

SMITH M., *"Economic Integration in the Asia Pacific Region: Is Open Regionalism an Oxymoron?"*, paper for the Bruges Conference, College of Europe, March 20-22, 1996.

YAMAZAWA I., *"Market Opening in East Asia: Implementation of the Uruguay Round, APEC Commitments and Trade Policy Reform"*, paper for the conference "Asian-European Trade Cooperation in a WTO Context", European Institute for Asian Studies, Brussels, Nov. 28/29, 1996.

Appendix 1

	AFTA	APEC
principles	. **GATT consistent** (Article XXIV?) . **Outward-looking** (Liberal rules of origin) . **Consensus-based** . **Co-operation**	. **GATT consistent** . **Non-discrimination** . **Open regionalism** (Concerted unilateralism) . **Transparency** . **Consensus-based** . **Co-operation**
Motives	. **Changes in external environment** (e.g. Globalisation; Competition with China) . **Policy changes in ASEAN countries** (e.g. Rapid Industrialisation based on outward orientation; Trade-FDI Nexus)	. **Uncertainty over the outcome of Uruguay Round** . **Reaction to deepning and widening of EU**
Basic Features	. **Binding** . **CEPT scheme** (1994-) Scheduled tariff reduction to 0-5%: Fast track by 1998 (<20%) by 2000 (>20%) Normal track by 2000 (<20%) by 2003 (>20%) Reducing "temporary exclusion" lists . **QRs on CEPT products to be removed** . **Other NTBs to be phased out in 5 years** . **40% cumulative rules of origin** . **Technical and other co-operation** (harmonistion of tariff nomenclatures; customs valuation; standards and quality; etc.)	. **Non-binding** . **Establishing "free and open trade and investment in the APEC region"** by 2010 (developed members) by 2010 (other members) . **Standstill on new protective measures** . **Trade and investment facilitation** . **Economic and technical co-operation**

Source: A table provided in the conference by the commentator to the Pelkmans paper, Dr. Kiichiro Fukasaku.

Although this table does not fully reflect the text of the paper (e.g. APEC has nine principles; the APEC motives were also growth oriented; etc.) it may serve as a convenient guide for the reader.

THE NORTH AMERICAN FREE TRADE AGREEMENT: ITS POSSIBLE EXTENSION TO SOUTH AMERICAN COUNTRIES

Donald R. MACKAY[1]

Special Trade Advisor,
Organization of American States, Washington

Introduction

Regionalism remains as strong a force in international trade policy as ever. From the mid-1980s to the early 1990s it was assumed, by some, that regionalism represented little more than international frustration with the pace and content of multilateral efforts aimed at trade liberalization. This, we now know, is clearly not true. Regional and multilateral trade liberalization efforts are here to stay, at least for the foreseeable future.

In the three major trading areas of the world (Europe, the Americas and Asia), regionalism is a strong, and perhaps, growing force. The Treaty of Rome launched a complex and far reaching program in Europe which is meeting the dual challenge of both deepening and expanding its ties of trade and economic integration. In Asia, the process remains somewhat more obscure and less formalized than elsewhere, nevertheless, the economic dynamism of that region is well-known to most. In the Americas — the principal focus of this paper — the goal of trade and

---

[1] The views in this paper are those of the author alone and do not represent the views of the Organization of American States, its Member Countries, or the Government of Canada.

economic liberalization remains a high priority for policy makers. The path(s) to such liberalization, however, are less well-known.

The negotiation of the North American Free Trade Agreement (NAFTA) had the effect of galvanizing the pursuit and practice of trade policy in the Americas. It cemented the view that the United States was prepared to enter into special arrangements outside of the multilateral context with a developing country[2]. The NAFTA, nevertheless, was greeted in the Americas with a mixed set of emotions. Envy on the part of some countries who quickly voiced their "interest" in participating, and concern on the part of others who sought to construct "counterbalancing" arrangements elsewhere in the Hemisphere.

The NAFTA has also had a major influence in the practice of trade policy within the region, especially at the technical level where we can see the NAFTA approach being duplicated at the subregional level. What are called "newer" Latin American integration efforts have generally adopted more of a "NAFTA-like" approach than the approach offered by the older Association for Latin American Development and Integration (ALADI). And while this is a positive development in straight trade policy terms, at the strategic level it nevertheless remains true that trade and economic integration in the Americas **cannot** be built around the NAFTA as the core.

This conclusion does not come easy, and will be difficult for some to accept. Nevertheless, there now exists a substantial enough body of evidence to support such a conclusion.

The Lay of the Land in the Americas

The Western Hemisphere[3] is a very different place in 1996 than it was a decade ago. The countries of the region have taken a series of great leaps over the past ten years, with bilateral and subregional trade agreements serving as vital complements to their domestic economic reforms. In contrast to many of the agreements that countries negotiated in the

---

[2] The arrangement between the US and Israel really falls into a set of very special and specific circumstances, so much so that it would be difficult to equate it on the same level as US willingness to enter into an arrangement with a developing country like Mexico. Naturally, the preexisting arrangement between Canada and the US also fits into a very specific set of circumstances.

[3] The Americas are understood to include the Caribbean as well as North, Central and South America, or the thirty-four Member Countries of the Organization of American States (excludes Cuba).

1960s, the agreements of the 1990s are based on an open and liberalizing trade regime.

The changes are largely a reaction to the situation faced by much of Latin America and the Caribbean in the 1980s which was characterized by misguided fiscal and monetary policies resulting in a debt crisis for some and a net outward transfer of financial and other resources for many. In the 1990s, efforts aimed at enhanced participation in the increasingly globalized marketplace, prompted many countries to revive many of their existing trade and integration arrangements and adopt policies aimed at trade liberalization through unilateral efforts to open domestic economic and trade regimes. In part, this revival was also a reaction to the perceived consolidation of trade blocs in other regions of the world, which have "called attention to the potential benefits of freer trade with existing partners."[4]

Meanwhile in North America, increased trade and economic linkages were built upon the foundation of the multilateral system embodied in GATT[5]. By 1987, however, the two countries had agreed that the sheer size and scope of bilateral trade had outgrown multilateral based trade instruments and the Canada-United States Free Trade Agreement was negotiated and came into force in 1989. In Mexico, domestic economic reforms began with that country's decision to join GATT in 1986, which set the stage for all three countries to open negotiations in 1991 on a North American Free Trade Agreement (NAFTA) that came into force in 1994.

Economic Integration: A Typology

One might distinguish six different types of economic-integration agreements:

- economic unions in which the members integrate all of their economic policies;
- common markets in which a customs union is supplemented by removal of all barriers to factor movements between members;
- customs unions in which member countries eliminate tariffs among themselves and establish a common external tariff on goods from third countries;

---

[4] LUSTIG Nora & BRAGA C.A. Primo, *"The Future of Trade Policy in Latin America"*, in: WEINTRAUB Sidney (ed.), **Integrating the Americas: Shaping Future Trade Policy**, Transaction Publishers, New Brunswick, N.J., 1994, pp.23, 17.

[5] The negotiation in 1965 of the Canada-US AutoPact, for which the US sought and received a GATT waiver, is considered in this paper, to confirm the rule.

- free trade agreements in which member countries eliminate substantially all tariff and non-tariff barriers among themselves;
- preferential agreements in which access to a larger market is offered without demands for reciprocity; and,
- sectoral agreements that provide for reduced-tariff or duty-free treatment among their members on a limited range of products[6].

Examples of the last four types of agreements can be found in the Western Hemisphere today. A significant number of customs unions and free trade agreements exist in the Americas. Canada, the United States, and some Latin American countries (e.g., Venezuela and Colombia) offer preferential non reciprocal access to their markets under various types of program and there are also numerous sectoral agreements on specific products negotiated within the framework of LAIA (Latin American Integration Association).

Customs Unions

Mercosur: The common market of the Southern Cone was created on March 26, 1991, when Argentina, Brazil, Paraguay and Uruguay signed the Treaty of Asunción. The two main instruments of the treaty were a four-year Trade Liberalization Program and the implementation of a common external tariff on January 1st, 1995[7]. Since then, Mercosur has completed a free trade agreement with Chile and in early September 1996 announced it intention to negotiate a similar arrangement with the Andean Group. Mercosur and the European Union have also held some tentative discussions[8].

The Andean Group (Bolivia, Colombia, Ecuador, Peru, and Venezuela) was established in 1969 when the Cartagena Agreement was signed[9]. The main objectives of the Andean Group were: to eliminate trade barriers within the Group; to create a customs union with a common external

---

[6] This typology is an elaboration of the scheme presented by BALASSA Bela, in: **The Theory of Economic Integration**, Richard D. Irwin, Homewood, 1961. Balassa's typology did not include preferential or sectoral agreements.

[7] Preceding the Asunción Treaty was the signature in 1986 by Argentina and Brazil of the Acta para la Integración Argentina-Brasileña. This new accord aimed at expanding bilateral trade among the two countries by adopting a sectoral approach. Two other accords preceded Mercosur: the Tratado de Integración in 1989, and the Acta de Buenos Aires in 1990.

[8] Concerning the agreement between Mercosur and the EU, see the García Jiménez's contribution in this book.

[9] Venezuela joined the Group in 1973.

tariff; to harmonize economic, social, and economic policies; and, to adopt a joint industrialization program. In the early years of the process, at the beginning of the liberalization program, intra-subregional trade increased between member countries whose markets had few preexisting links. However, shortly thereafter the deadlines for the fulfilment of the liberalization program and the adoption of a common external tariff were practically abandoned. In 1987, the Quito Protocol acknowledged this fact and modified the Cartagena Agreement by, *inter alia*, providing for more flexibility in the achievement of the Group's goals. In addition, a new safeguard clause and tariff quotas were introduced.

A revival of the Andean Group began in 1990, when the member states signed the La Paz Declaration which provided for the elimination of tariffs on intra-subregional imports by the end of December 1991, and the definition of a common external tariff. In December 1991, the Act of Barahona was signed in Cartagena. It provided for the establishment of a free trade zone by January 1st, 1992, and the definition of a common external tariff with four levels (from 5 percent to 20 percent). After some disagreements, free trade between Colombia, Venezuela, Ecuador and Bolivia went into effect as of February 1st, 1995. Simultaneously, a Common External Tariff (CET) was implemented by these same countries.

The Central American Common Market (Costa Rica, El Salvador, Guatemala, Honduras, and Nicaragua) also known as the Managua Treaty was signed in 1960, and entered into force in 1963. It provided for immediate free trade on 95 percent of all goods. The remaining tariffs were to be removed by June 1966. Other provisions of the treaty included an agreement on integration industries. Armed conflict between Honduras and El Salvador in 1969, followed by almost two decades of political and military instability meant that the CACM survived largely in name only in the 1970s and 1980s.

The agreement was reinvigorated in the early 1990s. In June 1990, a Presidential Summit in Antigua (Guatemala), the Plan de Acción Económica para Centroamérica (PAECA) called for the revival of economic integration in Central America. In 1992, Honduras was "readmitted", and created with El Salvador and Guatemala the Northern Triangle. This led to the establishment of a free trade area in 1993, which Nicaragua later joined to create the Group of Four. They agreed on a common external tariff with four sub-tariffs of 5, 10, 15 and 20 percent. These countries signed the Guatemala Protocol in October 1993, a program aimed at modernizing the Managua Treaty of 1960. Its main objective is the establishment of an economic union.

The five CACM members and Panama showed their commitment to integration by establishing a new organization, the Sistema de Integración Económica Centroamericana (SIECA), which began its work in February 1993. Since that time, SIECA has helped the Central American republics to modernize their trade relationships and perhaps as importantly has helped them to more effectively implement their obligations under the WTO[10].

The Caribbean Free Trade Association (CARIFTA) was created in 1967 as a limited free trade agreement. It was superseded by Caricom[11] when Barbados, Guyana, Jamaica, and Trinidad and Tobago signed the Treaty of Chaguaramas on July 4, 1973 to create the Caribbean Community. All Commonwealth Caribbean countries are members of the group. In July 1989, the Heads of Governments adopted several measures aimed at stimulating and promoting economic and political integration. One of the main objectives of the Organization is a phased common external tariff on most goods by 1998.

Free Trade Agreements

North American Free Trade Agreement (NAFTA): United States, Canada, and Mexico. The goal of negotiating a free trade agreement between the three North American countries grew out of a number of factors. Canada and the United States, partners in the single largest trading relationship in the world, successfully completed a bilateral FTA in 1988 that included goods, services, and investment, but did not deal in depth with intellectual property. For its part, Mexico had gradually come to be the third-largest trading partner of the United States, and had since the mid-1980s pursued a policy of economic and trade reform. The three countries also shared a view that the size and scope of economic and commercial ties in North America essentially required a unique agreement, one that could be customized to fit the specific circumstances of the region.

The negotiations were launched in Toronto (Canada) on June 12, 1991, and were completed fourteen months later on August 12, 1992 in

---

[10] SIECA has, for example, succeeded in drafting model legislation and regulatory procedures in the area of anti-dumping and countervailing duties, which have been incorporated into national legislation. Work has also taken place in the area of Rules of Origin and Standards and Technical Barriers to Trade.

[11] *Caricom* is composed of: Antigua and Barbuda, the Bahamas (not a member of the Common Market, only of the Caribbean Community), Barbados, Belize, Dominica, Grenada, Guyana, Jamaica, Montserrat, St. Kitts and Nevis, St. Lucia, St. Vincent and the Grenadines, and Trinidad and Tobago. Suriname joined the Organization in February 1995.

Washington D.C. The agreement was signed on December 17, 1992. It was supplemented in 1993 by the negotiation of "side agreements" on labor and the environment. Following the approval of the three countries' respective legislatures, NAFTA and its side agreements came into effect on January 1st, 1994.

The NAFTA is a comprehensive free trade agreement. In addition to establishing a 5- or 10-year schedule for the elimination of tariff barriers on most goods[12], it covers trade in services; provides protection for investment and intellectual property; applies rules to government procurement and the operation of government enterprises; and contains highly developed systems for the settlement of disputes. The agreement liberalizes market access conditions in a number of important sectors critical to the continued development of North America's infrastructure, such as in transportation, telecommunications, and financial services. It facilitates the movement of business people and professionals among the three countries.

The agreement contains an accession clause which has been the subject of much discussion. In December 1994, the three founding members of NAFTA announced their formal agreement to explore with Chile the basis of that country's accession to the agreement and formal negotiations were launched on June 7, 1995, in Toronto, Ontario. Since then, however, the United States was unable to secure "fast-track"[13] negotiating authority and the negotiations have become a bilateral Chile-Canada negotiation[14] — Chile already has a free trade agreement with Mexico.

Group of Three: Colombia, Mexico, and Venezuela. On June 13, 1994, Colombia, Mexico, and Venezuela signed the Group of Three Agreement entered into force on January 1st, 1995 and calls for the total elimination of tariffs over a 10-year period. Unlike most trade arrangements among Latin American countries, the Group of Three goes beyond tariff provisions, and deals with such matters as intellectual property rights, services,

---

[12] Most tariffs are eliminated long before the end of this phase-in period. Tariffs between Canada and the United States will be eliminated by 1997, as already established under the bilateral FTA between these two countries. For a small number of items, tariffs will be phased out over a period of up to fifteen years.

[13] "Fast-track", essentially, means that the Congress allows the Administration to negotiate tariff and other trade commitments on its behalf, with the further self-imposed promise not to seek amendments to the necessary implementing legislation in favour of a simple positive or negative vote.

[14] At the time of writing, it is known that negotiators are working towards an October 1996 deadline so that the agreement can be signed during the state visit of President Frei to Canada.

government procurement, and investment along lines not dissimilar from the NAFTA[15].

Bilateral free trade agreements: Led mostly by Chile and Mexico, the region also contains a number of important bilateral free trade agreements. Chile has negotiated a series of free trade agreements with Mexico (implemented on January 1st, 1992), Venezuela (implemented on July 1st, 1993), Colombia (implemented on January 1st, 1994) and Ecuador (implemented on January 1st, 1995) while Mexico has concluded agreements with Bolivia and Costa Rica.

In general, the Chilean bilaterals provide for trade liberalization in respect of trade in goods with some limited provisions in respect of maritime transportation. The agreements share a common structure although provisions in certain cases are customized to fit particular circumstances. Each contains well developed mechanisms for the settlement of disputes and the administration of the agreements, as well as clear timetables for the elimination of almost all tariffs and non-tariff barriers. Disciplines on trade-related measures are well developed and each also contains timetables for the further elaboration of such measures, as in the case of safeguards. The agreements do not cover other issues, such as trade in services, investment, protection of intellectual property rights or the harmonization of technical standards, although Chile's agreements with Colombia and Ecuador do contain some provisions in respect to sanitary and phyto-sanitary measures.

The Mexican bilaterals, on the other hand, take the NAFTA as their primary point of departure. The Costa Rica and Bolivia agreements, for example, contain structures similar to that of the NAFTA although some of the provisions do not have quite the same high level of trade discipline. In addition, Mexico is negotiating with Nicaragua to be followed by negotiations with El Salvador, Guatemala and Honduras.

Preferential Agreements

There are several preferential trade agreements in the Western Hemisphere which, for the most part, only need a brief mention in this paper. The *Caribbean Basin Initiative (CBI)* and the *Andean Trade Preferences Act (ATPA)*, provide preferential access to the US market for those

---

[15] Senior members of the Colombian negotiating team have confirmed to the author that the negotiations proceeded on the basis of the Spanish language NAFTA text as provided and explained by Mexico.

respective regions. In addition, the *Canadian-Caribbean Agreement (CARIBCAN)* also provides Caribbean countries with preferential access to the Canadian market. In addition, both Venezuela and Colombia have signed agreements with Caricom that provide temporary preferential access to the markets of those two countries[16].

Caricom-Venezuela: Antigua and Barbuda, the Bahamas, Barbados, Belize, Dominica, Grenada, Guyana, Jamaica, Montserrat, St. Kitts and Nevis, St. Lucia, St. Vincent and the Grenadines, and Trinidad and Tobago. This agreement was signed in October 1992, and provides for duty-free access for some imports from Caricom countries into Venezuela. After a five-year period, negotiations are to begin to make the trade agreement reciprocal.

Caricom-Colombia: Antigua and Barbuda, the Bahamas, Barbados, Belize, Dominica, Grenada, Guyana, Jamaica, Montserrat, St. Kitts and Nevis, St. Lucia, St. Vincent and the Grenadines, and Trinidad and Tobago. This agreement was signed in July 1994. It provides for the immediate elimination of Colombian duties on goods covering 86 percent of the Colombian imports from Caricom. Another 4 percent will be included by January 1998. Further negotiations will include the liberalization of the remaining Colombian tariffs and the trade concessions that the largest Caribbean countries will give to Colombia in reciprocity.

Sectoral Agreements
(Regional Scope and Partial Scope Agreements)[17]

Latin American Integration Association (LAIA): in 1960, the Latin American Free Trade (LAFTA) was established by the Treaty of Montevideo. The main goal of this treaty was to remove trade barriers among the member countries over a period of twelve years. However, this proved to be both controversial and difficult. By the end of 1978, the eleven signatories agreed that a restructuring of the Association was needed. The Treaty of Montevideo of 1980 set up LAIA as a successor

---

[16] Interestingly, after five years, the agreement with Venezuela calls for further negotiations aimed at making the agreement reciprocal, while the Colombia agreement also calls for negotiations in five years but with the aim of providing Colombia with reciprocal access only to the largest Caricom members.

[17] Besides the LAIA agreements, there exists another major sectoral in the Western Hemisphere, the *Canada-US AutoPact*. This bilateral agreement was signed by the two countries in 1965, and provides for duty-free trade in automobiles and automotive parts. This was the first significant departure that either the United States or Canada took in the postwar period from the rule of multilateralism. The *AutoPact* was incorporated in the *Canada-US Free Trade Agreement*.

to LAFTA. Its objective is to increase "bilateral trade among the member countries and between member countries and third countries through bilateral and multilateral agreements, with the goal of eventually achieving regional free trade."[18] LAIA members are Argentina, Bolivia, Brazil, Chile, Colombia, Ecuador, Mexico, Paraguay, Peru, Uruguay, and Venezuela. LAIA integration mechanisms are more flexible than those of LAFTA. They are based on a sectoral approach: regional scope agreements covering all members of the Association; and partial scope agreements which are trade agreements giving preferences on some specific products, signed by subgroups of members, normally two countries. Sometimes partial scope agreements are wider in scope and are called economic complementation agreements. There are currently thirty-two partial scope and economic complementation agreements in place, half of which have been signed in the 1990s[19].

Regional Liberalization: The Central Question

The question posed by this panel is related to the NAFTA and its possible extension to other South American countries. This is a slightly different question of whether accession to the NAFTA can constitute the mechanism by which the Western Hemisphere achieves true trade liberalization and economic integration.

Strictly speaking, the answer to the first question, at least from a technical perspective is yes. It has been determined, for example, that the NAFTA is the only agreement without a geographically defined accession clause, and to which all countries of the Hemisphere could theoretically adhere[20]. Membership in all the other agreements is subject to geographical or other limitations at the subregional level, none of which could theoretically encompass the entire Hemisphere. There are thus, certain practical difficulties, barring amendments being made to the agreements in question, in achieving Hemispheric free trade by the expansion in the membership of existing arrangements to other countries, with the exception, as noted, of the NAFTA.

---

[18] World Trade Organization, *Regionalism and the World Trading System*, WTO, Geneva, 1995, p.35.

[19] Economic Commission for Latin America and the Caribbean, *Desenvolvimiento de los procesos de integración en América latina y el Caribe*, ECLAC, Santiago, May 16, 1995, p.19.

[20] Organization of American States, Trade Unit, "*Trade and Integration Arrangements in the Americas: An Analytical Compendium.*", Washington D.C., September 9, 1996.

Nevertheless, we have already witnessed the delay encountered by a country as well "prepared" for NAFTA accession as is Chile. While the delay can objectively be attributed to political conditions in the United States, the difficulty encountered between Canada and Chile in concluding their bilateral agreement underscores the "high" admission price demanded by NAFTA accession[21].

Casting one's gaze beyond Chile for a moment, one is confronted with the fact that the next two most "attractive" countries in South America for "NAFTA membership" are Argentina and Brazil. Those two countries, however, constitute the core of the Mercosur customs union. Putting aside for a moment the difficulty in trade policy terms of reconciling a customs union and a free trade area[22], one may still recall that while Mercosur has itself greatly helped to expand trade and economic links in the southern part of the region, it nevertheless lacks a number of provisions that are found in the NAFTA. For example, the Mercosur Agreement lacks the sort of disciplines found in NAFTA's chapters on: government procurement; standards and technical barriers to trade; intellectual property; services and temporary entry. Nor does it contain the sorts of dispute settlement mechanisms found in the NAFTA, most particularly in the area of Review and Dispute Settlement in Anti-dumping and Countervailing Duty Matters (Chapter 19), a subject which alone could have been the focus of this paper.

Within the region encompassed by the Andean Pact, Colombia has gone perhaps the furthest in reforming its trade policy regime. While Colombian accession to the NAFTA is conceivable in technical terms strictly confined to trade policy, the political dimensions of such an accession are another matter entirely. Unfortunately, the process of trade and economic reform in Venezuela still remains very much in doubt which would make that country's "candidature" somewhat open to debate. Add to these already serious questions a question of institutional capacity[23] and it becomes obvious that NAFTA's extension to the rest of

---

[21] The Canada-Chile bilateral is a self-described "stepping stone" to NAFTA accession, nevertheless the Chileans are having difficulty reconciling some of their well know regulations of capital transfers with the disciplines in NAFTA's Chapter 11 (Investment). If such difficulties arise with a country that has undergone the sort of trade and macroeconomic reform as has Chile, then one must be less optimistic when considering a number of other Latin American countries.

[22] But without forgetting the need for consistency with Article XXIV of GATT 94.

[23] Unlike an agreement embodied in the European Union, implementation of the NAFTA rests solely with the national governments acting without the aid of a large and well funded international bureaucracy. As an example, the US Patent and Trademark Office has an estimated staff of 3,000 people to administer the domestic and

South America (not to mention the Caribbean or Central America), while perhaps possible, is not likely in the near term.

The Future of Trade and
Economic Integration in the Americas

Trade liberalization and economic integration in the Americas will be achieved by continued pursuit of a dual track approach. On the one hand, existing agreements and arrangements will continue to deepen and in some cases expand. This means, on the one hand, that many of the existing agreements will continue to evolve, in some cases along pre-planned lines. The NAFTA, for example, prefigures a range of future negotiations in areas such as services, government procurement and others. Other agreements, such as the Central American Common Market (CACM) have been reinvigorated and/or increased the importance of successful and effective implementation of existing obligations. In this same category, one may also add those agreements such as the Mercosur which are serving as engines to liberalization by their expansion outward. The successful conclusion of negotiations between Mercosur and Chile is one example.

The second track by which trade liberalization in the Americas is/will be accomplished is through the combined efforts of the thirty-four countries of the Hemisphere to build a Free Trade Area of the Americas (FTAA), which they have committed themselves to achieve by the year 2005. This process was launched at the Miami Summit in December 1994 and now is continuing at the level of Trade Ministers who have in turn established a total of eleven working groups.

The Free Trade Area of the Americas was officially launched in December 1994 at the Summit of the Americas when leaders from the thirty-four countries of the Western Hemisphere resolved to "begin immediately to construct the (FTAA), in which barriers to trade and investment will be progressively eliminated." They offered the following rationale for this undertaking: "Eliminating impediments to market access for goods and services among our countries will foster our economic growth. A growing world economy will also enhance our domestic prosperity. Free trade and increased economic integration are key factors for raising standards of living, improving the working conditions of people in the Americas and better protecting the environment."

---

international obligations of the US. El Salvador, it is estimated, has fewer than five people similarly employed.

Informal discussions of the FTAA often focus on two key questions: what will be the framework for a hemisphere-wide agreement and when will negotiations begin. Prior to Cartagena, the formal discussions of government officials have focused less on these broader issues and more on the need to gather the kind of technical information that ultimately fuels the negotiation process.

At the Ministerial in Cartagena, while much of the focus remained on the need for technical information, the Ministers made it clear that the time has arrived to consider the framework for the FTAA and how negotiations will occur.

On the issue of the framework for the FTAA, the Ministers noted that they had "examined approaches for constructing the FTAA which will build on existing subregional and bilateral arrangements in order to broaden and deepen Hemispheric economic cooperation and to bring the agreements together." Most importantly, they instructed the "Vice Ministers to discuss such approaches and to make specific recommendations before the 1997 Trade Ministerial Meeting."

As for negotiations, the Ministers said that they had "considered the timing and means of launching negotiations to establish the FTAA" and "agreed that substantial and additional preparatory work is necessary for productive negotiations."

"We also agreed that concrete progress must be achieved by the end of the century", the Declaration states. "Taking this into account as well as the progress achieved in the working groups, we direct our Vice Ministers to make an assessment of when and how to launch the FTAA negotiations and to make recommendations on these issues before the 1997 Trade Ministerial meeting."

In the preparatory work that preceded Cartagena, the Hemisphere's Vice Ministers played an increasingly visible role. By the time the Trade Ministers gathered around the conference table in Cartagena to begin their formal deliberations, their Vice Ministers had met three times to discuss how work should proceed on the FTAA.

As a result of decisions taken in Cartagena, the role of the Vice Ministers will continue to expand and they will have considerable influence over the shape and direction of the integration process.

In focusing on "approaches for constructing the FTAA" and "how to launch the FTAA negotiations" the Ministers delegated to their Vice

Ministers the responsibility for presenting formal proposals. Furthermore, the Ministers decreed that their Vice Ministers will "direct, evaluate and coordinate the work of all the working groups", and that any proposals from the working groups would be submitted first to the Vice Ministers "for their approval".

Finally, the Vice Ministers have been directed to meet "at least three times" in the next year, with Brazil, the host of the next Ministerial, acting as chair.

The Working Groups

Just as the Vice Ministers were directed to advance concrete proposals for the FTAA, the working groups also were instructed to give more thought to the negotiation phase.

The declaration states: "Each working group should identify and examine trade-related measures in its respective area, in order to determine possible approaches to negotiations. [...] We direct each of the working groups to submit to the Vice Ministers, for their approval, concrete proposals on areas for immediate attention in advance of the 1997 Trade Ministerial..."

The Ministers noted that, based on the reports received from the seven working groups established in Denver, "we are convinced that substantial progress on preparing for negotiations has been achieved and that the initial work program is well underway."

As was expected, the Ministers decided to create four new working groups covering, respectively, competition policy, intellectual property, services, and government procurement. They also agreed that a Working Group on Dispute Settlement would be created at the next Ministerial and instructed the Organization of American States to "start compiling information on the dispute settlement mechanisms being used in bilateral and subregional trade agreements in the Hemisphere."

Greater Focus on Small Economies

One recurring issue in the FTAA effort is the fact that the agreement will involve some of the world's largest economies and some of the world's smallest economies. Having already created the Working Group on Smaller Economies at the Denver Ministerial, the Ministers, in their Cartagena Declaration, broadened their effort to "facilitate integration of the smaller economies and increase their level of development."

"We call upon all working groups in their deliberations to take into account this commitment, as well as specific suggestions of the Working Group on Smaller Economies", the Declaration states. "Acknowledging the differences in levels of economic development among our countries in the Hemisphere, we recognize the need for technical assistance in order to facilitate the full participation of the smaller economies in the entire process leading to the FTAA."

COMMENTS

Sergio LÓPEZ-AYLLÓN[1]

Research Fellow, Institute of Legal Research,
National Autonomous University of Mexico

Introduction

Donald Mackay's report begins by pointing out that the American continent is a different place from what it was ten years ago. This starting point, which might seem trite, should not be underestimated because it is only by understanding the scope of transformations that one can understand the processes of regional integration that the American continent is currently undergoing. It is worth noting that these processes are not one-dimensional. In fact, they constitute the axis around which revolve a set of forces both economic and political in nature which are frequently contradictory. The North American Free Trade Agreement (NAFTA) is a paradigmatic example of this complex web of interests and, as is argued later on, sets a unique precedent whose ultimate consequences are still difficult to assess because of their intrinsic complexity.

Indeed, in the decades following the Second World War, the majority of Latin American countries adopted the import substitution model. This model was based on the development of a "closed" economy, with a correspondingly "closed" legal system. Changes in the world economic environment and the limits of the model itself[2] (such as foreign debt, high

---

[1] Suzanne STEPHENS prepared the English version of this commentary.

[2] During the period, CEPAL's conceptions played a significant role. According to the economist Raul Prebisch's theory, it was "necessary to strengthen the industrial sector with protection mechanism while a reinforced production structure was created to compete at the Latin American level, in markets that would be opened as a

inflation rates, public deficit, firms' lack of international competitiveness and the shortage of investment flows) forced most Latin American countries to change direction in the 1980s. At the beginning of this period, albeit with significant variations in each country, economic development policies and strategies were modified to make way for the liberalization of the economy, the sale of public firms, deregulation and the opening of trade[3]. All these policies converge in the reduction of the state's role and the strengthening of the market economy, in addition to movements towards democratization and respect for human rights.

As a result of the change in the economic model and the need for more open trade, Latin American countries gradually began to become integrated into the international economic and trade system, while at the same time they competed to attract foreign capital flows. At present, all the countries in the continent (with the exception of Panama, which has not yet been fully affiliated) are members of the World Trade Organization (WTO) and participate in the different agreements and organizations of multilateral economic cooperation[4]. At the same time, regional integration stopped being purely rhetorical and was instead expressed in different agreements that have been established or revitalized in recent years[5]. The replacement of the Latin American Free Trade Association (ALALC, 1960) by the Latin American Integration Association[6] (ALADI,

---

result of the integration and subsequently in international markets", quoted by VEGA CÁNOVAS Gustavo, *"México en las nuevas tendencias de la economía y el comercio internacionales"*, in: **Foro internacional**, Vol.XXVIII-1, 1987, p.66.

[3] See KAPLAN Marcos, **El Estado latinoamericano**, UNAM, México, 1996; BAER Werner & BIRCH Melissa, *"Privatization and the Changing Role of the State in Latin America"*, in: **New York Journal of International Law and Politics**, Vol.25-1, 1992, pp.1-25. For the case of Mexico, see ASPE Pedro, **El camino méxicano de la transformación económica**, FCE, México, 1993, 208 p. It is important to note that this process happens in other parts of the world. See for example GRINDLE Merilee S., **Challenging the State. Crisis and Innovation in Latin America and Africa,** Cambridge University Press, Cambridge, 1996, 243 p.

[4] See COLAS Bernard, **Global Economic Co-operation. A Guide to Agreements and Organizations**, (2nd ed.), Kluwer Law & Taxation Publishers-United Nations University Press, Deventer/Boston, 1994, 557 p.

[5] See ABBOTT Keneth W. & BOWMAN Gregory W., *"Economic Integration in the Americas: A Work in Progress"*, in: **Northwestern Journal of International Law & Business,** Vol.14-3, 1994, pp.493-527; KAPLAN Marcos, *"Derecho de la integración latinoamericana"*, in: SOBERANES Jose Luis (ed.), **Tendencias actuales del derecho**, Fondo de Cultura Económica, Mexico, 1994, pp.124-133; PIZARRO Roberto, *"Renovación y dinamismo de la integración latinoamericana en los años noventa"*, in: **Estudios internacionales**, Vol.XXVIII-110, 1995, pp.198-222.

[6] Established by the Treaty of Montevideo. Signed August 12, 1980. Entry into force on March 18, 1981. The objective of the ALADI is to increase "bilateral trade between the members, and between the members and other countries by the subscription of bilateral and multilateral agreements, with the goal of eventually integrating

1980) served as the prelude to a broader process. The North American Free Trade Zone[7] (NAFTA), the southern common market[8] (Mercosur), the Andean common market[9], the Group of Three free trade zone[10] (G3), the revitalized Central American common market[11] and the Caribbean community[12] (Caricom) have become reality. In addition to these large regional agreements, there are first, a profusion of bilateral accords that are either already operating or under negotiation, (e.g. those establishing free trade zones between Mexico and Costa Rica, and Mexico and Bolivia[13]; the bilateral investment or trade agreements between the US and several countries in the region[14] and the negotiations being conducted by Chile with Canada and Mercosur[15]) and second, intraregional

---

a regional free trade area." The members of ALADI are Argentina, Bolivia, Brazil, Chile, Ecuador, Mexico, Paraguay, Peru, Uruguay and Venezuela. The Treaty of Montevideo admits flexible integration mechanisms by way of different types of agreements: sectorial scope agreements and partial-scope agreements. Sometimes, the so-called partial-scope agreements have a broader scope, in which case they are called *de complementación económica*. See CARREAU Dominique, FLORY Thiébaut *et al.*, **Droit International Economique,** (3rd ed.), LGDJ, Paris, 1990, 725 p.

7 Established by the North American Free Trade Agreement signed December 17, 1992. Entry into force January 1st, 1994. The free trade area includes Mexico, Canada and the United States.

8 Established by the Treaty of Montevideo. Signed on March 26, 1991. Entry into force on January 1st, 1995. The Customs Union includes Brazil, Argentina, Paraguay and Uruguay.

9 Established by the Cartagena Agreement. Signed on May 26, 1969. Entry into force by the Quito Protocol on May 25, 1988. It establishes a free trade area with a common external tariff that includes Bolivia, Colombia, Peru, Ecuador and Venezuela.

10 The free trade area that includes Mexico, Colombia and Venezuela. The treaty was signed on June 13, 1994. Entry into force on January 1st, 1995.

11 Established by the instrument signed on December 13, 1960. Entry into force on June 3, 1961. The Central American common market was the most advanced example of regional integration until the late 1970s, when it experienced a profound crisis as a result of the political confrontation in the region and the economic factors resulting from recession in the world market. See PIZARRO Roberto, *"Renovación y dinamismo de la integración latinoamericana en los años noventa"*, in: **Estudios internacionales,** Vol.XVIII-110, 1995, pp.198-222.

12 The Caribbean Free Trade Agreement (CARIFTA) was formed in 1968. On July 4, 1973 the Caribbean Community and Common Market (Caricom) was established. The treaty provided for the establishment of a common external tariff, but the original timetable was not met. Even though a common tariff has been established, it is not uniformly applied.

13 The Free Trade Agreement between Mexico and Costa Rica was signed on April 5, 1994 and entered into force on January 1st, 1995. The Free Trade Agreement between Mexico and Bolivia was signed on September 10, 1994 and entered into force on January 1st, 1995.

14 For example the bilateral agreements signed with Argentina on November 14, 1991, Grenada on May 2, 1986 and Panama on October 27, 1982.

15 Chile has signed **new generation** agreements of *complementación económica* with Mexico (1991), Venezuela (1993), Colombia (1993), Ecuador (1994) and is currently negotiating a bilateral agreement with Canada.

agreements (Venezuela and Caricom, Colombia and Caricom, Central America and Mexico, to name just a few).

The most ambitious initiative is undoubtedly that seeking to create a large area of continental free trade, the Free Trade Area of the Americas (FTAA), negotiation of which is expected to be completed in 2005. The Cartagena Ministerial Declaration of March 1996 reiterates this goal, despite the enormous political and technical difficulties involved[16].

Throughout this process, the negotiation and passage of NAFTA constituted a point of inflection that, for various reasons, modified the horizon of the regional integration agreements[17]. Without seeking to provide an exhaustive account, I shall first point out the features of NAFTA that make it a unique agreement (Section 1) so as to be able to analyze its role in the future of the economic and trade integration of the Americas (Section 2). Like my colleague Donald Mackay, I shall conclude that NAFTA is unlikely to serve as an axis around which the process of trade integration in the American continent will revolve. However, NAFTA will undoubtedly mark this process and constitutes an inevitable point of reference, regardless of the future of regional integration.

1. NAFTA as a Unique Regional Integration Agreement

NAFTA is, for a number of reasons, an agreement with specific political and technical characteristics. I shall briefly indicate those which I regard as most relevant.

From a political point of view, NAFTA was the first free trade agreement between two of the most developed economies in the world, Canada and the United States, and a less developed country, Mexico. This was

---

[16] In the Final Cartagena Trade Ministerial Declaration on FTAA (Cartagena, Colombia, March 21, 1996) trade ministers stated: "We strengthened our commitment to conclude negotiations no later than 2005, and to make concrete progress towards the attainment of this objective by the end of this century."

[17] Theorists of economic integration typically rank the regional integration agreements as follows: **Preferential Trade Agreements**, or areas (PTAs, in which signatories impose lower tariffs on each others's imports than on imports from third countries); **Free Trade Areas**, or agreements (FTAs, involving not just lower but zero tariffs between member states, although typically not on all goods and services); **Customs Unions** (CUs, which are FTAs but with the same external trade measures for all member states); **Common Markets** (CMs, which allow free movement of factors as well as, products between member states); and **Economic Unions** (EUs, involving not only common factors markets and trade policies but also harmonization of other micro- and macroeconomic policies). See ANDERSON Kym & BLACKHURST Richard (eds), **Regional Integration and the Global Trading System**, Harvester Wheatsheaf, New York/London/Toronto, 1993, pp.4-5.

possible due to unusual political conditions, and implied a significant change in the way each of the three countries understood its role in the trade and geopolitical relations in the region and the world. For Mexico in particular, NAFTA represented a radical change of direction in its relations with the United States and, to a lesser extent, Canada[18].

From the time it was originally proposed, the agreement was conceived as one which would have universal coverage. Moreover, although the asymmetry between the economies was acknowledged, Mexico was not given special treatment *per se,* nor were there fiscal transfers in the form of financial aid funds for development. In this respect, NAFTA signified a new type of relationship between economies with different levels of development. As one observer has pointed out:

> the NAFTA approach, of a conventional free trade area supplemented by investment, services and carefully delimited temporary entry provisions (instead of full labor mobility) could prove more flexible in facilitating regional economic integration when countries have different income levels.[19]

It should be noted that the "cost" Mexico had to pay to prepare for and adapt to the new circumstances, including the negotiation and implementation of NAFTA, was very significant. Without going into details, suffice it to point out that between 1982 and 1995, most of Mexico's internal legal system was modified, particularly as regards economic, trade and financial issues. Thus 157 of the 203 federal laws (except for Federal District legislation) in force in 1995 were new or substantially modified. In other words, Mexico had to modify nearly 75% of its domestic legal system as a result of the new orientation of the economic growth model and opening of trade.

Technically speaking, a free trade agreement typically involves the elimination of tariffs and other regulatory measures between two or more

---

[18] See GUTIERREZ-HACES María Teresa, *"L'État mexicain et les États-Unis : du protectionnisme au libre commerce"*, in : PREVOT Marie France & REVEL-MOUROZ Jean (eds), **Le Mexique à l'aube du troisième millénaire,** Institut des hautes études de l'Amérique latine, Paris, 1993, pp.79-104; SERRANO Mónica, *"Reflexiones en torno a la iniciativa de una zona norteamericana de libre comercio",* in: ALCÁNTARA Manuel & MARTÍNEZ Antonia (eds), **México frente al umbral del siglo XXI**, Centro de Investigaciones Sociológicas-Siglo XXI, Madrid, 1992, pp.123-143.

[19] SMITH Murray, *"The North American Free Trade Agreement: Global Impacts",* in: ANDERSON Kym & BLACKHURST Richard (eds), **Regional Integration and the Global Trading System**, Harvester Wheatsheaf, New York/London/Toronto, 1993, p.85.

states[20]. NAFTA goes well beyond this. Indeed, based primarily on Canada-United States Free Trade Agreement (CUSFTA) and part of the Dunkel text, NAFTA negotiations produced an agreement of outstanding coverage and technical complexity. Let us examine why.

First, with very few exceptions[21], it includes all goods, including agricultural goods[22] and services. Second, NAFTA has a set of extensive, detailed disciplines regarding internal procedures. These include customs[23], safeguards[24], technical standards[25], government procurement[26], ad/cvd[27] and intellectual property[28] procedures. It also includes special provisions concerning transparency and administrative and legal procedures[29].

Third, and I think that this aspect has scarcely been analyzed, NAFTA integrates an investment agreement into a conventional trade agreement for the first time. Strictly speaking, NAFTA is both a trade and an investment agreement combined in a single instrument. This characteristic has important consequences as regards certain goods (e.g. automotive goods) but primarily as regards services since, as we know, commercial presence, the principal form of services trade, implies investment. The legal consequences of the inclusion of an investment chapter into NAFTA were evident even at the time of drafting the agreement[30]. In addition to the above, NAFTA also integrated specific disciplines concerning intellectual property.

---

[20] Experience shows that most of these agreements do not include all goods and services. See ANDERSON Kym & BLACKHURST Richard, *op.cit.*, p.5.

[21] Main exceptions are the following: the energy sector for Mexico (Annex 602.3), maritime cabotage and exports controls on logs for the US (Annex 301.3) and cultural industries for Canada (Annex 2106).

[22] An exception of this rule are dairy, poultry and egg products excluded from the Mexico-Canada agricultural bilateral agreement.

[23] See NAFTA Chapter V *Customs Procedures.*

[24] See NAFTA Article 803 and Annex 803.3 *Administration of Emergency Action Proceedings.*

[25] See NAFTA Chapter IX *Standard-Related Measures* and Chapter VI Section B *Sanitary and Phytosanitary Measures.*

[26] See NAFTA Chapter X Sections B *Tendering Procedures* and C *Bid Challenge.*

[27] See NAFTA Article 1904.15 and Annex 1904.15 *Amendments to Domestic Laws.*

[28] See NAFTA Articles 1714 to 1718.

[29] See NAFTA Articles 718, 909, 1019, 1306, 1411, 1604, and Chapter XVIII *Publication, Notification and Administration of Laws.*

[30] See NAFTA Article 1112.1 that established: "In the event of any inconsistency between this Chapter (Investment) and another Chapter, the other Chapter shall prevail to the extent of the inconsistency."

Fourth, most of the rules of origin in NAFTA respond to the criterion of change in tariff heading[31]. Nevertheless, it also contains a set of complex and controversial rules of origin applicable to certain sectors, particularly the automotive and textile sectors, which in turn respond to the interests of national industries and the economic characteristics of the region[32].

From an institutional point of view, the Free Trade Commission, made up of trade ministries, is a consultative and monitoring body, although its decisions must be adopted by the Parties through its internal procedures. The agreement contains three dispute settlement mechanisms[33] (inspired in international commercial arbitration) to ensure the fulfillment of obligations in the agreement. Compliance with the decisions of the dispute settlement panels is subject to certain rules and protection. However, NAFTA did not create bodies of a supranational nature whose decisions directly entail the Parties.

Finally, albeit in a limited and incomplete fashion, NAFTA and its side agreements include certain aspects of environmental, labor and competition issues. In the future, trade negotiations will include these issues, and while insufficient, their resolutions will serve as a useful point of reference.

Beyond these technical aspects, the negotiation of NAFTA constituted an encounter between two distinct legal traditions in an unusually intense interaction. Indeed, while one common language, that of economics, permitted the communication of economic interests, the same could not be said of law. The drafting, but above all, the implementation of the agreement entailed contact between the common and civil law systems, whose structure, concepts and practice are different. The effect of the contact between these systems permeates the whole text of the agreement

---

[31] During the NAFTA negotiations, a considerable effort was made in order to have clear and transparent rules of origin.

[32] See PALMETER David, *"Rules of Origin in Customs Unions and Free Trade Areas"*, in: ANDERSON Kym & BLACKHURST Richard (eds), **Regional Integration and the Global Trading System**, Harvester Wheatsheaf, New York/London/Toronto, 1993, pp.330-331; SMITH Murray, *op.cit.*, pp.89-94; KESSEL Georgina (ed.), **Lo negociado del TLC. Un análisis económico sobre el impacto sectorial del Tratado Trilateral de Libre Comercio**, ITAN/McGraw-Hill, México, 1994, 334 p.

[33] See HORLICK Gary & DEBUSK Amanda, *"Dispute Resolution under NAFTA: Building on the US-Canada FTA, GATT and ICSID"*, in: **Journal of World Trade**, Vol.27, No.1, 1993, pp.21-41; ENDSLEY Harry B, *"Dispute Settlement under the CUFTA and NAFTA: From Eleventh-Hour Innovation to Accepted Institution"*, in: **Hastings International and Comparative Law Review**, Vol.18, No.4, 1995, pp.659-711.

and achieves a compromise in several of its institutions. The effect is even more dramatic in view of the fact that, due to the way the reception of agreements operates in the Mexican legal system, these institutions are directly incorporated into Mexican law[34].

This encounter between legal systems and cultures is one of the reasons behind the scope and detail of the agreement. Added to the normal distrust concerning the operation and fulfillment of an agreement between the Parties was the accuracy and fondness for detail of the Anglo-Saxon legal culture, as opposed to the more general, principle-based style of writing of Latin culture. The result was a text of over 2,000 pages, contrasting sharply with other regional integration agreements which are far less lengthy.

The general detail of NAFTA contrasts notably with its accession clause, which, technically open to any other country in the world, contains just a few lines. Let us examine the scope of the latter from the perspective of its possible expansion to the south of the continent.

2. NAFTA and the Future of Trade Integration in the American Continent

During the NAFTA negotiations, two series of issues were raised regarding the agreement's relation to third countries. The first concerned the compatibility of NAFTA regulations with the multilateral system, particularly because the conclusion of the Uruguay Round negotiations was still uncertain. The second concerned accession by third countries. Both issues received a clear political response, raising technical problems that have yet to be fully resolved.

The first issue, which is not the subject of this commentary, was solved generically through Article 101 of NAFTA which declares its consistency with Article XXIV of GATT, and Article 103 where the Parties affirm their rights and obligations under GATT[35].

---

[34] See THOMAS J.C. & LÓPEZ-AYLLÓN Sergio, *"NAFTA's Extension of Specialized Dispute Settlement to Mexico: Challenges in Treaty Interpretation and Reconciling Common Law and Civil Law Systems in a Free Trade Area"*, in: **Canadian Yearbook of International Law,** 1996.

[35] The same article established as a general rule that, in the event of any inconsistency between NAFTA and GATT, NAFTA shall prevail to the extent of the inconsistency.

As regards accession, Article 2204 establishes the possibility that any country may join the agreement[36]. This situation was taken into account by those who drafted the agreement, who, particularly in light of the experience of CUSFTA, attempted to reduce the need to renegotiate the entire text of the agreement by means of a design that would minimize changes in the event of future accessions.

This design explains the structure of the agreement in chapters and annexes. Each chapter would contain the "core" of the obligations, leaving exceptions or specific provisions for each country in the annexes. Thus, in the case of the accession of a fourth country, the latter would theoretically have to indicate its commitments or applicable exceptions in specific annexes. The text of the chapters, in theory, shall not be modified in case of accession.

This scheme, designed on the road, was not perfect since, although it works in most cases, there are several provisions that would have to be modified in the event of the accession of one or more other countries.

An example of the above can be found, for instance, in Chapter XX which contains the general procedure for dispute settlement. This mechanism is primarily designed to operate on the basis of two or three contending countries. Although it might admit a fourth and perhaps even a fifth country, it would be unlikely to withstand more than five members. This situation would entail the need to redesign the operation of Chapter XX. Rules of origin are another, even more complex, example. These were designed to operate in a trilateral and regional context. The addition of a fourth country would probably require their revision, at least in certain sectors such as the automotive or textile sectors.

The institutional structure of NAFTA, which includes the Free Trade Commission, the secretariat and working groups, also contains features that, while permitting its operation in the sphere of North America, would have to be reviewed in a scenario with over five members.

---

[36] NAFTA Article 2204 reads as follows:
1. Any country or group of countries may accede to this Agreement subject to such terms and conditions as may be agreed between such countries and the Commission and following approval in accordance with the applicable legal procedure of each country.
2. This Agreement shall not apply as between any Party and any acceding country or group of countries if, at the time of the accession, either does not consent to such application.

Finally, the extension of NAFTA Chapter XIX[37], the binational review process in anti-dumping and countervailing duties, and the so-called side agreements on labor and environment matters, raises even more interesting problems since all these proceedings were designed in light of particular concerns and problems of the trade relations between Canada, Mexico and the United States.

The problems indicated here are magnified if, instead of countries being considered individually, they are thought of as groups of countries forming part of other regional agreements (e.g. Mercosur).

Chile's possible future accession to NAFTA will test the agreement's ability to incorporate other members into its current structure without altering its make-up. From another point of view, as Donald Mackay has already noted, the price of accession to NAFTA is high. However, NAFTA has been exerting a direct influence by other means.

Before NAFTA's negotiation, the majority of regional integration agreements followed what could generically be called the "ALADI model". Partial-scope economic agreements, including those with broad coverage, such as the one signed by Chile and Mexico, contained only a few general provisions. Following the passage of NAFTA, the "NAFTA model" was adopted in all negotiations initiated by Mexico. Thus, the agreements signed by Mexico with Bolivia, Venezuela and Colombia and Costa Rica[38] are similar to NAFTA in both coverage, structure and content, as shown in the accompanying chart. Differences, although they do exist, are minimal[39]. The same model is being used in Mexico's current

---

[37] In this Chapter, based on the Canada-US Free Trade Agreement, binational panels will examine whether the decisions of the national investigative authorities were made in accordance with the national legislation of the importing country. Thus, arbiters coming from completely different legal horizons, will have to apply the same principles that a national court would apply. This involves the creation of spaces for legal interaction, absolutely unheard of from the Mexican point of view and the consequences of which are still unpredictable. The reality shows that Chapter XIX procedures are not only theory but practice. As of October 1996, 23 cases have been filed. The short but lively history of NAFTA Chapter XIX shows well the difficulties of the relationship between the legal systems. The differences in the way the legal arguments are presented and the interpretation of constitutional requirements in Mexico are, *inter alia*, some of the problems the system faces.

[38] In the case of Venezuela and Colombia (G3), and Bolivia the agreements are both "partial-scope agreements of economic complementarity" under ALADI and free trade agreements under GATT. The Costa Rica Agreement is a free trade agreement under GATT since this country is not a member of ALADI.

[39] None of the these agreements have an equivalent to Chapter XIX binational panel process (instead they have disciplines in adv/cv procedures) and in all cases the energy sector is excluded. Other differences are in the scope of the agreements. For example textiles are excluded from the G3, and financial services from Costa Rica.

negotiations with Ecuador, Peru, Panama and the countries from the northern triangle (Guatemala, Honduras and El Salvador) and it will probably be the route chosen in the future.

Thus, the NAFTA model has already been adopted by other countries in the region. Therefore, NAFTA's scope and possible expansion are not limited to other countries' accession possibilities, but also involve the agreement's influence on the process of regional integration seen as a whole.

Conclusion

As Donald Mackay has pointed out, the complexity of the regional integration process, particularly in light of negotiations concerning the Free Trade Area of the Americas (FTAA) and regional integration agreements, make it unlikely that NAFTA will become the hub of the American system currently being created. This is due as much to the peculiarities of NAFTA itself as to the technical difficulties involved in a process of FTAA's scope.

Nevertheless, I think that NAFTA will be an inevitable point of reference for at least the following three reasons: first, because NAFTA is a significantly more sophisticated and complete model than the majority of existing agreements in the region as regards both coverage and disciplines; second, because this model has already been accepted in negotiations within the region and, with modifications, has become an element that integrates the system of regional accords; and third, because the negotiators who form part of the North American region will have the NAFTA model in mind as a parameter. These negotiators will obviously play a specific, crucial role in the process. Apropos of this, it will be extremely interesting to see the results of the interaction between the European model and the NAFTA model in the negotiations shortly to be initiated between the European Union and Mexico.

The processes of regional integration and the agreements that shape them entail immense technical and political difficulties. Specific interests highlight the difficulties of harmonizing regional and multilateral systems. There is an obvious risk that the multiplication of regional agreements may create a spider's web, one of whose worst consequences would be to create uncertainty in trade. It will therefore be necessary to work using imagination and flexibility, seeking the most generous rules that are at the same time compatible with the multilateral system. Moreover, particular care will have to be taken with institutional aspects to create a simple, effective and flexible framework, capable of responding rapidly to trade needs. This is the challenge. NAFTA is not a perfect solution, but it does provide certain useful elements. Evaluating its operation and reflecting on it may prove advantageous in the difficult task awaiting us in the years to come.

Table 1: Comparative FTAs

NAFTA	MEXICO - BOLIVIA	MEXICO - COSTA RICA	MEXICO - G3
1.- Objectives	1.- Objectives	1.- Objectives	1.- Objectives
2.- General definitions	2.- General definitions	2.- General definitions	2.- General definitions
3.- National treatment and market access for goods 3A: Automotive sector 3B: Textiles and apparel	3.- National treatment and market access for goods	3.- National treatment and market access for goods	3.- National treatment and market access for goods and 4.- Automotive sector
4.- Rules of origin	5.- Rules of origin	5.- Rules of origin	6.- Rules of origin
5.- Customs procedures	6.- Customs procedures	6.- Customs procedures	7.- Customs procedures
6.- Energy and basic petrochemicals			
7.- Agriculture and sanitary and phytosanitary measures	4.- Agriculture and sanitary and phytosanitary measures	4.- Agriculture and phytosanitary and zoosanitary measures	5.- Agriculture and phytosanitary and zoosanitary measures
8.- Emergency action	7.- Emergency action	7.- Emergency action	8.- Emergency actions
	8.- Unfair trade practices	8.- Countervailing duties provisions	9.- Unfair trade
9.- Standards related measures	13.- Standards related measures	11.- Standards measures	14.- Standards measures
10.- Government Procurement	14.- Government procurement	12.- Government procurement	15.- Government procurement

263

11.- Investment	15.- Investment	13.- Investment	17.- Investment
12.- Cross-border trade in services	9.- Services. Scope and coverage	9.- Services. Scope and coverage	10.- Services. Scope and coverage
13.- Telecommunications	10.- Telecommunications		11.- Telecommunications
14.- Financial services	12.- Financial services		12.- Financial services
15.- Competition policy, monopolies and state enterprises			16.- Policy in state enterprises
16.- Temporary entry for business persons	11.- Temporary entry for business persons	10.- Temporary entry for business persons	13.- Temporary entry for business persons
17.- Intellectual property	16.- Intellectual property	14.- Intellectual property	18.- Intellectual property
18.- Publication, notification and administration of laws	17.- Transparency	15.- Publication, notification, and due process	21.- Transparency
20.- Institutional arrangements and dispute settlement procedures	18.- Treaty administration	16.- Treaty administration	20.- Treaty administration
19.- Dispute settlement	19.- Dispute settlement	17.- Dispute settlement	19.- Dispute settlement
21.- Exceptions	20 - Exceptions	18.- Exceptions	22.- Exceptions
22.- Final Provisions	21.- Final provisions	19.- Final provisions	23.- Final provisions

THE NEW COMMERCIAL STRATEGY OF THE EUROPEAN UNION TOWARDS LATIN AMERICA: IN SEARCH OF MARKET ACCESS THROUGH A REGIONAL AND SPECIFIC APPROACH

Gonzalo GARCÍA JIMÉNEZ

Research Fellow,
Institut d'Études Juridiques Européennes (IEJE),
University of Liège

I. INTRODUCTION

Following a study of the World Trade Organization (WTO), the increase in terms of international trade during 1995 has been three times quicker than that of production and this trend seems to continue in prospects for the near future. Similarly, the increase of foreign direct investment has been quicker than that of trade and production[1].

Latin America (LA), by virtue of the outstanding records in terms of economic and political stability and the success of open schemes of integration, has been the region which has witnessed the quickest increase in terms of intra-regional trade as well as in terms of the value of imports in extra-regional trade. It has therefore become one of the most important and fastest-growing emerging markets for the United States (US) and for the European Union (EU)[2]. Both economic powers, highly

---

[1] World Trade Organization, *International Trade - Trends and Statistics*, 1995.

[2] Although the Common Commercial Policy is enshrined in the first pillar — EC — of the Treaty of Maastricht, and the conclusion of international agreements — in the absence of legal personality of the European Union — can only be carried out

dependent on exports, are confident about the region's long-term economic prospects and both see significant mutual benefits from greater commercial ties with the region. At the same time, when applying strategies to increase trade and investment flows with this region, both are also aware of trade and investment diversion that the, so-called, "South Cone Option" could bring about for them by virtue of a huge increase in intra-regional trade and investment flows.

In 1995 commercial exchanges between LA and the EU reached $80 billion[3] — doubling the amount reached in 1990 — and investment have also considerably increased. However, one should bear in mind that, regarding the total amount of trade, the US is, in general and in quantitative terms, better placed than the EU. It is therefore the main objective of the EU to create the conditions that might allow it to take advantage of the quantitative and qualitative advantages which it enjoys *vis-à-vis* the most dynamic, integrated and economically performing regions of LA. The already well established economic cooperation and the long-standing political dialogue between the EU and LA will contribute to facilitate, speed up and strengthen the rapprochement between both regions.

Because circumstances are different, the nature of the instruments governing economic and commercial relations must also be different from that of the past. Neither the third generation agreements, nor the application of the General System of Preferences any longer provides the appropriate framework to deal with the highest performing economies of LA. More effective and higher-profile instruments are needed in order for the EU and LA to gain the maximum profit from the new birregional context.

Therefore, on the one hand, facing LA's option for open regionalism, and, on the other, the dynamism of the US in this region, the EU has recently taken a new attitude. The purpose is to use the common commercial policy as an instrument to penetrate and get access to foreign markets. This new attitude focuses on a regional and specific approach and tends to apply variable geometry when dealing with LA. It is put into action by taking into account the national and regional realities in the economic and political fields as well as in the degree of regional

---

by the European Community, reference will be made in this paper to the EU. In this regard, it should be noted that in the Joint Declaration on political dialogue annexed to the Framework Agreements with Mercosur and Chile, reference is made to the EU and not to the EC.

[3] See **Europolitique**, No.2123, April 13, 1996, p.9.

integration. This should allow an important qualitative step forward in UE-LA relations as the new "fourth generation" agreements will lead to liberalize trade on a reciprocal basis in the future.

The instruments used are framework agreements leading to the creation of an inter-regional association and the establishment of a political and economic association, or to a new economic partnership and political concertation. The targets are the three most important emerging markets with the greatest **potential** for growth in the next century: Mercosur, Chile and Mexico. The formula used in these agreements consists on, first, establish an enhanced political dialogue, promote economic cooperation and closer cooperation in trade and other issues of mutual interest to, then, pave the way for progressive and reciprocal liberalization. Trade liberalization taking place, either, within the same agreement, or after a second one. From a commercial standpoint, they will gradually allow the EU and LA, through a gradual liberalization of trade in both directions, to obtain a better reciprocal market access which will be translated into an unprecedented intensification and diversification of exchanges between both regions.

Of course, this new approach can only take place by the shared view that the flourishing of regional integration agreements in the international scene is based on the principles of open regionalism. Thus, becoming the driving forces in the pursuing to trade liberalization efforts at the multilateral level.

II. THE OBJECTIVES

A. *In Search of New Markets to Increase Trade and Investment Flows ...*

The great economic and political mutations experienced in the Southern Hemisphere of the continent and, in particular, the abandoning of traditional protectionism to open itself, without hesitations, to the global trading system, are factors that amount to the fact that LA possesses a huge internal market and a great potential for expansion[4]. These factors

---

[4] Compare, during the period 1993-1994, the increase of 15.9% in the total percentage of worldwide exports of members countries of the Latin American Integration Association (Argentina, Bolivia, Brazil, Chile, Colombia, Ecuador, Mexico, Paraguay, Peru, Uruguay, Venezuela) to the increase of 19.3% in regard to the total percentage of worldwide imports. See "*Latin America at a Glance: A Comprehensive Guide to Markets and Operating Conditions*", in: **The Economist Intelligence Unit**, Annual Update, 1996, p.26.

have allowed this region to become a strategic area for investment and for the development of future commercial relations. Its constantly growing and expanding economy[5] justifies the increasing economic and political role it plays in the international scene and the interest of major trade actors in these new markets.

In terms of **trade**, the dynamism of its emerging markets justifies the increasingly important position that LA plays in EU foreign policy. Between 1990 and 1993 the total expansion of European exports towards industrialized nations amounted to 2%; towards the Mediterranean Basin 16.1%; and towards the rest of the world 16.2%. Nevertheless, during the same period, European exports to LA have grown up by 50%, making it one of the most dynamic regions for European exports. Since 1990, European exports to LA represented more than 25% of the total growth of European exports to developing countries[6]. Even though European exports to LA only represent 6% of its global exports, the EU occupies a privileged position. The EU is LA's second largest trading partner and the first for certain nations and regions. The six most dynamic economies of the region, which include Argentina, Brazil, Chile and Mexico, represent 84% of Latin American exports and absorb more than 80% of European exports to LA. Furthermore, as will be discussed later, prospects for the future provide for a quantitative and qualitative step forward in birregional relations in both trade and investment.

In the last ten years the estimated value of annual global **Foreign Direct Investment** (FDI) outflows has increased from $60 billion to $315 billion, and during 1995 outflows of foreign direct investment grew more rapidly than world trade[7]. Similarly, in the early 1990s, developing countries attracted nearly 55% of direct investment from abroad. The sharp increase of foreign investment to LA has been one of the most significant signs of the improved performance and optimistic expectations for the region. In light of these factors, and acknowledging the importance of FDI as a means of generating trade, the European Commission

---

[5] Despite the effects of Mexico's 1995 Peso crisis, of an average of 3.5%, during the period 1991-1996 for the eight largest economies which together account for more than 90% of the region's GDP (Argentina, Brazil, Chile, Colombia, Ecuador, Mexico, Peru and Venezuela). *Id.,* p.4.

[6] See Álvaro CALDERÓN, *"Mecanismos de cooperación financiera entre la Unión Euoropea y América Latina"*, paper presented at the II° Congreso Eurolatinoamericano sobre Integración, Granada, November 1995, p.3.

[7] See R. BLACKHURST & A. OTTEN, *"Trade and Foreign Direct Investment"*, in: **WTO Press Release**, October 1996, pp.3-7, 52.

(Commission) has recently affirmed[8] that, in order for Europe to consolidate a competitive position in the world economy, it is critical for the EU to ensure a permanent presence of business operators through direct investment in the new emerging markets such as LA's.

Although until 1994 the US supplied almost three-quarters of all investment flows to LA and the EU less than a quarter[9], figures from 1994 show a significant increase in EU's flows, representing now more than one-third of the total. Again, as in the case of trade, the most important growth, in relative (an increase of 40% over the preceding year) and absolute terms, has taken place in those countries with the greatest expanding internal markets: Mexico, Brazil, Argentina and Chile. Not surprisingly, this result is partly due to the EU's support — since the early nineties — in encouraging and promoting European FDI flows to LA through the implementation of mechanisms such as the European Community Investment Partners (ECIP), the recently expanded EU-LA program for business cooperation and investment promotion (AL-INVEST), and the access to large-scale lending from the European Investment Bank (EIB)[10].

The prosperity of the EU highly depends on foreign trade and investment. Many jobs within the European economy depend directly, and a larger number indirectly, on exports[11]. According to the Commission's White Paper on Growth, Competitiveness and Employment[12], the opening up of the world market is one way of accelerating the economic growth and the creation of jobs in Europe. In the light of this, the

---

[8] See European Commission Communication, *"A Level Playing Field for Direct Investment World-Wide"*, COM (95) 42 final, pp.10-13.

[9] A number of diversionary pressures might explain European reluctance to invest in LA during the early 1990s: first, economic recession from 1992-1994; second, the strong growth of intra-EU flows with the consolidation of the Single European Market; third, FDI flows were temporarily diverted towards Eastern Europe and the Mediterranean Basin. See Institute for European-Latin American Relations (IRELA), *"Aid, Trade and Investment Flows to Latin America: Differences Between EU and US Strategies"*, July 1995, pp.5-6.

[10] For a detailed analysis of EU policies in support of European investment in LA, see F. BATALLER, *"The European Union's New Relations with Latin America, Economic Cooperation and the Promotion of European Direct Investment"*, in: **Foreign Direct Investment in Developing Countries: The Case of Latin America**, IRELA, Madrid, 1994, pp.217-233.

[11] In fact, the economic prosperity of the EU is more dependent on the increase of international trade than that of the US. From 10 to 12 million of jobs are directed linked to exports markets.

[12] European Commission, *"Growth, Competitiveness, and Employment: The Challenges and Ways forward into the 21st Century"*, White Paper, Brussels/Luxembourg, 1994, Chapter B.II.6.

Commission has just defined a European strategy for international market access[13], deriving from a defensive attitude towards an offensive one. With this in mind, the purpose is to use the European trade policy as an instrument to penetrate foreign markets[14]. The underlying reason is to recognize the opening of international markets — arising from the liberalization at the multilateral and regional level — not as a threat, but as an opportunity to benefit from.

B. ... by Means of Free Trade Agreements...

Once the complementary nature of liberalization efforts at the multilateral and regional level has been clarified[15], two different approaches can be used by the EU as instruments for market opening: the multilateral and the bilateral/regional level[16]. The choice depending to a large extent on the objective.

At the **multilateral level**, with regards to trade, European concessions in the Uruguay Round have offered significant new possibilities for further strengthening commercial relations. After full implementation of the Uruguay Round Agreements more than half of all Latin American exports to the EU will enter Europe duty free. Conversely, although LA has taken decisive steps towards the multilateralization of trade in goods, the path towards further liberalization is still significant[17]. Similarly, the

---

[13] European Commission Communication, *"The Global Challenge of International Trade: A Market Access Strategy for the European Union"*, COM (96) 53 final, 1996.

[14] Following the reading of Article 110 of the Treaty which establishes that the aim of the Common Commercial Policy of the Community is to "... contribute, in the common interest, to the harmonious development of world trade, the progressive abolition of restrictions on international trade and the lowering of customs barriers." Therefore, what is at stake is the use of this Commercial Policy to concentrate efforts in the opening of foreign markets together with the progressive opening of the Community's market and due respect to the principles of multilateralism. See COM (96) 53 final, *supra*, note 13, p.3.

[15] See WTO Secretariat, *"Regionalism and the World Trading System"*, Geneva, April 1995.

[16] See COM (96) 53 final, *supra*, note 13, pp.5-7.

[17] After the full implementation of the Uruguay Round Agreements, more than 70% of both industrial and agricultural imports into LA will have bounded duties at rates lower than those prior to the Uruguay Round. Another 19% of industrial imports and 12% of agricultural imports will have newly-bound, even though, unchanged duties. However, despite these efforts, as regards MFN duties on industrial products, LA is a high protected region: only 2% of industrial imports into LA will be exempted from duties (compare to 37% in the EU), 87% will be subject to high import duties (compare to 2% in the EU), 7% will be subject to very high duties (compare to 1% in the EU). Therefore, although the liberalization efforts have tended to reduce the biggest peaks, the room for improvement is still high. See F. BATALLER, *"Liberalization efforts of the European Union and Latin America at the Uruguay Round"*, 1995, (unpublished).

steps taken towards liberalization of trade in services, while encouraging, are still relatively timid.

The EU is a strong supporter of the promotion of regional cooperation and integration efforts **among** developing countries[18]. In this field, by virtue of the unique experience of European integration, the EU has a great comparative advantage *vis-à-vis* other commercial blocs. In the trade field, support is provided both in the form of tariff-concessions and through cumulation arrangements for the rules of origin favoring trade between members of particular regional groupings. On the other hand, the use of development cooperation policy through financial, technical and institutional assistance for regional integration initiatives, has also proved to be of paramount importance. The EU efforts have therefore played a decisive role in the strengthening and successful achievement of open regional integration schemes in LA, thereby contributing to economic growth and political stability, facilitating better integration of the partner economies in the world economy and setting in place the conditions for sustainable development[19].

Nonetheless, the use of EU trade policy as a way of promoting regional integration has recently taken a qualitative step forward. Whereas until recently, the support to regional integration efforts among developing countries has been mostly external, now, by promoting free trade agreements **with** developing countries, it goes much further with the EU becoming directly involved, as a partner, in the initiative.

Therefore, willing to improve trade liberalization and market access records already achieved at the multilateral level, and in order to achieve quicker results in the opening of the most interesting integrated markets of LA — that will, consequently, create new opportunities for European business — the EU is also interested in the application of **bilateral instruments**. This level relies on the effective implementation of agreements leading to free trade — in compliance with WTO rules[20] — with

---

[18] See European Commission Communication, *"European Community Support for Regional Economic Integration Efforts among Developing Countries"*, COM (95) 219 final; F. BATALLER, *"Regional Integration Initiatives among Developing Countries: their Nature, Past Performance and Current Challenges"*, in: *The European Community as a World Trade Partner*, **European Economy**, No.52, 1993, pp.47-60.

[19] COM (95) 219, *supra*, note 18, pp.6-7, 12-13, 17. The reasons for the EU being: to pursue the objectives and comply with the procedures laid down in the Union Treaty for cooperation with the developing countries (Articles 130u and 130x of Title XVII "Development cooperation"), the need to address LA's problems, and the need to make cooperation more effective and give it a higher profile.

[20] See COM (96) 53 final, *supra*, note 13, p.7.

the highest performing individual third countries, such as in the case of Chile and Mexico, or regional groupings, such as that with Mercosur.

Hence, once economic and political changes are well-rooted, LA's competitive insertion in the global market is ensured, and the process of regional integration and liberalization is consolidated, the time has now arrived for the EU to **apply** this new commercial strategy[21]. The latter, taking into account Latin American diversity and using a regional and specific approach[22], tends to give primacy to the establishment of "fourth generation"[23] agreements with the regions or countries offering the most dynamic markets for European exports[24]. This approach being based, in the midterm and for the first time, on a reciprocal basis[25].

---

[21] See COM (95) 495 final, *infra*, note 22, pp.8-9; COM (95) 219 final, *supra*, note 18, p.12.

[22] See European Commission Communication, *"The European Union and Latin America. The Present Situation and Prospects for Closer Partnership: 1996-2000"*, COM (95) 495 final.

[23] Over the years, the EU has signed three types of, the so-called, "generation" agreements with LA. In the 1960s, "first generation" agreements consisted either of a general trade agreement or of more specific commercial agreements. In the second half of the 1970s and the early 1980s, "second generation" agreements were more substantial encompassing, in addition to commercial, economic, financial and technical cooperation. Since the early 1990s, "third generation" agreements changed on the quality level, containing a clause on the respect of human rights and democracy, they covered more cooperation sectors and, through the evolutive clause, were open to further extension in the future to new sectors. For a detailed analysis of the content, purpose and scope of these agreements, see Club de Bruxelles, *"Relations between the European Union and Latin America"*, 1994, pp.132-165.

[24] It should be noted that this flow was not unanimously supported within the EU. France, for instance showed worries in regard of the *emballement* of the European Commission during the last months, which led it to multiply in a confused manner free trade projects with other partners. See C. GOYABET, *"Les zones de libre-échange : nouveau sujet de tension entre les Quinze ?"*, in : **Revue du Marché commun et de l'Union Européenne**, No.395, February 1996, pp.77-80. As a result of these tensions, the opening of negotiations with Mexico was slowed down. See **Europolitique**, Section V, February 21, 1996, p.4.

[25] It is worth mentioning that in the context of the unilaterally-offered by the EU, "second and third" generation cooperation agreements with LA, there was no tariff preference. In addition, within the framework of the Lomé Convention, given the need for further development of the trading partners and following the principles stated in Part IV of the GATT, the EU did not demand reciprocity in the commercial exchanges based on a preferential basis with ACP countries. Finally, the General System of Preferences (GSP) is an instrument through which the EU unilaterally grants non-reciprocal customs concessions in favor of imports coming from the developing countries concerned, the purpose being to foster industrial and agro-food exports from developing countries. Neither the third generation agreements nor the GSP are nowadays the most adequate instruments to deal with the most dynamic emerging economies of LA. In addition, as regards the GSP, the new regulation, by making the system more conditional on the income level of developing countries, tends to harden the "gradual approach" in detriment of the most developed potential recipients. See J. LEBULLANGER, *"La rénovation des relations commerciales de la Communauté européenne avec les pays en développement"*, in : **La place de**

However, the EU is not offering close-at-hand free trade, but rather, a framework to strengthen relations and identify obstacles leading, in a second step, to a progressive and reciprocal liberalization[26] of markets, services and investment, with due allowance for the "sensibility" of certain products (such as agriculture for the case of Mercosur). Concerning Mexico and Chile, should the former finally adhere to NAFTA, the agreements will have to be accompanied by strict rules of origin in order to prevent "commercial triangulation" from American and Canadian producers.

Although the term free trade appeared in the first proposals of the Commission[27], it does not appear as such in the final agreements with Mercosur and Chile, contrary to the will of both. Instead, there appears a broader term: "progressive and reciprocal liberalization of trade". Nevertheless, despite this more neutral provision, the meaning and the nature of the framework agreements remain the same.

C. ... and Counterbalance
the North-American Dynamism in the Region

The movement that has taken place in favor of free trade within the European Union in the last few years is multifacetted.

Whereas regarding Central and Eastern countries the association agreements[28] provided for the creation of free trade areas, however they were mainly concluded for political reasons. The purpose was to prepare a smooth integration of these countries within the EU through the strengthening and reinforcement of democracy and market economy principles. Regarding the countries of the Mediterranean Basin and the

---

l'Europe dans le commerce mondial, Institut Universitaire International Luxembourg, July 1994, pp.221, 240-253; WTO Secretariat, *supra*, note 15, pp.19 and 34.

[26] Obviously, as will be analyzed later, the offer of a free trade area agreement must generally be supplemented by a series of actions aiming at legislative convergence, harmonization of standards and easing the restructuring of the partner economies so as to avoid major distribution imbalances among the countries. See COM (95) 219 final, *supra*, note 18, p.13. This is why, for instance, the policy package in regard of Mercosur includes the promotion of European investment in the region, technological cooperation, the encouragement of small and medium enterprises, as well as assistance for the alleviation of the social impact of liberalization policies and for the improvement of regional infrastructures.

[27] See COM (94) 428 final, *infra*, note 50.

[28] Concluded in 1992 with Hungary, the former Czech and Slovak Republic, and Poland. Followed in 1993 by Bulgaria and Romania, and by the three Baltic States and Slovenia in 1995.

Middle East, the purpose for establishing economic agreements leading to a free trade area[29] — that should enter into force by 2010 — is, in broad terms, to ensure peace and stability in the region[30] in order to give confidence to foreign investors and contribute to growth and economic integration. Finally, regarding Asia, the world's fastest-growing economic region, the EU is far behind *vis-à-vis* the US[31]. This is despite the new strategy launched by the Commission in 1994[32], the current efforts to revitalize and strengthen European links with Asian countries within the framework of the first Asia-Europe Meeting (ASEM)[33] held in Bangkok

---

[29] Three association agreements including free trade at the short term or for the 2010 horizon have been signed in the second half of 1995 with Tunisia, Israel, and the Kingdom of Morocco. In addition, in November 1995, during the Euro-Mediterranean Summit of Barcelona, the EU agreed to conclude these kind of agreements with all Mediterranean partners. Moreover, negotiations are being held with Egypt, Jordan, and Lebanon. See Euro-Mediterranean Conference held in Barcelona on November 27-28, 1995, Barcelona Declaration and work program, **Bulletin of the European Union**, 11-1995, pp.137-146; **Agence Europe**, February 9 and 14, 1996; European Commission, *"Renforcement de la politique méditerranéenne de l'UE : propositions pour la mise en œuvre d'un partenariat euro-méditerranéen"*, COM (95) final, March 8, 1995. As regards Turkey, after twenty years of preparation, the customs union has been finally entered into force in December 31, 1995.

[30] In this regard, one should bear in mind that the EU is dependent on this region for 24% of energetic supply, and has around five million of immigrants (compare to 700.000 coming from East Europe).

[31] During the ASEM Meeting, Commissioner Brittan said that better access to trade and investment will be prioritizing targets of the EU. Indeed, it seems that the EU has underestimated growth potential in this region. Therefore, as Asia's economic becomes increasingly apparent, the EU is desperate not to lose potential markets to its major competitors. European businesses have been diverted from Asia by opportunities closer to home, such as successive enlargements and changes in Central and Eastern Europe. However, at the same time US and Japanese businesses had developed in the Asiatic growing market a competitive edge over their European counterparts which had relied more on direct exports than establishing extensive marketing networks. Whereas during the periods 1985-87 and 1990-93 European exports to the emerging economies of Asia were not over 5% of its total exports, during these periods, US placed 8% and 10% and Japan 24% and 35%. Similarly, the EU is far behind its trade competitors as regards foreign investment. Between 1988 and 1993 FDI in the region doubled. Japan and the US are the main sources of FDI. However, in 1993, for nine east and southeast economies, the EU had the smallest share accounting for 13%. Of particular concern is also the EU's 4% share in China's total FDI, which is far less than in other emerging markets and far behind the US and Japan. See **Financial Times**, March 20, 1996; **European Report**, Section V, No.2150, July 1996, p.3.

[32] See European Commission Communication, *"Towards a New Asia Strategy"*, COM (94) 314 final.

[33] Despite US efforts to boycott this initiative, this first Asia-Europe Meeting held between the fifteen EU Member States, the seven countries of ASEAN, and Japan, South Korea and China, was successfully achieved and called for the establishing of a new partnership based on the promotion of political dialogue, the deepening of economic relations and the reinforcement of cooperation. A number of initiatives and a firm agenda for the deepening of the dialogue and a concrete follow-up were established. However, one of the most important outcomes has been the rapprochement of Asean countries as a bloc towards the EU, without the presence of the US

in March 1996, and the recent endeavor to implement this strategy by establishing a framework to create a new dynamic in EU-ASEAN[34] relations[35]. And what is potentially of greater importance, in the future, the gap will be the same, given the fact that the EU is not a member of the Asia Pacific Economic Cooperation (APEC)[36] — a forum providing for the creation of a free trade area and open investment area by 2010/2020, accounting for almost one-half of world trade growth.

Therefore, at the present moment, the fastest-growing, integrated and kin emerging markets at the EU's disposal are those of LA. However, the EU has also to face here the paramount influence of the US, as, on the one hand, it is the most important trade partner for the region as a whole, and, on the other, there is, for certain regions, a logical two-way rapprochement: North-South and South-North.

The North-South rapprochement because the US, the driving force behind NAFTA, set 2005 as the target for achieving a hemispheric free trade agreement under a free trade area of the Americas at the 1994 Summit of the Americas. The reason for the US to expand regional trade liberalization is basically very simple: a combination of economic, market and export growth is the only way for the US to get its trade deficit under control[37]. The theory being that, in the long run, breaking down barriers and pushing American exports, should generate enough opportunities for American firms so that exports and export-related jobs can grow in the US[38]. The facts are, that LA and the Caribbean now form the second fastest-growing region in the world, and the US Commerce Department projects[39] that by 2010 the US will export more goods and services to LA than to Europe and Japan combined. As a result over the next

---

and face to Japan and South Korea. See European Commission *"Regarding the Asia-Europe Meeting (ASEM) to be held in Bangkok on March 1-2, 1996"*, COM (96) 4 final; **Agence Europe**, March 4-5, 1996, pp.6-7; **Financial Times**, March 4, 1996.

[34] The Association of South-East Asian Nations is composed of: Brunei, Indonesia, Malaysia, the Philippines, Singapore, Thailand and Vietnam.

[35] European Commission Communication, *"Creating a New Dynamic in EU-ASEAN Relations"*, COM (96) 314 final.

[36] APEC groups the seven members of ASEAN, Australia and New Zealand, Canada, Mexico and the US, and Chile, China, Hong Kong, Japan, South Korea, Papua New Guinea, and Taiwan.

[37] See Comisión Económica para América Latina y el Caribe (CEPAL), *"Las políticas comerciales entre América Latina y Estados Unidos"*, in: **Notas sobre la economía y el desarrollo**, No.594, September 1996.

[38] See S. SPIELMAN, *"America's Plan for Regional Trade: Where Will it lead?"*, in: **European Business Journal**, No.7 Issue 2, 1995, pp.31-36.

[39] United States Department of Commerce, *"U.S. Global Trade Outlook 1995-2000"*, Washington D.C., 1995, p.64.

fifteen years, annual US exports to the region will increase by $144 billion — each $1 billion in new exports meaning 17.000 new US jobs[40]. In addition, it should be noted that the four Mercosur members, Chile and the three NAFTA members together represent 95% of the Hemisphere's market. The instruments to build on NAFTA[41] are mainly two: either by accession, adding countries one at a time, or by merging with existing groupings of countries.

As regards the South-North rapprochement, it mainly concerns the Caribbean and Central America due to trade, services and investment diversion prompted by NAFTA. However, North America is not necessarily the most logical focus of Mercosur's attention as they export more to other Latin American nations and to Europe than to the US. As will be discussed later, they are, together with Chile and members of the Andean Community, more interested in building up a strong and autonomous model of integration in the South Cone, convergence with NAFTA being only envisaged in the long term.

Therefore, LA has become one of the main commercial battlefields for the two most important economic powers of the world. However, it is not, any longer, a confrontation of a pattern of trading blocs but a building of such[42]. In addition, within this commercial confrontation, LA is no longer the target but, by virtue of achieving its integration process, a partner playing a new and active role. Moreover, it is not only the commercial "dialogue" which is at stake, but also the political, social, cultural and historical, for which the EU is better placed.

Hence, combining all these arguments — the success of certain schemes of integration in LA, the slow down of hemispheric liberalization promoted by the US as regards the South Cone, the natural tendency of certain regions and countries to get closer to the EU than to the US, the concentration in the last years of European investment and trade flows

---

[40] See P. STERN & R. PARETZKY, *"Engineering Regional Trade Pacts to Keep Trade and U.S. Prosperity on a Fast Track"*, in: **The Washington Quarterly**, Vol.19 No.1, Winter 1995, pp.211-233.

[41] For a more detailed analysis of possible scenarios to expand NAFTA and the pros and cons therein, see, for instance, R.L. BERNAL, *"From NAFTA to Hemispheric Free Trade"*, in: **Columbia Journal of World Business**, Vol.39 No.3, Fall 1994, pp.23-31.

[42] The EU recognized that the perspectives of the extension of the NAFTA and the establishment of a WHFTA following the results of the Miami Summit, can provide a positive contribution to the process of liberalization from a global perspective. See *"Déclaration finale de la Vème réunion ministérielle institutionnalisée entre l'UE et le Groupe de Rio"*, Paris, March 17, 1995.

within certain markets, and the new commercial strategy of the EU, which based on a gradual and progressive liberalization of trade, privileges a regional and specific approach — the consequence is clear: there is at the present moment a logical and mutual rapprochement between the EU and certain regions and countries of LA, specifically those with the best economic performances, political stability, and with the greatest prospects for growth.

III. THE TARGETS AND THE INSTRUMENTS

As already predicted in the Basic Document on European Union and Latin America and the Caribbean countries[43] adopted by the Council of Ministers in October 1994, a dynamic increase in the volume of trade between Europe and the new emerging markets of LA has taken place. In this document, the EU reaffirmed its intention to open discussion about new and more ambitious agreements which were to take into account the economic potential and the degree of regional integration among prospective partners.

In LA, more than two-thirds of the population, territory and production are concentrated in Argentina, Brazil, Mexico and Chile. Mexico made its choice by joining NAFTA. Argentina and Brazil have created, together with Paraguay and Uruguay, the Mercosur. Chile is open to the four directions: NAFTA, the EU, LA and Asia.

This is why the EU has recently adopted a new and much more active commercial and investment strategy towards the most performing emerging markets of LA. The reasoning behind this approach is clear: following a study of the Commission, without a free trade agreement with Mercosur, it could loose, in the long run, important sectors of this market. Conversely, the signing of such an agreement would allow the EU to, besides reinforcing its presence in this market, take advantage of an export increase in their bilateral trade balance of around 11.5% per year[44]. Much of the same reasoning can also be applied to the case of Chile, as well as that of fear from trade diversion brought by an eventual accession

---

[43] As reprinted in IRELA, *"Europa y América Latina: una cooperación para la acción. Documento básico sobre las relaciones de la Unión Europea con América Latina y el Caribe"*, 1994. For the first steps towards variable geometry in EU/Latin American relations, see also, Conclusions of the Corfu European Council, June 24-25, 1994; Conclusions of the Essen European Council, December 9-10, 1994.

[44] See, COM (94) 428 final, *infra*, note 50, p.11.

to NAFTA[45]. Finally, regarding Mexico, a free trade agreement is the only possible way for the EU to promote FDI and to protect commercial links from erosion brought by trade diversion induced by NAFTA[46].

A. The European Union and Mercosur: The First Step of New Birregional Relations

1. The Strategic Importance of Mercosur

a) A Dynamic and In-Growth Pole

Since the conclusion of the Treaty of Asuncion in March 1991, Mercosur members have made exceptional progress towards integration. Against most expectations, in five years they have established a free trade area, created a customs union, established an intergovernmental legal and institutional framework for Mercosur and agreed, in December 1995, on a five-year program to go forward with a common market.

With a GDP in 1995 of $984 billion, the potential and dynamic economic growth of Mercosur places it as the fourth economic region of the world, after the EU, NAFTA and Japan. With a population of more than 200 million, it represents 46% of LA's population and 59% of its territory. In 1995, the total amount of the region's trade with the rest of the world went beyond $120 billion: around $65 billion in exports (one third of total LA's exports) and $55 billion in imports.

Without any doubt, Mercosur is one of the new economic regions which offers the most potential for economic growth, is the most interesting area for foreign investment and has the highest attraction for businesses[47]. In addition, coupled with its demographic potential, this region is clearly becoming a market capable of rapid and huge increases of production and consumption levels of goods and services.

---

[45] In May 1995, faced to a possible rapid accession of Chile to the NAFTA, the European Commission stated that it would have as immediate result trade diversion affecting European exports on equipment and consumer goods. See, COM (95) 232 final, *infra*, note 74, p.8.

[46] See, COM (95) 3 final, *infra*, note 84, p.13.

[47] A recent US Congress report places Brazil and Argentina among the ten economies with the best growth economic prospects for the next decade. See US Congress, Joint Economic Committee, *"US-Latin America Economic Relations: Hearings before the Joint Economic Committee"*, May 1993. See also, G. FURIOL & S. WEINTRAUB, *"US Policy, Brazil and the Southern Cone"*, in: **The Washington Quarterly**, Vol.19, Summer 1995, pp.123-134; J. GRANDI, *"Le Mercosur en période de transition : évaluation et perspectives"*, in : **Problèmes d'Amérique Latine**, No.17, April-June 1995, pp.73-87.

The EU is Mercosur's largest market. In 1995, exports to Europe accounted for a quarter of the total — ahead of intra-bloc trade (20%), NAFTA (17%) and the rest of LA (11%) —, amounting to $17.8 billion, and representing 45% of total European imports from LA[48]. Notwithstanding the fact that the trade balance is positive for Mercosur, starting in 1990, the EU strongly increased exports to this market. In fact, during the first half of the 1990s EU exports to Mercosur have grown on average by more than 34% per year. EU exports to Mercosur have also grown much faster than EU exports to ASEAN or the Mediterranean countries, and considerably faster than its exports to the US, Japan and other developed countries[49]. In 1995 they grew by 50% more than the preceding year, making it the most dynamic market for European exports. The EU has traditionally been the main trade partner of Mercosur accounting for 30% of the total trade. This privileged rapport is also found in exchanges with member countries taken in isolation. Likewise, during the last years, the EU has also been the largest foreign investor in this region, which absorbs around 70% of the total European FDI to LA[50]. Similarly, the amount of European aid to Mercosur represents more than half of the total destined to LA.

b) An Open and Expanding Process

The dynamism and consolidation of Mercosur's integration scheme transforms it in a pole of attraction for neighboring countries[51] sharing common integration objectives and willing to take part in and profit from the outstanding economic growth prospects.

At the IXth Summit of Mercosur, held in December 1995 in Punta del Este (Uruguay), the Mercosur Action Program — setting the conditions

---

[48] See IRELA, "The European Union and Mercosur: Towards a New Economic Relationship?", Brussels, June 1996, p.28.

[49] Higher export growth rates were only achieved in trade with China (35%) and with the Central and Eastern European Countries (37%). EU exports to ASEAN grew only by 19%, to the Mediterranean Countries by 7.4%, to the US by 6.2%, to Japan by 4.6%. See F. BATALLER, "The Relations between the European Union and Mercosur: Policies, Achievements and Prospects", in: **EU - LDC Network Committee**, Vol.3 No.4, December 1996, pp.2-3.

[50] See European Commission Communication, "The European Community and Mercosur: An Enhanced Policy", COM (94) 428 final, pp.7-11; "Echanges commerciaux UE-Mercosur", Note from the Council's General Secretariat 34/95, May 29, 1995.

[51] At the same time of the Presidential Summit of Mercosur held in Buenos Aires on August 5, 1994, Bolivia and Chile expressed their will to start negotiations with Mercosur, establishing the basis for a number of agreements of economic complementarity aiming at the creation of a free trade area. Bolivia formally presented candidacy for accession even before the five years period fixed by the Treaty of Asuncion (Chapter IV, Article 20) for new incorporations.

to deepen integration and the agenda for external economic links — was approved. In this meeting, Bolivia and Mercosur signed an economic complementary agreement — the first ever negotiated by the Mercosur with a third Party — leading to the establishment of a free trade area as from the second semester of 1996 and the liberalization of all bilateral trade within ten years. Similarly, it was not until June 1996 that an economic association agreement, providing for the establishment of a free trade area through the elimination of tariff barriers in ten years and the harmonization of technical and sanitary standards, was signed with Chile. In September 1996 the Andean Community agreed on an accelerated timetable for negotiations **group-to-group** with Mercosur[52], and exploratory talks about a free trade agreement linking three-quarters of LA have begun. Bilateral discussions with Peru and Venezuela are also underway.

Also of paramount importance is the Brazilian proposition — immediately supported by the other three partners — to create a South American Free Trade Area (SAFTA) in the South Cone. It would encompass the Andean Community, Mercosur and Chile, and would be achieved by means of liberalization of goods, for approximately 80% of regional trade, during a period of ten years between 1995 and 2005. Further to the obstacles to a *de facto* realization[53], the importance relies on the new conception of LA *vis-à-vis* the NAFTA in a moment where, in the economic geography of the continent, it is easy to distinguish three poles centered in North, Central and South America. Indeed, in contrast to the revitalization of the dynamism of North-American economic integration, the achievement of a SAFTA would allow the formation of a hemispheric free trade area with the North based on a balanced convergence of economic blocs[54], rather than on bilateral agreements with the United States.

Needless to say that this approach benefits the interests of the EU, opening up new perspectives and placing it, namely, after the signing up

---

[52] Negotiations are under way, rather than on a traditionally country basis on a bloc to bloc one. See *"Andean Group Seek to Make up for Lost Time in Joint Negotiations with Mercosur"*, in: **Latin America Regional Reports**, October 1996.

[53] See IRELA, *"Las relaciones entre el Gran y el Mercosur: hacia un espacio económico integrado en América del Sur?"*, Rapport of the Conference No.3, June 1995.

[54] See, *"Área de Libre Comercio Sudamericana (ALCSA): una nueva iniciativa de integración latinoamericana"*, in: **Integración Latinoamericana**, March-April 1994, pp.1-2; F. PEÑA, *"New Approaches to Economic Integration in the Southern Cone"*, in: **The Washington Quarterly**, Vol.19 No.1, Summer 1995, pp.113-122. In addition, one of the purposes would also aim to avoid the problems that may arise with a "hub and spoke" system, in which the US would be in the center, benefiting from a variety of bilateral agreements, and the branches, constituted by countries from LA, would not benefit from free trade among them.

of the Inter-regional Framework Cooperation Agreement with Mercosur, in a privileged position in regard of the South Cone and LA in general. At any rate, should the SAFTA be achieved or not, the crux is the political will to establish it by ways of impulsion of inter-regional liberalization and with a view of creating a model of integration strong and independent from the US.

2. The Inter-regional Framework Cooperation Agreement: Towards the Establishment of a Free Trade Area[55]

a) Analysis and Essential Elements of the Framework Agreement

This agreement, based on a balanced and joint collaboration in the political, economic and commercial fields, is the first ever to have been signed between two custom unions of different continents[56].

The signing of this agreement shows the commitment of both regions, engaged in the dynamic of open regionalism[57] — which implies integration objectives going beyond a simple free trade area — to establish an inter-regional association through which almost all exchanges, in accordance to the WTO rules, will be liberalized. On the other hand, due respect to human rights and democratic principles are some of the essential elements.

It is a **non-preferential, provisional, transitional and evolving agreement**[58] in the way that, on a first stage it provides for the necessary mechanisms to reach compromise positions and jointly defines strategies to solve trade obstacles, and then, on a second stage a gradual trade liberalization will be carried out. However, the entry into force of the inter-regional association will need a new agreement between both

---

[55] *"Inter-regional Framework Cooperation Agreement between the European Community and its Member States, of the one part, and the Southern Common Market and its Party States, of the other part"*, **OJ** L 69/4, March 19, 1996.

[56] See *"EU-Mercosur: Ground Breaking Deal to Create World's Largest Trade Bloc"*, in: **European Intelligence**, January 1996, Section V, pp.1-2.

[57] "... both Parties consider the process of regional integration to be an instrument of economic and social development which makes it easier for their economies to become part of the world economy ... Reaffirming the desire to uphold and strengthen the tenets of international free trade, in compliance with the World Trade Organizations rules, with a particular emphasis on the importance of open regionalism..." See Preface of the Agreement; see also, *"Open Integration: the European Union and the Mercosur and the International System"*, in: **Euro-Latin American Forum**, March 1995, pp.32-35.

[58] See the evolutive clause in Title VI, Article 23.

Parties. The date remaining to the Parties' discretion[59] depending on how quickly negotiations progress.

The principal goal is commercial cooperation and the preparation of liberalization of trade with the perspective of establishing the conditions enabling the creation of an inter-regional association[60]. A four axis plan will serve to achieve this goal.

At first instance, the purpose is to establish a reinforced and regular institutionalized **political dialogue** in order to accompany and consolidate the rapprochement between both regions and coordinate positions in international fora. The Framework Agreement provides for the establishment of a dual scheme. On the one hand, there is the proposal to create a new mechanism of political dialogue and a reinforcement of cooperation between their respective institutional bodies[61]. On the other, a Joint Committee is established with the tasks of assisting the Council of Cooperation in supervising the achievement of the agreement and follow the improvements occurred within the economic and commercial dialogue with the purpose of establishing trade liberalization[62].

In addition, the purpose is to **cooperate in trade issues** in order to progressively prepare for trade liberalization. The agreement provides for the creation of a Joint Subcommittee on Trade[63] as well as for the establishment of working groups to conduct preparatory work, identifying obstacles in the tariff and non-tariff fields and exchanging information on services, in order to facilitate the promotion and diversification of exchanges between both regions. These organisms shall also make proposals regarding the schedule and scope of the subsequent liberalization of trade. The Framework Agreement also provides for cooperation on standards and certification, statistical matters, customs and intellectual property. The goal is therefore, to pave the way for gradual and reciprocal inter-regional trade liberalization[64] which will take into account the sensibility of certain sectors[65] with due respect to WTO rules.

---

[59] "The Parties shall determine the suitability, timing and conditions of the start of negotiations for Inter-regional Association in accordance with their own procedures and in the light of the work carried out and the proposals made within the institutional framework of this agreement." See Title IX: "Final Provisions", Art.34 §3.

[60] Id. Title I.

[61] Id. Title V: "Interinstitutional Cooperation", Article 19.

[62] Id. Title VIII: "Institutional Framework", Articles 25-30.

[63] Id. Title VIII, Article 29.

[64] Id. Title II: "Trade", Articles 4-9.

[65] This mainly refers to the industrial and agricultural sectors for which a transitional schedule for trade liberalization should be negotiated. Accounting for 60% of

As regards the **promotion of economic cooperation**, the aim is to contribute to economic expansion and improve international competitiveness, encourage technological and scientific development and, more generally, to diversify and tighten economic ties[66]. It is worth mentioning that the Framework Agreement provides for the enlargement of economic cooperation, already dealt with in the "third generation" bilateral agreements[67], to the regional level[68]. The encouragement and promotion of investment, and the closing together of economic actors of both regions, are the essential elements of economic cooperation projects encompassing, for instance, the transport, industrial, energy, infrastructure, science and technology, telecommunications and environmental fields.

Finally, the promotion of cooperation in the field of **regional integration** aims at making Mercosur take advantage from the European integration experience. This cooperation focuses on training, exchange of information and technical assistance in order for Mercosur to achieve legislative harmonization and the development of common policies in the commercial, macroeconomic and social cohesion levels[69].

b) Effects on the Prospects for EU-LA Relations

The reinforcement of relations between the EU and Mercosur is based on mutual and reciprocal interests[70], both at the economic and political level.

Mercosur's exports to the EU, the liberalization of the key agricultural sector may represent the biggest obstacle both in regard of the protection of EU's Common Agricultural Policy (CAP) and preferential schemes with Central and Eastern European and Southern Mediterranean associates. However, the reform of the CAP and the application of the Uruguay Round agricultural commitments would certainly diminish difficulties. See IRELA, *"El acuerdo interregional entre la UE y el Mercosur: Una nueva estrategia de la UE en América Latina?"*, September 1995, pp.6-7.

[66] See, Title III: "Economic Cooperation", Articles 10-17.

[67] The agreements were signed with Argentina in April 4, 1990 (**OJ** L 295/66, October 26, 1990); with Brazil in June 26, 1992 (**OJ** L 262/53, November 1st, 1992); with Paraguay in February 3, 1992 (**OJ** L 313/1, October 29, 1992); and with Uruguay in November 4, 1991 (**OJ** L 94/2, April 8, 1992).

[68] The provisions of the Framework Agreement shall not affect bilateral cooperation resulting from existing cooperation agreements. See Title VII: "Resources for Cooperation", Article 24 §3. Coexistence will be ensured in regard of all aspects which do not present conflict with the Framework Agreement, however, notwithstanding that action will be led to the most appropriated level (bilateral or regional), the Inter-regional Association will replace in due time all bilateral and regional existing agreements. See SEC (95) 481 final, April 4, 1995.

[69] See Title IV: "Encouraging Integration", Article 18.

[70] See COM (94) 428 final, *supra*, note 50, pp.3-5; F. ALDECOA, *"El acuerdo entre la Unión Europea y el Mercosur en el marco de la intensificación de relaciones entre Europa y América Latina"*, in: **Revista de Instituciones Europea**, Vol.22 No.3, Sept-October 1995, p.785; IRELA, *supra*, note 65, pp.8-9.

For Mercosur the purpose is to gain political support and assistance in order to conclude economic reforms and achieve the on-going integration process in the Southern Cone, thus allowing to counterbalance the US influence in the region. From an economic viewpoint, the perspective of achieving free trade with the EU will consequently raise exports towards an attractive and relatively easy-access market, create jobs, as well as ensure an important source of investment, technology and cooperation. The final establishment of the inter-regional association will mean a qualitative and quantitative step forward in the process of open regionalism, which will allow the Mercosur to reach a full partnership status on the international scene.

For the EU, in addition to the reinforcement of historical, cultural and social ties, the purpose is to consolidate Mercosur's political and economic reforms as well as the regional integration process. By this means, the EU will obtain privileged access to an important emerging economic zone which offers flourishing perspectives for European exports. More accurately, the establishment of the future liberalization of exchanges will offer a huge market for the industrial and services sectors. All this contributes to reinforce the presence of the EU in the South-Cone, this being of paramount importance either in the case a SAFTA was eventually established or the prospects for a hemispheric free trade area became reality.

As this agreement sets out the beginning of a new commercial strategy in the region, based, first, on an economic, commercial and political collaboration, and then on a gradual and reciprocal liberalization of exchanges through the establishment of an inter-regional association, the pioneer character of the agreement will appreciably influence the prospects of UE-LA relations.

This is the reason why this new strategy should not be regarded in isolation but inserted in an overall strategy. This framework of regionalized relations, which privileges the variable geometry in EU-LA relations[71] can, in the future, inspire a widespread basis to deal with other prospective partners presenting similar characteristics. Chile and the

---

[71] "... this strategy ... cannot be seen as an alternative to the dialogue with the Rio Group. It should instead be considered a means of deepening and extending that dialogue, within which the Community's interests demand that it recognizes and takes account of regional specificities." See COM (94) 428 final, *supra*, note 50, p.3. Indeed, this variable geometry strategy was already promoted in the 1994 EU's Basic Document on relations with Latin America and the Caribbean. In addition, it is worth mentioning that the negotiations of "third generation" agreements began also on the basis of this distinguished approach.

ongoing negotiations with Mexico are the next steps. The Andean Community might be the next in the future.

B. Strengthening Relations between the European Union and Chile

1. Chile: a *Colour Bearer* of Open Regionalism

a) Strategic Importance of Chile

This country has always been one of the main activists of open regionalism. On the one hand, regarding NAFTA, despite US and Chilean efforts to make Chile become the fourth member of this free trade agreement, in the absence of fast-track negotiating authority, the issue is at the present moment on hold. However, in order to face this ticking over, in November 1996 Chile and Canada signed a bilateral free trade agreement. Largely patterned after the North American Free Trade Agreement[72] and aiming at establishing vast free trade encompassing goods and services, investment and the establishment of a dispute settlement mechanism, the agreement would eliminate duties for 80% of bilateral trade. The main purpose is to ensure Chile's market access to the North-American market and ease Chile's eventual entry into the NAFTA. In this regard it is worth mentioning that Chile has, since 1991, a free trade agreement with Mexico that has doubled the amount of trade in the last four years. Since January 1996 Chile has zero tariffs on most trade with Mexico.

In addition to this North-oriented approach, and despite withdrawal from the Andean Pact in 1976, within the framework of the Latin American Integration Association (LAIA), Chile has several economic complementary agreements with Argentina, Colombia, Venezuela, Bolivia and Ecuador. As regards Mercosur, even though Chile showed reluctance to join this model of integration due to Mercosur's higher external tariff and different structure, in June 1996 it finally signed an association agreement providing for the establishment of a free trade area[73] with the subregion.

---

[72] Five trade policy areas included in NAFTA were nevertheless left out of the bilateral pact. Intellectual property, product standards and sanitary and phytosanitary measures because both Parties committed themselves to WTO obligations; government procurement and financial services because both Parties were not prepared to negotiate new access. In addition, there are a number of areas, such as anti-dumping and rules of origin, in which there are significant differences with the NAFTA Agreement. See **Inside US Trade**, November 29, 1996, pp.8-10.

[73] See **Agence Europe**, April 24, 1996, pp.8-9; June 25/26, 1996, p.12.

Finally, Chile has highly developed commercial links with the Asia-Pacific region, which absorbs a third of Chile's total exports. Besides being a member of the APEC, with a view to reinforce its presence in this region, Chile is also negotiating a bilateral free trade agreement with New Zealand.

b) Economic Importance of Chile[74]

With a constant and stable economic growth and an active policy of integration into the global economy, Chile is, at the present moment, one of LA's most interesting countries for the establishment of a political and economic association.

In terms of trade, exports are the main resource for Chile's economic development, absorbing more than 40% of production activity. As a result of the application of open regionalism, trade flows with major economic regions have significantly increased. With 26% of the total, the EU is Chile's main trade partner, closely followed by LA (23%), Asia (22%) and the US (18%). Notwithstanding the first place of the US as supplier of the Chilean market, European exports have witnessed, in recent years, a regular and constant increase. Conversely, the EU is by far the country's main market, taking over a quarter of Chilean exports.

Drawn by strong economic growth, FDI has risen sharply in recent years. European investment occupy a privileged position, accounting for 45% of the total FDI flows in the non-mining sector and surpassing the US (22%) and Latin Americas (17%). In percentage terms, Chile has witnessed the most important increase of european investment in any Latin American country.

2. The Framework Agreement on Trade and Economic Cooperation with Chile[75]

The general evaluation of commercial and economic relations between the EU and Chile is positive for both. The EU occupies a privileged

---

[74] See European Commission Communication on the strengthening of relations between the European Union and Chile, COM (95) 232 final, pp.2-6 and Annexes I-II; COM (95) 495 final, *supra*, note 22, Annexes III-IV; Commission's working document on present relations between the EC and Chile, SEC (95) 563 final.

[75] *"Framework Cooperation Agreement leading ultimately to the establishment of a political and economic association between the European Community and its Member States, of the one part, and the Republic of Chile, of the other part"*, **OJ** L 209/5, August 19, 1996.

position in terms of trade, investment and cooperation. It is of paramount importance for Chile, a country highly dependent on exports, to find and ensure new markets in order to diversify and increase production. In addition, cultural, political and economic links between the EU and Chile are strong, making the latter a close European ally, despite the geographical distance.

Therefore, on the basis of all these considerations, in the interest of both Parties and following the sample of EU-Mercosur's Framework Agreement, the signing of a fourth generation agreement took place in Florence on June 21st, 1996. This Framework Agreement intends to lead to an association of a political and economic nature which will provide for trade liberalization in two progressive steps.

As in that with Mercosur, we can find in this agreement the same transitional and evolving character as well as the same goal of preparing free trade by means of commercial and economic cooperation, support for the process of Chile's insertion in a regional integration strategy[76] and reinforcement of political dialogue with a view to achieving closer consultation on matters of common interest. Similarly, in order to give the framework agreement a preparatory status, there are no specific commercial concessions in the agreement itself. The agreement provides, rather, for the establishing of general conditions that will ease the passage to free trade[77], the move to liberalization of trade depending on an agreement reached by the Parties in accordance with their respective procedures following circumstances and progress made under the framework cooperation agreement.

Given the degree of liberalization achieved by Chile in some areas, the Framework Agreement provides for a more detailed cooperation in fields such as intellectual property[78], services[79], investment and in areas not provided for in the agreement with Mercosur, such as cooperation on reciprocal liberalization of public procurement and regulated sectors. Contrary to the agreement with Mercosur, the agreement provides for

---

[76] See Article 31.

[77] *Id*. Article 5 §3 a) of the Agreement.

[78] Article 10 of the Framework Agreement is written in a more detailed manner, listing each of the intellectual property rights envisaged and providing for a scheme of consultations in the case of commercial disputes. In order to reinforce cooperation in this field, it also provides for the conclusion of complementary agreements in issues such as geographic indications.

[79] See Article 14.

the elimination of the "third generation" agreement in place[80] once the new agreement has entered into force.

However, once the Association Agreement between Mercosur and Chile has been signed, the "bridge" envisaged for this purpose in a joint declaration annexed to the EU-Chile's Framework Agreement is due to enter into force, and the agreement has to converge towards the EU-Mercosur's one[81].

C. Towards Closer Relations between the European Union and Mexico

1. Mexico and the EU: In Search of a New Partnership

a) Strategic Importance of Mexico

During the last years, by virtue of the participation to major international multilateral bodies (to the GATT in 1986 and to the OECD in 1994) and of the establishing of an important net of regional integration agreements, Mexico has progressively affirmed and reinforced its economic weight and credibility in the international economic arena. In terms of trade and investment, these processes have led to a sharp increase in the economic importance of Mexico's market, making it one of paramount importance for the new commercial strategy of the EU.

As regards LA, Mexico together with Venezuela and Colombia, all three countries representing 35% of LA's GDP, created in June 1994 the Group of Three, a free trade agreement intended to be fully achieved by 2004. In 1991, it signed an agreement of economic complementation with Chile. In 1992, a free trade framework agreement, leading in the beginning of the century to the establishment of a free trade area for 120 million people, was signed with the countries of Central America. In 1994, Mexico had an important role for the creation and consolidation of the Association of Caribbean States (AEC), signed another agreement with Bolivia, and further negotiations are in course with other countries.

In 1993, Mexico became a member of the APEC[82]. In 1994, by the entry into force of NAFTA, a free trade agreement accounting for more

---

[80] The current agreement was signed in December 12, 1990 (**OJ** L79/1, May 26, 1991).

[81] See Annex III of the Agreement.

[82] However, it should be noted that, despite the importance of this region in the search of diversifying export markets, trade has remained rather weak. Therefore, the need

than 20% of global trade and with prospects of enlargement, Mexico became a founding member of one of the two largest markets of the world.

b) *Economic Importance of Mexico for European Interests*

After decades of strong protectionism and a highly regulated economy, the modernization and liberalization of Mexico's economy is nowadays a reality, despite certain recent distortions[83]. The EU has not remained aside of this process.

As regards the trade balance between the EU and Mexico, there has been a change in the trend during the period 1985-1993, deriving from a deficit situation for the EU towards a surplus one[84]. Thus, whereas in 1985 European exports to Mexico represented 18% of the total average to LA as a whole, in 1993 they amounted to 24%. The European exports market share in Mexico represented 11% as compared to 73% of North-American origin. Therefore, whereas the EU is Mexico's second largest export market, Mexico is, in absolute terms, the most important Latin-American trade partner for the EU. One should, nevertheless, bear in mind that in 1994, during the first year after the entry into force of NAFTA, which boosted the figures in trade and investment among the members, the outcomes were rather negative for the EU as its exports share was reduced by 39%.

In addition, over the last decade, European direct investment flows in Mexico have shown great dynamism, growing faster than those from any other source. Although somewhat contracted after the entry into force of NAFTA, the EU's direct investment represent 20% of the total and are the second most important source for Mexico. This stagnation in investment trends after 1994 showed that the risk of European operators being marginalized was a very real one.

This is why in February 1995, the Commission launched a recommendation: if a new framework of European-Mexican relations was not to be set out as soon as possible, trade and economic relations risked to be

---

to look for more kin markets becomes a necessity. See A. GUILLÉN, *"Las relaciones de México con la Cuenca del Pacífico en el marco del TLC"*, in: **Comercio Exterior**, July 1995, p.513.

[83] For an analysis of the reasons and consequences of the Peso crisis and the "Tequila" effect, see IRELA, *"Mexico: Economic and Political Uncertainty"*, November 20, 1995.

[84] See European Commission Communication, *"Towards Closer Relations between the European Union and Mexico"*, COM (95) 3 final, pp.9-10.

hampered or even eroded in the midterm because of trade-diversion induced by NAFTA[85]. In addition, the adherence of Mexico to several free trade agreements in a regional and bilateral level in the North, South and Central America, in the Caribbean Basin and the Asia-Pacific region, could also contribute to reduce European exports by almost 80%[86].

Therefore, the entry into force of a new strategy, made possible through a new agreement of economic partnership and political concertation which will lead to a progressive and reciprocal liberalization, would allow to reinforce the exchanges of goods and services, as well as to stimulate investment.

2. Towards an Economic Partnership and Political Concertation Agreement

Notwithstanding the importance of the third generation agreement signed between the EU and Mexico in 1991 in promoting closer economic relations[87], both Parties have recognized that this framework is no longer appropriate to face the new challenges. Therefore, the strengthening of relations between the EU and Mexico, rooted on reciprocal political and economic interests[88], needs the establishment of another instrument.

For the EU, the purpose is to consolidate Mexico's opening towards democracy, and to share and take advantage of historical, economic, political and cultural ties, as well as, to reinforce its presence in LA. From an economic viewpoint, despite the 1995 financial difficulties, Mexico has become, by virtue of trade liberalization, improvements in the legal context and the reinforcement of its position at the regional level, a market with a high potential of consumption and a very interesting

---

[85] Mainly in the textile and telecommunications sectors. *Id.*, p.10.

[86] The same argument also applies with regard to certain US exports. For instance, whereas Chilean wine enters into Mexico with a 0% tariff due to the 1991 free trade agreement between Mexico and Chile, US wine (namely Californian) is still subject to higher tariff. See, **The Economist**, February 1996, p.92. In addition, in order to show the importance of a new EU strategy, it should be borne in mind that, in 1995, for the first time, trade balance between the US and Mexico showed deficit: Mexican exports grew (25%) more than imports (9%) from the US. This has been, of course, one of the consequences of the 1995 Peso's crisis (the price fall allowed Mexico to increase exports and at the same time reduce more expensive imports), however, at the same, Mexico's free trade agreements in LA gave rise to an increase of intra-regional imports, thus changing to a certain extent the main source of supply for the Mexican market. See **The Economist**, March 9, 1996, p.56.

[87] The agreement was signed in April 26, 1991 (**OJ** L 340/1, November 11, 1991).

[88] See, COM (95) 3 final, *supra*, note 84, p.3.

destination for foreign investment. In the background, the goal is to avoid, or at least to hamper, the establishment of a hemispheric free trade area without European involvement. This would certainly represent an important risk for the EU as it could lose important market shares by the fact that European products would be submitted to tariffs contingencies which would not be applied to products coming from North, Central and South America.

Provided that an appropriated contractual framework is established, prospects for the development of future commercial relations are encouraging. Drawing from its experience within NAFTA, Mexico should be prepared to cope with the economic implications of liberalizing its trade with the EU. In addition, since Mexico's membership in NAFTA offers greater guarantees for investment and consolidates Mexico's position as a bridge to Western Hemisphere markets, European investment and trade flows will continue to grow in the future. Conversely, it would allow Mexico to boost bilateral trade with the EU and profit the most from advantages brought about by NAFTA integration.

From a political viewpoint, the goal **for Mexico** would be to preserve and promote economic and political rapports with the EU, serving this rapprochement to balance dependence on NAFTA partners. In addition, from an economic perspective, the European market is one of great attraction for Mexican products, with a relatively easy access and an important source of resources, technology and cooperation. Furthermore, a deeper and wider opening of the Mexican market to the EU would enable the former to cope with increased international competitiveness. Nevertheless, Mexico and the EU are not only looking for a mere liberalization and opening of markets. As inserted in the Solemn Declaration signed by both Parties in May 2, 1995, the agreement to be negotiated will cover, besides trade liberalization of goods and services, investment rules, a mechanism for dispute settlement, as well as cooperation in science, industry, education, information technology, and regional integration.

If the reasons underlying the need for a new partnership are clear, the way to create the instrument for achieving it has not been free from obstacles. Mexico has been at the heart of a dispute within the EU over the issue of free trade agreements with other regions. After long debates concerning the effects of such an agreement[89] in respect of WTO

---

[89] France raised the need to study the compatibility of the agreement with both factors. The study concluded that the prospective agreement would have enough margin of

provisions, third countries and European agriculture, and despite divergences among Member States[90] regarding the shape and the content of the commercial dispositions of the agreement, a final compromise was reached and the Council of Ministers finally agreed, on June 1996, to a mandate to open negotiations with Mexico.

Without either using the terms "free trade area", or directly foreseeing the ways to accomplish the liberalization, the proposed agreement would cover economic, commercial and other cooperation and political concertation. Regarding trade cooperation, the objective is to gradually establish a framework to encourage the development of trade in goods, services and investment, leading to a progressive and reciprocal liberalization and taking into account the sensibility of certain products, as well as WTO's provisions. It is therefore a compromise and a different approach from that used with Mercosur and Chile because the two steps of liberalization will be dealt within a single agreement. As provided for, a EU/Mexico Joint Committee will be assigned the task of carrying out negotiations in order to establish the conditions, the schedule and the *modus operandi* for the subsequent liberalization. Therefore, in a first step, both Parties will recognize that the goal is to set out a general favorable framework to gradually and reciprocally promote free trade, the purpose being to attain in the long term a global solution. The final agreement could only be approved and the *de facto* liberalization enter into force once an agreement on the whole is achieved. The agreement will also be unlimited in character and would replace, contrary to the Mercosur's framework agreement, the present third generation agreement from 1991.

---

conformity with the WTO rules, would not have important effects regarding EU's trade partners (Mediterranean basin, Eastern and Central Europe, and ACP countries), and would affect the common policies (agriculture, fisheries and industry) less than free trade with closer markets (i.e. Central and Eastern Europe and Mediterranean Countries). It was also concluded that the impact on EU agriculture would not represent an obstacle because Mexico was mainly an importer of such products and also because only 1.2% of European products were to be treated as sensible products. Therefore, the study concluded that, contrary to the Mercosur's case, there was no reason to exclude agriculture from the agreement. See **Agence Europe**, February 1996, pp.7-8; **Europolitique**, March 1996, Section V, p.13.

[90] Difficulties dealt with the modes in which the establishment of a free trade agreement would be drafted. Whereas for Spain, United Kingdom and Sweden this should be realized in a single phase, for France, Denmark, Netherlands and Portugal, it should be realized in two phases: the first one should prepare the conditions leading to free trade that would be realized in the second one — the main element being that in order to pass to the second phase a new decision should be required. See **Agence Europe**, March 23, 1996, p.9; **Europolitique**, February 26, 1996, Section V, p.13.

IV. CONCLUDING REMARKS

The economic growth of the EU is highly dependent on foreign trade performances. The work already carried out in favor of liberalization at the multilateral level can be reinforced and complemented by the same efforts at the bilateral/regional level. The EU needs to ensure future access to major and growing markets. Taking further steps in this direction, the EU is aware that trade policy has to be used as a more effective and sharp instrument to increase and ensure access to foreign markets. Other major economic actors are already moving in this direction.

Certain regions and countries of LA offer the EU emerging and dynamic markets. The interest of the EU is driven not only by actual trends in terms of trade and investment flows, but also, and overall, by the great **potential** economic growth prospects for these dynamic and constantly expanding markets. Likewise, the EU represents for them an important point of reference in terms of integration know-how, destination of exports and investment sources. This strong reciprocal interest is the result of a long-standing economic cooperation and political dialogue.

The Mercosur, Chile and Mexico are an important part of the EU's new global commercial strategy. The 1995 Framework Agreement with Mercosur, the first ever between two customs unions of different continents, and the foreseen inter-regional association, are ambitious efforts to strengthen relations and set up the conditions for a new birregional context.

However, the final achievement of these fourth generation agreements faces a number of **challenges**. The flexible character and the nature of these agreements, the capacity of the counterparts to deal with internal conflicts, and the compatibility to the WTO rules, are elements that will have to be carefully considered.

Some of the challenges rely on the evolving and preparatory character of these agreements. The goal is to prepare conditions paving the way to a second stage which will provide for reciprocal liberalization. However, the transition to the inter-regional association or the political and economic association is not automatic, but rather will depend on progress and work carried out. The lack of a precise clause establishing the ways and the moment to initiate free trade liberalization might make them become **too** flexible.

Others rely on the nature of the agreements themselves. As they are mixed agreements — they have been signed by the EC **and** its Members

States — Member States reticent of further liberalization will retain a decisive tool to give way or block the final purpose of the Framework Agreements[91]. Differences appeared before the Commission was given the task of opening negotiations with Mexico are an illustrative example.

The capacity of Mercosur to manage the existing asymmetries among its Member States in terms of their economic and political power, and the position of Chile *vis-à-vis* the NAFTA will also determine the rhythm of the second agreement.

Finally, given the more stringent multilateral rules as regards the content and the more cautious monitoring as regards the implementation of free trade agreements, compatibility with WTO rules would need to be carefully assessed. Problems may arise as regards some excluded sectors, such as agriculture in the agreement with Mercosur.

At any rate, even if negotiations leading to trade liberalization come about gradually, these new agreements represent the long-term economic and political commitments between two regions that share an important number of interests, economical and political, but also social and cultural.

---

[91] The Framework Agreements with Mercosur (Article 34 §3) and Chile (Article 42 §2) make the start of negotiations towards liberalization dependent on the Parties' **own procedures**. In this regard it should be noted that as regards liberalization of goods, as it is a Community field, no major problems should appear. However, as regards liberalization of services, a field of mixed competences following Opinion 1/94, problems and deadlocks may arise.

Transatlanticism in Support of Multilateralism? Prospects for Great Power Management of the World Trading System[*]

Richard H. STEINBERG

Acting Professor of Law,
University of California, Los Angeles

A. Introduction: Transatlantic Management of the World Trading System — Prospects and Problems

1. Alternative Paths to "Liberal Multilateralism"

The principle of "liberal multilateralism" has anchored US trade policy since the end of World War II, but it is now a contested term. There is no consensus when US trade policy discussions turn to the question of how to pursue liberal multilateralism and whether regional agreements (or transregional agreements) can further liberal multilateralism.

Fundamentally, disagreement among those engaged in and by US trade policy is not rooted in the concept of "liberalism". In the trade policy context, most agree that the term suggests that trade and investment should be conducted relatively free of governmental controls or restraints and that existing barriers to trade and investment should be reduced. This

[*] The author appreciatively acknowledges useful comments on earlier drafts from Eileen DOHERTY, Arthur ROSETT, John SETEAR, and Phillip R. TRIMBLE.

does not suggest that there is perfect agreement about the extent to which trade should be liberalized, how to liberalize, what to liberalize, and when to liberalize it[1] — but there is basic agreement on what it means.

Nor is there disagreement over the **outcome** suggested by the principle of "multilateralism". To international trade policy-makers, "multilateralism" suggests that all public international trade rules (including all bilateral and plurilateral arrangements) should be consistent with World Trade Organization (WTO) rules and that it is preferable that most new international trade rules be adopted in and applied through the institutions of the World Trade Organization.

But multilateralists are split over questions of **process**: whether and how regional or transregional arrangements might be used to facilitate a liberal multilateral outcome. There are three sets of views on the question, reflecting a contest over: "Who is truly a "liberal multilateralist"?"

In one ideal-typical view, which might be called "traditional multilateralism", the outcome-oriented dimension of multilateralism described above is complemented by a commitment to the **traditional multilateral process**, which entails participation in the negotiation, drafting and adoption of trade rules by all WTO Members on an equal basis[2]. Such

---

[1] Disagreements in the United States about these aspects of liberalization may be attributed to several factors, including whether one's economics more closely resemble a neoclassical approach or a strategic trade theory approach, and whether one is a purist about liberalization or more politically pragmatic about it. As will be discussed below, disagreements between the US Government and other governments about these liberalization issues are further complicated by different national "styles" of capitalism. For examples of the neoclassical approach, see, e.g., RICARDO David, *"On the Principles of Political Economy and Taxation"*, in: STRAFFA Piero (ed.), **Works and Correspondence**, Cambridge University Press, Cambridge, 1951, pp.133-49; and KINDLEBERGER Charles P. & LINDERT Peter, **International Economics**, (6th ed.) R.D. Irwin, Homewood, Ill., 1978. For an introductory discussion of strategic trade theory, see KRUGMAN Paul (ed.), **Strategic Trade Theory and the New International Economics**, MIT Press, Cambridge, 1990. For a discussion of pragmatic deviations from a pure neoclassical approach to liberalism, see RUGGIE John Gerard, *"International Regimes, Transactions and Change: Embedded Liberalism in the Postwar Economic Order"*, in: **International Organization** Vol.36 No.379, 1982. For discussions of different national "styles" of capitalism, see, e.g., ZYSMAN John, **Governments, Markets and Growth**, Cornell University Press, Ithaca, N.Y., 1983, especially Chapter 2; GERSCHENKRON Alexander, **Economic Backwardness in Historical Perspective,** Belknap Press, Cambridge, 1962, especially 5-30.

[2] For examples of the traditional approach, or suggesting a commitment to it, see KAHLER Miles, **Regional Futures and Transatlantic Economic Relations,** Council on Foreign Relations Press, New York, 1995, especially 61-73; BHAGWATI Jagdish, *"Aggressive Unilateralism: An Overview"*, in: BHAGWATI Jagdish & HUGH T. Patrick (eds), **Aggressive Unilateralism**, University of Michigan Press,

participation, traditionalists might suggest, is necessary if all members are to consent to the body of public international law[3]. Any trade negotiation which excludes some countries from it — instead of a traditional multilateral negotiation — could render trade solutions that excluded countries find impossible to accept. In recent policy debates over the wisdom of deepening transatlantic trade ties, some traditional multilateralists have suggested that in a transatlantic trade negotiation there will be some serious EU-US disagreements that will be hard to resolve; for some of those issues, the multilateral process might offer diplomatic allies to the United States to help pressure a change in the EU's position, but that process will have been foregone. More broadly, this author has argued that the traditional multilateral negotiating process might offer shifting diplomatic coalitions of nations on an issue-by-issue basis, creating multiple political cleavages that cut across each other, making it difficult for trading countries to group themselves into persistent political or economic blocs; in that way, the traditional multilateral process may forestall the creation of trade blocs and support the perpetuation of a system of global trade rules[4]. From the traditional multilateralism perspective, regional trade agendas are a source of concern; to the extent that traditional multilateralism has anything good to say about regionalism, it is that regional trade creation usually exceeds trade diversion and that the politics of regionalism appears to be relatively benign thus far[5].

Ann Arbor, Mi., 1990; JACKSON John H., **World Trade and the Law of GATT**, The Michie Company, Charlottesville, Va., 1969; and, more recently, JACKSON John H., **Restructuring the GATT System**, Royal Institute of International Affairs, London, 1990.

[3] On the notion of consent, generally, see, e.g., VAN BYNKERSHOEK Cornelius, *Quoestionum juris publici libri duo*, 1737 ed., Book I, (trans. Frank Tenney), **Classics of International Law**, Oxford University Press, New York, 1930; AUSTIN John, **The Province of Jurisprudence Determined**, Murray J., London, 1831, 1-31, 138-39; HALL William E., **A Treatise on International Law**, (3rd ed.), Clarendon Press, Oxford, 1890.

[4] This is analogous to Seymour Martin Lipset's arguments about the importance of crosscutting cleavages in social structure for the success of democracy. LIPSET Seymour Martin, **Political Man: The Social Bases of Politics**, Johns Hopkins University Press, Baltimore, 1981, especially 29-182.

[5] For the proposition that regionalism seems relatively benign thus far, see KAHLER, **Regional Futures**; EICHENGREEN Barry & FRANKEL Jeffrey A., *"Economic Regionalism: Evidence from Two 20th Century Episodes"* (paper presented at the Conference on Globalization and its Implications for the Newly Industrialized Economies of East Asia, East-West Center, Honolulu, Hawaii, August 15-17, 1994) (on file with author). On trade diversion generally, see VINER Jacob, **The Customs Union Issue**, Carnegie Endowment for International Peace, New York, 1950. See also DAM Kenneth W., *"Regional Economic Arrangements and the GATT: A Legacy of Misconception"*, in: **University of Chicago Law Review** Vol.30, 1963, p.615.

There are, however, serious critiques of a religious devotion to traditional multilateralism. Most prominently: it no longer exists and maybe never has[6]. Article XXIV of the General Agreement on Tariffs and Trade (GATT)[7] has permitted the establishment of free trade areas and customs unions. The proliferation and deepening of those preferential trade areas appear to be accelerating, most commonly along regional paths[8]. Trade liberalization is no longer taking place through purely multilateral processes and no one believes that it is possible to end regional trade liberalization. To the extent that traditional multilateralism precludes regional trade liberalization, traditional multilateralism is mere fantasy. To the extent that traditional multilateralism merely tolerates the regional liberalization efforts undertaken to date, it fails to conceive of a positive political role for the world's currently fastest and most dynamic form of trade liberalization.

A second ideal-typical view pursues regional arrangements simultaneous with multilateral efforts to yield a process of "competitive liberalization" — a competition between the regional and multilateral processes in which each regional integration effort creates pressure for multilateral results. Some US trade analysts have argued that regional trade groupings could serve as "stepping stones" to multilateral liberalization, with regional liberalization somehow "ratcheting upwards"[9]. While advocates of competitive liberalization have neither fully specified all of the assumptions nor fully detailed the logic of the approach, the main idea seems to be that the widening and deepening of each regional trade arrangement brings otherwise reluctant actors to the multilateral bargaining table because they fear that they will be left out of the alternatives to a multilateral solution — markets defined by large regional arrangements with substantial discrimination and adverse trade diversion

---

[6] Similarly, Ruggie has argued that pure "liberalism" has not really existed in the post-War period. See RUGGIE, **International Regimes**.

[7] General Agreement on Tariffs and Trade, October 30, 1947, T.I.A.S. No.1700, 55 U.N.T.S. 187 [hereinafter GATT 1947]; General Agreement on Tariffs and Trade, April 15, 1994, Agreement Establishing the World Trade Organization, Annex 1A in Final Act Embodying the Results of the Uruguay Round of Multilateral Trade Negotiations, Marrakech, April 15, 1994.

[8] See OECD, *Regional Integration and the Multilateral Trading System: Synergy and Divergence*, OECD, Paris, 1995.

[9] See, e.g., BERGSTEN C. Fred & HENNING C. Randall, *"Europe's Role in the World Economy: An American View"*, paper presented at the Joint Conference of the Institute for International Economics and Austrian National Bank, Vienna, Austria, October 18-19, 1993. See also STERN Paula, *"Is Regionalism Spoiling World Trade?"*, speech and comments to the Pacific Council on International Affairs, Los Angeles, California, February 14, 1997.

effects[10]. A common illustration of this process has been President Clinton's "Triple Play" of late 1993: conclusion of the NAFTA and upgrading the November 1993 APEC meeting to the summit level in order to pressure the EU into a solution to the Uruguay Round impasse on agriculture[11]. Moreover, some of those advancing the competitive liberalization approach suggest that the regional arrangements might create precedents for multilateral solutions[12].

There are several concerns about competitive liberalization. Instead of begetting multilateral liberalization, the formation, widening, and deepening of a regional trade area could beget the formation, widening, and deepening of other regional trade areas — a process that may be seen as "competitive regionalization"[13]. Interest groups in each regional area could begin opposing multilateral liberalization to the extent that it would reduce their enjoyment of trade diversion effects[14]. Each regional

---

[10] SCHOTT Jeffrey J., *"More Free Trade Areas?"*, in: **Free Trade Areas and US Trade Policy**, SCHOTT Jeffrey J. (ed.), Institute for International Economics, Washington D.C., 1989, 11; LUYTEN Paul, *"Multilateralism Versus Preferential Bilateralism: A European View"*, in: SCHOTT (ed.), **Free Trade Areas**, 277; PATTERSON Gardener, *"Implications for the GATT and the World Trading System"*, in: SCHOTT (ed.), **Free Trade Areas**, 353-65; FRANKEL Jeffrey A. & WEI Shang-Jin, *"European Integration and the Regionalization of World Trade and Currencies: The Economics and the Politics"*, **Working Paper** No.C95-053, Center for International and Development Economics Research, June 1995, 32-35; BERGSTEN C. Fred, **Competitive Liberalization**, Institute for International Economics, Washington, 1995.

[11] See, e.g., FRANKEL & WEI, **European Integration** No.33.

[12] SCHOTT, **More Free Trade Areas?**, 11; DIEBOLD William Jr., **Bilateralism, Multilateralism and Canada in US Trade Policy**, Ballinger, Cambridge, 1985, 91.

[13] Many political scientists and historians (many of whom would consider themselves realists) have argued that the world trading system is becoming competitively regional. See, for example, KRASNER Stephen, *"State Power and the Structure of World Trade"*, in: **World Politics**, April 1976, 28; GILPIN Robert, **War and Change in World Politics**, Cambridge University Press, Cambridge, 1981. See also KRUGMAN Paul, *"Is Bilateralism Bad?"*, in: RAZIN Assaf (ed.), **International Trade and Trade Policy**, MIT Press, Cambridge, 1991; WEBER Steve & ZYSMAN John, *"The Risk That Mercantilism Will Define the Next Security System"*, in: SANDHOLTZ Wayne (ed.), **The Highest Stakes**, Oxford University Press, Oxford, 1992. For more popular treatments, see KENNEDY Paul, **The Rise and Fall of the Great Powers**, Random House, New York, 1987; THUROW Lester, **Head to Head: The Coming Economic Battle Among Japan, Europe, and America**, Morrow, New York, 1992. Compare FRANKEL & WEI, **European Integration**, 33; SCHOTT, **More Free Trade Areas?**, 51-52.

[14] For examples of this argument and related arguments, see BHAGWATI Jagdish, *"Regionalism vs. Multilateralism"*, in: **The World Economy**, Vol.15, 1992, 535-56; WONNACOTT Paul & LUTZ Mark, *"Is There a Case for Free Trade Areas?"*, in: SCHOTT (ed.), **Free Trade Areas**, 59-84; SAXONHOUSE Gary, *"Pricing Strategies and Trading Blocs in East Asia"*, in: FRANKEL J. & KAHLER M. (eds), **Regionalism and Rivalry: Japan and the US in Pacific Asia**, University of Chicago Press, Chicago, 1993.

trade area could travel down its own path of regional regulations, developing its own regional "style" of capitalism[15], making it difficult to reconcile differences between regions in the multilateral forum. Worse still, regional trade areas could develop an "incentive to protect", causing them to raise trade barriers against those outside the region[16]. Some rational choice theorists have modelled the likelihood that competitive liberalization would slip into competitive regionalism; these analyses often make unrealistic or inappropriate assumptions[17], but many of them suggest that member states in regional trade areas will be willing to add new members until they reach a critical size, after which there are disincentives to add more countries or deepen liberalization multilaterally[18].

A third ideal-type, only some pieces of which have been articulated elsewhere, would pursue great power management of the multilateral trading system. By entering into transregional arrangements with each other, great trading powers with similar interests in liberalization could bring to bear the power inherent in their combined market size to yield global liberalization. This transregional approach might be referred to as the "great power management" approach to liberal multilateralism. As discussed in more detail below, the approach is consistent with the basic principles of the traditional realist school of international relations. And it is consistent with the intuition implicit in competitive liberalization that combined market power may have a potentially liberalizing political

---

[15] For an argument about how institutional features of a national economic system may interact with the international economy, see ZYSMAN John, *"National Roots of a "Global" Economy"*, paper presented at the Conference on Globalization and Regionalization: Implications and Options for the Asian NIEs, East-West Center, Honolulu, Hawaii, August 15-17, 1994.

[16] KRUGMAN Paul, *"The Move Toward Free Trade Zones"*, in: **Policy Implications of Trade and Currency Zones**, Federal Reserve Bank of Kansas City, Jackson Hole, 1991, 7-42.

[17] For example, these analyses assume implicitly that states seek to maximize welfare. See FRANKEL & WEI, **European Integration**, 35. But many empirical studies of trade negotiations suggest that states actually seek to maximize producer surplus in trade negotiations. For arguments supporting the latter point, see PUTNAM Robert, *"Diplomacy and Domestic Politics: The Logic of Two Level Games"*, in: **Intl. Org.** No.42, 1988, 427; AGGERWOL Vinod, **Liberal Protectionism: The International Politics of Organized Textile Trade**, University of California Press, Berkeley, 1985, especially 33-35. Some of these analyses also assume unrealistically that the "style" of capitalism among potential member states does not matter in predicting the critical size of a preferential trade area. For arguments suggesting the importance of considering the style of capitalism, generally, see ZYSMAN, **Governments, Markets, and Growth**; GERSCHENKRON, **Economic Backwardness**.

[18] See, e.g., SAXONHOUSE, **Pricing Strategies**; STEIN Ernesto, *"The Welfare Implications of Asymmetric Trading Blocs"*, in: **Essays on the Welfare Implications of Trading Blocs With Transport Costs and on Political Cycles of Inflation**, Ph.D thesis, University of California, Berkeley, 1994.

influence on those threatened with incomplete access to the combined market — but great power management goes further because it specifies two crucial historical-contextual factors left out of the competitive liberalization model: it considers which of the world's preferential trade regions could combine enough market power to pressure all (or almost all) other countries into liberalizing, and which regions have views of liberalization that are similar enough to make such transregional cooperation feasible.

2. Exploring the "Great Power Management" Alternative: Transatlantic Cooperation or Competition?

Once those factors are specified, transatlanticism suggests itself as the obvious candidate for the job. Transatlantic cooperation in closing the Uruguay Round exemplifies the kind of cooperation contemplated by the great power management approach. By withdrawing from the GATT 1947 and joining the WTO (that includes GATT 1994), the transatlantic powers forced the rest of the world to join the WTO (and all the associated Uruguay Round Agreements) or lose their Most-Favored-Nation (MFN) access to Europe and the United States, which no GATT Contracting Party could afford[19].

This chapter explores the prospects for transatlantic cooperation to further liberal multilateral outcomes. It is argued below that the combined market power of the European Union and United States is unmatched: a transatlantic economic region, or other forms of transatlantic trade cooperation, would be so powerful that it effectively could set the liberal rules of the multilateral system. Moreover, EU and US views of the appropriate substance of liberalization are similar, and so are their views of the main challenges to liberal multilateralism, largely because their respective versions of capitalism are so similar. But it is also shown below that barriers to transatlantic cooperation seem likely to limit the effectiveness of the approach — and could even render it completely unfeasible. Indeed, it is shown below that some realist thinkers — and some trade policy analysts — suggest that EU-US competition is more likely than cooperation. Four contemporary transatlantic policy initiatives that might be consistent with the great power management paradigm are analyzed below to better understand which is likely to prevail: transatlantic interests in cooperatively managing the global trading system or

---

[19] For more detail on this power play, see STEINBERG Richard H., *"Trade-Environment Negotiations in the EU, NAFTA, and WTO: Regional Trajectories of Rule Development"*, in: **Am. J. Intl. Law** No.91, 1997, 231, 241.

barriers to cooperation. The analysis suggests that EU-US cooperation on trade policy matters relating to third countries is proving difficult in the short term, but that it may become easier in the next decade or so. In the meantime, the analysis suggests great uncertainty over the prospects for great power management of the multilateral trading system.

3. Organization of this Chapter

Part B of this chapter will use realist international relations theory to elaborate the assumptions, logic, and operationalization of a transatlantic approach to liberal multilateralism. A traditional realist framework is applied to the contemporary political-economy to suggest that among the world's great economic powers, the European Union and the United States uniquely share a common interest in further multilateral liberalization on a Western model and buttressing the world trading system in the face of its strains and fractures. One manner of operationalizing the realist approach also suggests that the transatlantic powers have the combined market power necessary to yield such a result.

Part C considers barriers to transatlantic cooperation, many of which are suggested by rationalist versions of realist theory, rationalism more broadly, and the recent history of transatlantic relations. The list of potential barriers is daunting.

Part D evaluates contemporary transatlantic arrangements and proposals in terms of the great power management approach, considering the common interests and cooperation problems that will have been identified, and international legal constraints. There are several transatlantic policies that have been considered in the last few years, which the European Union and the United States could use to bring their power to bear on third countries in the interest of liberal multilateralism. The primary contemporary transatlantic trade initiative — the piecemeal effort to create a New Transatlantic Marketplace, described below — is not likely to substantially advance liberal multilateralism. Alternative initiatives — including proposals to create a Transatlantic Free Trade Area (TAFTA), and to modify WTO decision-making rules to better reflect EU and US power, also described below — are potentially useful means of advancing liberal multilateralism. But the analysis suggests that transatlantic cooperation to advance liberal multilateralism through these mechanisms probably will not be feasible politically in the short term. However, a less ambitious transatlantic policy, EU-US cooperation on select third country issues, may be feasible and could strengthen the liberal multilateral system in the short term.

Part E concludes by considering the future of the multilateral system in terms of the great power management paradigm, considering feasible transatlantic policies, as well as regional and bilateral policies that the European Union and the United States are likely to continue to pursue. It suggests that, in the near term, uncertainty about the future of liberal multilateralism will prevail: the current combination of bilateral, regional, and multilateral trade policies being pursued by the transatlantic powers could either evolve into increased transatlantic cooperation that will buttress liberal multilateralism, or decay into reduced transatlantic cooperation and catalyse competitive regionalism.

B. Traditional Realist Theory and the Logic of Transatlanticism

1. The Realist Basis of "Great Power Management" and the Logic of Transatlanticism

Both great power management and competitive liberalization may be seen as consistent with some principles common to realist approaches to international relations theory[20]. In the United States, there are several strands of postwar realist theory, including "traditional realism" (perhaps best represented by the work of Hans Morgenthau[21]) and a more formal deductive-axiomatic version known as "neorealism" (best represented by the work of Kenneth Waltz[22]). Both strands of realism treat nation-states, and regional groups of states endowed with sovereignty, as the fundamental units of analysis; neorealism does so expressly, while traditional realism does so implicitly[23]. Neorealism treats these units as rational and unitary[24]; traditional realism generally treats states as if they were rational and unitary, but also considers other factors such as domestic politics, ideology and international law[25]. For traditional realists, international

---

[20] Realism has its roots in the sometimes brutally and bluntly power-oriented analyses of writers like Thucydides, Clausewitz, and, more recently, Aron. See, e.g., THUCYDIDES, **The Peloponnesian War**, (the Crawley translation), The Modern Library, New York, 1982; VON CLAUSEWITZ Carl, **On War**, (trans. Col. J.J. Graham), Routledge & Kegan Paul Ltd., London, 1968; ARON Raymond, **On War**, (trans. Terence Kilmartin), W.W. Norton & Co., New York, 1968.

[21] See, e.g., MORGENTHAU Hans, **Politics Among Nations**, Alfred A. Knopf, New York, 1978.

[22] WALTZ Kenneth N., **Theory of International Politics**, Addison-Wesley, Menlo Park, Ca., 1979.

[23] See WALTZ, **Theory of International Politics**, especially Ch.5.

[24] *Ibid.*

[25] See, e.g., MORGENTHAU, **Politics Among Nations**, especially Part 5.

law and norms may have an impact on political behavior; whereas for neorealists, anarchy describes the political condition that prevails outside of and between those political units[26]. For realists (traditional and neo), powerful states determine international outcomes. In so far as international law enjoys compliance, that compliance depends largely (for traditional realists) or completely (for neorealists) on the powerful states of the system deciding that it is in their interest to comply, or in their interest to ensure that weaker states comply. International law with teeth therefore exists largely or completely only to the extent that the great powers find it in their interest. From this viewpoint, international law is epiphenomenal of the underlying power and interests of political units in the system endowed with sovereignty (i.e., nation-states and any regional group of nation-states endowed with some sovereign powers, such as the EU)[27].

Traditional realism is used here as the primary theoretical vehicle for explaining the relationship between power and liberal multilateralism, and for prescribing a transatlantic policy to support liberal multilateralism. At times, however, the analysis expressly borrows assumptions and deductions from neorealism and other rationalist approaches in order to add clarity to the analysis, to suggest alternative hypotheses, and to shed light on the feasibility of great power management.

Traditional realism may be seen as descriptive, explanatory, and prescriptive. It offers a description of and explanation for international behavior and international law. It is prescriptive in at least three related respects. First, it helps define the limits of political feasibility that constrain international law and international policy alternatives. Second, it suggests that an international legal system that stands in contradiction to the underlying distribution of state power and interests may collapse, although sociological factors (e.g., norms and legitimacy) may buttress such a system, and negotiated linkages across issue areas may yield mismatches between law and power in any one issue area[28]. Third, if a

---

[26] Compare WALTZ, **Theory of International Politics**, especially Ch.5, with MORGENTHAU, **Politics Among Nations**, especially Part 5.

[27] See KRASNER Stephen, *"Structural Causes and Regime Consequences: Regimes as Intervening Variables"*, in: KRASNER Stephen (ed.), **International Regimes**, Cornell University Press, Ithaca, N.Y., 1983, 1-22; KRASNER Stephen, *"Regimes and the Limits of Realism: Regimes as Autonomous Variables"*, in: KRASNER (ed.), **International Regimes**, 355-68.

[28] For more on this latter point, see STEINBERG Richard H., *"Consensus Decision-Making at the GATT/WTO: Linkage and Law in a Neorealist Model"*, **Working Paper** No.72, Berkeley Roundtable on the International Economy, Berkeley, California, February 1995.

policy-maker is from a hegemonic power or a great power, the framework — once operationalized — suggests how rules can be established to pursue that state's interests.

Hence, the traditional realist framework — once operationalized — can be used to prescribe strategies and tactics that facilitate the promotion of liberal multilateralism. Thus, for example, the approach can suggest pursuing a multilateral outcome through a process that does not entail participation by all affected countries: in any given regime — whether it is the multilateral system or a regional system — the great powers can set liberal rules and give lesser powers strong incentives to sign on.

Operationalization of the traditional realist framework to uncover alternative prescriptions for (and predictions about) setting rules that advance liberal multilateralism requires: (1) understanding the extent to which nation-states and regional units endowed with sovereignty have power to set rules in the international trading system; and (2) specifying the interests of the most powerful states and regional units. Failure to elaborate these elements is one of the analytic weaknesses of competitive liberalization: by failing to take this step, competitive liberalization can not prescribe which states or regions are most likely to cooperate so as advance liberal multilateralism. That analytic effort is made here, first by considering power, then interests.

2. The Power of Transatlanticism
   in Global Trade Negotiations

Many realists have operationalized "power" as a function of power across several dimensions (e.g., economic, security, and geographic dimensions) and have characterized the global distribution of state power in terms of how many "great powers" exist in the international system (e.g., hegemonic, bipolar, multi-polar, etc.); that approach is not taken here, for several reasons. First, most realists have operationalized "power" and characterized it in that way in order to predict how the balance of power will operate and how great powers will behave towards each other in general[29]. That goal is different from the narrower purpose

---

[29] To the father of neorealism, Ken Waltz, if the current geopolitical system were characterized as bipolar, and the European Union and the United States were the world's two great powers, then they would balance against each other instead of cooperating with each other; each power would represent a threat to the other, so they would balance against each other instead of cooperating. WALTZ, **Theory of International Politics**, especially Ch.6. To traditional realists, a bipolar system is also likely to

here of operationalizing power to understand how the rules of the international trading system are (or should be) established and maintained[30]. Second, a determination as to how many "great powers" exist may be nearly impossible, especially for a traditional realist: operationalizing "power" with precision is extremely difficult; in a traditional realist model, material indicators of power are modified by "softer" factors such as norms and law, further complicating the calculation; and it is hard to convert measures of state "power" (a continuous variable) into an expression of how many "great powers" exist (which is based on the dichotomous determination of whether a particular state should be characterized a "great power"). Third, for a traditional realist, norms and the embodiment of those norms in international law could lead to transatlantic cooperation despite a neorealist deduction to the contrary. Therefore, instead of attempting to determine how many great powers exist in the current geopolitical context (and inferring from that predictions and prescriptions about international trade rule-making and maintenance), this analysis uses rough indicators of power in the trade negotiation context to suggest which countries have the most influence over the rules of international trade.

For the purpose of evaluating the relative power of states to set the rules of international trade, power may be seen as a function of market size. Market access has been the primary goal of trading nations in every round of trade negotiations since establishment of the GATT in 1947. The sovereign powers that have set the rules of that system have been those with the largest markets. Those powers have used access to their markets to coerce and compensate lesser powers into accepting rules of the system[31]: they have compensated others with promises of increased market access (e.g., promising tariff reductions or elimination and quota expansion or elimination) and coerced others with threats of closure (e.g.,

---

result in balancing, *ceteris paribus*, but that prediction is qualified by attention to other factors that may induce cooperation, such as shared norms, international law, international institutions and common threats to both great powers in a particular issue area. See, e.g., MORGENTHAU, **Politics Among Nations**, Parts IV and V.

[30] There are good reasons to believe that an analysis of politics and outcomes in a particular issue area requires a measure of "power" that differs from that used to understand balancing behavior. For example, "power" may not always be fungible across issue areas. See KEOHANE Robert & NYE Joseph, **Power and Interdependence**, Little Brown, New York, 1977, especially 26-29. Moreover, even if two great powers can be expected to balance against each other generally, it is conceivable that they might cooperate with each other in a particular issue area in which they perceive common interests.

[31] This approach to power in the trade context bears some similarities to Albert Hirschman's. HIRSCHMAN Albert, **National Power and the Structure of Foreign Trade**, University of California Press, Berkeley, Ca., 1946.

threatening unilateral action by means of Section 301 of the Trade Act of 1974, as amended[32]).

By this measure, the United States and the European Union are the world's greatest powers when it comes to setting the rules of international trade: they have the world's biggest markets. Table 1 presents two rough indicators of market size for each of the ten countries with the biggest retained merchandise imports in the world: (1) gross domestic product, and (2) retained merchandise imports as a percentage of worldwide retained merchandise imports. The data suggests that the European Union and United States are by far the largest markets in the world; together their imports account for almost forty percent of all retained merchandise imports in the world. Considering both merchandise import shares and GDP, Japan is the next biggest market, but its annual GDP and annual retained merchandise imports are each less than half that of either transatlantic power.

The combined and coordinated economic and political capacity of Europe and the United States — deriving from the size of their markets — could be used to provide incentives for multilateral adoption of liberalizing rules and principles agreed upon by the two powers. Transatlantic coordinated action offers a greater probability of successfully resolving trade problems with third countries than is offered by the independent action of either power. Transatlantic cooperation in closing the Uruguay Round attests to that.

3. Transatlantic Interests

Such cooperation would not be possible if transatlantic interests were not similar and the transatlantic powers did not perceive a common external challenge. The European Union and the United States may share a commitment to a particular version of liberal multilateral outcomes[33] that

---

[32] Trade Act of 1974, secs 301-310, Pub. L. No.930618, 88 Stat. 1978 (current version as amended at 19 USC.A. sec. 2411 (West Supp. 1996)) [hereinafter Trade Act of 1974].

[33] Even for a neorealist, it is internally consistent for a state to advance liberal political or economic goals (e.g., democracy or free trade) by realist means, since neorealism takes interests as determined exogenously. See generally, WALTZ, **Theory of International Relations**. There are several useful analyses that combine liberal state policy preferences with a realist model of politics at the international level. See, for example, KRASNER Stephen, **Defending the National Interest**, Princeton University Press, Princeton, 1978; and GARRETT Geoffrey, *"International Cooperation and Institutional Choice: The European Community's Internal Market"*, in: **Intl. Org.** No.46, 1992, 533. Some analysts have combined a realist model of international behavior with a different kind of liberal factor — a liberal

Table 1
Indicators of Market Size, by Country, for the Ten Biggest Importing Countries

	1994 Merchandise Imports as Share of World Merchandise Imports*	1994 GDP (Est.) (Billions of $US)
USA	19.9	6738
European Union**	18.8	6806
Japan	8.0	2527
Canada	4.5	640
China	3.3	2979
Republic of Korea	3.0	508
Chinese Taipei	2.5	257
Mexico	2.4	729
Switzerland	2.0	148
Singapore	1.9	57

* Data reflects only retained imports (i.e., imports less re-exports), except for Mexico (which includes imports that may have passed through processing zones — maquiladoras).
** EU 12, excluding intra-EU trade.

Sources: World merchandise trade import shares are from WTO, International Trade: 1995 Trends and Statistics (Geneva: WTO, 1995), table II.3 at 26. 1994 GDP figures are from CIA, The World Fact Book 1995 (Washington, D.C.: CIA, June 1995), except for the EU GDP figure, which is from WTO, International Trade: 1995 Trends and Statistics, table III.30 at 54.

other countries do not share. Their common interest in liberalization may be derived from the theory of comparative advantage[34], ideology[35], or from realist theory[36]. To the extent they share a common interest in a **particular version** of liberalization and regulation, however, it is derived largely from their Western style of capitalism and regulation. "Liberalization" means different things to different states. Several political-economists have shown that "styles" of capitalism[37] and regulation[38] vary from country to country. Capitalist economies display different relationships between the state and society in economic affairs and these relationships may be seen in terms of different policies — for example, variance in the level of and manner in which subsidies are provided[39]; in the stringency of competition policy and its enforcement[40]; and in the means by which trade protection is afforded[41]. Accordingly, capitalist economies often disagree with each other about appropriate liberalization rules. While the styles of capitalism in Europe and North America are not identical, they are similar to each other relative to the styles of capitalism in Asia, the transitional economies of Eastern Europe and the former Soviet Union, and the developing countries of Africa and Latin America. Compared to the policy positions of most third countries, the policy positions of the EU Member States and the United States are more similar to each other across a broad range of issues that are on (or coming onto) the trade agenda — intellectual property protection, competition policy, environmental protection, labor laws, and services liberalization, to name a few.

The EU and US interest in a similar version of liberal multilateral outcomes may also be seen in a legal-historical perspective. Just after the Second World War, with the world split into two blocs, and the

---

domestic political model of preference formation. See, e.g., MORAVCSIK Andrew, *"Negotiating the Single European Act"*, in: **Intl. Org.** No.45, 1991, 19.

[34] See RICARDO, **Principles of Political Economy**.

[35] See, e.g., HARTZ Louis, **The Liberal Tradition in America**, Harcourt, Brace, New York, 1955.

[36] See, e.g., KRASNER, **State Power**.

[37] ZYSMAN, **Governments, Markets, and Growth**; GERSCHENKRON, **Economic Backwardness**.

[38] VOGEL David, **National Styles of Regulation: Environmental Policy in Great Britain and the United States,** Cornell University Press, Ithaca, N.Y., 1986.

[39] See, e.g., TYSON Laura D'Andrea, **Who's Bashing Whom?,** Institute for International Economics, Washington, 1991, Ch.5.

[40] See, e.g., GREEN Carl J. & ROSENTHAL Douglas E. (eds), **Competition Regulation in the Pacific Rim**, Oceana Publications, New York, 1996.

[41] See, e.g., TYSON, **Who's Bashing Whom?**.

United States dominant economically and militarily in the West, the United States was able to build a Western trading system in its image. The United States authored the text that became the GATT 1947[42]. That text constructed a liberal multilateral system, built largely on assumptions that the constituent economies were structured similarly to that of the United States and Western Europe — that they were Western liberal economies, composed of price-sensitive and profit-maximizing firms, with little government intervention except for purposes of solving market failures (such as the provision of public goods and competition policies intended to ensure that sectors remained relatively unconcentrated) and engaging in modest income redistribution. GATT rules have acknowledged that state trading enterprises[43], anti-competitive behavior[44], and other non-liberal governmental intervention might play a role in some economies, but the GATT-system did not contemplate that those features would be anything other than exceptions[45]. This system made sense as long as the constituent economies were essentially liberal[46]: liberal multilateral rules affected liberal economies similarly.

But national economic systems structured very differently from those envisioned in the Western liberal model are increasingly important actors in the world trading system. Reflecting that broader scope of national systems, the world trading system built in the Western image is suffering significant strains and lines of fracture[47].

To varying degrees, policy-makers in the European Union and the United States are likely to agree that several Asian economies, with industrial structures and government-business relationships that are fundamentally different from those in the West, pose challenges to the WTO system[48]. Strong industrial policies in some of these Asian economies

---

[42] See JACKSON, **World Trade**, especially 35-58.

[43] GATT 1947, Art.XVII.

[44] GATT 1947, Art.VI. In theory, anti-dumping rules are aimed at anti-competitive practices. See generally, DEARDORFF Alan V., *"Economic Perspectives on Antidumping Law"*, in: STERN Robert M. (ed.), **The Multilateral Trading System: Analysis and Options for Change**, University of Michigan Press, Ann Arbor, Mi., 1993.

[45] See WILCOX Claire, **A Charter for World Trade**, Arno Press, New York, 1972.

[46] For more analysis of this point in the context of China, see CLARKE Donald C., *"GATT Accession for China?"*, in: **University of Puget Sound Law Review** No.17, 1994, 517.

[47] Sylvia Ostry and others have called this problem, "systems friction". See the discussion in KAHLER, **Regional Futures**, 43-44.

[48] For analyses of Japan's trade and industrial policies and their relationship to world trade, some of which are relatively popular treatments, see JOHNSON Chalmers, **MITI and the Japanese Miracle**, Stanford University Press, Stanford, Ca., 1982;

are seen by some as having denied benefits to the West expected from tariff concessions and other WTO guarantees[49]. Weak competition policies in these Asian economies, mirroring concentrated industrial structures and inaccessible distribution systems, have served to limit imports in favor of domestic production[50] and limited the "contestability" of those markets[51]. Together, these policies have aided the development in Asia of sectors that many would consider strategic[52] and many see as having undermined the competitiveness of those same sectors in Europe and the United States[53]. In conjunction with macroeconomic savings and investment imbalances, some argue that these policies may also help explain chronic trade imbalances — particularly in specific sectors — between the United States and Europe, on one hand, and Japan, for example, on the other, regardless of whether the yen has been at 250 or 100 to the dollar[54]. And there is some evidence that those trade imbalances — particularly in specific sectors — may be understated: the regionalization

---

TYSON, **Who's Bashing Whom?**; VOGEL Steven, *"The Power Behind 'Spin-Ons': The Military Implications of Japan's Commercial Technologies"*, in: **The Highest Stakes**; WOLFF Alan W. & HOWELL Thomas R., *"Japan"*, in: HOWELL Thomas R. *et al.* (eds), **Conflict Among Nations: Trade Policies in the 1990's**, Westview Press, Boulder, Co., 1992.

[49] See, e.g., ABELS Tracy M., *"The World Trade Organization's First Test: The United States-Japan Auto Dispute"*, in: **UCLA Law Review** No.44, 1996, 467; and DEWEY Ballantine for Eastman Kodak Company, *"Privatizing Protection: Japanese Market Barriers in Consumer Photographic Film and Consumer Photographic Paper"*, Memorandum in Support of a Petition Filed Pursuant to Section 301 of the Trade Act of 1974, as amended, May 1995 (on file with author).

[50] See, e.g., LAWRENCE Robert Z., *"Do Keiretsu Reduce Japanese Imports?"*, paper prepared for the Eighth International Symposium of the Japanese Economic Planning Agency's Economic Research Institute on External Adjustments and Changing Trade Structure of Manufactured Goods since 1985, Tokyo, Japan, January 22-23, 1991; TATE John Jay, **Driving Production Home: Guardian State Capitalism and the Competitiveness of the Japanese Automobile Industry**, Berkeley Roundtable on the International Economy, Berkeley, Ca., 1995.

[51] On "contestability" in the trade policy context, see LAWRENCE Robert Z., *"Towards Globally Contestable Markets"*, in: **Market Access after the Uruguay Round**, OECD, Paris, 1996. This usage of "contestability" must be distinguished from its use by the "Chicago School" in the antitrust context; for that usage, see, e.g., STIGLITZ Joseph E., *"The Meanings of Competition in Economic Analysis"*, Publication No.328, Center for Economic Policy Research, Stanford, Ca., November 1992.

[52] On strategic trade theory, see KRUGMAN (ed.), **Strategic Trade Theory**.

[53] See, e.g., COHEN Stephen S., *"Geo-Economics: Lessons From America's Mistakes"*, in: CARNOY Martin *et al.*, **The New Global Economy in the Information Age**, Penn State Press, University Park, Pa., 1993, 100-105. But see KRUGMAN Paul, *"Competitiveness: A Dangerous Obsession"*, in: **Foreign Affairs**, March/April 1994, 28.

[54] See generally, JOHNSON, **MITI and the Japanese Miracle**.

of the *keiretsu* system in the face of *endaka* may be simply offshoring Japan's chronic trade imbalance with the West to the rest of Asia[55].

At the same time, transatlantic trade policy-makers are likely to agree that WTO rules do not fully address developing country issues. Many thoughtful policy-makers in the European Union and the United States want to integrate the developing countries more fully into the liberal trading system, largely for political purposes: to enhance the prospects for democracy and to "lock-in" those countries while they are in the midst of economic and political liberalization. The effort faces problems. Unstable macroeconomic histories in some developing countries limit EU and US business support for further integration. Many developing countries have a relatively weak administrative and legal infrastructure, making it difficult for them to administer and adjudicate customs issues, intellectual property protection, environmental protection, labor protection, and other Western-style regulatory systems that are now seen as important trade-related issues by various groups in Europe and the United States. Moreover, the level of development affects the value that polities place on building and maintaining such systems[56]. At the same time, the GATT's MFN principle, combined with the developed countries' political need for reciprocity, makes it difficult for the developing countries to bargain successfully for tariff concessions that favor their products[57]. As a result, North-South tension at the WTO persists and efforts to more fully open trade with developing countries face serious obstacles.

EU and US policy-makers also agree that now the transitional economies of China, the former Soviet Union, and Eastern Europe that are entering the world trading system pose new challenges to it. State or political party authorities, which still play an important role in most transitional economies (e.g., through state enterprises, state trading enterprises, and administration of investment requirements and trading rights schemes) inevitably make decisions that are based on considerations

---

[55] See generally, DOHERTY Eileen M. (ed.), **Japanese Investment in Asia: International Production Strategies in a Rapidly Changing World**, Berkeley Roundtable on the International Economy, Berkeley, Ca., 1995.

[56] WILDAVSKY Aaron, **Searching for Safety**, Transaction Books, New Brunswick, 1988.

[57] For economic projections suggesting that the developing countries will benefit less from the Uruguay Round results than the developed countries, see GATT Secretariat, *An Analysis of the Proposed Uruguay Round Agreement With Particular Emphasis on Aspects of Interest to Developing Economies*, MTN.TNC/W/122, MTN.GNG/W/30, Nov. 29, 1993, Special Distribution UR-93-0126, Table 16, at 31; GOLDIN I., KNUDSEN O., & VAN DER MENSBRUGGHE D., **Trade Liberalization: Global Economic Implications**, OECD and World Bank, Paris, 1993.

other than price and may thereby non-transparently defeat the GATT cornerstones of MFN, national treatment, tariff concessions, and quota bans[58]. The relative weakness of legal systems and central government authority in the transitional economies makes compliance with WTO rules difficult. At the same time, political and social dislocations in those countries require a delicate balance between liberalization and continuity.

With so many different interests and national economic systems represented at the multilateral bargaining table, and with economic and political power more dispersed than it was at the founding of the GATT-system, it is not surprising that progress through the traditional multilateralism approach has been moving to face these broad and fundamental challenges more slowly than regional liberalization efforts. The Uruguay Round was a great victory for world trade but it raises questions about the ability of the traditional multilateralism approach to respond quickly or fully to new issues facing the system. More than twenty years will have passed from the US decision to launch what became the Uruguay Round until partial multilateral solution of the problems identified underlying that decision[59], and the next round of multilateral challenges[60] will not be any simpler.

Partly in reaction to frustration at the multilateral level, and partly in response to the preferences made possible by free trade agreements, many countries have turned to regional trading schemes. The consequent regional trade groupings, and the emergence of competition between them, are further straining the WTO system. The European Union is joined by NAFTA, MERCOSUR, the FTAA initiative, APEC, and ASEAN's AFTA, each diverting (or threatening to divert) some trade and investment from countries outside its boundaries — much to the political chagrin of those countries[61]. While low MFN tariffs dampen the

---

[58] See JACKSON John H., *"State Trading and Non-Market Economies"*, in: **The World Trading System**, MIT Press, Cambridge, 1989, especially 283-98. See also CLARKE, **GATT Accession for China?**.

[59] The US Government identified issues for multilateral resolution in 1980; the European Union agreed to a new round in 1982; the Uruguay Round was not concluded until 1994; and the transatlantic powers will have to wait for even partial solutions to key problems like agriculture and intellectual property protection to be implemented after the year 2000. For general background on the history and results of the Uruguay Round, see SCHOTT Jeffrey J., **The Uruguay Round: An Assessment**, Institute for International Economics, Washington, D.C., 1994.

[60] See generally, OECD, *Market Access After the Uruguay Round*.

[61] See generally, OECD, *Regional Integration and the Multilateral Trading System*, especially Ch.VI; STEINBERG Richard H., *"Antidotes to Regionalism: Responses to Trade Diversion Effects of the North American Free Trade Agreement"*, in: **Stanford Journal of International Law.** No.29, 1993, 315, 322-25.

diversion effects of these arrangements[62], tariff peaks and other forms of protection still threaten diversion in certain sectors. Moreover, preferential rules of origin intended to enhance trade and investment diversion exacerbate the associated political tension. Each time a free trade agreement is concluded or expanded, those left outside express concern and complain[63].

For liberal multilateralists, these are disturbing trends, yielding a system facing increasingly serious strains and fractures. And among the world's great powers, Europe and the United States uniquely share many of the same interests in solving common problems with Asian economies whose industrial structures and government-business relationships are fundamentally different from those in the West, integrating the transitional economies into the world trading system, solving trade problems with developing countries, and reducing trade-distorting effect of regionalism. In so far as EU and US policy-makers views their interests along these lines, perceiving these developments as a common external threat, there is a potential for strengthening liberal multilateralism through a transatlantic approach.

C. Barriers to Transatlantic Trade Policy Cooperation: Suggestions from Neorealism, Rationalism, History, and Other Sources

While EU and US interests may be similar, and their combined power great, Europe and the United States face serious cooperation problems in attempts to advance free trade. To neorealists, a lack of cooperation on trade rule-making between great powers in a bipolar system might be a corollary of the deduction that they will balance against each other — but that corollary would have serious weaknesses[64]. To others who have called themselves "modified neorealists," barriers to cooperation among great powers in a multi-polar system would not be surprising; hegemonic stability theory has long predicted that multilateralism would decay into competitive regionalism as global political-economic power has diffused since the close of the Second World War and the new multiple centers of power find it hard to cooperate[65]. More broadly, rational choice theorists have also identified several types of problems that might

---

[62] See STEINBERG, **Antidotes to Regionalism**.
[63] See generally, OECD, *Regional Integration*, especially Ch.VI.
[64] See discussion above at pp.306-307.
[65] See, for example, KRASNER, **State Power**; GILPIN, **War and Change**.

interfere with great power cooperation efforts[66]. In short, there are good reasons to believe that transatlantic cooperation will not be simple and recent history seems to bear that out.

1. Interests in Third Countries Revisited: When Objectives or Salience Differs

When transatlantic efforts have been made to solve third country problems or system-wide problems, cooperation has frequently broken down. The analysis in Part B, above, suggested that US and European interests in third countries are similar, they are, however, rarely identical. These differences in interests often have been exploited by third countries.

For example, from 1994-95, the European Union and the United States each campaigned for further opening of Japan's automobile market. But the specific problems faced by the two auto industries were quite different. European auto-makers had invested substantially in the establishment of dealership and distribution, and their biggest concerns were about Japanese auto parts testing requirements, border inspection procedures that delayed and increased the price of importation into Japan, and other technical regulations[67]. In contrast, US auto-makers had not yet invested substantially in distribution and sales networks and wanted changes in Japanese regulatory business practices that would enable Japanese auto dealers to carry US cars[68]. The United States Government pressured Japan for these changes and Japan resisted. As US pressure was mounting, the Japanese Government reached agreement with the European Union on changes which were of little value to US auto-makers. The European Union simultaneously backed Japanese diplomatic challenges and legal threats against US unilateralism[69]. Eventually, the US Government struck its own deal with Japan[70]. However, there was no transatlantic cooperation in the automobile negotiations with Japan.

---

[66] For examples of analyses of cooperation problems from the rational choice perspective, see SCHELLING Thomas, **The Strategy of Conflict**, Harvard University Press, Cambridge, 1980.

[67] *"Brittan Says EU, Japan Reach 'Breakthrough' on Auto Imports"*, in: **International Trade Report (BNA)** No.12, June 7, 1995, 970.

[68] *"US, European Executives' Views Differ on Framework Agreement"*, in: **Intl. Trade Rep. (BNA)** No.12, Oct.25, 1995, 1769.

[69] *"EU, Japan Reach 'Breakthrough'"*, in: **Intl. Trade Rep. (BNA)** No.12, 970; *"EU Threatens Complaint in WTO if US, Japan Agree on Import Plan"*, in: **Intl. Trade Rep. (BNA)** No.12, May 31, 1995, 918.

[70] *"Japan, US Report on Auto Accord, Say Dispute Is Now Removed from WTO"*, in: **Intl. Trade Rep. (BNA)** No.12, July 12, 1995, 1176.

While the transatlantic powers shared a common goal of liberalizing Japan's auto market, there was little similarity of objectives.

Similarly, cooperation may break down when the transatlantic powers share identical objectives on a third country issue, but the salience of those objectives (relative to objectives on other issues) differs. For example, US negotiators have complained that in the Uruguay Round TRIPs[71] negotiations, the transatlantic powers had agreed to jointly pursue enhanced protection for pharmaceuticals in the regulatory approval pipeline, but the EU abandoned that position in exchange for other concessions from India that it considered more important; the US bargaining position on that issue was thereby ruined and the TRIPs Agreement does not offer the enhanced protection[72].

2. Interests in Third Countries Revisited: The Preferential Liberalization Alternative

A second problem for transatlantic cooperation is that the United States, or European governments, might rather liberalize on a preferential than a multilateral basis. In some circumstances, European countries might prefer to make arrangements with third countries by means of a bilateral arrangement between the European Union and that third country, instead of through the WTO or on an MFN basis. The European Union may offer an attractive alternative to multilateral liberalization for some European producers, in so far as liberalization on that basis enables those producers preferential access to the third country market. Similarly, for US producers, liberalization through NAFTA or on a bilateral basis may be more attractive than multilateral liberalization. In short, this preferential alternative offers some producers in each great power more **absolute** gains than would be enjoyed if liberalization were to take place on a multilateral basis, and more gains **relative** to that of producers from the other great power[73].

For example, the European Union's automobile arrangement with Japan, described above, could be seen as an attempt to secure improved

---

[71] *"Agreement on Trade-Related Aspects of Intellectual Property Rights"*, April 15, 1994, reprinted in: **International Legal Materials** No.33, 1125, 1197.

[72] Julius KATZ, former Deputy United States Trade Representative, interview with author, Washington, D.C., May 1995.

[73] A concern by nation-states with achieving relative gains — in addition to or instead of absolute gains — has often been associated with realism. See, e.g., WALTZ, **Theory of International Relations**, 105; GRIECO Joseph, **Cooperation Among Nations: Europe, America, and Non-Tariff Barriers to Trade**, Cornell University Press, Ithaca, N.Y., 1990, 40-49.

access to Japan's market on a basis that would put Europe's auto-makers on a better footing than US auto-makers. The European Union's association arrangements may be seen in a similar light. Potentially more dangerous, the EU and United States appear in some respects to be rivalling each other to establish preferential arrangements liberalizing substantially all trade with third countries or regions: while the United States is pursuing liberalization with Asia through APEC, the European Union has been arranging its own set of meetings with ASEAN countries, China, Japan, and South Korea; a similar game is being played with Mercosur.

3. Public Goods, Free Rides, and Preferential Third Country Negotiations

A free rider problem — resulting from providing negotiated results on an MFN basis — also inhibits cooperation and may exacerbate the demand for preferential third country negotiations. The European Union and the United States face many trade problems which if resolved on an MFN basis would have the qualities of a public good. When one transatlantic power acts alone to resolve such a problem, and the resolution is on an MFN basis, the other power may simply free ride on the result. For example, in 1994, the European Union refused US requests for help in negotiating improved intellectual property protection in China. In 1995, US negotiators' unilateral tactics resulted in China agreeing to protect intellectual property on an MFN basis and EU negotiators rushed to China to confirm that they would be able to free ride off the US action[74].

One transatlantic power may also adopt the risky tactic of providing diplomatic backing to a third country against the other transatlantic power on an issue, in exchange for some negotiated compensation, and still free ride on the results achieved by the other power. For example, US negotiators were frustrated by EU condemnation of US unilateral pressure on China over intellectual property issues in both 1995 and 1996 and the coincidental announcement of multi-billion dollar Chinese Government contract awards to European companies instead of their US competitors, which some in the United States perceived as Chinese decisions based on non-commercial diplomatic considerations[75].

---

[74] *"China To Apply US Agreement Equally to All Trading Partners, Brittan Says"*, in: **Intl. Trade Rep. (BNA)** No.12, April 26, 1995, 741.

[75] See, e.g., BARNATHAN Joyce, ROBERTS Dexter, BORRUS Amy & EINHORN Bruce, *"China vs. America"*, in: **Business Week**, July 24, 1995, 30.

This free-rider problem creates bilateral diplomatic resentment and is an incentive to fashion deals of interest to both transatlantic powers on a preferential basis. Thus, it is not surprising that some Europeans have expressed concern that the United States may have concluded a preferential bilateral agreement with Korea on access for beef[76] and with Japan on access for semiconductors[77], and some Americans interpreted the EU Commission's 1995 green paper on ways to improve commercial ties with China[78] as an effort by the European Union to achieve preferential access and relationships there.

4. Bilateral Issues and the Infrequency of Linkage: Diverting Attention from Common Third Country Problems

The transatlantic dialogue may be diverted to bilateral issues instead of focusing on shared problems in third countries. Producers on both sides of the Atlantic have plenty of gripes about governments on the other side[79]. This long list of bilateral disagreements might be associated with the fact that EU-US bilateral trade disputes are usually raised one at a time, usually in reaction to a trade measure taken by one side or as an existing practice rises in domestic political importance. Treating each issue independent of others forgoes the possibility of cross-issue linkages that can turn disputes that are seen in zero-sum terms when viewed individually into a positive-sum gain for both sides when considered

---

[76] The agreement is focused on "high quality beef", the definition of which has the effect of including most US beef and excluding most EU beef. Exchange of Notes and Record of Understanding Between the Government of the Republic of Korea and the Government of the United States of America on Beef, April 26, 1990 (on file with author).

[77] *"Arrangement Concerning Trade in Semiconductor Products"*, Sept. 2, 1986, US-Japan, reprinted in: **I.L.M.** No.25, 1986, 1409. For the EU view of the Japan-US semiconductor arrangements, see *"Brittan Says US-Japan Chip Pact Must Go Before ITA Can Arrive"*, in: **European Report**, April 24, 1996.

[78] The green paper is described briefly in *"China To Apply US Agreement"*, in: **Intl. Trade Rep. (BNA)** No.12, 741.

[79] Examples of such bilateral disputes abound: agricultural subsidies and protection, which are not resolved but merely in a cease-fire "peace treaty" period by the terms of Art.13 of the Uruguay Round Agreement on Agriculture, (Agreement on Agriculture, in Final Act Embodying the Results of the Uruguay Round of Multilateral Trade Negotiations (1994)); the EC Broadcast Directive (Council Directive Concerning the Pursuit of Television Broadcasting Activities, Oct. 3, 1989, **I.L.M.** No.28, 1989); subsidies for steel, shipbuilding, and aerospace; intellectual property protection for appellations of origin; shipping services regulations; trade diversion effects of preferential rules of origin; recurrent EU enlargement compensation issues; technical regulations and standards; ecolabelling; and the EC Beef Hormones Directive (Council Directive 88/146/EEC, March 7, 1988, OJ (L 70) 16).

simultaneously[80]. Whatever the cause, the long list of unresolved bilateral trade issues in each power's dossier on the other distracts from a focus on common third country problems.

5. Social Norms and the Black Box of Domestic Politics

The foregoing cooperation problems are generally consistent with the neorealist assumptions that the territorial actors in international relations are each unitary and rational; neorealists recognize that domestic politics and social norms exist, but choose to ignore them for purposes of theory-building[81]. As suggested above, traditional realism does not adhere as strictly to the assumptions that states are unitary and rational actors[82]. Considerations that deviate from those assumptions reveals additional cooperation problems.

First, suspend any assumption that the United States and the European Union are each rational: consider norms. It is not implausible that normative or ideological differences, for example, might explain differences in the tactics by which the European Union and the United States each negotiate with third countries on trade issues (i.e., US use of Section 301[83] versus Europe's less facially confrontational approach). Those differences in tactics might make it difficult to reach transatlantic agreement on an appropriate modality for trade negotiations with third countries.

Second, suspend any assumption that the United States and the European Union are each a unitary actor: open the black box of domestic politics. There are big, powerful interests within each great power that may be able to stop any particular cooperative act between the European Union and the United States. For example, the agriculture lobby in the European Union might well be powerful enough to stop any act of transatlantic cooperation — either bilaterally or with third countries — that were to entail complete agricultural liberalization. This is suggested by the failure to achieve complete agricultural liberalization in the Uruguay

---

[80] To see how the injection of a second issue into a multi-party negotiation may change the prospects for cooperation between the parties, see generally, RAIFFA Howard, **The Art and Science of Negotiation**, Harvard University Press, Cambridge, 1982, especially Parts III and IV.

[81] WALTZ, **Theory of International Relations**, Chs 4 and 5.

[82] See, e.g., Morgenthau's discussions of ideology and domestic politics. MORGENTHAU, **Politics Among Nations**, Ch. 7 (ideology), 134-45, 152-55 (some domestic political factors).

[83] Trade Act of 1974.

Round and by the near collapse of the round over the issue of even partial agricultural liberalization[84].

D. The Prospects for Transatlantic Trade Policy Cooperation: Evaluating Contemporary Transatlantic Trade Policy and Proposals

These cooperation problems could discourage the efficient combination of European and American power necessary to solve third country problems. The view taken here, that the European Union and the United States have market power sufficient to set international trade rules, and that they are the only great powers that share a Western view of liberal multilateralism, suggests that transatlantic cooperation is crucial to advancing liberal multilateralism. Failure to cooperate in advancing that goal, combined with the pursuit by each transatlantic power of its own regional and bilateral policies, would undermine the multilateral system and could well decay into competitive regionalism. However, cooperation problems often can be solved through various mechanisms or institutional arrangements. For example, as suggested above, linkage across issues can turn zero-sum games into positive sum games[85]. Similarly, it is well accepted that prisoners dilemmas may be overcome by arrangements that ensure repeated rounds (a shadow of the future)[86] or that reduce information costs[87]. Hence, transatlantic trade policies could be structured to facilitate liberal multilateral outcomes.

This suggests that it would be useful to evaluate contemporary transatlantic trade policy and proposals from a great power management perspective[88]. Is current transatlantic trade policy consistent with a great power management strategy? What would alternative great power

---

[84] See generally, SCHOTT, **The Uruguay Round**; STEINBERG Richard H., *"The Uruguay Round: A Legal Analysis of the Final Act"*, in: **International Quarterly**, April 1994, 1; PATTERSON Lee Ann, *"EC Agricultural Policy Reform"*, in: **Intl. Org.** No.51, 1997, 135.

[85] See discussion above.

[86] AXELRÓD Robert, **The Evolution of Cooperation**, Basic Books, New York, 1984; SETEAR John, *"An Iterative Perspective on Treaties: A Synthesis of International Relations Theory and International Law"*, in: **Harvard International Law Journal** No.37, 1996, 139.

[87] See, e.g., MILGROM Paul, NORTH Douglass C. & WEINGAST Barry, *"The Role of Institutions in the Revival of Trade: The Law Merchant, Private Judges, and the Champagne Fairs"*, in: **Economics and Politics**, March 1990, 1.

[88] A complete evaluation or test of realism's heuristic power and its application to the postwar history of transatlantic relations would be interesting, but is beyond the scope of this chapter.

management strategies look like? Are such strategies feasible given the kinds of cooperation problems identified above?

1. The State of Play: Current Transatlantic Trade Policy

For the past few decades, Europe and the United States have organized their trade relations and cooperation on common trade problems through summit meetings (now regularly scheduled twice annually), transatlantic cabinet meetings (which used to be regularly scheduled), relatively frequent ministerial and sub-cabinet meetings, normal diplomatic channels, *ad hoc* bureaucratic contacts, and plurilateral vehicles such as Quadrilaterals, G-7 meetings, and OECD activity. This approach has constituted a broad transatlantic trade dialogue that has often successfully resolved trade issues.

But in 1995, in the context of the fiftieth anniversary of the end of the Second World War, leaders on both sides of the Atlantic began championing initiatives to deepen EU-US trade relations. Some called for increasing joint work by civil servants and ministers in Washington and Brussels on specified EU-US trade issues; others called for the negotiation of a Transatlantic Free Trade Agreement (TAFTA); still others for a EU-US "economic space" or "New Transatlantic Marketplace" (NTM) that would progressively eliminate tariff and non-tariff barriers to trade, and would presumably address deeper trade-related policies such as standards, subsidies, intellectual property protection, investment measures, services, and competition policy[89]. There have been two main rationales offered for this flurry of proposals, but the approaches suggested by those rationales have not offered much guidance on how to reconcile a transatlantic initiative with a continued commitment to multilateralism.

Several geostrategic thinkers, particularly foreign ministry-types — including former US Secretary of State Warren Christopher, former British Foreign Secretary Malcolm Rifkind, German Foreign Minister Klaus Kinkel, former British Prime Minister Margaret Thatcher, and Henry Kissinger — have emphasized broad geopolitical and security arguments for deepening transatlantic trade relations (while also employing

---

[89] For examples of this flurry of proposals, see RIFKIND Malcom, *"Practical Steps to Take Toward Global Free Trade"*, in: **Wall Street Journal**, Nov. 30, 1995, A20; *"EU/US: Action Plan Fine-Tuned Before Transatlantic Summit"*, Europe Information Service, Dec. 5, 1995, available in WESTLAW, MAGSPLUS file; GREENHOUSE Steven, *"US to Seek Stronger Trade and Political Ties With Europe"*, in: **New York Times**, May 29, 1995, 3.

other arguments)[90]. Many of them perceive or fear "transatlantic drift" in light of the dissolution of the cold war glue that has helped bind together Europe and the United States and hope to use new economic arrangements to infuse the bilateral relationship with a dose of formal cooperation. Most of them have argued that the increased political commitment by the United States to Europe implicit in NATO expansion will require an economic counterpart to bind together the allies. Many of the Americans among them have suggested that efforts at deeper economic integration will help provide a broad context in which to generate US domestic political support favoring NATO expansion. All of these geostrategic thinkers have endorsed negotiation of a TAFTA (although former Secretary Christopher later backed off of his endorsement).

Several trade and commerce government officials — including former US Commerce Secretary Mickey Kantor, the late US Commerce Secretary Ron Brown, EU External Economic Affairs Commissioner Sir Leon Brittan, and Canadian International Trade Minister Roy Maclaren — as well as EU Commission President Jacques Santer, have focused their arguments for deepening transatlantic economic relations on potential bilateral trade benefits (while acknowledging and supporting other arguments, as well)[91], yet their trade policy recommendations usually have been less ambitious than those of the geostrategists. Economic policy analysts Clyde Prestowitz, Lawrence Chimerine, and Andrew Szamosszegi have estimated that direct static gains from EU-US free trade would equal approximately a half percent increase in the GDP of both the United States and the EU[92] — a modest figure. Yet US and EU trade and commerce ministers have not been willing to commit to the serious negotiations to completely end protectionism bilaterally that

---

[90] See, e.g., Secretary of State Warren CHRISTOPHER, *"Charting a Transatlantic Agenda for the 21st Century"*, address at Casa de America, Madrid, Spain, June 2, 1995, in: **Dispatch**, US Dept. of State, Bureau of Public Affairs, Washington, D.C., July 1995, 1; German Foreign Minister Klaus KINKEL, speech to the Council on Foreign Relations, Chicago, Illinois, April 19, 1995, in: **Germany Suggests Euro-NAFTA Trade Zone**, The Reuter European Community Report, April 19, 1995; BRIMELOW Peter, *"TAFTA?"*, in: **Forbes**, July 1, 1996, 52.

[91] See, e.g., The Right Honorable Sir Leon BRITTAN, *"The EU-US Relationship: Will It Last?"*, speech to the American Club of Brussels, April 27, 1995 (on file with author); Ambassador Michael KANTOR, *"Talking Points"*, American Chamber of Commerce, Brussels, May 22, 1995 (on file with author); Canadian Trade Minister Roy MACLAREN, *"Transatlantic Free Trade?"*, speech to the Royal Institute of International Affairs, May 22, 1995 (on file with author).

[92] PRESTOWITZ Clyde, Jr., CHIMERINE Lawrence & SZAMOSSZEGI Andre Z., *"The Case for a Transatlantic Free Trade Area"*, in: STOKES Bruce (ed.), **Open For Business: Creating a Transatlantic Marketplace**, Council on Foreign Relations, New York, 1996.

would be required to realize even these modest gains. To most veterans of the Uruguay Round, calls for negotiating a TAFTA need to be sobered by the reality of serious domestic political barriers to concluding a TAFTA, particularly in sectors like agriculture, broadcasting, and maritime services. Nonetheless, trade ministry types do see some potential for concluding transatlantic trade arrangements on topics where there is likely to be agreement between businesses on both continents.

The net result of these policy discussions has been the development of a relatively modest program for action in the short term and more ambitious talk about what might be possible in the longer term. In the December 1995 Madrid Summit, the European Union and the United States Government agreed to a New Transatlantic Agenda[93], one part of which commits the Parties to "Contributing to the Expansion of World Trade and Closer Economic Relations"[94]. This recited the Parties' mutual commitment to multilateralism — support for the WTO and the principle of multilateralism generally, and for successfully concluding the WTO Ministerial in Singapore in December 1996, the WTO services negotiations, and the OECD Multilateral Agreement on Investment, in particular.

Perhaps more concretely and substantively, the New Transatlantic Agenda launched several bilateral trade activities, many of which had been recommended by the Trans Atlantic Business Dialogue (TABD), a group of business leaders convened at the behest of EU Commissioners Brittan and Bangemann and the late US Commerce Secretary, Ron Brown. Specifically, the transatlantic powers agreed to: support the negotiation of an Information Technology Agreement, which now has been concluded successfully; reduce technical and non-tariff barriers to trade associated with business regulations in Europe and the United States, including through conclusion of a mutual recognition agreement on conformity assessment; conclude a bilateral customs cooperation and mutual assistance agreement; and establish a joint working group on employment and labor issues.

---

[93] US Information Agency, **The New Transatlantic Agenda**, December 3, 1995 <http://www.usia.gov:80/topics/atlinit/aganda.html>.

[94] The three other planks relate to: *"Promoting Peace and Stability, Democracy and Development Around the World"* — initiatives concerning human rights, Central Europe, Russia, and the Middle East; *"Responding to Global Challenges"* — initiatives concerning terrorism, crime, global environment, and health; and *"Building Bridges Across the Atlantic"* — cultural initiatives. **The New Transatlantic Agenda**.

Most broadly, instead of immediate negotiation of a TAFTA, the New Transatlantic Agenda called for the creation of an NTM that will "progressively eliminate" transatlantic tariff and non-tariff barriers. But the Parties were conveniently vague about the time span for completing liberalization and which barriers will be eliminated. Moreover, some policymakers seem to envision a piecemeal negotiation in which the NTM is built slowly over the course of a decade or more, with successive arrangements concluded issue-by-issue as solutions become feasible. The transatlantic powers are now studying jointly how to build the NTM.

Since the Madrid Summit, work on these areas has moved forward steadily. All of the promised negotiations, studies, and actions have been launched. Progress reports have been issued. But for the most part, little of magnitude has been concluded. The brightest lights have been conclusion of the ITA and the extent of consensus reached among businesses leaders engaging in the TABD, reflected most clearly in their May 1996 Progress Report, which offers dozens of recommendations for reducing transatlantic trade barriers. But even the TABD process will be limited in its impact by virtue of its membership, which by definition excludes other interests — such as organized labor, consumer and environmental groups, and lawyers — that could oppose various recommendations, such as those relating to automobile safety and environmental standards, product liability laws, and pharmaceutical regulation.

While these initiatives for deepening transatlantic trade ties are more modest than the TAFTA or full-scale NTM negotiations advocated by several foreign ministers, developments in 1997 may breathe new life into the transatlantic agenda. As the Clinton Administration considers a course for its second term, it may embrace new trade liberalization initiatives. More significantly, by mid-1997, European and US Heads of State likely will have met to bless NATO enlargement; the need to build and sustain political support for that action is likely to create new demands for improved transatlantic trade ties. The ensuing debate will likely join the familiar geostrategic and bilateral trade-improvement arguments raised in 1995.

These may be useful efforts, reducing inter-regional tension and slowly converging the two powers' positions on some trade issues of multilateral interest (to the extent that transatlantic arrangements approximate or harmonize the EU and US approaches). But the great power management paradigm suggests that transatlantic trade relations should be structured to more effectively and directly address common problems with third countries and manage the multilateral trading system[95]. To date, the policies — and the associated policy debates over reorganizing transatlantic trade relations — have not fully articulated a relationship between transatlanticism and multilateralism. Declarations of support for transatlanticism have been prefaced with a recitation of EU and US commitments to the multilateral system and to the successful conclusion of on-going multilateral negotiations, but there is no plan about how to get there. Transatlantic arrangements can be designed in such a way that they could undermine the multilateral system — or they could be designed to support it. The advancement of liberal multilateralism is not central to the architecture of current transatlantic trade policy. Several alternative policy proposals (which are variants of proposals that have been floated in the last few years) should be evaluated.

2. Alternative One: A Transatlantic Deep Integration Package, Quickly Negotiated

Deep transatlantic integration could serve as a cornerstone of enhanced cooperation and could be structured so as to advance liberal multilateralism. "Deep integration" entails liberalizing substantially all transatlantic trade in goods and services. It includes not only the elimination of **international** trade barriers, such as tariffs and quotas, and the conclusion of agreements on dumping, anti-dumping, subsidies, and countervailing duties issues, but would also address topics often considered **domestic** in nature, such as product standards, domestic regulatory policies, environmental policies, intellectual property, investment rules, competition policy and other domestic trade-related measures[96]. Some proposals for a TAFTA seem to have had transatlantic deep integration in mind[97]. It is shown below that such an exercise in transatlantic deep integration would likely improve transatlantic cooperation in third country

---

[95] Thus far, this set of goals has received only secondary consideration — at best — by EU and US leaders. The objective of improving transatlantic trade cooperation in the WTO and on problems of common interest in third countries has received more serious (though not central) attention in Canadian International Trade Minister Roy Maclaren's speeches. See, for example, Minister MACLAREN's speech to the Royal Institute of International Affairs, May 22, 1995. The third countries problem also received some attention in the EU Commission., Communication from the Commission to the Council, *Europe and the US: The Way Forward,* COM (95) 411, July 1995.

[96] "Deep integration" has been used in the way defined above by many trade analysts. See, e.g., LAWRENCE, **Towards Globally Contestable Markets**.

[97] See, e.g., RIFKIND, **Practical Steps**; Minister MACLAREN's speech to the Royal Institute of International Affairs, May 22, 1995.

negotiations and could be structured to maximize the chances that EU-US deep integration arrangements may become multilateral rules.

The process of negotiating deeper transatlantic integration could offer a means of resolving outstanding bilateral trade disputes. The process of concluding a deep integration package would entail the simultaneous negotiation of outstanding bilateral trade issues, potentially transforming the transatlantic dialogue from a serial bilateral dialogue to a dialogue with cross-issue linkages. As suggested above, this would be significant because a multi-issue trade negotiation (like the NAFTA negotiations or any trade round) can be shaped to yield a political resolution of several problems even when those problems could not be resolved if addressed individually[98].

Successful conclusion of a deep integration package could reduce EU-US trade tension that often inhibits cooperation on third country issues. Deeper transatlantic integration could offer through liberalization not only increased efficiency and welfare, but also a substantial decrease of tension-producing trade and investment diversion associated with the powers' respective regional free trade arrangements, and a resolution of the outstanding EU-US trade disputes that divert EU and US attention from more serious strains on the multilateral system. Conclusion of a transatlantic deep integration package would permit governments to appeal more easily to broad transatlantic political considerations and commitments in rejecting domestic pressure for trade-closing proposals and in efforts to further liberalize trade.

Independent of establishing other mechanisms or institutions to help address common problems with third countries, a transatlantic deep integration package would help make it easier for the two powers to cooperate in efforts to liberalize trade with the rest of the world. By reaching transatlantic agreement on most major trade issues, the two powers will have effectively harmonized their positions and interests on those issues for purposes of negotiations with countries outside the transatlantic region. After complete implementation of a transatlantic deep integration package, bureaucrats and industry in the European Union and the United States will have conformed to the arrangement's rules. There would be relatively few differences in transatlantic interests for other countries to exploit.

---

[98] See text above accompanying note 80.

Perhaps most significantly, a transatlantic deep integration package could be used to build a similar multilateral deep integration package in a relatively passive, non-aggressive manner by simply making the package open for accession (through negotiation) to any country willing to adopt all the arrangements' obligations, an offer to effectively end the risk of trade diversion from the giant transatlantic market in exchange for transforming other national economic systems into conformity with the Western liberal model implicit in the transatlantic package. To be consistent with current WTO rules, a transatlantic deep integration package could offer conditional MFN treatment (i.e., MFN treatment only to signatories which undertake its obligations) only to the extent that the package meets the criteria of GATT Article XXIV and to the extent not otherwise inconsistent with WTO rules. Since a crucial goal should be the establishment of deep integration on a multilateral basis, in negotiating the transatlantic deep integration package, the European Union and the United States should take into account the position of countries outside the transatlantic region before finally agreeing how to resolve each issue.

Ultimately, a transatlantic deep integration arrangement could serve as a means of ratcheting regional liberalization towards multilateral liberalization through joining the world's two most important sets of "hub and spokes" trade regimes. It is possible to see US regional negotiations help liberalize the Western Hemisphere; EU regional negotiations help liberalize Central and Eastern Europe, the Mediterranean, and parts of Africa; and a transatlantic deep integration package eventually might be shaped to serve as a vehicle for merging the two sets of regimes.

In other words, a great power management solution to the apparent contradiction between multilateralism and regionalism might be provided in this manner. But a deep integration arrangement between the European Union and the United States will not be successfully concluded in the short-term. The biggest problem is agriculture: EU intransigence on the topic in the Uruguay Round, France's apparent willingness to invoke the "Luxembourg compromise" to block substantial agricultural liberalization[99], and the EU-US "peace treaty" on agricultural issues through 2004 (embodied in Article 13 the Uruguay Round Agreement on Agriculture) all suggest the difficulty of agreeing on transatlantic agricultural liberalization in the short term. While it is not clear that agriculture needs to be fully liberalized in a deep integration package to satisfy GATT's

---

[99] See *"EC Ministers Instruct Negotiators to Clarify Blair House Accord With US"*, in: **Intl. Trade Rep. (BNA)** No.10, Sept. 22, 1993, 1564.

definition of a "free trade area"[100], it is certain that agricultural issues create a transatlantic political problem that is not easily solved: a deal without agriculture probably will not be acceptable to the US Congress, and a deal with agriculture probably will not be acceptable in Brussels. This does not mean that eventual negotiation of a transatlantic deep integration package is hopeless. Continued US pressure on the subject may help, and as Central European countries join the European Union — especially Poland and Hungary — the continued viability of the CAP will be questioned. Further long-term decline in the value of the dollar would put additional pressure on the CAP. Eventually, the agriculture problem may become more easily solved. However, in the short-term, conclusion of a deep integration package is of questionable feasibility, at best.

3. Alternative Two: A Transatlantic Deep Integration Package, Negotiated Piecemeal

Some policy-makers, recognizing the political constraints on agreeing now to completely eliminate tariff and quota protection on transatlantic trade, are considering deepening transatlantic integration in a piecemeal fashion, element-by-element over time, with no clear establishment of a free trade area at the outset. This appears to be what some policy-makers have in mind when they endorse the negotiation of an NTM that would "progressively eliminate" transatlantic tariff and non-tariff barriers[101].

The current transatlantic attempt to establish stand-alone bilateral agreements on topics that offer mutual benefit — many of which have been recommended by the TABD — will reduce transatlantic tension, facilitate trade, and could be considered part of a piecemeal deep integration process. For example, the effort to reach agreements on mutual recognition of product certification and testing[102] has been partly

---

[100] GATT Article XXIV.8(b) requires that, in creating a free-trade area, trade barriers be eliminated on "substantially all" the trade between the constituent territories. But "substantially all" is not defined and never has been. Moreover, the GATT Contracting Parties consistently approved European Free Trade Area agreements with third countries that expressly excluded agricultural products from liberalization. GATT, *Analytical Index: Guide to GATT Law and Practice*, GATT (6th ed.), Geneva, 1994, 766-69.

[101] See, e.g., *The New Transatlantic Agenda*, adopted in the December 1995 Madrid Summit, especially *"Contributing to the Expansion of World Trade and Closer Economic Relations"*.

[102] See, e.g., *"US, EU Agree on Mutual Recognition of Electronic Products"*, in: **Intl. Trade Rep. (BNA)** No.13, June 19, 1996, 1016.

successful and beneficial to both the European Union and the United States. The same may be said of efforts to negotiate "rules of the road" on relatively technical issues, such as on-going sectoral efforts to harmonize certain technical standards and on-going negotiations on customs matters[103]. Agreements on these topics should be relatively easy to negotiate (compared to topics like agriculture or the EC Broadcast Directive), which is another attraction of the piecemeal deep integration approach.

To a very limited extent, the transatlantic powers could negotiate agreements on important topics not yet covered by the WTO and try to use those elements of a piecemeal deep integration exercise as a basis for further liberalization of world trade and investment. To the extent not inconsistent with WTO rules, each element (presumably established in a stand-alone instrument) could offer MFN and national treatment to third countries only on the condition that they agree to accede to the instrument and undertake its obligations.

The OECD negotiations to create a Multilateral Agreement on Investment (MAI)[104] offer an analogous opportunity: Europe and the United States are intensively negotiating with others in the OECD, an agreement that they intend to sign and use as a basis for later WTO negotiations on the subject. To the extent permitted by WTO rules (the GATS[105] MFN obligation and TRIMs[106] constraints, in particular), the agreement could promise MFN and national treatment on investment only to signatories, thereby creating an incentive for other countries to negotiate accession.

Similarly, a transatlantic agreement on competition policy would not only resolve relatively minor EU-US differences on the topic, it would also coordinate a position that the European Union and the United States could use as a basis for negotiation with third countries and serve as a basis for action against anti-competitive behavior throughout the world.

---

[103] See generally, *"Business Leaders Draft Proposals for US-EU Trans-Atlantic Summit"*, in: **Intl. Trade Rep. (BNA)** No.13, May 29, 1996, 884; *"US, EU Agree to Move Ahead With Information Technology Pact"*, in: **Intl. Trade Rep. (BNA)** No.13, June 19, 1996, 1016.

[104] On the OECD Multilateral Agreement on Investment negotiations generally, see, GRAHAM Edward M. & SAUVE Pierre, **Investment and the New Trade Agenda**, Institute for International Economics, Washington, D.C., December 8, 1995. See also, OECD, *Multilateral Agreement on Investment: Progress Report By the MAI Negotiating Group*, OCDE/GD(96)78, Paris, 1996.

[105] General Agreement on Trade in Services, in Final Act Embodying the Results of the Uruguay Round of Multilateral Trade Negotiations, Annex 1B (1994).

[106] Agreement on Trade-Related Investment Measures, in Final Act Embodying the Results of the Uruguay Round of Multilateral Trade Negotiations, Annex 1A, 1994.

The transatlantic powers might consider building off the EC-US Cooperation Agreement[107], and if a new agreement should embody provisions establishing rules on the extraterritorial application of competition policy[108], define as impermissible specific types of anti-competitive behavior faced by both EU and US exporters, establish special obligations for the extra-jurisdictional production of evidence in competition policy cases, and establish certain presumptions where evidence is not produced or is otherwise difficult to obtain. The US Government would likely have to agree to modify its anti-dumping laws in exchange for a meaningful agreement on competition policy.

But the biggest problem with a piecemeal transatlantic deep integration approach is that it precludes evaluating when the package would constitute a free trade area as defined under Article XXIV, which makes it difficult to determine the extent to which it could deny benefits to non-signatories. In contrast to a quickly concluded deep integration arrangement, which would create a free trade area with WTO-legal preferential arrangements, a transatlantic deep integration package negotiated piecemeal would not become a free trade area within the meaning of GATT Article XXIV until it schedules the liberalization of "substantially all trade" between the EU and the United States. Until it met the terms of Article XXIV, it could offer preferential treatment for US and EU production only to the limited extent that goods, services, investment and competition policy are not covered by WTO MFN obligations; each piecemeal negotiated outcome often would have to be offered to other WTO Members on an MFN basis.

The resulting free-ride would make it difficult to conclude transatlantic deep integration in this manner; many in the United States will be loathe to engage in a process that will allow free-riders. Moreover, the application of unconditional MFN treatment to many of the deep integration elements as they were concluded would be inconsistent with a tenet of the great power management approach: to the extent of the free-ride, the transatlantic powers would not be using their market power to yield multilateral solutions. Unlike the quickly-negotiated deep integration package described above, the piecemeal negotiation of an NTM would have difficulty offering the arrangement's benefits to third

---

[107] Agreement Regarding the Application of Competition Laws, Sept. 23, 1991, US-European Community, reprinted in: **I.L.M.** No.30, 1991, 1491.

[108] For an example of this approach, see *Department of Justice Antitrust Enforcement Guidelines for International Operations*, Department of Justice, Washington, D.C., 1995. On the US approach to extraterritoriality generally, see *Restatement (Third) of the Foreign Relations Law of the United States,* 1987, Secs 400-433.

countries on the condition that they undertake its obligations. Thus, a deep integration package negotiated piecemeal between the transatlantic powers would be far less likely to advance liberal multilateralism than a quickly completed transatlantic deep integration package.

4. Alternative Three: Trilaterals and Other Arrangements Aimed Largely at Third Country Issues

In an effort to reduce strains on the liberal system, the European Union and the United States could consider launching a **set** or **series** of trilateral negotiations in which the transatlantic powers would cooperate in resolving trade tensions they have with various third countries. These negotiations could complement or substitute for the other transregional liberalization strategies described above. A program of trilateral negotiations would have three elements: (1) identification of topics on and countries with which the transatlantic powers should jointly negotiate; (2) identification of whether and how to create linkages across various trilateral negotiations in an effort to enhance the prospects for transatlantic cooperation; and, (3) an effective modality for coordinated action.

Initial topics might include: access to Japan's automobile and electronics industries, competition policy issues in certain countries, bringing China into the WTO, piracy of intellectual property, accelerated implementation of the TRIPs Agreement in certain developing or transitional economies, or liberalization of investment measures in third countries. EU and US interests in these and other issues should be studied further before concluding that these are appropriate for the trilaterals described here, but the potential for the topics identified above to become the focus of trilateral negotiations may be inferred from the substantial agreement among TABD participants that these are third country issues in which European and US businesses have similar interests[109]. For the longer term, the powers should decide on a process for identifying topics appropriate for trilaterals.

Since EU and US interests in these (and other) topics appear to be similar but not identical, and since there is a historical record of transatlantic cooperation problems in negotiating together with third countries, it would be advisable for the European Union and US Government to better understand the cooperation problems they are likely to face in the trilateral negotiation of those topics and then determine how to overcome

---

[109] See *Transatlantic Business Dialogue*, **Progress Report**, Brussels, May 23, 1996 (on file with author).

them. For example, a simultaneous or serial negotiation on several topics may help ensure continued cooperation between the transatlantic powers should either be tempted otherwise to cut its own preferential arrangement with a third country in any particular trilateral negotiation. The wisdom of transatlantic issue linkage across a **set** of trilateral issues, or transatlantic agreement to engage in a **series** of trilateral negotiations on different issues, will vary depending on the transatlantic cooperation problem that has to be resolved. Agreeing in advance to cooperate on a **series** of trilateral negotiations may be useful if the cooperation problem facing any single trilateral may be described as a prisoners' dilemma[110]. Similarly, agreeing in advance to cooperate on the simultaneous negotiation of a **set** of trilateral issues may be useful if the European Union and US Government can create linkages of issue positions across negotiations that assure mutual EU and US support for positions each of which one power would otherwise have little or no interest in supporting[111].

The hardest part will be agreement on an appropriate modality for coordination, given US attachment to Section 301[112] and Europe's disdain for it. One possibility is US agreement to refrain from using Section 301 during a period when the European Union and the United States are effectively coordinating action on a particular topic and country. The USTR could be required to certify occasionally that such coordination is producing positive results; failure to so certify would then require the USTR to treat (or consider treating) the problem under Section 301. This approach likely could be adopted by means of administrative action, requiring no formal Congressional action[113], provided

---

[110] See AXELROD Robert, **The Evolution of Cooperation**, Basic Books, New York, 1984.

[111] See RAIFFA, **Art and Science**.

[112] Trade Act of 1974.

[113] Courts will usually defer to an agency's interpretation of its own statutes, provided that the interpretation does not conflict with a record of Congressional views on the precise issue in question and the interpretation is "permissible." *Chevron v. Natural Resources Defense Council*, 467 US 837 (1984). The proposed approach to administering of Section 301 would not conflict any known record of Congressional views on the precise question and there is no good reason to think that it is an impermissible interpretation of the statute. See Section 301 of the Trade Act of 1974. Moreover, since Section 301 — and the proposed approach to it — involves foreign affairs, the courts might be even more deferential to the Executive Branch than on questions about the administration of statutes involving domestic matters exclusively. On the President's implied constitutionally based power to conduct foreign relations, see generally, *US v. Curtiss-Wright Export Corp.*, 299 US 304, 319 (1936). The US Trade Representative's administration of the "Special 301" statute, which entailed adding two categories of countries under investigation to the single category contemplated by the statute, might also be a useful precedent

that key Congressional leaders could be convinced that the approach is worth a try[114]. Both the European Union and the country that is the focus of the liberalization effort would have incentives to make the negotiations work, since they both dislike the Section 301 approach.

While trilaterals would be the norm, transatlantic cooperation in plurilateral negotiations might be appropriate in some cases. For example, transatlantic cooperation in plurilaterals might be appropriate in cases requiring a coordinated solution among several producer countries; arguably, this is the case in steel[115] and semiconductors[116]. Similarly, plurilateral talks may be required where a sector operates or a product is made across more than one country. Cross-national production networks, and intergovernmental arrangements bolstering those networks, are of increasing importance, particularly in Asia[117]. Two clear examples are the "China circle" of investment and production and the results of ASEAN's brand-to-brand complementarity schemes. These new patterns of production suggest the advisability of negotiating solutions to associated trade problems with more than just the country that is designated as the country of origin. Plurilaterals might also be appropriate when a third country, like Japan, holds significant power with respect to a fourth country; for example, EU-Japan-US cooperation on fourth country issues might be appropriate on issues like investment policy in certain Asian countries

---

for the proposed action. See "Special 301", sec.182 of the Trade Act of 1974, as amended, added by sec.1303 of the *Omnibus Trade and Competitiveness Act of 1988*, Pub. L. 100-418, Aug. 28, 1988, 102 Stat.1107. On the Office of the US Trade Representative's "practice" of maintaining two categories of countries for investigation that are not mentioned in the "Special 301" statute, see Committee on Ways and Means, US House of Representatives, *Overview and Compilation of US Trade Statutes, 1995 Edition*, USGPO, Washington, D.C., August 4, 1995.

[114] Convincing Congressional leaders of the worthiness of the approach is likely a political prerequisite to trying it. Before adopting its creative interpretation of "Special 301", the US Trade Representative consulted carefully with Congressional leaders. Michael BROWNRIGG, former Chief of Staff to US Trade Representative Carla A. Hills, interview with author, Los Angeles, California, April 4, 1997.

[115] Alan W. Wolff and others have argued that most of the world steel market has been effectively cartelized by producers from Europe, Japan, and Korea, and that any solution to the resulting problems for US producers will have to be resolved with representatives from all four countries. See generally, *Volume I: Executive Summary, Prehearing Brief on Behalf of Petitioners (Armco Steel Co., et al.), Certain Flat-Rolled Carbon Steel Products*, before the International Trade Commission, June 18, 1993, final investigation Nos 701-TA-319-332, 334, 336-342, 344, and 347-353, and 731-TA-573-579, 581-593, 594-597, 599-609, and 612-619.

[116] The effort by Korea to participate in the newly-created Semiconductor Council (with the European Union, Japan, and the United States) is consistent with this point. See *"Korea Pledges Tariff Cuts In Bid to Join Semiconductor Council"*, in: **Intl. Trade Rep. (BNA)** No.14, April 9, 1997, 615.

[117] See DOHERTY (ed.), **Japanese Investment in Asia**.

(since Japan is such an important source of investment) or eco-labelling of natural resources from Asia (since Japan is a big consumer of such products).

Where the transatlantic powers can not agree how to jointly solve a common problem in a third country, they could have "rules of the road" to ensure that they do not undercut each others' initiatives there. These rules might include: a commitment to conclude agreements on an MFN basis; a promise to support the goals of a negotiation, even if they disagree on methods; a promise not to formally attack specified approaches that may be used by a transatlantic power in negotiations; and a commitment to continuously consult with each other on the process and progress of negotiations.

5. Alternative Four: Transatlantic Cooperation in the WTO

Europe and the United States might consider reorganizing their cooperation in the WTO on a basis consistent with the great power management paradigm. Their activity could focus on third country problems, which would require deciding the same three issues raised in the context of trilateral negotiations outside the WTO: (1) the topics on which they could cooperate in the WTO (such as, China's accession; competition policy rules; the relationship between GATT 1994 Article XX and multilateral environmental agreements; and accelerated application of TRIPs to developing countries); (2) how to link or sequence negotiations on those topics so as to reduce the chance that third countries could entice one of the great powers into breaking ranks with the other; and, (3) the appropriate modality of coordination.

The most ambitious modality would be initiation of a "deep integration" trade round, building off of a transatlantic deep integration arrangement. More specifically, the transatlantic powers might launch a "deep integration trade round", using their own transatlantic deep integration package as the set of proposed texts to be modified upon better understanding of third country preferences. After appropriate modification, the transatlantic powers could close the deep integration trade round in much the same manner that they closed the Uruguay Round: withdrawing from GATT 1994 (thereby disengaging from its MFN obligation) and signing a new GATT, with its MFN obligation and an associated deep integration package. However, trade ministers and others have emphasized repeatedly of late that "political exhaustion" resulting from a flurry of trade agreements concluded in the last few years preclude launching a new round anytime soon.

In the longer term, the European Union and the United States might consider alternatives to the WTO consensus decision-making practice[118]. The consensus tradition does not reflect the underlying power of the European Union and the United States in world trade affairs. Moreover, it slows the process of further multilateral liberalization and necessitates the kind of power play used to conclude the Uruguay Round and suggested above as a means of concluding a deep integration trade round. Creation of an executive committee could provide a useful forum for regularized management of the WTO[119]. And adoption of a UN Security Council-style voting system[120] — majority rule, with specified members having a veto — could speed up the decision-making process and formalize efficient governance of the WTO[121]. These approaches recognize that the multilateral system has been managed effectively in the last twenty years only through close transatlantic cooperation and coordination. However, such a change is likely to be resisted by third countries that would lose formal power under such rules and by bureaucrats from the WTO and some WTO Members who are part of the epistemic community wed normatively to the consensus decision-making practice.

---

[118] Described in Art.IX.1 of the Agreement Establishing the World Trade Organization.

[119] Proposals for an "executive committee" or "advisory council" of powerful Contracting Parties or member states to lead decision-making in the GATT/WTO were made in 1990-91 in bilateral proposals by the United States to the European Community, and by the United States in Quad country meetings. KATZ, interview. There is precedent for such a decision-making structure: the Governors of the World Bank have delegated many of their powers to a group of Executive Directors. See Articles of Agreement of the International Bank for Reconstruction and Development ("the World Bank"), Art.V, sec.2(b), T.I.A.S. No.1507, 2 U.N.T.S. 134, as amended effective Dec. 17, 1965. Moreover, in conjunction with negotiation of the GATT 1947, the negotiators drafted a charter for an Organization for Trade Cooperation (OTC), which never came into being; the OTC charter provided for an "executive committee" of specially elected members. See JACKSON, **World Trade and the Law of GATT**, 51.

[120] Such a system was proposed to high-level EU negotiators by high-level US negotiators in 1990-91 bilaterals, but was rejected. KATZ, interview.

[121] In contrast to the WTO's consensus decision-making rule, the International Monetary Fund and the World Bank employ weighted voting, which reflects underlying power more accurately. See, e.g., Articles of Agreement of the International Monetary Fund, Art.XII, sec.5, 60 Stat.1401, T.I.A.S. No.1501, 2 U.N.T.S. 39 (1947) [original articles], as amended July 28, 1969, 20 UST. 2775, T.I.A.S. No.6748, 726 U.N.T.S. 266 (1976) [first amendment], and April 1, 1978, 29 UST. 2203, T.I.A.S. No.8937 (1978) [second amendment]; Articles of Agreement of the International Bank for Reconstruction and Development, Art.V, Sec.3.

E. Conclusions:
Answering Traditional Multilateralism's Critiques of Great Power Management and Alternative Futures for Policies and Outcomes

1. Answering Traditional Multilateralism's Critiques

The great power management approach to advancing liberal multilateralism articulated here has engendered objection from some traditional liberal multilateralists[122]. Traditionalists often view the full participation of all countries on an equal footing in the negotiation and adoption of trade rules as linked inextricably to a multilateral outcome and may be nervous about an exercise in great power management. For example, while a transatlantic deep integration package might be structured to encourage the adoption of its rules on a multilateral basis, the contemplated negotiating process clearly does not involve all countries of the world on an equal footing. Hence, traditionalists argue, it would forego the prospect of obtaining consent from third countries to multilateral rules and of obtaining diplomatic support from third countries on bilateral disputes between the European Union and the United States.

While the great power management approach to liberal multilateralism sees little need for participation by less powerful states on an equal footing with great powers, the approach values acceptance of trade rules by all WTO Members — and values participation by all members in the negotiation and drafting of multilateral rules, in so far as rules developed by powerful states should be fine-tuned to account for the domestic political needs of less powerful states. Realism suggests that the United States could not expect important help from diplomatic allies in the WTO on EU-US trade disagreements: to the extent that the European Union and the United States are dominant states in the WTO system, allies matter little[123], since players other than the European Union and the United States will have limited power to affect change[124]. And the idea that the multilateral process might create crosscutting cleavages that would forestall the coalescence of blocs in the WTO assumes that

---

[122] These objections were made in a spirited debate at a meeting on transatlantic economic policy issues at the Council on Foreign Relations, September 27, 1995 in Washington, D.C.

[123] See generally, WALTZ, **Theory of International Relations**, especially 204-209.

[124] However, as suggested above, on some issues, such as investment, Japan is also a powerful player. Hence, it might be useful to pursue trilateral cooperation on those issues.

interests are more or less randomly distributed across WTO Members, which is not the case: countries with similar styles of capitalism, and countries that are members of the same customs union or free trade area, tend to have similar interests in the WTO.

The great power management approach to liberal multilateralism might be preferred over traditional multilateralism on the ground that it is likely to be a more effective way of achieving multilateral outcomes and pursuing liberalization. A realist analysis of power changes in the post-War period supports that argument. Fifty years ago, at the genesis of a GATT system with twenty-two Contracting Parties, few preferential trade areas embedded in it, and the United States as the world's most powerful economic actor, it may have been feasible to pursue multilateral outcomes exclusively through a traditional multilateral process — which the United States could dominate (or afford not to dominate). But the system has evolved. The need for both EU and US support for the Uruguay Round results in order to conclude the Round attests to that.

Moreover, few European or US policy-makers are now in a position to assert that traditional multilateralism is the only appropriate path to follow: they conceived of the power play that closed the Uruguay Round and most of them are championing regional approaches through the EU or NAFTA — simultaneously declaring their support for multilateralism. The traditional multilateral liberalization approach is running a serious risk of being outpaced by the proliferation and deepening of preferential trade areas and by the inclusion of broadly varied types of national economic systems into the liberal multilateral system.

2. Alternative Futures for Policy and the World Trading System

This analysis suggests two alternative futures for the world trading system: great power management or competitive regionalism. Under one scenario, transatlantic cooperation does not move forward, EU-US trade relations become strained increasingly by continuing competition for preferential advantage in negotiations with third countries and by finger-pointing over the slow pace of success in the WTO, and failure by the European Union to help the United States advance liberal multilateralism leaves US trade policy with little choice other than to resort to a unilateral and regional strategy. The multilateral trading system fractures into competitive regionalism.

Under a happier scenario, the transatlantic powers cooperate in the short term on a set or series of third country problems, agreeing on appropriate topics and modalities for such negotiations. In a decade or so, when political roadblocks may have been lifted, they negotiate a deep integration package between them and present it (subject to fine-tuning) as a *fait accompli* to the rest of the world; either as the basis of a WTO deep integration round or as open to third countries conditioned on their willingness to undertake its obligations. EU-US deep integration would thus become the basis of deeper liberalization on a multilateral basis and would diffuse or eliminate the tension associated with inter-regional competition. In the future, the transatlantic powers might also champion changes in WTO decision-making rules to reflect transatlantic power. The current policy initiative — piecemeal negotiation of deep transatlantic integration, suggested by the NTM — is unlikely to leverage the concerted transatlantic power necessary to affect third country liberalization.

Thus, this analysis suggests the importance of reorganizing the ways the European Union and the United States can cooperate to advance liberal multilateralism. But it also suggests the difficulty of sustaining the cooperation required to do so. In the near term, uncertainty about the future of multilateralism will prevail: the transatlantic powers will find it in their interest to pursue simultaneously bilateral and regional policies, as well as liberalization efforts in the WTO and through some transatlantic action. In that context it will remain unclear what the future holds: transatlantic cooperation that will buttress liberal multilateralism or a decay in cooperation that will catalyze competitive regionalism.

PART II

REGIONAL AND MULTILATERAL TRADE RULES: SELECTED ISSUES

The second chapter of the book presents a comparative analysis of the treatment of selected issues under the major regional trade agreements in the world and their relation with existing or emerging multilateral rules: rules of origin; dumping, subsidies and anti-competitive practices; government procurement; services and investment; intellectual property rights; social protection and social clause; environmental standards; national treatment, mutual recognition and legislative harmonization; dispute settlement mechanism.

For those "new issues" likely to be on the agenda of future WTO rounds, the contributions seek to determine whether some of the solutions found at the regional level could be applied at the multilateral level.

Rules of Origin
in Regional Trade Agreements

David PALMETER

Graham & James LLP, Washington, D.C.

Overview

Regional trade agreements are proliferating for important economic and political reasons, and possibly for less important reasons as well. There does seem to be an element of a craze or a fad in the seemingly never-ending stream of new regional acronyms. The regional "bandwagon" is nothing if not popular.

Regional agreements are not new, however. They have been around for a long time. The United States of America (US) is a customs union, although it is much more than that as well. The European Union (EU) is also a customs union, though it is not a political union in the sense of the United States. Nevertheless, the EU is far more than a free trade area, and far more than the free trade area established by the North American Free Trade Agreement (NAFTA). Using just these three examples, we may say that there is a continuum from a free trade area, such as NAFTA, to a political union such as the United States and that the European Union is somewhere between them. At some point on that continuum, the relevant inquiry is as much, if not more, political as economic. Insights on the advantages and drawbacks of being at one point rather than at another on the continuum are more likely to come from political philosophers like Locke and Montesquieu than from economists like Smith and Ricardo. Decisions by governments to join or establish regional agreements may be based more on perceived political advantage, and less on perceived comparative advantage.

When governments establish a minimalist regional agreement, a free trade area (FTA), a prosaic but important detail takes on a degree of importance which is not as significant in more complex, or deeper, forms of regional integration. This detail is the need for rules of origin.

Since the sole purpose of a free trade area is to confer a tariff preference for the products of its members, rules are needed to determine whether products are indeed products of its members and, therefore, entitled to the preference. These rules — rules of origin — determine whether a product "originates" in the territory of a member of the free trade area for purposes of this preference.

Rules of origin take on a high degree of importance in free trade areas because, in FTAs, each member retains its own external tariff. If rules did not specify the steps needed to confer origin, goods from nonmembers would enter the territory of a higher tariff FTA member through the country with the lowest tariff, a process sometimes called "trade deflection". Customs unions avoid deflection by maintaining a common external tariff.

Since FTAs confer tariff preferences only on the products of their members, they also, of necessity, discriminate against the products of nonmembers. A more accurate term for an FTA, therefore, would be "PTA" for "preferential trade area" — or, perhaps, "DTA" for "discriminatory trade area". Similarly, a more accurate term for "rules of origin" in an FTA would be "rules of preference" because these rules are used to determine origin for purposes of the preference only. When it is necessary to determine origin for non-preferential purposes, different rules are usually used. International non-preferential rules of origin are the subject of the harmonization negotiations presently under way in the World Customs Organization (WCO) (originally, Customs Cooperation Council) which will give substance to the World Trade Organization's Agreement on Rules of Origin.

Although FTAs require rules of origin, there is a problem: there is no completely satisfactory rule of origin. Every methodology used has its shortcomings, and there are advantages and disadvantages for each method. Adoption of one particular rule of origin simply amounts to acceptance of one set of shortcomings rather than another. Some rules of origin, however, have more shortcomings than others.

Section A of this paper will examine different rules or methods used to determine origin. Section B outlines the rules of origin contained in some important regional agreements. Section C will discuss harmonization of rules of origin, while Section D will address some of the policy issues that arise in the context of rules of origin.

A. *Methods of Determining Origin*

1. Change in Tariff Classification

Under a rule based on the change in tariff classification, an article completed in one country from materials originating in another will be deemed to originate in the country of completion if the processing there is sufficient to change the tariff classification of the imported materials to a specified degree.

This method — sometimes called "tariff-shift" or Change in Tariff Heading (CTH) — appears to be the wave of the future in rules of origin, at least insofar as international agreements are concerned. It generally is the basis of the WCO harmonization effort, and it is the basis of most important regional agreements.

CTH is based on the widely-used Harmonized Commodity Description and Coding System ("Harmonized System" or "HTS"), which classifies articles at a two-digit chapter level, a four-digit heading level, a six-digit subheading level, or an eight-digit statistical level. Origin will be conferred if the final product is classified in a tariff category that differs in a specified way from the classification of the imported input.

A prosaic example from the Canada-US FTA (CUSFTA) and its NAFTA counterpart will illustrate the process, and some of the problems with the tariff-shift system:

> Tomato catsup is classified in Chapter 21 of the HTS, under item 2103.20, while tomato paste is classified in Chapter 20, under HTS item 2002.90. The FTA rule of origin provides that the operations necessary to convert a product classified in any chapter other than Chapter 21 into a product classified in that chapter will confer preferential origin on the Chapter 21 product. Thus, tomato catsup (Chapter 21) produced from imported tomato paste (Chapter 20) originates where the catsup is produced for FTA preference purposes.

> Under NAFTA, however, the rule is different. Conversion of tomato paste imported from outside NAFTA into tomato catsup within NAFTA will not confer origin on the catsup for preferential purposes. The formulation of the rule is that a change to item 2103.20 (tomato catsup) from any other chapter — except

subheading 2002.90 (tomato paste) — will confer origin. Thus, if fresh tomatoes (item 0702) are converted to tomato paste within NAFTA, and the paste then is made into catsup, also within NAFTA, the catsup would qualify for the preference; but if the paste is imported, the preference for catsup will be denied.

These two different rules demonstrate some of the advantages and some of the disadvantages of the tariff-shift system. Among the advantages is the fact that once a rule is decided, it can be stated clearly and unambiguously, and it is easy for those in the trade to learn. The disadvantage lies in the method by which the substance of the specific rule is decided. With tariff-shift there is no single "rule" of origin, such as a rule that states that any change at the two-digit, or the four-digit, or the six-digit level will confer origin. The CUSFTA and the NAFTA use changes at all of these levels, and at the eight-digit level as well, to determine origin, depending upon the product. Instead of a general rule or principle of origin, there are hundreds of individual rules in each of the agreements[1].

This absence of a general rule or principle for determining origin is perhaps the major shortcoming of tariff-shift, one that would be no surprise to political "realists" or to economists of the public-choice persuasion. It renders rules of origin susceptible to capture by industries interested in minimizing their exposure to competition. In NAFTA, in the case of tomato catsup, it was apparently easy for an industry interested in minimizing competition from tomato paste outside the three-country area to fashion a product-specific rule denying the preference to catsup made from the imported tomato paste. There is no other apparent reason for the change in NAFTA from the CUSFTA rule. In 1992, it so happens, Chile was the leading foreign supplier of tomato paste to the United States. Thus Chilean tomato paste can be used in catsup that will enjoy preferential treatment under the FTA, but none of it will have that privilege under NAFTA. It so happens that Mexico was the second leading supplier of tomato paste to the United States in 1992[2].

---

[1] By one count, the CUSFTA contains 1,498 separate rules of origin spread among the twenty pages of the relevant annex to the FTA. See, PALMETER David, *"The FTA Rules of Origin: Boon or Boondoggle?"*, in: DEARDEN, HART & STEGER (eds), **Living with Free Trade: Canada, the Free Trade Agreement and the GATT**, Institute for Research on Public Policy and Centre for Trade Policy and Law, Ottawa, 1989, 41, 47. There appears to be no public count of the number of separate rules of origin in the NAFTA, but the number of pages in the relevant annex (Annex 401) listing the specific rules is 148 (pp.3-150). Extrapolation would suggest, therefore, that the number is in excess of 11,000.

[2] In 1992, according to statistics published by the US Department of Commerce, the United States imported 22,112 metric tons of tomato paste, 8,754 (39.6% of the total) from Chile and 61,634 (30.0% of the total) from Mexico.

These facts would seem to justify the tentative assumption that the rule was changed at the behest of the Mexican producers of tomatoes or tomato paste, who presumably would benefit at the expense of their competitors in Chile. But this assumption depends upon further assumptions, such as the assumption that most tomato catsup in the NAFTA is made outside Mexico, that the Most Favored Nation (MFN) duty rate in Mexico for catsup is significant compared to the advantages the NAFTA preference would offer, and that the Mexican market is important to the catsup producers in Canada and the United States. Otherwise, Canadian and US producers of catsup might not find the NAFTA benefits significant enough to switch from their current Chilean suppliers of tomato paste.

The very fact that we are only able to speculate about the "policy" behind this particular rule illustrates the ease with which rules of origin based on tariff-shift may be captured by specific companies or industries. The stated rules are, superficially, comprehensible to all, but their rationale rarely is. The rules of origin for tomato catsup in the FTA and the NAFTA are stated clearly and unambiguously, but the rationale is apparent for neither. And, while we may speculate, we do not know, and probably would have difficulty learning, the rationale for the change from the FTA rule to the NAFTA rule.

Tariff schedules are lengthy, complex, tedious documents. A section of a tariff schedule generally will be comprehensible only to those familiar in detail with the products, processes, and economics of the industry. The hundreds of pages and thousands of lines of a tariff schedule offer countless opportunities for similar rules, rules that sometimes may amount to a covenant not to compete.

The tariff-shift rule also presumes that origin can be determined by a quick glance at the tariff schedule. Very often this will be the case. The rule for tomato catsup is clear, even if its rationale is not. But sometimes a glance at the tariff schedule will not produce a clear answer because it is not always apparent where in the tariff schedule a particular item should be classified. Tariff classification disputes have been a mainstay of the practice of customs lawyers for generations, and they are likely to continue their support of the legal profession so long as preferences make classification economically important.

Another problem with tariff-shift is its tendency to become outdated if the underlying tariff schedule is not kept up-to-date. When dealing with a particular product area, tariff schedules usually specify the major products within the area, and then provide a "basket" heading for all other related products. In rapidly developing product areas, there is a tendency for the trade to move into the basket category as newly-developed products replace those listed in the schedule. This problem can be remedied by keeping the tariff schedule up-to-date, but if the tariff schedule involved requires international negotiation, this may not always be easy. What industries in one country may see as "updating", industries in another may see as a threat. It seems unlikely that any significant change would be made in a tariff schedule without the concurrence of the industries concerned, effectively giving a veto to those who believe they would face increased competition as a result of the change.

Finally, the tariff-shift methodology can be burdensome and expensive. Producers must maintain records establishing the tariff classification not only of the finished product, but also of all raw and intermediate materials imported from third countries. A study in the 1980s estimated that the costs of the border formalities needed to administer this system amount to at least three percent of the value of the goods concerned, while the total economic cost amounted to at least five percent of that value. This burden was enough to lead European exporters of up to 25 percent of presumably EC-EFTA eligible trade to forego the preference and simply pay the MFN duty[3].

2. Value Added

The requirement that a minimum value be added to imported materials to confer origin for the finished product on the importing country may be employed as a separate rule of origin or in conjunction with another rule. Because processing and assembly operations often do not result in meaningful tariff changes when parts and components are assembled into a final product, value added often is used to supplement tariff-shift.

Like tariff-shift, value added has the advantage of being a rule that may be stated plainly and unambiguously, but also, like tariff-shift, value added may be more certain in its statement than in its application. And, while tariff-shift is subject to capture by special interests, value added may avoid capture by anyone, including governments, and that, too, can be a problem.

---

[3] HERIN Jan, *"Rules of Origin and Differences between Tariff Levels in EFTA and in the EC"*, **Occasional Paper** No.13, European Free Trade Association, 1986.

346

The statement of a value added "rule" is simple; for example, 40 percent of the value must be added in a country before origin will be conferred on that country. But calculation of value added frequently depends upon resolution of complex or controversial accounting issues. This adds both cost and uncertainty. Lengthy and costly audits are an inherent part of any rule based on value added since the claims of exporters must be verified. These impose a continuing administrative cost well beyond that which prevails with other rules of origin. Uncertainty is heightened under a value added system because origin is never finally determined until audits are completed — a process that can take years. If the auditors disagree with the calculations of the parties, enormous, unexpected demands for payment of duties may result. Whatever else value added may be as a rule of origin, certain and efficient it is not.

Perhaps most importantly, under value added rules of origin may change in unpredictable and uncontrollable ways. It may change from one day to the next because of fluctuations in exchange rates or in materials costs. Moreover, operations that will confer origin when performed in one country may not do so when performed in another because of different labor costs. In NAFTA, for example, origin — and preference eligibility — will be conferred more easily under value added on higher-wage Canadian and United States operations than on lower-wage Mexican operations. In this way, a value added rule may distort economic efficiencies and divert investment from where it might otherwise occur, and where it may be most needed.

3. Specified Process

Under a specified process system rules are drawn in terms of particular industrial operations. The system shares with tariff-shift the advantages of a clear and unambiguous statement of individual rules, but it also shares with tariff-shift the problem of obsolescence, as technical developments may tend to overtake the texts of specific rules. More importantly, specified process shares with tariff-shift a susceptibility of capture by those industries that do not always view trade expansion as a worthy goal. When governments base rules on the details of industrial processes, the industries concerned are likely to have a major influence in the formulation of these rules. Industries, after all, will have more expertise than governments in their own processes.

Specified process rules are dissimilar to tariff-shift rules in at least one important respect; they are not based on an agreed set of descriptions, such as a common tariff schedule. Therefore, they are likely to be even more difficult to negotiate in a multilateral context. To the extent that specified process rules of origin are used in free trade agreements, they seem to be used, as they are in NAFTA, primarily as a supplement to other rules.

4. Substantial Transformation

The basic rule of origin used in the United States is the "substantial transformation" rule. Strictly speaking, all rules of origin are substantial transformation rules — the substantiality of a transformation being defined by change in tariff heading, or by value added, or by specified processes. As the term "substantial transformation" is used in the United States, however, it has come to mean the determination of origin on a case-by-case basis, a methodology congenial to common-law legal systems. Its advantages are those of that system; the slow, incremental development of the rule built upon its application to specific factual situations, and reasoning from case to case[4].

By building upon precedent, reasoning by analogy, and taking one step at a time, such a system can establish sound, predictable rules. Nevertheless, the system has been criticized as inherently imprecise and subjective[5]. This debate, however, is irrelevant to the question of a rule of origin for a free trade area. Regardless of whether the substantial transformation case works well within a particular national legal system, it would be difficult to use as an international standard[6]. A substantial transformation rule based on the common-law case method will succeed only if there is, at the top of the system, a court charged ultimately with deciding appealed cases, thereby creating the case law upon which the system depends. No such international court exists, nor is one likely to

---

[4] "It is a three-step process described by the doctrine of precedent in which a proposition descriptive of the first case is made into a rule of law and then applied to a next similar situation. The steps are these: similarity is seen between cases; next the rule of law inherent in the first case is announced; then the rule of law is made applicable to the second case.", in: LEVI Edward H., **An Introduction to Legal Reasoning**, Chicago, 1949, at 1-2.

[5] SIMPSON John P., *"Reforming Rules of Origin"*, in: **Journal of Commerce**, October 4, 1988, p.12A, col.2.

[6] However, on May 24, 1996 Chairman Philip CRANE of the House Ways & Means Committee Subcommittee on Trade, in a letter to Acting United States Trade Representative (USTR) Charlene BARSHEFSKY, was critical of the US emphasis on the tariff-shift approach to rules of origin in the harmonization exercise and suggested that the traditional US test might be advanced instead, although he acknowledged that such an approach is "problematic at the international level". **Inside US Trade**, Vol.14 No.23, June 7, 1996, p.11.

be established for a free trade area. Consequently, substantial transformation is likely to be unworkable as a rule of origin for a free trade area.

B. Examples of Rules of Origin in Regional Agreements

1. Andean Group

The signatories of the Cartagena Agreement, establishing the Andean Group (Bolivia, Colombia, Ecuador, Peru, and Venezuela) have established rules of origin based on tariff-shift, supplemented generally by a 50 percent value added rule[7].

2. ASEAN Free Trade Area

The 1992 Agreement on the Common Effective Preferential Tariff (CEPT) scheme for the ASEAN Free Trade Area provides that a product shall be deemed to be originating from ASEAN member states if at least 40 percent of its content originates from any member state[8].

3. Australia-New Zealand Closer Economic Relationship

The 1983 Australia-New Zealand Closer Economic Relationship (CER) relies on a 50 percent value added standard. It also requires that the last process performed in the manufacture of the eighteen goods involved to be performed in the territory of the exporting member state[9].

4. Canada-United States Free Trade Agreement

The primary rule of origin in the Canada-United States Free Trade Agreement is change in tariff heading. This is supplemented by a 50 percent value added test for many products[10].

---

[7] Andean Group, Commission Decision 293 — Special Norms for Determining the Origin of Goods (March 21, 1991), **International Legal Materials** Vol.32, 1993, p.172. The value added rule specifies that "In the case of Bolivia and Ecuador this percentage shall be 60 percent." (Article 1(e)). It is not clear from this translated text whether goods from Bolivia and Ecuador shall be subjected to this higher amount, or whether Bolivia and Ecuador may apply this higher amount to goods from other members of the Group.

[8] Fourth ACP-EEC Convention, Protocol 1 Concerning the Definition of the Concept of "Originating Products" and Methods of Administrative Cooperation, **OJ** (1990) L84/8.

[9] STEELE Keith & MOULIS Daniel, *"Country of Origin: The Australian Experience"*, in: BOURGEOIS, VERMULST & WAER (eds), **Rules of Origin in International Trade: A Comparative Study**, University of Michigan Press, 1993.

[10] Canada-United States Free Trade Agreement, Part II, Chapter 3.

5. European Communities Association Accords

The EC has a variety of preferential trade arrangements which may be considered regional, such as the agreements with the countries of the European Free Trade Area (EFTA), the African, Caribbean and Pacific Countries (ACP), the Mashreq countries (Egypt, Jordan, Lebanon, and Syria) and the Maghreb countries (Algeria, Morocco, and Tunisia). The rules of origin vary somewhat from agreement to agreement, but in general they are based on tariff-shift supplemented by specified processing requirements and, in some cases, value added[11].

6. European Free Trade Association

As noted above, the rule of origin used by EFTA is based on specified process supplemented by a 50 percent value added test for certain products. The EFTA rule is a liberal tariff-shift system because most of the specified processes are described in four-digit HTS terms. Conversion of materials not falling within a four-digit classification into an article in that classification generally will suffice to confer preferential EFTA origin[12].

7. Israel-United States Free Trade Agreement

The 1985 Israel-US FTA uses the common-law substantial transformation test, apparently the only free trade agreement to do so. It also contains a 35 percent value added requirement. For purposes of calculating the 35 percent, the value of products of the other party may be counted for as much as 15 percent of the final value, thereby reducing the value added requirement to as low as 20 percent[13]. These rules parallel the rules of origin for the Caribbean Basin Initiative[14].

8. *Mercado Común del Sur* (Mercosur)

The Treaty of Asunción, establishing Mercosur among Argentina, Brazil, Paraguay, and Uruguay, establishes an origin rule based on tariff-

---

[11] WAER Paul, *"EC Rules of Origin"*, in: BOURGEOIS, VERMULST & WAER (eds), **Rules of Origin in International Trade: A Comparative Study**, University of Michigan Press, 1993.

[12] Convention Establishing the European Free Trade Association (Stockholm, January 4, 1960), Article 4, Annex B, Schedule I.

[13] Israel-United States: Free Trade Agreement, in: **International Legal Materials** Vol.24, Annex 3:5, p.653.

[14] Caribbean Basin Economic Recovery Act, Pub. L. No.98-67, tit.III, subtit.A, 97 Stat.369, 384-395 (codified as amended at 19 U.S.C.A. §§2701-2706).

shift, supplemented with a 50 percent value added requirement for processing operations. The Mercosur tariff-shift rule is based on the tariff nomenclature of the Latin American Integration Association[15].

9. North American Free Trade Agreement

NAFTA, as discussed, uses tariff-shift as the primary rule of origin, supplemented by value added and — particularly in textiles, apparel, and electronic products — by specified process.

C. Harmonization of Rules of Origin

The proliferation of different rules of origin has led to a number of attempts to harmonize them, but virtually no progress was made until the Uruguay Round. In 1976, the Organization for Economic Cooperation and Development (OECD) produced a compendium of rules of origin used by OECD countries. This compendium was followed by the United Nations Conference on Trade and Development in preparing a 1982 compendium dealing with rules of origin applicable to developing countries under different preference arrangements. In 1982 the Customs Cooperation Council (CCC) produced a comparative study of rules of origin[16].

Earlier, in 1973, the CCC approved the Kyoto Convention which was designed to simplify and harmonize general customs procedures, including rules of origin. However, the Kyoto Convention merely describes origin systems in use and does not set forth mandatory requirements. In 1981, the Secretariat of the General Agreement on Tariffs and Trade (GATT) prepared a note on rules of origin, and, in 1982, ministers agreed to study the rules of origin used by GATT's Contracting Parties[17].

Not much more was heard of rules of origin internationally until well into the Uruguay Round negotiations, but in the late 1980s, developments in three important areas served to focus more attention on the problems posed by rules of origin: (1) increased use of preferential trading arrangements, including regional arrangements, with varying rules of origin; (2) an increased number of origin disputes growing out of quota

---

[15] See, Argentina-Brazil-Paraguay-Uruguay: Treaty Establishing a Common Market, in: **International Legal Materials** Vol.31, Annex II, p.1041.

[16] See, United States International Trade Commission, *The Impact of Rules of Origin on US Imports and Exports*, **USITC Pub.**, May 1985, p.1695.

[17] *Ibid.*

arrangements, such as the Multifibre Arrangement and the "voluntary" steel export restraints applicable to the United States; and (3) increased use of anti-dumping laws and subsequent claims of "circumvention" of anti-dumping restraints through the use of third-country facilities.

In September 1989 the United States submitted a comprehensive proposal concerning rules of origin in GATT[18]. The Uruguay Round Agreement on Rules of Origin basically follows the procedures outlined in the US proposal. It establishes a three-year work program to harmonize non-preferential rules. The technical work is presently being conducted by a WTO Technical Committee, in conjunction with the World Customs Organization, on a product-sector basis, following the nomenclature of the Harmonized System. The agreement, of course, applies to all rules of origin used in non-preferential commercial policy instruments, thus retaining the distinction between rules of origin and rules of preference.

D. Policy Issues

1. Rules of Origin and "Directly Unproductive Profit-seeking" (DUP) Activities

Brian Hindley has observed that: "persons who are in favor of an active and "strong" trade policy are likely to favor rules of origin that foreign producers can satisfy only with difficulty and considerable expense. Protectionist policies will not hit their targets squarely without such rules of origin."[19]

"Strong" rules of origin have been used increasingly in recent years for trade restricting purposes[20]. Frequently this has been in the context of anti-dumping investigations. At other times the issue has been quota eligibility, particularly for textiles, apparel, and steel products. As production has increasingly become globalized, rules of origin have increasingly become an effective protectionist weapon.

Free trade areas, however, are not intended to be protectionist. Their very purpose is to create trade, not restrict it. Yet free trade areas can be

---

[18] This is described in PALMETER N. David, *"The US Rules of Origin Proposal to GATT: Monotheism or Polytheism?"*, in: **Journal of World Trade** Vol.24 No.2, April 1990, p.25.

[19] HINDLEY Brian, *"Foreign Direct Investment: The Effects of Rules of Origin"*, **Discussion Paper** 30, Royal Institute of International Affairs, 1990, at 13.

[20] See, PALMETER N. David, *"Rules of Origin or Rules of Restriction: A Commentary on a New Form of Protectionism"*, in: **Fordham International Law Journal** Vol.11, 1987, p.1.

more trade-diverting than trade-creating, and rules of origin can further trade diversion at the expense of trade creation. It is possible, for example, that producers of tomato catsup in the United States and Canada will import more tomato paste from all sources than they do now and, thereby, increase overall trade. It is also possible, however, that they will merely substitute Mexican tomato paste for Chilean tomato paste and, thereby, simply divert trade.

Whether trade diversion was or was not the intended result of the catsup-tomato paste rule of NAFTA, the potential for trade diversion in regional arrangements is very great. The formulation of product-specific rules of origin is, by its nature, very much out of the practical control of generalists, which is to say government officials at the policy level, and very much in the practical control of specialists, which is to say the representatives of concerned industries. An industry will support a preferential trade pact only if its particular rule of origin is to its liking. Rarely will there be any effective opposition. The most likely opposition to one country's advocates of a trade restrictive or diverting rule is another country's industry which would benefit from a liberal rule. No doubt at times supporters of a liberal rule have prevailed. But often the solution is likely to be the one reached in the CUSFTA, which holds that the transformation of fresh milk into aged cheese does not substantially transform the milk and, therefore, does not confer origin. Here, the Canadian and US dairy industries effectively said to each other: you stay on your side of the border and we will stay on ours. And the governments ratified that agreement.

Rules of this kind result from what Jadish Bhagwati calls "Directly Unproductive Profit-seeking (DUP) activities". Quite appropriately, he pronounces "DUP" as "dupe"[21]. Examples of DUP activities given by Bhagwati include:

(1) tariff-seeking lobbying that is aimed at earning pecuniary income by changing the tariff and, therefore, factor incomes;

(2) revenue-seeking lobbying that seeks to divert government revenues towards oneself;

(3) monopoly-seeking lobbying whose objective is to create an artificial monopoly that generates rent;

---

[21] BHAGWATI Jadish, *"Directly Unproductive Profit-Seeking (DUP) Activities"*, in: EATWELL J. (ed.), **The New Palgrave Dictionary of Economics**, Stockton Press, 1987, pp.845-847, reprinted in: IRWIN Douglas A. (Ed.), **Political Economy and International Economics** MIT Press, 1991, p.129.

(4) tariff-evasion or smuggling that *de facto* reduces the tariff (or quota) and generates returns by exploiting the subsequent price differential between the tariff-inclusive legal and the tariff-free illegal imports[22].

To this list might be added rules of origin lobbying in free trade agreements, the objective of which is to: (1) increase one's own exports at the expense of more competitive suppliers outside the free trade area; (2) block increased competitive imports from within the free trade area; (3) tailor the rule so that one's own specific multi-country operations benefit from the preference, while those of one's competitors do not (this may be particularly easy to do with complex, high-technology products); and, (4) if all else fails, support a rule that effectively blocks trade.

Of the various methods for formulating origin rules, tariff-shift and specified process are particularly susceptible to this kind of manipulation. Unfortunately, tariff-shift is otherwise the most practical basis for establishing rules of origin for free trade areas. Consequently, governments, whose interest is in liberalizing trade through free trade areas, must guard against the frustration of their policies by those who do not share their interests. As Ambassador Richard Gardner has observed: "For political reasons, the reduction in trade barriers which takes place in [preferential trade areas] will probably do more to give the participating countries sheltered markets against the outside world than it does to stimulate vigorous competition between them."[23] Rules of origin are a major weapon in the arsenal of those who wish to do this.

2. Freer Trade through Complexity

Rules of origin can be used to divert or limit trade in free trade agreements only to the extent that origin is important economically. If MFN tariffs are high, origin is important; if quotas restrict imports from outside countries, origin may be even more important.

By the same token, rules of origin add complexity to the trading system, and complexity serves only to add cost and to inhibit trade. In the preferential EC-EFTA trade, as we have noted, the total economic cost of rules of origin has been estimated at five percent of the value of the

---

[22] *Ibid.*

[23] GARDNER Richard N., **Sterling-dollar Diplomacy in Current Perspective**, Columbia University Press, 1980, p.14.

traded goods, leading exporters of up to 25 percent of the presumably eligible trade to forego the preference and simply pay the MFN duty[24].

This suggests that the way to reduce the risk that rules of origin will do more than "give the participating countries sheltered markets against the outside world" than they do "to stimulate vigorous competition between them" is to continue with multilateral efforts to reduce MFN trade barriers, even as regional free trade agreements are being pursued. If the multilateral effort is undertaken successfully, at some point, more and more exporters in the free trade area will take the option some of the EC and EFTA exporters have taken and will simply ignore the preference as something that costs more than it is worth. The free trade area then would become irrelevant, and that — paradoxically — would be the result most in line with the trade-creating goals of the designers of free trade areas.

Summary and Conclusion

Rules of origin — or, more accurately, rules of preference — are necessary for free trade areas. They establish which goods are entitled to the preference and which are not. No method of determining origin is completely satisfactory, but for free trade areas, tariff-shift is probably the best. Tariff-shift, however, is particularly susceptible to influence by special interests who prefer to divert or restrict trade and, therefore, frustrate governmental policies behind the negotiation of free trade agreements — freer trade among the members of the agreement, and, therefore, freer trade overall. Rules of origin also add to the cost of trade by adding further administrative complexity to the process. The best way to overcome these problems and to further the goals of a free trade agreement is, paradoxically, to reduce the importance of that agreement and, consequently, the importance of rules of origin by also reducing barriers to trade from sources outside the free trade area.

---

[24] HERIN, *supra*, note 3.

COMMENTS

Edurne NAVARRO VARONA

Boden, de Bandt, de Brauw, Jeantet, Lagerlöf & Uría,
Brussels

Introduction

As a compliment to the overview on the rules of origin regulations throughout the world provided by Mr. Palmeter, some further comments will be added in the following paper on two issues which deserve a closer look.

Firstly, the harmonization of rules of origin agreed in the Uruguay Round, and particularly both how such agreement was influenced by preexisting preferential rules of origin and how preferential rules of origin may in the future be affected by the World Trade Organization (WTO) agreement; and secondly, the origin of services.

Harmonization of Rules of Origin Agreed in the Uruguay Round; Preferential Rules of Origin

In the framework of the discussion on which this seminar is focusing, that is the interaction between regional trade agreements and multilateral rules it is interesting to recall how the agreement on rules of origin was reached in the Uruguay Round[1].

---

[1] See E. NAVARRO VARONA, *"Rules of Origin in the GATT"*, in: E. VERMULST, P. WAER & J. BOURGEOIS (eds), **Rules of Origin in International Trade**, 1993, p.364.

The said agreement established the basis for a harmonization of rules of origin at a multilateral level. The scope of the harmonization was however limited to the non-preferential rules of origin, that is those applying in the commercial relations between countries not benefiting from preferential treatment. However, it is interesting to note that the model of rules established for the harmonization was to a large extent inspired in the model of rules of origin which were being applied in preferential agreements.

Indeed, the change of tariff classification position, on which the WTO harmonization system is based, was mostly being applied in preferential agreements, both by the US and the EC.

However, no consensus was reached at the Uruguay Round to harmonize preferential rules of origin. This is understandable to the extent that preferential rules of origin are basically diverse to the extent that they reflect particular relationships between certain states. However, an annex to the agreement included some nonbinding general principles for preferential rules of origin, which were basically inspired from the principles which had been set for non-preferential rules.

It is, however, interesting to note that while the negotiations to establish the harmonized non-preferential rules of origin are still undergoing (the agreement established a three-year period to reach the harmonization), some countries have already expressed their desire to bring their preferential rules of origin to some extent in line with the principles established in the Harmonization Agreement.

In this sense, the EC is analysing the possibility of harmonizing its preferential rules of origin, bringing them all under the same set of principles which would simplify the current situation, and are likely to be influenced or follow the principles set in the Harmonization Agreement. Similar discussions are underway in the US.

Although the harmonization process is still far from being complete, it is a clear example of circular influences, in which the regional agreements have inspired the multilateral rules and these, at the same time, will influence rules set in regional agreements.

Origin of Services

Another interesting question is that related to the origin of services. The issue is to a large extent an academic one, since no "rules of origin for services", as such, have yet been adopted.

The issue has been addressed by several scholars[2], and was even the object of a study circulated by the GATT Secretariat as an internal document during the Uruguay Round[3]. Furthermore, some rules, although not defined as "rules of origin", in fact seek to solve the problem of identifying the origin of services.

The question has, so far, arisen essentially in the framework of regional agreements[4], but should be expected to be dealt with at a multilateral level, particularly as a progressive liberalization of services has been agreed within the WTO (General Agreement on Trade and Services, GATS).

Indeed, when faced with a liberalization from which only certain countries may benefit, the problem of determining who should benefit therefore arises. This was the situation which originally lead to the need to establish rules of origin for goods. The same question has appeared in relation to services although only to a limited extent, so far, given the traditional local scope of services.

The progressive expansion of international trade in services has lead to the establishment of certain rules which could be called "of origin" for services in regional agreements. Such has been the case, for instance, in the audiovisual services in the EC, where Directive 89/552/EEC[5] established certain quotas for European television programmes to be shown on TV in the EC. In order to determine which programmes are to be considered "European" certain principles are established in Article 6 of the directive; according to the nationality of the participants in the production, the nationality of the producers, etc. Similar principles have been

---

[2] B. HOEKMAN, *"Rules of Origin for Goods and Services; Conceptual Issues and Economic Considerations"*, in: **Journal of World Trade**, No.4, 1993, p.81; E. NAVARRO VARONA, *Las Reglas de Origen para las Mercancías y los Servicios en la CE, EE.UU. y el GATT*, Civitas, Madrid, 1995, pp.183 ff.

[3] *"Rules of Origin and Services: Conceptual Issues"*, MTN.GNS/W/140, October 15, 1991.

[4] The EC, US-Israel FTA, US-Canada FTA, NAFTA or the Australia-New Zealand Trade Agreement on Closer Economic Relations (ANZCERTA) have included provisions on the liberalization of services at a regional level. See E.H. FRY & L.H. RADEBAUGH (eds), **The Canada/US Free Trade Agreement: The Impact on Services Industries**, 1988; Ch. JOLIVET, *"Traitement national : pilier de la réglementation du commerce des services dans l'Accord canado-américain de libre-échange"*, in : **Canada-US Business Law Review**, No.3, 1991, p.209; H.G. BROADMAN, *"International Trade and Investment in Services: A Comparative Analysis of the NAFTA"*, in: **The International Lawyer**, 1993, p.623; G. THOMSON, *"A Single Market for Goods and Services in the Antipodes"*, in: **World Economy**, No.2, 1989, p.207.

[5] **OJ** 1989 L 298/23; see Proposal for amendment, **OJ** 1996 C 221/10.

established in Canada for TV and radio programmes. Rules have also been established in relation to air carriers, for which liberalization has been set in the EC, in order to limit the scope of those who can benefit therefrom[6].

It should, however, be noted that the question has also been addressed in a non-preferential framework, in the context of anti-dumping and countervailing duties[7]. Indeed, to the extent that anti-dumping duties may be imposed on services[8], it may become relevant to determine the origin of the service on which such duties should be imposed.

Generally, the principle followed to determine the "origin of a service" has been based on the **person** (natural or legal) who renders the service, and its link to a particular country. This would imply that, for instance for legal persons, the constitution of a subsidiary in a certain country would be sufficient to grant that company a right to benefit from the liberalization to which the nationals of that country are entitled.

However, in some cases, precisely in order to avoid abuses, reciprocity requirements have been established in order to impede the nationals of a country which keeps its doors closed, from benefiting from the liberalization which is taking place elsewhere. In this sense, the EC Second Banking Directive (89/646)[9] and Second Life Insurance Directive (90/619)[10] allow restrictions on the establishment in the EU of third country banking or insurance undertakings if reciprocity is not

---

[6] Regulation 2343/90, **OJ** 1990 L 218/8; Regulation 294/91, **OJ** 1991 L 36/1.

[7] See H. KUBO, *"Can Antidumping Law Apply to Trade in Services?"*, in: **Michigan Journal of International Law**, 1991, pp.868-869.

[8] In relation to maritime transport see EC Regulation 4057/86 (**OJ** 1986 L 378/14), which has however received limited application (Regulation 15/89, Hyundai Merchant Maritime Company Ltd., **OJ** 1989 L 4/1). In this respect see also P. BENTLEY & M. RONAYNE, *"Anti-Dumping Extended to Shipping Prices"*, in: **European Law Review**, 1987, p.212; W. ESLNER, *"Unfair Pricing Practices in Maritime Transport"*, in: **European Transport Law**, 1988, p.590; J.F. BELLIS, E. VERMULST & Ph. MUSQUAR, *"The New EEC Regulation on Unfair Pricing Practices in Maritime Transport: A Forerunner of the Extension of Unfair Trade Concepts to Services?"*, in: **Journal of World Trade**, No.1, 1988, p.47; D.S. SMITH, *"The EEC's Unfair Pricing Practices Regulation: New Wave of Competition or Protectionism in Community Shipping?"*, in: **Fordham International Law Journal**, 1988, p.883; S.D. YI & Ch.J. CHOI, *"The Community's Unfair Pricing Practices in the Maritime Transport Sector"*, in: **European Law Review**, 1991, p.279.
As to the problems arisen in other sectors, see C. HOSKINS, R. MIRUS & W. ROZEBOOM, *"US Television Programs in the International Market: Unfair Pricing"*, in: **Journal of Communications**, 1989, p.55.

[9] **OJ** 1989 L 386/1.

[10] **OJ** 1990 L 330/50.

granted to EU undertakings in that third country. So, for example, if Japan did not grant EU banks free access into Japan, restrictions could be applied on the establishment in the EU of a subsidiary of a Japanese bank, even though the subsidiary will otherwise be treated as a EU national.

Another problem that may arise is that related to some kind of "circumvention" in services, for instance, would a US subsidiary of a Japanese bank have free access to the EU or would it face restrictions because of the nationality of its holding company? In this respect the US-Canada FTA (Article 1406) and the Australia-New Zealand Closer Economic Relations Trade Agreement (ANZCERTA) (Article 14 of the Protocol on Trade of Services) included a provision which allowed the denial of preferential treatment (and, therefore, free access) to services which, although apparently rendered by an undertaking from one of the member states, were in fact being provided from a third country. Under such provisions it may be necessary to determine when a service is actually provided "from" one of the Party states entitled to preferential treatment.

In some cases, where several persons intervene to provide a service, it could be useful to identify certain key roles according to which origin could be determined (as it has been done in the determination of the origin of audiovisual services).

However, criteria different from the one related to the person rendering the service could be taken into consideration. In this sense, criteria related to the instruments used for providing the service could be considered, such as the country in which a boat or an aeroplane used for a transport service are registered (such criteria having also been used in order to determine the origin of fisheries)[11].

At a multilateral level, the question remains open and will have to be faced in coming negotiations. It could again be expected that the experience from regional agreements determining the "origin" of services will be of use to establish multilateral rules.

---

[11] See EC Regulation 4055/86, **OJ** 1986 L 378/1 and Regulation 3577/92, **OJ** 1992 L 364/7, on maritime transport.

The Treatment of Dumping, Subsidies and Anti-competitive Practices in Regional Trade Agreements

Jean-François BELLIS

Maître de Conférences, University of Liège;
Partner, Van Bael & Bellis, Brussels

As traditional trade barriers have come down as a result of the successive GATT Rounds, anti-dumping has taken on an increasing importance in international trade relations. The number of anti-dumping measures in force has considerably increased in the last fifteen years. The club of anti-dumping users is no longer confined to the four traditional users — the US, the EC, Australia and Canada — but now encompasses an increasing number of newly industrialized countries. This worldwide explosion in anti-dumping activity explains why anti-dumping turned out to be such a controversial issue in the Uruguay Round negotiations, even assuming for a few days in December 1993 the status of a potential "deal breaker". The result of these negotiations has been a revised Anti-Dumping Agreement which has introduced a number of technical changes but has left largely untouched the basic foundations of the anti-dumping instrument.

The second subject discussed in this paper — subsidies — has been much less controversial. Probably reflecting the more limited use of anti-subsidy proceedings as a trade policy instrument, the Uruguay Round negotiations on the Agreement on Subsidies was much smoother. It produced a definition of the term "subsidies" largely inspired by the countervailing duty practice of the US, the dominant user of anti-subsidy proceedings, but, at the same time, it legitimized certain forms of subsidization in which the EC had a keen interest, in particular regional subsidies.

In contrast to dumping and subsidies, which are covered by multilateral WTO rules, the third subject discussed in this paper — anticompetitive practices — is still characterized by a multilateral legal vacuum. Since the abandonment of the Havana Charter, whose Chapter V dealt with "restrictive business practices", no attempt has been made to introduce binding multilateral competition rules. This situation might change soon as the last few years have witnessed renewed interest in developing a multilateral framework for competition policy. Interestingly enough, some of the proponents of multilateral competition rules openly advocate the replacement of anti-dumping laws with competition laws which they consider to be a superior instrument to deal with the issue of dumping.

Despite their diversity, the rules governing dumping, subsidies and anti-competitive practices have one common object: they all seek to define the boundaries of what constitutes "fair competition". In that sense, they are interrelated.

The purpose of this paper is to analyze the treatment of dumping, subsidies and anti-competitive practices in a few selected regional trade agreements, namely, the network of regional trade agreements entered into by the EC[1], the North American Free Trade Agreement (NAFTA) and the Australia-New Zealand Closer Economic Relations Trade Agreement (ANZCERTA or CER). Apart from presenting a comparative perspective, the main object of this paper will be to discuss to what extent these various attempts to define rules of fair competition at the regional level provide lessons that could be used to deal with the emerging issue of trade and competition rules in the WTO context.

I. DUMPING, SUBSIDIES AND ANTI-COMPETITIVE PRACTICES IN SELECTED REGIONAL TRADE AGREEMENTS

A. *The Network of Regional Trade Agreements Entered Into by the EC*

Over the years, the EC has entered into a large number of regional agreements providing for the liberalization of trade usually in the form

---

[1] In view of its highly specific nature, the EC itself is not analyzed as a regional trade agreement for the purpose of this study.

of a free trade area or, for example, in the case of Turkey, that of a customs union[2]. All those agreements contain provisions dealing with dumping, subsidies and anti-competitive practices. The analysis below will focus on four agreements:

i) the early free trade agreements of the type entered into, for instance, with the EFTA countries in the seventies;

ii) the more ambitious free trade agreements conceived as a forerunner to possible accession to the Community concluded with Eastern European countries, the "Europe Agreements";

iii) the European Economic Area Agreement (EEA);

iv) the final phase of the Customs Union with Turkey, which entered into force on December 31, 1995.

1. The Early Free Trade Agreements with the European Free Trade Association Countries

The free trade agreements concluded in 1972-1973 between the EC and the European Free Trade Association (EFTA) countries[3] contain provisions on dumping, subsidies and anti-competitive practices which have been reproduced in many subsequent agreements.

As regards anti-dumping, the agreements authorize the adoption of anti-dumping measures in accordance with Article VI of GATT subject only to a simple consultation procedure within the Joint Committee entrusted with the implementation of the agreement[4].

On the issue of anti-competitive practices and subsidies, the agreements contain a provision declaring that the following practices are "incompatible with the proper functioning of the agreement in so far as they may affect trade between the Community (and the EFTA country concerned):

(i)   all agreements between undertakings, decisions by associations of undertakings and concerted practices between undertakings

---

[2] Customs union agreements have also been concluded by the EC with Cyprus, Malta, Andorra and San Marino.

[3] *Austria*, signed on July 22, 1972, **OJ** (1972) L 300/2; *Finland*, signed on October 5, 1973, **OJ** (1973) L 328/2; *Iceland*, signed on July 22, 1972, **OJ** (1972) L 301/2; *Norway*, signed on May 14, 1973, **OJ** (1973) L 171/2; *Portugal*, signed on July 22, 1972, **OJ** (1972) L 301/165; *Sweden*, signed on July 22, 1972, **OJ** (1972) L 300/97; *Switzerland*, signed on July 22, 1972, **OJ** (1972) L 300/ 189.

[4] Article 27 of the agreements with the EFTA countries except Portugal (Art.30) and Iceland (Art.28).

which have as their object or effect the prevention, restriction or distortion of competition as regards the production of or trade in goods;

(ii) abuse by one or more undertakings of a dominant position in the territories of the Contracting Parties as a whole or in a substantial part thereof;

(iii) any public aid which distorts or threatens to distort competition by favouring certain undertakings or the production of certain goods."[5]

In the event that practices incompatible with the proper functioning of the agreement are entered into in the territory of one Contracting Party, the other may refer the matter to the Joint Committee. If the Contracting Party concerned fails to eliminate the practice within the period fixed by the Joint Committee or if no agreement can be reached by the Joint Committee within three months of the referral, the other Contracting Party may adopt safeguard measures and in particular withdraw tariff concessions[6].

The provision on anti-competitive practices in the agreements with the EFTA countries was not frequently relied upon. The Community apparently referred to this provision in one instance only. At the 5th June 1995 meeting of the EC-Switzerland Joint Committee, the Community delegation expressed concern over the difficulties encountered by the Commission in the course of its investigations in the *Hoffmann-La Roche* Case as a result of Article 273 of the Swiss Penal Code relating to business secrets. The Community delegation stated that Article 23 of the EC-Switzerland Agreement imposed upon the Contracting Parties a duty to ensure the accessibility of the other Party to information concerning

---

[5] Article 23 of the agreements with the EFTA countries except Portugal (Art.26) and Iceland (Art.24). Note that the Community, when signing the agreements with the EFTA countries and Israel, made a declaration on the restrictive practices clause. That declaration, which was annexed to each of the agreements, reads as follows:

"The European Economic Community declares that in the context of the autonomous implementation of Article 23(1) of the Agreement which is incumbent on the Contracting Parties, it will assess any practices contrary to that Article on the basis of criteria arising from the application of the rules of Articles 85, 86, 90 and 92 of the Treaty establishing the European Economic Community."

See also on this matter the Commission's *Second Report on Competition Policy* (April 1973), pp.16-17.

[6] Article 27 of the agreements with the EFTA countries except Portugal (Art.30) and Iceland (Art.28).

possible antitrust violations. The Swiss authorities, however, were not asked to take any specific action with respect to the matter[7].

It is interesting to note that the free trade agreements with the EFTA countries approach the issue of subsidies, referred to as "public aid", as a form of anti-competitive practice to be treated in the same way as restrictive agreements or abuses of a dominant position without any reference to the procedures organized by the GATT Subsidies Agreement. Relatively few cases of public aid have been dealt with in the context of the free trade agreements with the EFTA countries, however. The most spectacular one has been that involving subsidies granted to Chrysler by the Austrian authorities in which the European Commission proposed in 1992 the imposition of a countervailing duty of 22 percent on imports of Chrysler Voyager minivans[8]. As a result of a compromise arrangement concluded at the last minute with the Austrian authorities, the EC eventually refrained from imposing any countervailing duty[9].

2. The Europe Agreements

The Europe Agreements have substantively taken over the provisions concerning anti-competitive practices, public aid and dumping found in the free trade agreements of the type concluded with the EFTA countries[10]. The main difference is the amount of detail introduced into the

---

[7] European Parliament Debates, Jan. 12, 1977, p.111, cited by HUNNINGS, *"Enforceability of the EEC-EFTA Free Trade Agreements"*, in: **European Law Review** No.2, 1977, pp.163-170. The circumstances under which the Community delegation had recourse to Article 23 (the so-called "Adams affair") are described in Mr. Hunnings' article at pp.169-171.

[8] *European Report*, September 9, 1992. The Commission investigated this matter as a result of a complaint lodged by Renault. The complaint alleged that the Austrian government had lured the Chrysler investment project away from Portugal and Spain which were constrained by the EC's strict state aid rules. The Commission proposed to impose a countervailing duty of 22% corresponding to the difference between the 33% subsidy granted to Chrysler and the 8-10% EC-permitted ceiling on investment aid. This figure was reduced to 10% to take account of parts originating in the EC that were incorporated in the Chrysler minivan.

[9] The compromise reached on November 25, 1992 between the EC and the Austrian government provided that Chrysler would put in escrow 43 million of the 100 million USD subsidy received from the Austrian government. This amount could be used by Chrysler only if it decided to double the capacity of its plant. If not, the money would go to the Austrian government. The amount of 43 million USD is based on the rationale that Austria should be allowed to provide a subsidy to Chrysler not exceeding 14.4% of the investment amount. This figure is itself the result of a compromise since the Commission's initial determination was that the subsidy could not exceed 10% of the investment. See **Associated Press**, December 2, 1992.

[10] *Poland*, signed on December 16, 1991, **OJ** (1993) L 348/1; *Hungary*, signed on December 16, 1991, **OJ** (1993) L 347/1; *Czech Republic*, signed on October 4, 1993, **OJ** (1994) L 360/1; *Slovak Republic*, signed on October 4, 1993, **OJ** (1994) L 359/1;

Europe Agreements concerning the implementation of competition rules by the Parties.

For instance, Article 62(4) of each agreement provides that during the first five years after the entry into force of the agreement, any public aid granted by the Eastern European country concerned shall be assessed taking into account the fact that such countries shall be regarded as an area identical to those areas of the Community described in Article 92(3)(a) of the EC Treaty. Each Party is also required to report annually to the other Party on the total amount and the distribution of the aid given. Unlike the free trade agreements with the EFTA countries, the Europe Agreements make it clear that, as long as no specific rules for the implementation of the provisions on public aid are adopted, the provisions of the GATT Agreement on Subsidies will be applicable.

As regards anti-competitive practices, the Europe Agreements provide for the adoption of implementing rules[11]. Such rules have already been adopted in the context of the Agreements with the Czech Republic, Poland and the Slovak Republic[12]. They define the respective competences of the European Commission and the competition authorities of the Eastern European country concerned but make it clear that both authorities shall settle the cases in accordance with their own substantive rules.

The rationale for the higher degree of detail found in the Europe Agreements with respect to anti-competitive practices and state aids is that these agreements have been designed as a first step toward accession of these Eastern European countries to the Community in a relatively near future. An attempt has therefore been made to integrate these countries to some extent within the scope of the existing Community competition policy, including the state aid rules. This objective was not present when the free trade agreements with the EFTA countries were concluded in the early seventies: these agreements were conceived as an alternative to the common market rather than as an antechamber to accession to the Community by the EFTA countries.

Romania, signed on February 1st, 1993, **OJ** (1994) L 357/1; *Bulgaria*, signed on March 8, 1993, **OJ** (1994) L 358/1; *Latvia*, signed on June 12, 1995, not yet published; *Estonia*, signed on June 12, 1995, not yet published; *Lithuania*, signed on June 12, 1995, not yet published; *Slovenia*, signed on June 10, 1996, not yet published.

[11] Article 62(3).

[12] *Czech Republic*, **OJ** (1996) L 31/21; *Poland*, **OJ** (1996) L 208/24; *Slovak Republic*, **OJ** (1996) L 295/25.

3. The European Economic Area (EEA)

The first, and thus far, only regional trade agreement concluded by the EC in which anti-dumping and countervailing duty rules were substituted for by competition rules is the EEA Agreement which entered into force on January 1st, 1994.

Article 26 of the EEA Agreement states that:

> Anti-dumping measures, countervailing duties and measures against illicit commercial practices attributable to third countries shall not be applied in relations between Contracting Parties unless otherwise specified in this agreement.

Protocol 13 on "the non-application of anti-dumping and countervailing measures" provides that:

> The application of Article 26 of this Agreement is limited to the areas covered by the provisions of this Agreement in which the Community *acquis* is fully integrated into this Agreement.

> Moreover, unless other solutions are agreed upon by the Contracting Parties, its application is without prejudice to any measures which may be introduced by the Contracting Parties to avoid circumvention of the following measures aimed at third countries:
> - anti-dumping measures;
> - countervailing duties;
> - measures against illicit commercial practices attributable to third countries.

a) "Community acquis"

Initially, the Community was not prepared to abandon a possible recourse to anti-dumping measures in the event that dumped imports from EFTA countries caused injury to a Community industry[13]. The EFTA countries' position was that dumping is the result of price discrimination between national markets made possible by the existence of a protected domestic market. Since, due to the provisions of the free movement of goods, import duties and charges having equivalent effect as well as quantitative restrictions and measures having equivalent effect would

---

[13] In fact, the Commission has initiated several proceedings against EFTA countries in the last few years, e.g. the 1991 *Silicon Carbide* proceeding against Norway, **OJ** (1991) C 279/11, and the 1992 *Ferrosilicon* proceeding against Norway, Iceland and Sweden, **OJ** (1992) C 115/2.

disappear with respect to originating products, domestic markets would no longer be closed off so as to enable dumping. With regard to restrictions on market access resulting from anti-competitive practices of domestic producers, the EFTA countries argued that these should be dealt with in the same way as the Community would deal with intra-Community dumping, that is, by the application of competition rules.

Since the EEA Agreement, apart from certain institutional aspects, was designed to create within the EEA almost the same degree of economic integration as within the Community itself, the Community eventually accepted the principle of the non-application of anti-dumping measures against EEA originating products[14]. The only sector not to benefit from this exemption was the fisheries sector in which the Community regulatory regime was not integrated into the agreement. As a matter of fact, the Commission initiated in August 1996 an anti-dumping and a countervailing duty proceedings concerning imports of salmon from Norway[15].

b) Anti-circumvention

The second paragraph of Protocol 13 to the EEA Agreement states that Article 26 does not prevent the Contracting Parties from adopting anti-circumvention measures. If the non-application of anti-dumping measures to EEA originating products were to enable third country producers to circumvent anti-dumping measures against direct imports from the third country concerned, the Community would thus be free to take measures. It is not clear whether this provision was absolutely necessary since Article 26 is restricted to EEA originating products. Since, as illustrated by the criteria set out in Article 13 of the EC Anti-Dumping Regulation, "circumvention" in the context of anti-dumping refers to practices whereby products subject to anti-dumping measures are exported in the form of parts for ultimate assembly in the Community or a third country, it is unlikely that products meeting the severe preferential origin requirements of the EEA Agreement could ever be found to "circumvent" EC anti-dumping measures in that sense.

---

[14] All pending anti-dumping measures involving EFTA countries were suspended as of January 1st, 1994 (Regulation No.5/94 of December 22, 1993 on the suspension of the anti-dumping measures against EFTA countries, **OJ** (1994) L 3/1). The proceeding against *Silicon Carbide* from Norway was later terminated (**OJ** (1994) L 94/32).

[15] **OJ** (1996) C 253/18 and 20.

c) Competition Rules

The EEA Agreement contains rules on competition which are identical to those in the EC Treaty. They prohibit, as incompatible with the functioning of the agreement, all agreements between undertakings, decisions by associations of undertakings and concerted practices which may affect trade between the Contracting Parties and which have as their object of effect the prevention, restriction or distortion of competition within the EEA. The rules also prohibit any abuse by one or more undertakings of a dominant position on the EEA market or a substantial part of it in so far as it may affect trade between the Contracting Parties[16].

In addition, concentrations of undertakings, which create or strengthen a dominant position through which effective competition would be significantly impeded within the EEA or a substantial part of it, shall be declared incompatible with the agreement[17].

Rules are also laid down on public undertakings, obliging the Contracting Parties not to enact or maintain any measures contrary to the rules in the agreement and in particular to the competition rules thereof[18]. Complex rules are also provided for the division of competences between the surveillance authorities within the EEA, i.e. the EC Commission and the EFTA Surveillance Authority (ESA), the institution equivalent to the European Commission for the EFTA pillar of the EEA[19].

Finally, the agreement contains rules of competition in the field of state aid, providing, *inter alia*, that aid which distorts or threatens to distort competition by favouring certain undertakings or the production of certain goods shall, in so far as it affects trade between the Contracting Parties, be incompatible with the functioning of the agreement[20].

---

[16] Article 53(1) and 54. See CHARLTON Helen, *"EC Competition Law: The New Regime under the EEA Agreement"*, in: **European Competition Law Report** No.2, 1994, p.55; ROUAM Claude, *"Remarques générales sur les règles de concurrence dans l'EEE"* and *"Aides d'Etat"*, in : JACOT-GUILLARMOD Olivier (ed.), **Accord EEE - Commentaires et réflexions**, 1992; RUSSOTTO Jean, *"Le régime des règles de concurrence (Art.53-56 EEE)"*, in: *ibidem*; MACH Olivier, *"Droit des ententes (Art.85 CEE/Art.53 EEE)"* and *"Le contrôle des concentrations (Art.57 EEE)"*, in: *ibidem*; NORBERG Sven *et al.*, **EEA Law - A Commentary on the EEA Agreement**, 1993, Chapters XIV-5.7 and XX.

[17] Article 57(1).

[18] Article 59.

[19] Articles 55, 56, 57(2) and 58.

[20] Articles 61 to 64.

4. Customs Union with Turkey

a) The Association Agreement with Turkey

On September 12, 1963, the European Economic Community, on the one hand, and Turkey, on the other hand, signed an agreement establishing an association between the two Parties[21]. The agreement entered into force on December 1st, 1964. While the preamble and text of the agreement expressly provide for possible future accession of Turkey to the EC at a later date, the aim of the agreement is to promote trade and economic relations between the Parties through the progressive establishment of a customs union.

With a view to the establishment of a customs union, the agreement provides that the association between the Parties comprises:

i) a preparatory stage, during which Turkey strengthened, with aid from the EC, its economy so as to enable it to fulfill the obligations of the following stages;

ii) a transitional stage, during which the Parties should progressively establish a customs union between them and closely align their economic policies; and,

iii) a final stage, based on the customs union and during which the Parties should closely coordinate their economic policies.

Under the Association Agreement, each Party retains its capacity to adopt anti-dumping measures during the transitional period. The agreement, however, provides for a specific information and consultation procedure between the Parties. According to Article 47 of the Additional Protocol[22], if, on application by a Party, the Association Council finds that dumping is being practised in trade between the Community and Turkey, it will address recommendations to the person or persons with whom such practices originate for the purpose of putting an end to them.

However, where the Association Council has taken no decision within three months from the date of the application or despite the issue of recommendations the dumping practices continue, the injured Party may,

---

[21] **OJ** (1964) L 217.

[22] For the purpose of implementing the transitional stage during which a customs union was to be progressively established, the Parties signed on November 23, 1970 an Additional Protocol determining the conditions, arrangements and timetables for such implementation. The Additional Protocol, which is annexed to the agreement, entered into force on January 1st, 1973.

after notifying the Association Council, take appropriate protective measures. In addition, where the interests of the injured Party call for immediate action, that Party may, after informing the Association Council, introduce interim protective measures which may include anti-dumping duties. Such interim protective measures cannot remain in force more than three months from the date of the application or from the date on which the injured Party takes protective measures.

When protective measures or interim protective measures have been taken, the Association Council may at any time decide that such measures shall be suspended pending the issue of recommendations or may recommend their abolition or amendment.

b) The Decision Implementing
   the Final Phase of the Customs Union

On 6 March 1995, the EC-Turkey Association Council adopted Decision No.1/95 laying down the rules for implementing the final phase of the customs union foreseen in the Association Agreement ("the Decision")[23]. The Decision entered into force on December 31st, 1995.

The Decision lays down a principle of harmonization whereby, in areas of direct relevance to the operation of the customs union, Turkish legislation must be harmonized as far as possible with Community legislation. The Decision regards as areas of direct relevance to the operation of the customs union the following: commercial policy and agreements with third countries comprising a commercial dimension for industrial products, legislation on the abolition of technical barriers to trade in industrial products, competition and industrial and intellectual property law and customs legislation[24].

With regard to trade protection measures, the Decision provides that, upon the request of either Party, the Association Council will review the principle of application of trade defence instruments other than safeguard measures by one Party in its relations with the other. The Association Council may decide, during such review, to suspend the application of these trade defence instruments provided that Turkey has implemented competition, state aids control and other relevant parts of the Community *acquis* which are related to the Internal Market and has also ensured

---

[23] **OJ** (1996) L 35/1.

[24] The Association Council may decide to extend the list of areas where harmonization is to be achieved in the light of the progress made by the association between the Parties.

373

their effective enforcement, thus providing a guarantee against unfair competition comparable to that existing inside the Internal Market[25].

This means that the applicability of trade defence instruments (other than safeguard measures) in trade between the Community and Turkey will only be questioned once Turkey can show that: (i) it has adopted; and, (ii) it is actually enforcing all the Community provisions and case law which ensure that competition will not be distorted within the customs union. Until such moment, either Party may resort, where warranted, to the application of trade defence instruments (such as antidumping measures) in accordance with the Decision in their bilateral trade relations.

As far as anti-dumping measures are concerned, and pending the above-mentioned review by the Association Council of the applicability of trade defence instruments in trade between the Parties, the Decision provides that the modalities of implementation of anti-dumping measures set out in Article 47 of the Additional Protocol remain in force[26].

Given that anti-dumping measures may still be applied, the Decision further provides, by derogation of the principle of free movement of goods within the customs union, that where one Party has adopted antidumping measures (or other measures pursuant to other trade defence instruments) in its relations with the other Party or with third countries, that Party may make imports of the products concerned from the territory of the other Party subject to the application of those measures[27]. The authorities of the importing Party will, for that purpose, ask the importer to indicate the origin of the products concerned on the customs declaration and request, where necessary, additional evidence in order to verify the true origin of the product in question[28]. This means that each Party will collect the anti-dumping duties it has imposed on imports of products originating in the territory of the other Party or in a third country this being made possible because the origin of the product concerned will be checked at the border between the two Parties.

It is, however, important to note that a statement by the EC attached to the Decision states that the Commission, without prejudice to the

---

[25] Article 42(1) of the Decision.

[26] Article 42(2) of the Decision.

[27] In these cases the relevant Party must inform the Customs Union Joint Committee accordingly; see Article 44 of the Decision.

[28] Article 45 of the Decision.

position of the Council, in the exercise of its responsibilities for anti-dumping and safeguard measures, will offer information to Turkey before the initiation of the proceedings. To this effect, appropriate modalities of application of Article 47 had to be set out jointly before the entry into force of the Decision. In accordance with the same statement, the Community will give, on a case by case basis, where appropriate, a clear preference to price undertakings rather than duties in order to conclude anti-dumping cases where injury is found.

B. NAFTA

1. The NAFTA Chapter 19 Bi-national Panel Review

The enforcement of anti-dumping and countervailing duty laws with respect to Canadian-US trade has been a major concern behind the negotiation of the Canada-US Free Trade Agreement. One of the principal goals of the Canadian Government in entering into this negotiation was to protect Canadian exporters from what it perceived to be an increasingly protectionist application of the US anti-dumping and countervailing duty laws. The US, for its part, was interested in subjecting Canadian subsidies to a greater degree of discipline. As attempts to develop a new body of trade rules applicable to Canadian-US trade eventually failed, the two sides agreed upon a temporary compromise solution: the setting up of a bi-national panel review mechanism that would replace national judicial review of final anti-dumping and countervailing duty determinations[29]. The NAFTA took over this mechanism with only relatively minor modifications[30]. Unlike the Canada-US Free Trade Agreement, however, the NAFTA does not envisage the ultimate development of a substitute system of rules for dealing with unfair pricing and government subsidization. Parties to the NAFTA are allowed to retain their own anti-dumping and countervailing duty laws which they may modify provided that they comply with the notification rules set out in the agreement.

---

[29] On this matter, see GREENBERG Michael, *"Chapter 19 of the US-Canada Free Trade Agreement and the North American Free Trade Agreement: Implications for the Court of International Trade: United States Court of International Trade Annual Judicial Conference"*, in: **Law & Policy International Business** No.25, 1993, p.37.

[30] See GASTLE Charles M. & CASTEL Jean-G., *"Should the NAFTA Dispute Settlement Mechanism in Antidumping and Countervailing Duty Cases Be Reformed in the Light of Softwood Lumber III?"*, in: **Law & Policy Int'l Bus**. No.26, 1995, p.823; ABA Section of Int'l Law and Practice; *"Dispute Settlement Under a North American Free Trade Agreement"*, in: **International Lawyer**, No.26, 1992, p.855; MOYER Homer E., Jr., *"Chapter 19 of the NAFTA: Binational Panels as the Trade Courts of Last Resort"*, in: **Int'l Lawyer** No.27, 1993, pp.707, 715.

A NAFTA bi-national review panel is composed of five members selected from rosters submitted by the Parties. All panellists must be citizens of the US, Canada or Mexico and be familiar with international trade law. There is a preference for the appointment of judges or former judges. Each Party may name two panellists from the roster. The fifth panellist is selected by consensus between the Parties. The panellists themselves elect the chair who must be a lawyer.

As NAFTA bi-national panels are a substitute for domestic judicial review, they are required to apply the domestic trade laws of the country whose determinations are under review, including the standard of review of that particular country. The standards are as follows:

i) in the case of Canada, that the agency failed to observe a principle of natural justice, erred in law when making its decision or based its decision on an erroneous finding of fact;

ii) in the case of the US, that the agency decision is unsupported by substantial evidence on the record or unsupported otherwise by rule of law; and,

iii) in the case of Mexico, the standard set forth in Article 238 of the *Código Fiscal de la Federación*, or any successor statutes, based solely on the administrative record[31].

In cases where the applicable domestic law is unsettled or contradictory, panels are obliged to construe and apply the law as well as possible on the basis of existing legal authorities, just as a domestic court would do.

Bi-national panel reviews of final anti-dumping and countervailing duty determinations may be requested by a NAFTA Party on its own, or on the request of a person who would otherwise be entitled under domestic law to request judicial review. NAFTA bi-national review proceedings are subject to a tight timetable which requires the issuance of a final decision within 315 days of the request for a panel. The panel decisions are final and binding on the Parties. The only avenue to challenge a panel decision is to submit it to the Extraordinary Challenge Committee but, as has already been made clear by a few cases, the Committee is not designed to act as an appeal court: the Committee may only review a decision of a bi-national panel in exceptional cases involving issues of impropriety[32].

---

[31] Quoted in APPLETON B., **Navigating NAFTA**, p.138.

[32] In order to bring an Extraordinary Challenge, the requesting Party must allege: (1) one of the following narrow grounds; and, (2) that it has materially affected the

The NAFTA also provides for bi-national panel review of proposed amendments to a Party's anti-dumping or countervailing duty laws whenever another Party alleges that such amendments are inconsistent with the NAFTA or the GATT.

An analysis of the cases handled by Chapter 19 bi-national panels would appear to indicate that, even though the standard of review applied by the bi-national panels is that set out in the domestic laws of the Party whose determinations are reviewed, the degree of scrutiny exercised by the panels tends to be higher than that exercised by domestic courts. Put in different words, the NAFTA bi-national panels are less inclined to showing deference to the determinations made by the national authorities and tend to frequently overrule them. Some commentators have attributed this state of affairs to the fact that the bi-national panels are usually composed of trade experts who may be less inclined to recognizing a wide margin of discretion to administrative authorities in matters which less specialized judges may consider to be too technical. The higher degree of scrutiny may also simply be the result of the bi-national composition of the panel. Even though the NAFTA ostensibly leaves unchanged the domestic trade laws of the Parties, the substitution of the domestic judicial review by a bi-national panel review has *de facto* modified the substantive treatment given to NAFTA exporters in anti-dumping and countervailing duty proceedings conducted by NAFTA Parties.

2. Competition Policy

The NAFTA does not include any competition rules. It only contains a provision requiring the Parties to introduce measures against anti-competitive business practices. This provision was mainly directed at Mexico which did not have any antitrust policy. For the rest, the NAFTA sets out a number of obligations concerning monopolies and state enterprises. The Parties have also agreed to establish a "Trade and Competition" Working Group which must report within five years on relevant issues concerning the relationship between competition laws, competition policies and trade. This task is similar to that attributed to another working group under the Canada-US Free Trade Agreement which was

---

panel's decision and threatens the integrity of the bi-national panel review process:
a. gross misconduct on the panel: such matters as bias, a serious conflict of interest or other material violations of the rules of conduct;
b. serious departure from a fundamental rule of procedure;
c. when the panel manifestly exceeded its powers, authority or jurisdiction such as failing to apply the appropriate standard of review.

requested to examine the possibility of using competition law as a means of harmonizing differences between anti-dumping and countervailing duty laws of the Parties. No agreement on this issue was ever reached.

C. Australia-New Zealand Closer Economic Relations Trade Agreement

Australia and New Zealand have embarked upon a process of economic integration, the first step of which was the conclusion of a free trade agreement, the New Zealand-Australia Free Trade Agreement ("NAFTA"), which came into force in 1966. NAFTA was replaced on January 1st, 1983 by a more ambitious project, the Australia-New Zealand Closer Economic Relations Agreement ("ANZCERTA", also referred to as "CER"). The essential objective of CER is to develop closer economic relations between the two countries through the expansion of free trade by the elimination of barriers to trade[33].

On August 18, 1988 the Australian and New Zealand Prime Ministers signed three protocols to CER containing binding commitments to move towards the creation of a single trans-Tasman market from July 1st, 1990. One of these protocols, the Protocol on Acceleration of Free Trade in Goods, provided for the abolition of anti-dumping procedures on goods originating in the free trade area and their replacement by remedies under the Parties' respective competition laws. This decision reflected the Parties' view that "the maintenance of anti-dumping provisions in respect of goods originating in the other Member State ceases to be appropriate as the Member States move toward the achievement of full free trade in goods between them and a more integrated market."

The abolition of the anti-dumping regime between the two countries was accompanied by an amendment of the Australian and New Zealand competition laws under which the scope of both laws was extended to the other country's territory[34]. Thus, the prohibition on the misuse of market power in Section 46 of the Australian Trade Practices Act was extended to cover the misuse of market power in a New Zealand market

---

[33] Closer Economic Relations Trade Agreement, March 28, 1983, Australia-New Zealand, **Australian Treaty Series** No.2, 1983 **New Zealand Treaty Series** No.1, reprinted in: **International Legal Materials**, Vol.22, p.948, Article 7.

[34] See VAUTIER K., *"Trans-Tasman Competition and Trade Law"*, in: VAUTIER et al., **Business of the CER**; AHDAR Rex J., *"The Role of Antitrust Policy in the Development of Australian-New Zealand Free Trade"*, in: **Int'l L. Bus.** No.12, 1991, pp.317, 325.

or a combined Australian and New Zealand market[35]. New Zealand likewise extended the prohibition of abuses of a dominant position in Section 36 of the New Zealand Commerce Act to dominant positions in a
market in Australia or in New Zealand and Australia[36]. New investiga-
tory powers were granted to the Australian Trade Practices Commission
and the New Zealand Commerce Commission to obtain information and
evidence in the other country for the purpose of enforcing the new prohibition of anti-competitive conduct affecting trans-Tasman trade. The
Australian and New Zealand Courts entrusted with competition law litigation were also given the power to direct subpoenas, injunctions, judgments and orders to persons in the other country which are enforceable
by the Courts of that other country. They are also authorized to conduct
proceedings in the other country[37].

Even though it was officially represented that the enforcement of competition laws would be a substitute for the protection previously afforded
to domestic industry under the anti-dumping legislation, the entry into
force of the protocol on July 1st, 1990 has radically altered the rules governing competition in the trans-Tasman market. Prior to July 1st, 1990,
local producers in Australia or New Zealand could request the imposition of anti-dumping duties with respect to goods exported from the other
country by simply showing the existence of price discrimination between
the two markets and the resultant material injury to the industry in the
importing country. Since that date, local producers qualify for protection
against a particular competitor in the trans-Tasman market only where

---

[35] Section 46 of the Trade Practices Act (as amended by the Trade Practices (Misuse
of trans-Tasman Market Power) Act 1990) provides that:
"A corporation that has a substantial degree of market power in a trans-Tasman
market (being a market in Australia, New Zealand or Australia and New Zealand)
must not take advantage of that power for the purpose of:
- eliminating or substantially damaging a competitor of the corporation ... in an
impact market (being a market in Australia that is not exclusively for services); or
- preventing the entry of a person into an impact market; or
- deterring or preventing a person from engaging in competitive conduct in an
impact market."

[36] Section 36A of the Commerce Act 1986 prohibits any person who has a "dominant
position" in a market in New Zealand or Australia from using that position for the
purpose of:
(i) restricting the entry of another person into that or any other market;
(ii) preventing or deterring a person from engaging in competitive conduct in a
market; or
(iii)eliminating a person from that or any other market.

[37] For more detailed descriptions of coordination in judicial procedures, see Mr. Justice
Ian BARKER & Mr. Justice A.A. BEAUMONT, *"Trans-Tasman Legal Relations -
Some Recent and Future Developments"*, in: **Australian Law Journal**, No.66, 1992,
p.566.

they prove that such competitor has a dominant position or a substantial degree of market power in the trans-Tasman market and is acting with a predatory purpose. This burden of proof has turned out to be so high that, thus far, no anti-competitive practice affecting the trans-Tasman market has yet been investigated under either Australian or New Zealand competition laws[38].

The CER integration process involves an effort of harmonization of business law which encompasses competition law. In its July 1992 Report[39], the Steering Committee of Officials presented recommendations on a number of trans-Tasman competition law issues warranting special examinations. One of the issues raised by the Committee was the possible extension of the prohibitions of trans-Tasman anti-competitive use of market power to markets for services: the new competition law provisions which have replaced the Australian and New Zealand anti-dumping regime only apply to locally originating products. Other issues considered by the Committee included the possible joint investigation of mergers and takeovers with a trans-Tasman impact, the prohibition of export cartels in trans-Tasman trade as well as the desirability of extending the extraterritorial reach of other prohibitions in the Australian and New Zealand competition laws.

One issue considered by the Committee with particular attention concerned the ostensible difference in the thresholds for anti-competitive use of market power in the Australian and New Zealand legislations. Whereas Section 46 of the Australian Trade Practices Act refers to the misuse of a "substantial degree of power" in a market, Section 36 of the New Zealand Commerce Act refers to the use of a "dominant position" in a market[40]. Some concern was expressed in New Zealand that the requirement of proving the existence of a "dominant position" laid down by the New Zealand legislation would make it more difficult for

---

[38] See KEWALKAM Ravi P., *"The Australia-New Zealand Closer Economic Relations Trade Agreement"*, in: **Journal of World Trade**, Vol.27 No.5, 1993, p.111.

[39] Report to Governments on Competition Law by Steering Committee of Officials, July 1992. The Steering Committee was set up pursuant to the signing by the Australian and New Zealand Governments on July 1st, 1988 of the Memorandum of Understanding on the Harmonization of Business Law and is assigned the task of examining the scope for harmonization of business law and regulatory practices in a number of areas.

[40] "Substantial degree of market power" according to the Federal Court of Australia could mean as little as 30 percent; "dominant degree of market power" has been interpreted by the New Zealand courts as meaning something in the vicinity of 80 percent. See DOWNER Alexander, *"Closer Economic Relations with New Zealand: the Next Steps"*, in: **A Coalition Policy Paper**, August 8, 1991.

New Zealand industry to obtain protection against anti-competitive practices as compared to the Australian industry which, under the Australian
legislation, only needs to show a "substantial degree of power". The
Steering Committee found that this divergence of approach had neither
impeded trans-Tasman trade nor affected the competitiveness or efficiency of the two respective economies. It only proposed that the application of the two tests should continue to be monitored. One reason why
no practical problem has yet been identified in the application of the two
tests is that, as stated above, no case has yet been brought under the provisions concerned in either Australia or New Zealand.

It should be noted that the Australia-New Zealand CER provides only
for the abolition of anti-dumping laws as between the Parties but not for
the abolition of countervailing duty laws which remain applicable. Some
commentators have explained that this does not have significant practical consequences as countervailing duty laws have rarely been used between Australia and New Zealand.

II. LESSONS FROM THE REGIONAL EXPERIMENTS

A. *The Resilience of Anti-Dumping and Countervailing Duty Laws in Regional Trade Agreements*

Even though regional trade agreements constitute the most advanced
form of economic integration short of the creation of a full-fledged common or "single" market, it is remarkable to observe that, with few exceptions, they continue to authorize the adoption of anti-dumping and
anti-subsidy measures among the Parties. With the sole exception of the
EEA, all the regional trade agreements entered into by the EC limit themselves to subjecting the imposition of trade policy measures to a consultation procedure. The NAFTA only provides for an *ad hoc* bi-national
panel review mechanism for final anti-dumping and countervailing
determinations but otherwise leaves the Parties free to enforce their trade
laws *vis-à-vis* exports from another Party. This illustrates the political
difficulty of eliminating the anti-dumping and anti-subsidy laws even
within a context of advanced regional integration.

The only two exceptions to this pattern, namely the EEA and the
Australia-New Zealand CER, can be regarded as exceptional cases.

The abolition of anti-dumping and anti-subsidy laws in intra-EEA
trade occurred after the EFTA countries had been linked by free trade
agreements to the EC for more than twenty years. The rationale which

was invoked to justify this abolition, namely the absence of trade barriers, was to a large extent already applicable when trade between the Community and the EFTA states was governed by these free trade agreements which became effective in 1973 and provided for the gradual total elimination of customs duties and other trade barriers between the Contracting Parties. The decision to replace anti-dumping and countervailing duty rules with competition rules in the EEA was essentially a political decision motivated by the objective to treat the EFTA members of the EEA as quasi-Member States of the EC. As a matter of fact, all the EFTA members of the EEA except Norway, Liechtenstein and Iceland joined the EC only one year after the EEA entered into force. The EC has, thus far, refused to extend the same treatment to any other regional partner, including Turkey, with which it has formed a customs union. Even though one would expect the degree of integration in a customs union to be greater than in a mere free trade area such as the EEA, it is striking that anti-dumping and anti-subsidy measures remain applicable to trade between the EC and Turkey. This highlights the truly exceptional nature of the EEA arrangement on anti-dumping and anti-subsidy measures.

The Australia-New Zealand CER is an equally exceptional arrangement. Here also, it took the Parties many years of close economic cooperation to finally take the decision of exempting one another from the scope of their anti-dumping laws. This decision was also a largely political one which can only be understood in a context of increasing economic and political cooperation between the two countries. Some commentators have also observed that, as a practical matter, the number of anti-dumping cases between Australia and New Zealand had significantly come down in the years preceding the entry into force of the decision to abolish anti-dumping measures on trans-Tasman trade.

All of this suggests that the proposals which are sometimes floated to abolish the anti-dumping laws on a worldwide basis are unlikely to succeed in any foreseeable future. Anti-dumping and countervailing duty laws will continue to be part of the world trade system even in the context of advanced regional integration. Abolition of anti-dumping and countervailing duty laws can be expected only between countries which will have reached such a degree of economic integration that will have the necessary confidence to accept each other's exports without the safety valve provided by the trade laws. It is noteworthy that this far-reaching step has been taken thus far only by countries which happened to share similar cost and social structures. The difference in cost and social structure between the EC and Turkey may be one of the reasons why anti-dumping and anti-subsidy measures have not yet been abolished in the EC-Turkey Customs Union.

B. The Replacement of Anti-Dumping Rules by Competition Rules

The EEA Agreement and the Australia-New Zealand CER Agreement present a common characteristic. In both cases, the elimination of anti-dumping rules was accompanied by the introduction of competition rules covering the entire territory of the free trade area. Only the technique used to achieve this objective differed: in the case of the EEA, the EFTA countries were invited to organize themselves along the same lines as the EC by subjecting themselves to competition rules taken from the EC Treaty and setting up a supranational surveillance authority patterned after the model of the European Commission. In the case of the CER, no new rules and no new institutions were created: the setting up of a trans-Tasman competition regime was achieved by extending the geographical scope of the existing Australian and New Zealand competition laws to the other Party's territory and giving the Australian and New Zealand enforcement authorities extraterritorial powers within the free trade area.

In both cases, the competition rules were presented as a substitute for the anti-dumping laws eliminated by the agreement. The experience under both the CER and the EEA, however, has been quite revealing. Not a single case of anti-competitive abuse of market power has been investigated by either New Zealand or Australia since the entry into force of the new CER competition law regime in 1990. This total absence of cases stands in stark contrast to the relatively active, though apparently diminishing, use of anti-dumping proceedings in trade between Australia and New Zealand in prior years.

It is more difficult to draw any conclusions from the relatively short experience with the EEA which became effective in 1994 and lost most of its EFTA members in the following year. It is clear, however, that those EFTA industries which were involved in EC anti-dumping proceedings in the pre-EEA days have not found themselves the target of investigations for predatory pricing under the EEA competition rules. Thus, for instance, the Norwegian ferrosilicon industry which was involved in several EC anti-dumping proceedings was referred to in the 1995 Report of the ESA only in connection with a nonexclusive distribution agreement between two ferrosilicon producers which the ESA proposed to approve[41].

---

[41] At p.61.

The substitution of competition rules for anti-dumping rules has only been formal: the anti-dumping rules which were previously applicable have simply disappeared and have been replaced by rules which are so different that it is more realistic to consider that they have been replaced by nothing. Since situations of "dumping" can be dealt with in the context of the CER or EEA (and EC) competition rules only when relatively strict requirements are met — in particular the need of establishing the existence of a dominant position or a substantial degree of market power — most, if not all, of the cases dealt with under the anti-dumping rules fall outside the scope of the competition rules.

Anti-dumping and competition rules do not share the same notion of what constitutes "fair competition". Anti-dumping rules are based on a *per se* condemnation of injurious international price discrimination (whether actual when actual export and domestic prices are compared or imputed when the export price is compared to a constructed normal value, that is, a determination by the authority of what the domestic price in the exporting country would have been if profitable domestic sales had been made). The notion of "fair competition" on which competition rules rest is radically different: they define "fair competition" as competition undistorted by restrictive agreements or abuses of a dominant position. The only area of overlap between the two sets of rules is limited to a relatively exceptional situation, that of "predatory" pricing which is normally dealt with by competition policy in the context of abuses of a dominant position or monopolization. The concern about excessive competition which underlies the prohibition of predatory pricing is so alien to the normal objective of competition policy that competition law actions against predatory pricing are extremely rare.

That competition rules could be a replacement for anti-dumping rules is therefore nothing but a fiction. The reality is that anti-dumping and competition policies are so inconsistent that the replacement of the former by the latter simply means the abolition of anti-dumping.

C. The Replacement of Anti-Subsidy Rules by State Aid Controls

The only regional trade agreement thus far in which anti-subsidy rules have been replaced by a state aid control mechanism is the EEA Agreement. As discussed above, the other regional trade agreement in which trade law rules have been replaced by competition law rules, the Australia-New Zealand CER Agreement, has limited itself to abolishing anti-dumping procedures on locally originating goods.

From a substantive viewpoint, the substitution of trade rules by competition rules in the field of subsidies does not raise the same difficulties as in the field of dumping. The substantive content of anti-subsidy and state aid rules is fundamentally identical. Both sets of rules share a common notion of "fair competition" defined as competition undistorted by unjustified state support to domestic producers.

Anti-subsidy and state aid rules only differ in the form of the remedy used: countervailing duties unilaterally imposed on imported products in the former case; a prohibition mechanism in the latter case. This is where the difficulty lies when one seeks to replace anti-subsidy procedures with state aid control mechanisms. Such mechanisms imply the creation of a supranational authority empowered to take decisions binding on the state that would grant an illegal aid. The characteristic feature of the EEA Agreement is that it has provided for the creation of an ESA which stands in relation to the EFTA states in the same position as the European Commission in relation to the EC Member States. In the absence of such an international authority, it is difficult to see how a state aid control mechanism could be enforced and act as an effective substitute for countervailing duty proceedings.

D. Anti-competitive Practices:
A Problem in International Trade?

In its Communication to the Council entitled *"Towards an International Framework of Competition Rules"*[42] the Commission put forward a number of reasons why, in its view, the adoption of international rules on competition should be considered. One of these reasons is set out as follows :

> ... anti-competitive practices are keeping our firms out of third country markets but they cannot, in the absence of appropriate domestic enforcement measures, be tackled effectively without international rules. European firms also face a competitive disadvantage if they have to compete with foreign producers operating from markets that are subject to less vigorous competition policies.[43]

In the light of the experience with regional trade agreements, one may wonder to what extent anti-competitive practices constitute a serious

---

[42] COM (96) 284 final, of June 18, 1996.
[43] At p.3.

problem in international trade. As noted above, no complaint was raised during the several decades in which the free trade agreements with the EFTA countries have been in force. Yet, these agreements contained provisions allowing the Parties to deal with anti-competitive agreements or abuses of a dominant position affecting trade between the Parties. Notwithstanding the pending *Kodak/Fuji* dispute[44], it might be worthwhile to conduct a thorough study of the actual impact of anti-competitive practices on international trade before embarking upon a process of negotiation of multilateral competition rules.

Another justification put forward for the adoption of multilateral competition rules is that such an initiative would lead to increasing convergence of competition laws, thus reducing the costs of compliance of firms operating in multiple jurisdictions. Once again, there is no clear evidence that differences in competition policies in different parts of the world would constitute a significant obstacle to trade deserving of the WTO attention. Here also, further study is needed especially since a worldwide coordination of competition policies could not be expected to proceed along the lines of the harmonization effort within the context of the EEA, the Europe Agreements or the customs union with Turkey in which the EC's regional partners were requested to take over the EC competition law wholesale. The differences in competition policies in different countries which are very visible in certain specific areas such as, for instance, vertical restrictions, may make it quite difficult to arrive at a high degree of convergence of competition rules. A cost/benefit analysis should be undertaken before the initiation of any such negotiation.

CONCLUSION

Trade laws have thus far largely succeeded in surviving the development of regional integration. Anti-dumping laws have been abolished only in exceptional cases of very advanced regional integration — the EEA and the Australia-New Zealand CER. In an increasingly open world

---

[44] Japan - Measures Affecting Consumer Photographic Film and Paper, complaint by the US (WT/DS44). On June 13, 1996, the US requested consultations with Japan concerning Japan's laws, regulations and requirements affecting the distribution, offering for sale and internal sale of imported consumer photographic film and paper. The US alleges that the Japanese Government treated imported film and paper less favorably through these measures, in violation of GATT Articles III and X. The US also alleges that these measures nullify or impair benefits accruing to the US (a non-violation claim). The US requested the establishment of a panel on September 20, 1996 and it was established on October 16, 1996. The US presented its formal submission on February 20, 1997.

trading system, domestic industries are clearly reluctant to abandon one of the last instruments of trade protection still authorized by GATT. In all the cases in which trade laws have remained applicable to regional trade, various solutions have been developed to mitigate the impact of trade law proceedings on regional producers. One of the most innovative formulae is the NAFTA bi-national panel review system which gives NAFTA exporters the benefit of a standard of review different, and perhaps *de facto* higher, than that enjoyed by non-NAFTA exporters under purely domestic judicial review mechanisms.

In contrast to the significance given to the issue of trade laws in regional trade agreements, anti-competitive practices have received much less attention. As noted above, the EEA, the Europe Agreements and the Customs Union with Turkey have led to the adoption of the EC competition policy by the regional partners concerned but these arrangements must be seen as steps towards a potential accession of these partners to the EC. For the rest, there has not been any indication that anti-competitive practices have been identified as a significant obstacle to regional trade.

COMMENTS[*]

Petros C. MAVROIDIS

Professor, Law Faculty, University of Neuchâtel

Introduction

Bellis (1997) clearly shows how varied practice has been in the treatment of dumping, subsidies and Restrictive Business Practices (RBPs) in regional trade agreements. An interesting supplementary question is what this tells about the state of multilateral trade law under the World Trade Organization (WTO) in this field. The diversity of approaches in Regional Agreements (RAs) could be explained in one of two ways: either the WTO rules in this area are too weak, or governments have been less than diligent in observing their WTO obligations. This paper briefly explores these questions and concludes by examining the status of the law in this area as a result of the entry into force of the Agreement establishing the World Trade Organization (WTO).

The Rule of Law

As Oliver (1996, p.4) states, both the opinion of the Permanent Court of International Justice on the "Customs Union between Germany and Austria", as well as Article XXIV of GATT define a Customs Union (CU), in contrast to a Free Trade Area (FTA), as an arrangement that does not merely involve liberalization of trade between Parties but which

---

[*] The author would like to thank Bill DAVEY and Patrick LOW and the participants in the Liège Conference on "Regionalism and Multilateralism" (October 3-5, 1996) for very helpful comments on an earlier draft.

also "entails the establishment of essentially uniform rules for goods coming from third Parties".

RAs, of whatever type, are an exception to the most fundamental obligation of the GATT-system: the Most-Favoured-Nation (MFN) clause. Any analysis of an Article XXIV-issue should consequently, be contextual[1] in the sense that it should be understood to operate as an exception to the MFN-clause. Some twenty-four years ago Hudec wrote:

> The seeming collapse of the MFN rules is probably the single most important cause of the present day pessimism about the GATT substantive rules. It is also the largest obstacle to renegotiation, for no other rules could have impact if the EEC practice were generalized.[2]

The "seeming collapse" is a reality now, since, depending of course on the assumptions, most of the trade is not conducted on a MFN-basis. A number of reasons have contributed to this situation and GATT's tolerance with respect to the formation of RAs is certainly one of them. And all this happened against the ongoing cry of economists that trade liberalization on a MFN-basis is the first-best policy (Bhagwati, 1993). The recently revived discussion on the conditionality/unconditionality of the MFN-clause — the terms of which are yet to be defined — will eventually further complicate matters.

There is a clear legal consequence that stems from this context: Article XXIV, being an exception to the MFN-rule, has to be construed narrowly. Article XXIV essentially comprises two aspects: an "external" aspect which regulates the relations between the members of an RA and the rest of the world (XXIV:5-6); and an "internal" aspect which regulates the relations of the members of an RA *inter se* (XXIV:8). Only the latter is of interest to us for the purposes of this commentary. Article XXIV:8(a) reads:

...

(a) A customs union shall be understood to mean the substitution of a single customs territory for two or more customs territories, so that:

(i) **duties and other restrictive regulations of commerce** (except, where necessary, those permitted

---

[1] Article 31.2 of the Vienna Convention on the Law of Treaties (VCLT) reads: "The **context** for the purpose of the interpretation of a treaty shall comprise, **in addition to the text,** including its preamble and annexes..." (emphasis added).

[2] HUDEC, 1972, at p.1362.

under Articles XI, XII, XIII, XIV, XV and XX) **are eliminated** with respect to substantially all the trade between the constituent territories... (emphasis added).

A similar provision is contained in Article XXIV:8(b) GATT that refers to FTAs. As a matter of fact, the problem treated in this note is much more of a problem in FTAs. (The EC has abolished anti-dumping duties among its Member States; there is, however, no clear indication that Mercosur will do so as well). Were we to apply the customary rule of interpretation of treaties embodied in Article 31 VCLT — as we have to, in conformity with Article 3.2 of the WTO Understanding on Rules and Procedures Governing the Settlement of Disputes (DSU) — we should end up concluding that the wording of Article XXIV GATT excludes the possibility of having recourse to either Anti-Dumping (AD) or Countervailing Duties (CVDs), since no reference is made to either Article VI or XVI GATT[3]. We reach the same conclusion when we place the wording in its context: Article XXIV GATT, being an exception to Article I GATT, should be construed narrowly and consequently, no GATT articles should be added to those figuring in the parenthesis in Article XXIV:8 GATT. The object and the purpose of the treaty certainly support such an interpretation since the purpose of the GATT is to maximize welfare based upon multilateral trade liberalization. Subsequent practice deviates from our conclusion at this point and it reflects a move from trade liberalization to "sustainable trade liberalization".

Article XXIV:8 GATT imposes an obligation of result on RAs: WTO Members have to abolish ADs and CVDs between them; the **means** used to achieve such a result is an issue not prejudged at all by Article XXIV:8 GATT and consequently, is left entirely within the discretion of those aspiring to establish an RA. This means that harmonization of competition laws is not a legal condition for the elimination of ADs or CVDs within RAs under Article XXIV:8 GATT. It is true, however, that, as Bellis notes, such elimination has occurred within RAs that have moved towards some form of harmonization of competition laws.

---

[3] The analysis in this paper is confined to the GATT. The issue will, eventually, be relevant also in the GATS-context. For the time being though, there are ongoing discussions and no final decisions on this issue in the GATS-context. Moreover, it seems — contrary to suggestions by economists — that an Article V GATS Working Party (WP) examining the compatibility of a RA with the GATS rules shall be dissociated from an Article XXIV GATT WP dealing with the same issue but with respect to goods. If this proves to be true, then one could imagine a CU or a FTA only on services or only on goods. Such an approach would further undermine the basic obligation, the MFN-rule, since it would make departure from the MFN-rule easier.

With respect to RBPs the following can be observed: there is nothing in the GATT that specifically addresses RBPs. The only indirect reference to RBPs is to be found in Article XXIX GATT. This article refers to, *inter alia*, Chapter V of the Havana Charter, the general principles of which WTO Members "undertake to observe to the fullest extent of their executive authority". The wording of Article XXIX GATT suggests that WTO Members are merely under a "best-endeavours" and not a strict legal obligation and it has generally been viewed by WTO Members as a dead letter. This is not to suggest that RBPs are altogether excluded from the scope of GATT. It has been suggested elsewhere (Hoekman & Mavroidis, 1994) that, under specific circumstances, claims based on RBPs can be brought before the WTO dispute settlement system provided that a governmental link can be established (in other words, provided that the allegedly illegal behavior can be attributed to a government). The recent dispute between the US and Japan which has been recently notified to the WTO (the *Kodak/Fuji* Case) reflects this perception.

The Relevant GATT Practice

Finger (1993, p.131) notes: "Rules are one thing; convincing countries to keep their policies in line with them is another." As is well-known, all RAs that involve WTO Members have to be reported to the WTO (Article XXIV:7 GATT). It is maybe less well-known that, with the exceptions mentioned in Bellis' article (the EC, the EEA and the ANZCERTA)[4], all notified and currently existing RAs have not yet abolished ADs and CVDs between their constituents[5]. What is disturbing is that no substantial discussion has ever been undertaken in the multilateral context to explain this tolerance. Hudec, again, puts things in perspective by noting that "the GATT's somewhat benign attitude toward RAs is merely one part of this larger tolerance toward departures from MFN in general."[6] In fact, there are GATT cases with AD and CVD actions between members of an RA.

Two reasons may be deduced as to why the GATT has shown indulgence towards RAs. First, GATT had to face, in its early years, the formation of the EC. That led to a number of pragmatic adjustments. This had repercussions on the legal nature of the reports of Working Parties

---

[4] With respect to the treatment of ADs and CVDs in the ANZCERTA, see DELLOW & FEIL, 1991.

[5] On this issue see MARCEAU, 1994, pp.147ff.

[6] See HUDEC, 1993, p.154.

(WPs) that examine, in the context of GATT, the compatibility of a notified RA with the relevant GATT rules. In a nutshell, such a report is
not a "green light" for the formation of an RA[7]. Those who want to proceed with the establishment of an RA will proceed anyway, independent
of questions suggesting doubts about the compatibility of the scheme
with the relevant multilateral rules that may be established by the members of a WP. On the other hand, those questioning the compatibility of
the noted scheme with Article XXIV GATT will spell out their differences in the final report, perhaps because of the fear that silence will be
interpreted as acquiescence. At the end of the day, a typical WP report
looks like an inventory for future disputes. The overall legal value of an
Article XXIV report is unclear. This is precisely why such a report cannot be used as a shield against future actions challenging the compatibility of the noted scheme with the relevant GATT rules; in general, WTO
Members preserve their Article XXIII GATT rights independently of the
adoption of a WP report. Eventually a decision on the compatibility can
only be taken by GATT/WTO panels (and now, as a last resort, by the
WTO Appellate Body).

Second, the timing of the notification of an RA is crucial.
Article XXIV:7(a) reads:

> Any Contracting Party **deciding to enter** into a customs union or
> free trade area, or an interim agreement leading to the formation
> of such a union or area, shall **promptly** notify the Contracting
> Parties and shall make available to them such information regard-
> ing the **proposed** union or area... (emphasis added).

Again there is variance between what the wording suggests and how
GATT practice evolved. In practice, WPs have typically examined RAs
that had already been signed and sometimes entered into force; they were
presented with a *fait accompli*[8]. Were we to take into account the fact
that decisions were taken in GATT-practice by consensus, along with the
reigning pragmatism of GATT, it is easy to understand GATT tolerance
in this context.

---

[7] JACKSON (1969, p.588) states: "... the international community was not prepared
to make compliance with the technicalities of Article XXIV the *sine qua non* of
eligibility for the exception from other GATT obligations."

[8] The WP on the FTA between Canada and the US for example, examined the consistency of the notified RA with Article XXIV GATT two years after the establishment of the notified RA, see GATT Doc. BISD 38S/47ff.

Concluding Remarks:
The Road Ahead

The WTO Understanding on the interpretation of Article XXIV of the General Agreement on Tariffs and Trade 1994 (hereinafter "the WTO Understanding") reaffirms that customs unions and free trade areas, "to be consistent with Article XXIV, must satisfy, *inter alia*, the provisions of Paragraphs 5, 6, 7 and 8 of that article."

One can only wonder at such a statement. Does it amount to an explicit approval of past GATT practice? According to Article 1b(iv) GATT 1994, GATT 1994 comprises more than just the text of GATT 1994, all "other decisions of the Contracting Parties to GATT 1994". Arguably, decision to adopt an Article XXIV GATT WP report could come under this provision. And as mentioned above, there is no reported case where a notified RA was not approved because of the treatment of ADs and CVDs between its members. Moreover, Article XVI of the Marrakesh Agreement establishing the WTO stipulates that:

> 1. Except as otherwise provided under this Agreement or the Multilateral Trade Agreements, the WTO shall be guided by the decisions, procedures and customary practices followed by the Contracting Parties to GATT 1947 and the bodies established in the framework of GATT 1947.

As argued above, the decisions in this field look typically like an inventory of future disputes and lack the necessary rigour that would enable them to be perceived as authentic statements revealing the GATT-practice on this issue. As far as the customary practice is concerned, it is divergent and, consequently, inconclusive: as Bellis (1997) notes, three RAs have abolished ADs between their members and two of them (EC and EEA) have also abolished CVDs.

Does it mean a change of direction? The wording of Article XXIV GATT has not changed. The WTO Understanding reaffirms adherence to the provisions of Article XXIV:8 GATT for an RA to be deemed consistent with the relevant GATT rules. And, as we pointed out earlier, the legal nature of an Article XXIV GATT WP report is unclear while state practice in this field is inconclusive.

It is suggested that, the way things have evolved so far, the answer can only come from more active use of the WTO dispute settlement procedures for questions touching upon the so-called "systemic interest"[9]. The WTO Understanding reaffirms that the multilateral dispute settlement procedures can be used to this effect. It relevantly provides:

> The provisions of Articles XXII and XXIII of GATT 1994 as elaborated and applied by the Dispute Settlement Understanding may be invoked with respect to **any** matters arising from the application of those provisions of Article XXIV relating to customs unions, free trade areas or interim agreements leading to the formation of a customs union or free trade area. (emphasis added).

WTO Members normally litigate only when trade interests are affected. Trade interests are normally defined very narrowly. Any non-MFN trade, in principle, affects the trade interests of those not participating in the RA. On the issue under discussion, however, things can be more complicated. Suppose countries A and B notify an RA to the WTO whereby, contrary to the wording of Article XXIV:8 GATT, they preserve the possibility to impose ADs and CVDs against each other. Country C is definitely losing its MFN-rights towards A and B as a result of the formation of the RA. At the same time, it faces a dilemma: should it contest the compatibility of the notified RA with Article XXIV:8 GATT? (systemic and maybe trade interest, since it depends on the volume of trade between C on the one hand and A and B on the other); or should it forget altogether about it? (trade interest, since in case C has trade with A and B, C is better off when A and B impose ADs and CVDs against each other than when they do not).

Were we to add to all this Bellis' point concerning the strength of the AD lobby, especially on the two sides of the Atlantic (by far the most active players in the WTO), one can easily understand why so far systemic interest has not prevailed. The picture is changing though. The multiplication of agreements concluded in the WTO-context will inevitably lead, if it has not done so already, to a more global awareness of what is really at stake. Moreover, the rule of "negative consensus", now applicable in the adoption of dispute settlement reports, has removed some of the reticence to submit cases to the WTO dispute settlement process. The first two years show that developing countries are becoming

---

[9] The term "systemic interest" is meant to cover the interest of WTO Members to see the rules observed, independently of whether their trade interests *stricto sensu* have been affected. As an example, one could imagine a situation where country X litigates against country Y that has unilaterally, and thus in violation of Article 23:2a DSU, imposed a quantitative restriction prohibited by Article XI GATT against country Z. It is true that sometimes the borderline between trade and systemic interest is hard to define.

active users of the system. If the WTO dispute settlement process can respond to the new challenges it faces and, thus, justify the increased confidence that WTO Members show to it, then, maybe, it will have given WTO Members the extra incentive they need to eliminate once and for all the artificial distinction between trade and systemic interest.

Bibliography

BELLIS Jean-François, *"The Treatment of Dumping, Subsidies and Anti-Competitive Practices in Regional Trade Agreements"*, in: BELLIS, DEMARET & GARCÍA JIMÉNEZ (eds), **Regionalism and Multilateralism after the Urugay Round**, IEJE, European Interuniversity Press (EIP), Brussels, 1997 (this volume).

BHAGWATI Jagdish, *Regionalism and Multilateralism: An Overview*, in: DE MELO Jaime & PANAGARIYA Arvind (eds), **New Dimensions in Regional Integration**, CEPR, Cambridge University Press, 1993, pp.22-51.

DELLOW Tony & FEIL John, *Competition Law and Trans-Tasman Trade*, in: ADHAR Rex J. (ed.), **Competition Law and Policy in New Zealand**, The Law Book Company Ltd, Sydney, 1991, pp.24-43.

FINGER Michael J., *GATT's Influence on Regional Agreements*, in: DE MELO Jaime & PANAGARIYA Arvind (eds), **New Dimensions in Regional Integration**, CEPR, Cambridge University Press, 1993, pp.128-148.

HOEKMAN, Bernard M. & MAVROIDIS Petros C., *Competition, Competition Policy and the GATT*, in: **The World Economy**, No.17(2), 1994, pp.121-150.

HUDEC Robert E., *GATT's Influence on Regional Agreements: A Comment*, in: DE MELO Jaime & PANAGARIYA Arvind (eds), **New Dimensions in Regional Integration**, CEPR, Cambridge University Press, 1993, pp.151-155.

HUDEC Robert E., *GATT or GABB? The Future Design of the General Agreement on Tariffs and Trade*, in: **The Yale Law Journal**, No.80(7), 1972, pp.1299-1386.

JACKSON John, H., **World Trade and the Law of the GATT**, The Michie Co., Charlottesville, Va., 1969.

MARCEAU Gabrielle, **Antidumping and Antitrust Issues in Free Trade Areas**, Oxford University Press, New York, 1994.

OLIVER Peter, **Free Movement of Goods in the European Community**, (3rd ed.), Sweet & Maxwell, London, 1996.

GOVERNMENT PROCUREMENT IN A MULTILATERAL CONTEXT

Pierre DELSAUX[*]

Maître de Conférences, University of Liège;
Administrator DG-XV/B4,
European Commission, Brussels

I. INTRODUCTION

1. Public procurement concerns the purchase by governments and public authorities of any good, construction services or services by any contractual means. Most governments, however, do not subject purchases of defence equipment to public procurement rules, for reasons of national security.

2. For a long time, public procurement remained outside the international stage. Though many realized its importance from an economic viewpoint, most countries preferred to remain silent on this issue because protectionism was the rule in this highly sensitive sector. An evolution has taken place in recent years, since a new plurilateral agreement was concluded during the Uruguay Round negotiations. Furthermore, despite the fact that this agreement has only recently entered into force, many voices are already asking for new steps to be taken in this field at a multilateral level.

3. This paper will study this evolution but will also try to examine the role played by the European Community.

---

[*] The opinions expressed in this article are strictly personal.

II. PUBLIC PROCUREMENT RULES
IN SOME REGIONAL AGREEMENTS

A. *The European Community*

1. Evolution of Public Procurement Rules in the European Community

1. The words "government procurement" or "public procurement" are not mentioned in the EC Treaty. At first sight, only two provisions can be directly associated with the question of public purchase. They are Articles 132 §4 and 223(a). Article 132 is very specific and only deals with the overseas territories. Article 223 is more important since it spells out an exception for reasons of national security. This provision has a general scope. It can be used by Member States to exclude from the application of the EC rules the purchase of some products and services linked to their security. The exact scope of Article 223 is still vividly debated, as shown by the need felt by the Commission to present recently a communication on the defence sector in Europe.

The absence of any specific provision on government procurement in the treaty can be explained for several reasons. Some have underlined that times were not ripe, when the EC Treaty was negotiated, to have detailed provisions on an issue that so much involves Member States' direct behaviour and interests. Another explanation certainly lies in the nature of the EC Treaty, which does not intend to regulate, but is rather a framework agreement.

2. That led to a consequence which might not have been foreseen by all when the treaty was negotiated. Since no specific exception, but Article 223, did exist for government procurement, the conclusion was that the general rules of the treaty were fully applicable even when public authorities were purchasing goods and services. This consequence quickly came to light.

3. Many of the EC rules are relevant to government procurement.

When public authorities purchase goods and services, they have to comply with the rules on the **free movement of goods** and on the **freedom of services**. This implies that they cannot create any obstacles to imported products or services and that no protectionism is permitted. For instance, a Member State is not allowed to reserve some of its government procurement to firms established in certain area of its territory. The Court considers that such a preference is an infringement of Article 30 of the EC Treaty when it relates to the purchase of goods. Similar case-law has been developed when the purchase of services is involved and when a Member State tries to reserve it to local firms.

Furthermore, to the extent that the supplies of these goods and services would compel the firms to establish themselves in another Member State, the articles on the **freedom of establishment** are also pertinent. For instance, the Court of Justice has condemned on this basis, a Member State where a public authority has, as a selection criteria, required the suppliers to be a national.

Last but not least, the **principle of nondiscrimination and the principle of equality of treatment** must also be complied with. These principles are fundamental and can have potentially very far-reaching effects. On this basis, the Court of Justice can investigate the details of a call for tender and can, for instance, sanction a Member State creating some kind of preference for a particular supplier. These principles have a very wide application and even exceed the concept of discrimination on the basis of nationality. For instance, in the Storebaelt Decision, the Court of Justice had to examine whether Denmark had infringed the EC Treaty by negotiating with only one supplier a modification of its offer after the opening of all submissions. This practice was condemned by the Court because it granted an undue advantage to one bidder to the detriment of the others.

4. As shown by the examples above, the EC Treaty has an important impact on the government procurement practices in the Member States. Some of the most important decisions of the Court of Justice in the field of public procurement have indeed been adopted on the basis of the treaty itself.

5. Very soon however, it became clear that this approach was not fully satisfactory. Infringement procedures can be taken only once a violation has occurred, which is often too late if a contract has been signed. Acting on the basis of the EC Treaty does not really have a preventive effect. Furthermore, the practical consequences of the existence of the EC Treaty on the actual purchasing practices were not transparent enough as long as the jurisprudence was not well established. The Commission therefore considered that it was preferable to increase predictability and to adopt a more preventive approach. This led to the adoption of two draft directives in 1965. They were finally approved in 1971. One dealt with public works and the other with the supplies of goods. Both covered only public authorities, but at all levels of the state (central and sub- central). This is the so-called "classic sector".

6. Several years after their entry into force, the Commission conducted an analysis of the directives' impact. The results demonstrated that it was necessary to modify them and to supplement them because cross-border purchases were still very limited. This was the reason for the adoption of more directives. To clarify the situation in this sector and to minimize the discrepancies, these texts were consolidated and completed in 1993.

7. The legal situation in the Community is presently as follows.

The two directives on **public works and public supply** already mentioned were amended but kept the same coverage with respect to the entities concerned.

A new directive was adopted concerning the **purchase of services**. These are not defined in the text, but the annexes contain two lists of services: one for which all the provisions of the directive are applicable and another for which only some transparency obligations exist.

A more decisive step was the extension of public procurement rules to the **"utilities" sectors**. These are the water, transport, energy and telecommunications sectors. Such evolution was accomplished in two steps. A first directive was agreed on in 1990 but did not cover procurement of services. That was the result of a second directive in 1993 (Directive 93/38), which also incorporates the provisions of the 1990 directive. The Directive 93/38 indicates a widening of the concept of government procurement because it includes bodies that are not part of the government of the Member States. It not only covers public bodies but also private entities enjoying exclusive or special rights. The logic behind such a move is economic. Some argue that the decisive criterion for the application of public procurement rules should be the ownership of a particular body. However, such a formalistic approach does not take into account the economic reality. For the Community the question is rather whether the concerned entity is faced with effective competition on the market. If the answer is positive, then the external pressures should be sufficient to compel this entity to purchase efficiently. On the other hand, in the absence of such competition, nothing would prevent the purchasing entity from buying inefficiently and passing the extra-cost onto the customers who have in any case no other alternative source of supply. This is true even in the case of private entities. One provision of the utility directive must be highlighted because it has had an effect on the evolution at the multilateral level. Article 36 of Directive 93/38 obliges a purchasing entity to give preference to products originating from the Community or from a country where Community products have been given comparable and effective access.

Finally, two directives have been adopted in order to harmonize to a certain extent the **remedies** available before the national jurisdictions. They represent an important step towards guaranteeing a more effective enforcement of the suppliers' rights. Even the most developed rules will remain a dead letter without the means for their effective application. Though the EC was more advanced than many countries in this respect, much was still needed. Indeed, the Commission has the right to bring an infringement case before the Court of Justice against a Member State, but is not sufficiently staffed to follow-up all the infringements which might occur during the purchasing procedures throughout the Community. Therefore, the awareness of the interested suppliers is indispensable, even it might seem difficult for them to "bite the hand that feeds them". To improve this, a certain degree of harmonization was needed. This was achieved by the two directives (one for the classic sector, the other for the utilities sector). However, both texts still leave many options open to Member States and do not regulate many aspects of this issue.

2. Motivations for Public Procurement Rules

1. There are two closely linked reasons for the adoption of a complete set of rules in the Community.

2. To understand the context it is useful to give some figures relating to government procurement. For a long time, public authorities have spent huge amounts of money for their purchase. According to the latest estimates, public purchasing in the European Community amounts to approximately 750 billion ECU per year; in other words, the equivalent of the gross national product of UK, or approximately 12 percent of the total gross national product of the Community.

The figures explain why it is impossible to avoid interfering with the use of such sums. The need for some kind of regulation is obvious especially since public procurement is decentralized in many countries and one cannot deny the fact that there is often a clear tendency to buy on a national basis. This results in inefficiencies of great cost. The Cecchini Report on the Cost of Non-Europe estimated that governments were paying about 22 billion ECU extra per year.

3. The need to improve this situation by adopting certain rules on public procurement is obvious. However, two different philosophies could be the basis of legislation on public procurement.

The first one tends to inject socioeconomic aims into public procurement. This approach favours interventionism. For instance, one could imagine that a public authority, when purchasing goods or services, would be obliged to give a preference to the suppliers whose offer is the most favourable towards protecting the environment or fighting more efficiently unemployment. In such a scheme, the entity does not choose the cheapest offer but the offer permitting the achievement of a particular objective. Public purchasing is then used as a policy instrument to support national or regional firms or industries. This may be done for strategic reasons (e.g. defence goods, telecommunications, aerospace), to support employment in declining industries, to compensate local communities near environmentally damaging public industries, to support emerging high technology industries and/or for more general political reasons (e.g. highly visible goods like cars). The risk is, however, that public procurement might sometimes be used for less respectable or generous reasons, involving misuse of public money, abusive favours, corruption, etc.

The second approach is competition driven: the offer which brings the best value for the money will be preferred. Procurement must be done on commercial grounds. Best value for the money does not automatically mean that the lowest bid will be chosen. Indeed, nothing prevents the purchasing entity from insisting on some technical criteria to be met by the offers and from choosing the offer which combines the best technical value with the best price. The objective is then to increase competition to a maximum extent so that the purchaser receives many offers and is able to choose the one that suits him best. Besides best value for money, a competitive public procurement system can deliver other benefits. When public purchasers demand the delivery of goods and services at the right price, at the right place, and at the right time, suppliers are forced to meet those demands. Competitive tendering therefore encourages the competitive delivery of goods and forces efficiency improvements in industry. It also has an impact on the rate of innovation in industry and encourages investment and growth. Additionally, as domestic industry becomes more competitive, it is better able to win contracts abroad and increase its share of world markets. Such an approach is more liberal economically. Its effects are more important if the market is broad and open.

4. The second option has been preferred at the Community level. This is hardly surprising since the whole EC Treaty is inspired by a competitive approach to the economy. The primary objectives of the EC public procurement policy have been to create competitive conditions in which public contracts are awarded without discrimination and to inject financial management disciplines and the awareness of value for money into the public sector and utilities. However, some room is still left to pursue other objectives. Even in the Community, a public authority may impose specific conditions when a contract is awarded in order to meet some other objective, provided there is no discrimination.

5. There is another reason why rules have been adopted at the Community level. Not regulating such huge spending by EC rules would have meant that a substantial part of the European economy would have remained closed or, at least, subject to protectionism without much control. It did not seem satisfactory to establish economic integration amongst the Member States without covering the possibility for them to maintain national preferences for their purchase. It is no secret that many public authorities could be tempted into giving some kind of preference to a local supplier.

It can therefore be considered that the adoption of public procurement rules lies at the core of the creation of a Single Market in Europe. Some kind of integration in the field of public procurement was necessary to fight against the direct effects of protectionism but also against the spillover effects on the rest of the Common Market. A firm benefiting from local contracts from its government, without any objective justifications, obtains a competitive edge which could lead to distortions of competition in the rest of the market. This is especially true due to the large sums involved.

6. There are other benefits of a more open procurement policy. The absence of fair, nondiscriminatory and transparent procurement procedures can facilitate and conceal fraud and corruption in public administration. Whilst transparent public procurement procedures are not sufficient in themselves to eradicate fraud and corruption totally, a system of procedural checks and balances helps to protect against breaches of public trust. However, such an argument has never been put forward to justify public procurement rules in the Community.

3. The Main Features of the EC Public Procurement Rules

1. One often tends to forget that EC public procurement rules are contained not only in the directives but also in the EC Treaty itself. The directives are only applicable above certain thresholds, which have been fixed so that a majority of contracts in the Community should normally be covered. However, below these thresholds, the EC Treaty is fully applicable, as is obviously also the case above these thresholds. The relevant EC principles have already been explained above.

2. The directives lay down rules on the procedures to be followed by the purchasing entities. They do not regulate the contract once a bidder has been chosen.

3. Because they have to deal with very specific questions, one must acknowledge that the EC directives might be seen as complicated. Furthermore, one could even argue that those directives bear little difference to a regulation, without however bringing about the benefits resulting from the latter. Politically, it was more feasible to adopt directives rather than regulations. As a practical consequence, the texts applicable to procurement can be found not only in the Community law but also in all the implementing national legislation. This creates another problem since the rate of transposition of the public procurement directives is the lowest of all texts being part of the Single Market programme. There is one important qualification: since most provisions have direct effect, any possible contradiction between a national provision and the Community text may be solved through the primacy principle. Some argue that the whole situation does not create, at the legislation level, the transparency that the directives would like to achieve in the procurement practices. This criticism is certainly relevant but not specific to procurement.

4. Despite an apparent complexity, and without entering into all the details, some of the main features can be underlined.

Transparency is a key to the system. Because of the fundamental reasons which justify an action of the Community in this field, several rules aim to achieve the wider publicity possible when a call for tender is launched in order to attract the best offers.

The means chosen for this is the *Official Journal* where all notices concerning call for tenders above the thresholds must be published. Several types of notices are provided. Their content is also harmonized to a large extent so that any supplier in the Community (and outside) is able to find easily the type of products or services concerned. Translation is done by the Commission itself. Furthermore, a database called TED (Tender Electronic Daily) has been created and the Commission is now working on a system to gather and disseminate electronically information. This system is called SIMAP. Another example of this search for transparency is the strict limits which are set forth for the use of restricted procedure of tendering. Contracting entities must normally choose an open or selective procedure, rather than a restricted one, involving real competition.

Nondiscrimination and equality of treatment are two other important elements. Several rules aim at ensuring that no supplier unduly benefits from a preference over its competitors. For instance, technical specifications may not be based on local standards. Another example is the obligation to respect a certain delay between the publication of the call for tenders and the beginning of the award procedure so as to guarantee that non-nationals are not disadvantaged because they get this information later than nationals.

Detailed rules are provided with respect to selection and award criteria. From this standpoint, the directives admit that the chosen bid is not the lowest one provided that the contracting entity has indicated in advance the technical criteria that will be used.

B. The NAFTA Agreement

1. Provisions on government procurement can be found in Chapter 10 of the NAFTA Agreement. This chapter is rather voluminous and contains relatively detailed provisions on the procedure to be followed by specific entities of all three Parties (Mexico, Canada and the USA). The NAFTA was signed in November 1993. This date is important because, as we shall see, at that time an agreement already existed within the GATT framework and a new one was almost finalized. In this context, one provision must be underlined: Paragraph 7 of Article 1002 states that Chapter 10 of the NAFTA Agreement shall prevail over the GATT procurement agreement in the case of inconstancy between the two texts.

2. The structure of Chapter 10 of the NAFTA Agreement is very similar to the WTO Agreement described hereafter, which explains why we will not enter into details.

The NAFTA Agreement is based on a threshold approach. Only contracts above certain sums are covered by its rules. Most of the thresholds are lower than those existing in the Community.

These rules cover all forms of contracts (goods, services and construction) awarded by federal entities and government enterprises listed in annexes. Sub-federal entities are not included. Furthermore, contrary to the situation in the Community, these lists are exhaustive.

The benefits of this agreement are open to firms of one of the three signatories. However, a Party may deny them to an enterprise that is a supplier of services of another Party if nationals of any non-Party own or control that enterprise and that enterprise has no substantial business activities in the territory of the Party under whose laws it is constituted.

III. THE DEVELOPMENT OF PUBLIC PROCUREMENT RULES AT THE MULTILATERAL LEVEL

A. *The GATT Agreement*

1. Contrary to the EC Treaty, the GATT Agreement contains an explicit provision on government procurement. Article 3 provides that:

> III:8 (a) The provisions of this article shall not apply to laws, regulations or requirements governing the procurement by governmental agencies of products purchased for governmental purposes and not with a view to commercial resale or with a view to use in the production of goods for commercial use.

Since Article 3 of the GATT Agreement concerns the national treatment obligation (NT), and not the Most-Favoured-Nation clause (MFN), one could try to argue that the exclusion is limited to the former. However, for all the negotiators, it is clear that the exclusion is general.

Another ambiguity stems from the fact that this text only mentions governmental agencies, but does not give a definition. An unadopted Panel Report on *"United States Procurement of a Sonar Mapping System"* clarified the scope of this concept and limited it to products paid by the government for its use or benefit and over which it has control.

The reason for the exclusion of government procurement from the GATT Agreement can be found in the fear of many countries that their purchasing practices would be substantially altered if they were obliged to follow more open procedures.

B. The Tokyo Round Agreement on Government Procurement

1. The solution adopted by the negotiators of the GATT Agreement was an open door to protectionism, perceived by some countries as unsatisfactory. One of the starting points for an evolution was the according of national preference by the US Government for the purchase of defence products. In reaction, some countries asked for cancellation before the Trade Committee of the OCDE. The result was the establishment of a working group in this organization to create a common framework for government procurement.

Some dates are meaningful since the working group finalized its first draft in 1965, at the same time as the preparation of the first EC draft directives. The working group resumed its talks in 1969 on the basis of a new US draft proposal. The talks went on until the end of 1975 when it was finally decided to continue the whole process within the framework of the Tokyo Round discussions. This led to the transmission by the OECD to the GATT of a document summarizing the conclusions of fifteen years of talks. This document was transmitted on October 15, 1976 to the first meeting of the Tokyo Sub-Committee on government procurement. It is certainly not a complete coincidence that this occurred just when the second phase of the EC harmonization was achieved.

2. The Text of the Tokyo Round is based upon the Works of the OECD.

The agreement entered into force on January 1st, 1981 and was subsequently revised in 1988. Its membership was limited to the EC, the US, Japan, Canada, Norway, Finland, Sweden, Austria, Switzerland, Israel, Hong Kong, Korea and Singapore.

The Tokyo Code is applicable to contracts above certain thresholds. It is limited to the central authorities of each signatory but only to the extent that they are mentioned in the list provided by each Party. These lists are contained in the annexes of the agreement, they are the result of a negotiating process and were agreed by all Parties.

The agreement is also limited to the procurement of products. Services are only covered to the extent that they are incidental to the supply of products and cost less that the products themselves.

The agreement spells out the principle of national treatment and of the most-favoured-nation but also lays down detailed operational rules concerning the tendering process.

This agreement is still in force despite the fact that all its members have decided to join the new government procurement agreement.

C. The Uruguay Round Agreement

1. Negotiations to adopt a more ambitious agreement were carried out during the cycle of the Uruguay Round. After many ups and downs, they were successfully concluded in December 1993. The agreement itself was finally signed on April 15, 1994 in Marrakech, after the Community and the US managed to conclude a separate bilateral agreement. The new Government Procurement Agreement (GPA) entered into force on January 1st, 1996. Contracting Parties to the 1996 GPA are the European Community, the USA, Canada, Japan, South Korea, Norway, Switzerland and Israel. A number of other countries are considering joining the new GPA (for instance Singapore and Hong Kong).

2. The final history of the negotiation is particularly interesting. One of the main reasons for beginning the negotiations was the willingness of both the Community and by the United States to reach an agreement on the opening of their telecommunications markets. As explained above, in Europe, this sector was under the scope of Directive 93/38 which contained an explicit Community preference. This was perceived by the Americans as a major obstacle in one key sector. The Europeans, for their part, had also the feeling that this sector was not open in the US. To some extent, the same was also true in the electricity sector.

Both partners decided to start negotiations to solve these issues on a bilateral basis, with the clear intention that any bilateral agreement between them on these outstanding issues would facilitate an agreement on a new code. The objective was to reach a balanced and comprehensive agreement on procurement at a sub-central level and in the utilities sectors. This agreement was to be integrated in a new code.

A bilateral Memorandum of Understanding (MoU) was agreed between the EC and the US in May 1993, opening up the Community's and the United States' power-generating ("electrical") procurement markets. This deal expired on May 30, 1995.

3. The momentum created by this memorandum of understanding was decisive for the amendment of the Tokyo Round Agreement. All the other Parties of the old agreement (except Singapore) consented to an expansion of the old agreement in December 1993. As regards the outcome of the December negotiations, the EC and the US reconfirmed the coverage of central government procurement ("Category A") to which they had already committed themselves the previous year in the Memorandum of Understanding on Government Procurement. However, they could not agree to open sub-central ("Category B") and utilities' ("Category C") procurement to each other. The EC (as most other Parties) considered the US offer of December 15, 1993 in both categories as insufficient (the US offered procurement by certain contracting entities in twenty-four states and procurement by the federally owned electric utilities).

Therefore, negotiations between both Parties continued beyond the December 15 deadline and, as had been agreed in the MoU, they were conducted on the basis of an independent study, financed by both sides, in order to appreciate the value of the respective offers. The study was completed in March 1994 and bilateral negotiations between the EC and the US recommenced immediately thereafter.

4. Alongside the signing ceremony in Marrakech of the Uruguay Round accords and the Government Procurement Agreement (GPA) in April 1994, the EC and US agreed on a further bilateral deal (the "bilateral") on procurement, which has been almost wholly incorporated into the GPA. This bilateral deal is a far-reaching agreement, concluded after seven years of negotiations, which opens state and city-level procurement to EU firms for the first time. In addition to access to procurement for some ports and airports, the deal also removes significant portions of "Buy American" legislation and "Buy American" federal funding programmes. The deal also opens the public electrical sector of both sides. Because the GPA did not enter into force until January 1st, 1996, the bilateral deal also extended the validity of the MoU from May 30, 1995 to the end of 1995.

No agreement was reached on procurement of telecommunications equipment which was one of the main US negotiating objectives. This was mainly due to problems of transparency related to procurement of private telecommunications operators in the US and to the fact that the US was unable to remove sufficient "Buy America" clauses from federally-funded programmes. Consequently, the EC maintained the application of Article 36 towards US bids in sectors such as telecommunications, public transport, water and airports. Furthermore, the US adopted sanctions against the Community which in its turn adopted counter-sanctions.

5. The government procurement agreement is not a real multilateral agreement whose adhesion is mandatory to be part of the WTO. The GPA is one of the GATT plurilateral agreements or codes. Its membership is limited, even though it is potentially open to all WTO Members.

6. Compared to the previous code, the GPA, which entered into force on January 1st, 1996, covers central government and sub-central governments (i.e. regional and local agencies) that are listed in Appendix I to the GPA submitted by each Party. The GPA also covers public utilities operating in ports, airports, water, electricity and urban transport sectors with the major exception of telecommunication.

The GPA does not define what is meant by government procurement. It covers the award of goods, service and construction contracts above the thresholds. In the GPA, these thresholds vary depending on the status of the contracting entity in question (whether central or regional) and on whether a good or service is being procured. In addition, some Parties to the GPA have chosen to apply differential thresholds. That means that they are able to have higher thresholds than other Parties, and thus reduce the number of contracts that they have to put out to international competition.

All goods are in principle covered by the GPA, except those specifically exempted for defence or other reasons. The services that are covered by the GPA are listed individually by Parties in Annexes 4 and 5 to Appendix I.

It has been estimated that the new GPA will open to international bidding, contracts worth around 350 billions ECU every year.

7. Article III of the GPA sets out the two basic principles governing the GPA: **national treatment**, which prohibits discrimination between foreign and domestic sources, and **most-favoured-nation**, which prohibits discrimination between foreign sources. Article III also prohibits discrimination between locally-established suppliers on the basis of degree of foreign ownership or on the basis of the country of origin of the goods or services being supplied. However, the national treatment provisions of Article III are modified to provide for reciprocity in the award of service contracts, and for all contracts awarded by utilities. In effect, the GPA is a series of bilateral agreements coexisting under a multilateral roof (i.e. a common set of rules). Indeed, the GPA allows Parties to derogate from Article III in order to secure reciprocity as regards coverage of entities, sectors and as regards thresholds.

These principles are supplemented by detailed rules on procedures. They are articulated along certain lines.

Discrimination is one of them. An example of the nondiscrimination principle may be found in the way technical specifications are defined in tender documents. Specifications may be used to define the performance requirements of the goods or services to be procured. These may include safety features, methods of production or conformity assessment procedures. Specifications could be used to favour a particular supplier. That is why reference should always be made to a commonly agreed international standard — where one exists — or other recognized standard. However, procurement rules may provide for certain exemptions to the nondiscrimination principle. For example, some Parties to the GPA provide for a certain number of contracts to be "set aside" for small and medium sized enterprises. One GPA Contracting Party also has a special provision relating to offset (i.e. technology transfer or buy-back arrangements), requiring suppliers to work with local industry.

Transparency is also essential for an open public procurement system; it is most often achieved by advertising contracts in official gazettes or newspapers. There are three types of advertisement, or notice:

- tender notices, which are used to invite bids for a particular contract;
- indicative notices, which are used to announce future contracts and to invite suppliers to express their interest in bidding for those contracts. They can also be used to advertise details of qualification procedures for purchasers that keep lists of qualified suppliers;
- post-award notices, which are used to advertise details of the winning supplier and the price at which a contract was awarded.

There are also three types of tendering procedures, which must also be announced at the start of the contract award process:

- the open procedure, in which all interested suppliers may submit tenders;
- the restricted procedure, in which only qualified suppliers are invited to submit tenders;
- the negotiated procedure, in which the purchaser consults the suppliers of its choice and negotiates the terms and price of the contract with one or more of them. The use of this procedure is often restricted and must be justified.

The operation of the entire procurement system must be **objective and fair**. Sufficient time must be given to bidders to prepare and submit their bids; tender documentation must be explicit and accessible; selection and award criteria must be objective and nondiscriminatory; and remedies must be available to bidders in order to prevent or correct infringements of procurement rules by purchasers:

- time-limits for submitting tenders are provided;

- tender documentation (i.e. the detailed information which the purchaser prepares on the goods or services it intends to buy and the procedure it will follow) should be explicit enough to enable suppliers to submit eligible tenders and should be sent to suppliers upon request. Tender documentation usually sets out the address to which tenders should be sent, the closing date for submitting bids and other deadlines. It should also make clear any relevant technical specifications, selection and award criteria and terms of payment;

- selection criteria concern the general suitability of suppliers. Proof of financial and technical reliability, supported by bank references, are objective indicators of a supplier's suitability for carrying out government work;

- bidders who meet objective selection criteria can then be assessed against award criteria. These may be the lowest price, or may involve a qualitative analysis, enabling purchasers to identify the economically most advantageous offer. That qualitative evaluation must be carried out fairly, and involve objective criteria such as delivery date, running costs, functional characteristics, technical merit, cost-effectiveness, after-sales services, or security of supply.

Public procurement procedures should also be supported by effective **remedies**, enabling bidders to challenge the improper award of contracts in national courts or before an independent tribunal. These remedies should provide for the suspension of the contract and for the award of damages to the injured Party.

8. One of the most difficult questions in practice is the exact scope of the agreement. Despite the MFN provision, each Party has defined in several annexes which of its entities will be covered by the agreement. These entities are not automatically offered to all other Parties since the coverage was negotiated on a bilateral basis. As a consequence, the listed entities are not obliged to accept the same types of bids from all Parties. The main differences occur mostly with respect to the utility sectors although some of them also exist at the sub-central level. Furthermore, most offers are accompanied by general notes modifying their scope. Finally, there is no parallelism between the different offers. For instance, the Community might have exchanged the electricity sector against the transport sector by railways of one country. A different approach was difficult because all Parties tried to measure the economic impact of their proposal and endeavoured to strike a balance with the other offers.

IV. COMPARISON BETWEEN
THE EC APPROACH AND THE GPA

1. When comparing the evolution in the Community with the developments under the GATT and now the WTO, many points of convergence appear even though some important differences remain. Even from a superficial viewpoint, it is obvious that the EC experience has had a decisive impact on the achievements so far in the multilateral context.

2. The philosophy supporting the GPA is similar to that contained in the EC directives. In both cases, the objective of public procurement rules is to obtain the best value for money. The best way to achieve this is through the adoption of very detailed rules of procedure besides the general principle of nondiscrimination. As in the Community, such rules are only applicable above certain thresholds, which are very close to those contained in the EC texts.

3. As for coverage, large similarities exist. The GPA covers for most countries goods, works and services, as well as the major utilities sectors.

4. A detailed examination of the provisions of the GPA also shows a clear influence from the EC directives. However, as shown by the brief historical description above, this influence was partly indirect. Actually, the EC members had a strong influence on the OECD draft text which served as a basis for the Tokyo Round Agreement. When the new GPA was discussed, the model of the EC directives was particularly relevant.

The contents of the GPA as well as the solutions chosen are very close to the EC approach. Transparency is also a key element of the system and several provisions aim to ensure fairness amongst all bidders. In many provisions, the GPA shows similarities to the directives. For instance, the information which must be given in the published notices is almost identical in both systems.

Despite these links between the GPA and the directives, some differences do exist.

5. The main difference results from Article 3.8 of the GATT Agreement and its consequences. As already mentioned, under the EC Treaty, the principles of discrimination and of equality of treatment are applicable to all kinds of government procurement. These principles have been given a wide interpretation and can be applied to many situations. Under the GATT, there is no such equivalent. The principle of national treatment is contained within the GPA. However, this does not cover all kinds of government procurement since thresholds are applicable. Outside the scope of the GPA, it is impossible to control the purchases made by public authorities. National treatment under the GATT Agreement also differs from the principle of nondiscrimination under the EC Treaty. The latter has a broader scope. The principle of national treatment in the WTO obliges equal treatment of both nationals and non-nationals. However, a legislation could provide for an identical treatment and at the same time create obstacles for a non-national. For instance, legislation could oblige a purchasing entity to wait for a certain period of time between the publication of the call for tender and the award of the contract. If the delay is identical for nationals and non-nationals, the principle of national treatment is probably not violated. From a practical point of view, however, if the delay is very short, nationals will be in a favourable position compared to their foreign competitors. Such a situation would probably be more difficult to condemn under the WTO system than under EC law.

6. With respect to coverage, one important difference must be underlined: private firms are not covered by the GPA. Despite many efforts by the EC negotiators, the approach followed in the Community in that respect has not been shared by the other Parties to the agreement. Only public entities are included, even in the utility sector. However, the question of privatization is not totally absent from the GPA. It is indeed very likely that ownership of some listed entities changes over time. The effects of such a privatization are somewhat surprising. One could have imagined that no compensation would be needed in such a case because the privatized entity would buy efficiently because of the market pressure and no need for legal constraint would then exist. However, Article XXIV clearly states that the privatized entity must be replaced by an equivalent entity offered by the Party. This example demonstrates once again that the GPA is based on reciprocity.

7. The GPA grants national treatment to products, services and suppliers. This implies that not only the nationality of the supplier is relevant, whereas within the Community the situation is different. The directives can be invoked by all suppliers established in the Community even

414

though their products originate from a third country. Once they are put into trade in the Community, they can freely circulate within the EC. The only qualification is Article 36 of the directives on the utilities sector which provides for a Community preference under some specific circumstances. The discrepancies in the approaches could lead to potential conflicts. If a supplier based in the Community participates in a call for tender with a product originating from a GPA country, he could theoretically benefit from both the EC directives and the GPA. However, when the content of the directives will be made consistent with the GPA, such situations will have almost no practical effect except for the fact that a panel might be required in case of violations of the GPA.

V. WHY ARE THERE SO MANY LINKS BETWEEN THE GPA AND THE EC RULES?

1. The influence of the EC experience on the GPA is hardly surprising. The need for harmonization in the Community was mainly explained by the necessity to avoid any trade distortions resulting from protectionism. The same logic can apply at the multilateral level.

2. Furthermore, the EC experience has shown how to achieve some kind of market integration in this sector. The EC was in a position to put forth to its partners a detailed set of rules both transparent and more easily readable than those existing elsewhere. In most other countries, procurement rules can only be found in numerous legislation and regulations. This is even true in the Community itself, where national legislation of Member States is often lengthier and more complicated than the directives.

3. Finally, the history of the negotiation process shows that the impulse was at the start mainly bilateral (US and Community) with other Parties being, to a certain extent, in the position of followers. This has had its disadvantages. Many countries perceived the GPA as an elitist club for some developed countries and have for this reason decided not to join.

VI. THE EFFECTS OF THE MULTILATERAL EVOLUTION ON THE REGIONAL INTEGRATION

1. The relationship between regional integration and the multilateralism is not a one way street. Even though there are clear links between provisions contained in regional agreements on public procurement and the

GPA, the contents of the latter has some direct consequence on the former.

2. In the case of the Community, the opinion that has been adopted by the Community institutions is very straightforward. After its ratification by the Community institutions and its entry into force in the beginning of 1996, the GPA is part of the Community law.

One has to clearly distinguish this with the question of the direct applicability of the GPA. A text can be part of Community law and not have direct effect. This means that Member States must adopt implementing measures, if needed, to comply with the obligations stemming from the international text being incorporated in the community law. In the case of all the Uruguay Round agreements (including the GPA), the Council has clearly stated that the texts resulting from this round were not supposed to have direct effect. However, one must admit that this statement only clarifies the intent of the Parties once ratifying the agreements, but would not in itself prevent the Court of Justice from giving a different analysis if it so wishes. Indeed, only the Court of Justice is competent to decide on the exact effects of a text in the Community legal order.

The failure for Member States to comply with the GPA could therefore lead to an infringement procedure brought under Article 169 of the EC Treaty.

3. However, even though the GPA is part of the Community law without any need for implementing measures at the Community level, the Community has felt the need to modify the public procurement directives. Indeed, to the extent that some provisions of the GPA give more rights to non-EC suppliers compared to the rights given by the directives, the Commission has proposed certain amendments to the directives in order to avoid inverse discrimination. An alignment of both texts will also facilitate the preparation of calls of tenders by purchasing entities. Otherwise, two different types of calls for tenders will have to be prepared each time.

4. Finally, one can not deny that the multilateral framework constitutes an important limitation on what can be done at the regional level. Members of the GPA are no longer free to change their legislation if that means a contradiction with international obligations. This is true even in the case of the Community because it is not realistic to have two contradictory regimes in the same area, one for the international calls for tenders and another for the members of the regional integration.

VII. THE FUTURE

1. The GPA is not a real multilateral agreement: few countries are members and reciprocity is a key element. Two reasons are mainly advanced for explaining such limited success. On the one hand, public procurement rules are often perceived by less developed countries as a one way street. By opening their government procurement they will be giving access to suppliers of the most developed nations whilst their suppliers will not be, in any case, in a position to obtain contracts in the most developed countries. On the other hand, there is a perception that the GPA is a complicated agreement which is not applicable as such in less developed countries.

2. Both arguments have their merits. It certainly holds true that suppliers from less developed countries will be faced with new competitors. However, one must not forget that public procurement rules are procedural rules. They aim to guarantee the transparency and the fairness of the purchasing process but they do not oblige to buy foreign products if national suppliers have better offers. From this viewpoint, the EC experience can be very enlightening. All statistics in the Community show that the amount of cross-border purchasing is still limited in the case of government procurement. Several reasons can explain this situation. One of them stems from the fact that most suppliers feel that being close to the purchasing entities is preferable and, accordingly, they decide to participate in calls for tenders through their local subsidiaries. This is especially true for public works. An opening of a public procurement market could therefore be an incentive for foreign firms to establish themselves in other countries, which will also increase the competitiveness of local firms.

It is true that the reading of the GPA is a difficult exercise and its application can raise many questions. As it has been explained, this is partly due to the influence of Community law. However, the GPA is aimed at developed countries, already familiar — some for a while — with rules on government procurement. Even within the EC, the application of the directives is sometimes difficult. This is shown by the difficulties existing in the transposition of the directives into national law or by the infringements resulting not always from bad intentions but from ignorance. If this model could not be followed by the present Parties of the GPA, it is unlikely that it could become in its present form a true multilateral agreement in the short run. However, from this viewpoint, the EC experience is also pertinent. People tend to focus only on the directives, but EC law on public procurement also contains the rules and

principles of the EC Treaty. For a long time, only these rules and principles were applied in the case of government procurement. This could be
a solution for the future.

3. Three different paths are now envisaged to expand abidance to some
kind of rules on public procurement at the multilateral level.

Public procurement of services is not covered under the GATT Agreement. However, one of its provisions states that negotiations on this subject should begin within two years after its entry into force. The discussions have already started in Geneva on this basis. The GATT's being a
true multilateral agreement constitutes certainly a useful forum.

The GPA itself provides for a review before the end of a three year
period (i.e. in 1999 at the latest). Several delegations in Geneva including the EC have been vocal for an early review of its provisions. During
the Singapore Ministerial Conference, it was agreed that such a process
will start in 1997. This review should also look into taking into account
within the GPA the evolution resulting from the development of the information technology.

Finally, the US and the Community had launched the idea of negotiating a true multilateral agreement based on certain principles. A paragraph of the Singapore Ministerial conference declaration concerns government procurement. It states that the ministers agree to "establish a
working group to conduct a study on transparency in government procurement practices, taking into account national policies and, based
on this study, to develop elements for inclusion in an appropriate
agreement."

This text is less ambitious than the papers submitted by the EC and
the US in preparation for the conference. According to these proposals,
the principles on which this agreement could be based are transparency,
openness and due process. For the Community, nondiscrimination is also
very important but one has to recognize that few countries are ready as
yet to open their procurement markets completely. An approach based
on principles is not completely unfamiliar to the Community since for a
long time, procurement in the Community was covered only by the principles of the EC Treaty. One could establish a parallel between the situation in Europe thirty years ago and some countries now with one important difference: the Court of Justice has played a major role in the
development of Community law on the basis of the treaty. If such a
scheme were to be followed at the multilateral level, it would be

important that the resolution of conflicts at the multilateral level were also organized efficiently.

The Singapore Declaration is explicit only on two points: a working group is established and it should launch a study on transparency. On the other hand, this text does not rule out the idea that other principles should be incorporated in a true multilateral agreement.

The main challenge for the future will be to coordinate these three approaches and in the future, envisage their merger in order to form one set of rules. This is certainly the key for a true multilateral agreement in the field of public procurement.

COMMENTS

Nicolas MICHEL

Professor,
University of Fribourg, Switzerland

Introduction

The report presented by Mr Pierre Delsaux gives an excellent over-view of the emergence of the respective rules of the European Union and the World Trade Organization (WTO). It shows how much Commu-nity law has influenced the plurilateral rules of the Government Procure-ment Agreement (GPA). It brings out the essential points of convergence and divergence.

The following comments aim to underline and highlight certain spe-cific aspects. Emphasis will be given to the implementation of respec-tive instruments, more particularly to the various means of guaranteeing effective implementation and to one aspect of the social consequences of opening markets.

1. The Effect of EU and GPA Rules in the National Legal Orders

Basic substantial EC Treaty rules, which are also applicable regard-ing public procurement, and many provisions of Community "public pro-curement" directives are considered by Community jurisprudence as di-rect effect rules. In addition, by virtue of the principle of primacy, they take precedence over conflicting national rules. Direct effect and primacy confer great effectiveness on EC rules.

As far as the GPA rules are concerned, it is still premature to assert what effect they will have with certitude. On the one hand, the experience relating to the application of the former GATT rules, in numerous countries, teaches that the tribunals were only prepared to recognize a direct effect as applicable in very rare circumstances; even if a consequential application of the ordinary criteria for recognition of direct effect were to lead to recognition of such an effect in a good number of the GPA rules, it would still be risky to claim that, in practice, this direction will be followed. On the other hand, nothing enables us either to affirm that the principle of primacy will be applied outside the European Community in as efficient a way as in the relations between the Community legal order and that of Member States. Moreover, it has been established that primary Community law affects public procurement procedures even below the directives' application thresholds, but that the GPA has no effect whatever on purchases which are not included in its field of application, for instance on those below the application thresholds of the agreement.

If one wanted to ensure better convergence between Community law and GPA law in the field of public procurement, then the latter should be developed along the lines of potential recognition of direct effect in certain rules, of primacy as well as of the application of the major fundamental principles of transparency, openness and nondiscrimination in all procurement procedures. By simply listing these aims one realizes that this type of development is improbable in the short term, and even in the middle term.

2. Remedies at National Level

Legal remedies play a major role as far as public procurement is concerned because, in the absence of any efficient control mechanism, the opening of public procurement markets with its fundamental principle of nondiscrimination might risk not becoming very effective.

The fact that international or supranational instruments impose on states that they make provision for effective legal protection systems is relatively recent. The first Community Directive in this field was passed in 1989 (Directive 89/669/EEC). As far as the WTO is concerned, the requirement of a proper jurisdictional protection system appears for the first time in the GPA adopted in Marrakech at the conclusion of the Uruguay Round. The significance of the respective measures justifies the following remarks :

a) Applicable Measures

In Community law, there are two directives which concern legal protection regarding public procurement:

- Council Directive 89/665/EEC of December 21, 1989 on the coordination of the laws, regulations and administrative provisions relating to the application of review procedures to the award of public supply and public works contracts *(The Public Remedies Directive)* (OJ L 395/33 of December 30, 1989); the field of application of this directive has been extended to cover the sphere of services by Article 41 of the Public Services Directive, modifying paragraph 1 of the Public Remedies Directive.
- Council Directive 92/13/EEC of February 25, 1992 coordinating the laws, regulations and administrative provisions relating to the application of Community rules on the procurement procedures of entities operating in the water, energy, transport and telecommunications sectors *(The Remedies Utilities Directive)* (OJ L 76/14 of March 23, 1992).

According to Article 1(1) of the Public Remedies Directive, the Member States shall take the measures necessary to ensure that, as regards contract award procedures falling within the scope of the Public Works Directive, the Public Supplies Directive and the Public Services Directive, decisions taken by the contracting authorities **may be reviewed effectively and, in particular, as rapidly as possible** on the grounds that such decisions have infringed Community law in the field of public procurement or national rules implementing that law.

The GPA deals with challenge procedures in its Article XX, paragraph 2 of which reads as follows:

Each Party shall provide nondiscriminatory, timely, transparent and effective procedures enabling suppliers to challenge alleged breaches of the Agreement arising in the context of procurements in which they have, or have had, an interest.

b) The Field of Application

It should be recalled that measures of organization and procedure established respectively by the directives and the GPA are only applicable within the limits of the fields of application of these instruments.

Concerning Community law, one might wonder, however, whether the principle of fair cooperation, as established in Article 5 of the EC Treaty, does not oblige Member States, also in the sphere of public procurement, to ensure legal protection of rights conferred by Community legal order, regardless of the application thresholds of the directives.

c) Grounds for Challenge

According to the Review Procedures Directives, challengers may make a complaint about an infringement of **Community law** in the field of public procurement or of **national rules implementing that law** (Public Remedies Directive Art.1(1), Remedies Utilities Directive Art.1(1)).

On the other hand, according to Article XX §2 of the Government Procurement Agreement, the suppliers may assert breaches of the agreement but not breaches of national rules implementing the agreement.

It is worth noting that the Community directives provide that the challenger may cite a violation of the national execution clauses, whereas the GPA does not offer the challenger this possibility.

d) Interim Measures

According to the two remedies directives, the challenge authority must be able to take, at the earliest opportunity and by way of interlocutory procedure, interim measures with the aim of correcting the alleged infringement or preventing further damage to the interests concerned, **including measures to suspend or to ensure the suspension of the procedure for the award of a contract or the implementation of any decision taken by the contracting entity.** Under EC law interim measures include the suspension of execution of a concluded contract. In the *Wallonia Buses* Case (Ruling of April 22, 1994, *Commission v. Belgium* C-87/94 R, ECR 1994), the President of the Court discussed, in application of Article 186 of the Treaty, the question as to whether it should take interim measures even though the contract had been already concluded. Consequently, it would be surprising if it did not also interpret the remedies directives in the sense that the "suspension of [...] the implementation of any decision taken by the contracting authority/entity" also encompasses the suspension of execution of the contract.

According to the terms of Article XX §7(a) of the GPA, challenge procedures shall provide for: rapid interim measures to correct breaches of the agreement and to preserve commercial opportunities. Such action may result in suspension of the procurement process. However the GPA does not require the possibility of suspension of execution of the contract through interim measures.

It follows that, as far as interim measures are concerned, the Community system would appear to offer better protection than the GPA system. In fact, legal protection is more effective if there is the possibility of suspending, not only the process of conclusion, but also the execution of the contract.

e) The Scope of the Ruling

According to the EC directives, the challenge authorities must be empowered to either set aside or ensure the **setting aside of decisions taken unlawfully**, including the removal of discriminatory specifications in documents relating to the contract award procedure (Public Remedies Directive and Remedies Utilities Directive Art.2(1)(b)). It is up to Member States to determine in their internal regulations the effect of the setting aside of a decision on a **concluded contract**; furthermore, a Member State may provide (except where a decision must be set aside prior to the award of damages) that, after the conclusion of a contract following its award, the powers of the body responsible for the review procedures shall be limited to awarding damages to any person harmed by an infringement (Public Remedies Directive and Utilities Remedies Directives Art.2(6)). In this last hypothesis, the challenged decision is not set aside.

Under the GPA, however, according to the terms of Article XX §7(c), challenge procedures shall provide either for correction of the breach of the agreement **or** for compensation for the loss or damages suffered. In other words, the legislation of a state may provide that in case of breach of the agreement the unlawful decision will not be annulled, even in cases where the contract has not yet been concluded.

f) The Damages

Article 2 §1(c) of the Public Remedies Directive and Article 2 §1(d) of the Remedies Utilities Directive specify that the legal protection mechanism to be established by Member States must provide the power to award **damages to persons harmed by an infringement**, without stipulating which elements of damage must be taken into account in the calculation of damages. Can the total amount of damages therefore be limited for example to the costs for tender preparation or protest, following the example of Article XX §7(c) of the GPA?

In view of the most recent case law, it seems that this question must be negated. In fact, in *Brasserie du pêcheur* and *Factortame* (Ruling of

March 5, 1996, *Brasserie du pêcheur SA v. Bundesrepublik Deutschland and The Queen/Secretary of State for Transport, ex parte: Factortame Ltd. e.a.*, C-46/93 and C-48/93, §90, ECR 1996), the Court declared that "national regulations which, generally speaking, might limit repairable damages to those damages caused to certain specially protected individual property, with the exception of the income loss sustained by the individuals, are not in conformity with Community law" (non-official translation). This question deserves to be given deeper thought.

According to Article XX §7(c) of the GPA, states are free to limit the damages which may be limited to costs for tender preparation or protest.

From what has been said so far, it would appear that, regarding damages, Community law is more favourable to the ousted tenderer than the WTO law.

In conclusion to these remarks on remedies at national level, it should be noted that in spite of appearances, the GPA rules do not necessarily ensure effective application of the agreement since award of the contract can be maintained and the amount of damages can be considerably limited.

3. Case Law of the European Court of Justice

On the subject of legal protection, it is important to emphasize yet another aspect mentioned in Mr. Delsaux's report: legal protection at the Community level. In fact, the European Court of Justice has rendered over forty rulings and eight orders for interim measures, following action for failure to comply with obligations under the treaties or preliminary ruling procedures. Although the Court's decisions are interesting regarding interpretation of provisions of directives, their essential potential for development lies in the interpretation of the basic substantial rules of primary law and of general principles such as the principle of equality of treatment, as well as in the development of interim measures, parallel to on-going national procedures, including more particularly the suspension not only of the procurement process but also of the execution of a concluded contract.

As for control of the application of the WTO law, the mechanisms of the organization still have to prove themselves. Considering the influence Community law has on the GPA, it will be interesting to note to what extent the case law of the European Court of Justice will be taken into account within the WTO.

4. Social Protection

One of the most controversial aspects of the implementation of Community directives and the GPA is the effect opening up public procurement markets will have both on employment and on the level of social protection for workers in states which enjoy a more advanced social system. Deep concern has sometimes been expressed about the risk of social imbalance arising from the pressures of international competition and disregard for respect for collective agreements or other social prescriptions in force in the Member State where the contract is executed. The question is more particularly urgent regarding public works procurement.

These concerns were the centre of lively debate not only within several Member States, particularly in Germany, but also within the European Union institutions. At the end of a controversial legislative process, the Council of the European Union has just adopted, December 16, 1996, a Posting of Workers Directive. The Directive requires, whenever there is cross-border movement of workers in the framework of a transnational provision of services, that the undertakings concerned guarantee the workers they have posted the terms and conditions of employment which are applicable in the Member States where the work is carried out, in as far as these prescriptions are mandatory for national undertakings. The notion of "terms and conditions of employment" includes minimum rates of pay, work periods, paid holidays, as well as health, safety and hygiene at work. The directive will be applicable, in principle, as of the first day of the posting, but the national legislator will, in certain cases, provide a time limit of up to one month. The way had already been opened up by the European Court of Justice (Ruling of March 27, 1990, *Rush Portuguesa*, C-113/89, ECR 1990 (§§ 12 and 18) .

The new directive sets rules which, for social reasons, limit competition. No doubt that this development will influence debate within the WTO.

Conclusion

In way of conclusion, here are two final remarks:

Community statistics according to which cross-border purchases are still limited deserve critical attention. On the one hand, implementation of such an ambitious set of directives necessarily requires a good many years. On the other, it is imperative to try to draw the lessons from experience acquired over the past years. I am all in favour of Mr. Delsaux's conclusion that it is important to work towards optimal coordination on the measures regulating public procurement, and to try to concentrate on a certain number of essential principles, even if it means giving up very detailed provisions, as long as the legal protection mechanisms function effectively.

Regional *versus* Multilateral Approaches to Services and Investment Liberalization: Anything to Worry About?[1]

Pierre SAUVÉ

Principal Administrator,
OECD Trade Directorate, Paris

A. Introduction

Much has been made of the proliferation of regional trade and investment liberalization agreements and the systemic challenges such agreements might potentially pose for the future of the multilateral trading system. The political economy of regional *versus* multilateral approaches to liberalization has been nothing short of a growth industry in trade policy circles in recent years, contributing a vast amount of scholarly literature on the subject[2].

This paper seeks to add to this burgeoning literature by focusing on a subject matter that has, *à la marge*, received slightly less attention in policy circles: a comparison of regional and multilateral approaches to

---

[1] The views expressed in this paper are personal and should not be attributed to the Organization for Economic Cooperation and Development (OECD) or its member countries. The author is grateful to Malcolm BOSWORTH, Michael HART, Bernard HOEKMAN , Richard SELF and Richard SNAPE for helpful discussions.

[2] See, for instance, *Regional Integration and the Multilateral Trading System: Synergy and Divergence*, Organization for Economic Cooperation and Development, Paris, 1995; and *Regionalism and its Place in the Multilateral Trading System*, Organization for Economic Cooperation and Development, 1996.

liberalizing services and investment[3]. As the subtitle of this paper suggests, the author believes that there are strong grounds to argue that services and investment are areas where the relationship between regional and multilateral attempts at regime formation is likely to display not only broad convergence but also strong complementarity.

There are perhaps three main reasons for coming to this conclusion. A first reason owes to **novelty**. Notwithstanding the fatigue that services negotiators may currently (and somewhat deservedly) feel, the development of rules on services and investment in a trade policy setting remains in its infancy. With the advent of the General Agreement on Trade in Services (GATS), the issue of trade in services has only just graduated from its former status as one of the Uruguay Round's "new trade issues". What's more, the GATS is still very much a work in progress, with negotiations ongoing in a large number of sectoral and substantive areas (hence the fatigue noted above). Much, therefore, remains to be "discovered" in the services area. Meanwhile, investment probably ranks first amongst the post-Uruguay Round's crop of so-called "new" trade challenges, thanks in no small measure to the inherently complementary links between trade and investment in a globalizing environment and the decision by OECD countries to launch negotiations on a proposed Multilateral Agreement on Investment (MAI)[4].

A second reason owes to the political economy of **recurring headaches**. Regardless of the negotiating setting in which they have taken place (i.e. bilateral, regional, plurilateral or multilateral level), attempts at services and investment liberalization have with few exceptions tended to run up against the same sectoral constraints and sensitivities[5]. In plain language, some sectors (e.g. audiovisual services and related "cultural" products, maritime or air transport, basic telecommunications) have to date proven more or less immune to liberalization, whatever the negotiating forum. This broad symmetry in negotiated **outcomes** obviously lessens the scope for policy segmentation (i.e. an incipient multi-tiered

---

[3] For a more complete consideration of regional approaches to services trade liberalization, see HOEKMAN Bernard & SAUVÉ Pierre, *Liberalizing Trade in Services*, **Discussion Papers**, No.243, The World Bank, Washington, D.C., 1994.

[4] For more background on both of these contributing factors, see *Market Access after the Uruguay Round: Investment, Competition and Technology Perspectives*, Organization for Economic Cooperation and Development, Paris, 1996.

[5] Civil aviation being one such example, given the spate of more liberal bilateral agreements negotiated recently throughout the world, as well as the comprehensive liberalization package underway within the European Community. Such liberalization, however, remains highly sector-specific, and has not, to date, found its place within the broader remit of a trade and investment policy environment.

trade and investment regime), a fear that underpins much of the debate over the potentially negative systemic effects of regionalism.

A third reason relates to the numerous advantages of **laboratory testing**. Regional attempts at regime formation in the services and investment areas have, in recent years, proven excellent testing grounds for developing what could (and ideally should) be tomorrow's integrated multilateral architecture of rules in both areas. Regional agreements have also allowed for a degree of experimentation in rule-design and policy dialogue that is often (and most unfortunately) not possible in a World Trade Organization (WTO) context. Seen in this light, and because the operation of existing regional agreements affecting services and investment has to date proven fairly benign, regionalism may actually be viewed as performing an essential early signalling task in both policy domains.

The rest of this paper highlights the positive policy interaction between regional and multilateral approaches to services and investment liberalization. It does so by recalling the treatment of services and investment in what stand out as the most relevant regional arrangements: the European Union (EU), the North American Free Trade Agreement (NAFTA), and the Australia-New Zealand Closer Economic Relations Trade Agreement (ANZCERTA). Many other recent or ongoing regional experiments could of course be looked at, chief among which are Mercosur, the proposed Free Trade in the Americas Agreement (FTAA), the Asia-Pacific Economic Cooperation forum (APEC), or the proposed ASEAN Free Trade Agreement (AFTA). The latter are not discussed in this paper, either because such arrangements do not currently cover services and/or investment or because the development of binding rules likely to influence the design of multilateral disciplines is not (or not yet) a defining feature of otherwise very useful policy dialogues.

This paper goes on to explore **whether** and **how** developments in the three regional arrangements noted above might actually provide useful guidance to governments as they seek to develop new and improved rules of the game for services and investment at the multilateral level. However, before determining whether "regional" medicine can be prescribed at the multilateral level, it is perhaps useful to diagnose what the patient is allegedly suffering from. This paper, therefore, turns its immediate attention to some of the "architectural" challenges that flow from the design and operation of current multilateral disciplines affecting services and investment.

B. In Need of a Fix?
WTO Rules on Services and Investment

1. Services[6]

Of all the landmark agreements reached in the Uruguay Round, GATS tends to be viewed as perhaps the weakest. Whether in terms of the structure of its core provisions, the means that were developed for securing liberalization commitments or the market access opportunities its rules and commitments have afforded, to date, to end-users, GATS is often regarded as an agreement that has failed to deliver on its promises[7]. This perception has not been much improved by the protracted difficulties encountered in the sectoral negotiations conducted since the WTO's entry into force (e.g. on movement of people, financial, basic telecommunications and maritime transport services). These substantive and procedural weaknesses make it all the more interesting to see whether and how regional approaches to services trade liberalization might inform the debate over the GATS' evolution.

Despite all the criticism that is levelled at GATS, the Agreement may still be viewed as having anticipated many of the policy- and rule-making challenges posed by the process of deepening economic integration. Indeed, in many respects, one of the key rule-making challenges confronting the multilateral trading system today is how best to respond to some of the lessons taught by GATS. These are lessons which the globalization process is revealing as quite often generic in nature. That is, applicable beyond services trade to all areas that are (or should perhaps be) subject to WTO disciplines. Such lessons include, *inter alia*, a recognition that:

> (i) trade and investment — access and presence in markets — are indissociable means of doing business, hence the futility of treating them as discrete policy domains requiring distinct rules;

---

[6] The following discussion draws on SAUVÉ Pierre, *"Services and the International Contestability of Markets"*, in: **Transnational Corporations**, 1996.

[7] See HOEKMAN Bernard, *"Assessing the General Agreement on Trade in Services"*, in: MARTIN W. & WINTERS L.A. (eds), *The Uruguay Round and the Developing Economies*, **Discussion Papers**, No.307, The World Bank, Washington, D.C., 1995, pp.327-364; SAUVÉ Pierre, *"Assessing the General Agreement on Trade in Services: Half-Full or Half-Empty?"*, in: **Journal of World Trade**, Vol.29, No.4, August 1995, pp.125-45; and SNAPE Richard H. & BOSWORTH Malcolm, *Advancing Services Negotiations*, Paper presented at an Institute for International Economics Conference on "The World Trading System: Challenges Ahead", Washington, D.C., June 24/25, 1996.

(ii) the distinction between goods and services, which lays at the root of the Uruguay Round's "two-track" approach, is of equally dubious merit, particularly from a broad market access perspective and at a time when technology is rendering many more services internationally tradable through their bundling with goods[8];

(iii) disciplines on private anti-competitive conduct form, alongside those targeted at the removal of public trade and investment impediments, form an essential ingredient of effective access and presence in markets;

(iv) "competition-friendly" domestic regulatory conduct is key to securing and enhancing — and not nullifying — the market access and market presence opportunities that flow from trade and investment liberalization;

(v) a wide variety of nondiscriminatory measures, both quantitative and regulatory in nature, may impair market access and presence opportunities; and,

(vi) reaping the full benefits of globalization requires that more be done to facilitate the international mobility of business people, who are key agents of deep integration and whose reasons for crossing borders span a broader universe than that addressed by GATS.

Despite the fact that GATS negotiations represented the first truly multilateral attempt to confront the numerous policy challenges deriving from globalization, the agreement suffers from a number of shortcomings. It is useful, therefore, to reflect on some of the "architectural" or rule-design challenges left outstanding (or addressed in an unsatisfactory manner) by the Uruguay Round and on the best means of addressing them, some of which may well draw on lessons learnt at the regional level. Three such challenges come to mind most vividly:

(i) the fact that **the agreement is unduly removed from other parts of the WTO family of agreements**. While this reflects the (by now hackneyed) North-South divide that permeated the Punta del Este Declaration, it imparted a significant "reinvent-the-wheel" dimension to the services negotiations, a problem that was compounded by the novelty of the subject matter. The result is an agreement that is not designed to exploit the real world synergies (including from a negotiating point of view) that flow

---

[8] See WYCKOFF Andrew, *"The Growing Strength of Services"*, in: **The OECD Observer**, No.200, June-July 1996, pp.11-15.

from the increasing convergence between goods, services, investment and intellectual property-related issues (e.g. the link between product standards affecting telecommunications equipment and the services sold using such equipment). Duplication is another side-effect, for example when GATS calls for (multilateral) services-specific rules on government procurement (at a time when the WTO's (plurilateral) Government Procurement Agreement already covers services and construction);

(ii) the fact that **the agreement contains so few obligations that are of truly general application** (only in respect of the agreement's provisions on transparency and most-favored-nation treatment). This comes in marked contrast to **all** other constituent parts of the WTO and gives GATS a distinct (and distinctly weakening) *à la carte* flavor[9]. The question arises of why so many of GATS' core disciplines, for example on domestic regulatory conduct or on payments and transfers (which already governed by multilateral disciplines under the International Monetary Fund (IMF) articles of agreement) should be conditioned on the *bon vouloir* of a member's scheduled commitment?; and,

(iii) the fact that **GATS uses a highly unsatisfactory approach to scheduling liberalization commitments**, through its combination of a positive list approach to coverage and recourse to scheduling by sector **and** mode of supply. This scheduling technology has introduced a number of shortcomings, chief among which is the generation of schedules of commitments that lack significantly in user-friendliness. In turn, this:

- seriously complicates attempts at measuring — and hence marketing — the tangible liberalization benefits accruing to the GATS' core constituency: business users;

- generates insufficient transparency (the most precious of commodities given the regulatory nature of impediments to services trade), especially in non-scheduled sectors (where restrictions typically abound);

- allows for the maintenance of potentially significant gaps between the nature and level of country bindings and the actual regulatory situation prevailing in any given services market; and,

---

[9] See SNAPE & BOSWORTH, *op.cit.*, (1996) for a more complete discussion of this issue.

- introduces a scheduling/liberalization bias against the cross-border supply of services in favor of the commercial presence mode of supply[10].

On this latter issue, it is worth recalling that the scheduling approach adopted in GATS does not derive from any specific provision found in the agreement. Rather, the "hybrid" approach was adopted in a somewhat *ad hoc* manner in the final stages of the Uruguay Round[11]. What this means, then, is that it can (and should) be revisited in the context of the GATS' built-in agenda on rule-making matters, though negotiators have so far shown a disquieting aversion to doing so.

An opportunity to re-examine the scheduling technology of GATS would however present itself if and when WTO Members were to agree to address investment-rule-making in a more comprehensive manner. This is so, given the numerous overlaps that would arise between the commercial presence-related provisions of the GATS and an overarching set of disciplines on investment liberalization and protection that would need to be embedded at the very core of the WTO's architecture. Though the GATS contains by far the largest number of investment-related provisions found in the Final Act of the Uruguay Round, the need to address potentially overlapping obligations — hence to achieve greater coherence and complementarity between multilateral rules on trade and investment — would also arise in regard to a number of other WTO Agreements, e.g. the Trade-Related Investment Measures (TRIMs) and Trade-Related Aspects of Intellectual Property Rights (TRIPs) Agreements, the Agreement on Subsidies and Countervailing Measures, as well as the WTO's integrated Dispute Settlement Understanding.

---

[10] For more on the TRIM-like outcome generated by the GATS' hybrid approach to scheduling commitments, see SAUVÉ Pierre, *"A First Look at Investment in the Final Act of the Uruguay Round"*, in: **Journal of World Trade**, Vol.28, No.5, October 1994, pp.5-16.

[11] The political economy of this decision is most interesting. Two main reasons, one substantive, one more procedural, led to the adoption of a hybrid approach. In substantive terms, many countries (and not only developing ones) were of the view that the adoption of the alternative top-down/negative list approach would result in greater pressure to liberalize than they were prepared to undertake, and would leave them "naked" (i.e. bound at "free") in sectors where regulatory regimes were weak or undeveloped. A positive list approach was preferred because it allowed considerably more selectivity in market opening and did not (perversely) generate an automatic standstill in prevailing regulatory regimes. Procedurally, resistance to negative listing owed mainly to the prevailing sentiment that such an approach could prove particularly burdensome for developing country administrations, particularly if the Uruguay Round had to be completed by the time of the Brussels Ministerial meeting in December 1990.

As regards more specifically the GATS, the incorporation of a comprehensive set of investment disciplines within the WTO would provide an opportunity to effect four broad types of architectural reforms[12]. These are:

(i) **doing away with the need for a modes-of-supply approach** both to defining trade in services and to scheduling liberalization commitments;

(ii) **adopting a negative list approach to scheduling commitments**[13], which presupposes an overarching set of general obligations as a point of departure;

(iii) **replacing the commercial presence dimension of the GATS by a generic set of investment disciplines applicable to all substantive areas subject to WTO disciplines** (i.e. no more services-specific rules on investment); and,

(iv) **going generic, as well, with regard to matters governing the cross-border mobility of business people.** As for investment, there are few if any compelling reasons to confine matters relating to the temporary movement of people solely to a GATS pigeonhole.

The fourfold reform agenda outlined above suggests that GATS should ultimately apply only to cross-border trade in services. Establishment-related "trade" would be governed for its part by a horizontal (i.e. undifferentiated as between goods, services, or Intellectual Property Rights (IPRs)) set of investment disciplines, as would measures governing the temporary movement of service suppliers. More broadly, such an approach would contribute to equipping the multilateral trading system with a more coherent architecture of trade and investment (and hopefully competition disciplines) with which to promote the greater openness of markets for goods, services, ideas, and investment while enhancing the cross-border mobility of business people.

2. Investment

For all the design flaws one may find in the GATS, the agreement may surely not be faulted for lacking in ambition. By comparison, the

---

[12] This may indeed present the only real opportunity to remedy the GATS' key architectural weaknesses given the difficulties inherent in (and the general undesirability of) attempting to reform the GATS from within, i.e. perform what political scientists call "regime reversal".

[13] See SAUVÉ (1996) for a more complete discussion of the economy-wide and negotiating benefits of negative listing.

TRIMs Agreement, the main instrument through which investment matters were supposed to integrate the multilateral trading system during the course of the Uruguay Round, fails even to appear on trade-policy radar screens (though a number of complaints against alleged non-conforming measures, particularly in the automobile sector, have recently been lodged by WTO Members).

As noted earlier, the bulk of WTO provisions dealing directly with investment matters are found in GATS, and not the TRIMs Agreement. While the GATS negotiations have brought out quite vividly the central importance of investment to trade in services and generated far more by way of commercial presence commitments than may have been expected, its treatment of investment-related matters is embodied in provisions which display a number of deficiencies: they lack definitional clarity, do not generate adequate transparency, do not generate an across-the-board standstill, and afford weak and insufficient protection to investors and their investment (as compared to provisions found in most investment agreements or NAFTA). The TRIMs Agreement, for its part, remains extremely limited in scope, and is largely attuned to the concerns of an era in policy-making characterized more by suspicion of — and the need to control — foreign investment than by keenness to compete for and attract such investment. The latter agreement's shortcomings are by now well known and need not be described in any great detail. These include the fact that :

(i)   the agreement governs measures affecting trade in goods only, reflecting once more the "partial equilibrium" approach taken in the Uruguay Round;

(ii) its Illustrative List of prohibited measures covers only a limited subset of trade-distorting performance requirements;

(iii) the agreement does not discipline the granting of investment incentives, to which the undertaking of voluntary or mandatory performance requirements is often closely tied;

(iv) it essentially codifies existing GATT jurisprudence, namely the application of Articles III (National Treatment) and XI (General Elimination of Quantitative Restrictions) to covered measures; and most perversely;

(v)   it grants members the right to temporarily deviate from — indeed enjoy a waiver — from GATT obligations to which they are already bound.

To suggest that much remains to be done multilaterally in the investment field therefore borders on the understatement[14]. This means that negotiators aiming to develop WTO-bound rules on investment have little choice but to seek inspiration from the various "rule-models" provided for by the complex web of existing (or planned) investment agreements, be they bilateral, regional (e.g. NAFTA) or plurilateral (Energy Charter Treaty, MAI). That being said, it bears recalling that the TRIMs Agreement (Article 9) foresees the need, **before the year 2000**, for WTO Members to consider the need for more encompassing work and possible disciplines on investment and competition policy within the multilateral trading system. This is an important means — indeed a major anchor — through which to achieve the overall coherence in rule-design called for above[15].

C. Services and Investment: A Look at Regional Attempts at Regime Formation

An important question underlying this paper's analysis is whether regional agreements and the multilateral process are complementary or

---

[14] Of course, WTO provisions other than those found in GATS and the TRIMs Agreement affect investment-related matters. The TRIPs Agreement, for instance, while containing no detailed provisions dealing specifically with the treatment of investment, may nonetheless be viewed as generating positive investment protection externalities for firms investing in, producing and trading research- and intellectual-property-intensive goods and services. Such protection, however, operates indirectly, insofar as it targets products (investment or services) embodying intellectual property, rather than the investment through which such production takes place (or the investors involved). Similarly, the Uruguay Round Agreement on Subsidies and Countervailing Measures contains a number of disciplines that may potentially relate to the granting of investment incentives.

[15] One of the most compelling reasons for including a comprehensive agreement on investment in the WTO — and one that is particularly germane to the debate over regional *versus* multilateral approaches to liberalization — is the need to establish common multilateral rules for the complex and overlapping web of bilateral (of which there are an estimated 900 such agreements), regional e.g. (APEC, NAFTA), plurilateral (e.g. Energy Charter Treaty) and multilateral (e.g. OECD Instruments, WTO) agreements currently in existence. The existence of these different agreements brings with it the risk of conflicting approaches to emerging investment. More fundamentally still, the inherent complementarity between trade and investment requires an integrated approach to investment and trade. For more on the rationale for placing investment on the WTO's agenda, see WOOLCOCK Stephen, *"An Agenda for the WTO: Strengthening or Burdening the System?"*, paper presented at a joint LSE/RIIA Conference on *"The New Commercial Policy Agenda: Strengthening or Burdening the WTO?"*, London, May 30, 1996. See also GRAHAM Edward M., *"Direct Investment and the Future Agenda of the World Trade Organization"*, paper presented at an Institute for International Economics Conference on *"The World Trading System: Challenges Ahead"*, Washington, D.C., June 24-25, 1996; and BRITTAN, Sir Leon, *"Investment Liberalization: The Next Great Boost to the World Economy?"*, in: **Transnational Corporations**, Vol.4, No.1, April 1995, pp.1-10.

substitute paths to liberalizing barriers affecting services and investment. One way of addressing this question is to compare the effective degree of liberalization achieved under regional auspices as opposed to existing multilateral disciplines. If the magnitude of liberalization — understood in terms of the quality both of **agreed rules** and of **binding commitments** — achieved under regional agreements is limited, the effects on both member and nonmember countries will be small, and the issue of the relationship between regional agreements and the WTO loses much of its potential for controversy. Conversely, if intra-regional liberalization is more extensive, or if there are substantive differences in the nature of the trade and investment liberalizing rules and disciplines, the relationship between regional and multilateral agreements becomes more interesting. An important issue, then, concerns the differences between regional agreements and the WTO, as this will determine the degree of effective discrimination of regional agreements against nonmembers.

1. The European Union

The European Union is unique among the agreements discussed in this paper in that it goes beyond intergovernmental cooperation. This is reflected, *inter alia*, in the fact that the EU has its own prerogatives and resources and that binding decisions on certain issues are taken on the basis of a majority vote. A major objective of the Treaty of Rome, which established the European Economic Community, was the realization of the "four freedoms" of free internal movement; goods, services, labor, and capital, including the right of establishment. In principle, the freedom to provide services applies to all services, with the exception of transportation services for which the primacy of national policies was recognized until a common EU-wide regime was established. As a result, there has been, to date, more limited intra-EU competition in transportation services, with governments frequently setting tariffs (e.g. in rail), imposing and enforcing quotas (road transport), or agreeing to bilateral market-sharing arrangements (air transport).

Although EU Member States abolished border tariffs and quotas affecting intra-EU trade in goods on schedule, until recently very little progress had been made in effectively liberalizing intra-EU trade and investment in services. In the financial services sector, Article 61 of the Treaty of Rome stated that liberalization was to be affected in step with the progressive liberalization of capital movements — on which little progress has been made. Liberalization of the medical and pharmaceutical professions was made contingent upon the harmonization of licensing and certification requirements. Rulings by the European Court of Justice in the mid-1970s reaffirmed that, as of the end of the transitional period (1970), all other services in principle were subject to the relevant provisions of the Treaty of Rome. The main liberalizing principles of the Treaty of Rome in this area are the freedom to provide services (i.e. the freedom to engage in cross-border trade) and the freedom of establishment. These principles proved to be insufficient to lead to a significant increase in the openness of many EU service markets because differences in national regulations — rather than policies that explicitly discriminated between domestic and other EU firms — constituted the major barriers to market access. Not surprisingly, the prevailing view up to the mid-1980's was that progress to achieve the liberalization of services transactions was so slow as to raise serious doubts as to whether it would ever arrive at its destination.

Lack of progress appeared to be due to a lack of enthusiasm on the part of many EU members. Many Member States argued in the Council that a necessary precondition for liberalization was the adoption of common regulatory policies for specific services, and that in the absence of harmonization, the principle of national treatment should continue to be applied. However, repeated efforts at agreeing to harmonized policies proved relatively unfruitful. In part, this failure reflected a disinterest on the part of service industries to expand beyond domestic markets and to form a unified EU Internal Market. To the extent that service industries desired to compete in other EU markets, establishing branches or subsidiaries appeared to be the preferred option. Foreign direct investment within the Union by EU service companies has generally been allowed without significant restrictions. Once established, affiliates are, of course, subject to host country standards and regulations. The Council's harmonization practice prior to the adoption of the Single European Act implied that freedom to establish and freedom to provide services were regarded as closely linked, if not equivalent.

The liberalization that occurred during the 1970s and early 1980s was, thus, mostly the result of **unilateral** initiatives by certain countries to deregulate specific industries. This changed with the adoption of the Single Market or EC-1992 program, which represented an attempt to achieve the original objectives of the Treaty of Rome, although by going beyond the original treaty by introducing the concept of the "Internal Market". Among other things, the Single European Act led to the adoption of qualified majority voting in the Council on most issues relating to the establishment and functioning of the Internal Market, agreement to open up public procurement markets — including services — to

EU-wide competition, and the introduction of the concepts of minimum standards, mutual recognition and "home country control" for regulatory regimes. The principle of mutual recognition — which originated in decisions of the European Court of Justice — requires Member States to allow products lawfully introduced into the commerce of one EU country to be sold in all other Member States. While relatively straightforward when applied to goods, the intangibility of services often implies that mutual recognition procedures need to be complemented by common EU-wide minimum "quality" standards. This requires the negotiation and adoption of directives or regulations. Much of the EC-92 program thus consisted of directives related to specific service industries.

The EU also imposes disciplines on state aids, public procurement and competition within industries. The adoption of the Single European Act led to more frequent targeting of service industries by the European Commission's competition authorities. Investigation of the value-added telecommunications service industry and the air transportation sector underlay to some extent the adoption of directives aimed at progressive liberalization in both industries. The European Commission has the right to monitor state aids and require Member States to oblige firms to repay such aids. It may even impose fines on those Member States that do not comply.

The European Court of Justice played a pivotal role in the adoption of the mutual recognition principle in the Single European Act. As befits a fully integrated economic region, the dispute settlement provisions of the EU are, as well, far-reaching. Community law has primacy over the national law of Member States, and has direct effect. Thus, private parties may invoke EU law in national courts. In conjunction with the power of the Commission to initiate legal proceedings against a Member State which it perceives as not implementing EU directives or regulations, this ensures that violations of EU rules are frequently contested and thus made transparent. However, the Court does not have the power to enforce judgments, and, in contrast to most other international trade agreements, there are no provisions for Member States to retaliate against each other.

The EU's Single Market initiative has clearly exerted far-reaching effects in terms of liberalizing intra-EU service markets. This is reflected, *inter alia,* in the great increase in merger and acquisition activity since the late 1980s. Firms operating within the Single Market increasingly face common standards and are becoming progressively freer to choose the economically optimal mode of supplying their services in other Member States' markets. At the same time, the EU experience illustrates how difficult it can be for countries to liberalize access to service markets in a cooperative manner. It also reveals the limits of principles such as national treatment and Most-Favored-Nation (MFN). Nondiscrimination must be complemented by other measures, such as the application and enforcement of competition rules, liberal conditions on establishment, the harmonization of standards, the establishment of mutual recognition arrangements for the certification and licensing of professional service-providers, and the acceptance of a certain degree of competition in regulations.

2. The North American Free Trade Agreement

The North American Free Trade Agreement (NAFTA) was completed on August 12, 1992 and entered into force on January 1, 1994. Marking a significant departure in economic relations between developed and developing countries, NAFTA extended to Mexico the rights and obligations of the 1989 Canada-United States Free Trade Agreement (CUSFTA). It also expanded on the CUSFTA, both by **broadening** its coverage and by **deepening** the treatment applying to sectors and issues already covered under the bilateral pact. Services and investment are good examples of a policy area whose treatment was both significantly broadened and deepened by NAFTA. While drawing on the earlier and more limited provisions of the CUSFTA, NAFTA is noteworthy for having provided the three countries' services and investment negotiators with the first opportunity to apply a number of the lessons learned in developing GATS (and described earlier).

The services and investment provisions of NAFTA differ from those of the CUSFTA and GATS in a number of significant ways, making NAFTA arguably the most comprehensive package of services trade and investment liberalization achieved in an intergovernmental trade agreement to date. NAFTA negotiators opted to treat services in as generic and integrated a way as possible. NAFTA's services package is thus made up of — and draws its overall consistency from — several parts of the overall agreement, many of which relate to trade in goods in which services are often embodied. These include: (i) a comprehensive set of **disciplines on investment protection and liberalization embedded at the agreement's core** (since much of services "trade" takes place through an established presence); (ii) liberal rules on **cross-border trade in services**, including those pertaining to local presence, the right of non-establishment and a more generic treatment of matters relating to licensing, accreditation and professional services; (iii) sector-specific disciplines and/or liberalization timetables for **financial services, telecommunications and transportation services**; (iv) new protection for **intellectual property-intensive goods and services** (e.g. telecommunications, computer services); (v) disciplines on — and significant liberalization of — **government procurement of services and construction** (predating the Uruguay Round's Government Procurement Agreement (GPA) outcome); (vi) recognition of the nexus between goods-related non-tariff barriers and services trade liberalization through the establishment of **work programs on standards harmonization** for land transportation (bus, truck and rail services) and telecommunications equipment; and, (vii) border facilitation in respect to the **temporary entry of business people** and their "tools of the trade".

NAFTA introduced significant changes to the CUSFTA as regards the treatment of investment, resulting in a considerable clarification of the rules governing the treatment of all foreign investment in North America[16]. Two key differences distinguish the CUSFTA and the NAFTA investment chapters: (i) the coverage of the NAFTA chapter has been extended to a much larger group of investment, including various forms of non-equity interests, and to a greater number of sectors, among which **all** service sectors (the provisions do not distinguish between goods or services and also apply to intangible assets such as IPRs); and, (ii) the security of investment has been enhanced through the development of extensive provisions regarding the settlement of disputes and the protection of international investors and their investment. The innovations contained in NAFTA's investment chapter seem destined to have multilateral ripple effects, prompting many to argue that such a body of rules should ultimately replace the hodgepodge of rules currently scattered around the WTO family of agreements[17]. Not surprisingly, NAFTA's investment provisions have provided the main blueprint to negotiations of an OECD-based MAI.

A major architectural change introduced by the NAFTA relates to its approach to coverage. Unlike the CUSFTA (or GATS), NAFTA's complementary chapters on cross-border trade in services and investment do not take a positive list approach to coverage, but rather, apply to all

---

[16] See GESTRIN Michael & RUGMAN Alan M., *"The NAFTA Investment Provisions: Better Rules but New Problems"*, in: **The NAFTA Papers: C.D. Howe Commentary**, No.42, C.D. Howe Institute, Toronto, March 1993; and, HUFBAUER G. & SCHOTT J.J., **NAFTA: An Assessment**, Institute for International Economics, Washington, D.C., 1993.

[17] See HUFBAUER & SCHOTT, *op.cit.*, 1993; and, SAUVÉ, *op.cit.*, 1994.

measures affecting trade and investment in services and not specifically excluded from coverage. NAFTA does not make use of mode-of-delivery distinctions, whether in defining services or investment or as a means to achieve progressive liberalization. With the exception of most air transport services (i.e. all services except aircraft repair and maintenance and speciality air services), the sectoral coverage of NAFTA's cross-border services chapter is universal in scope. An important consequence of the negative list approach to coverage is that, unlike the CUSFTA, there is no general grandfathering of non-conforming measures under NAFTA. Rather, the agreement compels Parties to list all non-conforming measures at both the national and sub-national levels within prescribed time limits. Failure to list non-conforming measures within these limits entails their full and automatic liberalization. The obligation of NAFTA Parties to provide detailed information on remaining regulatory impediments to trade and investment in services yields a much greater degree of transparency than that achieved in GATS.

NAFTA's services and investment-related rules and disciplines carry forward elements that are common to most regional or multilateral agreements, namely the core liberalizing principles of national treatment, MFN and nondiscrimination, the latter being defined in NAFTA as the best of national treatment or MFN. The agreement does, however, draw a distinction between discriminatory (i.e. national treatment or MFN-related measures) and nondiscriminatory measures that restrict access to a service market. The latter are called "quantitative restrictions" in NAFTA. While Parties are unconstrained with respect to the latter measures, these must nonetheless be listed in an annex for transparency purposes and are subject to periodic negotiations. Drawing from the CUSFTA, NAFTA provides for an explicit right of non-establishment by outlawing all future measures requiring the local presence of firms or service providers (i.e. residency requirements for professionals) as a precondition for the delivery of a service. Both national treatment and MFN are general obligations under NAFTA. NAFTA, moreover, incorporates a "ratcheting" provision whereby a Party's commitments under the Agreement are automatically adjusted to reflect any liberalization of domestic measures.

The negative list approach adopted under NAFTA required the production of a set of annexes pertaining to reservations and exceptions to the investment and cross-border services disciplines. NAFTA allows reservations to be lodged against a number of obligations common to — or found in either — the cross-border trade in services or investment chapters; national treatment, MFN treatment, local presence (cross-border trade in services), as well as obligations relating to performance requirements and to requirements on the nationality of senior management and boards of directors (investment). The annexes to the NAFTA Agreement are substantial. What is relevant, however, is not so much the number of such annexes but their content, i.e. what they reveal about the degree to which North American service markets have been rendered more open and the extent to which intra-regional liberalization exceeds what may be achieved at the multilateral level. A review of the annexes shows that, with a few notable exceptions (i.e. land transportation, speciality air services, professional services), the degree of liberalization agreed to in NAFTA by Canada and the United States closely approximates — albeit in a now fully transparent manner — what had been achieved under the CUSFTA. The situation is quite different for Mexico which, while lodging the largest absolute number of reservations, also undertook significant liberalization commitments in the greatest number of service sectors under NAFTA. "Unbound" reservations were, moreover, lodged in those sectors — basic telecommunications, air and maritime transportation, government services — where the frontiers of liberalization have traditionally proven most difficult to nudge, regardless of the negotiating forum (including the EU). Still, NAFTA is noteworthy for registering progress in a number of complex and/or highly regulated service sectors where liberalization has so far proven difficult to achieve in regional and/or multilateral settings. Such sectors include professional services, telecommunications, transportation (bus, truck and speciality air services), as well as financial services.

As noted earlier, an essential ingredient of NAFTA's integrated approach to rule-making is its provisions governing the temporary movement of business people (and found in Chapter 16 of the agreement). The generic nature of these business-facilitating provisions set them apart from their services-specific treatment under the WTO. Like the CUSFTA, NAFTA identifies four categories of people that are eligible for temporary entry; business visitors, traders and investors, intra-company transferees and professionals[18]. NAFTA, moreover, extends duty-free privileges to the tools of the trade (e.g. computers, software, samples, promotional material) imported on a temporary basis by professionals covered by the agreement's temporary entry provisions.

NAFTA includes no disciplines on services-related subsidies, owing to the three countries' position that such matters are best addressed in a multilateral setting (such discussions are currently underway in the

---

[18] The latter comprise some sixty-three professional activities that are listed in the chapter.

GATS). NAFTA does, however, break important new ground in the area of government procurement. Disciplines of openness, transparency and competitive bidding are to apply to the purchases by public entities of goods **and** services, including construction services. NAFTA's expanded coverage brings the total North American market covered by the agreement's procurement disciplines to some $78 billion US (half of which is estimated to consist of services and construction contracts), up noticeably from approximately $20 billion US of goods-only procurement subject to CUSFTA disciplines. Such expanded coverage is significant in that it typically represents the most direct and immediate means of liberalizing the provision of many services — such as computer services, consulting, engineering, or construction — that are, otherwise, subject to few or no cross-border impediments. For such services, the trade-disciplining rules contained in the agreement's cross-border services chapter may on the whole be less important from the point of view of securing effective access to other countries' markets. While the detailed new rules and market opportunities afforded by NAFTA's procurement chapter are significant, it should be borne in mind that the agreement liberalizes access to slightly less than a tenth of North America's estimated $800 billion US civilian procurement market[19].

Like the CUSFTA and the WTO, NAFTA does not feature services-specific dispute settlement procedures but rather subjects potential disputes to a generic set of procedures applying to all matters covered by the agreement. NAFTA innovates by making binding dispute settlement available to determine whether one country's retaliation in response to another country's failure to comply with a panel report is itself "manifestly excessive". Another significant improvement borrows from procedures common to the bilateral investment agreements that the US and Canada have with other countries and establishes a regime of mixed — or investor-state — arbitration for the enforcement of obligations under the investment chapter of the agreement.

Two final features of NAFTA that are worthy of note are its provisions on matters relating to competition policy and its accession clause. Reflecting both the (then) incipient nature of the trade and competition debate, and the bureaucratic and political sensitivities in the United States in this area (and its link to the administration of US trade remedy laws),

---

[19] See HART Michael & SAUVÉ Pierre, *"Does Size Matter? Canadian Perspectives on the Development of Government Procurement Disciplines in North America"*, in: HOEKMAN Bernard & MAVROIDIS Petros C. (eds), **Law and Policy in Public Purchasing: The WTO Government Procurement Agreement**, University of Michigan Press, Ann Arbor, (forthcoming).

NAFTA achieved relatively little in this area, other than to subject the activities of monopolies and state enterprises to nondiscrimination in the purchase and sale of goods (where the latter have a monopoly). The agreement also features hortatory calls for positive comity-type consultations on competition-related matters and saw the establishment of a Working Party on trade and competition whose mandate is to address competition matters in the more integrated market created by the free trade rules. Similar in design and intent to that contained in GATT, the aim of NAFTA's accession clause is to allow other countries or groups of countries, within or outside the Western Hemisphere, to join NAFTA by accepting the same obligations as other member countries. Viewed by proponents of the trilateral pact as a clear commitment of signatory governments to a process of "open regionalism", the accession clause would ensure that expansion of NAFTA membership would not require that negotiations start from scratch. It would also provide a ready-made vehicle to lock in the agreement's negotiating advances — in terms of both trade rules and disciplines and of liberalization commitments — made in the areas of services and investment.

3. The Australia-New Zealand Closer Economic Relations Trade Agreement

Australia and New Zealand negotiated a trade agreement during the mid-1960s which entered into force in January 1966. The structure of this agreement was similar to that of other trade agreements negotiated during this period; a commitment to abolish tariffs for "scheduled" commodities over an eight-year period, accompanied by a number of safeguard clauses. Essentially a tariff agreement, its coverage was carefully designed to exclude sectors where reciprocal liberalization might have a significant impact[20]. A positive list approach was taken to determine the coverage of the agreement. The stated intention of the two governments was to gradually expand the agreement's coverage over time. However, no time frame or binding procedures were established within which this expansion would be completed. As the two governments proved unable to significantly increase the coverage of the agreement — potentially affected import-competing industries were indeed quite successful in preventing their inclusion — its impact was quite limited. Indeed, trade-weighted average tariffs on intra-area trade flows actually **rose** over time.

---

[20] A 1966 Article 24 GATT Working Party Report noted that the agreement covered only about 50 percent of trade between the two countries, some 90 percent of which was already duty-free!

Reflecting a change in trade policy thinking and consequent dissatisfaction with the provisions of the agreement, the bilateral pact was superseded by the Closer Economic Relations Trade Agreement in 1983. In contrast to the earlier agreement, the initiating objective of the ANZCERTA was substantial trade liberalization. It took a negative list approach to coverage — all products being included except those explicitly mentioned for exclusion — and imposed much greater disciplines on quantitative restrictions. Time limits were set for the abolition of tariffs, quotas and export subsidies. Export subsidies were eliminated by 1987, tariffs at the beginning of 1988, and quantitative restrictions by July 1995. Free trade in commodities (goods) was achieved on July 1, 1990 — five years ahead of schedule — by which time all three of these instruments no longer applied to trade within the region (intra-Tasman trade). The 1983 Agreement included a first attempt to liberalize government procurement of goods and harmonize product standards and related regulations. However, the magnitude of liberalization of government procurement was rather limited as Australian states were excluded from coverage and were allowed to maintain preferential practices.

The ANZCERTA Agreement was renegotiated in 1988, at which time it was agreed to include a Protocol on Services, eliminate anti-dumping provisions for intra-Tasman trade, as well as industry-specific subsidies that affected intra-Tasman competition, extend the coverage of nondiscrimination in government procurement of goods to preferences of Australian states, and harmonize a number of regulatory policies, including product standards and competition laws affecting trade in goods.

The goal of the Protocol on Services, which came into force in 1989, was to establish a framework of transparent rules, liberalize barriers to trade in services and facilitate competition in the provision of services. The protocol contains no references to concepts such as progressive liberalization, reciprocity, or fair trade. Nor does it make explicit use of modes of supply. As in NAFTA, a negative list approach was followed to determine the coverage of the agreement (i.e. all service sectors are covered unless specifically exempted). As in virtually all services-related agreements, whether at the regional or multilateral level, excluded sectors include a fairly predictable list of "sensitive" areas; basic telecommunications, broadcasting, air transport, maritime cabotage and postal services. Australia reserved restrictions on the establishment of foreign-owned banking branches, subsidiaries or representative offices, as well as legislative limits on shareholdings in Australian banks. Also excluded were federal government procurement preferences for construction, engineering and general consultancy, and preferences in Australian states for basic health and third-party insurance.

In a notable achievement, however, and in contrast to other regional agreements, these sectoral exclusions are not of indefinite duration. The agreement contains provisions aimed at bringing these sectors within the scope of the protocol through periodic reviews. Thus, in the 1992 review of the agreement, Australia removed its reservations relating to banking and government preferences for Australian companies in construction, engineering and general consultancy. New Zealand removed its reservations for radio and television broadcasting, short-wave and satellite broadcasting, stevedoring and part of the reservation relating to aviation services. Both countries amended their reservations on telecommunications and postal services. In addition to removing sectors from reservations lists, the two governments also agreed to work towards the full integration of their aviation markets[21]. In the ANZCERTA's 1995 review, Australia agreed to liberalize its reservations on postal services and telecommunications, while New Zealand did so in respect to aviation services and coastal shipping.

Parties are required to provide national treatment, MFN treatment for excluded sectors (unlike GATS or NAFTA), and market access for covered services. Market access is defined as granting persons and services of the partner country access rights no less favorable than those allowed to domestic providers. National treatment is defined conventionally, except that allowance is made (as in the other agreements) for differences in treatment that nonetheless result in effectively equal treatment between foreign and domestic service providers, and for differences that are motivated by prudential, health or safety considerations. While there is no mention of nondiscriminatory regulations (quantitative restrictions) as impediments to market access, the market access article implicitly allows such restrictions to be maintained.

The principles and rules of the agreement apply to any measure — existing and future — that relates to or affects the provision of a covered service by or on behalf of a person of one Party within or into the territory of the other Party (Article 2). Both measures taken at the federal and the state level in Australia are covered by the protocol, although

---

[21] Although a Memorandum of Understanding was signed in 1992 to form a single aviation market across the Tasman, including the right to operate in each others' markets from November 1st, 1994, Australia decided in October 1994 not to proceed. Discussions between the two governments resumed in July 1996, with a view to sealing an agreement on a single aviation market by the end of the year.

sub-national (i.e. state-level) measures were excluded in an annex. There is, therefore, no grandfathering as in the Canada-United States Free Trade Agreement (CUSFTA), except indirectly in respect of the excluded sectors mentioned above. Also excluded from the national treatment obligation are taxation measures, subsidies and government procurement. As far as the latter two policies are concerned, disciplines for goods greatly exceed those for services under the ANZCERTA.

Service providers originating in a member state are free to choose their preferred way of doing business, including through means of an established presence. In what amounts to its single greatest weakness, the ANZCERTA does not deal with investment (an issue that was left for future negotiations). Thus, although the agreement does include a right of establishment — this being recognized as a critical element of the provision of many services — such establishment is subject to the foreign investment policies maintained by each country. As in the CUSFTA and NAFTA, but unlike GATS, the agreement incorporates the principle of non-establishment. Measures requiring establishment are forbidden if the measure constitutes a means of arbitrary or unjustifiable discrimination or a disguised restriction on trade between the member states in services. Unlike the CUSFTA and NAFTA, but as in the European Union, Australia and New Zealand form a common labor market. Nationals from one country are free to seek employment in the other. As with the EU, the establishment of a common labor market obviates the need for CUSFTA- or NAFTA-type provisions on temporary entry, as well as on the removal of citizenship and/or permanent residency requirements associated with the licensing of service providers. Such freedom of movement by people remains, however, a key component of the ANZCERTA's treatment of services.

While the two countries agreed to adopt similar competition laws, as for intra-EU trade, and to abolish the application of anti-dumping laws to intra-bloc trade flows in the 1988 renegotiation of the Agreement, these provisions apply to merchandise trade flows only. The protocol on services imposed a standstill on export subsidies and other direct assistance affecting trade in covered services, and required Member States to work towards the elimination of all such measures by July 1990. To date, and pending the completion of ongoing negotiations under the GATS , the ANZCERTA is the only trade agreement to contain disciplines on trade-related subsidies for services. The ANZCERTA also contains "best efforts" language regarding licensing and certification requirements. And unlike in GATS and NAFTA, MFN treatment must still apply to excluded sectors. The "best efforts" commitment was all that was feasible given the authority of Australian states with respect to numerous licensing and certification matters. Under the ANZCERTA (as in NAFTA and GATS), Parties endeavor to ensure that such measures do not act to discriminate against persons of another Party when these seek access to licensing or certification. Parties are also encouraged — but not required — to recognize qualifications obtained in the other Member State, though the agreement contained no specific procedures aimed at facilitating such recognition. The lack of binding EU-type mutual recognition disciplines may be viewed as inhibiting the ability of both countries' professional communities to reap the full benefits of a common labor market.

Enforcement procedures under the ANZCERTA are informal and non-binding. There is a requirement to enter into consultations if one Party considers that an obligation is not being fulfilled by the other Party, or the achievement of an objective is being or may be frustrated. No panel proceedings or binding arbitration — let alone a EU-type supranational court — are foreseen. The lack of binding dispute-settlement procedures sets the ANZCERTA apart from the other agreements reviewed in this paper and may generally be seen as weakening the effects of an otherwise innovative and fairly liberalizing instrument. Finally, it should be noted that, as with NAFTA, ANZCERTA has an accession clause providing for the future association of other countries on terms to be negotiated jointly between the potential entrant and existing members.

D. Retooling the GATS?
Regional Lessons in Rule-design

Among the regional arrangements reviewed in the preceding section, the European Union quite clearly involves a degree of liberalization that is unlikely to be matched at the multilateral level in the near future. The same conclusion holds if the EU is compared to NAFTA or the ANZCERTA (let alone to agreements such as Mercosur, Asian-Pacific Economic Cooperation (APEC), or the proposed Free Trade Area of the Americas (FTAA)). In prescribing regional medicine for what allegedly ails the multilateral trading system, one must accept that the process of European integration is in a quite different category, involving as it does a degree of supranationality (and a degree of political union) that go much beyond what is contemplated in either the WTO or other regional trade/investment agreements. Indeed, the provisions of the Treaty of Rome and the Single European Act aim at a degree of market integration — and involve recourse to a range of (necessarily) sovereignty-impairing instruments — that go far beyond what has emerged, to date, from all other regional arrangements or could be contemplated in a WTO context (e.g. a single world market for labor).

Still, the EU experience remains highly relevant for consideration of the possible evolution of the multilateral trading system's architecture, particularly in light of its integrated approach to the cross-border movement of goods, services, capital and people and the central complementary role of competition in disciplining public and private restraints to trade and investment. The EU experience also illustrates quite vividly how the liberalization of service markets may be difficult to achieve in practice, and how far-reaching the policy instruments required to do so may need to be.

Potentially more promising, therefore, from the point of view of its practical adoption in an evolving WTO setting (if only because such rules emanate from the narrower confines of trade policy), would appear to be the generic and complementary approach to services-related matters found in NAFTA (and, in some regards, the ANZCERTA, though the latter agreement's lack of investment disciplines remains a crippling prescriptive shortcoming). In addressing some of the multilateral trading system's key architectural deficiencies in the areas of services and investment, both of the above agreements provide, *à divers degrés*, some useful guidance to Geneva-bound negotiators. Thus:

- both NAFTA and the ANZCERTA highlight the fact that using modes of supply distinctions as a basis to define trade in services and, especially, as a means to secure liberalization commitments, is not only unnecessary but likely counterproductive (resulting in a degree of policy segmentation that reduces the economies of scope that flow from a broader approach to market access)[22];

- reliance in both the NAFTA and the ANZCERTA on a negative list approach to coverage has yielded considerable gains in transparency and user-friendliness, is more inherently liberalizing (by locking in the regulatory *status quo* in all sectors), does not bias the scheduling of commitments against any particular way of transacting services, lends itself more easily to formula-based liberalization, and typically generates positive regulatory reform externalities. In contrast, the freedom of GATS members not to list particular service sectors virtually excludes "sensitive"

---

[22] It also tends to result in what SNAPE & BOSWORTH (*op.cit.*, 1996, p.7) have called a "made-to-measure" approach to liberalization which limits commitments to "where, and to the extent that, it does not hurt".

industries from its coverage without shedding light on the discriminatory practices they maintain in such sectors;

- reliance on a negative list approach in both agreements has also allowed Parties to affirm their adherence and commitment to an overarching set of general obligations, chief among which is the core national treatment principle. The hybrid approach to scheduling adopted in GATS, in contrast, encourages "selective/*à-la-carte*" commitment to nondiscrimination. The scope for lodging MFN exemptions under GATS (and NAFTA) lessens that commitment further and has led to greater sectoral specificity (and the search for sectoral, as opposed to overall, reciprocity)[23];

- the development of generic rules on investment and the temporary entry of business people in NAFTA is more responsive to the doing-business needs of internationally-active firms in today's rapidly globalizing environment. Such an approach moves away from a sector- or issue-specific approach to rule-making, results in a leaner, more rational and coherent set of horizontal disciplines and offers the possibility of achieving greater overall balance in the multilateral system's treatment of factors of production; and,

- NAFTA's incorporation of a comprehensive set of investment disciplines provides firms with a significantly greater degree of ease and security of market presence than that provided by existing multilateral disciplines. Incorporating a similar body of rules into the WTO could provide the central means (indeed perhaps the only means) of reviewing the operation and design of existing investment-related provisions in the WTO.

More broadly, all three regional agreements reflect their member government's growing recognition that effective conditions of access and presence in markets require the adoption of a broad and more coordinated approach to the multiplicity of factors that determine such access. Hence the need to devise policy instruments that progressively break down artificial or bureaucratic distinctions between the treatment of

---

[23] The ANZCERTA Agreement (as well as arrangements within the EU, though talks of a possible two-speed Economic and Monetary Union (EMU) could be argued to represent a conditional MFN-type approach to monetary integration) and the GATT (with the exception of waivers and the Article XXXV provision for non-application between particular Parties) do not specifically provide for sectoral exemptions from MFN among the Parties. As SNAPE & BOSWORTH (1996) have noted: "When under GATT such [MFN] exemptions have been allowed — the Multifibre Arrangements being the prime example — the results have been trade restricting and competition impairing rather than liberalizing."

goods and services, between the trade and investment modes of doing business, and ultimately between public and private forms of anticompetitive conduct (to which only the EU has, so far, provided an articulated policy response). Seen in this light, regional experiments in rule-design help lay the basis for tomorrow's more integrated architecture of WTO rules.

Notwithstanding the substantive architectural differences noted above, NAFTA, the ANZCERTA and GATS tend to be broadly similar as regards the sectoral coverage of liberalization commitments for services and investment. Indeed, these agreements show a tendency to exclude — or encounter recurring headaches in — the same broad range of sectors; among which are basic telecommunications, broadcasting, air and maritime transport, and government services. These are sectors where the EU has also met particular difficulties in liberalizing market access opportunities. The fact that, with few exceptions, the same sectors seem to remain immune to liberalization regardless of the negotiating setting would appear to suggest that regional agreements are not generally viewed by member countries as a substitute path to faster or significantly more comprehensive liberalization of trade or investment in services. The incremental nature of liberalization in both the regional and multilateral contexts further supports the proposition that both negotiating settings may exhibit strong complementarity.

The issue of whether or not regional agreements are building blocks for multilateral liberalization is also, in large measure, a question of the extent to which the formation of a regional trading area implies discrimination against nonmembers. Agreement to negotiate GATS was influenced by the emergence of the EC-92 program and NAFTA (though less so by the ANZCERTA), and it can be argued that progress made in the multilateral discussions was, in part, driven by the existence of regional liberalization agreements and negotiations. Not only did the threat of trade and investment diversion increase the incentives to engage in — and ultimately complete — the multilateral talks, but the regional developments constituted a source of information and know-how for both participants and outsiders. There has indeed been a substantial amount of cross-fertilization between the regional agreements and the GATS. The core instruments of liberalization that are embodied in all agreements are, indeed, broadly similar. Sectoral annexes are also frequently comparable. In the case of NAFTA, for instance, the wording of disciplines on financial services and telecommunications was drawn in large part from GATS. GATS, in turn, clearly built upon the experiences gained in achieving progressive liberalization within the EU, the earlier CUSFTA and the ANZCERTA. Thus, it followed (unfortunately) the CUSFTA in adopting a positive list approach to coverage, and the ANZCERTA with respect to the distinction between national treatment and market access. All of the agreements drew upon the EU experience, recognizing to a greater or lesser extent the importance of disciplines on licensing, accreditation, mutual recognition, standards harmonization, as well as the need for a right of establishment. These links suggest that the two institutional approaches share strong complementarities.

All this is not to say, of course, that there are no sources of concern from a systemic perspective. A key question in this connection is whether the conditions imposed by Article V of GATS (i.e., the substance of the disciplines regarding the formation of regional integration agreements) are adequate to safeguard the interests of nonmembers. The answer to this is arguably no. The relatively weak requirements regarding the extent of internal liberalization that must occur under Article V imply only a limited constraint on "strategic" violations of the MFN obligation and the specific commitments on market access and national treatment made under GATS. It could indeed be argued that many types of agreements, including some with only limited coverage in sectoral or mode of supply terms and no more than a standstill commitment, could satisfy the conditions imposed by GATS[24]. Very much, therefore, depends on the intentions and objectives of the countries that negotiate integration agreements that cover services and investment. In addition to the weakness of the disciplines imposed by GATS in this regard, the absence of any requirement in Article V that integration agreements be "open" in principle (i.e., contain an accession clause) is an important shortcoming. Given the difficulty of determining simple, quantifiable criteria with which to ensure that integration agreements liberalizing both trade and factor flows are not detrimental to nonmembers, adoption of a requirement of such an accession clause could have helped ensure that the systemic effects of economic integration agreements remain positive[25].

---

[24] A prime example of this is the debate over whether the proposed MAI represents a regional integration agreement under the terms of GATS Article V, as this could be construed as providing a solution to the free-rider problem arising from the application of GATS Article II to services-related measures covered by the MAI. On this issue, see WIMMER A. M., *"The Impact of the General Agreement on Trade in Services on the OECD Multilateral Agreement on Investment"*, in: **World Competition**, Vol.19, No.4, June 1996, pp.109-120.

[25] For a more complete discussion of the application of GATS Aricle V, see HOEKMAN & SAUVÉ, *op.cit.,* 1994, pp.56-63.

COMMENTS

Karl FALKENBERG

Head of Unit, DG I/M/1,
European Commission, Brussels

Introduction

Pierre Sauvé has facilitated my task as a discussant by choosing a very academic presentation. I would like to comment from a more down-to-earth negotiator's perspective, gained during the last twenty years of multilateral trade negotiations.

The views expressed are my own and do not necessarily reflect positions of the Commission of the European Communities.

Pierre Sauvé's fundamental point is that the relationship between regional and multilateral attempts at regime formation is unproblematic: it shows not only broad convergence, but also strong complementarity. The underlying view of the world seems to be Fred Bergsten's brave new world: a totally free and fully integrated world market, towards which regional experiments might usefully contribute for the few years still needed.

I do not share these basic premises. I do see the merits of an integrated multilateral trading system, rules-based and as open as possible. We have just created it: it is the World Trade Organization (WTO). But this will not, for decades to come, be a fully integrated economic policy-making system. I do, therefore, see regional integration as an objective in its own right aiming at creating a far higher level of economic integration than would be achievable or tenable at world level, for a long time to come.

The relationship of regional and multilateral rules, therefore, is more relevant as I see long term coexistence of the two approaches. Potentially, there is also room for conflict as competing systems emerge.

In the areas of both trade and investment, preferential regional rules will have a distorting effect on the optimum allocation of resources. That is an academic common place. But this effect, will be more than balanced by the wealth induced trade effects, provided that regional integration does not lead to increasing trade barriers towards third countries. This is the experience drawn from almost forty years of European integration.

That brings us to the relevance of GATT Article XXIV and the strict respect for the conditions that it establishes for free trade area or customs union qualification. As Pierre Sauvé indicates, in the past respect has not always been paid to the requirement to cover "substantially all trade".

The question one may then ask is whether greater respect would have led to better agreements, or to fewer free trade agreements, or perhaps simply to even less respect for multilateral rules?

Acceptance of rules is enhanced by the reasonableness of their interpretation. When, in GATT, the Working Party on the European Community (the original six) could not come up with a finding of conformity, the tone was set. No agreement would meet the threshold. If none meets the threshold, then why respect the rule anyway?

One can only hope that the WTO will not repeat the mistakes of GATT in relation to regional integration. That would require Members to actually seek to recognize a number of agreements as being in conformity. The necessary flexibility exists in both the relevant GATT and General Agreement on Trade in Services (GATS) articles, if the political will can be found.

1. Services

Of all the agreements reached in the Uruguay Round, GATS is probably the most relevant. Relevant in that it brings the most dynamic sector of the world economy under a set of agreed, open rules and that it seeks to introduce predictability for market access to all members' markets. Not only for the Hong Kongs of this world are services the most important economic sector. For Hong Kong, services represent 90 percent of the GDP and 80 percent of employment. In the EU and the US, too, the importance of the service sector as a contributor to GDP and employment is growing rapidly, and not only for low-wage bicycle delivery services. In 1990 services accounted for 49 percent of GDP in the EU and 42 percent of employment.

GATS is basically a modern revisited version of GATT revisited with improved provisions on transparency, domestic regulation, national treatment and regional integration. It also establishes the key Most-Favoured-Nation (MFN) provisions.

Criticism that GATS is an *à la carte* approach, because all provisions do not apply to all sectors, misses the point.

National treatment under GATT only relates to imported goods not domestic goods. The foreign producer has no national treatment, only its product. National treatment, therefore, only comes into effect once a product has passed through the tariff and non-tariff barriers, which are negotiated individually and sectorally by members.

For GATS, the national treatment provision covers the service provider, not only the service. If it had been extended without restriction to the market access commitments made, it would have amounted to completely free access.

What has been negotiated in GATS is equivalent to the approach followed in GATT: where market access is granted, there should be national treatment.

Could one have gone further and established national treatment on a market-access basis? I doubt it. Where this has been attempted, long lists of reservations have been the consequence.

Take Article V on regional integration. Pierre Sauvé argues that it is insufficiently precise. I would contest this and point out that it is far more precise than its GATT counterpart Article XXIV.

Notably, it establishes an Article 58 Rome Treaty equivalent to the national treatment obligation for any third-party service provider lawfully established in one of the countries to an Economic Integration Agreement.

As proof for his contention on Article V, Pierre Sauvé refers to the Organization for Economic and Cooperation and Development (OECD) which is apparently considering using Article V as an MFN exemption for the Multilateral Agreement on Investment (MAI). He omits to say that the vast majority of OECD members have rejected such a broad and distortive interpretation of Article V.

Among the many myths often referred to in academic papers, let me just highlight the following:

- GATS is removed from other parts of the WTO family of agreements: in fact GATT, GATS and Agreement on Trade-Related aspects of Intellectual Property rights (TRIPs) form the three substantive agreements covered by the WTO Agreement and its integrated dispute settlement system. They form a single package which Members can only take in totality, including new members.

- GATS duplicates existing provisions, e.g. in government procurement: the existing government procurement agreement has developed such elaborate rules, that no one, except the present happy few, wants to accede to the ivory tower. GATS will, at least for services, provide an MFN-based approach to government procurement, applicable to all Members. In fact, similar ideas for goods have led to efforts to negotiate a transparency and due-process based agreement alongside the existing Government Procurement Agreement (GPA).

- GATS does not provide transparency on regulatory matters: wrong, Article III on transparency sets a general obligation to publish all regulations affecting all services. The EU will therefore have to be transparent by publishing all laws, even in sectors where it has not taken specific commitments, such as on audiovisual services, for example.

- The approach chosen for scheduling has led to fewer than possible commitments: this is a particularly ill-founded criticism as it seems to imply that countries would have allowed more binding commitments through a simple trick. Does anyone believe that Canadian equity restrictions in telecommunications, Malaysian restrictions on maritime transport or Indian reservations on financial services would not have been introduced? Whether you have a so-called bottom-up approach or negative listing, the end result will be the same.

- Finally, the modes of supply. I agree with the statement that trade and investment — access and presence in markets — are indissociable means of doing business. Unfortunately, those that believe this are in a clear minority. If the negotiators had not been exhaustive by listing the four modes, trade in services would, today, only be cross-border trade, i.e. a very limited portion, as any movement of persons linked to it would already disqualify a service as cross-border supply. The modes were a good way to better understand regulations governing the supply of services. Maybe they have served their purpose. But there is no provision under GATS which requires scheduling according to the four modes.

The modes do complicate GATS, but I fear they have been relevant as educational tools for policy makers in areas not traditionally covered by trade rules: transport, telecommunications, banking, etc.

A short word also on the four suggested "architectural" changes to GATS:

i) Doing away with the modes; only if trade in services is defined as incorporating the four modes could one attempt to eliminate the distinction for scheduling purposes; this can be done without any change.

ii) Adopting a negative-list approach; I do not believe that countries will make commitments they do not intend to make by a simple presentational trick. I believe rather on the contrary that the approach followed in GATS has allowed many countries to list commitments which would otherwise have taken no commitment at all. It is the best means to achieve progressively higher levels of liberalization which is the major GATS objective.

iii) Replacing commercial presence with an investment agreement; for services, commercial presence is an essential element. Very few services are traded in a pure cross-border mode, therefore, commercial presence must remain an integral part of a meaningful services agreement.

iv) Mobility of business people; trade in goods may also require physical presence here or there. Trade in services, however, requires it almost as a general rule. Therefore, having these provisions in GATS makes a lot of sense.

My own suggestion for improvement: complete the sectoral market access negotiations rapidly and begin preparations for the first round of comprehensive, progressive market-access negotiations. GATT would never have been successful over the years in opening up markets if a zero for zero approach had been sectorally applied from the outset.

2. Investment

The criticism on the Agreement on Trade-Related Investment Measures (TRIMs) is largely justified. Its scope is too narrow to deal with the trading reality in today's world economy. As said before, the distinction between trade and investment is increasingly artificial. This said, a few positive elements of the TRIMs Agreement are:

- it is a first and fair attempt to consider the impact of investment on trade under the WTO;
- existing GATT provisions have been reinforced;
- it establishes that neither Article XVIII nor Part IV of GATT constitute derogations for Lesser-Developed-Countries (LDCs);
- the disciplines on incentives can be found extensively in the Subsidies Agreement.

It is clear, however, that far more extensive rules for investors are necessary, ranging from investment protection to market access and national treatment.

As pointed out, GATS contains extensive rules on investment in its modes 3 and 4 commitments. These go further, in theory, than the OECD approach based simply on the notion of national treatment. Indeed, national treatment for market access protects all monopolies. The EU has no interest in this.

GATS does not address investment protection in any explicit way, a lacuna that should be addressed.

Much of the investment discussion today turns around the right forum: the Energy Charter, OECD, WTO, UNCTAD, the choice is considerable. In addition, the protection aspect is addressed, traditionally, in bilateral investment agreements.

A rational approach to choosing a forum can only point to the WTO for its evident links to trade and large geographic coverage.

Unfortunately, international decision-making is not always governed by ratio. Some developing countries feel that investment is too development related to accept any form of disciplines being negotiated in forums like the WTO, still perceived as the industrialized countries' club. At the other extreme, the US position is not to negotiate in a relatively broad "democratic" forum, but among a select few: the OECD. One can only hope that once the OECD negotiations have been completed next year, the WTO will be allowed to establish a set of truly multilateral rules.

The OECD Multilateral Agreement on Investment (MAI) will raise two kinds of problems with regard to the issue of multilateralization *versus* regionalism. First, the OECD Agreement will have to contain a regional integration clause, unless it establishes a full set of complete market access commitments. The more limited the OECD Agreement is, the more members of smaller integration agreements should be entitled to liberalize further without extending the benefit on an MFN-basis. Secondly, the OECD itself will be a regional agreement, but not a complete one (as it will not deal with cross-border trade and consumption abroad). Its members will, therefore, have MFN obligations for all market access and national treatment commitments in services. These obligations flow from the GATS Agreement.

This overlap will create a free-rider problem, if commitments in the MAI go beyond the GATS commitments. If the OECD countries grant each other full access in financial services, telecommunications or other service sectors, developing countries will benefit from these rights under the GATS MFN-clause.

Pierre Sauvé has made a plea for a coherent transparent international system. The overlap created by several regional agreements, from the Energy Charter, to the MAI to the existing GATS rules and potential WTO investment rules, is, quite obviously, not going in the right direction.

Conclusion

Let me conclude by going back to the question of regionalism *versus* multilateralism for services and investment. It is my belief that, for many years to come, regional integration agreements will open up these two aspects of economic activity more rapidly and more thoroughly than will be possible on a universal basis. This is not only a problem, but a necessary limitation for the functioning of the world economy. The dramatic monetary problems of Mexico after the creation of NAFTA should be a warning against seeking to merge very different economies rapidly into a single market, even as imperfect as NAFTA is. German unification provides another example of the costs involved in such efforts.

So regional integration can precede multilateral solutions and serve as a testing ground. It should, however, be forced to respect the fundamental obligation of not raising the level of protection towards nonmembers and, therefore, be subject to strict conditions and criteria as we have designed under GATS. Only then will their wealth creating effects be beneficial to all.

CONVERGENCE, DIVERGENCE AND INTERACTION OF REGIONAL TRADE AGREEMENTS AND THE AGREEMENT ON TRADE-RELATED ASPECTS OF INTELLECTUAL PROPERTY RIGHTS (TRIPs)

Inge GOVAERE

Lecturer, Law Department,
College of Europe, Bruges

Introduction

In the field of intellectual property rights, the Agreement on Trade-Related Aspects of Intellectual Property Rights (TRIPs), as it results from the Uruguay Round negotiations, occupies a very special place. For the first time, it is acknowledged on a worldwide level that intellectual property rights are clearly linked to, and have an important role to play in, international trade. The TRIPs Agreement goes far beyond the aborted Tokyo Round negotiations on the introduction of a code on counterfeit products. It introduces a comprehensive set of minimum standards of intellectual property protection, as well as enforcement mechanisms. The application of the World Trade Organization (WTO) dispute settlement mechanism to TRIPs is revolutionary in this respect. A closer reading of the TRIPs Agreement, moreover, reveals a fundamental departure from the traditional approach taken under GATT. The following findings are illustrative[1]. First and foremost, TRIPs adopts a coercive approach

---

[1] On these and other examples, see GOVAERE, I., *"Trade-Related Aspects of Intellectual Property Rights: The EC Dichotomy Uncovered"*, in: **La place de l'Europe dans le commerce mondial**, Institut Universitaire International Luxembourg, Session de juillet 1994, pp.161-215, pp.182-191, as well as the works referred to there.

instead of the prior permissive approach to intellectual property rights under GATT. This reflects the conceptual change that has taken place concerning the role of intellectual property rights in international trade. Whereas before the existence of intellectual property protection was perceived as an indispensable barrier to trade, nowadays it is rather the absence of, or deficiencies in, intellectual property protection that are regarded as being detrimental to trade. TRIPs is, furthermore, not so much concerned with trade liberalization as with trade regulation and securing export markets. This is perfectly illustrated by the approach taken to the issue of exhaustion of intellectual property rights[2]. TRIPs also acknowledges that intellectual property rights are "private rights", whereas GATT usually is not concerned with the granting of property rights to individuals. Finally, TRIPs, contrary to GATT practice, does not make concessions for the least-developed countries in terms of substantive derogations but only introduces some flexibility in so far as the transitional period is concerned.

The initiative to include TRIPs in the Uruguay Round negotiations came from the US, therein rapidly followed by the EC and Japan. The need to establish a clear linkage between trade issues and intellectual property rights in the framework of GATT was not universally shared from the outset. The developing countries, in particular, were initially strongly opposed to this exercise arguing that the World Intellectual Property Organization (WIPO) offered a more suitable forum to negotiate changes in intellectual property laws worldwide. The history of the negotiations, in particular the antagonism between the industrialized and developing countries, as well as the outcome of the TRIPs Agreement have already been the topic of much debate so that they will not be dealt with here in detail[3]. The difficult question that needs to be addressed is whether one can establish convergence, divergence and interaction between regional trade agreements and the TRIPs Agreement. The

---

[2] On this issue, see *infra*, pts B.1 and D.1.

[3] Specifically on the TRIPS Agreement, see for instance ULLRICH, H., *"TRIPS: Adequate Protection, Inadequate Trade, Adequate Competition Policy"*, in: **Pacific Law & Policy Journal**, 1995, pp.153-210; O'REGAN, M., *"The Protection of Intellectual Property, International Trade and the European Community: The Impact of the TRIPS Agreement of the Uruguay Round of Multilateral Trade Negotiations"*, in: **Legal Issues of European Integration**, 1995, pp.1-51; RINGO, F., *"The Trade-Related Aspects of Intellectual Property Rights Agreement in GATT and Legal Implications for Sub-Saharan Africa"*, **Journal of World Trade**, 1994, pp.121-139; COTTIER, T., *"The Prospects for Intellectual Property in GATT"*, in: **Common Market Law Review**, 1991, pp.383-414. On the WTO Agreement, see for instance DEMARET, P., *"The Metamorphoses of the GATT: From the Havana Charter to the World Trade Organization"*, in: **Columbia Journal of Transnational Law**, 1995, pp.123-171.

interaction between regional and multilateral trade rules is most apparent in the field of intellectual property rights. Both sets of rules seem to be interwoven to such an extent that it leads to wonder whether one would have been possible without the other. Any attempt at creating a coherent structure to deal with this topic is, therefore, necessarily a somewhat artificial, if not hazardous, exercise. This paper mainly addresses the following questions: when did the linkage of trade and intellectual property occur; what is the impact of regional trade agreements on TRIPs and *vice versa*; to what extent may TRIPs lead to a convergence of norms and standards of intellectual property protection between Parties to different regional agreements and third Parties; and finally, does the existence of TRIPs render the insertion of intellectual property provisions in (new) trade agreements obsolete.

Regional agreements and preferential trade agreements are legion. However, in view of the opposition of the developing countries to the linkage of intellectual property rights and trade, it seems legitimate to focus on a possible interaction with regional trade agreements concluded by those who pushed for change most, namely the US and the EC. Japan can easily be discarded, together with Hong Kong, as it is one of the few WTO Members that had not yet become a Party to a preferential type of trade agreement notified to GATT by the end of 1994[4]. With respect to the US particular attention needs to be given to the NAFTA provisions on intellectual property rights. NAFTA, which was concluded before the WTO Agreement, was the first agreement which introduced comprehensive and substantive provisions on intellectual property rights in a free trade agreement between industrialized countries (the US and Canada) and a developing country (Mexico)[5]. As the EC qualifies as a customs union under Article XXIV GATT, both the EC internal rules on intellectual property rights and the intellectual property provisions in its free trade agreements concluded with third countries, will be taken into consideration in view of establishing possible interaction with TRIPs. In order to better understand the relationship between regional trade agreements and TRIPs it is necessary first to open up the debate and to look for the policy considerations underlying the linkage of intellectual property rights to trade.

---

[4] See *GATT Activities 1994-1995*, WTO, Geneva, April 1996, p.99.

[5] See *infra*, pt B.3.

A. The Linkage of Intellectual Property Rights to Trade

The TRIPs Agreement is, of course, not a lone-standing fact inspired by a sudden impulse on behalf of the US Government. Some point to the important, although apparently not necessarily so intended, impetus given to the linkage of trade and intellectual property rights in an address to the nation delivered by President R. Reagan in 1983. He pledged "to maintain America's technological superiority into the next century", however, "when asked for his program, the White House admitted that the President's pledge was a last minute addition without backup papers."[6] Others point to the 98th Congress, whereby a series of measures were enacted that required the examination of the "adequacy and effectiveness" of the intellectual property laws of US trading partners as part of the trade assessment process, as the first publicly evident linkage of intellectual property rights and trade issues[7]. If it is difficult to agree on what the first clear policy statement on this linkage was, it is undisputed that the eventual acceptance of intellectual property rights as a trade-related issue by policy-makers, was mainly a response to the specific demands by private undertakings for more and better intellectual property protection on third markets. In other words, the integration of intellectual property issues in international trade relations over the last decades was a market-led evolution which was subsequently endorsed by policy-makers. This finding raises the question of how it is possible that the wishes of some industries in one country could, in such a relatively brief time span, be translated into worldwide applicable rules in the framework of the WTO.

The newly gained awareness by US policy-makers in the early 1980s about the economic and commercial implications of the absence of, or deficiencies in, intellectual property legislation of their trading partners, led to the inclusion of the issue of TRIPs on the agenda of the Uruguay Round at Punta del Este in 1986. The actual form and content the TRIPs Agreement was to take was, at that point, not yet fully established. The choice of a multilateral approach to deal with this issue may perhaps be explained by the apparent shortcomings of the bilateral approach previously adopted by the US. The US Trade and Tariff Act of 1984 opened

---

[6] GADBAW, R., *"Intellectual Property and International Trade: Merger or Marriage of Convenience?"*, in: **Vanderbilt Journal of Transnational Law**, 1989, pp.223-242, at pp.234-235.

[7] KASTENMEIER, R. & BEIER, D., *"International Trade and Intellectual Property: Promise, Risks and Reality"*, in: **Vanderbilt Journal of Transnational Law**, 1989, pp.298-307, at pp.288-289.

the door to the use of unilateral measures in order to ensure the adequacy of intellectual property protection in third countries. Not only did it clarify that Section 301 could be applied in order to try and remedy deficiencies in intellectual property protection in third countries[8]; it also made it possible to link the granting of General System of Preferences (GSP) to the adequate protection of intellectual property rights. If this was considered to be a step in the right direction, a major drawback was that this method only had an impact on certain US trading partners while having virtually no impact on others[9]. As long as the necessity to link trade and intellectual property rights was not a generally recognized objective, it proved difficult to use trade as a point of leverage to ensure intellectual property protection, in particular with regard to the most important trading partners of the US[10].

The inclusion of TRIPs on the agenda of the Uruguay Round eventually forged a breakthrough in the worldwide perception of intellectual property rights as an important trade-related issue. It seems that this was an indispensable step towards making it a subject of negotiation also within the framework of regional integration and free trade agreements. In spite of its initial reluctance to widen the scope of GATT involvement in intellectual property rights beyond the issue of counterfeit and piracy, the EC soon joined the US in its claim for the elaboration of substantive norms of intellectual property protection[11]. Like the US, the EC also began to use unilateral measures, such as the New Commercial Policy

---

[8] Section 301 was amended by the 1988 *Omnibus Trade and Competitiveness Act*. The latter introduced Special 301 which specifically targets the absence and deficiencies in intellectual property protection in third countries. On the legal history and GATT-compatibility of Section 301, see BELLO, J. & HOLMER, A., *"The Heart of the 1988 Trade Act: A Legislative History of the Amendments to Section 301"* and HUDEC, R., *"Thinking About the New Section 301: Beyond Good and Evil"*, in: BHAGWATI & PATRICK (eds), **Aggressive Unilateralism: America's 301 Trade Policy and the World Trading System**, Harvester Whetsheaf, New York, 1991, respectively at pp.49-89 and pp.113-159.

[9] See KASTENMEIER, R. & BEIER, D., *op. cit.*, at pp.289-290; GADBAW, R. *op. cit.*, at p.230.

[10] Intellectual property disputes are not alien to the industrialized countries. See for instance JACKSON, DAVEY & SYKES, **Legal Problems of International Economic Relations**, (3th ed.), West Publishing Co., 1995, at p.850 where the following figures are reported: "For example, a US software manufacturers association recently alleged that Japan was the 'worst country for software piracy', and further asserted that such piracy was costing the US industry $3 billion a year. The same association estimated losses from piracy in Europe as a whole at $4.5 billion a year. The President of the Motion Picture Association of America recently claimed that the industry's losses due to unauthorized showing of films were greatest in Italy, and put them at $225 million annually."

[11] PAEMEN, H. & BENSCH, A., **Du GATT à l'OMC : La Communauté Européenne dans l'Uruguay Round**, Leuven University Press, 1995, pp.88-89.

Instrument and GSP, in order to force third countries and, in particular, developing countries to raise the level of intellectual property protection granted to EC industries[12]. It is, nonetheless, only around 1990 that the insertion of provisions in bilateral agreements, aimed at raising the level of intellectual property protection, became a common practice. It is significant, for instance, that the Canada-US Free Trade Agreement (CUSFTA) of 1988 did not mention this issue, whereas, it is a major chapter in the NAFTA Agreement of 1992[13]. Similarly, the trade and cooperation, as well as the Europe Agreements concluded by the EC and Central and Eastern European Countries (CEECs) from 1990 onwards contain provisions which are, clearly, aimed at raising the level of intellectual property protection offered in the CEECs. This stands in contrast with the earlier trade and cooperation agreements concluded with, for instance, Poland and Hungary which only mentioned the need to comply with previously contracted international obligations, mainly those within the framework of WIPO[14]. The reason for this could be twofold. Whereas in 1988 the negotiations on TRIPs still seemed destined to end in a dead-lock, the Dunkel Initiative of 1989, which was largely inspired by the EC position, re-launched the discussion on TRIPs. It was apparently a secret statement by the EC negotiator to India and Brazil, to the effect that the future TRIPs Agreement would not necessarily be part of GATT from a legal point of view. That made progress possible, not only in so far as counterfeiting was concerned, but also with regard to the elaboration of adequate norms and enforcement of intellectual property protection[15]. Although the EC negotiator was eventually proved wrong, in so

---

[12] For more details see GOVAERE, I., *"Intellectual Property Protection and Commercial Policy"*, in: MARESCEAU (ed.), **The European Community's Commercial Policy after 1992: The Legal Dimension**, Martinus Nijhoff Publishers, 1993, pp.197-222, at pp.201-203. It seems that the EC adopted this autonomous approach from 1987 onwards. It is interesting to note that the New Commercial Policy Instrument was also initiated in 1987 in the *AKZO* Case against the US, on the grounds that Section 337 of the 1930 US Tariff Act infringed upon Article III GATT by according less-favourable treatment to patent-based imports as compared to domestic goods. On this case, see the GATT panel decision of November 7, 1989 (L/6439), **GATT Basic Instruments and Selected Documents**, 36th Supp. 1990.

[13] See DESCHAMPS, I., *"L'accord de libre échange nord-américain : une nouvelle voie pour l'Amérique"*, in : **Revue Trimestrielle de Droit Européen**, 1993, pp.461-484, at p.475. The FTA was ratified in 1988 and implemented in 1989. NAFTA was signed on December 17, 1992 and entered into force on January 1st, 1994.

[14] For an analysis of the intellectual property provisions in the agreements with the CEECs, see GOVAERE, I., *"The Impact of Intellectual Property Protection on Technology Transfer between the EC and the Central and Eastern European Countries"*, in: **Journal of World Trade**, 1991, pp.57-76.

[15] See PAEMEN, H. & BENSCH, A., *op. cit.*, at p.147.

far as the legal nature of the TRIPs Agreement is concerned[16], the fact remains that, for the first time, it was accepted by all Parties that the issue of elaborating substantive norms and enforcement of intellectual property protection could be negotiated in the context of a multilateral trade agreement. Having acquired this new understanding worldwide most likely made it easier for the industrialized countries to make a similar link between trade and intellectual property rights in regional and free trade agreements. The trading partners of the US and the EC already faced the threat of autonomous retaliation in case of inadequate protection of intellectual property so that, from their point of view, negotiating a bilateral package deal including intellectual property rights was most likely to be preferred over being the potential target of a carrot-and-stick approach.

It thus seems possible to discern some interaction between the development of the TRIPs negotiations and the elaboration of agreements including provisions on intellectual property rights. The former seem to have somehow paved the way for the inclusion of intellectual property provisions in regional trade agreements. The next section looks at whether the proliferation of the latter from the 1990s onwards may, in turn, have contributed towards the successful conclusion of the TRIPs Agreement in its actual form.

B. Impact of Regional Trade Agreements on TRIPs

1. Intellectual Property Rights in the EC and the EEA

The purpose of this section is not to analyse the place of intellectual property rights in EC law in detail but, rather, to establish in what manner the approach of the EC towards intellectual property rights, which was later extended to the European Economic Area (EEA), may have influenced the outcome of the TRIPs Agreement. Considering the success of the European integration model, establishing not only a customs union but a fully-fledged internal market, it may seem surprising that intellectual property rights are, even nowadays, after the Treaty on the European Union, only mentioned in Article 36 EC as indispensable barriers to trade. This implies that, in so far as EC law is concerned, it is in principle still a permissive approach that prevails in the intra-Community context, allowing but not obliging Member States to adopt adequate and

---

[16] By virtue of Article II, 2 WTO the TRIPS Agreement, which is annexed to the WTO Agreement (Annex 1C), forms an integral part of the WTO Agreement and is binding on all members.

effective measures of intellectual property protection[17]. The contrast with the coercive approach adopted in the TRIPs Agreement is striking[18].

In the absence of harmonization it essentially remains up to the Member States to determine the level of intellectual property protection they want to grant, provided that the national intellectual property measures respect the principle of nondiscrimination as laid down in Article 6 EC, and do not amount to a disguised restriction on intra-Community trade or an arbitrary discrimination under the second sentence of Article 36 EC[19]. It is apparent, however, that intellectual property rights are closely linked to both trade in products and services. On the basis of the principles of territoriality and exclusivity, intellectual property rights may, in principle, be used to close down national borders to the importation of products that were legitimately put on the market in other Member States. Such a practice is difficult to reconcile with the Community objective of establishing a Common Market. The EC Court of Justice (ECJ), therefore, introduced the principle of Community exhaustion of intellectual property rights[20]. This implies that if the product was first put on the Community market by the intellectual property owner, or with his consent, then the latter may no longer invoke his intellectual property rights in order to prohibit parallel importation. A peculiarity of the Community understanding of exhaustion is that it applies regardless of whether or not the intellectual property owner has a parallel intellectual property right in the Member States of exportation[21]. It might be because of the apparent far-reaching, not to say unwarranted, effect for intellectual property owners that this trade liberalising principle was not extended to

---

[17] However, see *infra* point C.1. on the implications of the TRIPS Agreement for the EC.

[18] On this contrast, see GOVAERE, I., *op. cit.*, (Session de juillet 1994), pp.161-215.

[19] These restrictions ensue from relatively recent case law of the European Court of Justice, whereby the existence/exercise dichotomy was somewhat revisited. See, respectively, the *Phil Collins* Case of 1993 (Joined Cases C-92/92 and C-326/92) and cases concerning the grant of compulsory licences of 1988 (Case C-30/90 *Commission v. UK* and Case C-235/89, *Commission v. Italy*). On these cases, see GOVAERE, I., **The Use and Abuse of Intellectual Property Rights in EC Law**, Sweet & Maxwell, 1996, at pp.168-194.

[20] For the first time in the *Deutsche Grammophon* Case (Case 78/70).

[21] See Case 187/80, *Merck v. Stephar*. This was recently confirmed in Joined Cases C-267/95 and C-268/95, *Merck v. Primecrown* and *Beecham v. Europharm*, although the ECJ added the qualification that the principle of exhaustion would not apply in the absence of parallel protection if "the holder of the patent can prove that he is under a genuine, existing legal obligation to market the product" in the Member State of exportation.

trade relations with third countries[22]. The only exception is the Agreement on the European Economic Area which expressly extends the Internal Market, including the principle of **regional** exhaustion, to the EFTA states concerned.

As in the Community context, the principle of exhaustion is stringently linked to the need to safeguard the Internal Market and the Community has been, from the beginning, strongly opposed to the inclusion of such a principle in the TRIPs Agreement[23]. This transpired in Article 6 TRIPs which reads as follows:

> For the purposes of dispute settlement under this Agreement, subject to the provisions of Articles 3 (NT) and 4 (MFN) nothing in this Agreement shall be used to address the issue of the exhaustion of intellectual property rights.

The EC, thus, firmly rejected the insertion of this trade liberalising principle in the TRIPs Agreement and was also, at first, reluctant to elaborate norms and standards of intellectual property rights within the context of GATT. The initial EC position was that the TRIPs negotiations should not lead to a harmonization of national intellectual property laws[24]. This may also be explained by the problems faced with regard to intellectual property rights in an intra-Community context. The position of the EC Member States with respect to intellectual property rights was traditionally closer to that of the developing countries than to that of the US[25]. They had always been reluctant to give up their sovereignty in this field, in favour of the EC, by virtue of harmonization. Even after the EC and its Member States endorsed the US view on the need to elaborate norms and standards of protection, the Member States continued to contest the exclusive competence of the EC on the matter, an issue which was eventually brought before the EC Court of Justice and settled in its well-known Opinion 1/94[26].

---

[22] See in particular Case 270/80, *Polydor v. Harlequin*. For an evaluation of the impact of the principle of exhaustion in the absence of parallel protection, see GOVAERE, I., *op. cit.* (1996), in particular at pp.164-168.

[23] See also *infra*, at pt D.1.

[24] See *"Guidelines and Objectives Proposed by the European Community for the Negotiations on Trade Related Aspects of Substantive Standards of Intellectual Property Rights"*, reproduced in BEIER & SCHRICKER, **GATT or WIPO**, IIC Studies Vol.11, VCH, 1989, pp.323-332, at p.324.

[25] See also PAEMEN, H. & BENSCH, A., *op. cit.*, at p.88.

[26] See *infra*, point C.1.

This does not mean that there was no harmonization of intellectual property laws in the EC prior to the TRIPs Agreement. There were indeed a certain number of intellectual property harmonization measures which the EFTA countries were required to adopt as part of the *acquis communautaire*[27]. EC harmonization proved to be more difficult with regard to the "traditional" aspects of intellectual property rights which were already firmly rooted in national laws, than with regard to the relatively new areas of intellectual property protection, such as lending and rental rights, and new technologies, such as computer software and cable re-transmissions[28]. For instance, there is an EC harmonization directive on copyrights in cable re-transmissions whereas, there is, as of yet, no basic EC harmonization of copyright laws, thus leaving the definition of crucial concepts such as "the protected author" subject to national legislation. If the EC did not offer an overall example of how the TRIPs Agreement could be shaped, the experience gained in the EC with certain areas of intellectual property harmonization did, nonetheless, have an effect on the TRIPs Agreement as it stands today. It should be underlined that the EC Draft on TRIPs served as the basis for discussion for it was, to a large extent, taken over in the Dunkel Draft. It is not surprising, therefore, to encounter similarities between parts of the TRIPs Agreement and some EC harmonization measures which were, at that time, either already adopted or in the pipeline.

The best known example is, of course, the provisions on geographical indications which were inserted under pressure from the EC. Although EC legislation is much more extensive in this field it lays at the basis for Articles 22-24 TRIPs. Article 23 TRIPs, dealing with the protection of geographical indications for wine and spirits, is a clear indication of the impact of EC achievements in the field of harmonization of intellectual property laws in TRIPs. Furthermore, Section 2 of Part II of TRIPs dealing with trademarks, to a large extent corresponds to EC harmonization Directive 89/104 on the approximation of trademark legislation. For example, the definition of protected subject-matter in Article 15 TRIPs and the rights and limitations of trademark rights as laid down in Articles 16 and 17 TRIPs correspond to Articles 2 and 4 to 6 of EC Directive 89/104 respectively. Similarly, Article 22 (3) TRIPs, which prohibits the registration of geographical indications as trademarks, finds its counterpart in Article 3(1) of EC Directive 89/104. In so far

---

[27] See Article 65(2) EEA, Article 1 of Protocol 28 and Annex XVII.

[28] On the state of EC intellectual property harmonization measures, see GOVAERE, I., *op. cit.*, 1996, at pp.52-58.

as copyrights are concerned, it is for instance illustrative to point out that Article 10 TRIPs, which expressly provides that "computer programs, whether in source or object code, shall be protected as literary works under the Berne Convention", corresponds to the approach adopted by the EC in Council Directive 91/250 on the Legal Protection of Computer Programs (Article 1)[29]. Also Council Directive 92/100 on Rental and Lending Rights and Certain Rights Related to Copyright[30] is, be it to a minor extent, reflected in Articles 11 and 14 TRIPs[31].

It is, thus, possible to pinpoint some kind of "spillover" effect from internal EC harmonization to TRIPs. However, the TRIPs negotiations, in turn, proved to be a means for the EC Commission to try to accelerate the internal EC harmonization process. In some of its proposals the EC Commission pointed to the TRIPs negotiations as an additional argument for EC harmonization. Sometimes this was explicitly stated, as in Council Decision 94/700 on the extension of the legal protection of topographies of semiconductor products to persons from Canada, which was expressly motivated by the need to comply with the TRIPs Agreement once it entered into force[32]. Or it was implied, as in the proposals on the legal protection of industrial design rights which are still under discussion today, where it is merely stated that "the provisions of the Regulation are fully consistent with the provisions on industrial designs in the draft TRIPs Agreement at present under negotiation."[33] Under both approaches adopted by the EC Commission the interaction of internal and worldwide harmonization endeavours in the field of intellectual property rights was most apparent. This has, nonetheless, not necessarily been the decisive argument prompting the Member States to adopt EC harmonization measures. Safeguarding national sovereignty in the field of intellectual property rights has remained an important preoccupation of the latter, as the following test-case perfectly illustrates.

The most obvious, although partly unsuccessful, attempt to use the TRIPs negotiations as leverage for provoking a change in the attitude of the Member States can be found in the Commission's *Proposal for a Council Decision concerning the accession of the Member States to the*

---

[29] **OJ** 1991, L 122/42.

[30] **OJ** 1992, L 346/61.

[31] Article 11 TRIPS, for instance, only deals with rental rights in respect to computer programs and cinematographic works and even then the granting of rental protection is not always obligatory.

[32] **OJ** 1994, OJ L 284/61.

[33] COM (93) 342 Final of December 3, 1993.

Berne Convention for the Protection of Literary and Artistic Works, as revised by the Paris Act of 24 July 1971, and the International Convention for the Protection of Performers, Producers of Phonograms and Broadcasting Organizations (Rome Convention) of 26 October 1961" of 1991[34]. The Commission explained that in its view:

> ... any Community action should be two-pronged, being carried out both at the internal level with a view to the formation of the single market in 1993, and at the international, multilateral level with a view to the creation of a world environment favourable to copyright and neighbouring rights and affording them an adequate and effective minimum level of protection from which right holders from the Community can then also benefit.[35]

In particular, the interaction between EC and TRIPs harmonization was underlined. On the one hand, it was pointed out that "the position of the Member States and of the Community would give an example, an "impetus" capable of bringing about greater international support for the Berne (Paris Act) and Rome Conventions." On the other hand, the Commission spelled out that in the Draft TRIPs Agreement, as submitted by the Community, Contracting Parties would be required to comply with the fundamental provisions of the intellectual property conventions concerned[36]. This requirement indeed found its place in Article 9 TRIPs with respect to the Berne Convention (1971). Internal EC harmonization was, thus, needed to back up the TRIPs proposal made by the EC, whereas the eventual international harmonization by way of TRIPs was invoked in order to make the proposal for internal EC harmonization seem less far-fetched, and thus more acceptable to the Member States. If, in so-doing, the Commission convinced the Member States of the need to harmonize their copyright laws, through the adherence to the said intellectual property conventions, it failed in its objective to achieve this through a binding EC harmonization measure, which would amount to acknowledging the competence of the EC in this field. Instead of a Council Decision, the Council adopted a **resolution** in which it merely **took note** of the fact that the Member States undertook to adhere to the

---

[34] COM (90) 582 Final of January 11, 1991. For the amended proposal see COM (92) 10 final of February 14, 1992. Of the twelve Member States, only Belgium and Ireland were not yet Parties to the Paris Act of the Berne Convention so that it was the Brussels Act (1948) that still applied to them. Only Belgium and Portugal had not yet ratified the Rome Convention.

[35] *Id.*, Explanatory Memorandum, pt 2.

[36] *Id.*, see respectively at pts 18 and 21.

intellectual property conventions concerned, by 1995 at the latest[37]. This later became a legally binding obligation by virtue of the explicit inclusion of the objective for all Contracting Parties, thus including the Member States, to adhere to specified intellectual property conventions in the EEA Agreement[38]. However, because of the mixed nature of the latter, it was not clear whether or not this provision fell under the concurrent competence of the Member States[39]. In the same resolution the Council, nonetheless, proceeded to invite the Commission to pay particular attention to the adherence to, and respect of, the Berne (1971) and Rome Conventions by **third countries** when negotiating agreements[40].

2. Intellectual Property Provisions in Bilateral Agreements

Whereas in an intra-Community context the Member States remained reluctant to fully harmonize their intellectual property legislation by virtue of EC harmonization, in measures from the nineties onwards it became a common practice, for both the EC and the US, to insert provisions in trade agreements aimed at raising the level of intellectual property protection offered by third countries. The approach adopted by the US and the EC, although sharing a similar objective, may be distinguished in so far as the practical implementation is concerned. Their respective agreements concluded with the CEECs are illustrative in this respect.

In the bilateral trade agreements concluded by the EC and the CEECs two types of intellectual property provisions may be found, sometimes in one and the same agreement. A first type of provision inserted in the Europe Agreements stipulates that the CEEC undertake to adhere to intellectual property conventions, specified in an annex to the agreement, to which the EC Member States are Parties or which are *de facto* applied by the latter[41]. This list usually includes, but is not necessarily limited to, the Berne (1971), Paris and Rome Conventions. A second type of provision puts the obligation on the associated country to approximate "as far

---

[37] **OJ** 1992, C 138/1, pt 1.

[38] **OJ** 1994, L 1. See Article 5 of Protocol No.28 (combined with Article 65(2) EEA), which contains in principle the obligation for all Contracting Parties to adhere to various intellectual property conventions by 1995, among which the Berne Convention (1971) and the Rome Convention.

[39] On this issue, see also *infra*, at pt C.1.

[40] **OJ** 1992, C 138/1, pt 2.

[41] See for instance Article 66 §2 and Annex XIII of the Europe Agreement with Poland, **OJ** L 348/1 of 31.12.1993.

as possible" its intellectual property legislation to that of the EC, or to "use its best endeavour" to do so[42]. If, from the point of view of the CEECs and in the absence of EC harmonization measures, the question arises of whether or not it would be sufficient to adopt the lowest level of protection provided for in a Member State it is clear that, from the point of view of the EC, the overall objective is to "export" high norms and standards of intellectual property protection in order to secure export markets[43].

Contrary to the EC approach, which aims at provoking general changes in the intellectual property legislation of the CEECs, the provisions inserted in bilateral agreements between the US and the CEECs seem to be more tailor-made to serve the specific and immediate interests of American industries abroad. For instance, in the economic agreement signed with Poland in March 1990, the Parties undertook, *inter alia,* to provide copyright protection for software and to introduce patents for both products and processes in the chemical and pharmaceutical sectors[44]. Those issues carried much weight for the US during the TRIPs negotiations and were finally endorsed in Articles 10 and 27 TRIPs, respectively[45]. Similar provisions may, for instance, also be found in the commercial agreement signed with the Soviet Union in 1990 and in the trade agreement signed with Ukraine in 1992[46]. It should, nonetheless, be pointed out that contrary to the agreements concluded by the EC, which put an obligation only on the associated country and not on the EC or its Member States, the agreements concluded by the US placed obligations on both Parties. The US apparently does not require third countries to adopt intellectual property measures that it itself does not, or cannot, enforce domestically as is the case for the EC.

Despite those differences it is clear that both the EC and the US adopted a bilateral package deal approach whereby the prospect of better trade relations was used as leverage to obtain the required improvement

---

[42] See, for instance, the Europe Agreement with Poland, *op. cit.*, Articles 66, 68 and 69.

[43] For more details, see GOVAERE, I., *op. cit.,* 1991.

[44] **PIBD**, No.484/90, p.II-119, as cited in C.U.E.R.P.I., **Actualités des droits de Propriété intellectuelle dans les Pays de l'Est**, No.8, 1990, at p.7. See also **International Review of Industrial Property and Copyright Law**, 1990, pp.763-764.

[45] In spite of the opposition by the developing countries, Article 27 TRIPS provides for the grant of patents for both products and processes in all fields, thus including pharmaceutical drugs.

[46] On the agreement with the USSR, see **PIBD** No.482/90, as cited in C.U.E.R.P.I., *op. cit.*, at pp.11-12 and **I.I.C.,** 1990, pp.908-909. On the agreements with the Ukraine, see **I.I.C.,** 1992, p.724.

of intellectual property protection for Community and US industries in third markets. Considering the sometimes conflicting views of the latter, which also became apparent during the second stage of the Uruguay negotiations on TRIPs, the in-between position of third countries that were required to live up to the requirements of both the US and the EC was not always an easy one[47]. The EC and the US already early on in the TRIPs negotiations acknowledged that in order not to undermine the multilateral trading system, problems encountered with regard to trade-related intellectual property rights should, whenever possible, be dealt with under the dispute settlement mechanisms provided for by the agreement, rather then by having recourse to unilateral and bilateral action[48]. The proliferation of bilateral package deals, including provisions on intellectual property rights in the course of the TRIPs negotiations, as well as the continued use of unilateral measures by the EC and the US to provoke changes in intellectual property protection abroad, undoubtedly contributed towards making the inclusion of substantive norms of intellectual property protection in a multilateral set of rules, even if legally binding and subject to dispute settlement, an acceptable if not almost appealing alternative. At the same time, it became clear that if the multilateral rules were to be effective in replacing bilateral and unilateral pressures then a relatively high level of protection should be provided for. However, as more and more developing countries had already modified their intellectual property legislation subsequent to pressure from the US and the EC, the further changes required by the TRIPs Agreement "became less significant for many of them."[49] One may only wonder whether the TRIPs Agreement would have existed in its current form if it had not been for the "groundwork" function fulfilled by the bilateral approach adopted by both the US and the EC.

3. Intellectual Property Provision in NAFTA

NAFTA is a prime example of the interaction between regional agreements and the TRIPs Agreement. Chapter 17 of NAFTA, which deals

---

[47] For instance, the US successfully used Section 301 to secure better intellectual property protection for American industry in the Korean market. Yet Korea was subsequently suspended from the EC list of countries benefiting from GSP in retaliation for the discriminatory treatment of EC industry, in comparison with American industry, in the field of intellectual property protection.

[48] See the *"Guidelines and Objectives Proposed by the European Community for the Negotiations on Trade Related Aspects of Substantive Aspects of Intellectual Property rights"* of 7 July 1988, in: BEIER & SCHRICKER, *op .cit.*, pp.323-332, at p.325.

[49] See JACKSON, DAVEY & SYKES, **Legal Problems of International Economic Relations**, (3rd ed.), West Publishing Co., 1995, at p.887.

with intellectual property rights, largely owes its existence to the TRIPs negotiations, as the 1991 Dunkel Draft on TRIPs formed the basis for the NAFTA negotiations on intellectual property rights. Conversely, NAFTA could be considered as a test-case for the TRIPs Agreement as it was the first time that such a comprehensive set of provisions, relating to both substantive norms and enforcement of intellectual property rights, was included in a regional agreement let alone in an agreement between industrialized countries (the USA and Canada) and a developing one (Mexico). This is not to say, however, that only Mexico needed to change its intellectual property legislation accordingly. Canada was also required to make important changes, for instance it had to adhere to the Berne Convention (1971)[50] and eliminate its discriminatory compulsory licensing regime as applied to the pharmaceutical sector[51]. The US, for its part, had to, for example, amend its patent law with respect to inventions made in Canada and Mexico in order to eliminate the discrimination inherent in its system of "first-to-invent". The discriminatory factor consisted in the determination of the date of the invention, using the actual date of invention for inventions made in the US and the date of filing a patent application for inventions made outside the US[52].

Seeing that Chapter 17 of NAFTA is almost identical to the Dunkel Draft in almost all essential issues, only the main differences will be highlighted[53]. For instance, NAFTA does not make a distinction between copyright and neighbouring or related rights, as TRIPs does, but rather introduces one general scheme of protection covering both. This is not merely a formal difference. Article 3 §1 of the Dunkel Draft stipulated that the principle of National Treatment (NT) in respect to performers, producers of phonograms, and broadcasting organizations would only

---

[50] By virtue of Article 1701 NAFTA, each Party shall make every effort to accede to the Geneva Convention for the protection of producers of phonograms against unauthorized duplication of their phonograms (1991), the Berne Convention (1971), the Paris Convention (1967) and the UPOV Convention (1978 or 1991).

[51] For an overview of the main implications of Chapter 17 NAFTA for the three countries concerned, see HUFBAUER, G. & SCHOTT, J., **NAFTA: An Assessment**, Institute for National Economics, 1993, pp.85-90.

[52] See ABBOTT, F., **Law and Policy of Regional Integration: The NAFTA and Western Hemispheric Integration in the World Trade Organization System**, Martinus Nijhoff Publishers, 1995, at pp.94-95.

[53] For a more detailed comparison, see LEVY, C. & WEISER, S., *"The NAFTA: A Watershed for Protection of Intellectual Property"*, in: **International Lawyer**, 1993, pp.671-689. However, as Abbott points out, only few meaningful distinctions are found between the Dunkel Draft and Chapter 17 NAFTA. See ABBOTT, F., *op. cit.*, at p.93 footnote 80.

apply in respect of the rights provided by the TRIPs Agreement[54]. Whereas the principle of national treatment as laid down in Article 1703 NAFTA, in principle, applies to all intellectual property rights alike, including copyright and related rights. Two important exceptions, however, need to be mentioned[55]. First, because of a fundamentally different approach by the US and Mexico to performers' rights, secondary uses of sound recordings may be applied on the basis of reciprocity[56]. Secondly, the Canadian cultural industries exemption, which was already embodied in the Canada-US FTA, has, in NAFTA, been extended to include copyright[57]. Although the latter seems to be a far-reaching exception, in practice its impact should be minor due to the fact that the US has retained its right to retaliate in case Canada actually invokes the cultural industries exemption[58]. In so far as patent protection is concerned the text of NAFTA remains very close to the Dunkel Draft. It is noteworthy that NAFTA does not go any further than the Dunkel Draft in so far as the protection of biotechnology is concerned[59]. NAFTA is, however, more strict on the matter of dependent compulsory licensing than the Dunkel Draft[60]. Whereas the latter allowed this practice when the second patent involved an important technical advance or considerable economic significance in relation to the invention claimed in the first patent, the former forbids dependent compulsory licensing except as a remedy for an adjudicated violation of competition law[61]. A difference should also be noted in so far as the so-called "pipeline" protection is concerned. Whereas the Dunkel Draft limited this to patents filed after the entry into force of the TRIPs Agreement, NAFTA provides for pipeline protection for pharmaceutical and agrochemical products already patented elsewhere[62]. For

---

[54] This was maintained in the final version of Article 3 §1 TRIPS. See also *infra*, at pt D.3.

[55] On these exceptions, see also *infra*, at pt C.2.

[56] Article 1703 §1 NAFTA. See HUFBAUER, G. & SCHOTT, J, *op.cit.*, at p.86, where it is pointed out that contrary to the US, Mexico took the view "that the original performer holds the right to the secondary use of a sound recording in a public performance or a broadcasting context."

[57] Article 2106 and Annex 2106 NAFTA.

[58] See HUFBAUER, G. & SCHOTT, J., *op.cit.*, at p.87.

[59] This has been subject to criticism. See for instance HUFBAUER, G. & SCHOTT, J., *op.cit.*, at pp.89-90; LEVY, C. & WEISER, S., *op.cit.*, at p.680, where they forward the view that in this respect "the NAFTA repeats the Dunkel TRIPS Text's mistake".

[60] See LEVY, C. & WEISER, S., *op.cit.*, at pp.682-683.

[61] Compare Article 31(l)(i) Dunkel Draft (maintained in the final TRIPS Agreement) and Article 1709 §10(l) NAFTA.

[62] Compare Article 70 §8 Dunkel Draft (as maintained in TRIPS) and Article 1709 §4 NAFTA. On this issue, see HUFBAUER, G. & SCHOTT, J., *op.cit.*, at pp.88-89; LEVY, C. & WEISER, S., *op.cit.*, at p.685.

trademarks and service marks. The main difference between the Dunkel Draft and NAFTA is that the former takes a permissive approach towards requiring the use of a trademark to maintain registration whereas the latter mandates this[63]. In the field of geographical indications it is apparent that NAFTA fails to include the Dunkel Draft provisions for wine and spirits[64]. In so far as trade secrets are concerned it has been pointed out that "it is one of the few areas where the protection provided under the NAFTA is less than that contained in the Dunkel TRIPs Text."[65] NAFTA allows the Parties to protect trade secrets only when evidenced in a tangible form whereas the Dunkel Draft did not refer to such a requirement[66]. On the whole, these are only minor differences considering the wide scope of the provisions concerned.

The impact of the Dunkel Draft on NAFTA is, however, not limited to substantive norms and standards of intellectual property protection which are substantially the same in both texts. The NAFTA provisions on enforcement of intellectual property rights were also, to a large extent, copied on the Dunkel Draft, an innovative issue which was considered to be of a great importance, in particular for Mexico[67]. Conversely, NAFTA also had an impact on the TRIPs Agreement for not only did it set a practical example for the latter, it also showed the determination to go ahead with the enforcement of intellectual property standards even in the absence of multilateral rules to that end.

C. Impact of TRIPs on Regional Trade Agreements

If the insertion of intellectual property provisions in bilateral and regional trade agreements by the US and the EC undoubtedly had both a contextual and a substantive impact on the TRIPs Agreement, so did the conclusion of the TRIPs Agreement have an impact on the bilateral and regional trade agreements. With the globally acknowledged linkage of trade and intellectual property rights, it is no longer uncommon, nowadays, to find that intellectual property provisions have been inserted in

---

[63] Compare Article 19 Dunkel Draft (as maintained in TRIPS) and Article 1708 §8 NAFTA.

[64] Articles 23 and 24 Dunkel Draft (as maintained in TRIPS), which were inserted under the impulse of the EC, see *supra*, pt B.1.

[65] LEVY, C. & WEISER, S., *op.cit.*, at p.678.

[66] Compare Article 1711 §2 NAFTA and Article 39 Dunkel Draft (as maintained in TRIPS).

[67] See HUFBAUER, G. & SCHOTT, J., *op.cit.*, at p.90.

bilateral and regional trade agreements[68]. It is interesting to see whether and to what extent the conclusion of the TRIPs Agreement may, furthermore, have served to remedy problems encountered previously in regional agreements with a high level of integration such as the EC and NAFTA.

1. The European Community (and European Economic Area)

At first sight it seems paradoxical that, although the TRIPs Agreement may to a large extent be traced back to the EC Draft on TRIPs, it managed to achieve something which proved most difficult in an EC context, namely establishing a basic harmonization of intellectual property legislation among the EC Member States. The reason for this is not so much to be found in the unwillingness of the Member States to harmonize their intellectual property legislation as in the consequences this potentially entails. Internal EC harmonization of intellectual property legislation necessarily implies a shift of competence from the Member States to the EC and thus, concurrently, a loss of national sovereignty in the matter[69]. External harmonization of intellectual property legislation, by virtue of the conclusion of international agreements, does not necessarily have the same effect.

The reluctance of the Member States to harmonize their intellectual property legislation by way of EC harmonization is best illustrated by reference to the method used to harmonize the patent laws of the Member States. The Community Patent Convention was, as the name suggests, concluded in the form of an international agreements between the Member States rather than through the EC harmonization provisions[70]. Another example is the previously mentioned response given to the Commission's proposal concerning accession to the Berne (1971) and Rome Conventions[71]. The Member States were unwilling to do this on the basis of an internal EC harmonization measure, although a similar obligation was later written into the European Economic Area (EEA)

---

[68] See *infra*, pt E.

[69] As the ECJ held in the *Denkavit* Case (Case 251/78), Member States may not invoke Article 36 EC in order to derogate from EC harmonization measures. The situation is somewhat different for the EFTA countries which are members of the EEA even though they are required to take over EC harmonization measures as part of the *acquis communautaire*. As the ECJ noted in its Opinion 1/91 the EEA does not imply a transfer of sovereignty on their part but is merely an international agreement under public international law.

[70] **OJ** 1996 L17/1; **OJ** 1989 L 401/1.

[71] See *supra*, at pt B.1.

agreements. The EEA Agreement is, however, of a mixed nature and Protocol No.28, on intellectual property rights, explicitly states that "the provisions of this Protocol shall be without prejudice to the competence of the Community and of its Member States in matters of intellectual property."[72]

Similarly for the Member States it was easier, as a matter of principle, to accept external harmonization by virtue of multilateral rules established in TRIPs rather than by the use of internal EC harmonization measures, as long as this did not threaten their competence in the field of intellectual property protection. They, therefore, strongly opposed the Commission's view that all trade-related matters dealt with in the WTO, including TRIPs, fell within the exclusive competence of the EC[73]. The dispute was eventually settled by the ECJ in its famous, albeit controversial, Opinion 1/94. With respect to TRIPs it held that the EC and its Member States are jointly competent, except for border measures relating to counterfeiting which belong to the Community's exclusive competence under the Common Commercial Policy heading. This qualified statement by the ECJ paved the way for the adoption of Council Regulation 3295/94 on counterfeiting and piracy[74], as required by Part III, Section 4 TRIPs, which was previously blocked because of the divergence in views about the proper legal basis. On the other hand, Opinion 1/94 did not prompt the Member States to implement the rest of the TRIPs Agreement by virtue of internal EC harmonization measures. The fact that the external harmonizing effect of TRIPs is not necessarily followed up by internal EC harmonization, but rather is implemented by the individual Member States, may only further emphasise the fundamental importance of the TRIPs Agreement for the EC. Whereas the special relationship between the EC and its Member States has proved to be an obstacle to obtain significant progress in the field of intellectual property harmonization, the TRIPs Agreement is an indirect, but indispensable, tool to achieve the same objective.

---

[72] See Article 9 of Protocol 28 to the EEA Agreement.

[73] According to the EC Commission the Community was exclusively competent by virtue of the common commercial policy. See EC Commission proposal for a Council Decision concerning the conclusion of the results of the Uruguay Round of Multilateral Trade Negotiations (1986-1994), COM (94) 43 final of 15.04.1994. In the proceedings leading up to ECJ Opinion 1/94 the EC Commission reiterated this view, pleading in subsidiary order that the EC was exclusively competent by virtue of its implied powers. On this dispute and ECJ Opinion 1/94, see GOVAERE, I., op.cit., 1994, at pp.191-205.

[74] **OJ** 1994 L 341/8. For the implementing regulation, see **OJ** 1995 L 133/2.

2. The North American Free Trade Area (NAFTA)

The impact of TRIPs on NAFTA is of a totally different order. Internal harmonization of intellectual property legislation in NAFTA was already achieved by the insertion of Chapter 17 which, as mentioned above[75], was negotiated on the basis of the Dunkel Draft on TRIPs. Since the TRIPs Agreement remains close to the Dunkel Draft, almost all the essential issues of the Dunkel Draft were taken over in NAFTA, it is clear that the conclusion of the TRIPs Agreement does not have a fundamental impact on the latter. It is nonetheless interesting to consider whether the TRIPs Agreement, because it involved negotiations and the need to find compromises with other trading partners, may lead to external harmonization in the two problem areas which gave rise to the insertion of exceptions to the NT clause of NAFTA[76].

First of all, there was the problem with performers' rights in secondary uses of a sound recording in a public performance or a broadcasting context. Mexico grants these rights to the original performers whereas the US only recognizes the right of the copyright owner in this respect. Even though the copyright owner may or may not be the performer, the latter is not *per se* protected[77]. Reciprocity was introduced as an exception to the NAFTA principle of national treatment as Mexico was unwilling to unconditionally extend its protection to US nationals without a counterpart for its own nationals in the US. Article 14(1) TRIPs seems to have resolved this issue by stipulating that **performers** shall have the possibility to prohibit the unauthorized secondary use of their performance. The TRIPs Agreement thus seems to call for a modification of the US legislation which would make the NAFTA reciprocity requirement more important in the future, if not equivalent to the principle of NT[78].

Secondly, there was the — at least theoretical — cultural exemption which allowed Canada to discriminate, including the field of copyright protection, against Mexican and US industries[79]. The need for a cultural exemption, in particular in relation to the audiovisual sector, was also a highly debated topic in the framework of the Uruguay Round

---

[75] See *supra*, at pt B.3.

[76] See *supra*, at pt B.3.

[77] See HUFBAUER, & SCHOTT, *op.cit.*, p.86,

[78] Compare to HUFBAUER & SCHOTT, *op.cit.*, at p.86 where they write that under NAFTA "the right of US and Canadian performers in Mexico will be subject to reciprocity, which for the foreseeable future means no protection."

[79] See *supra*, at pt B.3.

negotiations on General Agreement on Trade in Services (GATS). It finally led to the implied recognition of some kind of "cultural specificity" under that agreement in the sense that NT and market access may be restricted by not listing any commitments for the audiovisual sector[80]. However, no similar concession specifically for the cultural sector was made under the TRIPs Agreement. It thus seems that the multilateral rules established by the latter, including the principle of national treatment, are fully applicable also to the cultural sector and, if inconsistencies were found, could be invoked by the other WTO Members, including Mexico and the US[81], under the WTO dispute settlement procedure[82].

The TRIPs Agreement, thus, also has the potential to overcome certain problems faced in a NAFTA context, although the external harmonization that it may bring about is likely to be far less important for NAFTA than it is for the EC.

D. Convergence and Divergence

1. Basic WTO Principles and Regional Integration Agreements

Besides the effect of the TRIPs Agreement on regional trade agreements as such, it is also important to consider to what extent the TRIPs Agreement may lead to a convergence of intellectual property norms and standards between Parties to different regional agreements and third Parties. The TRIPs Agreement by itself has a harmonization effect as the minimum norms of intellectual property protection it lays down should, in principle, be adopted by all WTO Members. Yet may all WTO Members also rely on the TRIPs Agreement, and in particular on the principles of NT and Most-Favoured-Nation (MFN), in order to benefit from intellectual property provisions specific to regional agreements? This

---

[80] For more details on this issue see FALKENBERG, K., *"The Audiovisual Sector"*, in: BOURGEOIS, BERROD & GIPPINI FOURNIER (eds), **The Uruguay Round Results: A European Lawyers' Perspective**, The Bruges Conferences N.S.8, European Interuniversity Press, Brussels, 1995, pp.429-434.

[81] See Article 2005 §1 NAFTA which provides the following with respect to dispute settlement: "Subject to Paragraphs 2, 3 and 4, disputes regarding any matter arising under both this Agreement and the General Agreement on Tariffs and Trade, any agreement negotiated thereunder, or any successor agreement (GATT), may be settled in either forum at the discretion of the complaining Party."

[82] Abbott, however, is of the opinion that "the NAFTA reservations with respect to audiovisual services and products are unlikely to be considered inconsistent with the WTO Agreement" because of the inconclusive outcome of the Uruguay negotiations with respect to the audiovisual sector. See ABBOTT, F., *op.cit.*, at p.96.

question arises in particular where divergences in intellectual property protection remain due to the adoption of higher norms of intellectual property protection, or due to the regional nature of answers given to inconclusive issues under the TRIPs Agreement, such as the first-to-invent *versus* first-to-file debate in the field of patent protection.

A peculiarity of the TRIPs Agreement is that the general principles of NT and MFN refer to intellectual property protection granted to **nationals**, similar to the NT principle laid down in the World Intellectual Property Organization (WIPO) conventions on intellectual property rights. In essence, each WTO Member should not grant less favourable treatment to nationals of other Members than to its own nationals (Article 3 TRIPs — NT), and any advantage, privilege or immunity granted by a WTO Member to the nationals of any other country should immediately and unconditionally also be granted to the nationals of all other Members (Article 4 TRIPs — MFN). If the cornerstone of the TRIPs Agreement is nondiscrimination, the cornerstone of regional integration agreements is precisely discrimination *vis-à-vis* third Parties[83]. During the Uruguay Round TRIPs negotiations some confusion, therefore, arose over an early proposal from the EC negotiators which was understood, by some, to mean that regional integration agreements would not be subject at all to the principles of MFN and NT as laid down in the TRIPs Agreement[84]. The position of the EC was soon clarified in the sense that it was only the principle of exhaustion, which essentially deals with the parallel importation of **goods**, that could not be accepted as a topic to be dealt with in the TRIPs Agreement[85]. In principle it was thus decided that regional integration agreements would also be subject to the TRIPs principles of NT and MFN. The exceptions to those basic principles, however, merit particular attention.

---

[83] See SAMPSON, G., *"Compatibility of Regional and Multilateral Trading Agreements: Reforming the WTO Process"*, in: **American Economic Review**, 1996, pp.88-92, at p.88.

[84] See **News of the Uruguay Round**, 19 April 1990, at p.13, where it is reported that the EC draft on TRIPS "affirms the principles of national treatment and most-favoured-nation treatment/nondiscrimination, with exceptions for customs unions and free trade areas."

[85] For the text of Article 6 TRIPS on the principle of exhaustion, see *supra*, at pt B.1. As Demaret pointed out, Article 6 TRIPS implies that "it should be permissible to apply the exhaustion of exclusive rights only to domestic trade and not to external trade, provided that the national and foreign holders of the exclusive rights are treated in the same manner", see DEMARET, P., *"The Metamorphoses of the GATT: From the Havana Charter to the World Trade Organization"*, in: **Columbia Journal of Transnational Law**, 1995, pp.123-171, at p.168.

2. Most-Favoured-Nation Treatment

Consistent with the Swiss Draft[86], Article 4 (d) TRIPs allows for derogations from the MFN principle in international agreements relating to the protection of intellectual property which entered into effect prior to the WTO Agreement, on the condition that these "are notified to the TRIPs Council and do not constitute an arbitrary or unjustifiable discrimination against nationals of other Members."[87] A notification to this effect was completed on December 19, 1995 relating to both the EU Treaty and the EEA Agreement. The notification apparently did not only cover those two treaties but also any present or future secondary legislation issued by the EU or its Member States[88]. NAFTA also qualifies for this exception[89]. This implies that advantages granted to nationals of other EC or EEA Member States, on the one hand, and of other NAFTA states, on the other hand, do not have to be extended automatically to nationals of all other WTO Members. The latter could, nonetheless, still rely on the TRIPs principle of NT in order to receive treatment not less favourable than that accorded to the nationals of an EEA or NAFTA state, respectively, and thus indirectly also benefit from intellectual property provisions in regional integration agreements.

3. National Treatment

Contrary to the MFN principle, the impact of the principle of NT as laid down in Article 3 TRIPs may not be limited to the entry into force of the WTO Agreement. However, Article 3 TRIPs does not always and unconditionally apply. In respect to performers, producers of phonograms, and broadcasting organizations the application of the principle of national treatment is expressly limited to the rights provided under the TRIPs Agreement[90]. This implies, for instance, that nationals of other WTO Members will not be able to claim national treatment with respect to many of the rights covered by EC Directive 92/100 on *"Rental and Lending Rights and Certain Rights Related to Copyright"* which contains detailed rules on performers' rights. Furthermore, Article 3 TRIPs makes the principle of NT "subject to the exceptions already provided in, respectively, the Paris Convention (1967), the Berne Convention

---

[86] See **News of the Uruguay Round**, June 1, 1990, at p.8.

[87] For the other exceptions to MFN, see *infra*, at pt E.

[88] On this issue see **I.I.C.**, 1996, p.581.

[89] See also ABBOTT, F. *op.cit.*, at p.95.

[90] See also *supra*, at pt B.3.

(1971), the Rome Convention, or the Treaty on Intellectual Property in Respect of Integrated Circuits." This implies that WTO Members may, exceptionally, substitute NT for a reciprocity requirement if this is in conformity with the intellectual property conventions mentioned[91]. In so far as the EC is concerned, the ECJ made clear in the *Phil Collins* Case that Member States may not discriminate against nationals of other EC Member States regardless of the fact that the imposition of a reciprocity requirement was in conformity with an intellectual property convention[92]. However, under the same conditions it seems that, by virtue of a combination of the exceptions laid down in Article 3 and 4 TRIPs, nationals of other WTO Members could continue to be discriminated against[93].

The basic TRIPs principle of NT will, nonetheless, allow third Parties to benefit to some extent from intellectual property provisions laid down in regional integration agreements. It has been pointed out that the principle of NT in TRIPs has little in common with the principle of NT in intellectual property conventions for it has become part of a *quid pro quo* deal instead of granting privileges to foreigners on a non-reciprocal basis[94]. Because of the rather high level of harmonization required by the TRIPs Agreement it may be expected that the difference between NT and reciprocity requirements, in the exceptional cases where this is still allowed, will eventually become less significant in practice. Also, the quasi-automatic insertion of reciprocity requirements with respect to nationals of third countries, and in particular those countries which had not yet adhered to specific intellectual property conventions as is the practice in EC legislation[95], will need to be reconsidered in view of compliance with the NT obligation under TRIPs. For instance, EC Council Regulation 40/94 on the Community trademark had to be amended to

---

[91] Pursuant to Article 3 TRIPS a notification has to be made to the TRIPS Council if a Member avails itself of the possibilities provided in Article 6 of the Berne Convention (1971) or Paragraph 1(b) of Article 16 of the Rome Convention.

[92] Joined Cases C-92/92 & C-326/92.

[93] This is not merely a theoretical construction. See for instance Article 18 §2 of the Commission proposal on an EC Directive concerning the protection of industrial designs, where it is pointed out that the possibility to invoke Article 2(7) Berne Convention with respect to nationals of other **EC Member States** is contrary to the nondiscrimination principle of Article 6 EC (COM (93) 344 final of 3.12.1993). In its amended proposal the Commission proposes to delete this paragraph not because it would be contrary to the TRIPS Agreement but, simply, because it has become superfluous subsequent to the clear statement on the applicability of Article 6 EC to intellectual property rights by the ECJ in the *Phil Collins* Case (COM (96) 66 final of 21.02.1996).

[94] See ULLRICH, H., *op.cit.*, at p.180.

[95] See also DEMARET, P., *op.cit.*, at p.165.

the extent that it subjected "the granting of NT to nationals of states not Party to the Paris Convention to the requirement of reciprocal national treatment in their country of origin for nationals of the Member States", regardless of whether or not it concerned WTO Members[96]. Another significant example of the impact of the TRIPs principle of NT is the fact that the US also had to eliminate the discriminatory feature of its first-to-invent system for patents, as it already had with regard to Mexico and Canada pursuant to NAFTA[97], with respect to the other WTO Members[98]. Although the TRIPs Agreement did not do away with the divergence in approach to patents, leaving it up to the WTO Members to adopt a first-to-file or first-to-invent system, from a practical point of view for patent owners it does render the coexistence of the two systems more compatible than before.

E. Does TRIPs Render Intellectual Property Provisions in International Agreements Obsolete?

With the successful conclusion of the TRIPs Agreement, which harmonizes intellectual property protection almost worldwide, the question may be posed whether the inclusion of intellectual property provisions in free trade and regional integration agreements continues to serve a useful purpose. There are several reasons why the latter may prove to be complementary to the former.

Bilateral trade agreements may still be used in order to provide an additional incentive to ensure the proper implementation of the TRIPs Agreement[99], or to speed up its implementation[100]. In most

---

[96] See Uruguay Round Implementing Legislation, COM (94) 414 final, 5.10.1994, Part 7 pt II (this was followed by EC Regulation 2868/95, **OJ** 1995 L 303/1). Other EC implementation measures identified in the field of intellectual property rights concerned geographical indications and layout-designs of integrated circuits.

[97] See *supra*, at pt B.3.

[98] See Section 531 of the 1994 Uruguay Round Agreements Act, H.R. 5110.

[99] See for instance, in relation to the US, the recommendation expressed in the Report on *"WTO Implementation from the President's Advisory Committee for Trade Policy and Negotiations: Cementing and Improving Existing Agreements"* of March 11, 1996, Trade-Related Aspects of Intellectual Property Rights, point 4. In relation to the EC, see for instance the Proposal for an inter-regional framework cooperation agreement between the EC and Mercosur, COM (95) 504 final of 23.10.1995, Article 9(2) which reads: "Within the bounds of their laws, regulations and policies, and in line with the undertakings made within the TRIPS Agreement, the Parties shall ensure that there is suitable and genuine protection of intellectual property rights, if necessary by arranging for such protection to be stepped up."

[100] See for instance the Commission Proposal for a Council Decision concerning the conclusion of a framework agreement for trade and cooperation between the EC

cases, however, the purpose of such agreements will be to raise the level of intellectual property protection beyond what has been established by the TRIPs Agreement, either in order to secure export markets or to respond to specific market situations. It may already be inferred from the wording of the TRIPs Agreement that it is not meant to be a final stage in the development of intellectual property protection worldwide. Article 1 TRIPs emphasises that TRIPs only lays down **minimum** standards of protection. Whereas, with respect to geographical indications for wines and spirits express reference is made to the possibility of concluding bilateral or multilateral agreements aimed at increasing intellectual property protection[101].

The current proliferation of bilateral and regional trade agreements, embodying intellectual property provisions which are aimed at raising the standard of intellectual property protection beyond the level established by TRIPs, may essentially be explained by the continued search for higher intellectual property standards abroad in order to secure export markets for domestic industries[102]. Such provisions will, however, no longer be in the sole interest of the negotiating countries. It should be noted that the previously mentioned exception to the MFN clause for international agreements only applies to those which entered into force **prior** to the WTO Agreement and were duly notified[103]. In principle any advantage, favour, privilege, or immunity granted under new trade agreements should also, therefore, immediately and unconditionally be extended to the nationals of all other WTO Members. The only exceptions to that rule are the advantages:

[...] granted in accordance with the provisions of the Berne Convention (1971) or the Rome Convention authorising that the treatment accorded be a function not of national treatment but of the treatment accorded in another country;
[...] in respect of rights of performers, producers of phonograms and broadcasting organizations not provided under this agreement.[104]

---

and the Republic of Korea, COM (96) 141 final of 27.03.1996, which provides in Article 9 that "the Parties agree to implement the WTO Agreement on TRIPS not later than 1 July 1996".

[101] See Article 24 TRIPS.

[102] On the different US agreements containing intellectual property provisions and their underlying rationale, see the *"1996 Trade Policy Agenda and 1995 Annual Report of the President of the United States on the Trade Agreements Program"*.

[103] See *supra*, at pt D.2.

[104] Article 4(b) and (c) TRIPS. Other exceptions concern advantages "deriving from international agreements on judicial assistance of law enforcement of a general

It should be recalled that the principle of NT may not be invoked in this respect either[105]. Besides those exceptions, nationals of all WTO Members should thus be able to benefit from the higher standards of intellectual property protection negotiated in an international trade agreement, not only indirectly by virtue of the NT principle as is the case for "old" and notified agreements, but directly by virtue of the principle of MFN[106].

In other cases, in particular in the framework of free trade or regional integration agreements, the minimum protection provided by TRIPs may not be considered as sufficient to respond to the specific market situation[107]. This is certainly the case for both the EC and NAFTA which aim at a high level of integration. In light of safeguarding the Internal Market the former faces the additional problem that it is the Member States which are, to a large extent, responsible for the implementation of TRIPs. Whereas under TRIPs a Member State could decide to offer a higher level of protection than the other WTO Members, including other EC Member States, such a situation would be prejudicial to the Internal Market objective. Similar considerations, for instance, led to the adoption of an EC Directive harmonizing the duration of copyright law at seventy years *post mortem auctoris* whereas TRIPs only lays down a minimum term of fifty years *post mortem auctoris*[108]. It is, therefore, to be expected that in the future EC harmonization efforts will also continue in the field of

---

nature and not particularly confined to the protection of intellectual property" (Article 4(a) TRIPS) and "procedures provided in multilateral agreements concluded under the auspices of WIPO relating to the acquisition or maintenance of intellectual property rights" (Article 5 TRIPS, providing an exception to both NT and MFN).

[105] See *supra*, at pt D.3.

[106] However, see ULLRICH, H., *op.cit.*, at p.183, footnote 133, where he raises some pertinent questions in relation to the meaning of the MFN provision in relation to intellectual property.

[107] See for instance the Commission's *"White Paper on the Preparation of the Associated Countries of Central and Eastern Europe for Integration into the Internal Market of the Union"*, COM (95) 163 final/2 of 10.05.1995, at p.352, where it is stated that: "The TRIPS Agreement is a great step forward, but it has to be recognized that most of the multilateral conventions, and especially those revised in the late 60s or early 70s, do not give an answer — or at any rate not a complete answer — to all the questions which arise, particularly in connection with technological development. In the nature of things, too, the single market often calls for closer and more structured harmonization of national legislation than do the international conventions. So that although multilateral action is necessary, it is not sufficient to meet the needs of the Single Market."

[108] Council Directive 93/98 harmonizing the term of protection of copyright and certain related rights, **OJ** L 290/9 of 24.11.93. See also the "harmonization options" as mentioned by the Commission in its proposal, COM (92) 33 final of 23.03.1992, at pt 45 ff. Compare to Article 12 TRIPS.

intellectual property rights. An additional factor for further intellectual property harmonization by way of regional trade agreements might be that, under certain circumstances, it may be easier for individuals to enforce their rights ensuing from such agreements than from the WTO Agreement[109]. Furthermore, it might be considered appropriate to insert the principle of regional exhaustion into a regional trade agreement, an issue which is expressly left open by the TRIPs Agreement[110].

If there are numerous reasons why intellectual property provisions will continue to be inserted in regional trade agreements concluded by WTO Members, whose intellectual property laws are already to a certain extent harmonized by the TRIPs Agreement, then there seems to be all the more reason to insert similar clauses in agreements with countries who are not (yet) Members of the WTO. The US-China dispute over intellectual property rights, which was eventually settled by an agreement, is illustrative in this respect.

Conclusion

It is one thing to establish the interaction between the TRIPs Agreements and regional trade agreements and to point out convergence and divergence which ensues from the coexistence of multilateral and regional rules on intellectual property protection. It is a totally different, and much more difficult, exercise to find a globally acceptable justification for the reasons that have led to the linkage of intellectual property rights and trade in the first place. From a formal point of view the continuing search for higher standards of intellectual property protection than those embodied in the TRIPs Agreement, by way of regional trade agreements, may not be objected to. The question nonetheless remains whether the inflationary spiral of intellectual property protection worldwide may not eventually prove to be a price too high to pay for certain WTO Members, and in particular those who were already reluctant to agree on the "minimum" standards of protection laid down in the TRIPs Agreement. With the current proliferation of trade agreements embodying norms and standards of intellectual property protection which are higher than those set in the TRIPs Agreement it is to be expected that the latter will, eventually, be considered by some WTO Members to be insufficient and

---

[109] In the EC, for instance, the cases in which harmonization measures and provisions in agreements concluded with third countries may be held to have direct effect are far less controversial than with regard to the WTO Agreement.

[110] See *infra*, at pt B.1.

hence in need of renegotiation. In light of this foreseeable evolution it is all the more important that, this time, the WTO first elaborate a general policy on global competitiveness before engaging in negotiations aimed at further reinforcing the linkage of trade and intellectual property rights worldwide.

COMMENTS

Hanns ULLRICH

M.C.J. (NY University)
Professor, Bundeswehr University Munich

Introduction

International intellectual property protection is a special issue. But it
is a broad field of convergence, divergence and interaction between regional and multilateral trade rules. Inge Govaere has covered it with a
fair and balanced report which makes comments look either repetitive or
pedantic. It is only in her conclusion that she sheds some doubt on the
international trends in increased intellectual property protection. However, the relationship between intellectual property and international trade
seems fairly clear since the nature of the goods and services traded has
undergone, and still undergoes, a dramatic change from conventional
commodities to innovative products, and since the international allocation not only of manufacturing activities but also of research and development moves away from domestic roots to global presence and network-
building. As rapid as this evolution takes places, it develops gradually
via regional integration. These integrating regions grow into areas of
densified trade, they establish new and specifically regulated markets,
and they emancipate themselves more quickly from the nation-state to
become the new centers of gravity of industrial activities and interests.
Beyond convergence, divergence and interaction, their rules, therefore,
may directly or indirectly collide with multilateral trade rules. My comments relate to these conflicts and their resolution by exemption or distinction of the trade rules concerned.

A. Conflicts?

1. The Conflict Potential

When inquiring into the relationship between regional and multilateral trade rules regarding intellectual property rights, the principle guiding the analysis ought to be improvement of trade. Therefore, our interest should be in determining the effects international or regional rules of intellectual property protection produce rather than in examining the compatibility of such rules. But even so, what are the questions that need to be answered? The conventional lawyer's approach might still be to first state the multilateral rules, and then to ask whether the regional trade rules are in line with these multilateral rules because multilateral rules carry with them both a notion of supremacy — they are binding to all countries and they are intended to govern global trade which should not be interfered with regionally — and a notion of better, because free and equal trade that benefits all rather than a few countries only. However, even assuming that the multilateral rules essentially consist only of those embodied in the World Trade Organization (WTO)/Trade-Related aspects of Intellectual Property rights (TRIPs) Agreement and the main international intellectual property conventions[1], such an approach is not quite as simple as it appears at first glance. For one thing, the TRIPs Agreement does not only ask for implementation of its sometimes rather vague rules, notably in the area of exceptions to protection[2], but it also allows Members to provide for "more extensive protection"[3] than is required by

---

[1] While the WTO-TRIPs Agreement does make express reference only to some pre-existing Conventions of varying importance (Paris Convention for the Protection of Industrial Property of 1883 and Berne Convention for the Protection of Literary and Artistic Property of 1886 on the one hand, Rome Convention for the Protection of Performers, Producers of Phonograms and Broadcasters of 1961 and Washington Treaty on Intellectual Property in Respect of Integrated Circuits of 1989 on the other hand, see Arts 1-3 TRIPs), there are other conventions as well of international importance (e.g. Universal Copyright Convention of 1952 International Convention on the Protection of Plant Varieties of 1961) or vocation which are good law, but suffer from more or less insufficient membership. In addition, the principles of international public law relating directly or indirectly to the protection of intellectual property may be relevant.

[2] See UNCTAD, Financial and other implications of the implementation of the TRIPs-Agreement for Developing Countries, Geneva 1996, 57 et passim, REICHMAN, The TRIPs Component of the GATT's Uruguay Round: Competitive Prospects for Intellectual Property Owners in an Integrated World Market, 4 Fordh. Int. Prop. Media Entertainment L. J. 171, 185 et seq (1993).

[3] The concept of "more extensive protection" appears to be ambivalent: it may mean covering additional subject-matter, but it may also mean covering more protectable subject-matter by lowering the levels of access to protection (novelty, non-obviousness for patents, originality for copyright) or even raising these levels in order to upgrade the value of protection. As these criteria do determine the trade-off

the agreement itself, provided that such protection does not contravene the provisions of this agreement. Therefore, in addition to the question of correct implementation, there is that of unjustified overprotection. Assuming that these two questions can be answered correctly on the level of Members that individually grant protection, would any of these answers need to be modified when Members act concertedly on the regional level? This question really raises several issues:

a) First, does regionalization justify lesser protection either with respect to trade among Member States or with third countries? Members may be inclined to at least lessen protection available with respect to trade within their regional grouping with a view to achieve this grouping's objectives. The availability or non-availability of territorial protection against parallel imports and re-imports is a case in point[4]. Other cases which are more or less directly related to trade are easily conceivable, for example: rules on reverse engineering of computer-software that are intended to foster competitiveness; rules on the availability of protection that require applicants to take titles covering the entire region rather than only some national territories and which prevent territorially limited assignments[5]; or, rules that exclude know-how from protection that is only locally unknown[6] or that subject intellectual property rights to compulsory licences if only part of the region are not adequately supplied.

b) A second issue becomes particularly acute when Members belonging to a regional group concertedly strengthen protection, i.e. by way of regional harmonization of intellectual property laws, or with respect to regionally harmonized implementation of TRIPs Standards of protection or of exceptions. In both situations the mere fact of joint action necessarily produces "synergistic plus values" enhancing the operation and the

---

between incentives to innovate and competition for the diffusion of innovations, the authority to extend protection may easily create problems in view of the caveat, that the extension may contravene the TRIPs Agreement, e.g. by creating new barriers to trade (see Preamble of TRIPs); for the tradeoff-issue see recently MATUTES, REGIBEAU & ROCKETT, Optimal Patent Design and the Diffusion of Innovations, 27 Rand J. Ec. 60 (1996); for the criticality of these issues see ULLRICH, GATT: Industrial Property Protection, Fair Trade and Development in BEIER & SCHRICKER, GATT or WIPO? New Ways in the International Protection of Intellectual Property, Weinheim 1989, 127, 139 et seq.

[4] See GONZALEZ; An Analysis of the Legal Implications of the Intellectual Property Provisions of the North American Free Trade Agreement, 34 Harv. Int'l L. J. 305 (1993) comparing EC-rules with NAFTA.

[5] See Art.1(2) Community Trademark (OJEC 1994 L 11, 1); Art.2(2) Community Patent (OJEC 1989 L 401, 10) as compared to CJEC of June 22, 1994, Case C-9/93, *IHT Internationale Heiztechnik/Ideal Standard*, Rep 1994 I 2789.

[6] Comp. ULLRICH, Nationale Geschäftsgeheimnisse und Gemeinsamer Markt, RIW Supp 23/1990 at pp.10 et seq.

results of the protection or of the exception, quite apart from the standard-setting effects such joint action will produce on the multilateral level. This is so because intellectual property protection generally is justified on the rationale that it provides incentives for inventive, artistic or marketing activities within systems of competition[7]. TRIPs itself is based on this rationale (Art.7), and this rationale means, that if a group of Members does set identical standards within their — more or less-integrated economies — which differ from those followed by the rest of TRIPs Members, they will jointly achieve different economic results with competition enhancing the level of these results beyond what they would be in a purely national setting. In other words, joint intellectual property standards not only foster integration undertaken regionally but they also provide a competitive advantage to the region.

2. Regional Exceptions from or Regional Concentration of Protection

a) The common problem with these issues is that they may not be answered on the traditional basis of exceptions granted from international trade rules to free trade areas or custom unions[8]. First, such intellectual property harmonization need not occur only within these two types of exceptions. The harmonization effects of the European Patent Organization are independent from either the European Union or the European Economic Area[9]. Second, the rationale underlying these exceptions, namely that regional integration will increase trade beyond the levels afforded by general GATT rules, is not really pertinent in the TRIPs context or, at least, has to be drastically modified. Contrary to its name, the Agreement on Trade-Related Aspects of Intellectual Property is not trade-related, at least not directly, but protection-oriented. Its focus is on reducing trade distortions resulting from inadequate protection by

---

[7] See generally DAVID, Intellectual Property Institutions and Panda's Thumb: Patents, Copyrights and Trade Secrets in Economic Theory and History, in WALLERSTEIN (ed.), Global Dimensions of Intellectual Property Rights in Science and Technology, Washington 1993, 19, 24 et seq; critical ULLRICH, Lizenzkartellrecht auf dem Weg zur Mitte, GRUR Int 1996, 554, 561 et seq.

[8] See Art.XXIV GATT and the Agreement on the Interpretation of Art.XXIV GATT 1994, OJEC 1994 L 336, 16.

[9] Other examples are the Strasburg Convention on the Unification of Certain Points of Substantive Law on Patents for Inventions of 1963 or of the European Agreement on the Protection of Television Broadcasts of 1960 (with Protocols of 1974, 1983), both concluded within the framework of the Council of Europe; comp. also the ASEAN-Framework Agreement on Cooperation in the Field of Intellectual property Rights of December 15, 1995, GRUR Int 1996, 719.

granting effective protection, i.e. by limiting trade in the conventional, liberal sense. What it really represents is an attempt to transpose the operation and the rationale of national intellectual property systems on the global level because the kind of competition that used to be more or less limited to national markets now occurs on the world market, i.e. dynamic technological competition[10]. The relatively simple basic-idea is, therefore, that just as free imitation by individual competitors must be barred by intellectual property protection for innovating enterprises which, in the absence of protection, would have no interest in innovation, so must imitating "newly industrializing countries" be induced to provide protection or else industrialized countries would see the fruits of their efforts drained away and, ultimately, could and would not maintain their investment in technological lead, international distribution etc. Consequently, a new rationale for accepting regional exceptions from TRIPs ought to be developed; for instance, reinforcement of competition for innovation beyond TRIPs levels. But that would mean accepting precisely the kind of distortions TRIPs is intended to prevent: in the case of regionally lessened protection, foreign enterprises appear to be put at a disadvantage, and, in case of regionally improved protection, the rest of the TRIPs Members would suffer as well from the increased strength of the group members. What is more, the rest of the TRIPs Members may even be blamed for granting insufficient protection.

b) In reality, things are even more complicated because regions of harmonized intellectual property protection are not closed areas, and because their economic importance cannot reasonably be analyzed in terms of standards of intellectual property protection alone but only against the background of the overall regional integration. Thus, due to the principle of national treatment, which has been generally recognized long before the TRIPs Agreement[11], nationals of Member States not belonging to the regional grouping may benefit from all the regionally harmonized protection (or suffer from the harmonized exceptions). Consequently, whatever specific and arguably "protectionist" intellectual property rules are adopted by a regional grouping, unless the region is dominated by

---

[10] See ULLRICH, TRIPs: Adequate Protection, Inadequate Trade, Adequate Competition Policy, in HALEY & IYORI, Antitrust: A New International Trade Remedy, Seattle 1995, 153 = 4 Pac. Rim. L. Pol. J. 153, 173 et seq, 184 et seq (1995); *id.*, Technology Protection According to TRIPs: Principles and Problems, in BEIER & SCHRICKER (eds), From GATT to TRIPs, Weinheim 1996, ... = GRUR Int 1995, 623, 629 et seq.

[11] See Art.2 Paris Convention; Art.5 Berne Convention; Art.II Universal Copyright Convention; BEIER, One Hundred Years of International Cooperation - The Role of the Paris Convention in the Past, Present and Future. 15 IIC 1 (1984).

enterprises from the region, they will not produce regional effects, but they will simply allow (and probably for the worse) international enterprises to develop the same business strategies on the regional level which they used to apply on the national level, or, put differently, their global intellectual property strategies will be based on regions covered where formerly they had been based on states covered[12]. This, by the way, is a direct consequence of the logic of TRIPs, which is conceived in terms of states negotiating for the control of "wild" foreign markets by offering control of and protection in the domestic national markets which they control[13] whereas the means of market protection and control, i.e. intellectual property, are held by individual private enterprises acting independently on the international level. In fact the entire TRIPs deal makes sense only for the Member which, due to its control over the largest market and the lead and presence abroad of its domestic industry can be sure that its nationals will be able to gain control of foreign markets by intellectual property rights and to reap the benefits of a protection that they have made generally available by offering (or by withdrawing) trade concessions that give foreign nationals access to their domestic market and/or that provide them "equal" intellectual property protection.

c) In view of this permeability of regional intellectual property protection groupings to foreign interests, these groupings may be more properly described as "power poles" providing more efficient control over available harmonized and possibly intensified intellectual property protection than as regional extensions of national protectionism. This is not only true when granting procedures for patents[14], trademarks[15], plant varieties[16] or designs[17] become regionally centralized or when, due to the

---

[12] Comp. ULLRICH, loc. cit. 4 Pac. Rim. L. Pol. J. 169 et seq, 186 et seq.

[13] See STRAUS, The Importance of TRIPs for Patents, in BEIER & SCHRICKER (eds), From GATT to TRIPs, loc. cit. at ... = GRUR Int 1996, 179, 182 et seq. rediscovering a truism; comp. the critique by ULLRICH, loc. cit. BEIER & SCHRICKER, GATT or WIPO at 135 et seq; id., Technology Protection, loc. cit. GRUR Int 1995, at 634.

[14] Such as administered by the European Patent Organization, the African Regional Intellectual Property Organization (ARIPO), the *Organisation Africaine pour la Propriété Industrielle (OAPI)*, or under the recent Europe Asean Patent Convention of 1995.

[15] Such as available under the Madrid Agreement Concerning the International Registration of Trademarks of 1891 (and its Protocol of 1989 attempting to internationalize the *de facto* regional character of the agreement), the ARIPO and OAPI Conventions or the Community Mark Regulation.

[16] See Council Regulation (EC) No.2100/94 of July 27, 1994, OJEC 1994 L 227, 1.

[17] Such as under the Hague Agreement on the International Deposit of Industrial Designs of 1925 (*de facto* regional) or under the future Community Design Regulation.

extension of jurisdiction[18] and the mutual recognition of judgements, enforcement of protection against foreign acts of infringement is improved. Rather, the uniformity of substantive law as such, results in lessening the costs of managing intellectual property protection, in enhanced availability and reliability of protection and, in particular, in an enlarged overall scope of identical territorial protection which strengthens its reach and provides a safer basis for investment and marketing decisions with respect to the markets covered by intellectual property.

In fact, regional intellectual property rules may be classified; first, according to whether and to what degree they simply facilitate obtention of protection by harmonizing formalities, allowing application with or examination by central organizations, or provide for the centralized granting of titles to protection[19]; and second, according to whether, beyond procedure, they also provide for harmonization of substantive rules in various ways and, more importantly, with a varying degree of density of detail regulation[20]. In respect to the latter, regionally harmonized or unified intellectual property rules may simply implement TRIPs or go beyond the protection asked for by its multilateral rules[21]. The interesting distinction, however, is not between the implementation and extension of the protection the TRIPs Agreement provides. Rather it is, first,

---

[18] Gerichtshof den Haag of February 3, 1994, GRUR Int 1995, 253; BERTRAM, The Cross-Border Injunction in Dutch Patent Law, 26 IIC 618 (1995).

[19] To the difference of procedural rules that have been harmonized internationally e.g. within the Patent Cooperation Treaty or the recent Trademark Law Treaty, regional centralization tends to extend to the centralized grant of the industrial property rights, see notes 14-17.

[20] Whereas the Central European Free Trade Agreement (Art.25, Annex VI) obliges Members only to upgrade their protection to the level of international conventions, (34 Int'l Leg. Mat. 1, 19 (1965), the Agreement Establishing a European Economic Area (Art.65(2), Protocol 28) requires Members to adopt more or less the international as well as the Community rules, and whereas the European Union is in part passing from advanced harmonization (trademarks, copyright, hopefully designs) to unification (Community mark, probably Community patent and Community designs), the Andean States grouped under the Cartagena Agreement do have agreed on uniform intellectual property rules as regards e.g. patents, utility models, industrial designs, industrial secrets, marks and trade names (Decision 344 of Oct. 21, 1993, 34 Int'l Leg. Mat. 1635 (1995), copyright (Decision 351 of Dec. 17, 1993, GRUR Int 1996, 713) and plant varieties (Decision 345 of Oct. 21, 1993, GRUR Int 1996, 938). Uniform intellectual property rules do exist since long in the Scandinavian countries.

[21] Thus, the North American Free Trade Agreement, in addition to implementing by anticipation TRIPs-rules in some detail (e.g. as regards trademarks - Art.1708 - or trade secrets - Art.1711) introduces the protection of encrypted program-carrying signals against decoding devices (Art.1707), see LEVY & WEISER, The NAFTA: A Watershed for Protection of Intellectual Property, 27 Int'l Lawyer 671 (1993); SIMON, GATT and NAFTA Provisions on Intellectual Property, 4 Fordh. Intell. Prop. Media Ent. L. J. 267 (1993).

whether, beyond formal negotiation and agreement, the regional rules have been defined jointly or have been predetermined by one or some Members, like in the case of the European Economic Area[22], of the European Agreements associating Eastern European countries to the EEC[23] or of NAFTA[24], and, second, whether these regional rules of intellectual property protection have been adopted within the framework of a specific system of regional economic integration. It is, indeed, the nature of this economic integration which, more than anything else, will determine the meaning and the effects of these intellectual property rules.

B. Coexistence!

1. The Impact of Regionalization on Intellectual Property Protection

a) Intellectual property rights are instruments of economic competition. The value of the exclusivity they provide depends on what the market is willing to pay for the products protected, i.e. on the competitive strength of these products or processes in terms of cost efficiency, quality, marketing and servicing, etc.[25]. The competitive strength, in turn, is determined by the markets available to the owner of the intellectual property as regards territorial scope, accessibility, uniformity or diversity of legal and economic conditions, etc. Clearly regional harmonization of intellectual property rights, therefore, does not affect their operation or alter their economic effects beyond what has been said above where the

---

[22] See note 20.

[23] See Art.66 and Annex XIII Europe-Agreement between the European Communities and the Republic of Poland (OJEC 1993 L 348, 1), requiring Poland to improve its intellectual property rules so as to afford a level of protection comparable to that existing in the EC. Similar provisions are to be found in the other Europe Agreements with Bulgaria, Romania, the Czech and the Slovak Republics, Hungary, Lithuania, Estonia, and even Russia, though in some the terms are more flexible. For those countries which actually want to join the Community the approach seems understandable, and the Community has it made clear that ultimately they have to adopt identical standards of protection (EC-Commission, White Book on "Preparing the Associated States of Middle and Eastern Europe for Integration into the Internal Market of the Union", Annex p.352 et seq - KOM (95) 163 final/2). The problem is that adoption of Common Market standards of protection are asked for, but corresponding free trade rules for parallel imports refused, see SOLTYSINSKI, International Exhaustion of Intellectual Property Rights under the TRIPs, the EC Law and the Europe Agreements, GRUR Int 1996, 316, 323 et seq.

[24] See references *supra* note 21.

[25] See for the interrelationship of competition and intellectual property UNCTAD, loc. cit. et 26 et seq, 31 et seq et passim; ULLRICH, European Standards of Patentability, Weinheim 1977, 193 et seq; *id.*, loc. cit. GRUR Int 1996, 565 et seq.

markets covered remain separated and heterogeneous. Factual uniformity of the markets[26], however, and, *a fortiori*, ease of access and territorial extension by virtue of regional integration will directly affect both the legal functioning and the economic importance of harmonized or even unified exclusive intellectual property protection, and the more so the more advanced the integration becomes as a matter of law and of economic fact[27]. Whether this benefits the domestic industry of the integrating markets or foreign enterprises competing with them in these markets and/or third-country(export)markets is a question of the original distribution of competitive strengths and of the readiness and determination of the respective industry to exploit the enlarged market opportunities, but not of regional integration as such. The important point, however, is that regional economic integration increases the value and importance of intellectual property, and that it does so regardless of what the intellectual property is, simply as a matter, or as a result of, achieving the objectives of integration: larger, more or less unified markets, improved competitiveness, economic growth and stability. Integration determines the markets within which an intellectual property system has to achieve its function as an incentive system, and, just as, due to integration, the incentives increase and, therefore, the benefits accruing to the intellectual property owner, so must the intellectual property rules conform to the necessities of integration[28].

b) Regional integration rules naturally correspond to the economic, social and political needs and interests that have spurred countries to integrate. The same is true for the harmonized intellectual property rules as regards the subject-matter and the standards of protection. Although, as a matter of positive law, the TRIPs Agreement has laid to rest much of the controversy on what the standards of protection are which are appropriate for a given economy[29], there appears to remain considerable room

---

[26] Such as in the case of the Scandinavian countries following uniform intellectual property rules.

[27] Attainment of economies of scale, improved allocation of resources and enlarged home market base do result in an interdependency of upgraded protection and enhanced value of intellectual property, see recitals 2 - 4 EC-Computer Programme Protection Directive of May 14, 1991 (OJEC 1991 L 122, 42); recitals 2, 3 EC-Directive on the Protection of Data Bases of March 11, 1996 (OJEC 1996 L 77, 20); see Report: Harmonization of Industrial Property and Copyright Law in the European Community, 18 IIC 303, sub II 3 (1987).

[28] Comp. CJEC of July 14, 1981, Case 187/80, *Merck/Stephar*, Rep. 1981, 2063, sub No.11; of January 20, 1981, Cases 55/80 and 57/80, *Musik-Vertrieb membran/ GEMA*, Rep. 1980, 147 sub No.25; ULLRICH, Patentschutz im Europäischen Binnenmarkt, GRUR Int 1991, 1, 5.

[29] But at least the academic debate goes on, see the summary of the papers submitted to a TRIPs-symposium by REICHMAN, Compliance with the TRIPs-Agreements-

for implementing rules adapted to the specific needs of Members[30], at least if the "correct" implementation of the TRIPs Agreement is controlled by the TRIPs Council on the basis of a rule of law[31] rather than as a matter of a power game. So, on the one hand, the TRIPs Agreement need not really block regionally adequate implementation and application of its standards. On the other hand, to the extent that the TRIPs Agreement contains a balanced set of intellectual property rights and standards where at least the major Members can find their basic interests represented in terms of intellectual property rights covering subject-matter that is important to their national industries[32], the agreement may even serve as a minimum balance of rights that regional Members must comply with when negotiating the intellectual property terms of integration.

2. Integrating Intellectual Property into Market Integration

a) A more intricate problem, however, is presented by the intellectual property rules which are specific to regional integration as such and which, generally, are related to the principle of territoriality. Thus, regional integration may require, or at least result in, an extension of national exhaustion of intellectual property rights to the entire integrated area[33]; it may exclude territorially limited assignments or probably even territorially limited licenses[34]; it may allow prior users of inventions to

---

Introduction to a Scholarly Debate, 29 Vanderbilt J. Transnat'l L. 363 (1996); McGRATH, The Patent Provisions in TRIPs: Protecting Reasonable Remuneration for Services Rendered - or the Latest Development in Western Colonialism? Eur. Int. Prop. Rev. 1996, 398.

[30] See references *supra* note 2.

[31] In this respect, the European Court of Justice's self-restraint when asked to control politically unconvincing national intellectual property rules, though based on the distribution of powers between Member States and the Communities as regards harmonization of laws, should serve as a guidance, and the more so as an internal market requires more uniformity than a global market; see for this self-restraint e.g. CJEC of June 30, 1988, Case 35/87, *Thetford/Fiamma*, Rep. 1988, 3585; of October 5, 1988, Case 53/87, *CICRA/Renault*, Rep. 1988, 6039; of November 30, 1993, Case C-317/91, *Deutsche Renault/Audi AG*, Rep. 1993 I 6227.

[32] See on the reciprocal dealings e.g. as regards indications of origin interesting the European countries GOVAERE, Intellectual Property Rights, *supra* in this book (text sub B.1 following notes 28 et seq).

[33] As is well known, the principle of Community-wide exhaustion is accepted in the European Union, but not in its relationship with third, associated countries, see the critique by SOLTYSINSKI, loc. cit. GRUR Int 1996, 316; as regards the NAFTA, see reference *supra* note 4.

[34] For the former proposition see *supra* note 5; the admission of territorially limited licenses by Art.43 (now Art.42) Community Patent Convention has been a highly controversial issue, see Die Luxemburger Konferenz über das Gemeinschaftspatent, Bericht der Deutschen Delegation: Die sogenannten Wirtschaftsklauseln (by Krieger), GRUR Int 1976, 187, 208, 212 et seq; DEMARET, Le brevet

exploit the invention throughout the region[35], and, arguably, it may permit conflicts of trademarks by accepting the honest national user's imports into the territories of other honest concurrent users[36]. The list of the conflicts, which are all known from the EEC, may easily be extended. They may arise as an immediate result of integration or as integration develops. The problem is that a balance always has to be found between the objectives of integration and the intellectual property owner's interests, since either available protection might be curtailed or expectancies, in the scope of existing protection, frustrated. Clearly, there is no inherent logic or preestablished principle that guarantees that the conflicts will always be decided along the lines marked by the European Court of Justice with respect to the specificities of the Common Internal Market[37] or that, in this respect, customs union must be distinguished from free trade areas or regular free trade areas from those set up as associations bound to be integrated into common markets[38]. As is well-known, international exhaustion of intellectual property rights is the rule in the Common Market, but is not yet accepted in free trade areas although it is vividly supported by many authors[39].

b) The question then is whether the TRIPs Agreement provides some guidance in this area at least with respect to such regional integration efforts that are being undertaken subsequent to its Members joining the WTO, because in such cases frustration of existing protection appears to be most obvious. The obvious rule to look to in TRIPs, of course, is the

---

communautaire après Centrafarm : un instrument dépassé ou inachevé ? Rev. trim. dr. eur. 1977, 1, 46 et seq. They are now admitted as a matter of intellectual property law, but strictly limited by antitrust rules, see Commission Reg.240/96 on Technology Transfer Agreements, Art.1 (OJEC 1996 L 31, 2).

[35] The issue is not yet decided and bound to be controversial, see ULLRICH, loc. cit. in BEIER & SCHRICKER, From GATT to TRIPs, loc. cit. sub III 1 = GRUR Int 1995, 636.

[36] See to the contrary CJEC of June 22, 1976, Case 119/75, *Terrapin/Terranova*, Rep. 1976, 1039; the issue has been controversial following CJEC of July 3, 1974, Case 192/73, *Van Zuylen Frères/HAG AG*, Rep. 1974, 731, overruled by CJEC of Oct. 17, 1990, Case C-10/89, CNL-SUCAL/HAG AG, Rep. 1990 I 3711. The Community Trademark Regulation, Art.107, accepts territorial loopholes of protection in favor of well acquired prior rights of local importance.

[37] For an overview see LOEWENHEIM, Intellectual Property Before the European Court of Justice, 26 IIC 829 (1995).

[38] Comp. the critical analysis by SOLTYSINSKI, loc. cit. GRUR Int 1996, 316. The truth of the matter is that the TRIPs Agreement itself is misbegotten in that it fails to simply accept international exhaustion (with exceptions being left to Members' national legislation), see ULLRICH in BEIER & SCHRICKER, From GATT to TRIPs, loc. cit. sub II 2 d (1) = GRUR Int 1996, 634 et seq.

[39] See references notes 37, 38.

exhaustion rule of the TRIPs Agreement itself, but it only gives poor advice. Whether or not it leaves the problem of exhaustion entirely to national legislation or only excludes it from dispute settlement[40], legislative history, at best, seems to support a non liquet with respect to acceptance of exhaustion within a customs union or a free trade area[41]. But that is only half of the problem, because regional exhaustion may be worse than national exhaustion to the extent that it also results in enlarging the territories from which outside parallel importers are excluded: following the EC-example, internal liberalization will tend to go hand-in-hand with reinforced protection against third country imports. The better rule would be that regional exhaustion may be practised only at the price of generally accepting international exhaustion, but that, of course, is not what is wanted by, e.g., the Common Market.

Be this as it may, whichever way the abstention rule of Article 6 is twisted, it relates only to the issue of exhaustion, not to the many other integration-specific issues of territorial intellectual property protection, and it may not even serve as an exemplary rule. The general principle underlying the TRIPs Agreement is that of territoriality, the major vice of which is that it not only allows Members to rely on it even though parallel protection, i.e. monopoly rewards, are guaranteed with respect to the first sale in the export market, but that the whole economic operation of the TRIPs Agreement as a mechanism of international trade is based on the principle of territoriality, this serving to separate the markets which are bargained for within WTO trade negotiations[42]. Whatever the merits of TRIPs may be, as far as its reliance on the principle of territoriality is concerned, it is an exercise in market segregation, not in market integration[43]. It aims at suppressing cross-border competition, especially competition based on lower factor costs.

---

[40] See STRAUS in BEIER & SCHRICKER (eds), From GATT to TRIPs, loc. cit. sub V d = GRUR Int 1996, 193; ULLRICH in BEIER & SCHRICKER (ed.), From GATT to TRIPs, loc. cit. sub II 2 d (i) = GRUR Int 1996, 635, both, however with opposite conclusions.

[41] Apparently, EC-opposition to international exhaustion was based on the idea of some sort of customs union-privilege rather than on genuine intellectual property considerations, see GOVAERE, loc. cit., this publication, *supra* sub B.1 (text following note 20).

[42] See ULLRICH in BEIER & SCHRICKER (ed.), From GATT to TRIPs, loc. cit., sub II 2 c = GRUR Int 1996, 633 et seq.

[43] Therefore, apart from telling only half of the story (see *infra* note 44), STRAUS, repetitive explanation of the TRIPs rationale largely misses the point, see STRAUS in BEIER & SCHRICKER (eds), From GATT to TRIPs, loc. cit. sub II = GRUR Int 1996, 180 et seq.

c) But the TRIPs Agreement does not outlaw economic integration either, not expressly and not by implication. The TRIPs Agreement is exclusively concerned with establishing, as a matter of legal institution-building, a system of intellectual property rights which meets certain standards and which is based on formal territoriality. Its *modus operandi* is not in any way altered when regional territories are substituted for national territories. Of course, the economic effects will be different. But the TRIPs Agreement is not concerned with economic effects. Such effects may have motivated negotiations[44], but they are not part of the rules that resulted from these negotiations. This is so because these economic effects depend, not only on the kind and size of the markets protected by intellectual property rights, but also on the way these markets are established and regulated by Members; and, because such regulation of the economic environment within which intellectual property rights have to play their role is left to the Members' sovereign determination. Article 8 § II and Article 40 of the Agreement, which both deal with antitrust control of restrictive or abusive intellectual property practices, are clearly evidence of this abstention in that they refer, even such an intellectual-property-related matter as are the antitrust rules of licensing, to national legislation with minimal reservations only[45]. All other matters of market regulation which, more or less, directly affect the yield and even the functioning of intellectual property (e.g. price control, product safety and quality standards, subsidies etc.) are entirely left to Members or at least entirely outside the TRIPs Agreement. If at all, they are controlled by other WTO Agreements. Similarly, regional integration and the strain it puts on intellectual property protection by limiting, modifying or superseding the principle of territoriality, is a matter of establishing and regulating the markets and the competitive conditions under which intellectual property rights may be exercised. It is not for the TRIPs Agreement but for the general WTO Agreements to allow for and control regional integration as a matter of general economic organization. Therefore, in

---

[44] This motivation was complex and ambiguous embracing counterfeiting concerns as well as dissatisfaction with the WIPO-administered Paris Convention, and worries of dwindling competitiveness that were home-made rather than due to imitative competition by low labour cost-countries, see EVANS, Intellectual Property as a Trade Issue, 18 (2) World Competition 137 (1995); O'REGAN, The Protection of Intellectual Property, International Trade and the European Community: The Impact of the TRIPs Agreement of the Uruguay Round of Multilateral Trade Negotiations, Leg. Iss. Eur. Integr. 1995 (1) 1, 8 et seq; ULLRICH in BEIER & SCHRICKER (eds), loc. cit., GATT or WIPO, at 131 et seq.

[45] Comp. UNCTAD, loc. cit. at 105 et seq; FOX, Trade, Competition, and Intellectual Property-TRIPs and its Antitrust Counterparts, 29 Vanderbilt J. Transnat'l L. 481 (1996).

contrast to general intellectual property rules[46], any integration-specific rules need only be justified under the general standards of international trade liberalization, but are not affected by the TRIPs Agreement. Put differently, where regional integration is accepted as such, the consequences that this entails in the judgement of the organization as regards the territorial operation, effects and necessities of intellectual property protection[47] must be recognized as well and are outside any control based on the TRIPs Agreement. More particularly, as regards parallel imports, this distinction means that Article 6 TRIPs Agreement is not even relevant to the issue of regional intellectual property exhaustion.

Conclusion

Inge Govaere's contribution to this symposium clearly shows the mutual reinforcement of international intellectual property protection by the TRIPs Agreement on the one hand, and by regional agreements on the other hand. In fact, regional and bilateral trade agreements are used to transport the intellectual property concepts of the major trading partners into other countries. However, as the TRIPs Agreement remains, for better or for worse, either vague (Arts 6, 13, 30) or altogether silent when it comes to determining the exceptions from protection, it is only the protection, not its limitation, that is so exported.

As far as regional integration is concerned, it does, in principle, justify more far-reaching harmonization of intellectual property protection than is appropriate on a global level. This is so for two related reasons. First, intellectual property has to be adapted to the economic environment within which it is supposed to have beneficial effects. Therefore, to allow regional integration as a matter of principle also means to allow appropriate and, for that matter, improved standards of protection not

---

[46] Such as the rules stating the requirements for the acquisition of intellectual property rights, their exercise and exceptions or the loss of the right. Thus, the example given above of how reverse engineering rules are shaped in view of fostering competitiveness of domestic industry are not outside the control of TRIPs, though, for good reason, the agreement leaves room for implementation (see Art.13 as regards copyright protection; reverse engineering of trade secrets is not directly dealt with by the agreement).

[47] The distinction will not always be easy to handle. Thus, calculating patent office fees according to the territories covered by a patent granted centrally such as European patents recently has come under attack, see ARMITAGE, Updating the European Patent Convention, GRUR Int 1990, 662; HELFGOTT, Why Must Filing in Europe Be So Costly, 74 JPTOS 787 (1994), and generally European Patent Office, The Costs of Patenting in Europe, 26 IIC 650 (1995); BERNIER, Global Patent Costs Must Be Reduced, 36 IDEA-J. L. Tech. - 473 (1996).

only as regards integration (specific rules of protection — as shown above they are outside the realm of TRIPs) but also as regards the means and levels of protection in general. After all, the TRIPs Agreement also purports fostering and developing procompetitive intellectual property protection, provided that this does not result in disguised restriction of trade. Second, multilateral harmonized standards of protection on as advanced a level as that reached by the TRIPs Agreement do propose general across the board rules even where differentiation is needed. Just as bilateralism is too efficient a tool for using the economic leverage of one country, multilateral rules, in the guise of establishing a rule of law, really may have a bias in that they tend to equally apply to all situations even though, in fact in a not yet globally equal world, the situations are different. Regionalism offers a highly flexible intermediate approach.

Which ever way regional rules are defined, however, it is important to be mindful of the fact that regional integration ought to be the forerunner of more advanced trade. Therefore, it should pioneer both as regards determining improved forms of protection and the limits of protection. The EU, in particular, has become the integration model for so many other regions, that it is most regrettable that it has come to restrict extraterritorial exhaustion of intellectual property protection to its internal trade only rather than to export its concepts to other regions and to world trade in general. This is not to say, that the same rules must apply worldwide, but an exhaustion doctrine that differentiates between regional exhaustion *à la Merck/Stephar*[48] and accepts international exhaustion at least in genuine re-import cases would have been a most welcome export article.

---

[48] See references *supra* note 28.

SOCIAL DIMENSIONS OF
INTERNATIONAL TRADE LIBERALIZATION

Anne TREBILCOCK

Principal Legal Officer, Office of the Legal Adviser,
International Labour Office, Geneva

What the Conference Programme has called "Social Protection and Social Clause" is known in the International Labour Organization (ILO) as the Social Dimensions of the Liberalization of International Trade. By whatever name it is called, the topic is a vast and controversial one. Before delving into it, however, I will first say a few words about the unique features of the ILO, because they have an influence on the debate.

The ILO was established by the Treaty of Versailles in 1919 to promote peace and social justice, and it became a specialized agency of the United Nations after the Second World War. Its unique feature is that representatives of workers and employers, as well as governments take part on an equal-footing in the decision-making bodies of the Organization. Tripartite delegations from the 174 Member States meet in Geneva each June at the annual International Labour Conference, where international labour conventions and recommendations are adopted. International labour conventions adopted in this way are treaties open to ratification by the ILO's Member States.

The focus of this book is on regional trade agreements and multilateral rules. The ILO itself offers a set of fundamental multilateral rules and a universal framework for monitoring their implementation. The ILO is the only universal intergovernmental organization that is directly involved in setting and monitoring international standards specifically concerning labour and related social rights. It has an extensive machinery for examining reports on the implementation of international labour standards and for entertaining complaints against governments that allege noncompliance with international standards. These can be lodged by organizations representing workers or employers, or by other member governments that have also ratified the convention in question. There are also special procedures for protecting the right of freedom of association; these apply to all ILO Members States by virtue of their acceptance of the ILO Constitution. I want not go into the detail of all the various procedures, but it is important to know that they have all been well-entrenched in the ILO for many years, they are actively used and there have been calls to strengthen how they operate. They exist to encourage respect for labour rights, and where that fails, what has been termed "the mobilization of shame" can be resorted to, in order to incite reform. It is important to recall that the ILO cannot impose any type of trade or economic sanctions.

With a topic as vast as this one, all I can hope to do is outline the ILO's perspective on the social dimensions of international trade liberalization. But first I will give you a bit of history leading up to the development of this perspective as it now stands. It is a dynamic topic, with the important defining actors being not only international organizations, regional arrangements, governments, but also trade unions, employers' organizations, business groups, consumer associations and other Non-Governmental Organizations (NGOs) as well. The initiative of FIFA to develop a voluntary code for manufacturing footballs without exploitation of child labour provides a recent example.

In a sense, the issue of a relationship between labour standards and trade has been an ILO concern since its founding. The Preamble to the 1919 Constitution of the ILO proclaims: "the failure of any nation to adopt humane conditions of labour is an obstacle in the way of other nations which desire to improve the conditions in their own countries." And it is one of the rationales for the adoption of international labour standards. The Havana Charter, as proposed after World War II, would have built upon this by stating that unfair labour conditions in export production create difficulties in international trade, although it was never adopted. Much more recently, the Director-General Hansenne of the ILO sparked debate on the question of a relationship between free trade and labour standards in his 1994 report to the International Labour Conference. In this report — which was finalized well before the sudden emergence of the social-clause issue in the final stages of the Uruguay Round — he brought to light the challenge that ILO normative action faced as a consequence of the fiercer competition resulting from the globalization of the economy and the liberalization of trade. He then asked for the views of ILO constituents on the role that the organization should play in the issue. Fears were expressed by some that the pressure of competition might turn the "virtuous circle" of social progress into a race to the bottom; others suspected that protectionism would keep them out of protected markets. Proponents and opponents of having a so-called "social clause" or a mandatory link between trade and labour standards were equally vehement about their positions — without, however, always defining very precisely just what they had in mind.

These considerations led the Governing Body of the ILO in June 1994 to set up its Working Party on the Social Dimensions of the Liberalization of International Trade. All members of the ILO Governing Body (representatives of governments, employers and workers) can participate in the Working Party. It has seen their active involvement at every full ILO Governing Body session held since that time. In the first document prepared for the Working Party[1], the ILO Secretariat attempted to focus the debate by outlining the legal parameters that exist not just within the ILO but in the GATT/WTO system as well. It explores the complexities of finding an intersection of international trade law and international labour law.

Some members of the Working Party initially pushed the idea of giving a mandatory dimension to the protection of internationally recognized workers' rights. The idea was that all countries engaged in international trade should have a legal obligation, not based on the voluntary ratification of particular conventions, to observe certain workers' rights, and that this obligation should be enforceable through trade sanctions. Not surprisingly, this proposal quickly sparked sharp polarization between its advocates — trade unions and some governments, mainly, though not exclusively, of industrialized countries — and its opponents — employers and the majority of governments, particularly those of developing countries.

The debate between the two sides became reduced to allegations of unfair competition or "social dumping" on the one hand and disguised protectionism on the other. When the idea of a so-called social clause did not get very far at the Ministerial Meeting in Marrakesh, discussion reverted to the ILO. With the upcoming Singapore Ministerial Meeting of the World Trade Organization, calls to discuss a possible linkage are in the press once again. In the meantime, discussion continues within

---

[1] See the ILO Governing Body documents relating to the Working Party on the Social Dimensions of the Liberalization of International Trade, November 1994.

the ILO and in other fora, such as the Organization for Economic and Cooperation Development (OECD) to engage in a policy dialogue with dynamic nonmember economies.

As the Director-General of the WTO, Mr. Ruggiero, remarked when he addressed European Trade Ministers in Dublin, this is a thorny subject. He added, however, that there has been real progress toward understanding in the area of labour standards and trade compared with where we were a few months ago. The terms of the debate have been clarified considerably. Promoters of a linkage of some sort between trade and worker rights have explained that they are **not** calling for global minimum wages, uniform working conditions worldwide or anything of the sort. The focus is now on how best to promote the very basic workers' rights that are prescribed in the ILO Constitution and fundamental ILO conventions: those on freedom of association, collective bargaining, nondiscrimination (including equal remuneration for men and women for work of equal value) and the abolition of forced labour and child labour. They have seen that developing countries are entitled to pursue their economic growth by making full use of their legitimate comparative advantages. At the same time, countries rejecting any type of link have also reaffirmed their recognition of the validity of these basic workers' rights and their own commitment to improving social conditions as economic development proceeds. And there is growing acknowledgement that the unilateral application of trade sanctions is probably not the best way to achieve social goals in most cases.

The ILO's role in this debate is not to put right distortions in international competition that may arise from the different levels of social protection that countries offer their workers. In any event, the political and technical difficulties of integrating such principles into the international trading system should not be underestimated. The liberalization of trade is the ILO's concern only in so far as it may affect both the ability and the will of states to pursue the social objectives embodied in the ILO Constitution. For the ILO, then, the issue is how to find an effective means of ensuring that social progress goes hand-in-hand with the liberalization of trade and the globalization of the economy. In other words, the challenge is how to ensure that all those members of the WTO which are also members of the ILO "play the game" of social progress fairly, despite the constraints and the temptations of fierce competition in a more rugged economic environment.

When I say that they must play the game fairly, I mean two things. In the first place, they must abide by certain **fundamental rules** which

514

apply to all countries in all regions irrespective of their level of development or societal priorities — and which in fact are a precondition for social development. But that is not all. Given the new opportunities afforded by the economic development that liberalization generates, they must also endeavour to improve in good faith the lot of workers within their countries by making sure that the economic progress that liberalized trade produces will go hand-in-hand with social progress.

What are these fundamental rules to be universally applied? In the first place, freedom of association, protection against discrimination and the ban on forced labour as a form of slavery appear in the Universal Declaration of Human Rights. The Social Summit held in Copenhagen in 1995 listed the following as basic workers' rights: the prohibition of forced labour and child labour, freedom of association and the right to organize and bargain collectively, equal remuneration for men and women for work of equal value, and nondiscrimination in employment. It invited all governments to protect and promote respect for these rights. This endorsement by the heads of state and government of virtually all countries around the globe both endorsed the notion of fundamental workers' rights and affirmed their universal validity.

These fundamental rights of workers can also be looked upon as a precondition for the exercise of all their other rights. They can be seen as the logical extension to the labour market of the principles that are inherent in the liberalization of the market in products and services — sort of basic "labour market access" rules. Indeed, the ban on forced labour, the recognition of freedom of association, the right to engage in collective bargaining, protection against discrimination, keeping children out of the labour market until they have had a chance to be educated, are merely the conditions that must be fulfilled for the labour market to function optimally. Unlike wage differentials, it would not be acceptable for a violation of such rights to give rise to a legitimate comparative advantage. The OECD recently took a look at core labour standards and trade; the "strongest finding [of its study was] that there is positive association over time between successfully sustained trade reforms and improvements in core standards."[2]

Taking a closer look at debate on this issue within the ILO, it is possible to identify — tentatively at least — several, largely interconnected developments.

---

[2] *"Core Workers' Rights and International Trade"*, OECD, Paris, 1996, p.13.

1) The first is a clear lack of consensus on a "punitive" linkage between international labour standards and liberalization of trade in the form of trade sanctions. Parallel to this, however, another consensus has emerged on the need for a positive linkage, or more accurately a process of positive interaction, between the economic progress resulting from trade liberalization and social progress. This is reflected in many ways, including increased ratification of fundamental ILO Conventions and their implementation, support for the ILO Programme for the Elimination of Child Labour, voluntary codes and inspection mechanisms developed by producers of goods for export, just to name a few examples.

2) Secondly, there has been recognition of the special significance of fundamental workers' rights, as defined in the ILO, for the purpose of trade. I have already mentioned the important conclusions of the Social Summit of Copenhagen, promoting voluntary adherence to the provisions of the relevant ILO Conventions, namely those on the prohibition of forced labour and child labour, freedom of association, the right to organize and bargain collectively and the principle of nondiscrimination. The recently published study of the OECD, *"Core Workers' Rights and International Trade"*, uses the same list. Quite recently, the Director-General of the WTO recalled that respect for core labour standards has been agreed by all its members in the Universal Declaration of Human Rights, and that all WTO delegations have recognized the primary role of the ILO in international labour issues. An element of concern for workers' rights can be seen in the regional arrangements of the European Union, NAFTA (with the Labor Cooperation Commission) and to some extent Mercosur (with its Economic and Social Council and Working Group on labour, employment and social security) as well. The ways in which this plays out reflects differences in their institutional structures as well as other factors. The ILO is of course watching all of these developments with considerable interest.

3) Thirdly, there has also been progressive recognition that, in their capacity as ILO members which have accepted the ILO Constitution, all those states which also participate in the international trade system already have a duty to ensure that the benefits expected from trade liberalization in terms of economic growth should somehow also be reflected in the field of social welfare. Defining the exact manner in which states would be expected to discharge this obligation remains to be explored. Certainly, there

516

has been a call for cooperation and coordination among various organizations concerned with the question. The ILO maintains both formal and informal contacts with the range of other international and intergovernmental organizations that are addressing various aspects of the issue. There has also been a call to strengthen the ILO's work on basic worker rights and to provide more assistance to countries for the purpose of achieving respect for these rights.

When the Director-General made the ILO's contribution to the G7 Employment Conference held in Lille on April 1-2, 1996, he set out three propositions: (1) it is for each country to determine the level and content of social protection according to its economic possibilities and its preferences; (2) there are some basic workers' rights that should be unconditionally recognized, irrespective of a country's level of development or its values and preferences; and, (3) the interdependence arising out of the globalization of the economy places the states concerned, as members of the ILO, under the obligation of promoting social progress parallel to the economic progress resulting from trade liberalization. He concluded by saying: "The Member States of the WTO are members of the ILO and cannot act in one organization inconsistently with obligations they have voluntarily assumed in the other. [...] The ILO, which throughout its history has displayed institutional inventiveness, affords effective means of action within its constitutional framework, provided there is the will to act."

To conclude, this is an issue that is not going away. The challenge ahead is to find a response that is acceptable to both developed and developing countries, both of which have workers' and employers' interests to take into account, and makes the best, most appropriate use of the distinct features of the various institutional structures as they continue to evolve.

List of Selected References

"Trade and Labour Standards: Can Common Rules Be Agreed?", Address by Michel HANSENNE, Director-General, ILO, Wilton Park Conference, Steyning, United Kingdom, March 6, 1996.

"The Social Dimension of the Liberalization of International Trade", Paper presented by Michel HANSENNE, Director-General, ILO, G7 Employment Conference, Lille, France, April 1-2, 1996.

Report of the Director-General (Part I), International Labour Conference, 81st Session, 1994, pp.56-63.

BEQUELE A., *"Child Labour and Minimum Social Standards: The Challenge for Asia"*, **Asia Papers** No.1, ILO, IPEC, Dec.1995.

MAUPAIN F., *"La protection internationale des travailleurs et la libéralisation du commerce mondial : Un lien ou un frein ?"*, in : **Revue Générale de Droit International Public**, Vol.1, janvier/février 1996, pp.45-100 (summary in English available).

ILO Governing Body (GB) documents relating to the Working Party on the Social Dimensions of the Liberalization of International Trade, November 1994.

"THE SOCIAL DIMENSIONS OF THE LIBERALIZATION OF WORLD TRADE" AND "TRADE AND LABOUR STANDARDS: CAN COMMON RULES BE AGREED?" THE VIEW FROM THE ILO — A COMMENTARY AND A REJOINDER

José A. CANELA-CACHO

Graduate School of Public Policy,
University of California Berkeley

A. A New Era of Expanded International Trade

World Trade: the First Two Years under the WTO

As the Twentieth Century comes to a close, the integration of world markets has reached levels hard to imagine as recent as ten years ago. The World Trade Organization (WTO), successor to the GATT by virtue of the Marrakech Agreement of April 15, 1994, will become a universal organization of 154 Member States once accession agreements with 31 applicant countries, among them the People's Republic of China and the Russian Federation, are fully negotiated. Surely, not even the most optimistic among the original 22 founding members of GATT in 1948 — for the most part the advanced market economies of the period — anticipated this extraordinary expansion in the membership of the organization fewer that fifty years later.

More revealing than the expansion in WTO membership is the evolution of world trade in recent years. Data from 1994 and 1995 suggest that we are in the beginning of a period of substantial expansion in world trade, comparable in volume to that ushered in by GATT around the time of the Kennedy Round of tariff elimination. From 1963 to 1973 the volume of world trade increased at an average annual rate of 8.9%, almost twice the annual growth rate of world output (5.1%) (Bhagwati, 1989:5). This was, until 1994, the best period ever in the history of GATT, but over the next decade that record may very well be surpassed. In the last two years world trade, measured in volume, grew at an annual rate of 8.2% even though world output increased by a mere 3% per year. The full significance of this data is revealed as one considers that from 1973 to 1983 world trade and world output experienced roughly the same sluggish annual growth rate (2.6%), whereas the rebound in world trade in the decade 1983-93 reached a yearly growth rate of slightly under 5% (WTO, 1996).

The remarkable expansion of world trade in the last two years and the high expectations for the remainder of the century correspond to various factors. First, with the creation of the WTO a new set of trade liberalizing measures will become fully effective over the next few years, notably in areas other than trade in goods; the Agreements on Trade in Services, Trade-Related Investment Measures, and Trade-Related Aspects of Intellectual Property Rights, embodied by the WTO Agreement, will bring down trade restrictions and eliminate other domestic regulatory disincentives to open trade. An early indicator of the enhancing effect of this new regime can be found in the area of commercial services; the **value** of commercial services traded in 1995 was 14% larger than in 1994, a rate of increase almost twice as large as that for merchandise trade (WTO, 1996).

A second important factor is the reinvigoration of the process of regional integration through agreements that include liberalization commitments well beyond those in the WTO regime. The leading instance is, of course, the European Union (EU) well on its way to achieving overall economic integration of 15 nation-states into a single market. While not in the same league, the Southern Common Market (Mercosur), in the making since at least 1985, was launched by Argentina, Brazil, Paraguay and Uruguay in 1991 under the Treaty of Asunción. This treaty provided for the implementation of a common market area among these four countries under ambitious deadlines. The first phase-in period was successfully completed by the end of 1994 and the Parties appear determined to fulfill implementation of the common market area according to schedule. Further, other Latin American countries, most notably Chile and Mexico, are seriously exploring trade liberalization agreements with Mercosur.

More recently, in 1994, Mexico, Canada and the United States inaugurated the North American Free Trade Agreement (NAFTA), perhaps the most ambitious free trade agreement ever, considering the Parties involved and their prior level of integration, particularly between Mexico and its two Northern neighbors. Over the next ten years NAFTA will eliminate most barriers to trade and investment flows among the three countries, including **all** goods and services; it will gradually open government procurement at the federal level to the competitive bidding of all providers in North America; it introduces minimum standards of protection for intellectual property rights and for the rights of foreign investors and investments; it mandates procedural transparency and the observance of due process in all aspects of domestic regulatory processes that have a bearing on trade and investment; and, it institutes binding dispute settlement mechanisms through which a Party can challenge another Party's actions — in procedure or in substance — as incompatible with the terms of the agreement. This is a long list of features, to which one must add two unprecedented side agreements that attempt to deal with labor and environmental concerns raised by regional integration (see Section C). Again, NAFTA contains an accession clause and other countries in the Americas are ready, eager in the case of Chile, to join the club.

A New Role for Developing Economies

It must be recognized that the dynamism of world economic integration today is, in no small measure, the result of a change of heart in the economic policy of a good number of countries in the developing world. In Latin America, in Central and Eastern Europe — including countries once part of the Soviet Union — and in Asia, one country after another has adopted over the past decade export-oriented growth and foreign-investment absorption strategies as the means for achieving high and sustainable overall rates of economic growth. International trade and investment agreements have become the tool of choice to gain international market access and to attract foreign investment, and thus the eagerness of so many developing countries to join preferential arrangements of the type previously mentioned. While this new economic policy may or may not ultimately succeed, recent data suggest that the strategy is yielding results insofar as involvement in world trade. The regions of the world with the largest increase in total dollar-value of exports are: first, Eastern and Central Europe (including the former Soviet Union), up 26% in 1995 from 1994 values, followed by China and the so-called six East Asian trader countries — Korea, Malaysia, Singapore, Taiwan, and Thailand — with a 23% increase, and third, Latin America with a 22% rise, most of it on account of Mexico's whopping 31% increase in exports in 1995 — the second largest increase among all countries (WTO, 1996).

It is in this context of developing countries emerging as powerful export regions that the debate about free trade becomes increasingly one about "fair trade". This is a term of art with various connotations, one of which is the idea that trade among unequal partners — in terms of their economic development, their safety social networks, and their levels of protection for the environment, workers, and consumers — may actually be detrimental for the more advanced country, unless lesser developed countries agree to "upward harmonization" provisions as a condition for joining a preferential trading arrangement. Politicians, advocates, and academics who define themselves as "fair traders", frequently point out that labor costs, including wages and benefits, can easily differ by a factor of eight to ten between developed and developing countries, and then ask: Can the developed countries afford to compete with the developing world? Are the developing countries deliberately exacerbating labor cost differentials so as to increase their market share and to what consequences? And if so, what can be done and who should be doing it?

These are the fundamental questions captured by the concept of "social dumping" which the two ILO documents motivating this commentary have set out to address. This rejoinder includes two parts. The first set of comments is contained in Section B and concentrates on the assessment by the ILO of the social dumping problem and the legal remedies that may be available to counteract it under existing international trade law. In Section C I briefly review the "social dumping" debate that surrounded the negotiation and passage of the NAFTA and highlight the major elements of the Labor Agreement through which the issue was addressed. This is an important precedent because it represents, to my knowledge, the first attempt to define a social dumping situation in the context of a free trade agreement that could lead to the imposition of trade sanctions. I also advance in that same section some arguments to the effect that some of the more serious labor issues faced by a number of countries are the result of domestic conditions peculiar to each individual country, for the most part unrelated to international trade. Nonetheless, in my final thoughts I invite the reader to consider whether international trade agreements, and more specifically trade sanctions, can be used to effect positive changes in countries with troublesome domestic labor situations.

B. The ILO View on "Social Dumping": When does it Exist? How can it be Remedied?

The bottom line of the legal, policy, and political analyses of the ILO on the question of social dumping seem to me right on target. On the political front, there is candid recognition that the social dumping debate will be increasingly framed as a North-South contentious issue, one that will neither be resolved shortly nor dismissed for good. We are in for a long process that will see slow and gradual accommodations, alternating perhaps with few and far between major shifts prompted by specific political situations. I argue later that the NAFTA process was one of those situations, although is not yet clear with what lasting effects, if any.

The Heterogeneity of Labor Conditions Worldwide: Wages and Benefits

On the policy analysis side, the ILO openly recognizes that labor standards and labor rights and benefits vary substantially among trading partners, and that those differences are often determinative of trade patterns. Justifiably, the ILO considers it infeasible, at this point, to define a core of labor rights that countries would be willing to adhere to as a precondition for joining a preferential trade agreement. (ILO, 1994:2). Bluntly put, to insist otherwise might well prevent countries from entering into beneficial trade arrangements, thus forgoing the economic growth thereby generated which, in turn, **could** improve the well being of workers.

To emphasize the degree of difficulty of a labor harmonization exercise, the ILO could have reminded us of the substantial wage differentials prevailing among entrenched trading partners. The wage differential between Mexican and US manufacturing workers has become a favorite example of the huge discrepancy in earnings that may result in unfair trading. Of course, that differential is anything but trivial. While comparisons of this type are inherently problematic and therefore should be taken with caution, the US Department of Labor estimated that in 1989 the average hourly compensation costs for manufacturing workers in the US was about 6.2 times the cost for their Mexican counterparts (US Department of Labor, 1990). Following the Mexican financial crisis of 1995 (see below), that relationship is probably in the order of 8 to 10 times. Not as commonly mentioned, however, is the fact that the same study found large wage differentials between US workers and their counterparts in Hong Kong (5.1 to 1), and in Singapore (4.6 to 1), even though these two Asian countries have per capita incomes four to five times that of Mexico and about two thirds the per capita income of the US. Moreover, the US Department of Labor study also showed that comparably large wage differences exist between some members of the European Union: German manufacturing workers were paid 6.3 times the wages of their Portuguese counterparts, about 12 times as much if one adjusts for purchasing power parity according to estimates provided by Flanagan (1993:183).

This data clearly illustrates that pronounced discrepancies in wages among trading partners are not rare. Such large wage differentials usually involve countries in different stages of economic development. Yet, large differences in work benefits also exist among countries with roughly equal per capita income, differences that have a significant impact in the total cost of labor. For example, union contracts for industrial workers in Germany provide for 40 days of paid vacation per year, whereas comparable contracts for US workers provide for only 23 days (US Bureau of Labor Statistics, cited in *New York Times*, 1994). Ehrenberg (1994:19) has compared many other work benefits among a large set of developed economies and, again, he finds that substantial dispersion is the rule rather than the exception. To cite another example, maternity leave is a maximum of 13 weeks in the US, 26 weeks in Norway, and 52 weeks in Australia.

I am not aware of any practicable plan to harmonize in the foreseeable future, the highly heterogeneous labor conditions prevailing worldwide, and the ILO is certainly not recommending a harmonization plan be developed and implemented. The experience of the European Community shows that convergence of wage levels, let alone other work benefits, cannot be taken for granted even two decades after the full removal of any formal barriers to labor mobility among member countries. As shown by Flanagan (1993), by the late 1980s the dispersion of hourly labor costs among the original six members of the European Community was very similar to that existing in 1960.

One then must ask: if substantial differences in labor costs are here to stay, under what conditions do those differences become an unfair advantage, a social dumping practice deserving the imposition of a compensatory duty or the application of some other form of trade sanction? Here I want to turn to the legal analysis that the ILO undertakes in the *"Social Dimensions"* document to answer that question in light of present WTO law and its interpretation as practised under GATT, where still applicable.

Possible Remedies against "Social Dumping" under Current WTO Regime

The ILO first considers the possibility that a social dumping case could be addressed under Article VI of the GATT. This article entitles countries to impose anti-dumping duties on imported goods when they are introduced into their markets at less than their "normal value... [and where such practice] causes or threatens injury to an established industry [in the importing country] or materially retards the establishment of a domestic industry." As an alternative compensatory duty, Article VI provides for the imposition of countervailing duties on an imported good that has benefited from a production or an export subsidy in its country of origin.

It is rather doubtful that Article VI could be successfully invoked to levy anti-dumping duties on goods exported by countries with low wage levels. If the price of a product accurately reflects the actual cost of labor involved in its production, it is difficult to imagine a persuasive legal argument showing that the good is being sold below "its normal price", a defining element of a dumping action.

Perhaps slightly more likely to succeed is the argument that a country's low wages constitute a form of subsidy under the purview of Article VI. As discussed in Section C, the claim has been made that some countries, deliberately and systematically, adopt wage containment policies — even wage suppression policies — to make their products more competitive internationally and to attract foreign investment. One could argue that reduced wages — relative to what they would be under free labor-markets — constitute a production subsidy, in part or in whole passed on to the consumer of the importing country and paid for by the workers of the exporting country. To my knowledge, no country has incorporated into its domestic unfair trade statutes a provision along these lines, a possibility one cannot rule out. "Aggressive unilateralism", as the ILO reminds us, is a serious risk that the world trading community continues to face. If such a statute were enacted it would most certainly be challenged before the WTO in what would become, arguably, one of the defining cases of the international trading system in the early twenty-first century. While the ILO text does not discuss the legal subtleties involved in the interpretation of Article VI, it seems to conclude that Article VI would have to be amended before a country could use it to level the "labor playing field" *vis-à-vis* its trading nations. Reaching a consensus on such an amendment is at present most unlikely.

The ILO points to another, much more intriguing, legal basis that a WTO Member could invoke to respond to alleged social dumping practices by another member, and that is the "non-breach" nullification and impairment mechanism pursuant to Article XXIII(b) of GATT. The argument is that social dumping by one country, while perhaps not a violation of any current WTO provision, may nonetheless frustrate the commercial benefits that another country could have reasonably expected as a result of joining the agreement. For example, a country's successful implementation of a policy that cut wages by 50% would most likely be followed by a reduction in that country's imports and an expansion of its exports. The trading partners of that country would experience the opposite effect, losing some opportunities to export which they were counting on at the time they became Parties to the agreement. Arguably, under Article XXIII(b) this situation would qualify as nullification or impairment of trade benefits and the affected countries would be entitled to withdrawing commercial benefits from the nullifying country, in an amount commensurate to their loss.

Of course, countries do not decree wage cuts, but sometimes they are forced to devalue their currencies to such an extent and with such consequences that the result is precisely a reduction in wages and an increase in the domestic price of imports relative to exports. In sum, a scenario in the end not much different from the hypothetical example and, unfortunately, one for which there is a recent historical precedent: Mexico's financial crisis of 1995.

Applying "Non-Breach" Nullification and Impairment in the Labor Context: A Bad Policy Idea

The following basic figures offer a partial basis to gauge the consequences of the Mexican financial crisis of 1995 that was set in motion by the devaluation of the peso on December 22, 1994. No implication of cause and effect should be attached to the order in which these figures are presented or discussed.

By the end of 1995, the peso to dollar exchange rate had more than doubled, from 3.5 pesos per dollar in December of 1994 to 7.7 a year later; the inflation rate, as measured by the national consumer price index, reached 53% compared to 7% in 1994; and, the average annual increase in nominal wages was under 20%. These figures combined suggest a major upward shift in Mexico's competitive position in the international market and, in effect, data on Mexico's external accounts conclusively reflect that. In value terms, merchandise exports in 1995 grew by 31% while the value of imports decreased by 9%, so that a deficit in the trade account of 18.5 billion dollars in 1994, turned into a surplus of 7.1 billion dollars in 1995. The adjustment in the current account was even more striking: a deficit of nearly 29 billion dollars in 1994, equivalent to 8% of the country's GDP, was reduced to 0.7 billion in 1995 (Banco de Mexico, 1996; BDINEGI, 1996; WTO, 1996).

In light of these figures, one can reasonably conclude that, at least in 1995, the expectations of Mexico's trading partners were not fully realized. A quick back-of-the-envelope calculation, based on the relationship between the inflation rate and the devaluation rate, suggests a reduction of about 27% in the dollar price of Mexican products; similarly, a calculation based on the percent increase in wages and the devaluation rate, points to a reduction of 40 to 50% in the dollar purchasing power of Mexican wage earners, while their peso purchasing power decreased in the range of 20% to 25%; certainly Mexico's trading partners had expected, as recently as early 1994, macroeconomic conditions in the Mexican economy conducive to higher demand for imports.

Yet, to suggest that Mexico's trading partners should be able to reinstate some custom duties, or other non-tariff restrictions, on Mexican products and services so as to cover their losses and to re-level the "playing field", would be just about one of the worst policy prescriptions one could provide. Withdrawing trade benefits here — which after all is the preferred form of trade sanctions — would plunge the Mexican economy into a deeper and longer recession, leading to a subsequent reduction in Mexican imports. Continued access to foreign markets is arguably the *sine qua non* condition to bring Mexico back to sustained growth and to restore benefits nullified or impaired to Mexico's trading partners. Preliminary data for 1996 compellingly make this point. By year's end GDP growth was in the order of 4% while merchandise imports experienced an increase of 23%. Remarkably, imports in 1996 were also 3% higher, in real terms, than imports during 1994 (BDINEGI, 1997).

There is no question that Mexico's crisis in 1995 improved the competitiveness of the country in international markets and that, as a result, Mexico is better off in regard to its external accounts while its trading partners perhaps are not. Yet, applying customs duties, or any other restrictions, on Mexican goods as compensatory measures would ultimately benefit no one. If moral hazard is a concern, and somehow that serves as the basis for recommending compensatory actions in cases like this, it need not be. While Mexico's external standing has improved markedly, Mexicans overall are much worse off; just consider that GDP per capita in 1995 decreased by about 8%. It is difficult to imagine that Mexico, or for that matter any other country, would devalue its currency by over 100% and lower its labor costs by a third, as strategies to expand its share of the world market. On the contrary, for various political and policy reasons, countries often resist to the eleventh hour a devaluation of their currency, even when the adjustment of the exchange rate is painfully clear and the costs of delaying it are huge.

The decision by the Worker's Group of the Governing Body of the ILO to stop pressing, at least for the time being, for mandatory trade sanctions linked to deterioration of labor conditions is a positive development. As Director-General Hansenne has reminded us, improving the well-being of workers is not possible in the absence of economic growth. The ILO has then adopted the sensible position that it should support policies that foster economic growth — and trade liberalization is one such policy — while also advancing policies that will give workers a fair share of the proceeds of that growth. The problem with mandatory trade sanctions in connection with shifts in labor conditions is that the instances in which those shifts are particularly pronounced, as in the Mexican case just described, applying trade sanctions would run counter to those fundamental objectives.

The question however remains, whether there are circumstances where mandatory trade sanctions linked to violations of labor rights would be an appropriate and fruitful policy response. I briefly review one agreement that seems to provide an affirmative answer to this question. I am referring to the North American Agreement on Labor Cooperation (NAALC)[1], subscribed to by Canada and Mexico as a complementary agreement to the NAFTA.

C. The North American Agreement on Labor Cooperation (NAALC)

The Fearsome Labor Effects of Trade Agreements

Much of the opposition to the NAFTA in the US stemmed from concerns that the agreement would mean lower wages for American workers and a permanent loss of a significant number of American jobs. Because of the six to one ratio between US and Mexican manufacturing wages, it was argued that many companies would relocate to Mexico,

---

[1] North American Agreement on Labor Cooperation, Sept. 14, 1993. US-Can.-Mex., 32 **I.L.M.** 1499.

where they could produce at much lower costs while still maintaining access to the US market for their products. Presidential candidate Ross Perot, to this day one of the most ardent opponents of the NAFTA, in 1992 coined the phrase "the giant sucking sound" to evoke the irresistible pull of "Mexican cheap" labor on American manufacturing firms leading to their relocation *en masse* to Mexico once NAFTA was passed.

The connection of NAFTA with lower wages can be attributed to the so-called "lowest common denominator" effect associated with trade agreements. The argument is that firms operating in the country with the lowest standards in the region — be it in labor conditions, environmental protection, consumer protection, and so on — would have a cost advantage that the firms in the other countries would have to meet lest they be driven out of business. For example, firms in the US would demand from workers, and obtain, reductions in wages on the basis that otherwise they could not compete with Mexican firms; legislatures and regulators in the US — at the federal and state levels — would eventually lower standards after being persuaded by management representatives that existing standards are pricing them out of the market because their Mexican competitors, facing lower standards or none at all, can offer a cheaper product. The result: a rush to the bottom, a "downward harmonization" of wages and standards, that cannot be avoided unless binding "upward harmonization" provisions are included in the agreement and the Parties ultimately comply or are forced to comply with them.

A number of studies were completed to assess the likely effects of NAFTA on trade, investment, and employment in the three participating countries[2]. Overwhelmingly, those studies projected a minuscule effect of NAFTA on US employment levels, positive or negative. For example, a study commissioned by the US Department of Labor (1990b:IX-A-1) estimated that by the year 2000 the US would add 65,000 jobs as a result of trade liberalization with Mexico, equivalent to about half of one percent of the US labor force. Some sectors of the American economy were expected to lose jobs (apparel and construction craftsmen) but it was estimated that the majority of the sectors would be unaffected or would experience minor gains. Up or down, the change in base employment levels as a result of NAFTA was estimated at under 0.6% for all occupations (US Department of Labor, 1990b:IX-A-2:A-13). Estimates of that order of magnitude seemed sensible because of the relative size of the two economies — about 21 to 1 in 1993 (World Bank, 1995) — and

---

[2] A compilation of some of this studies can be found in US International Trade Commission, 1992.

because of the already generally low barriers in the US to trade with and investment in Mexico.

Politically, however, the fear of substantial adverse labor effects dominated the debate. Fair trade became a buzz phrase among the Democratic leadership in the US House of Representatives; as a condition for approving NAFTA, they demanded a labor side-agreement, "with real teeth" a code term for trade sanctions, to ensure against downward harmonization and "social dumping" practices by Mexico[3].

Characterization of Mexican Labor Policy

One of the main concerns voiced in the debate was that the Government of Mexico, in violation of Mexico's own labor law, prevented unions from advancing the interests of workers, for example by co-opting the leadership of unions or by simply repressing the activities of independent unions. Shaiken (1993) argued that it was a myth that manufacturing wages in Mexico were low because of low labor productivity. He offered data from automobile engine plants in the US and Mexico showing that productivity of Mexican workers had been on the rise for ten years, reaching virtual parity with productivity levels of American workers by the early 1990s. For the entire Mexican manufacturing sector Shaiken cited estimates of a 30% increase in productivity between 1990 and 1992, and a 25% reduction in real wages over the same period. He surmised that "if real compensation had tracked productivity through 1990 [...] compensation would have been almost 80 percent higher" (Shaiken, 1993:13). He attributed the "decoupling" of wages and productivity largely to government policies restrictive of labor rights formally granted under Mexican law but unenforceable as a matter of reality. Therefore, by deliberately depressing wages the Government of Mexico was creating for itself an unfair comparative advantage. American workers could not compete under those circumstances: they would lose their jobs or they would have to accept wage cuts, perhaps substantial ones.

There is voluminous literature on the subject of Mexican labor relations in the twentieth century, in particular the alliance, Collier (1991) has called it a "contradictory alliance", that the government and unions

---

[3] A similar debate unfolded about "environmental dumping" and generally about concerns that free trade would seriously damage the environment, particularly in the border area. In the end, a North American Agreement on Environmental Cooperation was also signed by the three countries, with comparable structure to the NAALC. See MACGRAW, 1995.

worked out around the time of the Administration of President Lázaro Cárdenas (1934-40) which would become a cornerstone of Mexico's impressive economic growth and industrialization, especially after 1952 and through 1972. The historical record of that alliance is mixed and controversial, with substantial variation in rhetorical tone and actual labor policy (see Collier,1991). Sure enough, government control over union activities has been a recurrent theme, perhaps a defining element, in the study of Mexican labor relations. But the alliance has also meant stability and growth, increases in wages during some periods, and the implementation of many pro-labor policies, at least in the books, such as workers' entitlement to a share of the firms' profits. To describe the government-labor relationship exclusively as one of control and wage containment by the government to the detriment of labor would be inaccurate.

Shaiken, however, is right about the downward trend of wages, in particular minimum wage, after 1981. As Figure 1 shows, the minimum wage has been decreasing without interruption over the last fifteen years, its level sinking by mid-1996 to one-third the minimum wage level in 1980. By comparison, the median manufacturing wage has fared better, but there too the trend is hardly encouraging. The financial crisis of 1981, precipitated in part by the collapse of the oil markets, sent wages in a downward spiral, losing by 1988 30% of their 1980 value. That trend was reversed around 1989, with wages growing steadily for the next four years to the point that by 1994 they were less than 10% below their 1980 value. Unfortunately, as a result of the 1995 crisis, wages by the end of that year were thrown back to their 1983 level, a loss of about 20%, whereas by mid-1996 wage levels are estimated to be below their 1986 level, the lowest since 1980. Figure 1 also reveals a substantial rise in productivity since 1988, with a slight recovery of GDP per capita in the period 1988-1994, followed in 1995 by a sharp drop to 10% below the 1980 per capita GDP.

There is no question that the cyclical financial crises of the Mexican economy since 1976 (the first devaluation of the peso after a 22-year period of stability) have exacted a huge toll on wages, particularly in the mid-1980s, where wages were going down at a much faster rate than the reduction in GDP per capita. Here, it would appear that, the brunt of the cost of adjustment is being paid by wage earners, consistent with Shaiken's characterization of labor policy. But, the recovery of median manufacturing wages after 1988 is not what one would expect to see if Shaiken's views are right. Notice that after 1988 median wages increased steadily even though GDP per capita was fairly flat. This is the period

Figure 1

Productivity, GDP Per Capita, Median Manufacturing Wage, and Minimum Wage in Mexico, 1980-1996 (1980=100)

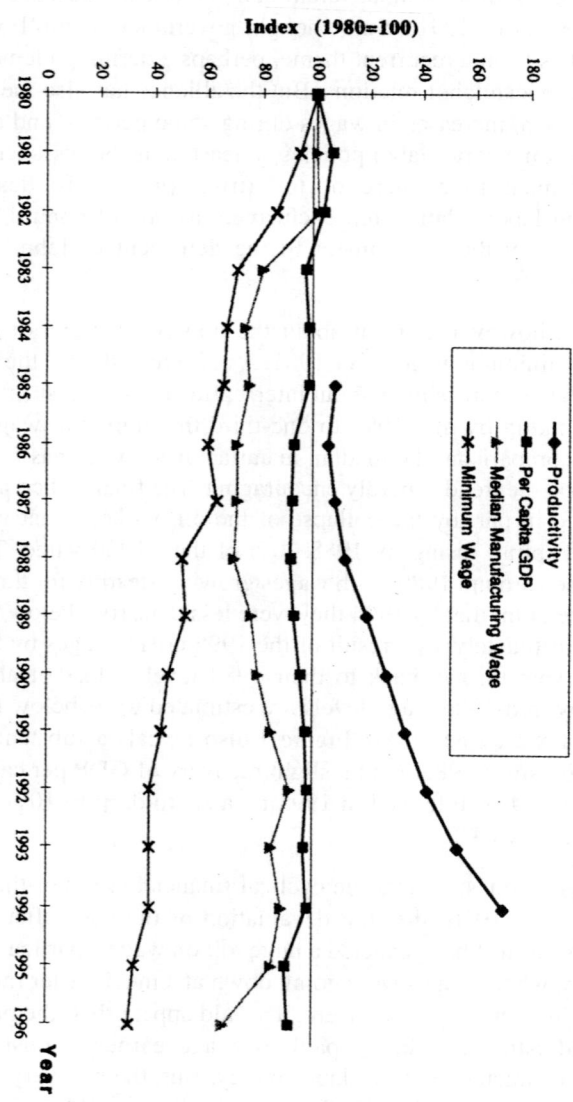

Source: Annual estimates calculated by the author from data in *Poder Ejecutivo Federal* (1996) and BDINEGI (1997).

when Mexico brought inflation under control, successfully renegotiated its foreign debt, and instituted reforms to encourage foreign investment. At the very least one can conclude that, institutional rigidities and all, real wages in Mexico do tend to increase when the economy grows. There is much more to wage setting than government fiat, in Mexico too.

Structure and Content of NAALC

The Democratic administration of President Clinton accepted the conventional wisdom in the US pro-labor community that the problem in Mexico was a lack of enforcement of labor laws not deficient labor rights being on the books. If those laws were effectively enforced, the argument went, social dumping practices and downward harmonization of labor standards would be precluded. Wages would rise *pari passu* with productivity; unions would be able to negotiate fair agreements on behalf of members, and so on.

Reflecting the conventional wisdom about enforcement, the North American Agreement on Labor Cooperation (NAALC), that the Parties finally signed on September 14, 1993, incorporated a novel aspect; an overall commitment of the Parties to enforce their own labor laws, whatever their terms. This may sound like a superfluous commitment, for after all it is a defining principle of all modern constitutional systems that government institutions and officials must uphold the law. Yet, the significance of this commitment is that a country's failure to enforce its labor law could trigger trade sanctions by one or both of the other two NAFTA countries. The actual cases where this would be possible is actually fairly restrictive, and even then many procedural hurdles must be overcome before sanctions could be imposed (see below), but it is nonetheless an important precedent because it is the first case where a free trade agreement incorporates a "labor clause" linked to trade sanctions.

The NAALC includes two other conceptually distinct parts which, because they do not provide for trade sanctions in any way, may be hastily dismissed as meaningless. The first important aspect of the agreement deals with cooperation activities that the Parties have agreed to promote regarding practically any labor issue. The agreement and the main body it establishes for its governance and implementation, the North American Commission on Labor Cooperation (the Commission), both bear the word cooperation in their name, so apparently the Parties expected cooperative activities to become the most frequent undertaking under the agreement, if not the most important. Article 11 lists a non-exhaustive list of areas for cooperation ranging from child labor, to wages benefits, to migrant workers, to equality of women in the workplace, and so on.

The Commission is composed of a ministerial Council (the labor ministers of the three countries), the highest decision-making organ of the Commission (Art.10), and a Secretariat, the executive and administrative organ of the Commission (Art.12), headed by an Executive Director with a support staff of fifteen, five from each country. The members of the Secretariat are specifically instructed "not to seek or receive any instructions from any government or any other authority external to the Council" (Art.12(5)). They are considered international officials working for an international organization with legal personality. The size of the Secretariat and the employment status of its members make it possible for an imaginative and committed executive director to spearhead the Council into potentially profitable cooperative endeavors. As secretariats go, this has been well funded.

The second part of the agreement, aside from enforcement, revolves around the National Administrative Office (NAO) that each country agreed to establish in its respective territory (Art.15). While the NAO's have a number of strictly administrative responsibilities, such as facilitating the exchange of information among the countries, each of the national offices has been charged with providing "for the submission and receipt, and periodically publish a list, of public communications on labor law matters arising in the **territory of another Party**." (emphasis added). They are further required to "review such matters, as appropriate, in accordance with domestic law." (Art.15(3)).

The language of this provision could be clearer, as its current phrasing leaves room for ambiguity. Still it seems to require that, for example, the NAO in Canada receive "communications" from the public — presumably anybody with a self-described interest — about matters related to labor law "arising" in either the US or Mexico. In this example, the NAO in Canada would have to review the matter communicated to it in accordance with Canadian law.

Not even two months after the entry into force of the NAALC, two submissions were filed by American labor unions before the NAO in the US. These submissions dealt with the dismissal of workers at two US *maquiladoras* plants in Mexico, and included allegations that the workers had been illegally dismissed because of their union organizing activities. The American Office accepted the cases, even though they pertained to activities that had taken place in 1993, before the NAACL had entered into effect, and that the cases dealt with actions by American companies in Mexico rather than policy or administrative actions directly by the Government of Mexico. The US Office conducted a public hearing where both cases were jointly considered, and where a number of trade union officials, dismissed workers, and a team of Mexican labor specialists testified. Ten months after the submissions were filed, the Office issued a report of its review, essentially stating that it had found no evidence that the Government of Mexico had failed to enforce applicable labor law in the two cases (see Compa, 1995, for a thorough analysis of these two initial cases).

What is important for the purposes of this paper, is to point out the emergence of fora where labor practices in one NAFTA country can be scrutinized by, essentially, government officials of another NAFTA country. It could be argued that these fora do not amount to much for once a case is accepted for review by a NAO office — and they seem to have enormous latitude to decide which cases to accept provided that they relate "to labor law matters arising in the territory of another Party" (Art.16(3)) — its powers are ultimately limited to issuing a report whose findings and recommendations are nonbinding. Yet, the moral persuasion of public reports could be considerable, especially if the body issuing the report is perceived as impartial and fair. Governments do not like to be embarrassed by negative reports, and when they are, changes in practices may follow after a while, sometimes a long while. The point is that a review process that lacks any form of mandatory trade sanctions at the end, may nonetheless contribute to positive change, if wisely applied. The ILO documents make exactly the same point about the review processes provided under many of the ILO-sponsored conventions, none of which contemplate trade sanctions as a possibility.

Labor Dumping and Trade Sanctions

Parts IV (Arts 20-26), V (Arts 27-41), and VI (Arts 42-49) of the NAALC, delimit the set of possibilities that could form the basis for a "labor dumping" case, although that terminology is not used in the agreement. There have been no actual cases litigated under these provisions of the NAALC so what follows relies solely on the text of the agreement.

The agreement indirectly recognizes that a country may derive an unfair trade advantage by engaging in a "persistent pattern of failure [...] to effectively enforce" its labor laws (Art.27(1)), and that such unfair advantage is actionable by the affected country, provided a number of additional requirements are met. First, the agreement explicitly states that one isolated instance of non-enforcement does not constitute a "pattern", and that the only actionable violations are those perpetrated by a country on a "sustained or recurring" basis (see Art.49). Obviously, there is a lot of room between an "isolated" event and a "sustained" practice, but the agreement does not make clear at which point in the continuum between those two extremes violations become actionable. Only through actual cases will we learn where the agreement draws the line between action-able and non-actionable violations. Secondly, the agreement recognizes (Art.49) that in some instances an agency or an official may reasonably decide not to enforce the law, for example for the sake of fulfilling a higher public policy objective which otherwise would be compromised. Situations like those are not considered "enforcement failures" and, thus, are non-actionable.

In addition, the agreement requires that the non-enforcement viola-tion refers to an issue that is "mutually recognized by the labor laws" of both the complaining country and the country complained against. To satisfy this requirement the labor laws of both countries must "address the same general subject matter [the one giving rise to the complaint] in a matter that provides enforceable rights, protections or standards." (Art.49).

Two additional requirements further limit the scope of potential ac-tionable cases: the matter under dispute can pertain only to technical labor standards that relate to occupational safety and health, child labor, or minimum wage (Art.27). All other areas of labor law are excluded. And, two, the alleged non-enforcement pattern must be "trade-related" (Art.29), by which is meant that the non-enforcement pattern must affect companies that produce goods or provide services which are traded among the Parties, or companies that are in competition in the territory of the country where the non-enforcement is allegedly taking place, with companies or persons of another country. In other words, the agreement requires that the pattern of non-enforcement ultimately provides a com-petitive advantage to local firms over their competitors from other countries.

Aside from these substantive limitations, there are also two procedural steps that must be exhausted before an arbitration panel can be formed to adjudicate a labor-dumping case. First, the Parties are directed to en-gage in ministerial consultations to attempt to resolve the dispute (Art.22), and second, if consultations fail, a Committee of Experts must be assembled to study the matter and issue a report — within 180 days of being formed — including "practical recommendations that may assist the Parties" in finding a resolution to the disputed matter (Arts 23 and 25). Only then, and assuming a resolution to the dispute has not been reached, would an arbitration panel be convened to determine if there is a labor rights violation which a country must correct or else face the possibility of trade sanctions and/or a fine, in the event of noncompliance with the decision by the arbitral panel.

It should be evident that the number of cases which could lead to trade sanctions is fairly limited and that the signatory countries have insured that an arbitration panel is convened only after a number of non-litigious opportunities to address the problem have been unsuccessfully tried. It is hardly surprising then that nearly three years into the life of the agreement not a single case has reached the stage of dispute settlement prior to arbitration and there are currently not any labor matters under consideration that could reach that stage in the near future. Does this mean that the agreement is irrelevant, at least in so far as labor dumping situation?

Time will tell, but I think not. First, the dispute settlement provisions could remain dormant for a long time and still exert some influence on government labor-practices. In designing their policies or administrative actions in the labor field countries now have to consider the possibility of a challenge before a North American arbitration panel. In light of that risk, countries may rule out certain courses of action that one could describe as unfavorable to labor and that in the past could have been easier to adopt. For example, a North American country may find it politically more difficult to reduce the budget for industrial safety inspectors now than it would have been before the passage of the NAALC. Such a move could subsequently be invoked as evidence of that country's neglect of its duty to oversee firms' compliance with labor standards.

Second, as other countries accede to the NAFTA in the next few years one should expect that those countries would also have to ratify the NAALC. As the membership to the Labor Agreement increases so will the likelihood that labor dumping cases are successfully initiated. Once cases are considered and resolved, the possibilities and pitfalls of the current regime will reveal themselves, perhaps eventually leading to a reconsideration of the terms of the "social clause" as currently contemplated by the NAALC.

Conclusions

The labor implications of trade agreements will only become a more pressing and contentious issue as the developing countries continue to capture a growing share of international markets.

I have stated my agreement with the International Labor Organization that, with the exception of prison labor policies, the current WTO regime does not provide a legal basis to require members countries to follow or refrain from following specific labor practices lest trade sanctions be imposed by their trading partners. The prospect of requiring countries to honor a set of labor rights as a condition for trading under WTO or other preferential trade arrangements are presently quite limited, but such a prospect is no longer unthinkable. I have argued that despite its extremely narrow scope, the North American Agreement on Labor Cooperation has set an important precedent in that regard. The NAALC represents the first attempt in the context of a free trade area in which trade sanctions have been adopted as a deterrent to, and a remedy against, the violation of a very restrictive set of labor rights. Political imperatives rather than sound policy reasons explain, in my opinion, this development. What direction the NAALC regime will follow and to what effects, is difficult to predict, although I have asserted the proposition that it would not be inconsequential, for better or worse. To improve the observance of labor rights the NAALC also includes mechanisms in which trade sanctions play no role. I have suggested that, in the end, those mechanisms, which include the possibility of cooperative undertakings under the direction of a well-funded and independent Secretariat, may prove more effective in the promotion of labor rights than the dispute settlement procedures.

Using Mexico as an example, I have illustrated that in some instances labor conditions in a country, especially wages, may suffer a considerable reduction concurrent to the country's greater participation in the stream of international trade. Yet my argument has been that the deterioration in labor conditions need not have resulted from international trade and that the use of trade sanctions as a means to prevent or redress a deterioration in wages might do more harm than good for workers. Trade sanctions could simply plunge a country into a deeper recession, ultimately leading to a further reduction in wages and employment levels.

I fully concur with the ILO that the main challenge today is the adoption and implementation of policies that help secure a share of the proceeds of economic growth for workers. Under most conditions, trade sanctions in conjunction with a labor clause may not be helpful in that effort.

References

BHAGWATI, Jagdish, **Protectionism**, MIT Press, Cambridge, MA, 1988.

COMPA, Lance A., *"The First NAFTA Labor Cases: A New International Labor Rights Regime Takes Shape"*, in: **US-Mexico Law Journal** No.3, 1995, pp.159-181.

BANCO DE MEXICO, *Información Económica Básica*, 1996, http://www.quicklink.com/mexico/bm/bm1.htm.

BDINEGI (Banco de Datos del Instituto Nacional de Estadística, Geografía e Informática), *Información Económica de Coyuntura,* 1996, http://dgcnesyp.inegi.gob.mx/bdine/bancos.htm

BDINEGI (Banco de Datos del Instituto Nacional de Estadística, Geografía e Informática), *Información Económica de Coyuntura,* 1997, http://dgcnesyp.inegi.gob.mx/bdine/bancos.htm

COLLIER, Ruth, **The Contradictory Alliance: State-Labor Relations and Regime Change in Mexico**, International and Area Studies, University of California Berkeley, Berkeley, CA, 1992.

FLANAGAN, Robert J., *"European Wage Equalization since the Treaty of Rome"*, in: ULMAN L., EICHENGREEN B., & DICKENS W.T. (eds), **Labor and an Integrated Europe**, Brookings Institution, Washington, DC, 1993, pp.167-187.

HANSENNE, Michael, **Trade and Labor Standards: Can Common Rules Be Agreed?** Address given at the 46th Wilton Park Conference on Liberalizing World Trade and Prospects for the Singapore Ministerial Meeting, Steyning, West Sussex, March 6, 1996.

INTERNATIONAL LABOUR OFFICE, **The Social Dimension of the Liberalization of World Trade**, Working Party on the Social Liberalization of International Trade, Geneva, /WP/SLD/1, 1994.

MACGROW, Daniel, **NAFTA & The Environment: Substance and Process**, American Bar Association, Section of International Law and Practice, Washington, DC, 1995.

"How Workers Fare: Comparing Wages and Benefits", in: **New York Times**, June 24, 1994.

PODER EJECUTIVO FEDERAL, *Segundo Informe de Gobierno de Ernesto Zedillo Ponce de León*, Anexo, México: Presidencia de la República, 1o. de Septiembre 1996.

ROBINSON, Ian, *"How Will the North American Free Trade Agreement Affect Worker Rights in North America?"*, in: COOK M.L. & KATZ H.C. (eds), **Regional Integration and Industrial Relations in North America**, ILR Press, Ithaca, NY, 1994, pp.105-131.

SHAIKEN, Harley, **Myths about Mexican Workers**, Democratic Study Center Series, Washington, DC, 1993.

US DEPARTMENT OF LABOR, *International Comparisons of Hourly Compensation Costs for Production Workers in Manufacturing, 1975-1989*, **Report** 794, Bureau of Labor Statistics, Washington, DC, 1990(a).

US DEPARTMENT OF LABOR, *Industrial Effects of a Trade Agreement between Mexico and the USA*, **Report** PB91-110627, Washington, DC, 1990(b).

US INTERNATIONAL TRADE COMMISSION, *Economy-Wide Modeling of the Economic Implications of a FTA with Mexico and a NAFTA with Canada and Mexico*, **Publication** 2508, ITC, Washington, DC, 1992.

ZAPATA, Francisco, **Mexican Labor in a Context of a Political and Economic Crisis**, El Colegio de Mexico, Mexico, (Unpublished manuscript), 1995.

WORLD BANK REPORT, **Workers in an Integrating World**, Oxford University Press, New York, NY, 1995.

WORLD TRADE ORGANIZATION, **World Trade Expanded Strongly in 1995 for the Second Consecutive Year. Robust Trade Expected this Year**, Geneva, Press/44, March 22, 1996.

Environmental Protection in Regional Trade Agreements: The European Community and NAFTA[*]

Daniel C. ESTY & Damien GERADIN

*Associate Professor of Environmental Law and Policy,
Yale School of Forestry and
Environmental Studies and the Yale Law School;*

*Associate, Coudert Brothers, Brussels;
Visiting Lecturer, University of Paris II (Panthéon-Assas);
Research Fellow, Institut d'Études
Juridiques Européennes, University of Liège*

INTRODUCTION

Free trade among nations is generally recognized to produce mutually beneficial results. Liberalized trade has a number of positive economic effects on domestic economies, such as an increased range of consumer choice, a reduction in the cost of inputs, and potential increased economies of scale and therefore higher returns on investment. Open markets may also stimulate social progress as contact among societies leads to the sharing of new ideas, more rapid diffusion of technological advances, and the development of a common base of experiences. Finally, by creating links among people and a prosperity based on interdependence, trade

[*] The present paper is a revised version of an article published in *"The Harvard Environmental Law Review"*.

enhances the prospect of harmony among societies and serves to promote peace. In the wake of the worldwide economic chaos of the 1930s and World War II, these considerations led to the establishment of the General Agreement on Tariffs and Trade (GATT). The GATT was designed to provide an institutional structure in support of liberalized trade negotiations at the international level. Similarly, the benefits provided by freer trade motivated the creation of a series of regional trade agreements, such as the European Community (EC), North American Free Trade Area (NAFTA), Association of South-East Asian Nations (ASEAN), Caribbean Community (Caricom) and Southern Common Market *(Mercado Común del Sur)* (Mercosur).

Largely in parallel with this movement towards trade liberalization, states have developed increasingly sophisticated policies to protect the environment. These policies have led to the adoption of various kinds of environmental standards and regulations. Environmental legislation may regulate the characteristics of products or the production methods by which products are made. Many environmental laws aim to internalize the costs of environmental degradation into the prices producers or consumers pay and thereby create an incentive to reduce air or water pollution. Environmental legislation also comprises waste management and disposal regimes, as well as programs to ensure the conservation of natural resources.

For most of the last half-century, trade liberalization and environmental protection have moved along separate tracks. Today they increasingly intersect and are seen by some to collide. We see both freer trade and a healthier environment as important contributors to social welfare that need not be traded off against each other.

This paper seeks to examine the relationship between trade liberalization and environmental protection with an eye toward alleviating conflicts between these important policy goals and making them more mutually reinforcing, especially in the context of regional trade agreements. In Part I, we spell out and categorize the various concerns that the parallel pursuit of trade liberalization and environmental protection has raised. In Part II, we suggest a taxonomy of the responses that can be used to address the concerns outlined in Part I. The nature and characteristics of these tools and strategies vary considerably, consistent with the diverse set of trade/environment tensions to which they respond. Such tools range from a *laissez-faire* approach to differences in environmental standards among jurisdictions in a free trade regime to total harmonization of environmental regulations. In Part III, we apply the theoretical framework outlined in Parts I and II to two regional trade agreements, the European Community (EC)[1] and the North American Free Trade Agreement (NAFTA)[2]. We examine the extent to which the trade and environment concerns discussed in Part I have arisen in these two agreements, as well as the degree to which the responses discussed in Part II have been used to address these concerns. In Part IV, we discuss the extent to which the experience of regional trade systems could be used to deal with trade and environment issues arising in the context of the World Trade Organization (WTO). Finally, in Part V, we offer some general conclusions.

PART I: THE CONCERNS

This part categorizes and spells out the various concerns that may arise from the intersection of trade and environmental protection policies in the context of regional free trade agreements. A first set of concerns relates to the issue of market access. Notably, free traders worry that environmental standards, especially those which regulate the environmental characteristics of products (**product** standards), may act as barriers to trade. Conversely, from an environmental standpoint, the concern is that trade liberalization entails market access commitments that could be used to override environmental product standards or that might lead to downward harmonization of such standards.

A second set of concerns relates to the issue of competitiveness. There is a fear that inappropriate differences in the level of stringency of environmental standards, especially those which regulate the production methods by which products are made (**process** standards), may create distortions of competition, give incentives for industrial relocation, and trigger a "race toward the bottom" in environmental policy-making.

---

[1] The reason why we refer to the European Community (EC) instead of the European Union (EU), is that, with respect to the matter at hand, the EC is the more precise term. Under the Maastricht Treaty, the Member States agreed to establish a "European Union". The institutional framework for the EU is based upon three pillars: (i) the EC; (ii) the common and foreign and security policy; and (iii) cooperation in the fields of justice and home affairs. Since trade and environment policies are exclusively dealt with in the context of the first pillar, the present paper will refer to the "EC", which represents the more relevant, more specific legal order.

[2] North American Free Trade Agreement, December 8, 11, 14, 17, 1992, Cor.-Mex.-US 32 **ILM** 289 605, Art.915.1 (1993).

A. Market Access

Worries about environmental standards acting as barriers to the free movement of goods between states take two primary forms. First, product standards may impede trade when they discriminate between imported and domestic products. Product standards are discriminatory when different requirements are imposed on imported and domestic products. The WTO recently found, for example, that the United States had discriminated against imported gasoline by imposing differential baselines for olefins (an impurity that causes pollution) on foreign producers[3]. Product standards discriminate in their effect when, although they superficially appear to apply equally to imported and domestic products, they bear more heavily on imports. An example of this kind of discrimination would be a regulation prohibiting the sale of a toxic substance that is largely imported from other nations while allowing a competing substance of similar toxicity that is mainly manufactured by domestic producers. Another example is the Ontario requirement that beer be sold in returnable glass bottles, which happens to be the way that Canadian brewers package their products, effectively barring US beers usually sold in (recyclable) aluminium cans from the market[4].

Second, even in the absence of protectionism, the adoption of different product standards may fragment the market, increase transaction costs and generate dis-economies of scale for all producers. For example, inconsistent motor vehicle emission standards impede trade in cars since they force producers to set up special production lines for each country in which they wish to sell.

Conversely, from an environmental standpoint, there is a fear that regional trade agreements ensuring the free movement of goods and avoiding the types of barriers to trade described above may prevent or discourage governments from adopting or maintaining certain kinds of environmental product standards. These agreements generally mandate that environmental standards not discriminate between domestic and imported products, not create "unnecessary" obstacles to trade and be based on scientific principles. Environmentalists fear that a strict application of these terms could result in a weakening of environmental regulatory programs.

---

[3] *"First WTO Ruling Goes Against US: Dual RFG Standards Discriminatory"*, in: **Air/Water Pollution Reports Environmental Week** No.4 Vol.34, Jan. 19, 1996.

[4] ESTY, **Greening the GATT**, Institute for International Economics, 1994, at 274.

B. Competitiveness

The second set of concerns raised by different environmental requirements in the context of trade liberalization relates to the issue of competitiveness. These concerns take several forms.

First, differences in the stringency of process standards may distort
competition. Some differences in environmental regulations represent an
appropriate response to variations in circumstances — e.g., strong winds
or fast rivers that dissipate pollution more quickly, less densely popu-
lated areas, lower levels of existing pollution, etc. Indeed, gains from
trade are made possible by such differences. But in other cases, less strict
requirements are not based on comparative advantage, and the advantage gained by producers facing lower pollution control costs might be
illegitimate or unfair. Intervention to eliminate the first type of difference would not be good policy. Where, however, the choice of sub-
optimal standards in one jurisdiction threatens to erode the competitive
position of producers in other places, policy intervention may be
appropriate.

Second, there is a concern that differences in the level of stringency
of process standards may induce industrial relocation. In order to lower
their environmental compliance costs, producers may be tempted to relocate from states enforcing strict standards to those with more lax standards. There is little evidence that such shifts toward "pollution havens"
occur[5]. The lack of empirical data probably reflects the fact that industrial relocation depends on a number of factors and, in general, labor
costs, transportation expenditures and access to markets generally swamp
the significance of environmental compliance costs. In addition, the costs
of moving production from one nation to another are often considerable.

Nevertheless, as other costs (e.g., capital, labor) equalize across jurisdictions, small differences in variables such as pollution control expenditures may grow in relative importance, exacerbating environmental
competitiveness concerns. Moreover, in certain industries (e.g., refining)
environmental costs already represent a significant share (10 percent) of
total costs, and in most industries, pollution prevention and control

---

[5] See, e.g., KALT, *"The Impact of Domestic Environmental Regulatory Policies on
US International Competitiveness"*, in: SPENCE & HAZARD (eds), **International
Competitiveness**, Cambridge University Press, 1988; LOW & YEATS, *"Do Dirty
Industries Migrate?"*, in: LOW (ed.), *"International Trade and the Environment"*,
World Bank Discussion Paper 159.

expenditures are rising[6]. Environmental competitiveness concerns are likely to be more pronounced in "commodity" products where small price differences can dramatically affect sales. In other goods, product differentiation is significant so that variations in pollution control costs pale in comparison to opportunities to innovate in ways that add value to the product and set it apart from the competition[7].

Finally, increased economic competition across jurisdictions may have an effect on environmental policy making. Faced with the prospect of having their industries suffer reduced sales, lost jobs and diminished investment in competition with companies whose costs are lower due to more lax environmental requirements, government officials may choose not to elevate environmental standards or even to relax enforcement of current standards. This environmental policy dynamic is known as the "race to the bottom", which has been described as "a race from the desirable levels of environmental quality that states would pursue if they did not face competition for industry to the increasingly undesirable levels that they choose in the face of such competition."[8] Note that the "race" is not really "to" the bottom but rather "towards" the bottom. In fact, governments rarely lower standards; the real effect is one of "political drag" or "regulatory chill", making it difficult for governments to move towards optimal environmental policies.

PART II: THE RESPONSES

This part surveys the various responses to the trade and environment concerns outlined above. These responses range from a *laissez-faire* approach pursuant to which trade and environment concerns are assumed to be adequately addressed by the "invisible hand" of the market to total harmonization strategies that mandate identical standards across jurisdictions.

A. *Laissez-faire*

One response to the market access and competitiveness concerns outlined above is to do nothing. A number of authors argue that the

---

[6] EPA, *Environmental Investments: The Cost of a Clean Environment*, 1990.

[7] See, e.g., PORTER & VAN DER LINDE, *"Green and Competitive"*, in: **Harvard Business Review**, Sept.-Oct. 1995, pp.120-34.

[8] REVESZ, *"Rehabilitating Interstate Competition: Rethinking the 'Race-to-the-Bottom' Rationale For Federal Environmental Regulation"*, in: **New York University Law Review** No.67, 1992, pp.1210.

competitiveness concerns simply reflect differences in circumstances and preferences playing out in the marketplace and deserve no more attention than differences in wage levels. More dramatically, advocates of regulatory competition suggest that attempts to mitigate or eliminate diversity in process standards will reduce social welfare by eliminating a dimension of comparative advantage and thereby reducing the benefits of specialized production and trade. If, however, varying environmental process standards do not reflect differences in circumstances, or the variations trigger strategic behavior in policy-making and a race toward the bottom, then a *laissez-faire* approach is likely to yield poor results. In addition, if transboundary environmental harms exist, decentralized (state-by-state) regulation cannot be counted upon to produce optimal outcomes. Because harms (or benefits) that fall outside the regulating authority's borders tend not to be counted, the regulatory cost-benefit calculus is skewed and governments systematically select sub-optimal levels of environmental protection. Whenever pollution externalities are present, some form of collective action will be required to avoid market failure and allocative inefficiency. At the very least, a regime that allows for the clarification and vindication of the rights of those who suffer pollution spillovers must be established. Other regulatory regimes might be preferable depending on the significance of transaction costs in the circumstances.

The *laissez-faire* response also does nothing to guard against protectionist abuses of product standards. Absent a mechanism for unmasking barriers to trade disguised as environmental rules, markets may be unfairly closed to imports triggering reciprocal barriers around the world[9]. Some commentators have recently suggested that such fears of beggar-thy-neighbors behavior are exaggerated. Al Sykes, for example, notes that protected markets are self-defeating[10]. They raise costs for one's own consumers and can competitively disadvantage one's own industries by forcing them to rely on more costly inputs. Sykes further observes that, with regard to product standards, market forces will yield an optimal degree of harmonization. Where consumers value diversity, they will pay the higher costs entailed by smaller production runs. Where price matters, the advantages of a common product across several markets permitting scale economies will result in harmonization.

---

[9] KENNEDY, *"Reformulating US Trade Policy to Protect the Global Environment: a Multilateral Approach"*, in: **Harvard Environmental Law Review** No.18, 1994, p.185.

[10] SYKES, **Product Standards for Internationally Integrated Goods Markets**, Institute for International Economics, 1995.

B. Trade Restrictions and Subsidies

To respond to competitiveness concerns, some policy-makers, including a number of industry and environmental interest groups, have called for the use of trade restrictions to penalize products from jurisdictions that apply lax environmental process standards[11]. If, for example, cement produced in the United States costs 30 percent more to make due to pollution controls than cement from Mexico (where environmental requirements are generally less stringent), they argue that the United States should impose a 30 percent "eco-duty" on Mexican cement. The rationale for imposing such charges on imported goods is that any cost differential arising from lower standards is unfair and distorts the price at which a product enters the marketplace. Even more radical is the call for a trade ban on products produced under conditions that do not meet the standards of the importing country[12].

Free traders object vehemently to the use of eco-duties, arguing that such policy instruments, far from equalizing the terms of trade, actually distort trade relationships by eliminating the comparative advantage of countries that are unable to set stringent environmental standards. Many trade theorists also suggest that any broad-based program of eco-duties would likely be captured by protectionists and would lead to mischief and inefficiency. Other critics note that it is difficult to evaluate cost differentials and, hence, to apply such eco-duties properly[13].

More fundamentally, trade restrictions seem inconsistent with the spirit of cooperation that is the essence of regional trade agreements. Such agreements must be premised on a sense of confidence in the basic values, democratic institutions, and governmental integrity of the partner jurisdictions. The greater the degree of integration, the stronger this baseline confidence must be.

Disruptive effects arising from differences in environmental standards might also be addressed by "green" subsidies. Governments that fear that their producers will be disadvantaged in markets with competitors with less strict pollution control obligations sometimes subsidize the environmental investment made by their companies. Traditional thinking

---

[11] See, e.g., Guy DE JONQUIERES, *"WTO Chief Fears Wave of Protectionism"*, in: **Financial Times**, July 7, 1995 p.5.

[12] See Ross PEROT, **Save your Job, Save our Country: Why NAFTA must be Stopped - Now!**, Hypherion, New York, 1993.

[13] See STEWART, *"International Trade and Environment: Lessons from the Federal Experience"*, in: **Washington & Lee Law Review** No.49, 1992, p.1329.

suggests that the use of subsidies to offset pollution costs borne by one's own industries is less offensive and less disruptive to an open trading system than comparable eco-duties[14].

But recent thinking casts doubt on the benign character of eco-subsidies. First, subsidizing polluters violates the Polluter Pays Principle, an accepted standard of good environmental policy[15]. By subsidizing the purchase of pollution control equipment, governments lower the cost of production and dull the incentive for consumers to look for less-environmentally-damaging substitutes. Second, subsidies are increasingly the tool of choice for governments seeking to lure industry. But the financial packages offered by one jurisdiction may be matched by others, starting another form of the race toward the bottom. The end result of such a competitive process may be that governments give away whatever benefits might have been obtained by the new facility[16]. Finally, subsidies, although not as aggressive a tool as eco-duties, increasingly are viewed as inconsistent with the spirit of cooperation that must animate a free trade agreement. Indeed, the EC has instituted strict controls on the types of subsidies that a Member State can offer in an attempt to influence a company's locational decisions[17].

C. Judicial Bounding

Regional trade agreements generally contain mechanisms designed to selectively invalidate trade restrictive environmental measures. These mechanisms, which we refer to as "judicial bounding", give a judicial or quasi-judicial body the power to strike down protectionist "environmental" measures and, even absent protectionist intent, those measures which unacceptably disrupt trade.

One advantage of judicial bounding is its flexibility. Judges or panellists do not usually apply trade disciplines strictly, but attempt to balance trade liberalization objectives with other goals such as environmental protection. There are, however, clear limitations on the exclusive reliance on courts or trade panels to unify markets and, simultaneously,

---

[14] Indeed, the GATT Uruguay Round Agreement authorizes the use of such green subsidies to some extent.

[15] Organization for Economic Cooperation and Development, *The Polluter pays Principle: Definition, Analysis, Implementation*, 1975.

[16] See, e.g., MYERSON, *"O Governor, won't you buy me a Mercedes Plant?"*, in: **New York Times**, September 1, 1996 sec.3, p.1.

[17] See Article 92 of the EC Treaty.

uphold environmental standards. First, judicial decisions have essentially a negative or corrective effect: they can only remove specific obstacles to trade, not prevent such obstacles from arising. This is a particularly serious handicap in the area of product standards where, because of growing consumer demands for environmental quality, governments enact increasing numbers of regulations governing the environmental characteristics of products, including the biodegradability or the environmental impact of their components, the size, weight and content of their packaging, etc. In this context collective action to harmonize product standards appears to be a surer and swifter strategy than selective judicial invalidation of trade restrictive environmental measures. Second, from the perspective of those interested in environmental protection, selective judicial invalidation of laws and regulations appears to condone the trumping environment by trade. This sense of injustice increases where the deciding body or judge comes from a trade-oriented institution or otherwise lacks legitimacy or authoritativeness. Thus, while there is little outcry when the US Supreme Court invalidates US state environmental laws as burdens on interstate commerce[18], NAFTA or WTO authorities doing the same thing produces great outrage[19].

D. Harmonization

Another way to deal with both market access and competitiveness concerns is harmonization of environmental standards. While there are good reasons to think that differences in standards across jurisdictions with diverse circumstances will increase social welfare, there are also cases where convergence might be more beneficial. Trade officials and economists too often dismiss "harmonization" as inefficient, treating **total** harmonization of standards as if it were the only available policy option. This section discusses a more refined set of harmonization approaches which allow some of the benefits of diversity and, at the same time, permit some of the advantages of coordinated policy.

Possible harmonization strategies fall into two groups. First, a number of harmonization techniques appear to be particularly appropriate to address market access concerns because they coordinate environmental **product** standards and seek to eliminate barriers to market entry. These

---

[18] See, e.g., *Fort Gratiot Sanitary Landfill, Inc. v. Michigan Dept of Nat. Res.*, 504 US 353 (1992); *Philadelphia v. New Jersey*, 437 US 617 (1978); *C&A Carbone, Inc. v. Clarkstown*, 511 US 383 (1994).

[19] See, e.g., the environmental outrage over the GATT tuna dolphin decision or the prospect of a judicial body under the NAFTA. See ESTY, *supra*, note 4.

are: (i) uniform standards; (ii) maximum standards; (iii) establishment of essential requirements; (iv) pre-standard harmonization; and (v) harmonized public information approaches. By contrast, a number of other harmonization techniques address competitiveness concerns by coordinating environmental **process** standards. These are: (i) minimum standards; (ii) multi-tier requirements; (iii) convergence of standards; (iv) differentiated standards; (v) goal harmonization; (vi) harmonization of options; and (vii) systems harmonization.

1. Market Access

a) Uniformity of Standards or Total Harmonization

Total harmonization suggests the adoption of uniform standards across all jurisdictions. Each regulating authority implements exactly the same environmental requirements. Neither higher nor lower standards are permitted. There are several advantages to total harmonization. First, total harmonization of product standards allows producers to realize economies of scale in design and production and generally prevents market fragmentation. Second, total harmonization prevents confusion about what the rules are. Because everyone must adhere to the same standards, any deviation in performance can easily be detected. Third, total harmonization facilitates enforcement of the rules because regulators can achieve economies of scale in their activities drawing on the work of other officials who are enforcing exactly the same requirements. Finally, there may be some administrative gains from "network effects" that arise where adherence to a common standard allows efficiency in developing control technologies, training programs, legal systems, or any other aspect of an environmental regime that would otherwise consume resources in each jurisdiction individually.

These advantages, however, come at a high price. A single standard across all jurisdictions does not allow for tailoring of the requirements to local needs, circumstances or preferences. To the extent that the world is heterogeneous, single standards have a tendency to reduce welfare. Under conditions of relative homogeneity, however, the advantages of uniform standards may outweigh the losses that arise from ignoring diversity in conditions and values.

b) Maximum Standards

Maximum standards impose a ceiling on the stringency of environmental requirements. Maximum product standards promote free trade because diminished variations in product requirements facilitate the entry of companies into new markets and may reduce regulatory administration costs as well. Because states are free to apply more lax standards, maximum standards provide no guarantee, however, that states will not maintain or adopt sub-optimal standards, with resultant environmental degradation.

c) Essential Requirements Harmonization

Under this approach, harmonization is limited to essential environmental requirements. The regulation of the detailed technical regulations necessary to achieve those basic requirements is generally left to individual jurisdictions or, as will be seen in the EC context, standardization organizations. The principal advantage of this approach is that it permits some diversity and yields some of the benefits of uniform standards. This form of partial harmonization may promote consensus among states and thus lead to optimally-harmonized standards.

d) Pre-standard Harmonization

Many of the benefits of product standards harmonization can be achieved if jurisdictions coordinate their regulatory systems so that they use common testing protocols, scientific methodologies, and risk assessment procedures. This type of harmonization offers substantial cost benefits for companies operating in multiple jurisdictions. For example, a pesticide maker that has met the testing requirements for selling its product in the German market would be able to have regulatory judgments made by French authorities on the basis of the data from Germany. With adequate quality controls, such an inter-jurisdictional system of mutual recognition ensures that the company does not need to go through additional years of product testing and reproving, thereby reducing the cost of regulatory review. Because one of the stumbling blocks to good environmental protection is the dearth of good science and analytic work on which to base regulations, ensuring that the technical efforts of one country are made available to other countries is an important advantage.

e) Public Information Harmonization

A final type of harmonization focuses on the information that the public is provided about the environmental qualities of products. If a common "eco-label" was developed for all states that are Parties to a trade agreement, companies would not have to go through separate analysis and label-development processes for each market. In addition, consumers would become well-versed in a specific set of environmental criteria and better able to make informed judgments.

552

2. Competitiveness

a) Minimum Standards

Minimum production process or method standards set a regulatory floor below which no jurisdiction can go. Such standards ensure that all governments require at least a baseline level of environmental protection from their industries. Under a program of minimum standards, jurisdictions remain free to impose more stringent requirements. By reducing environmental compliance cost differentials across jurisdictions, minimum standards constrain the possibility of distortions of competition, industrial relocation and a race toward the bottom. Indeed, game theory suggests that properly-structured minimum standards may diminish strategic behavior and thereby reduce the risk that interjurisdictional competition will yield sub-optimal results. A regime of minimum standards allows for some tailoring of standards to meet local conditions but not unlimited variations in environmental requirements. This approach provides some of the benefits of uniform standards, such as opportunities for scale economies in the administration of environmental regulations, without surrendering all of the welfare gains from having standards that match local requirements.

b) Multi-tier Harmonization

Multi-tier regulatory regimes with different standards for different groups of states also obtain some of the benefits of standards tailored to local conditions without losing all of the advantages of uniform requirements. Because one of the most important variables determining the optimal level of environmental protection is a state's wealth and level of economic development, a system of unified standards for those states with comparable levels of development may prove quite valuable. One could imagine, for example, a set of environmental standards developed for the most economically advanced states that would reflect a quite high degree of environmental protection. A second set of standards, with more modest requirements, might then be developed for less economically advanced states whose needs for environmental protection are great but that cannot afford high-level standards. Finally, a baseline set of standards could be defined for countries whose economic position is so modest that anything more than a limited set of environmental goals is unaffordable, and whose capacity to develop their own regulatory regime is limited. Such a multi-tier system would provide for economies of scale and network effects among the countries within each regulatory tier. At the same time, the existence of multiple tiers would ensure that standards would at least roughly correspond to the individualized needs of countries. Such a program would also allow countries to "graduate" into higher degrees of environmental protection as they develop.

Multi-tier standards could also be developed to correspond to varying baseline conditions. Under such a regime, jurisdictions with fast-moving rivers might permit more effluent to be discharged than those with waterways that have lower assimilative capacities. We discuss this variation on the multi-tier theme below.

c) Convergence

Another response to harmful competitive pressures created by varying environmental standards would be to promote a negotiated convergence of standards across jurisdictions. Eliminating wide variations in environmental standards limits the risk of a race toward the bottom. This "convergence" of requirements would also provide for some administrative efficiency while still permitting considerable tailoring of environmental programs to local conditions.

d) Differentiated Harmonization

Another approach to the uniformity-versus-diversity dilemma is a regulatory program that sets standards centrally but not uniformly. Under such a regime, central authorities identify environmental targets but provide for different degrees of stringency (in time tables for achieving the target or in the level of accomplishment itself) depending on the circumstances present in each subjurisdiction. The United States uses this sort of differentiated approach in its Clean Air Act[20]. Metropolitan areas are ranked based on the severity of their air pollution problems (extreme, severe, serious and moderate). The more severe an area's "non-attainment" problem, the more time the jurisdiction is given to comply with national clean air goals. Los Angeles, for example, has seventeen extra years to meet the established National Ambient Air Quality Standards.

Differential standards are more efficient than total harmonization, and yet the common goals ensure that wide variations in the rigor of environmental protection efforts do not persist over time. Again, this mechanism serves to balance the benefits of diverse standards set at the local level with the benefits of reduced competitiveness stresses obtained by more centralized standards.

---

[20] 42 U.S.C. §§ 7401-7642.

e) Goal Harmonization

Under this approach, harmonization is limited to the environmental goals that must be achieved by each jurisdiction. States are, however, free to choose the environmental strategies they deem most appropriate to attain the goals. Van den Bergh, Faure & LeFevere have proposed such a regulatory approach for the EC. They suggest that creating an "environmental margin", within which standards may fluctuate, offers the best balance between the benefits of standards that are purely tailored to local conditions and the advantages of uniform controls. Specifically, Van den Bergh and his co-authors argue for broad environmental quality standards and goals to be set at the EC-wide level[21]. Each Member State would determine for itself how to achieve the EC-wide target. In effect, the goals are harmonized but the implementation of specific environmental programs and the identification of precise emission standards would be decentralized.

Another variation on goal harmonization is the use of ambient standards. If a certain level of exposure to a specified type of pollution is identified as the safe threshold, this standard can be established as the baseline requirement in all jurisdictions. Of course, the difficulty of attaining this standard will vary across jurisdictions.

f) Harmonization of Options

An alternative to goal harmonization is to limit harmonization to a set of policy options among which jurisdictions can choose. For example, jurisdictions would be given the choice between several alternatives to deal with waste, such as landfilling under special conditions, incineration (again, under special conditions) or various recycling strategies. The advantage of this approach is that it facilitates consensus across jurisdictions with varying requirements and, hence, the adoption of harmonization legislation. Another advantage is that it allows a degree of experimentation.

g) Systems Harmonization

Another approach to the issue of divergent regulatory standards is to mandate conformity with certain established environmental systems or procedures, but not to insist that all jurisdictions adopt identical substantive standards. The development of set environmental management

---

[21] Roger VAN DEN BERGH *et al.*, *"The Subsidiary Principle in European Environmental Law: An Economic Analysis"*, (unpublished paper).

requirements (ISO 14000) by the International Standards Organization (ISO) is a type of systems harmonization[22]. ISO 14000 would impose basic management standards on participating companies, but not a strict set of substantive requirements.

By guaranteeing that at least a rudimentary environmental management structure is in place, such an approach might help to reduce the number of cases where divergent standards arise from public choice distortions or "regulatory" failure rather than variations in local needs and conditions. In doing so, a harmonized approach to environmental systems would reduce the risk of a race toward the bottom in the environmental regulatory domain. The disadvantage of relying on environmental systems is that there may be little convergence in the substantive requirements that are imposed from jurisdiction to jurisdiction. As a result, wide variations in environmental compliance costs may persist and competitiveness tensions may endure.

E. Enforcement Commitments

Rather than harmonizing standards in any form, Parties to a free trade agreement might simply agree to rigorously enforce their own national environmental rules. This non-harmonization allows for standards to be tailored to each country's individual circumstances and needs. The commitment to full enforcement of national laws might, however, be seen as a way of preventing derogations that would be unfair and potentially a trigger for a race toward the bottom in environmental policy-making.

PART III: CASE STUDIES:
THE EUROPEAN COMMUNITY AND NAFTA

In this part, we examine the extent to which the market access and competitiveness concerns outlined in Part I have arisen in two regional trade agreements, the EC and the NAFTA. In addition, we review the extent to which the responses outlined in Part II have been used to address these concerns.

Of course, the EC and NAFTA are only two of a large number of regional trade agreements now in place, including ASEAN, Caricom and Mercosur. The focus on the EC and NAFTA reflects the fact that these two agreements are the most sophisticated, and arguably the most

---

[22] See *"Euro-green: The Regs"*, in: **CFO Magazine**, Vol.12, No.9, 1996, p.22.

integrated, of the regional trade agreements. Moreover, trade and environment issues have been at the forefront of policy debates in these two agreements. Thus, the EC and NAFTA offer the most robust regional trade models for comparison.

A. *The European Community*

1. Market Access

The trade restrictive effects of product standards, including environmental product standards, have been a major source of concern in the EC. Indeed, the creation of a common market, where goods circulate freely between Member States, has always been the main purpose of European economic integration. The central strategy used by the EC to address market access concerns has been judicial bounding. The European Court of Justice has interpreted broadly the free trade provisions included in the EC Treaty. In recent years, however, the European Court of Justice has become increasingly sensitive to environmental objectives and has explicitly recognized in several cases that trade liberalization should not prevent Member States from adopting legitimate environmental standards. In Section a), we examine how the European Court of Justice has attempted to balance free trade with environmental protection. Another EC strategy to protect market access has been harmonization of environmental product standards. As we have seen, such harmonization allows companies to realize economies of scale and generally eliminates barriers to trade. In Section b), we review the various kinds of harmonization used by the Community to avoid environmental obstacles to trade. We also discuss whether the EC legislation has fully integrated environmental requirements in this harmonization process or whether the environment has been merely ancillary to the EC's economic objectives.

a) *Judicial Bounding*

Judicial bounding represents the heart of the EC effort to ensure that product standards do not unduly restrict market access. The textual basis of this strategy is found in Article 30 of the Treaty, which provides that all quantitative restrictions and "measures having equivalent effect" shall be prohibited. In the *Dassonville* Case, the Court of Justice interpreted the concept of "measures having equivalent effect" as "all trading rules enacted by Member States which are capable of hindering, actually or potentially, directly or indirectly, intra-Community trade."[23] As defined

---

[23] Case 8/74, *Procureur du Roi v. Dassonville et al.*, (1974) **ECR** 837, 852.

in *Dassonville*, Article 30 appears to prevent discriminatory **and** nondiscriminatory environmental measures affecting trade.

This sweeping free trade principle is, however, tempered by two exceptions. Article 36 allows Member States to adopt measures *prima facie* that are incompatible with Article 30 in pursuit of non-economic goals, among which are the protection of human health or life, animals, or plants. In addition, the "rule of reason", the origin of which is to be found in the *Cassis de Dijon* Case, allows Member States to adopt nondiscriminatory trade restrictive measures to protect a series of "essential requirements" including the protection of health and environmental protection[24]. In order to benefit from these exceptions, environmental measures must, however, be subject to a so-called test of "proportionality". Notably, they must (i) be pertinent; and (ii) they must be the least restrictive method of attaining their objective[25].

The question of the compatibility with the EC Treaty of environmental product standards affecting trade arose in the famous *Danish Bottles* Case[26]. In that case, the Commission challenged a Danish law that required manufacturers to market beer and soft drinks in "returnable containers". In addition, the size and shape of the containers had to be approved by the Danish National Agency for the Protection of the Environment (NAPE). Following protests from producers of beverages and containers in other Member States, the Commission urged the Danish Government to change the law. As a consequence of the Commission intervention, in 1984, the Danish Government amended the bottle law so as to allow the use of non-approved containers, either within well-defined limits (3000/hl per producer per annum) or to test the market, provided that in both cases a deposit-and-return system was established for the non-approved containers. The Commission was not satisfied with the 1984 amendments and in 1986 brought proceedings against Denmark to have both the compulsory deposit-and-return system and the NAPE approval system declared incompatible with Article 30 of the EC Treaty.

---

[24] Case 120/78 *Rewe-Zentral AG v. Bundesmonopolverwaltung für Branntwei*, (1979) **ECR** 649, 662.

[25] See, e.g., Case 125/81, *Commission v. United Kingdom*, (1983) **ECR** 203, 236: "whilst the protection of the health of animals is one of the matters justifying protection under Article 36, it must none the less be ascertained whether the machinery employed in the present case by the United Kingdom constitutes a measure which is disproportionate in relation to the objective pursued, on the ground that the same result may be achieved by means of less restrictive measures, or whether, on the other hand, ... such a system is necessary under Article 36."

[26] Case 302/86, *Commission v. Denmark*, (1988) **ECR** 4602.

With regard to the deposit-and-return system (i.e. the first aspect of the Danish legislation), the European Court of Justice found that, though it affected intra-Community trade, this system was:

> an indispensable element of a system intended to ensure the re-use of containers and therefore [...] necessary to achieve the aims pursued by the contested rules. That being so, the restrictions which it imposes on the free movement of goods cannot be regarded as disproportionate.

Hence, the returnable containers mandate was upheld as justified under the rule of reason. However, with regard to the NAPE approval system (i.e., the second aspect of the Danish measure), the Court found that by restricting the quantity of beer and soft drinks which could be marketed by a single producer in non-approved containers to 3000/hl a year Denmark had failed to fulfill its obligations under Article 30 of the Treaty. According to the Court:

> [t]he system for returning non-approved containers is capable of protecting the environment and, as far as imports are concerned, affects only limited quantities of beverage compared with the quantity of beverages consulted in Denmark owing to the restrictive effect which the requirement has on imports. In these circumstances, a restriction on the quantity of products which may be marketed is disproportionate to the objective pursued.

It is not easy to assess the potential impact of the *Danish Bottles* on the relationship between trade and environmental protection in the EC. On the one hand, some observers perceived that, by upholding the Danish deposit-and-return system, the Court of Justice gave a green light to pro-environment Member States to develop their own schemes of environmental protection even if at the expense of the unity of the Internal Market[27]. This freedom might in turn lead to a proliferation of inconsistent product standards with resulting risks of market fragmentation. On the other hand, the second part of the judgment, which deals with the NAPE approval system and the 3000/hl limit suggests that the Court of Justice is prepared to apply a certain degree of scrutiny to trade restrictive environmental measures.

The implications of the *Danish Bottles* Case are therefore rather uncertain. Although the Court of Justice made clear that environmental

---

[27] See, e.g., *The Freedom to be Cleaner than the Rest*, in: **The Economist**, October 14, 1989, p.21.

protection may, in certain circumstances, take precedence over the free movement of goods; the full extent of the Member States' regulatory discretion is not clearly limited. In this context, it will be the task of the Court in subsequent cases to better define the boundaries of Article 30 of the Treaty when this provision applies to environmental protection.

b) Harmonization of Member States Environmental Product Standards

Harmonization of environmental product standards has been seen by the EC as another instrument of prime importance in ensuring the free movement of products. Among the variety of harmonization strategies we have identified, the central focus of the EC has been on **uniform** standards. Since varying product requirements impede intra-Community trade, the adoption of uniform standards for all Member States has been perceived as the most effective method of ensuring unrestricted movement of products between Member States. Total harmonization regimes have, for example, been adopted in the areas of vehicle emission standards[28], chemical substances[29], pesticides[30], and batteries[31].

In a number of circumstances, the EC has, however, opted for other, less all-encompassing strategies of harmonization. In some areas of regulation, such as the regulation of noise-generating equipment[32], the EC has opted for **maximum** standards barring Member States from setting standards more stringent than the EC norm. As in the case of uniform standards, this strategy helps to eliminate barriers to trade by guaranteeing that a product which complies with the EC standard can circulate freely throughout the EC without fear of being held to more stringent national requirements. On the other hand, the adoption of maximum standards is often criticized as giving preference to economic interests

---

[28] See, e.g., Directive 94/62 amending Directive 70/220 on the measures to be taken against air pollution by gases from positive-ignition engines of motor vehicles, 1994 **OJ** L100/42.

[29] See, e.g., Directive 76/679 on the restrictions on the marketing and use of certain dangerous substances and preparations, 1976 **OJ** L262/201 and its amendments; Directive 67/548 on the classification, packaging and labelling of dangerous substances, 1967 **OJ** L196/1 and its amendment Directives.

[30] See, e.g., Directive 94/414 concerning the placing of plant protection products on the market, 1991 **OJ** L230/1; Directive 78/361 on the classification, packaging and labelling of dangerous preparation (pesticides), 1978 **OJ** L206/13.

[31] See Directive 91/157 on batteries and accumulators containing certain dangerous substances, 1991 **OJ** L365/14.

[32] See, e.g., Directive 84/534 on the permissible sound power level of tower cranes, 1984 **OJ** L300/130; Directive 84/533 on the permissible sound power level of compressors, 1984 **OJ** L300/123.

over environmental ones[33]. Under a regime bounded only by a "ceiling", Member States may indeed adopt less stringent national standards — perhaps creating pressure on others not to adopt strict standards.

The EC has also undertaken to harmonize certain forms of "pre-standards". For example, Directive 93/67 sets up an harmonized risk assessment procedure to be followed by manufacturers and importers for all new chemical substances they place on the market[34]. As noted above, such common procedures ease market entry for companies by ensuring that they do not have to carry out different tests and protocols for each of the Member States in which they want to market their substances. As expressly noted in the preamble to the directive, harmonized risk assessment procedures also guarantee baseline levels of public health and ecological protection throughout the EC.

In addition, in recent years, the EC has increasingly relied on a so-called "New Approach" to harmonization[35]. The central characteristic of this New Approach is that harmonization is limited to the adoption at the EC level of "essential requirements" necessary for ensuring the free movement throughout the Common Market of the product in question[36]. The task of drawing up detailed regulations, on the basis of those essential requirements, is left to European standardization organizations, such as the *Comité Européen de Normalisation* (CEN). If a product meets these specifications, it benefits from a presumption that it satisfies the EC's essential requirements and that it should be allowed to circulate freely throughout the EC. This New Approach avoids the need for the Community to have extremely detailed regulatory directives. It facilitates the decision-making process and allows the EC to move more quickly in the creation of an internal market.

---

[33] See, e.g., LOMAS, *"Environmental Protection, Economic Conflict and the European Community"*, in: **Mac Gill Law Journal** No.33, 1988, p.506.

[34] See Directive 93/67 laying down the principles for assessment of risks to man and the environment of substances notified in accordance with Council Directive 67/548, 1993 **OJ** L227/9. See also Regulation No.1488 laying down the principles for the assessment of risks to man and the environment of existing substances in accordance with Council Regulation No.793, 1994 **OJ** L161/3.

[35] The text of reference with regard to the "New Approach" is Council Resolution of May 7, 1985 on a New Approach to Technical Harmonization of Standards, 1985 **OJ** C136/1.

[36] The New Approach relies on the concept of "mutual recognition" according to which a product which is lawfully produced and marketed in one Member State must be admitted in another Member State except when the latter can refer to essential or mandatory requirements. See Case 120/78, *Rewe Zentral AG v. Bundesmonopolverwaltung für Branntwei*, (1978) **ECR** 649. The harmonization of those essential requirements would therefore be necessary and sufficient to ensure the free movement of goods throughout the Community.

Finally, in 1993, the EC adopted an eco-labelling scheme[37]. The scheme is designed to inform consumers about the environmental qualities products and to ensure that uniformly high levels of environmental performance are achieved by products bearing the eco-label. A Committee of Member States' representatives is in charge of adopting ecological criteria for a number of products. Once such criteria have been adopted for a specific product, competent bodies in each Member State assess individual applications by producers for a label and approve the use of the label by successful applicants. Contrary to the instruments described in the preceding paragraphs, the eco-label scheme does not really help to create an internal market. From a trade standpoint, one of the central weaknesses of the scheme is that it does not override the national eco-label schemes, such as the German Blue Angel or the Nordic Swan, which are entitled to operate alongside the EC eco-label. To satisfy consumer expectations, producers remain obliged to develop separate claims for label status for each Member State having an eco-label scheme.

If the EC harmonization process has been generally celebrated by free traders, it has often been criticized by environmentalists for leading to the adoption of sub-optimal standards. Environmentalists argue that, because of the complexity of the decision-making process and the existence of competing interests among Member States, EC harmonized standards often reflect the lowest common denominator. The Single European Act, which was adopted in 1986, introduced in the EC Treaty several provisions designed to address that concern. First, by replacing the traditional unanimity voting system by a system of qualified majority voting, Article 100A(1) has considerably simplified the decision-making process, thus helping the adoption of strict emission standards. Second, Article 100A(3) requires the Commission to "take as a base a high level of environmental protection" in its proposals concerning health, safety, environmental and consumer protection. Second, Article 100A(4) authorizes, in certain circumstances, Member States to apply more strict national standards than EC harmonized standards if they deem it necessary to protect the environment.

2. Competitiveness

Although the attention of the EC originally concentrated on the trade disruptive effects of environmental product standards, in recent years, the scope of EC efforts to minimize trade-environment tensions has

---

[37] Regulation No.880/92 on a Community eco-label award scheme, 1992 **OJ** L99/1.

grown. Member States have come to realize that deeper economic integration requires some degree of integration in other spheres such as environmental protection. There is also a growing awareness that wide variations in environmental process standards could have important trade effects. In particular, fears have grown that differences in pollution control requirements could generate distortions of competition and, hence, disrupt the functioning of the Common Market. The negative consequences of the distortions of competition created by inconsistent environmental process standards on the Common Market are abundantly illustrated in the preambles of related directives[38], Court of Justice judgments[39] and legal literature[40].

Against this background, the main approach used by the EC to address the distortions of competition that may be created by inconsistent environmental standards has been minimum harmonization of such standards[41]. The rationale for such an approach is that some variations in standards are legitimate and should be expected given the varying circumstances of the Member States. However, Member States with no environmental protection program or very low standards might well be seen as suffering from regulatory failure not careful matching of their standards to their circumstances. Minimum standards, moreover, reduce the pollution control cost disparities among and between Member States, narrowing the environmental-cost-based competitive advantage available to producers in low-standard jurisdictions. The adoption of minimum process standards while helping to maintain fair conditions for competition does not prevent any Member State from adopting more strict national standards.

---

[38] See, e.g., Directive 76/464 on pollution caused by certain dangerous substances discharged into the aquatic environment of the Community, 1976 **OJ** L129/23 ("(w)hereas any disparity between the provisions on the discharge of certain dangerous substances into the aquatic environment already applicable or in preparation in the various Member States may create unequal conditions of competition and thus directly affect the functioning of the common market.")

[39] See, e.g., Case C-300/89, *Commission v. Council*, (1991) **ECR** I-2867, 2901 ("provisions which are made necessary by considerations relating to the environment and health may be a burden upon the undertakings to which they apply and, if there is no harmonization of national provisions on the matter, competition may be appreciably distorted.")

[40] See, e.g., LOMAS, *supra*, note 33.

[41] See, e.g., Directive 87/217 on the prevention and reduction of environmental pollution by asbestos, 1987 **OJ** L85/40; Directive 80/778 relating to the quality of water intended for human consumption, 1980 **OJ** L229/11; Directive 78/176 on waste from the titanium dioxide industry, 1978 **OJ** L54/19; Directive 76/464 on pollution caused by certain dangerous substances discharged into the aquatic environment of the Community, 1976 **OJ** L129/23.

In certain circumstances, the EC has been forced to opt for alternative, more flexible, strategies of harmonization for production processes. For example, in Directive 88/609 for the regulation of air pollution from large combustion plants[42], the EC opted for a strategy of multi-tier harmonization, i.e., different rules applying to different groups of Member States. While Germany urged the adoption of strict minimum limits for SO_2 and NO_x from large combustion plants, consistent with its own unilaterally-adopted requirements, a number of other Member States, such as Greece, Ireland, Portugal and Spain, were concerned that strict emissions limits would have a negative impact on their industry and would generally impede their economic development. Directive 88/609 thus strikes a compromise. With regard to existing plants, the directive requires overall reductions of SO_2 and NO_x but with varying implementation dates. Not only are different reduction targets set, but a number of Member States, including Greece, Ireland and Portugal, are even authorized to increase their emissions for some period[43]. To increase the flexibility of this control regime, Member States have the discretion to allocate the permitted emissions among the various facilities within their territory[44]. With regard to new plants, Directive 88/609 establishes differentiated emission limits according to the size of the installation[45]. It also gives Spain special authorization, until 1999, to permit the entry into force of additional combustion plants[46]. Thus, ultimately a regime of minimum standards will be in place, protecting German industry from persistent, significant air pollution control cost disadvantages.

Additional controversy has emerged over what type of harmonization to pursue and whether standards should be differentiated not only on the basis of the level of development but also on the basis of differences in assimilative capacity of the ecosystem across Member States. The most extensive discussion over the choice of such techniques arose in the context of Directive 76/464 on water pollution caused by certain dangerous substances[47]. Directive 76/464 divides dangerous substances into two categories: a "black list" of substances considered to be dangerous for the aquatic environment and a "grey list" covering substances considered to have less harmful effects[48]. The point of contention in the

---

[42] 1988 **OJ** L336/1, amended by Directive 94/66, 1994 **OJ** L337/83.

[43] See Article 3 and Annexes I and II of the Directive.

[44] See Article 3.2.

[45] See Article 3.2.

[46] See Article 5.3.

[47] 1976 **OJ** L129/23.

[48] See lists I and II in the Annex of the Directive.

proposal originally made by the Commission concerned the control regime to be adopted with regard to black list substances. The Commission proposed specific effluent standards for each substance on the list. Those standards specified a level of maximum allowable emissions for each substance but did not take into account local environmental conditions.

All Member States agreed on the proposed method, except the United Kingdom, which proposed instead that ambient water quality standards be applied for the discharge of individual substances. Such standards would prescribe a level of water pollution which must not be exceeded, without specifying any maximum level of discharge by a particular industry. Harmonized ambient standards preserve the comparative advantage of industries located in regions that are less polluted or that are better able to absorb pollution. Hence, the use of water quality standards rather than effluent limits would allow the United Kingdom to exploit a locational advantage derived from its system of short, free-running rivers that permit water quality standards to be met in many locations even if industry is granted generous emissions permits.

The EC eventually opted for a strategy of harmonized options, whereby effluent standards would be the general rule but a Member State could, under strict conditions, opt for an alternative system of water quality standards[49]. The attitude taken by the United Kingdom during these negotiations was nevertheless severely criticized as self-interested and contrary to the requirements of a common market because it prevented equalization of the conditions of competition. On the other hand, the adoption of a system of effluent standards would have imposed costly burdens on the regions of the EC with waters having a high absorptive capacity and prevented them from exploiting their natural locational advantages.

The controversy over which regulatory technique should be used for the harmonization of industrial processes has never been totally resolved and has recently reappeared with force in the context of the negotiations over the proposed directive on integrated pollution prevention and control[50]. The objective of this directive, which contains the new EC strategy for the regulation of industrial processes, is the prevention of

---

[49] See Article 6 of the Directive.

[50] Common Position No.9/96 adopted by the Council on November 27, 1995 with a view to adopting Council Directive 96/_ concerning integrated pollution prevention and control, 1995 **OJ** C87/8.

industrial pollution at source. The directive sets up a prior authorization procedure whereby industrial installations would apply to the competent authority in the appropriate Member State for a permit to operate. The conditions of the permit would include emission limit values for the pollutant substances to be emitted from the installations authorized to operate.

As in the case of Directive 76/464, there existed a strong disagreement among Member States on how these limit values should be set. Certain Northern Member States argued that these limits should be fixed at the EC level on the basis of the "Best Available Techniques" or "BAT" (i.e. technology-based effluent standards). German industry and the German government insisted, in particular, on common technology requirements to ensure a level playing field across the EC. The German authorities wanted industries in other Member States to bear the costs of installing state-of-the-art pollution abatement technologies which German producers have already borne pursuant to strict domestic standards. On the other hand, Southern Member States and the United Kingdom argued that effluent limits should be adopted at the Member State level pursuant to more flexible environmental quality standards. These Member States suggested that ambient standards would permit them to take into account their environmental circumstances and, hence, their natural locational advantages.

The common position reached by the Council in November 1995 attempted to reconcile these competing positions. Emission limits in the permits granted by Member State authorities to the controlled installations would be:

> based on the best available techniques, without prescribing the use
> of any technique or specific technology, but by taking into account
> the technical characteristics of the installation concerned, its geo-
> graphical location and the local environmental conditions.[51]

This provision has been strongly criticized by the European Parliament on the ground that it will lead to different levels of environmental protection across in the EC[52]. In response to this criticism, the Environment Commissioner has, however, made clear that the Commission would not allow national permit authorities to abuse the flexibility built into this provision by setting low requirements designed to give local

---

[51] Article 9.4 of the common position.

[52] See *"Parliament Approves IPPC Proposal, Sends Measure to Council for Final Action"*, in: **International Environmental Report**, May 29, 1996, p.431.

companies a competitive advantage[53]. In this regard, the Commissioner indicated that she would not hesitate to propose uniform emission standards if it appeared that national authorities were failing to adopt appropriate pollution control standards.

The preceding paragraphs illustrate that there have been serious concerns in high-standard Member States about the cost differentials that arise from varying environmental process standards. By contrast, concerns that low standards in some Member States would create incentives for industrial relocation or trigger a race toward the bottom as high-standard countries were forced to roll back their environmental requirements to keep pace — the second and third types of competitiveness concerns we identified — have received less attention in the Community. As we discuss in Part IV, a number of reasons may be advanced to explain why the fear of industrial migration has not emerged in the EC with any real force.

It is more difficult to explain why the risk of a race toward the bottom arising from environmental cost differentials across jurisdictions has not been seen as a major issue in the EC. To the extent that Member States are concerned that high domestic environmental standards may affect the competitive position of their companies on domestic and international markets, a race toward the bottom could very well occur. In this regard, the negotiations of the *"Directive on Integration Pollution Prevention and Control"* have shown that there is a real concern in some Member States and EC institutions that some Member State authorities may seek to obtain competitive advantage by imposing inappropriately low standards on local companies. Though little data exist, it appears that high-standard Member States are increasingly reluctant to impose further pollution control efforts on their industries if comparable efforts are not being imposed in other Member States. This may explain, for example, why, despite pressure from environmental groups, pro-environment Member States such as Germany have, so far, hesitated to adopt energy taxation schemes to address climate change on a domestic basis.

Finally, it has been suggested that the strategy of harmonization has largely failed to ensure fair conditions of competition in the EC[54]. Though Member States are bound by similar or comparable standards, there are wide disparities in the levels of implementation and enforcement of such

---

[53] See *"Bjerregaard Defends Flexibility in IPPC Directive"*, in: **Environment Watch**, June 7, 1996, p.13.
[54] See VAN DEN BERG *et al., supra,* note 21.

standards among Member States. While a number of Member States, such as Germany, Denmark or the Netherlands, have established sophisticated implementation and enforcement mechanisms, others, such as Greece, Italy, Portugal or Spain, have failed to develop such mechanisms and generally have poor implementation and enforcement records. In general, the Commission is dependent on national environmental efforts. In fact, when the Commission learns that a Member State has not implemented or enforced EC standards, its only recourse beyond hortatory statements is to start legal proceedings against that Member State before the European Court of Justice, on a claim that the Member State in question has failed to comply with its obligations under EC law. This procedure is extremely slow and to date has proven to be a rather weak deterrent against slack environmental performance. In response, some commentators have suggested that the Commission play a more central role in implementation and enforcement. In the current political context, which is dominated by the principle of subsidiarity, it is, however, unlikely that the powers of the Commission will be increased in this respect.

B. NAFTA

1. Market Access

Two separate chapters deal with market access: Chapter 7B (sanitary and phytosanitary standards) and Chapter 9 (other technical barriers to trade, including environmental product standards). Each seeks to ensure the free movement of goods between Mexico, the United States and Canada.

One characteristic of NAFTA's market access provisions is their relative complexity and even seemingly contradictory requirements. For example, NAFTA guarantees each Party the right to set and maintain environmental health and safety standards consistent with the level of protection it alone deems appropriate (Article 715); but the agreement also mandates that such measures be based on scientific principles (Article 712). These provisions represent a compromise between two conflicting visions. Free traders argued that NAFTA should impose strict disciplines on standard setting by the Parties to ensure the unimpeded movement of goods among them. But environmentalists feared that such disciplines could be used to override legitimate environmental product standards. The NAFTA's market access provisions represent an effort to reconcile trade liberalization with environmentalist opposition to any relaxation of environmental standards.

A first discipline that is imposed on the Parties by Chapters 7B and 9 is that they should base their sanitary and phytosanitary rules and their environmental requirements more generally on international standards such as those adopted by the Codex Alimentarius Commission, the World Health Organization (WHO) and the International Standard Organization (ISO). Environmental regulations that conform with these international standards are presumed to be consistent with the market access disciplines imposed in Chapters 7B and 9. To respond to the environmentalist critique that international standards may be too low to ensure appropriate levels of environmental protection, Chapters 7B and 9 allow Parties to adopt, maintain or apply standards that are more stringent than international standards.

Chapter 7B recognizes that each Party is free to "establish its appropriate levels of protection"[55], subject to compliance with certain risk assessment procedures[56]. But, it imposes restrictive conditions on the type of standards that may be adopted. First, sanitary and phytosanitary standards must be "necessary" for the protection of human, animal or plant life or health[57] and can be applied only to the extent "necessary" to achieve the Parties' chosen level of protection[58]. Second, they must be "based on scientific principles" and "not maintained when there is no longer a scientific basis."[59] Third, sanitary and phytosanitary standards must not "arbitrarily or unjustifiably discriminate" against imported products "when identical or similar conditions prevail."[60] Finally, they must not create "disguised restrictions on trade between the Parties."[61]

Chapter 9 also recognizes the right of each Party to "establish the levels of protection that it considers appropriate."[62] This chapter, however, also imposes restrictive conditions on the type of standards that may be adopted. First, Chapter 9 provides that Parties should not apply standards that discriminate against products of other Parties[63]. It also provides that Parties may not prepare, maintain or apply standards "with a view toward or the effect of creating unnecessary obstacles to trade."[64]

---

[55] Article 712.2 of NAFTA.
[56] Article 715.3.
[57] Article 712.1.
[58] Article 712.5.
[59] Article 712.3.
[60] Article 712.4.
[61] Article 712.6.
[62] Article 904.2.
[63] Article 904.3.
[64] Article 904.4.

How well these provisions balance the need to ensure open markets with the goal of not overriding legitimate health, safety, and ecological programs is hotly contested. Trade commentators generally find the NAFTA to be a model for future regional trade agreements[65]. Other observers, especially some environmental analysts, are less impressed with the balance that has been struck[66].

2. Competitiveness

Concern about the possible competitiveness advantage of companies operating from Mexico, with its more lax environmental standards, was not the only trade-environment issue discussed during the NAFTA negotiations, but it got the most attention and generated the most political heat[67]. US environmentalists claimed that trade liberalization would cause industries to migrate from the United States to Mexico, attracted by Mexico's status as a "pollution haven". This migration would in turn increase the risks of pollution spillovers into the United States and fuel demands by US industry for lower US environmental standards.

NAFTA addresses these concerns in two different ways. First, NAFTA's investment chapter attempts to prevent Parties from lowering their environmental standards to attract investment. Specifically, NAFTA Article 1114 provides that:

> The Parties recognize that it is inappropriate to encourage investment by relaxing domestic health, safety or environmental measures. Accordingly, a Party should not waive or otherwise derogate from, or offer to waive or derogate from, such measures as an encouragement for the establishment, acquisition, expansion or retention in its territory of an investment or an investor. If a Party considers that another Party has offered such an encouragement, it may request consultations with the other Party and the two Parties shall consult with a view to avoiding any such encouragement.

There has been considerable debate over this "pollution haven" provision because where one Party believes another has induced investment

---

[65] See, e.g., ALTHAUS, *"Gore says NAFTA a Beginning; 'Community of Democracies' Seen for Hemisphere"*, in: **Houston Chronicle**, December 2, 1993 Section A, p.1.

[66] See, e.g., WALLACH, *"Hidden Dangers of GATT and NAFTA"*, in: **The Case Against Free Trade**, Earth Island Press, 1993.

[67] See ESTY, *"Making Trade and Environmental Policies Work Together: Lessons from NAFTA"*, in: CAMERON, DEMARET, GERADIN (eds), **Trade and Environment: The Search for Balance**, Cameron & May, 1994, p.373.

through a reduction in the rigor of its environmental program, the remedy provided by NAFTA is merely "consultations". These talks are to be undertaken "with a view of avoiding any such encouragement", but there is no threat of "snap back" tariffs, eco-duties, or other trade sanctions if consultations do not resolve the issue. Environmental critics of the NAFTA argued that this provision had no "bite" and would not deter Parties from pursuing strategies of competitive environmental deregulation. Ironically, many trade officials and some members of the business community expressed a contrary fear that this provision would open a potential protectionist point of attack on the NAFTA and would result in a flood of complaints, against US companies and practices[68].

As with other aspects of the NAFTA, this investment provision is ambiguous on key points. For example, the provision expressly mentions waiving or derogating from an existing law, but the meaning of "relaxing" environmental standards is not clear. Parties cannot provide waivers for the purpose of attracting investment, but can they relax enforcement? NAFTA Parties clearly remain free to lower their environment standards for purposes other than attracting or retaining investment. For example, they can relax their laws to overall increase export competitiveness[69].

Second, the North American Agreement on Environmental Cooperation (NAAEC), the NAFTA Environmental "Side Agreement", negotiated by the Clinton Administration with Canada and Mexico after the conclusion of NAFTA itself, has a number of provisions designed to try to ensure that Parties adequately enforce their environmental laws[70]. But, again, the negotiators had to balance the environmentalists' demands against fears that enforcement requirements might be captured by protectionists. The terms of NAAEC are thus diluted and contorted.

The Side Agreement established a trilateral North American Commission on Environmental Cooperation (NACEC)[71] designed to: (1) facilitate cooperation between the NAFTA countries on environmental issues;

---

[68] No such flood of cases has occurred.

[69] See CHARNOVITZ, *"The North American Free Trade Agreement: Green Law or Green Spin?"*, in: **Law & Policy International Business** No.25, 1994, p.1.

[70] See North American Free Trade Agreements: Treaty Materials, bklt.9, at 2, 36 (HOLBEIN & MUSCH (eds), 1994).

[71] North American Agreement on Environmental Cooperation between the Government of the United States of America, the Government of Canada, and the Government of the United Mexican States, September 13, 1993 in NAFTA, December 17, 1992 Con.-Mex.-US, 32 **ILM** 289, GOS (1993).

(2) serve as a forum for regular ministerial-level meetings; (3) provide an independent secretariat to report regularly on significant environmental issues confronting the NAFTA Parties; (4) ensure that environmental enforcement remains a priority in all three countries, including provision for an annual enforcement activity report; (5) coordinate with the trade officials in all three countries on any NAFTA-related environment issues; and (6) ensure that there are ample opportunities for public participation in the development and implementation of environmental laws and programs in all three NAFTA countries[72].

Any "persistent pattern of failure to effectively enforce" environmental laws or regulations can be brought to the NACEC for action[73]. The NACEC will accept complaints from Parties, individuals or non-governmental organizations and is charged with convening consultations to resolve disputes. If, however, no agreement is reached, a NAFTA Party may seek arbitration that could theoretically result in "monetary enforcement assessments"[74]. There are, however, several intervening steps that make the imposition of eco-duties most unlikely. In fact, in the three years since NAFTA went into effect, no "lack of enforcement" dispute has ever gone to arbitration much less resulted in penalties.

Of greater significance is the elaborate cooperative environmental programs established by both the United States and Canada with Mexico. In particular, the US Environmental Protection Agency (EPA) and Mexican environmental authorities developed an elaborate Integrated Border Environmental Plan and an action agenda of collaborative projects to implement it[75]. In addition to cooperative work under the Border Plan, a series of US-Mexican joint environmental efforts have been launched[76]. Hundreds of Mexican enforcement officials have participated in training programs in the United States. Thus, the essence of the NAFTA response to trade-environment tensions is found not in the Trade Agreement or even the Side Agreement but in the ongoing US and Canadian efforts to help Mexico enforce its own environmental laws.

---

[72] See Testimony of EPA Administrator Carol Browner before the US House Com. on Ways & Means, Sept. 4, 1993.

[73] NAFTA Side Agreement, Article 24.

[74] Side Agreement, Articles 35-6.

[75] See ESTY, *supra*, pp.376-78.

[76] See for example the work program developed under the US-Mexico-La Paz Agreement.

C. Comparative Analysis

1. Market Access

Regional trade agreements, like all trade liberalization efforts, focus on market access. The market access concerns outlined in Part I play a key role in both the Community and NAFTA systems. Both regimes seek to remove obstacles to trade, including the regulatory barriers that may be created by environmental standards. On the other hand, both the EU Treaty and NAFTA recognize that trade liberalization should not override legitimate environmental standards.

There are some important similarities between the Community and NAFTA approaches to trade-environment concerns. Both systems promote trade liberalization through a form of judicial bounding on environmental liberalization. The European Court of Justice has interpreted the prohibition contained in Article 30 of the EC Treaty extremely broadly to cover a large number of Member States measures, including environmental standards, affecting trade. Similarly, NAFTA Chapters 7B and 9 impose a set of disciplines designed to restrict the ability of NAFTA Parties to adopt environmental standards affecting trade. Both the EC and NAFTA market access disciplines rely on comparable legal concepts, such as the absence of discrimination between domestic and imported products and avoiding unnecessary obstacles to trade.

But the EC Treaty and NAFTA also contain language designed to ensure that legitimate environmental standards are not systematically sacrificed at the altar of trade liberalization. For example, Article 36 of the EC Treaty allows Member States to adopt trade restrictive measures to protect human, animal, and plant life. This provision could be used to justify a number of environmental product standards such as standards prohibiting products containing hazardous substances. Moreover, in the *Danish Bottles* Case, the European Court of Justice made clear that, to the extent they are proportionate, trade-restrictive environmental products standards, such as standards regulating the packaging of products, will be deemed legitimate under the rule of reason. The NAFTA provisions assuring Parties the right to choose the level of public health and ecological protection they desire and to adopt environmental requirements more strict than international standards provide similar assurances. In combination with the overriding objective of preserving sustainable development found in the Preamble and the investment provisions designed to blunt regulatory races toward the bottom, these "environmental" elements of NAFTA led the former EPA Administrator to call NAFTA the "greenest" trade agreement ever drafted[77].

Beyond judicial bounding, the approach to environmental protection varies quite considerably between the EC and NAFTA. In the EC, harmonization of product standards has emerged as another central tool to address market access concerns. As a result, a large number of harmonization directives have emerged from Brussels and a growing institutional structure supports the development of an EC supranational environmental law and regulatory system.

For several reasons, the creators of NAFTA did not pursue harmonization as a primary response to trade-environment tensions. First, NAFTA does not aim to achieve the deep level of economic integration envisioned by the Community. As a number of observers have noted, the deeper the economic integration sought, the deeper the integration that must be pursued in other realms such as environmental policy. In addition, in contrast to the EC Treaty, NAFTA does not create a set of institutions with broad regulatory powers. Second, at the time NAFTA was negotiated, US and Canadian environmentalists strongly opposed harmonization[78]. They shared the belief that US and Canadian environmental standards represented the highest levels of environmental protection and that any harmonization with Mexican standards would compromise domestic environmental protection[79].

This confidence (some might say arrogance) of the US and Canadian environmental communities resulted in a NAFTA focus on preserving national environmental policy prerogatives, not the creation of a new supranational environmental authority[80]. From an environmental perspective, this strategic choice appears to have been mistaken. Regardless of the standard set, many environmental problems go unattended to due to a lack of resources and meek commitment to policy development, implementation, and enforcement. NAFTA does little to supplement the

---

[77] See William Reilly quotation in Sector tells Bush to act on anxieties over NAFTA, **Financial Times**, August 12, 1992, p.4.

[78] See, in particular, the diatribes from Public Citizen decrying the threat of preemption of US environmental law.

[79] Fears of downward harmonization could have been dealt with by focusing on the adoption of minimum standards under NAFTA.

[80] See, in particular, the diatribes from Public Citizen decrying the threat of preemption of US environmental law.

existing national regulatory systems and represents a missed opportunity to advance the environmental cause[81].

2. Competitiveness

Fueled by Ross Perot's accusations that NAFTA would result in a "giant sucking sound" as factories and jobs moved to Mexico[82], there has been considerable concern in the United States about the impact of NAFTA on the competitiveness of US industry. An active coalition of anti-NAFTA labor and environmental[83] interests made fears about the disadvantage US industry would suffer in a unified North American marketplace, given Mexico's purportedly more lax environmental rules, the central trade-environment focus in the NAFTA debate. This concern played a major role in the broader political process surrounding NAFTA. The US Trade Representative made a major effort to win over environmental skeptics[84], EPA officials testified dozens of times before House and Senate Committees about NAFTA and the Environmental Side Agreement, and every discussion of the merits of the treaty included some consideration of the environmental competitiveness issue[85].

The investment provisions designed to deter shifts to pollution havens and the Side Agreement provisions on enforcement, discussed above, were introduced primarily to address these fears. The outgoing US and Canadian efforts to reinforce Mexico's regulatory capacity are also aimed at blunting the potential differences in environmental compliance costs that might induce industrial relocation or trigger a race toward the bottom. These provisions represent some of the most novel parts of the NAFTA. Indeed, there are no corresponding aspects in the EC Treaty. As investment flows become a more significant dimension of what is meant by an open market, these provisions may take on an even greater significance[86].

---

[81] Mexico, as noted earlier, has received some institutional reinforcement, but largely due to environmental programs running in parallel with the NAFTA, not because of the agreement *per se*.

[82] See, e.g., *"Free Trade, Faster Change"*, in: **Washington Post**, October 11, 1992, p.C7.

[83] Note that ultimately a significant number of US environmental groups supported NAFTA. See ESTY, *supra*, p.28 for an explanation of how NAFTA divided the US environmentalist community into "sustainable development" environmentalists who were pro-NAFTA and a "limits to growth" faction who opposed the agreement.

[84] See, e.g., HUFBAUER & SCHOTT, **North American Free Trade: Issues and Recommendations,** 1992.

[85] See ESTY, *supra*.

[86] See, e.g., the OECD effort to draft a Multilateral Agreement on Investment and the mounting pressure to include environmental provisions.

In contrast, competitiveness concerns have not been at the forefront of the EC policy debate. This is probably due to the fact that, even though competitiveness pressures exist in the Community context, these pressures have never raised the fear of major industry migration. It may also be due to the fact that there is no true "Europolitics". Broad policy issues, such as competitiveness, are generally discussed by EC bureaucrats rather than politicians and the public. As a result, although a debate exists in the Community over competitiveness, it is less passionate and public than in the NAFTA context. Moreover, interest groups are generally less analytically sophisticated and, therefore, less powerful in the EC than in the United States. EC environmental groups, in particular, have done little to raise concerns about competitiveness impacts on the environmental policy-making process.

To the extent that competitiveness concerns arise in the EC, they have generally focused on the issue of distortions of competition. Member States with high environmental process standards, Germany in particular, fear that such standards may represent a competitive disadvantage to their companies compared with the companies located in low standards Member States, such as the Southern countries. By contrast, in NAFTA, almost all the attention focused on the issue of industrial migration and the race toward the bottom. As we have seen, US environmentalists feared that less demanding standards would attract US industry to Mexico and that the threat of industrial relocation would force the United States to lower its environmental standards to prevent such migration.

Several questions must be answered to understand why the competitiveness issue took such different forms in the EC and NAFTA. Why has the prospect of environmental cost differentials leading to industrial migration and a race toward the bottom been less significant, or at least perceived as less significant, in the EC than in the NAFTA? Why has the focus in the EC context been on preventing distortions of competition, such as lost market shares or profits, rather than on other dimensions of the competitiveness problem?

Five factors seem to make industrial relocation less likely to occur in the EC than in the NAFTA context. First, because environmental standards tend to be less stringent in the EC than in the United States, environmental compliance costs represent a more modest fraction of the total cost structure for European companies. The potential gains of moving to low-standard jurisdictions are less significant for European companies than for American companies, reducing the threat of industrial relocation.

Second, in the EC, differences in environmental standards between high-standard EC countries, such as Germany and the Netherlands, and low-standard countries, such as Spain and Portugal, appear to be smaller than the differences in the stringency of standards between the United States or Canada, which have very high standards, and Mexico, which has less strict or poorly enforced standards. As a result, from a compliance costs standpoint, the potential gains that a German company can realize by moving to Spain are less significant than the gains that an American firm can realize by moving to Mexico.

Third, in the EC, there are a number of legal obstacles to migration that do not exist in the United States. For example, in most European countries, high severance pay and long-term notice must be given to workers by companies that close a production plant. To the extent that they render plant closures extremely difficult, such obstacles generally increase the transaction costs, and hence reduce the attractiveness, of moving from one European country to another one.

Fourth, the quality of transport and telecommunications infrastructure varies considerably among European countries. Infrastructure is generally far superior in the Northern Member States. The risk of problems in getting products to market mitigates against industry migration in the EC. This problem is less significant in NAFTA where production facilities can be located on the US-Mexico border. Products manufactured on the border can be relatively easily shipped to the major markets in the United States.

Finally, differences in legal systems, administrative traditions and language across the EC considerably increase the "search costs" for companies contemplating an intra-Europe relocation in pursuit of lower pollution control costs. In the NAFTA context, companies need only explore one alternative market, and information on Mexican standards is generally easy to obtain.

As discussed above, it is more difficult to explain why the risk of a race toward the bottom has not been seen as a major issue in the EC. The lack of real fear of industrial relocation has certainly been a factor limiting the gains that a Member State could anticipate from any attempt to relax environmental requirements. To the extent that Member States **are** concerned that high environmental standards may affect the competitiveness of their industries, a race toward the bottom could be triggered. Some recent events, such as the negotiations of the draft *"Directive on Integrated Pollution Prevention and Control"*, tend to demonstrate that they are circumstances where Member States are prepared to act strate-. gically. There are also a number of factors that indicate that a race-to-ward-the-bottom dynamic is likely to become a more serious concern in the EC. First, the completion of the Internal Market will intensify competition in the EC and, hence, put pressure on any cost difference across Member States. Second, the possible integration in the EC of a new set of countries from Eastern and Central Europe with poor environmental records, may exacerbate the fear of competitiveness pressures in the high-standard Member States.

There are three reasons why the concern that differences in the stringency of environmental standards would create distortions of competition and redistribution of market shares and profits has been more significant in the EC than in NAFTA.

First, while European companies usually face strong competition from companies located in other Member States, most US industries face relatively little competition from Mexican companies. Because many European companies operate in a number of EC Member States, more European companies face competition as a result of the EC than American ones as a result of NAFTA.

Second, the size of the Mexican economy, which is about one twentieth the size of the US economy, makes competition from Mexico unlikely to shift the competitive dynamics of most US markets. Any Mexican participation in the market is dwarfed by the pressure of other US importers. In contrast, no EC Member State has a dominant share of the European market, so EC companies often face significant intra-Community competition and even more significant potential competition.

Finally, many US companies saw NAFTA as an opportunity, not as a threat. Many large US firms set up facilities in Mexico to take advantage of lower production costs. The American auto industry, for example, welcomed the opportunity for co-production with Mexican facilities as a way of lowering their costs and making their vehicles more competitive in the North American and export markets. Some European companies are siting facilities across Europe to take advantage of such differential circumstances, but not many.

In addition to the differences in the nature of the concerns, significant variance can be seen in the responses by the EC and NAFTA to these concerns. The EC reaction to competitiveness pressures has centered on harmonization of standards in various ways. The NAFTA response to the same issue has been a commitment to strengthened enforcement of

national environmental standards. As a result, a significant EC environmental infrastructure, involving about three hundred officials, has been developed in Brussels and Copenhagen. This institutional commitment to the environment has proven to be important and has fostered the development of a growing body of EC environmental law. In the NAFTA, the transnational institutional commitment has been far more modest. The NACEC in Montreal has a staff of just a few dozen people. But the focus on enforcement and implementation of environmental commitments has been far stronger in the US-Mexico-Canada context than in the EC one.

The EC's emphasis on adopting supranational environmental rules has paid important dividends, but the EC's impact on actual environmental quality has been quite limited in some countries due to a lack of focus on implementation. Likewise, the limited institutional commitment in the NAFTA has constrained the potential environmental gains. A trade agreement that incorporated **both** law-building and enforcement/implementation strategies would be probably even more successful.

PART IV: TRADE AND ENVIRONMENT
IN THE WTO CONTEXT

Environmental issues have become a major preoccupation in the World Trade Organization (WTO). The WTO's Committee on Trade and Environment (CTE) has been meeting regularly to try to identify ways to lessen the tension between trade liberalization and environmental protection[87]. Reviewing the progress of the CTE will be a first-tier agenda item at the WTO Ministerial Conference in Singapore in December 1996. WTO Director-General Ruggierio has declared "trade and environment" to be one of the WTO's central post-Uruguay Round challenges.

Although five years have passed since the 1991 panel decision finding a US ban on the import of tuna products caught in a manner harmful to dolphins inconsistent with the principles of the international trading system[88], there has been little progress in making trade and environmental policies more mutually reinforcing. Environmentalists, who at the time of the "tuna dolphin" decision ran large advertisements in US newspapers

---

[87] For a full review of the CTE's efforts see the WTO website on the Worldwide Web.

[88] US-Restrictions on the Imports of Tuna, August 16, 1991, reprinted in **ILM** 1594 (1991).

decrying the threat from *"GATTzilla"*[89] and raising the specter of GATT disciplines systematically undermining national efforts to promote environmental protection, continue to raise questions about and to block in some cases further liberalized trade. In fact, the *Tuna/Dolphin* Case and other "trade and environment" incidents[90] have generated a wide-ranging policy debate, involving scholars, politicians, interest groups and international organizations, about the relationship between trade and environmental protection in the context of world trade rules[91].

The interface between global trade and environmental protection policies reflects both the market access and competitiveness concerns found in regional trade systems. Market access questions have always been at the heart of multilateral trade negotiations. Article III's national treatment clause prohibits WTO Members from adopting standards that discriminate against products from other members. Because of the major tariff reductions achieved over the last four decades, "non-tariff barriers" to trade, including environmental product standards, are now seen by many as the most significant obstacle to trade liberalization. The Uruguay Round Agreement considerably strengthened the disciplines contained in the Technical Barriers to Trade Agreement (the TBT Agreement) and has added a set of protection against trade-inhibiting Sanitary and Phytosanitary Standards (the SPS Agreement). But these new disciplines have also been seen by environmentalists as posing a threat to the freedom of states to adopt and enforce the environmental standards they deem appropriate.

Of course, the WTO also contains language designed to safeguard legitimate environmental regulations. In fact, GATT Articles XX(b) and (g) authorize the adoption of trade restrictive measures to further certain categories of legitimate environmental objectives. The TBT and SPS Agreements also contain language designed to preserve the freedom of WTO Members to adopt national legitimate environmental standards.

---

[89] See ESTY, *supra*, p.34.

[90] See, e.g., the EC ban on USD beef containing hormones, the US threat to the import of European wines revealing traces of the unlicensed pesticide procymidone, the US sanctions imposed on Taiwan for failing to control illicit trade in tiger bones and rhino parts in violation of the Convention on International Trade in Endangered Species (CITES), the Community challenge to the US fleetwide Corporate Average Fuel Economy (CAFE) mileage requirements for automobiles and the Venezuelan GATT case brought against the reformulated gasoline regulations issued under the US Clean Air Act. For a discussion of these trade and environment incidents, see ESTY, *supra*.

[91] See ESTY, *supra*.

In contrast to the EC, the WTO does not attempt to harmonize environmental product standards. Like Chapters 7B and 9 of NAFTA, the TBT and SPS Agreements merely urge WTO Members to base their own requirements on international standards. The weakness of this approach is that there are many substantive areas where standards have not been harmonized and tensions remain. A number of bilateral initiatives have, therefore, recently been initiated to develop transatlantic standards or at least some convergence between major trade partners. For example, two US government agencies have proposed the creation of an international forum to harmonize environmental and safety regulations for automobile engines. This would be done by extending an existing UN Economic Commission for Europe (UN/ECE) working party on vehicle construction[92]. Similarly, the EC Commission has proposed that the EC align its emission standards for non-road motor vehicles with US standards, so as to create a large transatlantic market in such vehicles[93].

As markets become global in scope, pressure for worldwide standards to facilitate access will increase. The adoption of identical standards may not be a feasible, or even desirable, objective. Looser forms of harmonization may, however, be appropriate. For example, the "essential requirements" (also known as "New Approach") harmonization strategy used in the EC could provide a useful precedent. As we have seen, the central characteristic of this approach is that harmonization is limited to the adoption of "essential requirements". The task of drawing up, on the basis of these essential requirements, the detailed specifications that must be respected by products is left to European standardization organizations. *Mutatis mutandis*, under the auspices of the WTO, high-level officials from Member countries might undertake to reach agreements on the essential requirements of selected products. Technical expert groups in the pertinent standardization organizations (ISO, Codex Alimentarius, etc.) might then undertake to draft standards that fulfill such requirements. To answer the traditional critique from environmentalists, that the work of international standardization organizations does not sufficiently take into account environmental considerations, one could imagine a system whereby such organizations would work under the supervision of a committee of independent environmental experts or even under the auspices of United Nations Environmental Program (UNEP).

---

[92] See *"Car Makers Search for Common Environmental Standards"*, in: **Europe Environment**, July 19, 1996, p.6.

[93] See *"Transatlantic Norms Agreed on for Mobile Machinery Emissions"*, in: **Environment Watch**, April 16, 1996, p.14.

The competitiveness effects of differential environmental requirements has also become a central issue in the WTO. In recent years, industry groups in industrialized nations have increasingly complained about what they perceive as unfair competition from low-standard developing nations[94]. These groups asked their governments to retaliate to level the playing field. Environmentalists also fear that competition from low-standard nations may trigger a race toward the bottom that will reduce environmental protection in high standards nations. To address these concerns, some policy analysts have argued for the opening of a new "green round" of multilateral trade negotiations to address competitiveness issues[95].

So far, the WTO has failed to address these competitiveness concerns and, indeed, many WTO officials dismiss competitiveness as a non-issue. The Tuna/Dolphin decision and the GATT 1992 trade and environment report[96] make clear that eco-duties and other forms of process-related trade restrictions are antithetical to the GATT true believers. This hostility cannot come as a surprise given the GATT's emphasis on market access and trade liberalization. But it is regrettable that the WTO does not recognize the need to strike an appropriate balance between trade and environmental protection goals. We believe that the rules of international trade must be structured in a way that recognizes that transboundary pollution spillovers and competitiveness-driven environmental policy dynamics that leave all the parties in sub-optimal positions threaten market failure in the international economic system.

If further worldwide economic integration is to occur, the WTO or entities working in conjunction with the WTO will have to develop mechanisms that permit a greater degree of environmental policy integration. Harmonization of environmental process standards is generally dismissed by economists on the ground that differences in local economic and geographical conditions would make harmonization highly inefficient. But the EC experience teaches that differences in local conditions can be taken into account through flexible harmonization strategies. Minimum standards, multi-tier harmonization, differential standards based on ambient exposure limits, or the establishment of common essential requirements are likely to prove more useful than rigid uniform

---

[94] See KOENIG, *"Experts Fear 'Eco-Dumping' by Nations with Less-stringent Environmental Laws"*, in: **New York Times**, March 27, 1996, Sec.A, p.4.

[95] See SABECOFF, **A New Name for Peace: International Environmentalism, Sustainable Development and Democracy**, 1996.

[96] GATT Secretariat, *Trade and Environment Report*, 1992.

standards[97]. These techniques balance the need to prevent a counterproductive race toward the bottom with the efficiency gains of allowing jurisdictions to exploit their natural advantages and different circumstances. The NAFTA experience also provides some useful guidance — demonstrating the value of a commitment to environmental enforcement and implementation in parallel with any effort to liberalize trade.

CONCLUSION

In this paper, we have identified two sets of concerns arising from the parallel pursuit of trade liberalization and environmental protection in the context of regional trade agreements. A first set of concerns relates to the issue of market access. On the one hand, free traders worry that environmental **product** standards may act as barriers to trade. Conversely, environmentalists fear that market access disciplines adopted in the context of trade agreements could be used to override environmental standards and might lead to a downward harmonization of such standards. A second set of concerns relates to the issue of competitiveness. Environmental advocates fear that inappropriate environmental differences in the stringency of environmental **process** standards may create distortions of competition, industrial relocation and a race toward the bottom.

We have identified a variety of responses that can be used to address these "trade and environment" concerns. The nature and characteristics of these responses vary considerably ranging from a *"laissez-faire"* approach to differences in environmental standards among jurisdictions to total harmonization of such standards.

In looking at the EC and NAFTA, we see that in both cases "trade and environment" concerns have been at the center of policy debates. Market access concerns have been a focus in both legal orders. In the EC, such concerns have been addressed through a mix of judicial bounding and harmonization of environmental product standards. The NAFTA has also relied on judicial bounding to address such concerns. By contrast, because of the lack of a proper institutional framework and the opposition of US and Canadian environmentalists, little attempt has been made in the NAFTA to harmonize product standards.

---

[97] The Montreal Protocol's different CFC phaseout timetables provides an example of how a multi-tier regime might work.

Competitiveness concerns have been particularly central in the NAFTA context. Environmental and industry interest groups raised the fear that cost differentials arising from varying levels of stringency of environmental product standards could lead to industrial relocation and a race toward the bottom. The risk of industrial relocation and a race toward the bottom has not received great attention in the EC. High-standard Member States have, however, expressed the fear that environmental cost differentials could give a competitive disadvantage to their industries compared with industries located in Member States enforcing less strict standards. The EC has addressed such distortions of competition through harmonization of environmental process standards. The effectiveness of this strategy of harmonization has, however, been reduced by the lack of proper implementation and enforcement procedures in some Member States. In contrast, NAFTA has not attempted to harmonize environmental process standards. Strengthened national enforcement and implementation of environmental commitments has been the focus in NAFTA.

Market access and competitiveness concerns have also received considerable attention at the WTO level. Because free traders fear that environmental standards may emerge as a new kind of non-tariff barrier, much of the WTO focus has been on disciplines on environmental regulations. Conversely, environmentalists have expressed the concern that the market access disciplines contained in the WTO might be used to challenge legitimate environmental standards. The WTO has addressed market access concerns through judicial bounding — the well-developed dispute panel process. As in the case of NAFTA, and contrary to the EC, the WTO does not attempt to harmonize product standards. But the globalization of product markets and the desire for deeper international economic integration may make some form of global harmonization necessary in the future.

Competitiveness pressures arising from environmental cost differentials have received attention in the WTO. Industries located in high-standard countries increasingly feel that they face unfair competition from industries located in low-standard countries. Environmentalists also fear that pollution created by lax production methods in such countries could threaten the global environment. But, to date, the WTO has done little to address these concerns. As the tuna dolphin decision makes clear, process-related environmental trade restrictions are contrary to the GATT as it is currently interpreted. Unfortunately, the WTO has failed to provide any alternative solutions to the competitiveness concerns. In this regard, the WTO could learn from both the EC and NAFTA experiences.

The EC experience demonstrates that differences in circumstances can be accommodated through flexible strategies of harmonization. The NAFTA illustrates that a focus on implementation and enforcement of local standards could also lessen competitiveness pressures and provide for a better environment.

Environmental issues are ineluctably linked to trade liberalization. Trade agreements that address the linkage expressly are more likely to achieve appropriate accommodation with environmental objections — and will likely prove to be more durable.

Towards an Equitable Relation between Trade and Environment: The EC, NAFTA and WTO Compared

Wybe Th. DOUMA & Mark JACOBS

Lecturer, Department of European and Economic Law,
University of Groningen

Research Fellow, T.M.C. Asser Instituut,
Institute for International Law, The Hague

Introduction

After having been neglected for many years, the discussion on trade and environment issues under world trade law started at the beginning of the nineties[1]. The developments within the European Community (EC)[2] and North American Free Trade Agreement (NAFTA) form an interesting reference point for a debate on the relationship between trade liberalization and environmental protection. Depending on the level of integration pursued, there are valuable lessons to be learned from both

---

[1] See for example S. CHARNOVITZ, *"Environmental Exceptions in GATT Article XX"*, in: **Journal of World Trade**, vol.25, No.5, 1991, pp.37-55, P.A.G. VAN BERGEIJK, *"International Trade and the Environmental Challenge"*, in: **Journal of World Trade**, vol.25, No.6, 1991, pp.105-115, and the GATT Report *"Trade and the Environment"*, Geneva, 1992.

[2] Like Esty & Geradin, we will also refer to the European Community (EC) instead of the European Union (EU). It should be noted that the first, intergovernmental pillar consists not only of the EC but also comprises the European Atomic Energy Community (Euratom) and the European Coal and Steal Community (ECSC).

regional integration processes where trade and environment issues are concerned[3].

The paper by Esty & Geradin offers a good illustration of this debate[4]. The authors provide an excellent analysis of the concerns of both free trade advocates and environmentalists while also examining responses which aim at integrating environmental concerns and liberalization of trade. They start off by sketching the existing concerns and summarizing the high variety of possible responses, ranging from a *laissez faire* approach, trade restrictions, subsidies, and judicial bounding, to various forms of harmonization. After that, they explore the developments within the European Community and NAFTA in this respect. In the case of the EC they describe how a mixture of judicial bounding and harmonization of environmental standards is employed. As for NAFTA, judicial bounding is relied upon. Their conclusion is that the WTO could learn from the experiences within the EC as well as NAFTA.

This article is not a mere reaction to their paper. It is meant to be supplementary by presenting some recent developments on the issues that Esty & Geradin have dealt with. In addition, some other topics which are felt to be of importance in the debate on trade and environment within the European Union, NAFTA and WTO are touched upon. For instance, it will be submitted that principles of environmental law, like the ones codified in the EC Treaty and NAFTA, are of essential importance to striking a just balance between trade and environment interests through judicial bounding. Another topic touched upon is public participation.

Part A of this paper discusses trade and environment issues within the EC. On the topic of judicial bounding, some judgments of the European Court of Justice other than the *Danish Bottles* Case will be scrutinized. As for the topic of harmonization, Esty & Geradin pointed out that the EC's flexible harmonization strategies could be an alternative for total harmonization in situations where differences in circumstances exist. We will discuss some possible disadvantages to this flexible approach, notably where the so-called "essential requirements" are concerned. In

---

[3] See for example Ernst-Ulrich PETERSMANN, **International and European Trade and Environmental Law after the Uruguay Round**, Kluwer Law International, London/The Hague/Boston, 1995; and, Martin HESSION & Richard MACRORY, *Balancing Trade Freedom with the Requirements of Sustainable Development*, in: Nicolas EMILIOU & David O'KEEFFE (eds), **The European Union and World Trade Law after the GATT Uruguay Round**, John Wiley & Sons Ltd., Chisester/New York/Brisbane/Toronto/Singapore, 1996, pp.181-217.

[4] *Trade and Environmental Protection in Regional Trade Agreements: The European Community and NAFTA*, October 1996.

addition, some comments are made on the way in which the EC Treaty provides Member States with strict environmental standards with the opportunity to hold on to their high standards in spite of harmonization.

Part B deals with NAFTA and the way in which it links the two policies aims trade liberalization and environmental protection. The system of judicial bounding will be discussed extensively, as well as the American legislation implementing the NAFTA Agreement.

In Part C we examine some of the latest developments within the framework of the WTO. First of all, the results of the Ministerial Conference of the WTO in Singapore in December 1996 where environmental issues are concerned will be discussed as well as the work of the Dispute Settlement Body in reports on Trade-Related Environmental Measures (TREMs). Another important subject discussed in this part is the legitimacy of trade restrictions taken pursuant to Multilateral Environmental Agreements (MEAs). Throughout this part, comparisons will be made with the two regional trade organizations discussed above. Finally, in Part D we present our conclusions.

A. *The European Community*

1. Introduction

In order to understand the functioning of the European Community (EC), first some comments on its basic goals and tasks will be made. The EC is based on a customs union, but it comprises far more. It also envisages the establishment of a common market, which should have been completed by December 31, 1969[5]. In this common market, the economies of the participating states are to be integrated by ensuring a free movement of goods, capital, services and persons (the "four freedoms"). To achieve this goal, the treaty itself laid down prohibitions with a very broad scope such as the one on quantitative trade barriers (Article 30)[6]. Where differences in national laws which were justified under Article 36 or the "rule of reason" existed, harmonization measures were to be adopted.

In an attempt to give a new impetus to the process of integration, the Commission in June 1985 published the White Paper[7] in which it outlined

---

[5] Article 8(7) of the original EEC Treaty, now Article 7(7) EC Treaty. It proved to be impossible to fully establish the Common Market by the prescribed time-table.

[6] The basic judgment in this respect is the *Dassonville* Case 8/74, [1974] **ECR** 837.

[7] COM(85) 310 final.

some 300 harmonizing measures which were to be adopted by December 31, 1992 in order to achieve what was now called an internal market[8]. The project succeeded in boosting the integration process, *inter alia* because the harmonization measures related to the Internal Market from then on could be adopted by qualified majority (Article 100A) instead of via unanimity voting (as was the case under Article 100). Thus, the Internal Market has created conditions which are similar to those inside a domestic market.

2. Primary EC Law

EC's Task

In the original EEC Treaty from 1957, protection of the environment was not mentioned. Nevertheless, the Community has developed a substantive set of rules on this subject since the beginning of the seventies, including a separate title on this subject in the EC Treaty itself[9]. Interestingly enough, this was made possible at first by interpreting the official goal of economic expansion as expressed in Article 2 EEC Treaty in such a way, that it also covered qualitative aspects such as the protection of the environment[10]. This line of reasoning resembles the concept of sustainable development which became well known through the report of the Brundtland Commission from 1987[11].

The Treaty on the European Union from 1992 codified the commitment to environmental protection by amending the article which sets out the EC's tasks. Strangly enough, Article 2 does not refer to "sustainable development" but to "sustainable and non-inflationary growth respecting the environment" which seems to be a somewhat weaker expression. It is doubted whether the difference in wording has any legal significance[12]. If the present Intergovernmental Conference would follow the suggestions to amend Article 2 by referring to the more common

---

[8] This new notion of an internal market was inserted in the EEC Treaty via the Single European Act as of July 1st, 1987.

[9] There exist over 300 EC directives and regulations which deal with all aspects of the protection of the environment.

[10] Paris Summit of October 19-20, 1972, **Bulletin EC** 1972, No.10 and Declaration of November 22, 1973, **OJ** 1973 C 112/1.

[11] World Commission on Environment and Development, **Our Common Future**, Oxford University Press, Oxford, 1987.

[12] See J.H. JANS, **European Environmental Law**, Kluwer Law International, The Hague/London/Boston, 1995, p.6; and, Ludwig KRÄMER, **EC Treaty and Environmental Law**, (2nd ed.), Sweet & Maxwell, London, 1995, p.63.

expression sustainable development[13], the Member States would definitely show a more wholehearted commitment than back in 1992.

The Title on the Environment

The title on environment policies consists of Articles 130R, S and T. Article 130S is to be used as a legal basis for measures which primarily aim at the protection of the environment[14]. In Article 130R(1), a number of objectives of environmental policy is expressed[15]. Article 130R(2) describes the environmental principles which the EC is to use as a basis for its action[16]. As we will show below, the principles are not only political aspirations but they have a legal significance in the process of judicial bounding as well. One particular focus point of this paper will be the precautionary principle, which influences the way in which the onus of proof of the necessity of environmental measures is set. It can thus determine the outcome of judicial bounding.

In the following Article 130R(3), it is stipulated *inter alia* that the Community in action relating to the environment shall take account of environmental conditions in the various regions of the Community and the economic and social development of the Community as a whole and the balanced development of its regions. In Part A.3 on harmonization within the EC, the way in which these conditions play a role in secondary EC law will be illustrated using the example of the Directive on Packaging and Packaging Waste. The same directive will also show how the New Approach of harmonization and the so-called essential requirements can look in practice.

---

[13] *Dublin II Treaty Draft*, December 5, 1996, Conf. 2500/96. See also R. HALLO (ed.), **Greening the Treaty II**, Stichting Natuur en Milieu, Utrecht, 1995; and, European Environmental Bureau, **Memorandum to the Dutch Presidency and the EU Member States**, Brussels, 1997. All these documents can be found on the European Environmental Law homepage, [http://www.eel.nl].

[14] By contrast, Article 100A is to be used when the functioning of the Internal Market forms the primary aim of an EC measure. The legal base is of importance to the decision-making procedure; only under Article 100A does the European Parliament have a veto right for instance.

[15] These objectives are preserving, protecting and improving the quality of the environment, protecting human health, prudent and rational utilization of natural resources and promoting measures at the international level to deal with regional or global environmental problems.

[16] The principles are a high level of protection, precaution, prevention, rectification at source, the polluter pays and integration. The latter principle requires that environmental protection requirements must be integrated into the definition and implementation of other Community policies.

Article 100A on the Internal Market

Since the Single European Act, the word environment also appears in Article 100A on the Internal Market, where it is stipulated that the Commission is to take as a base a high level of environmental protection[17]. This provision does not ensure that the adopted legislation will aim at the highest possible level of protection of the environment, or at the highest level which one or more Member States already employ. The fact that the Member States no longer have a veto right does not necessarily ensure the adoption of strict environmental standards, as Esty & Geradin seem to suggest. It is more likely that the outcome of the debate will be that a compromize is reached between countries pursuing a higher and those in favor of a lower level of protection[18]. This brings us to the exact reason why the exception of Article 100A(4) was created.

The Exceptions of 100A(4) and 130T

Article 100A(4) makes it possible for Member States to apply stricter national rules than the harmonizing EC measures where this is necessary "on grounds of major needs referred to in Article 36, or relating to the protection of the environment or the working environment." The exception forms a radical break from the whole idea behind harmonization. A Member State that wants to make use of the provision has to notify the Commission of its intentions. The Commission needs to approve of the national *"Alleingänge"*. In practice, the Commission has done so only three times[19].

The exception of Article 100A(4) EC Treaty leaves many questions unanswered. For instance, it is not certain whether it can only be invoked by Member States that voted against the harmonizing measure. As a Member State voting in favor of a measure is allowed to start a procedure against that measure[20], one might conclude that voting in favor of a

---

[17] The integration principle of Article 130R(2) is thus explicitly expressed here.

[18] This is in fact what happened with the Packaging and Packaging Waste Directive discussed below.

[19] Twice with regard to the German ban on PCP (Decisions of December 2, 1992, **OJ** 1992, C 334/8 and September 14, 1994, **OJ** 1994, L 316/43) which was stricter than the provisions of a directive on this substance and once with regard to a similar Danish ban (Decision of February 26, 1996, **OJ** 1996, L 68/30). The first decision on the German PCP ban was annulled by the ECJ in a proceeding initiated by France, but only because of the fact that the Commission had not substantiated its reasons (Case C-41/93, *France v. Commission*, [1994] **ECR** I-1829). The Commission thus was able to reissue its approval, this time with an extensive motivation.

[20] Case 166/78, *Italy v. Council*, [1979] **ECR** 2575.

measure should also not preclude resource to the exception of Article 100A(4). Another point of discussion is the question whether the word "applied" implies that only existing national standards can be upheld. An affirmative answer would mean that strict standards like the ones allowed for in Germany and Denmark would not be allowed in another EC Member State if the latter would want to introduce it at a later date.

The EC Treaty contains yet another exception which allows for national environmental measures stricter than the ones agreed upon in harmonizing EC measures. This exception is formulated in Article 130T. Article 130T ascertains that the measures adopted under Article 130S do not preclude the Member States from "maintaining or introducing protective measures compatible with this Treaty." From the fact that Article 100A(4) speaks of "apply", it is sometimes concluded that the exception can only be invoked where existing national legislation is concerned[21].

Both the exceptions of Article 100A(4) and 130T show that the EC Member States are allowed to strive for high levels of environmental protection, even when harmonization measures exist. States with a progressive environmental policy, under certain conditions, are thus prevented from having to lower their standards.

3. EC Harmonization

As explained above, the Internal Market cannot be achieved solely via the prohibitions which the EC Treaty contains and judicial bounding, as this still leaves the Member States with a considerable amount of discretionary power to adopt environmental protection measures. Harmonization is thus the only way to realize a true internal market.

The EC's environmental harmonization measures are not only influenced by the provisions of Articles 130R, S and T discussed above. They are also shaped within the framework of so-called Environmental Action Programmes. Since 1973, five of these have been made[22]. In addition, specific resolutions on policies with regard to specific sectors are regularly adopted[23].

---

[21] KRÄMER, p.109, *supra* note 12.

[22] **OJ** 1973 C 112/1, **OJ** 1977 C 139/1, **OJ** 1983 C 46/1, **OJ** 1987 C 328/1 and **OJ** 1993 C 138/1.

[23] For instance with regard to waste, where the Commission on 30.07.1996 presented a draft Council resolution on waste policy, COM(96)399 final, which is to replace the old waste strategy (Council Resolution of May 9, 1990, **OJ** 1990, C 122/2).

Esty & Geradin already gave a thorough overview of the different styles of harmonization which are currently employed within the EC. They concluded that the flexible approach might be a solution in situations where differences in the situations stand in the way of total harmonization, possibly also to be employed within the WTO framework.

An example of this flexible approach is Directive 94/62 on Packaging and Packaging Waste[24]. The directive can be regarded as a response to the *Danish Bottles* Case, from which it had become clear that EC law did not preclude obligatory deposit-and-return systems for bottles, nor did it preclude a ban on metal cans. The new directive leaves the Member States with fewer possibilities to pursue such strict standards. It even introduces maximum recycling percentages. However, if Member States can show that their higher standards do not hinder the functioning of the Internal Market and fulfill a number of other conditions, they may retain their national standards[25]. On the other hand, the Packaging Directive contains exceptions for Greece, Ireland and Portugal, allowing them to fulfill the requirements of the directive at a later date then the other Member States[26]. Thus, a multi-tier approach is followed.

The Packaging Waste Directive also follows the New Approach in the sense that it lays down the basic outlines of the "essential requirements" which packagings are to fulfill. For instance, the packaging volume and weight is to be "limited to the minimum adequate amount to maintain the necessary level of safety, hygiene and acceptance for the packed product and for the consumer." As for the incineration of packaging waste, "a minimum inferior calorific value to allow optimization of energy recovery" is to be ensured. Such requirements are, as far as the protection of the environment is concerned, all but essential. As for the functioning of the Internal Market, they are of importance, all the more since the directive contains a free movement clause, stating that as long as a packaging

---

[24] **OJ** 1994, L 365/10. In the preamble it states that "the differing national measures concerning the management of packaging and packaging waste should be harmonized in order, on the one hand, to prevent any impact thereof on the environment or to reduce such impact, thus providing a high level of environmental protection, and, on the other hand, to ensure the functioning of the Internal Market and to avoid obstacles to trade and distortion and restriction of competition within the Community." Article 100A forms the legal basis, which shows that aspect is the major focus point.

[25] The Commission is to confirm the measures, after having verified that they are consistent with the considerations and do not constitute an arbitrary means of discrimination or a disguised restriction on trade between Member States.

[26] Because of their specific situation, i.e. respectively the large number of small islands, the presence of rural and mountain areas and the current low level of packaging consumption, the directive explains.

fulfills the "essential requirements" a Member State is not allowed to ban it from its market[27].

Another aspect of the New Approach followed by this directive is the possibility of establishing more concrete essential requirements for specific types of packaging outside the framework of the EC itself. The Commission is asked to promote "European standards" for packaging. Two problems arise here. First of all, there is no more direct democratic accountability when private organizations determine the standards. Secondly, organizations such as CEN and CENELEC are only just beginning to incorporate environmental concerns into their work[28].

Esty & Geradin are right that the flexible harmonization methods and the New Approach allow the EC to move more quickly in the creation of an internal market. However, the example of the packaging waste directive shows that the risk exists that some states which pursue strict standards can be forced to take a step back. If the harmonizing measure does not contain exceptions for such countries, invoking the exception of Article 100A(4) — discussed above — might be the last option for states wanting to hold on to their strict norms[29].

4. Judicial Bounding

Environmental product standards which fall under the prohibition of Article 30 EC Treaty are allowed, provided that they are necessary, proportionate, and that they do not form arbitrary discrimination or a disguised trade restriction. These conditions are partly expressed in Article 36, and partly developed in the case law of the ECJ. The example discussed by Esty & Geradin is the *Danish Bottles* Case[30]. In this judgment, the ECJ on the one hand offered Member States the possibility to pursue their own environmental protection policies at the expense of the unity of the Internal Market. On the other hand, a certain degree of scrutiny to trade restrictive environmental measures was applied by the Court. The authors therefore underlined that other case law of the Court will

---

[27] Article 18 of Directive 62/94.

[28] The suggestions made by Esty & Geradin that such organizations should come to work under the supervision of independent environmental experts or of UNEP are interesting in this respect and should be elaborated upon.

[29] Denmark might find itself in this position where the ban on metal cans is concerned, especially since the Commission has started infringement proceedings against Denmark on this matter, **ENDS Environmental Daily**, Wednesday March 19, 1997.

[30] Case 302/86, *Commission v. Denmark*, [1988] **ECR** 4602.

need to be awaited to define the boundaries of Article 30 of the EC Treaty more clearly.

Several cases can shed some light here, both in the field of environmental protection and in related areas. From these cases, some conclusions can be drawn on the conditions which are of importance when the Internal Market interests are weighed against those of the protection of the environment.

After the *Danish Bottles* Case, the main case relating to trade and environment issues was the *Walloon Waste* Case[31]. The Walloon Region had prohibited the importation of waste from other Belgian regions as well as from other countries. This was necessary as the Walloon Region was facing an abnormal, massive influx of waste which constituted a genuine threat to the environment in view of its limited capacity to handle waste. These facts had not been contested by the Commission, which sought the annulment of the Walloon law as it violated Article 30. As the protection of the environment is not among the exceptions mentioned in the narrowly interpreted Article 36, the "rule of reason" exception had to be turned to. The Court submitted, that the Walloon measures were justified by mandatory requirements relating to the protection of the environment. Thus, the condition of necessity was met. The problem was, that normally only national measures which do not discriminate between domestic products and products stemming from other countries can be invoked under the rule of reason. As foreign waste is no more harmful for the environment than Walloon waste, the Commission brought forward, the measures were discriminatory and had to be considered as a violation of Article 30.

The ECJ, in what can be considered a novel approach to say the least, took this formal hurdle by the following line of reasoning. Waste, it was contested, is a special product to which special rules apply. The treaty itself in Article 130R(2) contains principles such as the rectification at source. This principle, the Court explained, means that each region, commune or other local entity has to take appropriate measures to receive, process and dispose of its own waste. Consequently, waste should be disposed of as close as possible to the place where it is produced in order to keep the transport of waste to the minimum practicable[32]. Consequently, waste produced in one place does differ from waste produced in

---

[31] Case C-2/90, *Commission v. Belgium*, [1992] **ECR** I-1909.

[32] The ECJ also pointed out that the EC had become a Party to the Basle Convention of March 22, 1989 in which the principles of self-sufficiency and proximity are set out.

another place and the Walloon measures cannot be considered discriminatory, the Court concluded.

The protection of the environment thus was given precedence over the free movement of goods. It was thus left up to the Belgium authorities to decide how they wanted to protect the environment. Does this mean that an EC Member State can freely set its environmental standards? Definitely not, as the general conditions of proportionality and necessity need to be met as well; the mere fact that a national measure is aimed at the protection of the environment does not suffice. In the *Walloon Waste* Case, the proportionality of the measure was not contested, as the Commission had focused on the discriminatory nature. If other measures had been brought to the attention of the ECJ which would achieve the same goal which hindered trade less, the result might have been different[33].

Just to illustrate how the proportionality argument influences the decisions of the ECJ, another example will be turned to. In the *Crayfish* Case, a German import ban on live crayfish was held disproportionate[34]. These measures were necessary, according to Germany, to protect domestic crayfish from diseases. However, there were other measures available, involving less serious restrictions for intra-Community trade, which "were capable of effectively protecting the interests pleaded" as the Court put it. Therefore, the German measure was held to be disproportionate.

The question remains, if Member States which set there environmental standards at a high level can upkeep that level, as long as they make sure that they employ only proportionate measures to reach these high goals. Or does the proportionality principle also mean, that even when no other, less trade-restrictive measure exists, the environmental goals are to be balanced against the trade restrictions? According to Advocate General Jacobs in his opinion to the *Danish Bottles* Case, the proportionality principle does indeed mean that a twofold test is applicable. If the level of protection sought is not reasonable, he submitted, than it has to be reduced[35]. It seems to us, that the ECJ never followed this line of

---

[33] See for a more extensive treatment of this case, W.Th. DOUMA, *"The* Walloon Waste *Case"*, in: **European Business Law Review**, vol.4, No.2, 1993, pp.32-43.

[34] Case C-131/93, *Commission v. Germany*, [1994] **ECR** I-3303.

[35] Also according to Stephen WEATHERILL & Paul BEAUMONT, **EC Law** (2nd ed.), Penguin, London, 1995, p.454, the question is not only whether there are alternative means available that are less restrictive of trade, but also whether or not the restriction stands in proportion to the risk presented by the import.

reasoning and thus leaves it to the Member States to define the height of their standards.

In doing so, they will have to demonstrate that their rules are "necessary to give effective protection to the interests referred to in Article 36."[36] Contrary to NAFTA (see part B.3 below), the burden of proof rests on the national authorities who wish to curtail the free movement of goods. The Court interprets the exceptions to the basic rules of the treaty in a narrow manner. Still, this does not mean that states have to come up with one hundred percent conclusive proof. If there exist genuine fears, the ECJ treads warily in rejecting national measures. Some cases in the field of the protection of human health can illustrate this.

The ECJ allows Member States to prohibit a substance in the interest of the protection of public health even if there is scientific doubt about the harmful effects of that substance. This was for instance shown in the Case 53/80 where the additive nisin (a preservative) was concerned[37]. Contradictory scientific evidence was presented, stemming from the FAO and other sources. The ECJ was of the opinion that, where genuine scientific doubt existed, the existence of a risk, even if disputed, is sufficient to invoke the exception of Article 36.

This decision implies that Article 30 does not drive protection down to the lowest common denominator[38]. What in fact is demonstrated here is a precautionary approach, which all Community institutions according to Article 130R(2) need to follow. In this respect, the EC system is similar to NAFTA.

5. Public Participation

The present Intergovernmental Conference shows, that the importance of a greater involvement of the public in the reshaping of the EC Treaty rules is gradually beginning to emerge. For instance, in January 1996, a hearing was organized by the Commission where interested Parties could express their opinions on the IGC and the environment. Furthermore, several NGO's have presented extensive reports expressing their views on the amendments necessary[39].

---

[36] Case 227/82, *Leendert van Bennekom*, [1983] **ECR** 3883.

[37] Case 53/80, *Officier van Justitie v. Koninklijke Kaasfabriek Eyssen BV*, [1981] **ECR** 409.

[38] Other cases which can be mentioned in this respect are Case 174/82 *Sandoz* [1983] **ECR** 2445; Case 94/83 *Heijn* [1984] **ECR** 3263; Case 247/84 *Leon Motte* [1985] **ECR** 3887 and Case 304/84 *Muller* [1986] **ECR** 1511.

[39] See footnote 13 above.

The most important way in which the public is involved in the environmental law of the EC is through its direct effect before the national judiciary, which is also obliged to interpret national law in the light of the wording and purpose of EC law which does not have direct effect. Access to the European Court of Justice itself is quite a different matter, as several examples have shown[40].

6. Concluding Remarks on the European Community

The EC uses a two track approach where the integration of trade and environmental issues is concerned: judicial bounding on the one hand and harmonization on the other hand. As for judicial bounding, we agree with Esty & Geradin that the ECJ in the *Danish Bottles* Case did not clearly define the boundaries to the regulatory discretion of the Member States pursuing environmental protection. The *Walloon Waste* Case clarified this matter only to a certain extent. The case showed first of all that the ECJ does not hesitate to give precedence to environmental interests, even when this means that an import ban disrupts the free movement of goods. It also forms an example of the way in which principles of environmental law can be of legal significance. Other examples on the protection of human health also show that the ECJ does put the onus of proof on the state wanting to invoke an exception to the free trade rules, but via a precautionary interpretation such states do not have to present full proof the necessity of their measures. In this way, a reasonable balance between trade and environment interests is struck by the judiciary.

It should also be stressed that in the EC system, the effect of such judgments is not as disruptive to the functioning of the Internal Market as it might seem at first. The reason for this is that trade and environment interests can still be balanced via harmonization. The flexibility which the New Approach offers is not always of advantage to the environmental interests, it was shown.

The remaining question which Esty & Geradin also asked themselves, is whether EC legislation has fully integrated environmental requirements in the harmonization process or whether the environment has been merely ancillary to the EC's economic objectives. It is submitted here, that the EC's environmental policy and law is quite advanced. Still, the general quality of the environment is not yet improving within the EC. Also,

---

[40] Notably the *French Nuclear Tests* Case T-219/95 R, *Danielsson v. Commission* [1995] **ECR** II-3051.

progress towards sustainable development is slow[41]. Thus, the main challenge for the EC lies in fully integrating environmental concerns in all Community policies. Apart from that, improved implementation and enforcement of EC environmental legislation[42] and increased public participation remain of importance.

B. NAFTA

1. Introduction

The early negotiations on the North American Free Trade Agreement show that NAFTA was intended to become purely a trade agreement, covering only the aspects of trade liberalization. However, the rapid growth of environmental consciousness, especially in the United States, but also in Canada and Mexico, led to the awareness that liberalizing trade would have an impact on the environment and the possibilities of environmental policy making.

Environmental organizations thus succeeded in putting environmental issues on the agenda of the NAFTA negotiations. The amount of discussion on environmental issues has tempted some commentators to note that NAFTA is the "greenest trade agreement" ever realized. The linkage between the issues of free trade and environmental protection during the talks on NAFTA has indeed been unrivalled in negotiations for any other trade agreement, but NAFTA is by no means greener than other agreements. There are, however, interesting lessons to be learned from NAFTA and its Side Agreements.

2. The Linkage of Trade and Environment

The political climate in the United States since the first *Tuna/Dolphin* Case of 1991[43] and the influence of environmental interest groups in the US have been the main reasons for the linkage of trade and environment in the negotiations on NAFTA. The need to gain congressional

---

[41] See among others European Environment Agency, *Environment in the European Union, 1995. Report for the Review of the Fifth Environment Action Programme*, Copenhagen, 1995; and, the Commission's Communication COM(95)624 final of 10.1.1996, *Progress Report on Implementation of the European Community Programme of Policy and Action in relation to the Environment and Sustainable Development "Towards Sustainability"*, January 1996.

[42] See for instance the Commission's Communication of October 22, 1996, COM(96)500, *Implementing Community Environmental Law*.

[43] **BISD** 38, D/155-205.

acceptance for NAFTA brought about a completely new feature in the discussions on trade and environment. For the first time, the discussion was not just a technical debate between economic, legal and environmental experts. This time, a much larger public was involved. Environmental interest groups were able to put their concerns about the effects of free trade on the environment high on the political agenda[44].

As a result, various exemptions on free trade have been made within the NAFTA provisions to accommodate national environmental protection policies and multilateral environmental agreements. The main provisions of NAFTA that deal with the relation between trade and environment are the following:

a) The preamble places the goal of trade liberalization in the context of sustainable development. It is stated that the development of world trade must happen in a manner consistent with environmental protection and conservation. The Parties also pledge to promote sustainable development, and to strengthen the development and enforcement of environmental laws and regulations[45].

b) Article 1114 NAFTA, in which the Parties "recognize that it is inappropriate to encourage investment by relaxing domestic health, safety or environmental measures." This provision is to avoid industrial relocation and investment flight because of lower environmental standards.

c) Article 104 NAFTA, states that in case of any inconsistency of NAFTA provisions with a number of Multilateral Environmental Agreements (MEAs) the latter shall prevail over NAFTA.

d) Chapter 7B, concerning sanitary and phytosanitary measures, and Chapter 9 on all other standards-related measures, underline that each Party has the right to set its own appropriate levels of protection and to apply them under certain conditions.

The amount of references to environmental issues in NAFTA provisions and the adoption of Side Agreements[46] reflect the importance for

---

[44] Annette BAKER FOX, *"Environment and Trade: The NAFTA Case"*, in: **Political Science Quarterly** Vol.110 No.1, 1995, p.49.

[45] As these provisions are placed in the preamble, their legal significance is limited. They find only limited echoes in the text of NAFTA itself.

[46] Parallel to NAFTA the Parties have set up structures for cooperation on environmental issues such as the Mexican-US Border Plan that deals with the specific environmental problems in this region and the North American Agreement on Environmental Cooperation (NAAEC), which creates institutions to advance environmental protection and (environmental) sustainability of trade flows stimulated by NAFTA.

the Parties of the protection of the environment. Nevertheless, the content of most of these provisions shows that the efforts to make the two policy objectives of trade liberalization and environmental protection more cohesive and mutually enforcing have not been very successful. The way NAFTA is to be implemented and the possibilities to enforce the provisions under its dispute settlement mechanisms also do not seem to enhance the chances for a more successful integration of the two policy objectives.

3. Judicial Bounding

Unlike the situation within the EC, NAFTA institutions are not authorized to adopt secondary legislation. Therefore, the NAFTA Parties must adopt internal legislation and rules that give effect to their commitments. Here in this paper, we will use the situation in the United States as an example to show what problems can occur in an intergovernmental system of integration for countries with a monistic approach to international law.

The principal legislation that has been adopted in the United States is the NAFTA Implementation Act[47]. This act expressly deprives NAFTA of direct effect on the law of the United States[48]. Private Parties have no possibility of bringing litigation in the federal or state courts on the basis of the agreements, unlike the situation in the EC described above.

Federal agencies are implementing the NAFTA Implementation Act through administrative regulations. Those regulations may be challenged in the federal courts by private Parties in the United States. However, these regulations will be challenged on the basis of the NAFTA Implementation Act, and not on the basis of NAFTA itself[49].

The fact that the act restricts the implementation of NAFTA in the United States does however facilitate the United States to maintain their own level of environmental protection. In addition to the understanding

---

[47] Pub. L. No.103-182, 107 Stat. 2057 (1993), codified at 19 USC, §3311 *et seq.* (1994).

[48] Paragraph 102(a) provides that "no provision of the agreement, nor the application of any such provision to any person or circumstance, which is inconsistent with the law of the United States shall have effect." Paragraph 102(c) further provides that no person other than the United States shall have any cause of action or defence under the agreement or any of the side agreements.

[49] This is yet another difference with EC law, where national judges are obliged to give precedence to EC provisions with direct effect and to interpret national law in the light of the wording and purpose of EC law which does not have direct effect.

that NAFTA must not be read as to modify national environmental legislation, the act also provides that federal and state agencies will not be prohibited from engaging in any activities relating to both sanitary and phytosanitary measures and technical standards, or to be limited in determining the level of protection of human, animal, or plant life or health the agency considers appropriate[50].

Judicial bounding within NAFTA and its Side Agreements takes place at four different levels. The first is the dispute settlement mechanism for disputes between the Parties. The second is the possibility for private Parties to challenge regulations implementing NAFTA. As we have described above, judicial bounding in this manner depends largely on the creation of national legislation implementing NAFTA as its Parties do not grant direct effect to the treaty.

The NAFTA dispute settlement system only allows the states to initiate procedures. The general procedure is explained in Chapter 20 of NAFTA and is largely the same as the WTO dispute settlement procedure. Article 2005 NAFTA even gives Parties the opportunity to have their case heard before both a GATT and a NAFTA panel. However, NAFTA provides that in disputes among the Parties concerning Multilateral Environmental Agreement (MEA) or an environmental, health or safety measure, the challenged Party has the right to have the case heard exclusively under the provisions of NAFTA[51].

NAFTA explicitly states that a Party challenging another Party's environmental, health or safety standards under Chapter 7B and 9 bears the burden of proof in the dispute[52]. In addition, NAFTA underlines the precautionary approach (Articles 907.3 and 715.4). Parties are allowed to adopt environmental, health and safety measures even if scientific evidence is not conclusive as to the risk which a product or service could pose. Once adequate scientific information becomes available, such national measures are to be re-examined. If no scientific basis can be found, the measure is to be repealed.

The Parties to NAFTA thus do not need to provide full scientific evidence for their measures. They only must show that the measures are based on scientific principles (Article 712.3) and are the product of an acceptable risk assessment process. A scientific basis is defined as "a

---

[50] NAFTA Implementation Act, § 351.

[51] NAFTA, Articles 2005.3, and 2005.4.

[52] NAFTA, Articles 723.6 and 914.4, 32 **ILM** (1993), pp.382, 391.

reason based on data or information derived using scientific measures" (Article 724).

A weaker point in the NAFTA dispute settlement procedure is the lack of public participation and transparency. Under NAFTA's provisions members of the public or non-governmental organizations cannot participate or have access to the hearings or consultations conducted during a dispute. It is even possible that the public will not have access to the final decision of the panel.

On two more occasions dispute settlement occurs in NAFTA. There is a separate consultation procedure for disputes that arise when a Party encourages investment by relaxing domestic health, safety and environment measures under Article 1114 and further. However, the lack of enforcement provisions has raised serious concerns whether this provision is able to discourage investment flight because of differences in environmental standards.

This procedure is in line with a potentially more important procedure under Article 22 of the Side Agreement on Environmental Cooperation. Under this provision an arbitrage panel decides on matters regarding a persistent failure by a Party to effectively enforce its environmental law.

The only right granted to private Parties or non-governmental organizations under NAFTA and its side agreements is the right to file a complaint with the Secretariat of the NACEC in case of a failure to enforce national environmental legislation[53]. The Council can decide to make the research in the matter available for the public. Another option is to start a procedure under Article 22 when the failure to enforce environmental law in question is part of a persistent pattern of non-enforcement.

4. Conclusion

The NAFTA dispute settlement mechanism reflects the degree of integration between the states in North America. The countries are very reluctant to lose control over their national legislation. The failure to translate the intensity of the political debate on trade and environment in the procedural rules on the implementation and enforcement within NAFTA shows that no agreement could be reached on the way in which these two policies should be integrated.

---

[53] NAAEC, Article 14.

The implementation of NAFTA and its Side Agreements is dependent upon a chain of national legislation that has to be adopted, and which in the case of the United States contains provisions that explicitly state that the NAFTA provisions cannot invalidate federal and state regulations. Furthermore, private Parties can only indirectly derive rights under the agreements and have almost no access to and insight in the dispute settlement mechanisms provided for in the agreements.

Thus, the political process towards the adoption of NAFTA, the active public participation and the involvement of environmental organizations contributed to the large amount of provisions to secure adequate protection of the environment, and in that way, a better balance between trade and environment has been created. However, the way the agreement has to be implemented and the lack of public participation and transparency could be improved.

C. A Comparison to WTO Practices

1. Introduction

The debate on the relation between trade and environment has been largely nonexistent under GATT, although several dispute settlement panels were confronted with questions on the compatibility of trade-related environmental measures with GATT provisions. During the Uruguay Round of negotiations on the establishment of a WTO, still no agreement could be reached on this issue. The WTO created a Committee on Trade and Environment that has been meeting on a regular basis to identify the intersections and collisions between trade liberalization and environmental protection. Since 1994, it has been the major forum where the debate on trade and environment has taken place. Furthermore, WTO General-Director Ruggiero declared that the debate on trade and environment would be one of the major items to be dealt with in the WTO.

At the WTO Ministerial Conference in Singapore in December 1996, trade and environment was supposed to be one of the major themes. However, although the conference has been called a major success because of the progress made in various other areas, it has been a disappointment from an environmental point of view. Hardly any attention has been paid to trade and environment issues, either at the conference or in the media.

The decision adopted at the conference concerning trade and environment merely underlined the importance of the work done by the Committee and directed the Committee to carry out its work under its existing terms of reference. The only interesting observation was that the conference welcomed the involvement of environmental as well as trade experts in the work of the Committee, thereby accepting that a more balanced approach to the issue should guide its work, by taking into account environmental concern as well.

In this part, we will first compare the decisions taken by the GATT dispute settlement panels on trade-related environmental measures with the EC jurisprudence and with the provisions NAFTA has provided for. After that we will discuss the importance of MEAs for a better coordination of environmental issues and their relationship with WTO.

2. Judicial Bounding

Since 1980 the GATT dispute settlement procedures have been used frequently for the settlement of international disputes over trade-related environmental measures. On eight occasions, a dispute settlement panel decided on matters involving environmental measures[54].

GATT made no direct reference to the protection of the environment as a legitimate reason for exceptions on the free trade principles. However, Parties in dispute settlement procedures and the established panels have used Article XX(b) and (g) GATT to justify measures in the interest of environmental protection[55]. This is contrary to the development in

---

[54] The reports of the GATT/WTO Dispute Settlement Body were the following:
 a. The 1982 Panel Report on the US prohibition of imports of tuna and tuna products from Canada, **BISD** 29 S/91-109.
 b. The 1987 Panel Report on US taxes on petroleum and other environmental taxes, **BISD** 34 S/136-166.
 c. The 1988 Panel Report on Canada's restrictions on exports of unprocessed herring and salmon, **BISD** 35 S/98-115.
 d. The 1990 Panel Report on Thailand's restrictions on importation of cigarettes, **BISD** 37 S/200-228.
 e. *Tuna\Dolphin I*, 1991, **BISD** 39 S/155-205.
 f. *Tuna\Dolphin II*, 1994, **GATT Document** DS 29/R of June 1994.
 g. The 1994 Panel Report on US taxes on automobiles, **GATT Document** DS 31/R of October 1994.
 h. The 1996 Panel Report and Appelate Body Report on US Standards for Reformulated and Conventional Gasoline, [http://www.wto.org/wto/dispute/gas1.htm]. March 14, 1997.

[55] Article XX reads: "Subject to the requirement that such measures are not applied in a manner which would constitute a means of arbitrary or unjustifiable discrimination between countries where the same conditions prevail, or a disguised restriction

the EC where the rule of reason allows for exceptions (such as the protection of the environment) not covered in Article 36 EC (which does cover "the protection of health and life of humans, animals and plants")[56].

The decisions of the different panels seem to indicate that the possibilities to pursue environmental objectives through trade measures are much more restricted under WTO rules than might be the case under NAFTA, and that they are more in line with EC jurisprudence.

Like in the EC system, and contrary to the situation under Chapters 7B and 9 of NAFTA, the Party that is seeking to rely on an exception to the rules of GATT and wants to invoke Article XX GATT bears the burden of proof. This has been done to cope with the concern of several states that there was a danger that unchecked exceptions would result in a proliferation of disguised protectionist policies.

The interpretation of Article XX(b) resulted in a very narrow meaning of the term "necessary", thereby marginalizing environmental considerations. In the *Thai Cigarette* Case of 1990, the panel decided that "the import restrictions imposed could be considered necessary in terms of Article XX(b) only if there were no alternative measure consistent with the General Agreement, or less inconsistent with it, which Thailand could reasonably be expected to employ to achieve its health policy objectives." This introduced a least-GATT inconsistency test that has been confirmed later in the *Tuna-Dolphin* Cases of 1991 and 1994, a proportionality test therefore.

This reasoning has been in line with the ECJ jurisprudence as is discussed in Part A. Like in the EC, it is not clear whether the proportionality test also includes balancing the environmental risk against the trade restrictions, i.e. finding out whether the level of protection sought is reasonable[57]. One can seriously doubt whether this should be left to judicial bodies, like the ECJ and WTO panels, instead of the legislative

---

on international trade, nothing in this agreement shall be construed to prevent the adoption or enforcement by any Contracting Party of measures:

(b) necessary to protect human, animal or plant life or health, [...] and,

(g) relating to the conservation of exhaustible natural resources if such measures are made effective in conjunction with restrictions on domestic production or consumption."

[56] See the *Danish Bottles* and *Walloon Waste* Cases discussed above. Compare also Article 100(4) EC, which differentiates "national provisions on grounds of major needs referred to in Article 36 **or** relating to the protection of the environment." (emphasis added, WTD/MJ).

[57] See also footnote 35 above.

institutions. Moreover, the question is whether the WTO panels in their present composition are qualified enough to perform such a balancing act.

Under GATT and EC law, the test of what is "necessary" is in principle in favour of a free trade policy. In the case of NAFTA, the fact that the burden of proof lies in the hands of the Party that challenges environmental protection already led to statements by NAFTA Parties that they do not expect that the necessity test under Chapters 7B and 9 lends itself to the development of a least trade restrictiveness jurisprudence under NAFTA.

We have to wait whether the interpretation of NAFTA provisions will struck a different balance than the decisions of the GATT panels and the ECJ have done, before we can decide whether the NAFTA system is more favourable to an equitable relation between trade and environment.

The effect of the dispute settlement mechanism of the WTO on the integration of trade liberalization and environmental protection must not be overestimated since only states can initiate procedures for WTO panels. It is very unlikely that these states will let a panel decide on matters for which so little international agreement exists. The same can be said for the dispute settlement procedures in NAFTA, that has much in common with the system used in WTO.

This is the major difference with the system of judicial bounding in the EC, which offers private Parties the possibility to invoke EC law before their national judiciary. The jurisprudence of the ECJ has been a major asset in the European integration process and the case law we discussed in Part A is proof of the importance of judicial bounding in the EC. To a certain extent, the ECJ has contributed in clarifying the relationship between trade and the environment. Since a similar style of judicial bounding on a global level will not be feasible in the near future, the WTO might learn from the dispute settlement procedures in NAFTA.

3. Multilateral Environmental Agreements

Multilateral Environmental Agreements (MEAs) based on international consensus are viewed by the international community as the best way of coordinating policy action to tackle global and transboundary environmental problems[58]. Above all, the EC integration process has

---

[58] Article 12 of the Rio Declaration.

shown that harmonization, or at least coordination in areas other than trade is necessary in order to reach a higher degree of economic integration and trade liberalization.

Therefore cooperation through international agreements, for example on standardization, sanitary and phytosanitary measures or environmental policies must be regarded as the best policy to reach the objective of integrating environmental protection with trade liberalization.

The question that then needs to be answered is what the relationship should be between WTO and MEAs. One of the most treated subjects in WTO's Committee on Trade and Environment (CTE) has indeed been the compatibility of MEAs with WTO provisions where these MEAs contain trade related measures to reach the environmental objectives of the agreement. These measures have been introduced to directly prohibit or regulate trade in for example ozone depleting substances, endangered species or hazardous wastes, as a sanction against noncompliance with the agreements, or to avoid free riders, who want to benefit from the environmental improvement without sharing its costs.

One solution to the compatibility problem is that Parties to both WTO and the MEA agree that one of the agreements takes precedence over the other. In the case of NAFTA, this is exactly what the countries have agreed upon. As we have seen in Part B, Article 104 NAFTA gives priority to certain widely accepted MEAs. For the WTO, this is not an option at the moment, as there is no MEA to which all WTO Member States are Parties, and non-Parties to the MEA would block a decision for this reason. Although amendments could be made to most WTO provisions on a two-thirds majority basis, the fact that decisions in WTO are generally taken unanimously makes it very unlikely that a same system that NAFTA employs will be adopted.

The other option is that WTO takes precedence over MEAs. In that case, every trade measure under the scope of an MEA must fulfill the demands of the WTO provisions. Any trade-related measure taken under an MEA may then be brought for a WTO dispute settlement panel, who will only consider the compatibility of the measure with WTO provisions. No suggestions to use this option have ever been made[59], and international law seems not to offer any possibility to give precedence over one of the agreements as well.

---

[59] See the report of the CTE to the WTO Ministerial Conference in Singapore, November 8, 1996.

Thus, the situation occurs that no clear hierarchy can be established between trade agreements and MEAs. Many proposals have been made in the CTE to deal with the compatibility problem this situation has brought about. In our opinion, the following suggestions should be considered.

First, we strongly advocate that policy coordination between trade and environmental policy officials takes place to try to avoid any conflicts. If a conflict nevertheless occurs, there must be agreement over the procedures to be followed to solve the conflict. In our view, the introduction of a clause that would not allow a WTO dispute settlement panel to examine either the legitimacy of the environmental objective or the necessity of the trade measure taken pursuant to an MEA, but rather only whether or not the measure constitutes a means of arbitrary or unjustifiable discrimination, could be a possibility to better balance free trade and environmental protection. In this case, however, a list of MEAs recognized by the WTO Members should be drawn up, an action that some Parties to the WTO will not easily agree to.

4. Concluding Remarks

At this moment, there is no real progress within WTO on the relation between trade and environment. The Singapore Conference did not pay attention to the subject because the discussions in the CTE already pointed out that no agreement could be reached yet on any of the aspects of the relationship. Therefore, the panel reports on trade-related environmental measures give the best review of the present status of the situation. The 1996 Panel Report and Appelate Body Report on US Standards for Reformulated and Conventional Gasoline did not differ substantially from the older reports on TREMs. The WTO Dispute Settlement Body does not have the same authority as the ECJ has in the EC, so it is not very likely that the a panel report will bring any important changes in the relationship of trade and the environment without any political sign that a different relationship is considered.

In the future, the debate in the CTE might provide some answers on issues like MEAs, standards related measures, environmental subsidies and taxes or on Production and Processing Methods (PPMs). For the time being, the subject has proven to be too difficult to come to political agreement on these issues. The experiences in NAFTA and the EU might provide the WTO with some significant materials and ideas to keep the discussions alive and offer some solutions as well.

D. Conclusion

The experiences in the EC show that the level of economic integration which the Member States pursue — the establishment of an internal market — necessitates harmonization of environment. The Community adopted many regulations and directives to remove trade barriers to the Internal Market, which at the same time set standards for an acceptable level of environmental protection.

In case of conflicts between trade and environment interests under the general rules of the treaty, Article 36 and the rule of reason provide for a test whether the trade-related environmental measures taken by an EC Member State are necessary, proportionate, and whether they do not constitute arbitrary discrimination or a disguised restriction on trade. The *Walloon Waste* Case showed that environmental principles can be decisive in balancing trade liberalization and environmental protection. From a number of other cases in the field of the protection of human health it was concluded that the effect of putting the burden of proof on the state which invokes the exception is not too harsh, when a precautionary approach is followed. Thus, in case of scientific doubt the protection of human health gets the benefit of the doubt. It is our opinion that the same should hold true for trade *versus* environment cases.

Although by no means perfect, the way the relation between trade and environment has been handled in the EU thus provides some valuable lessons for further integration efforts in other regions or on a global level.

The situation in the WTO and NAFTA is much more comparable. The cooperation in these trade agreements has been restricted to the removal of trade barriers. The main difference is that the North American countries have included much more possibilities in NAFTA and its Side Agreements to make exceptions on the grounds of environmental protection. They created another balance between trade and environment than in the EC or WTO, where more emphasis has been put on liberalization of trade. This has undoubtedly been the result of the public participation, for example the influence of environmental organizations on the decision-making process during the negotiations. These open discussions on the relation between trade and environment may also serve as an example for the future debate on this issue.

However, the implementation process in NAFTA can contribute less to the current debate. As for the system of judicial bounding, many imperfections are visible. Still, it will be interesting to see how NAFTA jurisprudence develops considering the stronger emphasis that has been put on environmental protection. It would be very valuable for the debate on Article XX GATT as well, since this provision remains to be explained in favour of free trade. The introduction of the use of the precautionary approach in NAFTA and the EC could be a valuable lesson from which the WTO can learn.

It has not been the intention of this paper to come with the answers on trade and environment issues that international organizations have to cope with nowadays. We hope that this article will be regarded as a useful supplement to the paper of Esty & Geradin and that the two articles together might contribute to the debate on a more cohesive and mutually supportive approach of trade liberalization and environmental protection.

STANDARDS OF TREATMENT, HARMONIZATION AND MUTUAL RECOGNITION: A COMPARISON BETWEEN REGIONAL AREAS AND THE GLOBAL TRADING SYSTEM

Giorgio SACERDOTI

Professor of International Law,
Bocconi University, Milan

1. Domestic Regulations as an Obstacle to International Trade

The increasing removal of barriers to international trade, which is both a sign and an element of the globalization of the world economy, has resulted in a low level of tariffs for most goods, limitations to the use of border adjustment and restrictions measures as to their import and to multilateral regulation and liberalization of trade in services.

Domestic regulatory policies, generally not bound by trade commitments, have, as a result, come to the forefront as the most relevant obstacles to the free flow of goods and services and a source of distortion of international competition.

The circulation of services is not hampered by tariffs or other custom barriers as has mainly been the case for goods. Barriers to trade in services are more complicated and less transparent. They consist mainly of government regulation of individual services and of the circulation of related factors of production, which are part of the governance of national economic systems according to national policy objectives reflecting social traditions and the structure of the economy of each country. Protection of local companies and of nationals engaged in the service sector from foreign competition is only one aspect of this structure, as it is clear in relation to key sectors when they are restricted to national monopolies.

Indeed, in most countries, both industrialized and developing, the extensive regulation of services, which has grown through the years in response to old and new concerns (though mitigated by the recent world-wide trend towards deregulation) has brought about a series of restrictions on access to many sectors and strict administrative control of the exercise of regulated activities and professions. The examples of infrastructure services (shipping, transport and communications), financial services (banking and insurance) and professions (legal, medical, architectural and engineering) are typical in this respect.

Foreigners, both individuals and companies, are sometimes barred altogether from these services, or they are subject to cumbersome requirements and limitations (such as residency, establishment, qualifications tests) which makes it difficult to gain effective access to these markets or sectors, both in industrialized and developing countries.

2. Most-Favoured-Nation Treatment

Traditionally, the most used standards of treatment internationally, such as the Most-Favoured-Nation (MFN) and national treatment standards, have been resorted to bilaterally, regionally and multilaterally in order to cope with these problems as they affect trade. Their inadequacy to ensure further effective liberalization in the current situation of low tariffs and extension of liberalization to services have prompted the use of other concepts and methods (such as transparency, mutual recognition, and harmonization) in order to fill the gaps between divergent domestic policies and multilateral trade liberalization.

MFN treatment has been pivotal in the regulation of the trade of goods in order to secure nondiscrimination between the Parties to a trade treaty and third Parties as to the subject matter of the agreement. When the Parties have negotiated mutually advantageous, i.e. substantial, reciprocal concessions, this clause ensures that these concessions will not be undermined by better conditions granted in the future by one of the trading partners to a third Party.

The clause does not bar the granting of such better conditions. It extends them (automatically under the prevailing unconditional MFN clause) to the Party or Parties of the agreement containing the clause thus enabling both future liberalization and the preservation of acquired benefits. By "benefit" the competitive opportunities are meant by which the goods, producers and suppliers of the benefiting Party may derive from being put on the same footing as third Party products or enterprises in regard to tariffs and border restrictions. No guarantee is included, or implied, that the granting of MFN benefits to other trading partners will not have an adverse economic impact on the actual or expected position in the target market by the exporting country[1].

From this point of view the MFN clause implies the interplay of market economies. By prohibiting discrimination by governments based upon the geographical origin of internationally traded goods, the MFN clause reduces the area of public interference with the economy for political reasons and enhances free market operation.

3. National Treatment

These advantages are limited to the competition of goods, services, investment, persons, as the case may be, of different foreign origin in a given market. This clause does not bring about more liberal market access for foreigners in contrast to nationals. It merely prohibits discrimination between foreigners and foreign goods irrespective of the actual degree of market openness, which could remain small. It also bars discrimination in respect to new restrictions and when they are admitted in special circumstances (i.e. to safeguard measures).

In pursuing the objective of eliminating generally discriminatory treatment in international commerce, enshrined in the preamble of GATT, the obligation of granting also **national treatment**, found in Article III, is therefore also of paramount importance.

As to trade of goods, national treatment is relevant once imports have gone through border barriers, except that measures affecting both imported and domestic goods but applied at the border to imported goods should be also dealt with. This requires as a rule special provisions as those found in the first Note to Article III and in Article VIII.1.a) of GATT.

The commitment to grant national treatment affects directly domestic policies. The extent of the ensuing obligations can be far reaching. This

---

[1] See generally ROESSLER, *"Diverging Domestic Policies and Multilateral Trade Integration"*, in: BHAGWATI & HUDEC (eds), **Fair Trade and Harmonisation**, 1996, V.II, 21 ff.

depends from the type and level of domestic regulation, whether *de jure* and also *de facto* differential treatment are covered and whether objective rules for a legitimate non-trade purpose affecting differently foreigners and foreign products are considered as falling under its purview. The formulation of the principle as "treatment no less favourable than that accorded to like products of national origin" while adding some flexibility for the importing country makes it more far reaching, in that it makes substance rather than form relevant.

A balance has been struck in Article III GATT limiting the full application of the national treatment to matters and state measures directly affecting the competitiveness of imported goods, which appear *prima facie* discriminatory. In other respects the principle applies only to measures not only resulting in but also having the intent of protecting the like domestic product. The definition of "like product" is fundamental to maintaining the value of the obligation for foreigners when substitution between different but competing products is economically possible and relevant.

Contracting Parties merely "recognize" in Article III.1 of GATT that "internal taxes and other internal charges and laws, regulations and requirements affecting the internal sale, offering for sale, purchase, transportation, distribution or use of products [...] should not be applied to imported products so as to afford protection."

As to measures directly affecting the equal treatment of imported and domestic goods, Article III.2 prohibits subjecting domestic products to internal taxes and charges in excess of those applied to like domestic products. Paragraph 4 mandates national treatment in respect to laws and regulations affecting the internal sale, offering for sale, purchase, transportation, distribution or use of imported products.

4. Services and Investment

The very nature of **services** makes exclusive reliance on MFN and national treatment inadequate when the liberalization of services is sought in an effective albeit progressive way.

Regulations by which the structure of the market is determined and which limit the access of foreigners are more important than protection at the border, which in the case of goods is the principal object of the MFN clause. In this respect one has to further consider that in the international movement of services their trans-border supply is, in many sectors, marginal and often technically impractical. The inherent immaterial nature of services requires dealing with the position, rights and duties of the service supplier whose activity is inseparable with the service itself. Commercial presence of the foreign supplier and the movement of natural persons are accordingly covered in GATS as a modality of trade in services. These two modes correspond by-and-large to the freedom of establishment and of services, including some aspects of the free movement of workers and capital, as these freedoms are enshrined in the Treaty of Rome and regulated within the European Community.

In view of the extensive regulation of most service sectors the obligation of national treatment by itself does not ensure access and competitive opportunities to foreigners either. This standard has to be supplemented by other general criteria and specific provisions.

The progressive liberalization intent of the WTO/GATS system, the same that characterized the EEC until the full establishment of the Internal Market, distinguishes this framework from other international regimes dealing with services and **investment** which rely only on the combination of MFN and national treatment obligations.

A typical example of the Friendship, Navigation and Commerce (FNC) Treaties, which the US used to enter into, one with Italy in 1948, brought before the International Court of Justice (ICJ) in the *Elsi* Case decided in 1989, grants to the national of either Party in the territory of the other one "upon terms no less favourable than those now or hereinafter accorded to nationals of such other Party" the right to "engage in commercial, manufacturing, processing, financial, educational, religious, philanthropic and professional activities, except the practice of law." (Art.I.2.a).

National treatment is combined with MFN treatment: according to Article II.4 "corporations and associations shall not in any case [...] receive treatment less favourable than the treatment which is or may hereinafter be accorded to corporations and associations of any third country."

Also, Bilateral Investment Treaties (BITs) rely on a combination of these two criteria in favour of the investors of either Party and their investment. Notwithstanding, the declared object of these agreements, that of promoting foreign investment besides protecting them, the right to make investment, that is to enter the other Party's market, is generally not covered, although BITs are of course entered into by countries that do admit foreign investment under their domestic laws and are interested in direct investment inflows. When the right of access is granted, as in recent US BITs, a negative list of restricted sectors is included in the agreement.

Instruments aimed at favouring effective market access in nondiscriminatory terms require further details and commitments. Thus the Organization of Economic and Cooperation Development (OECD) 1976 legally nonbinding Declaration on International Investment and Multinational Enterprises takes into account the fact that most investments from abroad are carried on through local subsidiaries. i.e. foreign controlled enterprises to which national treatment should be accorded as well.

In view of the existing domestic restrictions in this area, the OECD Council Decision, also adopted in 1976 and since revised, provides for notification of existing exceptions and for periodic reviews aimed at reducing them through "peer pressure". A new endeavour to liberalize access and treatment through a binding instrument is under way in OECD, where a Multilateral Agreement on Investment (MAI) is being currently negotiated.

5. MFN and National Treatment in the GATS

As for GATS, Article II provides for immediate unconditional MFN treatment for the services and service suppliers of other members in relation to all measures covered by the agreement, not only those subject to specific commitments[2].

As in GATT, this provision does not establish conditions for more liberal market access; it merely bars discrimination irrespective of the actual degree of market openness.

Moreover, Article II does not require elimination of existing preferential treatment as to services. Under Article II.2, members may maintain inconsistent measures provided these are listed in the annex. These measures should last, in principle, for not more than ten years and are subject to multilateral review every five years.

A different, more stringent regime is provided for sectors and modes of services which members of the WTO have listed in their schedules of

---

[2] See generally, WEISS, *"The GATS 1994"*, in: **Common Market Law Review** No.32, 1994, 1177 ff.; FOOTER, *"The International Regulation of Trade in Services Following Completion of the Uruguay Round"*, in: **The International Lawyer** No.29, 1995, 453 ff.; YI WANG, *Most-Favoured-Nation Treatment under the GATS*, in: **Journal of World Trade** Vol.1 No.30, 1996, 91 ff.

specific commitments as a result of the initial liberalization negotiations which have taken place in the Uruguay Round.

In this respect, members are subject to market access and national treatment obligations. Market access relates to market entry and presence conditions which in the service-sector pertain to the regulation of the domestic market and not to border controls on goods. Quantitative limitations of the number of foreign service-suppliers are a typical example of non-permissible restrictions in this respect (Art.XVI GATS).

National treatment relates to the conduct of operations after market entry. It has been supplemented by access requirements because national treatment applied to services is a necessary but not sufficient condition to ensure effective market access in view of the nature of the service industry and the stable presence in the market which is usually required in order to operate effectively.

Article XVII does not contain a list of incompatible measures, since this approach would be both problematic and ineffective. On the contrary the obligation concerns any measure. Article XVII.2 indicates explicitly that treatment no less favourable than that accorded to domestic services and their providers does not require and conversely is not satisfied by formally identical treatment. An evaluation of the competitive effect of the applicable regime is required instead.

Article XVII.3 specifies that: "Formally identical or formally different treatment shall be considered to be less favourable if it modifies the conditions of competition in favour of service or service suppliers of the Member compared to like service or service suppliers of any other Member."

This authoritative interpretation of the standard within GATS cannot be considered a general feature of the standard. It relates specifically to the structure of the service industry and to the features of foreigners' presence in such markets.

De facto and *de jure* discrimination are thus covered. The competitive effect is the only relevant to evaluate a given measure. A protective intent is not required in addition, which makes Article XVII of GATS more stringent than the corresponding Article III of GATT.

This provision is potentially very far reaching and even disruptive of established regulations and practice, including objectively justified requirements, such as residency and professional or other qualifications, which may affect nationals and foreigners differently.

Two other features of GATS tend, however, to limit this impact.

First of all, WTO Members did not intend to liberalize service markets fully and immediately, not even specific sectors. This is the object of future progressive liberalization efforts to be carried on through periodic rounds of multilateral negotiations much as has been the practice in GATT (Art.XIX.1 GATS). Specific commitments appear to have been carefully made not only with a view to the negotiating balance but also with the aim of binding only existing openings for foreigners in the domestic service markets.

GATS enshrines a "positive list" approach under which members list their commitments by sector and by mode. Commitments made tend to reflect the current legal situation of each member and incorporate basically a "stand still" obligation. If one looks at the EC and its Member States' schedules, these list, not only individual sectors and specific modes which are the object of their undertakings, but they contain a number of terms, limitations and conditions on market access and national treatment as authorized by Article XX, in order to safeguard existing regulations and restrictions.

6. The Relationship between Domestic and Trade Policies

The second aspect relates to the need to distinguish between regulations potentially or actually affecting foreign goods and services more severely than domestic ones, and between those that are objectively justified by the need to protect paramount general interests and objectives from those whose discriminatory effects are not balanced by those needs. Furthermore, one should consider whether those interests and objectives are internationally shared, if they are properly relevant from an individual country point-of-view and if the means to achieve those objectives are not unduly restrictive.

The conformity of the national measures to international yardsticks of a technical nature, where they exist, or the elaboration of such standards may offer a solution, in some domains, both in respect to goods and services. In other fields different methods may be pursued, taking into account the fact that in a world of sovereign states, having different policies, priorities and interests, the elaboration of common standards for trade liberalization purposes to be applied in the regulation of the domestic economy, when these regulations are meant to protect other interests and concerns can only be the result of negotiations based on shared values and aims.

Difficulties in reaching this goal increase when the equalization of requirements and conditions concerns areas where trade consideration, or the hindrance of trade is deemed of minor importance, in comparison with other domestic policies that would be affected by change and possibly loosened.

The ongoing debate on the setting of internationally agreed (minimum) standards in the field of environment and labour, as far as these are relevant to trade, is a good example. The absence of common standards can even be justified theoretically as an aspect of the different competitiveness of nations, which is a propellant to trade, due to differences in endowment of resources, or a combination thereof, or level of development. From this point of view no accusation of unfair trade advantage could be entertained against countries which refuse to accept agreed high standards when common welfare is not involved.

When common welfare is at issue, appropriate standards should be agreed within international organizations dealing with environmental global care or workers' worldwide minimum protection, as the case may be; and they should be adopted for trade purposes[3].

On the other hand, the increasing reciprocal interference of many uncoordinated domestic policies and their negative impact on global welfare has to be faced. The ensuing tensions and diseconomies justify the view that minimal harmonization of such policies is appropriate whenever national regulations cause distortions in foreign markets and in international investment patterns[4].

The problem is where to draw the line and whether pressure by leading actors can and should replace agreement by free consent. This discussion is just a piece, and a fundamental one, of the debate as to the merits of globalization *("mondialisation") versus* the preservation of national sovereignty entrusted to democratic governments ("accountability").

7. Divergent National Rules on Goods and Free Trade in the EC and in the GATT/WTO

In order to pursue the equalization of the legal conditions of domestic markets a variety of instruments may be used, depending on the nature

---

[3] Cf. HUDEC, *"Introduction to vol.2"*, in: BHAGWATI & HUDEC, *op. cit.*, 5 ff.

[4] See OECD, *"Reforming Regulations"*, doc. GD (96) 115.

of the subject matter, its connection with trade, the level of equalization required to avoid discrimination, also taking into account the relevance of non trade interests.

Article XX GATT and Article 36 EC address these matters. Article 36, which has to be viewed in connection with Article 30, which prohibits measures equivalent to quantitative restrictions, reduces the freedom of individual EC Member States in their reciprocal trade more severely than GATT rules. Under the *Cassis de Dijon* and *Dassonville* Case law of the European Court of Justice (ECJ)[5] national provisions concerning the features of products cannot be applied to like imported products which comply to the legislation of the exporting country when their application to such products is not justified under Article 36; so the principle of free flow of goods within the Community prevails. On the other hand, general rules equally applicable to domestic and imported products concerning the marketing and sale of the product can be successfully challenged only if they do not result in discrimination against imported products[6].

If the differences in national legislation are such that they directly hamper the free circulation of goods, the EC resorts to the "approximation of laws to the extent required for the proper functioning of the Common Market" (Art.3h of the Rome Treaty).

To deal at least partially with the matter of technical barriers to trade, in the GATT/WTO system, specific supplementary agreements were made in the Tokyo and Uruguay Rounds. The mutual recognition of national standards, which underlies the ECJ jurisprudence and was generally adopted in the EC after the Single European Act, is not found in GATT.

The WTO Agreement on Technical Barriers makes it clear in the preamble and in its basic provisions, that its purpose is to avoid that national measures in the area create unnecessary obstacles to international trade. A series of non-trade interests are fully preserved provided that those measures do not intend, or have the effect, of creating such obstacles (Art.2.2). Existing international standards are to be used as a rule and members are encouraged to participate in their preparation by appropriate standardising bodies "with a view to harmonizing technical regulations" (Art.2.6). "Unnecessary" has been defined as referring to

---

[5] Judgements of 20.2.1979, 120/78, and of 11.7.1974, 8/74, respectively.

[6] *Keck* Case, judgement of 24.11.1993, n.267/91. See generally MENGOZZI, **European Community Law**, 1992, 208 ff.

regulations which are more restrictive than necessary in fulfilling a legitimate objective, or when the objective itself is not legitimate[7].

In contrast to the EC, the WTO itself is not involved in standard-setting and harmonization; moreover many discretionary escape clauses are included in the agreement. The institutional framework to ensure compliance is also relevant. The dispute settlement system in the WTO has been improved from that of GATT but of course it does not match the compulsory and exclusive jurisdiction with binding direct effects of the EC.

In other areas the record of the multilateral trade system is even less satisfactory, though trade matters are directly concerned. This is the case in regard to rules of origin. Under the relevant WTO Agreement, harmonization of these rules, or rather direct international standard setting, will be undertaken. Negotiations will be based on the general criteria spelled out in the agreement and on the principle that they should be objective and "should not be used as instruments to pursue trade objectives directly and indirectly." (Art.9)[8].

Harmonization in the WTO/GATT system is basically limited to measures directly concerning goods. It does not concern domestic policies which may indirectly affect trade.

8. Harmonization and Mutual Recognition in the EC

Harmonization, in contrast, is a key element of the EEC Common Market and has been supplemented by the extensive use of mutual recognition of domestic regulations in order to speed up the establishment of the Internal Market under the Single European Act.

Harmonization is a general instrument for the establishment of the Common or Internal Market (Art.3h of the Rome Treaty). It does not relate only to the elimination of national barriers to trade, but is a mean of promoting, through progressive approximation of the economic policies of the Member States, their development, expansion and increased stability (original text of Art.2).

---

[7] VÖLKER, *The Agreement on Technical Barriers to Trade*, in: BOURGEOIS, BERROD & GIPPINI FOURNIER (eds), **The Uruguay Round Results**, European Interuniversity Press (EIP), Brussels, 1995, 331 ff.

[8] See KEIJZER, *GATT Agreement on Rules of Origin*, in: **The Uruguay Round Results**, *op. cit.*, 331 ff.

Article 100 provides for approximation through the unanimous adoption of directives by the Council of any provision which directly affects the establishment or functioning of the Common Market. Article 100A, added by the Single European Act of 1986 in order to speed up the establishment of the Internal Market, provides for approximation by majority voting in respect to relevant national provisions "as have as their object the establishment and operation of the Internal Market."

Harmonization is wide in scope but includes limitations both on subject matters and procedure which are relevant for our examination. It is carried out through directives (though this is not mandated by Art.100A), distinguishing it from normative uniformity which results from the use of EC regulations. The ensuing margin of freedom left to Member States is increased by the practice of drafting flexible directives that leave options open to national authorities. This facilitates agreement in the Council, albeit at the cost of reducing uniformity.

Article 100A is not applicable *inter alia* to fiscal provisions where, as a consequence, progress has been slow. The content of the harmonized provision is left open, except that: "The Commission's proposals for the approximation of laws on health, safety, environmental protection and consumer protection will be based on a high level of protection" (Art.100A.3). National derogations may be authorized by the Commission if they are necessary to protect major needs as recognized by Article 36 or relating to working or natural environment protection, provided that they are not a means of arbitrary discrimination or disguised restriction to trade between Member States (Art.100A.4).

As to specific matters, notably establishment, freedom of services and company law, harmonization is provided for with specific provisions. Coordination of the provisions relating to professions, including formation and access was considered a prerequisite of the mutual recognition of diplomas and was carried out by individual directives dealing with specific professions under Article 57.

The jurisprudence of the ECJ since the *Reyners* and *van Binsbergen* decisions of 1974 have held that the freedom of establishment is an individual right stemming from the EEC Treaty which the directives are only meant to facilitate. The former approach has been modified accordingly. Discrimination based on nationality is clearly inadmissible (Art.6 EEC); other requirements are severely tested under a standard-of-necessity to protect fundamental interest[9]. Directive 89/48 concerning a

---

[9] See ECJ, *Insurance* Case, judgement of 19.12.1986, 205/84.

general system of recognition of advanced professional degrees reflecting at least three years of study has effectively opened the respective markets of the Member States to the circulation of professional service suppliers and their services.

Reliance on mutual recognition of Member States' standards and controls even when harmonization is incomplete has also become, since the Single European Act of 1986, a major tool for the establishment of the Single Market in the field of such highly regulated and sensitive service industries as banking and insurance. Home-country control coupled with close cooperation between national regulators has become an innovative feature of the interpenetration of the economies and their regulation within the Community. Integration without full legislative uniformity or centralization of supervision is found in the US and in other federal systems. This feature underlines the radical difference between integration of the economies within the European Union and worldwide liberalization and removal of barriers pursued within the WTO.

Another basic features of the EC integrated and institutionalized system is also relevant, namely the principle of supremacy of Community law. Since harmonization is not complete and differences in the legal regimes and therefore in the economic conditions of production and marketing remain between national markets, some competition between the EC Member States' systems as a whole exists and must be taken into account.

9. The Limited Scope of Harmonization in the WTO

NAFTA, a much looser form of integration than the Community, lacks common effective organs, does not rely on harmonization, though its coverage is not limited to trade in goods. NAFTA protects national policies which may be an obstacle to trade as to sanitary and phytosanitary measures, by expressly disapplying Article XX.b GATT in this respect. It allows greater leeway for deviations from international standards than WTO/GATT rules[10]. In wider free trade areas harmonization is even more problematic[11].

---

[10] See ABBOTT, **Law and Policy of Regional Integration**, Kluwer, 1995, 73 ff. Harmonization programs are foreseen as landing transportation and telecommunication equipment which are directly relevant to trade in these products. A Committee on Standards Related Measures is provided, in NAFTA, with the task of facilitating the process by which the Parties make compatible their standards-related measures and of providing a forum for consultation

[11] See C. JACKSON, *The Free Trade Agreement of the Americas and Legal Harmonisation*, in: **American Soc. International Law Insight**, 12/1996.

NAFTA, however, follows a negative-list approach to services, whereby reservations to a liberalization commitment are admitted. This approach results in a more substantial across-the-board opening of the markets than the GATS approach.

Harmonization and mutual recognition is not generally within the scope and competence of the WTO though Articles VI and VII of GATS on "domestic regulation" and on "recognition" take into account the requirements that liberalization entails in this respect. The inherent absence of a cohesive institutional structure, i.e. of organs endowed with the competence to push ahead such a process, makes it cumbersome to pursue these objections generally. Intergovernmental negotiations which need consensus to be successful limit this approach to well-defined areas directly relevant to international trade, such as technical barriers, where agreement is possible also on the basis of industry common interest.

Unilateral autonomous harmonization of technical standards or adoption of such standards as developed by the producing countries and industries (e.g. as to high-tech products) is also a reality and a method. This approach does not entail international obligations and controls; it lacks therefore stability and predictability.

Under the GATS/WTO approach exporting countries are not limited as to the policies they pursue concerning the production of goods. On the other hand, the competence of the importing countries to impose restrictions on imports is allowed insofar as they affect the consumer and the environment of the importing state (destination principle). The focus is on products, not on the producer or on production methods. The use of trade restriction, to put pressure on exporting countries policies as an alternative to agreement or harmonization is contrary to this division of competencies.

Even when rules are laid down concerning the policy of the exporting country which may unfairly affect the competitiveness of imports, such as dumping and subsidies, GATT/WTO relies basically on permitting protective measures by the importing country. The focus is more on limiting the excessive use of this exceptional protection (i.e. anti-dumping and countervailing duties requirements), than on curtailing the competence of the exporting country.

The laying down of common principles and policies in the field of competition could undermine this approach and limit reliance on importing countries' countermeasures. Harmonization by itself does not seem sufficient; common policy management, international supervision and uniform enforcement would be required as in the EC, where *infra* community dumping and antisubsidy protection is accordingly inadmissible. The chart annexed to this paper seems to confirm that harmonization and mutual recognition, especially when non-trade domestic policies are affected, imply a strong (regional) institutional framework as found in the EC.

A change of approach in the direction of mutual coordination appears however in Articles VI and VII GATS on domestic regulation and recognition. These provisions are generally applicable and not limited to service sectors and modes where a state has entered in specific opening commitments.

Article VI on domestic regulations foresees the establishment of multilateral disciplines, based on objective criteria, "with a view to ensuring that measures relating to qualification requirements and procedures, technical standards and licensing requirements do not constitute unnecessary barriers to trade in services." With regard to professional services where commitments have been undertaken "each member shall provide for adequate procedures to verify the competence of professionals of any other member."

Article VII authorizes, but does not require, that a member recognize the education or experience obtained, requirements met, or licences or certification granted in a particular country for the purpose of the fulfilment of the member's standards or criteria for the authorization, licensing or certification of service suppliers.

Such recognition may be achieved through harmonization, based on an agreement with the country concerned or granted autonomously. The adoption of common international standards is recommended.

A kind of MFN clause covers the matter: the state that grants such recognition should afford any other country the opportunity to join the agreement, to negotiate a similar agreement, or to demonstrate that this country meets the autonomous requirements of the first state.

This piecemeal approach appears to be inspired by the example of the European Community. The cautious programmatic approach taken in Articles VI and VII GATS to harmonization and mutual recognition reflects the absence in the WTO of centralized common institutions endowed with the power to promote such development which is recognized as being necessary for effective access by professionals and other suppliers to the WTO Members' respective service markets.

10. Conclusions

1) Extensive harmonization and connected mutual recognition requires and is a feature of areas of advanced regional integration, such as the EC, which are not limited to trade and are endowed with adequate institutions.

2) Harmonization is not generally a prerequisite for free trade though uniform technical standards are appropriate to avoid national trade restrictions especially as to consumer goods and new high-tech products. Equalization of requirements for traded goods and a certain level of harmonization and mutual recognition of qualifications of service suppliers is necessary in order to make reciprocal market-opening effective. Reaching agreement on these issues on a global scale, even on a sectorial basis, has been and will be difficult.

3) Harmonization of predominantly non-trade domestic policies affecting freedom of trade should take those non-trade aspects and interests in account as a priority. Competent non-trade *fora* and organizations should be fully involved.

4) The globalization of economies is a tendency and a goal. Other values and interests both global and national cannot, however, be sacrificed to this end.

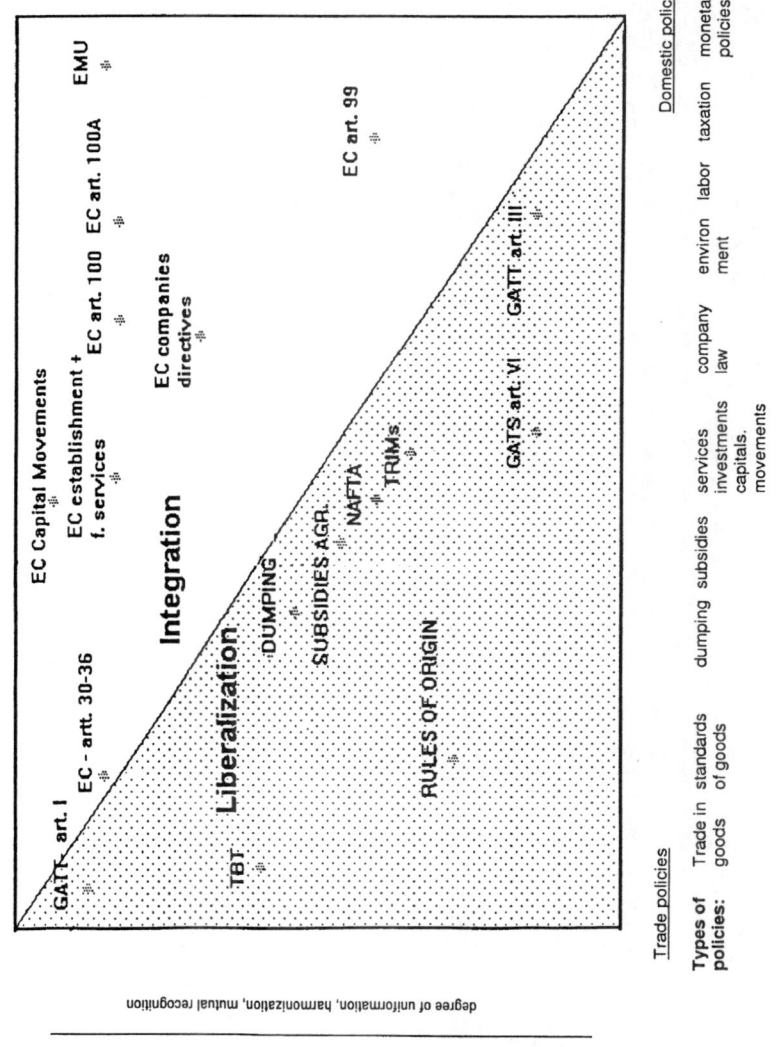

degree of uniformation, harmonization, mutual recognition

Multilateral traties + Org's   FTAs   Supranational organisations

Degree of institutionalization

Trade policies

Types of policies: Trade in goods   standards of goods   dumping   subsidies   services investments capitals. movements   company law   environ ment   labor   taxation   monetary policies

Domestic policies

Technical Standards in a Context of Regional Integration Agreements

Gonzalo GARCÍA JIMÉNEZ & Miguel GARDEÑES SANTIAGO

Research Fellow, Institut d'Études Juridiques Européennes, Faculty of Law, University of Liège

Faculty of Law, Autonomous University of Barcelona

1. Introduction

During the last decades, significant progress has been made in lowering barriers to international trade, in particular those barriers related to tariffs. Under the framework of the GATT, successive rounds of trade negotiations have significantly reduced tariffs for many industrial sectors to levels that have ceased to be a real impediment for the free flow of international trade. But as traditional tariffs have diminished, the importance of non-tariff impediments, including those related to standards and technical rules, have significantly increased. The proliferation of different standards and regulatory requirements, accompanied by diverse conformity assessment procedures, constitutes indeed one of the most serious constraints for international trade in goods.

At the multilateral level, the Uruguay Round represents an important improvement over the past. The Technical Barriers to Trade and the Sanitary and Phytosanitary Measures Agreements reinforce, clarify and extend the scope and coverage of rules and procedures on standards and conformity assessment. In addition, the new WTO Dispute Settlement system may considerably strengthen the effectiveness of the multilateral trading system.

At the regional level, the approaches of the European Union (EU) and of the North American Free Trade Agreement (NAFTA) to technical barriers to trade will be surveyed. Because they represent two different conceptions of regional integration agreements, the level of integration in this area is also different. The most far-reaching and comprehensive model is that of the European Union. Although obviously unique, for certain key aspects, such as harmonization of standards and technical regulations and mutual recognition of conformity assessment procedures, the European approach offers a model of reference for the rest of the world and serves as a springboard for future developments.

Improving transparency in conformity assessment procedures is one of the goals of the multilateral trade agreements. However, further improvement in this area is possible. Mutual recognition agreements on a regional or bilateral basis are important tools to facilitate international trade, as well as to establish the economic, legal and technical conditions necessary to ameliorate market access, promote trade liberalization efforts on a global basis and set a framework for improvements in future multilateral rounds. Recognizing the potential benefits of moving beyond the GATT framework at a faster pace than other signatories, the European Union and the United States are about to conclude a mutual recognition agreement in certain sectors. One of the most significant regional developments is also taking place in the framework of the Asia-Pacific Economic Cooperation.

2. The Multilateral Framework: The WTO Rules

a) The GATT General Principles

The principal GATT 1994 provisions affecting product standards are those relating to most-favored-nation treatment (Article I) and national treatment (Article III), together with the general exceptions relating to health, welfare, public morals (Article XX) and national security (Article XXI). These are complemented by two specific Agreements on Technical Barriers to Trade (TBT) and Sanitary and Phytosanitary Measures (SPS). While the TBT Agreement resulted from the revision of the 1979 GATT Standards Code, the SPS Agreement was drafted within the framework of the negotiations on agricultural issues[1]. In spite of these

---

[1] A detailed analysis of the history of the negotiations process can be found in STEWART T.P. (ed.), **The GATT Uruguay Round. A Negotiating History (1986-1992)**, (2 vols), Ed. Kluwer, Deventer, 1993, with the contribution of S.G. MARKEL on technical barriers to trade (pp.1067-1105) and J.M. BREEN on agriculture

different origins, both agreements embody the same basic principles. Although emphasis will be made upon the TBT Agreement, a parallel survey of the SPS Agreement will also be made.

These texts lay down a set of rules intended to discipline Member States' laws and regulations affecting trade in goods adopted for reasons such as public health or consumer protection, with the objective of reconciling the need for free world trade with other legitimate public interests[2]. Therefore, the WTO rules do not deprive Member States of their regulatory competence in these areas, though they pose some limits on the exercise of this competence, to prevent an abusive or unreasonable use of regulatory power. This is quite clearly expressed in the first Report issued by the Appellate Body[3], in which, after condemning some aspects of the US rules on gasoline for their inconsistency with Articles III.4 and XX of GATT, it stated that it did not mean "... that the ability of any WTO Member to take measures to control air pollution or, more generally, to protect the environment, is at issue", and added "WTO Members have a large measure of autonomy to determine their own policies on the environment — including its relationship with trade — their environmental objectives and the environmental legislation they enact and implement. So far as concerns the WTO, **that autonomy is circumscribed only by the need to respect the requirements of the General Agreement and the other covered agreements.**"[4] Therefore, the responsibility for legislating product conditions rests within the Member States, and the limits posed by WTO rules will come into play only when state regulations create unnecessary barriers to trade.

(pp.125-254). See also, E.L.M. VOLKËR, *"The Agreement on Technical Barriers to Trade"*, in: BOURGEOIS, BERROD & GIPPINI FOURNIER (eds), **The Uruguay Round Results. A European Lawyers' Perspective**, European Interuniversity Press, Brussels, 1995, pp.281-310.

[2] For a clarifying analysis on the balance between national regulatory objectives and WTO's purpose to establish a legal framework respecting the legitimate exercise of domestic regulatory autonomy whilst minimising regulatory differences between members, see F. ROESSLER, *"Increasing Market Access Under Regulatory Heterogeneity: The Strategies of the World Trade Organization"*, in: **Regulatory Reform and International Market Openness**, Organization for Economic Cooperation and Development (OECD), 1996, pp.117-129.

[3] Issued on April 22, 1996, and adopted by the Dispute Settlement Body on May 20, 1996 in the case of the United States Standards for Reformulated and Conventional Gasoline. WTO Appellate Body, AB-1996-1. **International Legal Materials** 1996, pp.603-634. See G. NOGUEIRA, *"The First WTO Appellate Body Review: United States-Standards for Reformulated and Conventional Gasoline"*, in: **Journal of World Trade**, December 1995, pp.5-30.

[4] Point V (Findings and Conclusions), last paragraph; underlining added.

b) Strengthening the Multilateral Trading System

As for the **scope** of the agreements, TBT deals with all types of product regulations and standards, adopted for reasons such as national security, prevention of fraud, public health and the protection of the environment (Article 2.2) and, therefore, has a general scope[5]. The concept of product specification includes not only those which refer to the product itself, but also those relating to processes and production methods[6], and this was one of the important improvements by comparison with the 1979 GATT Standards Code. Apart from governmental regulations, the agreement also covers voluntary standards issued by public or private standardization bodies (Article 4), including also a **"code of good practice"** to guide their activities (Annex 3). By contrast, SPS Agreement is limited to governmental sanitary and phytosanitary measures specifically intended to protect human and animal life and the preservation of plants (Article 2.2 and Annex A).

Notwithstanding their different scope, the basic rules embodied in both agreements are quite the same: when adopting and implementing product regulations, members must respect nondiscrimination (Articles 2.1 TBT and 2.3 SPS) and proportionality (Articles 2.2 TBT, 2.2 and 5 SPS). The **nondiscrimination** requirement should be understood in the light of Article III.4 of the General Agreement, which sets out the obligation to treat imported products no less favorably than like products of national origin when applying internal regulations, and Article XX, which lays down some general exceptions, subject to the requirement that they are not applied in a manner which would constitute a means of "arbitrary

---

[5] However, technical standards adopted for the purpose of purchase by governmental bodies are excluded, as they are covered by the WTO Agreement on public procurement (Article 1.4).

[6] See definitions in Annex A. In general, see G. FOY, *"Towards Extension of the GATT Standards Code to Production Processes"*, in: **Journal of World Trade** No.2, 1992, p.121. For the scope of the interpretation of the so-called PPMs (product characteristics and their related process and production methods), see R. QUICK, *"The Agreement on the Technical Barriers to Trade in the Context of the Trade and Environment Discussion"*, in: BOURGEOIS, BERROD & GIPPINI FOURNIER (eds), *supra*, note 1, pp.319-326. Significantly, in the US-Venezuela Gasoline Dispute, the Panel, when dealing with Article III:4 National Treatment, instead of applying the narrow interpretation of PPMs of the Tuna I Report (where the Panel, using a product-centered approach, determined that the US import restrictions against Mexican harvested yellowfin tuna on the basis that dolphins may be caught in the purse nets was a regulation that could not possibly affect tuna as a product), applied a broader approach, the like-product distinction, on the basis that a **highly subjective and variable treatment** of producer characteristics would create **great instability and uncertainty in the conditions of competition**. Therefore, the Panel found that imported gasoline was effectively prevented from benefiting from as favourable sales conditions as domestic gasoline. See §§ 6.11 to 6.13.

or unjustifiable discrimination between countries where the same conditions prevail, or a disguised restriction on international trade."[7]

The **proportionality requirement** means that measures and regulations must not be more burdensome than necessary. The basic idea is that, of the range of measures capable of attaining the desired level of protection, states should choose the least trade-obstructing one. This idea is clearly expressed in the footnote to Article 5.6 of the SPS Agreement, which reads: "…a measure is not more trade-restrictive than required unless there is another measure, reasonably available taking into account technical and economic feasibility, that achieves the appropriate level of sanitary or phytosanitary protection and is significantly less restrictive of trade."

Technical and sanitary regulations should be **based on available scientific evidence** and states must be able to demonstrate that their regulations are really justified, especially because other members have the right to demand explanations about them (Articles 2.5 of TBT and 5.8 of SPS). In addition, the Appellate Body has confirmed that **the burden of proving** that a measure is justified for one of the reasons under Article XX of GATT rests on the Party invoking the exception[8].

One of the TBT and SPS Agreements' key issues is the new role given to **international harmonization**, which is promoted as a means of reducing technical obstacles to trade in goods. This is done by encouraging members to base their product regulations on existing international models provided their adoption does not interfere with the pursuit of legitimate domestic policy. For instance, Article 2.4 of TBT says that states will base their technical regulations in existing international standards, unless these standards are inappropriate for "fundamental reasons". Furthermore, Article 2.5 adds that, when state regulations conform with international standards, it shall be presumed — unless the contrary is proven — that these regulations do not create unnecessary barriers to trade. As a consequence, the role of international standards is fostered in

---

[7] In its Report in the US gasoline standards case, the Appellate Body explained the conditions which a state measure found contrary to one of the obligations under the agreement must fulfill in order to be covered by one of the exceptions under Article XX (see, especially, the arguments relating to the introductory provisions of Article XX in Section IV). In the particular case, it found that some of the US standards were contrary to Article III.4 and, even though they were within the terms of Article XX(g), they did not meet the general requirements of Article XX.

[8] Section IV, Paragraph 3 of the US gasoline standards case. Another important obligation laid down in the agreements is the duty to notify projected regulations to the WTO Secretariat (Article 2.9 and 2.10 TBT and Annex B SPS).

a very important way, as a presumption of reasonableness is associated with them. Nevertheless, the concept of international standards is different in TBT and SPS. As far as TBT is concerned, international standards are voluntary standards emanating from international standardization bodies, namely ISO and IEC[9], whereas in SPS (Article 3) this expression refers to the norms and guidelines of international specialized agencies, such as the FAO/WHO Codex Alimentarius Commission in the field of food safety (Annex A)[10].

Apart from regulations and standards, the agreements deal also with **conformity assessment activities**, such as testing, inspection, type approval or certification. States are asked to conduct their activities in this field in accordance with the general rules of nondiscrimination and proportionality and, in addition, they must ensure procedural guarantees in favor of traders and importers in order to avoid arbitrary or protectionist attitudes, and which include, *inter alia*, the prohibition of unjustified delays or excessive fees, the duty of confidentiality, the right of applicants to be informed of any details of the procedure and the right to lodge appeals (Articles 5, 7 and 8 of TBT and Annex B of SPS). These provisions are of great importance, since it is quite clear that, even if regulations are neutral and in conformity with international rules, there is always the risk that they are applied in an arbitrary or unfair manner, and thus the importance of rules governing their practical implementation through assessment and control procedures[11]. The extension of rules and procedures on standards and conformity assessment plays therefore an important role in the strengthening of the multilateral trading system and market liberalization.

Finally, it should be taken into account that the rules laid down in the agreements **apply to central government authorities**, but do no affect

---

[9] International Standardization Organization and International Electrotechnical Commission; on the importance of voluntary standards in international trade, see A.O. SYKES, **Product Standards for Internationally Integrated Goods Markets**, The Brookings Institution, 1995.

[10] About the legal nature of Codex standards, see J.P. CHIARADIA-BOUSQUET, **Régime juridique du contrôle et de la certification de la qualité des denrées alimentaires : puissance publique et producteurs**, Ed. FAO, Rome, 1994, pp.24-27.

[11] An example of a controversy on assessment procedures is that of the dispute between the EC and Spain — not a member at that time — about the Spanish system of approval for domestic electrical appliances, which the EC claimed to be discriminatory. In its Recommendation of July 10, 1984 the Committee on Technical Obstacles suggested some changes in the approval procedure, which were followed and so there was no need for a panel to solve the dispute. See LÓPEZ ESCUDERO, in: **Los obstáculos al comercio en la Comunidad Económica Europea**, Ed. Universidad de Granada, 1991, p.103.

local authorities directly. However, they affect them indirectly, because Member States are obliged to take all possible measures to ensure that local authorities also comply with the agreements[12].

c) The Importance of the WTO Dispute Settlement Mechanism

To a large extent, successful application of WTO rules dealing with technical obstacles to trade, as that of any other WTO rule, will depend on the commitment of Member States to respect these rules and on the proper functioning of the new dispute settlement mechanism, which has been greatly improved[13]. Under the new system, complainants have the possibility of obtaining a dispute resolution panel and then an appellate review. As panel reports and appeals will be adopted as definitive unless the signatories decide not to do so by consensus, the authority for sanctions can no longer be blocked by the losing disputant. Therefore, non-compliance with TBT or SPS provisions found by WTO dispute settlement panels either will require reduction of the trade-distorting behaviour or will allow for cross-retaliation through increased tariffs if a signatory does not abide by the decision of the Dispute Settlement Body.

Because of these provisions, not only prospects for definitive legal interpretations of controversial or ambiguously worded GATT obligations are greatly enhanced, but also, signatories will have to carefully consider the use of technical barriers in a protectionist way so as to avoid WTO-authorized trade sanctions.

There is already some evidence that WTO rules in the area are going to be used and relied upon by member states. First, apart from GATT 1994, TBT and SPS Agreements have been the most invoked by the Parties in disputes raised so far[14]. Secondly, and quite significantly, the first case resolved by the Appellate Body dealt with a technical obstacle to trade in goods[15]. Finally, more cases are pending, for instance the

---

[12] This "best efforts" rule appears in Articles 3 and 7 TBT and 13 SPS, and applies also to non-governmental organizations (Articles 4 and 8 TBT and 13 SPS).

[13] Annex 2 of the WTO Agreement; see A. LOWENFELD, *"Remedies along with Rights: Institutional Reform in the New GATT"*, in: **American Journal of International Law**, No.88, July 1994, pp.477-488; and, P.T.B KOBONA, *"Dispute Resolution under the WTO- an Overview"*, in: **Journal of World Trade**, No.3, 1994, p.23.

[14] According to the report by WTO Director-General Ruggiero on the first year of operation of the WTO, up to November 27, 1995, the DSB had received twenty-one demands for consultations. All cases involved trade in goods and, therefore, came under GATT 1994. In addition the TBT Agreement was invoked on seven occasions and SPS on five. See **WTO Focus** No.6, December 1995, pp.5-6.

[15] The above mentioned case on US gasoline standards. This case was solved on the grounds of the GATT provisions alone, because the panel found that, as US measures

complaint of the US and Canada against the European Union's restrictions on meat treated with synthetic growth hormones[16]. Greater use of the WTO dispute settlement procedures will lead also to certainty, transparency and less reliance on unilateral measures to resolve disputes.

3. The European Union

The European Union's policy for dismantling technical barriers to trade in goods between Member States has developed since the early seventies[17]. Its basic instruments are the direct application of the provisions of the EC Treaty and the role of the judiciary when interpreting these provisions, the harmonization of national laws, the information procedure established by Directive 83/189, and the global approach to conformity assessment.

a) EC Treaty Provisions, Case Law and Mutual Recognition

The main treaty provisions are Article 30, on quantitative restrictions on imports and Measures having an Equivalent Effect (MEE), Article 34, on quantitative restrictions on exports and MEE, and Article 36, which lays down the exceptions that may justify a prohibition or restriction on imports, exports or transit. In fact, these provisions have given rise to a very rich case law from the European Court of Justice (ECJ).

As early as 1974, the ECJ gave in its *Dassonville*[18] judgment the general definition of a MEE under Article 30, which encompassed "all trading rules enacted by Member States which are capable of hindering, directly or indirectly, actually or potentially, intra-Community trade..."

---

had been found contrary to Articles III.4 and XX of GATT, it was unnecessary to determine whether they were consistent or not with TBT Agreement (paragraph 6.43 of Panel Report). As this particular point was not challenged in the appeal, the Appellate Body refused to examine the issue of the application of the TBT Agreement (II.C). Indeed, the finding of the panel was correct because the measure at stake was discriminatory. On the contrary, if it had been nondiscriminatory or equally applicable, the TBT Agreement should have been taken into account, in order to evaluate the proportionality and reasonableness of the measures.

[16] See **WTO Focus**, No.12, August-September 1996, pp.4-5. In this regard, it is noteworthy that because the issue involved production methods for beef, it was not covered under the 1979 Tokyo Round Standards Code. The United States used unilateral action and imposed sanctions against the European Union under Section 301. However, with the completion of the Uruguay Round, this kind of disputes can be addressed under the SPS Agreement.

[17] See the general program for the elimination of technical obstacles to trade (**Official Journal of the European Communities, OJ** C 76, of June 17, 1969), together with Commission Directive 70/50, of December 22, 1969 (**OJ** L 13, of January 19, 1970).

[18] Dated July 11, 1974 (8/74, R. 837).

This wide definition has been interpreted to include many different types of state regulations, insofar as they affect trade between Member States, such as those relating directly to imports, those establishing technical requirements for products, price regulations, regulations on advertising and sales promotion, administrative practices in the context of governmental purchases or even non binding practices by public authorities[19]. More recently, however, the ECJ has tried to limit the scope of Article 30 in its *Keck* judgment[20], in which it stated that the concept of MEE does not include regulations on "selling arrangements", an expression which compared to product "conditions" seems to include circumstances external to the product itself, such as shops' holidays and opening hours or types of establishments allowed to sell certain products, as long as these regulations are applied in a nondiscriminatory way.

In its well-known *Cassis de Dijon*[21] Case the ECJ laid down the criteria that determine whether state regulations affecting trade in products are justified or not. The Court recognizes that national regulations affecting trade between Member States — and, therefore, creating an obstacle — may be admitted if they are justified to protect a "mandatory requirement", such as consumer or environmental protection. In order to be justified, the measure must be applied in a nondiscriminatory way and must keep due proportionality. The proportionality condition has been interpreted in the sense that, within the range of measures permitting attainment of the objective pursued, states must choose those which are less trade-obstructing. Therefore, state measures should not be more

---

[19] A detailed analysis in A. MATTERA, **Le marché unique européen; ses règles, son fonctionnement**, Ed. Jupiter, Paris, 1990. By contrast with this broad interpretation of Article 30, the ECJ has interpreted Article 34 in the sense that it applies only to measures specifically affecting exports; See, for instance, the *Groenveld* Decision of November 8, 1979 (15/79, R. 3409).

[20] November 24, 1993 (C-267 and 268/91). Two very different views of the Court's judgment are those of A. MATTERA, *"De l'arrêt Dassonville à l'arrêt Keck : l'obscure clarté d'une jurisprudence riche en principes novateurs et en contradictions"*, in: **Revue du Marché Unique Européen**, No.1, 1994, pp.117-160; and, R. JOLIET, *"La libre circulación de mercancías: la sentencia Keck y Mithouard y las nuevas orientaciones de la jurisprudencia"*, in: **Gaceta Jurídica de la CE**, Vol.D-23, 1995, pp.9-38.

[21] Dated February 20, 1979 (120/78, R. 649). See also the interpretative Communication by the EC Commission in **OJ** C 256, of October 3, 1980. An early assessment of the practical importance of this ruling in A. MATTERA, *"L'arrêt "Cassis de Dijon" : une nouvelle approche pour la réalisation et le bon fonctionnement du marché intérieur"*, in : **Revue du Marché Commun**, 1980, pp.505-514; by the same author, see also *"L'Article 30 du Traité CEE, la jurisprudence Cassis de Dijon et le principe de la reconnaissance mutuelle"*, in : **Revue du Marché Unique Européen**, No.4, 1992, pp.13-71.

burdensome than necessary[22]. Discriminatory measures can be justified only on the grounds of one of the exceptions expressly listed in Article 36, which are public order, public morality, public safety, public health, protection of artistic and historical heritage and of industrial and commercial property[23], as long as these measures do not constitute — in wording very much reminding of Article XX of GATT — "an arbitrary discrimination or a disguised restriction on trade."

Hence, *Cassis* provides a tool by which the judiciary can compel Member States to mutually recognize their national regulations governing production and marketing of goods, as long as they offer an equivalent level of protection of the public interests at issue. This basic rule is one of the cornerstones of the new approach on technical regulations and standards in the European Union.

As stated earlier, these provisions have provoked a very important body of case law and have been very powerful instruments for liberalizing trade between Member States. Of course, one of the main reasons for their success is that they may be directly applied in any Member State and, consequently, they give rise to individual rights that interested Parties can invoke before national courts and authorities[24]. This individual-right-protection character has been reinforced in a very important measure by the ECJ decision in *Brasserie du Pêcheur*[25], in which the Court admitted that, in certain circumstances, a breach of Article 30 may even give rise to state liability for damages.

---

[22] For instance, in the field of food regulations, in numerous cases — Italian vinegar, German beer, Italian pasta... — the ECJ has confirmed that for the protection of aspects other than safety or health (names of products, composition and quality requirements not affecting human health...), sufficiently informative labeling would be an appropriate measure. More strict measures as, for instance, a marketing ban would only be justified where health or safety are at stake. See, in general, Commission Communication in **OJ** C 271, October 24, 1989.

[23] Nonetheless, in *Commission vs. Belgium* (July 9, 1992, C-2/90) the Court admitted the conformity with Article 30 of restrictions imposed by Belgium, for environmental reasons (not included in Article 36), on trade and transport of waste products, even if they applied only to imported waste. This solution, however, was due to the very special nature of the "merchandise" considered, waste products, and to the EC policy in this area (the general rule that waste should be eliminated as close as possible to its source of production). This decision should be considered as exceptional.

[24] For a general view of the obligations imposed on national judges by EC law, See D. RUIZ-JARABO, **El juez nacional como juez comunitario**, Ed. Civitas, Madrid, 1993.

[25] March 5, 1996 (C-46 and 48/93); See G. TESAURO, *"Responsabilité des Etats membres pour violation du droit communautaire"*, in : **Revue du Marché Unique Européen**, No.3, 1996, pp.15-34; and, A. RIGAUX, *"L'arrêt Brasserie du Pêcheur-Factortame III : le roi peut mal faire en droit communautaire"*, in : **Europe**, May 1996, pp.1-6.

b) The "New Approach": Accelerating Harmonization

Apart from the basic treaty provisions, it should be kept in mind that in the European Union context, especially after the completion of the Internal Market legislative program[26], there is a very high degree of harmonization of Member States' legislation. In the first place, very important general EU texts have been adopted such as Directive 84/450 (September 10, 1984), on misleading advertising, Directive 85/374 (July 25, 1985), on liability for damages caused by products and Directive 92/59 (June 29, 1992) on the general safety of products and, secondly, there are a large number of texts on specific goods, such as pharmaceutical products, foodstuffs and industrial products.

As far as industrial products are concerned, the so-called "new approach" to technical harmonization was adopted in 1985[27], in response to the shortcomings of former methods of harmonization[28]. The basic features of this new approach are: first, the scope of directives is defined through large categories of products (machines, construction products, toys...) rather than product by product; second, directives limit themselves to the basic safety requirements products must satisfy (performance standards rather than descriptive standards) and, third, EC Commission mandates standardization bodies with the task of elaborating voluntary standards that are in conformity with the regulatory goals of the directives. Therefore, products complying with these standards benefit from a presumption of conformity with the requirements of the directives, unless the contrary is proven. Consequently, given the role to be assumed by voluntary standards, an important effort has been made

---

[26] See the European Commission's *White Paper on the Completion of the Internal Market*, COM(85)310 final, June 14, 1985. Article 100(A), introduced by the Single European Act, permitted an acceleration of the EC lawmaking machinery, by introducing qualified majority voting in the EC Council, instead of unanimity required by Article 100. About the importance of European common standards for the international competitiveness of the European industry, see Commission's Communication *"Industrial Policy in an Open and Competitive Environment"*, COM(90)556 final, November 16, 1990, p.12.

[27] See Council Resolution of May 7, 1985 (**OJ** C136/1, June 4, 1985). See, for instance, J. PELKMANS, *"The New Approach to Technical Harmonization and Standardization"*, in: **Journal of Common Market Studies**, Vol.25 No.3, 1987, pp.249-269.

[28] In fact, the "old approach" to harmonization proved to be slow and inadequate. Aiming at highly detailed harmonization, this approach encountered many difficulties. For some products it took more than a decade to lay down harmonized rules, which were sometimes outdated by the time they entered into force. Moreover, the problem of divergent industrial standards, which are of private and voluntary nature, but are nonetheless able to act as a barrier to trade, was left largely unadressed. See P. EECKHOUT, **The European Internal Market and International Trade. A Legal Analysis**, Clarendon Press, Oxford, 1994, pp.265, 270-275.

to develop the activities of European standardization bodies, namely CEN, CENELEC and ETSI[29]. Accordingly, harmonization is no longer aimed at completeness. Only the essential requirements to which products have to conform become the object of common rules and, therefore, approximation of national laws is limited to these essential requirements.

c) The Mutual Information Directive: Avoiding the Creation of New Technical Barriers

The direct application of treaty provisions and harmonization of national legislations have played a very important role in dismantling technical barriers to trade. Nevertheless, their common weakness is that they apply only when an obstacle already exists, the effects of which may hinder free circulation for quite a long time, before it is "removed" by a judicial decision or a legal text. For this reason, the need arose for some instrument of a preventive nature, that would act at an early stage, before possible obstacles were created. This instrument came with Directive 83/189, of March 28, 1983[30], which requires Member States to notify the EC Commission of all projects of technical regulations they plan to adopt. It should be noted that, since its revision in 1994, the concept of "technical specification" for the purposes of the directive includes also those relating to processes and production methods, insofar as they affect the products' characteristics. When the notification is received, the Commission transmits the project to the rest of Member States, who have the opportunity to present their views. In the meantime, the author of the project is obliged to maintain a *statu quo* period during which it may not adopt the text.

This mechanism allows mutual information and transparency and, in practice, has proved to be very effective in avoiding potential obstacles at this early stage[31], the overall level of compliance by states being quite

---

[29] ETSI: European Telecommunications Standards Institute.
See the European Commission's "Green Book" published in **OJ** C 20 of January 28, 1991, followed by the Communication published in **OJ** 96 of April 15, 1992 and Council Resolution of June 18, 1992 (**OJ** C 173, of July 9, 1992).

[30] **OJ** L 109, April 26, 1983, modified in the last place by Directive 94/10, of March 23, 1994 (**OJ** L 100, April 19, 1994). The precedents for this type of mechanism may be found in the non-binding gentlemen's agreement published in **OJ** C 76 of June 17, 1969 and in the GATT Standards Code of 1979.

[31] On its functioning, see J. FRONIA & G. CASELLA, *"La procédure de contrôle des réglementations techniques prévue par la Directive 83/189; instrument de prévention des obstacles aux échanges et de politique industrielle cohérente"*, in : **Revue du Marché Unique Européen**, No.2, 1995, pp.37-85; as for statistical data on the implementation of the directive in 1995, see the notice published in **OJ** C 309 (October 18, 1996).

high. However, sometimes, states have failed to notify their product regulations and, of course, this constitutes a breach of EC law, as the ECJ has had the opportunity to point out on several occasions[32], but until very recently some doubts remained as to the situation of national regulations which were adopted disregarding the procedures laid down in the directive. Since 1986[33], the Commission held that these regulations are non-enforceable against third Parties, but the Court had not given an express confirmation on this point, despite having had the opportunity to deal with several cases involving Directive 83/189. Finally, in its *CIA Security International* decision, issued on April 30, 1996[34], the ECJ stated that Articles 8 and 9 must be interpreted to mean private Parties may rely on them before national courts and, consequently, technical regulations adopted without prior notification should not be applied[35], thus confirming the non enforceability of such regulations. Of course, the practical importance of this ruling does not need to be stressed.

Finally, it should be noted that, in line with this transparency policy, a new decision has been adopted[36] that requires states to notify to the Commission any measure restricting sales of goods coming from other EC Member States (marketing bans, withdrawal orders...) and, therefore, states will be required to demonstrate in all cases the reasons justifying their measures restricting trade in products.

d) The "Global Approach": Mutual Recognition of Conformity Assessment

However, mutual recognition and harmonization of essential requirements alone were not sufficient for the elimination of barriers to trade. The new approach did little to solve obstacles associated with conformity assessment, because, even when the underlying product requirements were the same, there was a lack of confidence in testing and certification conducted abroad. This led the European Commission to complete the new system by proposing a "Global Approach to Conformity

---

[32] See, for instance, its judgment of August 2, 1993 (C-139/92).

[33] Communication published in **OJ** C 245 (October 1, 1986).

[34] Case C-194/94.

[35] See §§ 47-55.

[36] Decision 3052/1995, of December 13, 1995 (**OJ** L 321, December 30, 1995). See E. GIPPINI FOURNIER & M. SERENA LA PERGOLA, *"La nouvelle procédure d'information mutuelle sur les mesures nationales dérogeant au principe de libre circulation des marchandises à l'intérieur de la Communauté"*, in : **Revue du Marché Unique Européen**, No.4, 1996, pp.145-180.

Assessment"[37], aimed at developing homogeneous certification structures throughout Europe[38] and at creating legal marks to prove conformity with EC directives[39]. This represents an innovative effort to develop mutual confidence in certification and testing conducted abroad, through a combination of reliance on international quality control standards and mutually acceptable procedures to ensure that they are followed.

4. The North American Free Trade Agreement

a) Background

On January 1st, 1994, with the entry into force of the North American Free Trade Agreement (NAFTA), the governments of the United States, Mexico and Canada established a framework to reduce barriers to trade between them[40]. For this purpose, the agreement deals with the most obvious barriers, namely tariffs and quota systems, which clearly limit the entry of foreign goods into each country. In addition, member states also recognized the need to limit other barriers to trade that unjustly treat foreign goods in an unequal or protectionist manner.

The NAFTA provisions on technical barriers to trade build upon earlier commitments established by the Canada-United States Free Trade Agreement. This predecessor to the NAFTA expanded upon the commitments of the 1979 GATT Standards Code and established additional procedural guarantees based on the principles of increasing compatibility and mutual recognition of standards[41].

To a great extent, NAFTA provisions are based on the two Uruguay Round Agreements[42], with similar or identical language in many

---

[37] See Commission's Communication in **OJ** C 267, of October 19, 1989. A general view of EC conformity assessment policy in J. McMILLAN, *"La certification, la reconnaissance mutuelle et le marché unique"*, in : **Revue du Marché Unique Européen**, No.2, 1992, pp.181-211.

[38] Mainly by promoting the use of EN 29000 and EN 45000 series of European standards and by creating in 1990 the European Organization for Testing and Certification (EOTC).

[39] See Directive 93/68 and Decision 93/465, both of July 22, 1993 (**OJ** L 220, August 30, 1993).

[40] "... reduce disruptions to trade; establish clear and mutually advantageous rules governing their trade; ensure predictable commercial framework for business planning and investment..." See the Preamble of the North American Free Trade Agreement (hereinafter the Agreement).

[41] See Chapter 6 of the Canada-US Free Trade Agreement.

[42] For further discussion on the relation of NAFTA with Uruguay Round Agreements, see J. JOHNSON, **The North American Free Trade Agreement: A**

provisions. The NAFTA provisions dealing with sanitary and phyto-sanitary measures are set out in Section B of Chapter Seven (Articles 709 to 724), and those dealing with technical regulations, standards and conformity assessment procedures are set out in Chapter Nine (Articles 901 to 915). In this section emphasis will be made on this last chapter.

b) Scope and Coverage

Article 915 defines standards-related measures to consist of three types of measures: standards, technical regulations, and conformity assessment procedures. The first term refers to voluntary product standards while the second refers to mandatory standards imposed by governments. Finally, the third refers to procedures which determine whether a product meets a standard or technical regulation and expressly excludes, unlike 1994 GATT TBT Agreement, "approval procedures".

Chapter 9 applies to all standards-related measures that, directly or indirectly, affect trade in goods or services, other than agricultural and procurement standards which are dealt with in their own NAFTA chapters[43]. Unlike the 1994 GATT TBT, which only applies to goods and not to services, services referred to in this chapter are land transportation and telecommunications. There is no exclusion of the human, animal and plant life and health exception of GATT Article XX(b) — as it is the case in NAFTA SPS provisions. Therefore, a standards-related measure may be justified under this GATT exception, which has been clarified by NAFTA as including environmental measures[44].

Unlike NAFTA provisions with regard to SPS, the obligation to ensure observance by state and provincial governments set out in NAFTA Article 105 does not apply to Chapter 9. National governments are only obliged "to seek through appropriate measures"[45] to ensure observance

---

Comprehensive Guide, Canada Law Book Inc., 1994, Sections 1.6 and 6.7.; F.M. ABBOTT, **Law and Policy of Regional Integration: the NAFTA and Western Hemispheric Integration in the World Trade Organization System**, Martinus Nijhoff Publishers, 1995, pp.55-56, 106-108.

[43] Respectively, Chapter 7 and Chapter 10.

[44] Article 2101(1). Here, it should be recalled that in the 1991 *Tuna/Dolphin* Case, a GATT panel interpreted a provision similar to Article 904, in the case Article XX(b) to apply only to measures necessary to protect the environment of the trade-restricting country but not outside its boundaries. NAFTA does not alter this limitation. See M. TREBILCOCK & R. HOWSE, **The Regulation of International Trade**, Routledge, 1995, p.352. For further analysis on the incorporation of GATT Article XX exceptions to the NAFTA, see J. JOHNSON, *supra*, note 42, Chapter 4.3(5)(b)(i); F.M. ABBOTT, *supra*, note 42, p.74.

[45] Article 902.

of the technical standards obligations[46] by states and provinces and non-government standardizing bodies. This obligation is much weaker than the general NAFTA Article 105 requirement — "... take all necessary measures..." —, and a lesser commitment than the GATT obligation — "...take such reasonable measures as may be available to them to ensure compliance...".

Each country must extend national treatment and MFN treatment in its standards-related measures[47]. Goods and services from another NAFTA country must be treated as favourably as those which are domestic or which come from non-NAFTA countries.

c) Encouraging Harmonization

As standards-related measures may interfere with free trade, NAFTA negotiators had to weigh the protection of national public policies — through the maintenance of high standards — against the objective of trade liberalization[48]. Therefore, NAFTA provisions contain strong language encouraging harmonization of domestic and international environmental, health, and safety standards, but also make clear that the Parties have broad discretion to reject harmonization if necessary to ensure that NAFTA will not interfere with the integrity of domestic regulatory systems.

Article 905(1) essentially **requires** NAFTA countries to use international standards as the basis for their standards-related measures[49]. Moreover, any country using an international standard as a domestic technical measure enjoys the benefit of a presumption[50] that its use of the standard is consistent with the basic NAFTA provisions respecting

---

[46] With regard to Article 904 (basic rights and obligations), Article 905 (use of international standards), Article 906 (compatibility and equivalence), Article 907 (assessment of risk), Article 908 (conformity assessment), and to some provisions to Article 909 (notification, publication and provision of information).

[47] Article 904(3). As for the nondiscrimination obligation in conformity assessment procedures, see Article 908.

[48] See, for instance, Article 906(1): "Recognizing the crucial role of standards-related measures in achieving legitimate objectives, the Parties shall, in accordance with this chapter, work jointly to enhance the level of safety and of protection of human, animal and plant life and health, the environment and consumers."

[49] Article 915 specifically mentions: the International Organization for Standardization (ISO), the International Electrotechnical Commission (IEC), Codex Alimentarius Commission, the World Health Organization (WHO), the Food and Agriculture Organization (FAO) and the International Telecommunications Union (ITU). In addition, the article specifies that NAFTA countries may designate other bodies.

[50] Article 905(2).

nondiscrimination and obstacles to trade. Article 906(2) further encourages each Party to act in the future to harmonize — **make compatible** — its governmental regulations — to the greatest extent practicable — with the standards of other NAFTA trading partners[51]. To facilitate this effort towards compatibility and equivalence, Article 913 creates a Committee on Standards-Related Measures[52]. In addition, when harmonization is absent, the agreement requires mutual recognition when a Party demonstrates the equivalence of its regulations and mutual recognition of conformity assessment procedures when Parties are **satisfied** as to their adequacy[53]. A decision by the importing Party not to afford mutual recognition is to be explained in writing on request by the exporting Party[54].

d) While Preserving Legitimate Protection

Despite this strong language encouraging harmonization, the NAFTA is also careful to guarantee that trade expansion does not come at the expenses of Member States' rights to establish legitimate TBTs.

On the one hand, Article 905(1) authorizes Parties to depart from international standards in instances where those standards would be "ineffective" or "inappropriate" to fulfill legitimate objectives pursued by governments, because of factors related to climate, geography, infrastructure, technology, science or level of protection. Article 905(3) also allows NAFTA countries to apply standards-related measures providing for higher levels of protection than international standards, therefore contributing to an "harmonization upward" effect on standards.

On the other hand, Article 904(1) expressly affirms that each country retains the basic right to adopt, apply, maintain and enforce its own standard-related measures, including measures relating to safety and the protection of human, animal or plant life or health, the environment[55]

---

[51] As for the harmonization of conformity assessment procedures, see Article 908(1).

[52] This committee has, among others, the task of facilitating the process by which the Parties make compatible their standards-related measures and to providing a forum for consultation on standards issues. In addition it establishes and determines the scope and mandate of various sub-committees (e.g. in Land Transportation, Telecommunications, Automotive and Labelling of Textile and Apparel Goods) and working groups. However, those bodies, although comprised of representatives of the Parties, cannot adopt measures on behalf of the Parties.

[53] Article 906(4), (6).

[54] Article 906(5).

[55] This provision goes beyond comparable language in Article XX of GATT, in that it explicitly mentions environmental measures. For an environmental oriented

and the consumer. In addition, making clear that NAFTA does not oblige its member states to harmonize their standards, each country may establish the level of protection it considers appropriate[56] when pursuing the legitimate objectives of safety, the protection of human, animal or plant health, the environment or consumers[57]. However, unnecessary obstacles to trade between the Parties can not be created. Therefore, measures will be admissible only if they are justified by a legitimate objective and do not exclude goods or services complying with this objective[58]. In this regard, it should be noted that the GATT "least trade-restrictive" requirement to qualify a measure as a necessary or unnecessary obstacle does not appear in Chapter 9 of the NAFTA. In addition, the definition of what constitutes a legitimate objective is a broad and permissive one[59].

Therefore, the problem arises when determining which TBTs are legitimate — and then justified —, and which are merely disguised attempts of unequal or discriminatory treatment against foreign goods or services. There is no doubt that determining whether the measure is legitimately based on a licit purpose or is merely a facade for protectionist purposes, is essential to establish an equilibrium between the right of member states to maintain some sovereign control in appropriate situations and the principles of free trade. In the absence of official complaints filed under the NAFTA provision dealing with TBTs, and drawing from experience on bi-national panels within the framework of the US-Canada

---

approach of technical standards and other "green" provisions in the NAFTA, see R.B. LUDWISZESKI & P.E. SELEY, *"'Green' Language in the NAFTA: Reconciling Free Trade and Environmental Protection"*, in: BELLO, HOLMER & NORTON (eds), **The North American Free Trade Agreement: A New Frontier in International Trade and Investment in the Americas**, pp.374-383.

[56] Articles 904(2) and 907.

[57] Article 907(2) provides essentially that NAFTA countries "should", when establishing a level of protection they consider appropriate and when conducting risk assessments, avoid distinctions between similar goods and services where the distinctions result in arbitrary or unjustifiable discrimination against goods or service providers from other NAFTA countries. It should be noted that the using of the ambiguous expression "should" instead of the unambiguous "shall", suggests that there are circumstances in which this obligation does not apply. See J. JOHNSON, *supra*, note 42, section 6.6(3)(b).

[58] Articles 904(4) and 907(2).

[59] "... legitimate objective includes an objective such as: a) safety, b) protection of human, animal or plant life or health, the environment or consumers, including matters relating to quality and identifiability of goods or services, and c) sustainable development, considering, among other things, where appropriate, fundamental climatic or other geographical factors, technological or infrastructural factors, or scientific justification but does not include the protection of domestic production", Article 915. However, it should be noted that, unlike the provision of the GATT, the NAFTA concept of "legitimate objective" does not include essential security or national security.

Free Trade Agreement — in two[60] of the three cases[61] the panel put into question the validity of the barrier and called, to a certain extent, for the reduction of the barrier — experience shows that the domestic "legitimate objective" has been interpreted in a restrictive manner to the benefit of the principles of free trade[62].

The agreement also provides for due process and transparency rights, imposing strict minimum requirements on the actions of governments related to the making of new standard-related measures. It requires, for instance, public notice identifying the good or service to be affected and the objectives and reasons for the measure, at least sixty days prior to the adoption or modification of standards-related measures that may affect trade in the NAFTA territory[63]. In addition, Parties are required to identify "inquiry points" to answer all reasonable inquiries and provide relevant documents[64]. They are required to provide complete and unambiguous information, technical advice and assistance at the request of another Party. Parties are also required to encourage their domestic standardization bodies to cooperate with other Parties' standardization bodies[65].

Finally, it should be noted that the agreement provides that a NAFTA country challenging the consistency of another country's standards-related measure has the burden of proving the inconsistency of that measure[66]. Such a provision does not exist in the GATT TBT Code.

---

[60] *In the Matter of Canada's Landing Requirement for Pacific Coast Salmon and Herring*, **North America Free Trade Agreement Dispute Resolution (FTAD)**, October 16, 1989 (concerning Canadian regulations which, on the basis of environmental reasons, forced all catches of pacific coast salmon and herring from Canadian waters to be landed on Canadian soil prior to processing for verification and processing); *In the Matter of Puerto Rico Regulations on the Import, Distribution and Sale of U.H.T. Milk from Quebec*, **FTAD**, June 3, 1993 (concerning a Puerto Rico ban on imports of milk from Quebec for failure to meet newly imposed standards). In both cases the Panel determined that the Canadian and the Puerto Rican regulations were not within the realm of a legitimate objective as defined under the FTA and called for a least-restrictive means test for domestic policy objectives as the appropriate standard of justification for trade restricting measures.

[61] *In the Matter of Lobster from Canada*, **FTAD**, May 21, 1990. In this case, the Panel examined under the national treatment provisions of the FTA United States' ban on the marketing and transport of sub-sized lobsters and acknowledged the fact that a legitimate objective existed.

[62] For a deep analysis of these cases and a critic of the bi-national panel's approach, See C.J. IAMARINO, *"Technical Barriers to Trade Under the NAFTA System: A Call for Legitimate Protection"*, in: **Journal of Legislation**, No.21, 1995, pp.111-124.

[63] Article 909.

[64] Article 910.

[65] Article 911.

[66] Article 914(4).

5. Completing the Multilateral Agenda: The Need for Mutual Recognition Agreements

a) The Concept and the Benefits of MRAs

While the use of tariff barriers has decreased, there has been a world-wide trend to use standards as barriers to trade. The lack of harmonized standards hinders the ability of enterprises to access foreign markets either on a multilateral or a regional basis. Economic actors are faced with the high costs inherent to the TBTs and cannot exploit all opportunities provided by trade liberalization and global competition.

In a **regional integration context** the most developed scenario when dealing with harmonization of standards and regulations has taken place in the European Union. Other regional groupings in Latin America[67], such as Mercosur[68], and in the Pacific Region, such as the APEC forum, are also moving in this direction and working groups on standards have been established. In NAFTA, despite the strong language encouraging harmonization, little has been accomplished as far as harmonization of regulations and standards is concerned[69]. However in an attempt to deal with the inconsistent application of standards and improve the flow of goods across the borders, discussions regarding harmonization between member

---

[67] For a description of the present situation of certain TBTs in Latin America, see Organization of American States, Trade Unit, "*Trade and Integration Arrangements in the Americas: An Analytical Compendium*", Washington D.C., September 9, 1996. Calling for the promotion of open regionalism in the region, preventing the use of technical standards as arbitrary barriers to trade, and for reduction of intraregional discrimination, see Economic Commission for Latin America and the Caribbean (ECLAC), United Nations, "*Open Regionalism in Latin America and the Caribbean: Economic Integration as a Contribution to Changing Production Patterns with Social Equity*", Santiago de Chile, 1994, p.8.

[68] Under the Treaty of Asunción, member states implemented a series of trade liberalization measures intended to ensure that a substantial proportion of intra-bloc trade was unrestricted by the end of the transition phase, on December 31, 1994. In the field of standards focus was mainly placed on packaging, dimensions and safety of traded products. Significant advances were made in the foodstuffs sector and in the vehicle and telecommunications industries. Common rules — mainly on the basis of internationally accepted norms — for a wide spectrum of goods were devised and an agreement to be bound by a plant and health accord, designed to prevent the use of health considerations as a *de facto* barrier to trade, was reached. See Institute for European-Latin American Relations (IRELA), "*The European Union and Mercosur: Towards a New Economic Relationship?*", Brussels, June 1996, pp.6-7.

[69] Some authors argue that, in the long term, if NAFTA is expanded to include other countries, a similar decision-making gridlock that paralyzed the EU harmonization process before the *Cassis de Dijon* approach may occur in NAFTA. See J.H. JACKSON, W.J. DAVEY & A.O. SYKES, **Legal Problems of International Economic Relations**, West Publishing Co., (3rd ed.), 1995, pp.546-547.

states are already being held within the framework of the North American Trilateral Standardization Forum[70].

At the **multilateral level**, in an effort to facilitate international trade, the 1994 GATT TBT Agreement requires members to participate actively in international standardization bodies and to use available international standards and conformity assessments systems unless they have a good reason not to use them[71]. As a second best solution, Article 2.7 of the TBT Agreement encourages WTO Members to recognize as equivalent technical regulations of other members, even if those regulations differ from their own, provided they are satisfied that these regulations adequately fulfill the obligations of their own regulations[72]. Furthermore, with the objective of facilitating trade, Article 6.3 encourages Members to conclude bilateral or plurilateral mutual recognition agreements regarding each other's conformity assessment procedures[73]. Therefore, the Uruguay Round TBT Agreement encourages harmonization where it is possible and mutual recognition where it is not[74].

So far, **Mutual Recognition Agreements (MRAs)** have been envisaged basically in the field of conformity assessment procedures for

---

[70] In addition to harmonization of standards, efforts are being focused on creating more efficient procedures for conformity assessment and certification of compliance of standards among the NAFTA countries in sectors such as construction and building regulations, medical devices and technology, safety equipment and foodstuffs. See *"Inconsistent Application of Standards called Problem for North American Trade"*, in: **International Trade Reporter**, November 11, 29, 1995, p.1957; *"Canada should push for Harmonization of Product Standards"*, July 7, 1996, p.1144; *"NAFTA Industries meet to harmonize Standards"*, February 12, 1997, p.263.

[71] Articles 2.6 and 2.4. Whereas the Tokyo Round TBT Code allowed signatories to deviate from international standards when formulating technical regulations whenever the international standards were "inappropriate", the Uruguay Round TBT Agreement requires Members to use international standards except when they would be an "ineffective or inappropriate means for the fulfillment of the legitimate objectives pursued", for instance because of fundamental technological problems. This is a significant change in language, as it forces Parties to articulate why international standards are inadequate in relation to domestic objectives. See A.O. SYKES, *supra*, note 9, pp.124-125.

[72] In similar terms, but with different wording, Article 4.1 of SPS Agreement.

[73] Article 6.3 of the TBT Agreement, states: "Members are encouraged, at the request of other Members, to be willing to enter into negotiations for the conclusion of agreements for the mutual recognition of the results of each other's conformity assessment procedures. Members may require that such agreements fulfill the criteria of paragraph 1 and give mutual satisfaction regarding their potential for facilitating trade in the products concerned." In similar terms, Article 4.2 of SPS Agreement encourages Members to conclude agreements recognizing the "equivalence" of their respective sanitary and phytosanitary measures.

[74] For further analysis, see A.O. SYKES, *supra*, note 9, pp.77-86.

industrial products[75]. These agreements function on the premise that if a product of a sector covered by the agreement is successfully tested in one country, the results of the test should also be respected by the other Parties, thus establishing a "once tested accepted everywhere" principle. A key element of these agreements is that acceptance of tests and certificates from the other Party is granted irrespective of whether the two Parties have or not equivalent regulations governing the products concerned[76]. Therefore, even if desirable, it is not necessary for countries to have harmonized their respective regulatory requirements prior to the conclusion of a MRA. This is particularly important in view of the traditional difficulties countries have encountered to achieve harmonization of their regulatory requirements.

The **benefits** of the MRAs are clear: first, under a MRA governments will agree to recognize the results of each other's product inspection, testing, or certification procedures issued by agreed bodies, thus eliminating double testing and certification in the importing country, and this will result in cost savings, elimination of delays and better market access. Second, the importing country will lose the possibility of applying domestic testing or certification procedures in a protectionist or discriminatory manner. As a result, trade will be facilitated, costs will be reduced[77] and competition and increased efficiency will be stimulated. Finally, MRAs will contribute to enhance transparency and promote harmonization of standards and regulatory systems.

Again, the most comprehensive and far-reaching approach to conformity assessment has taken place in the European Union. By developing transparent criteria for determining when conformity assessment procedures should be deemed comparable, such a regional process of implementing mutual recognition can be seen as a starting point of an expanding dynamic process to the rest of the world[78]. Having developed the concept of mutual recognition in the Internal Market as well as on a

---

[75] See S. FARR, **Harmonization of Technical Standards in the EC**, Ed. Chancery Law Publishing, London, 1992, pp.85-89.

[76] For a clear analysis on the concept and purpose of MRAs, see J. CLARKE, *"Mutual Recognition Agreements"*, in: **International Trade Law and Regulation**, No.2, 1996, pp.31-36.

[77] The US Commerce Department estimates that US companies can save over $100 million per year under these MRAs. See, **International Trade Reporter**, No.13, December 18, 1996, p.1956.

[78] See comments of K. NICOLAÏDIS, in: A.O. SYKES, *supra*, note 9, pp.139-153.

pan-European basis[79], negotiations to establish mutual recognition obligations with other countries have been launched[80].

b) European Union-United States Negotiations on Mutual Recognition and other Bilateral and Regional Developments

In its memorandum on the global approach to certification and testing the European Commission declared the intention to conclude agreements for mutual recognition of tests, reports, certificates and marks with third countries[81]. The Council in its resolution on the global approach, announced its intention to allow third country conformity assessment bodies to participate in the European system on the same basis as European bodies[82].

Exploratory talks between the European Union and the United States on mutual recognition of conformity assessment began in 1992. The final objective was to facilitate reciprocal access to markets for private business through the mutual acceptance of third Party product test results, inspections, and product certifications. Negotiations between the European Union and the United States officially began in 1994 and should be concluded by early 1997. Under these negotiations both Parties must assess in which cases mutual recognition can apply unconditionally and in which cases it must be conditioned on further regulatory convergence. Only the MRA with the United States is estimated to remove barriers on $40 billion worth of trade between both Parties and is expected to eliminate up to 80% of compliance and testing costs once it enters into force. Despite certain obstacles, due mainly to differences over the transition period on pharmaceutical products and medical equipment, it seems that the two sides have reached agreement in principle on

---

[79] The European Free Trade Association (EFTA) countries aligned themselves — through the European Economic Area Treaty — to the EU approach. A comprehensive view of the EEA Treaty in O. JACOT-GUILLARMOD (ed.), **EEA Agreement (Comments and Reflections)**, Ed. Schulthess Polygraphischer Verlag, Zurich, 1992. About the association of EFTA countries to the EU negotiations with third countries for the conclusion of MRAs, see Protocol 12 of the EEA Agreement.

[80] For a global assessment of these negotiations, see the EU Commission's Communication on external trade policy in the field of standards and conformity assessment, COM(96)564 final, of November 13, 1996.

[81] **OJ** C 267/26, October 19, 1989.

[82] Council Resolution on a global approach to conformity assessment, **OJ** C 101/1, January 16, 1990. For the Community's competence to conclude such agreements, their relationship with existing agreements providing for mutual recognition of certification and testing concluded by individual Member States with third countries and the proposed content of these agreements, see P. EECKHOUT, *supra*, note 28, pp.290-295.

standards for telecommunications terminal equipment, information technology, electrical products requirements, veterinary biologics and pleasure boats[83].

In 1994 negotiations on MRAs were also launched with Canada, Australia and New Zealand. Negotiations with Switzerland and Japan followed in 1995 and similar negotiations for MRAs with other countries in Asia[84], Central Europe and Latin America — namely with Mercosur[85], Chile[86] and Mexico — may follow in the near future depending on the fulfillment of a number of conditions[87]. As recognized by the European Commission, giving priority to standards and TBTs questions in bilateral trade relations is a major component of the recently launched New

---

[83] See **International Trade Reporter**, Vol.13, October 23, 1996, p.1642; Vol.14, January 29, 1997, p.193.

[84] See European Commission Communication, *"Creating a New Dynamic in EU-ASEAN Relations"*, COM(96)314 final; see also C. COSGROVE-SACKS (ed.), *"Implications of the Single European Market for Asia and the Pacific"*, Economic Commission for Europe, United Nations, Geneva, 1996, pp.68-74.

[85] One of the objectives of the Inter-regional Framework Cooperation Agreement between the European Union and Mercosur is cooperation on trade and economic matters as well as on standards and certification to facilitate market access. In order to achieve closer relations with the aim of encouraging the increase and diversification of trade, preparing for subsequent gradual and reciprocal liberalization of trade and promoting conditions which lead to the establishment of the Inter-regional Association, the Framework Agreement proposes to examine prospects for beginning negotiations for the conclusion of mutual recognition agreements. See *"Inter-regional Framework Cooperation Agreement between the European Community and its Member States, of the one part, and the Southern Common Market and its Party States, of the other part"*, **OJ** L 69/4, March 19, 1996, Articles 4 and 6.2. See also G. GARCÍA JIMÉNEZ, *"The New Commercial Strategy of the European Union towards Latin America: in Search of Market Access through a Regional and Specific Approach"*, earlier in this book.

[86] The Framework Agreement on Trade and Economic Cooperation with Chile, with the aim of preparation for liberalization of trade, provides also for cooperation on standardization, accreditation, certification, metrology, and conformity evaluation, as well as for the negotiation of a mutual recognition framework agreement. See *"Framework Cooperation Agreement leading Ultimately to the Establishment of a Political and Economic Association between the European Community and its Member States, of the one part, and the Republic of Chile, of the other part"*, **OJ** L 209/6, August 19, 1996, Articles 5 and 6(b).

[87] These conditions mainly refer to: membership of the GATT Agreement on TBT; obtaining guarantees that the competence of conformity assessment bodies in the partner economy are, and remain on a par with those in the European Union; confining the extent of mutual recognition to tests, certificates and marks of conformity; the agreements presenting a balanced situation concerning all aspects of conformity assessment; and the agreements having the status of formal treaties concluded between governments. See European Commission, DG-I, *"A Guide to European Community Negotiations with Third Countries concerning the Mutual Recognition of Conformity Assessment"*, Brussels, 1996. For a general view of the actual EU policy in this area, see the above-mentioned Communication of November 13, 1996.

Market Access Strategy[88], which, together with the strengthening of the multilateral trading system and the consolidation of WTO rules, proposes the use of the bilateral level in certain areas to achieve quicker results in market opening and set the starting point for further liberalization on a global basis.

In the NAFTA, besides harmonization of standards, a priority is also to create more efficient procedures for conformity assessment among member countries. For this purpose, discussions are underway on the scope for possible MRAs[89]. Likewise, in the context of the Free Trade Agreement between Canada and the United States, both are also strengthening inter-agency cooperation in mutual recognition. Also, in the framework of the Free Trade Area of the Americas, the working group on standards and technical barriers to trade established the conclusion of MRAs as one of the priorities[90] for achieving open trade in the region by 2005. The association agreement between Chile and Mercosur and negotiations between the latter and the Andean Community also contain provisions in this regard. Similarly, mutual recognition is also a concern for countries in Central and Eastern Europe[91] and for the ASEAN countries.

c) The Asia-Pacific Economic Cooperation Forum and MRAs

Alongside with the pioneer character of the European Union-United States MRA, one of the most advanced and ambitious of all these bilateral and regional developments has been the decision by a group of countries of the APEC[92] to begin in 1995 a major action plan to conclude

---

[88] European Commission Communication, *"The Global Challenge of International Trade: A Market Access Strategy for the European Union"*, COM(96)53 final.

[89] For instance, one of the main issues facing NAFTA trade in industrial safety equipment is mutual recognition. Whereas Canada and Mexico require that the equipment be certified, the United States does not. As a result a MRA to recognize certification bodies for safety equipment will be difficult because there is none in the United States. Other major concerns refer to food standards. See **International Trade Reporter**, January 12, 1997, Vol.13, p.263.

[90] See, **International Trade Reporter**, Vol.13, March 13, 1996, p.425.

[91] For an analysis on the need for Central and Eastern European Countries to dismantle non-tariff barriers, see Organization for Economic Cooperation and Development (OECD), *"Barriers to Trade with Economies in Transition"*, Centre for Cooperation with the Economies in Transition, 1994.

[92] The APEC members are the United States, Canada, Japan, Korea, Hong Kong, Australia, New Zealand, Singapore, Taiwan, Mexico, Chile, Brunei, The People's Republic of China, Thailand, Indonesia, Malaysia, the Philippines and Papua New Guinea.

wide MRAs among its members[93].

As part of the plan to foster trade growth in the region and accelerate the effective implementation of the Uruguay Round TBT Agreement, the Action Agenda focuses on the conclusion of regional MRAs in regulated and non-regulated sectors as a means to achieve the goals of free and open trade in the region — by 2010 for industrialized members and 2020 for developing-country members — of the Bogor Declaration. As recognized in the Joint Statement to the Action Agenda, this will act as a powerful impetus for further liberalization at the multilateral level.

The APEC member nations account for about half of the world economy and world trade[94] and are some of the world's most highly competitive exporters[95]. However, the differences in APEC members' standards and conformity assessment infrastructures, policies on testing and product certification, as well as national technical capacities are parallel to the diversity in their levels of economic development. In addition, it is also noteworthy that this forum does not have a dispute resolution mechanism to deal with this and other trade-related matters. In light of this, and acknowledging that, in order to overcome bureaucratic resistance to change among regulators, work is easier carried out on a bilateral rather than plurilateral framework, the Action Agenda recognized the importance of early bilateral arrangements between more advanced economies in the region as a first step to the long-term commitment of APEC-wide arrangements[96].

Because most serious barriers to trade are in regulated sectors[97], the first priority has been launching negotiations on MRAs in sectors such as electrical and electronic equipment, automotive and transportation

---

[93] Asia-Pacific Economic Cooperation (APEC), Committee on Trade and Investment, *"Medium and Long Term Action Plan on Standards and Conformance"*, Japan, November 1995. For an extensive and thorough analysis of TBTs developments and the need for MRAs in the APEC, see J.S. WILSON, *"Standards and APEC: An Action Agenda"*, Institute for International Economies, Washington D.C., October 1995.

[94] Over the last five years, trade within APEC has expanded by 87%.

[95] An annual growth of 8% over the next ten years has been predicted for East Asian developing economies. The United States is the largest exporter and importer within APEC. US exports in goods have risen by 60% during the last five years.

[96] The Action Agenda encourages the establishment of and participation in, by 2000 in the case of industrialized economies and 2005 in the case of developing economies, a network of mutual recognition arrangements in voluntary sectors. See Asia-Pacific Cooperation, The Seventh Ministerial Meeting, *"The Osaka Action Agenda. Implementation of the Bogor Declaration"*, November 16, 1995, Part I, Section C-5.

[97] See, J.S. WILSON, *supra*, note 93, pp.74-79.

equipment, medical devices, construction materials, chemicals, and also in toys and foodstuffs. Implementation guidelines on telecommunications equipment standards have also been agreed[98]. Upward harmonization of standards among APEC nations is also being promoted as well as technical assistance to enable the less developed countries to build conformity assessment infrastructure.

6. Conclusion

As tariff barriers decline with the advent of freer trade at the regional and multilateral level, TBTs have increasingly become one of the most significant non-tariff challenges for the next century.

The 1994 GATT TBT Agreement has significantly reduced the potential for use of technical regulations and standards as non-tariff barriers to trade. Apart from important improvements in transparency and extension of rules on technical regulations and standards, one of the fundamental changes is that, unlike the 1979 Standards Code, the agreement binds all WTO Members. To a great extent, the success on reducing TBTs will depend on the proper functioning of the new Dispute Settlement Mechanism. Obviously, the possibility of referring these barriers, first, to dispute panels and, second, to the Appellate Body should help governments to carefully consider multilateral rules embodied in TBT and SPS Agreements when adopting and applying technical regulations. As far as conformity assessment procedures are concerned, the developments currently underway at the regional and bilateral level can provide a very useful tool for liberalizing trade, thus complementing the general obligations laid down in the agreements and providing a model for future initiatives.

To the extent that trade liberalization in regional integration agreements follows an open policy of nondiscrimination, stronger economic ties within one region can advance economic prospects for all nations. This is particularly true in areas such as standards and conformity assessment in which the benefits of developing alternative models through regional trade talks can lay the foundation for new progress at the multilateral level. In a context of regional integration, two different models have been analyzed. Both the European Union and NAFTA contain provisions that go beyond the multilateral framework. In spite of its obviously unique nature, which makes it an unlikely model for the rest of the

---

[98] **International Trade Reporter**, Vol.13, July 2, 1996, p.201.

world, the EU offers very interesting experiences in dismantling technical barriers to trade, through the mutual recognition of national laws, harmonization of national legislation when mutual recognition is unworkable, the prevention of new barriers by establishing compulsory information mechanisms, and mutual recognition of conformity assessment procedures.

The Uruguay Round Agreements encourage harmonization where it is possible and mutual recognition, as a second best solution, where it is not. It should be noted, however, that at the multilateral level the concept of "harmonization" is very different from what is understood by harmonization in the European Union, and this difference should not be overlooked: whereas in the EU harmonization implies getting to work the complex EU lawmaking machine and enacting supranational legislation, at the multilateral level harmonization does not mean at all action by a supranational legislator. In fact, it only means that national regulators, when adopting national rules, should take into account available international models emanating either from specialized international agencies (in the case of measures covered by SPS Agreement) or standardization bodies (in the case of those covered by TBT Agreement).

As for mutual recognition, both TBT and SPS Agreements refer to it in quite general terms, encouraging Member States to take additional measures — basically MRAs — in order to put it into practice. In fact, one of the main instruments to reduce TBTs, facilitate trade and extend progress made in the Uruguay Round is the conclusion of MRAs. Based on the "once tested accepted everywhere" principle and the reciprocal benefits inherent in terms of reducing costs and promoting transparency, these agreements provide an attractive trade-opening tool for stimulating liberalization on a regional, bilateral or plurilateral basis that can, then, lead to promote trade liberalization efforts on a global basis. Following the European "global approach" to conformity assessment, many industrialized nations and regional groupings are also moving in this direction. Recognizing the potential benefits of moving beyond the GATT/WTO framework, the European Union and the United States are about to conclude a MRA. Other bilateral and plurilateral MRAs are also underway, as those being negotiated in the APEC forum.

All these MRAs now in progress represent an important step forward to complete and complement what has already been achieved at the multilateral level. They will have important implications for economic growth and trade liberalization in the next century and may set the path for improving the multilateral agenda in future rounds.

PART III

REGIONALISM AND MULTILATERAL TRADE RULES: AN INTERACTIVE RELATIONSHIP

The final chapter of the book discusses the extent to which multilateral rules act as a constraint on regional trade arrangements and the reciprocal influence of multilateral and regional rules from a broader perspective.

THE NEW WTO DISPUTE SETTLEMENT MECHANISM

Pierre PESCATORE

Former Judge,
Court of Justice of the European Communities,
Luxemburg

As a result of the Uruguay Round, the dispute settlement mechanism has been notably developed. At the same time care was taken to ensure continuity with the old practice: see Article XVI:1 of the World Trade Organization (WTO) Agreement and Article 3:1 of the Understanding on Dispute Settlement (DS). This suggests a comparison between new and old, which will form the first part of my report. This being done, I shall show that in spite of a systematic effort at attaining a reinforcement of the system, there remain a number of dubious aspects, which I shall discuss in a second part. Finally, in a third part, I have assembled the, as yet, scarce elements of practice under the new rules.

A. From GATT to WTO: Transition to a New Era of Dispute Settlement

The Marrakesh Agreements, embodying the results of the long-drawn Uruguay Round, have been hailed, and rightly so, as considerable progress in the field of international trade law. In this respect the Uruguay Round has entered into history as a unique achievement, indeed a *transitio ad alterum genus,* in comparison to all the preceding "rounds". This applies also to dispute settlement, which moved from its hitherto marginal position to become, as is said in Article 3.2 of the Understanding, a "central element" in the new trading system.

In this part of my report, I shall try to describe this transition through a comparative analysis of dispute settlement as it evolved from GATT to WTO. The strong points of the new regime appear to be the following: (1) the system has been in many respects brought up to a higher level of legal effectiveness; (2) the, so far, essentially normative provisions of the various agreements have been embedded into an institutional structure; (3) the unity of the system of dispute settlement, which had been breaking apart after the Tokyo Round, has been restored; (4) a bridge has been opened from sectorial isolationism of "GATT law" to general international law; (5) the system of sanctions has been reorganized in a multilateral framework; (6) finally, we may note that all those procedural devices which had proved to be essential for the effective functioning of the old GATT mechanism have been taken over integrally into the new system. This is an impressive record, which calls for some more explanation.

1. Creation of a Secure Legal Basis for DS

For almost half a century GATT has remained the most prominent example of the truth of a French saying: *"Il n'y a que le provisoire qui dure"*. Everything was frail and questionable in the old GATT system: the General Agreement itself rested on a protocol of provisional application; the whole procedure of dispute settlement, after a long period of pure pragmatism, had been brought only recently into the form of successive decisions, the authority of which had, however, remained uncertain. This state of uncertainty has been radically cured by the fact that the WTO Agreements have been negotiated in the form of regular international treaties, entered into in conformity with the constitutional provisions of the members. By this, the provisions relating to dispute settlement have benefited from *a double upgrade*: not only have they been embodied in a formal Understanding, but the same Understanding, in virtue of Article II:2 of the WTO Agreement, has received the same legal authority as the constitutive instrument itself, of which it makes an integral part.

It is to be hoped that the termination of almost fifty years of legal vagrancy will bring about a consolidation of the substantive provisions of the new WTO, not only in the mutual relations of the Contracting Parties, but also in the sphere of their *municipal law*. The idea of GATT being a mere forum for continuous negotiation and adjustment belongs now to the past. The WTO, in contrast to the old GATT, constitutes a system of binding legal obligations between the members. For this reason, the cause of direct applicability on the territories of the members —

of at least those provisions which fulfil the relevant criteria (i.e. to be unconditional and sufficiently precise) — finds now a solid legal basis. By saying this, I refer to provisions such as the rule of nondiscrimination, of which there is a great variety, the principle of national treatment, the specified obligations resulting from tariff bindings, the elimination of various obstacles to trade, notably quantitative restrictions, the freedom of transit and the like, all of which fulfil the criteria of direct applicability. Thus, there could be a convergent action of DS, at the international level, and of adjudication in the sphere of internal law of the members[1].

2. The Institutional Structure of WTO and DS

Unlike the old GATT, the WTO Agreements represent much more than a complex of contractual obligations. The obligations assumed in virtue of the WTO Agreements are embedded into a structure that can be rightly said to have an *institutional* and, more so, a *constitutional* character[2]. This development had already discreetly started when the Contracting Parties of GATT had mutated themselves into the GATT-Council, vested with a multifaceted decisional power. This mutation is now completed, as expressed by Article I of the WTO Agreement, creating a "World

---

[1] It is regrettable that the European Community, which has insisted throughout on direct applicability in its internal affairs, applies a reverse standard in relation to GATT and WTO. Thus, the EC Council, in its Decision 94/800 EC, of December 22, 1994 (**Official Journal** L 336/1, 1994), approving the Marrakesh Agreements, took care to insert a preambular declaration to the effect that "by its nature", the WTO Agreement could not be invoked directly in the courts of the Community or its Member States. The fact that this "clarification" had to be inserted in the Decision's Preamble proves by itself that the pretended lack of direct applicability is by no means evident from the agreements themselves. This attempt at altering *ex post* the effect of an international agreement is incompatible with good faith in international relations and with the principle of legal protection at home. — As for the Court of Justice, it has still in recent times sustained the same doctrine in relation to GATT. See the *Banana Judgement* of October 5, 1994, **ECR** I (1994), 4973, and the comment of Ulrich EVERLING, *"Will Europe slip on Bananas?"*, in: **Common Market Law Review**, 1996, pp.401-437. Everling suggests that the Court's attitude will have to be reconsidered in the light of the new legal situation created by the entry into force of the WTO Agreements (see p.422 and note 45).

[2] I have assembled some ideas of a rather philosophical character on these themes in my articles on *"La constitution nationale et les exigences découlant du droit international et du droit de l'intégration européenne : Essai sur la légitimité des structures supra-étatiques"*, in : **Revue de Droit Suisse**, 1992, pp.43-72; and, *"La interpretación del derecho comunitario por el juez nacional"*, in: **Revista de Instituciones Europeas**, Madrid, 1996, pp.7-31 (see especially pp.16-18). — The constitutional aspect is one of the central themes of the writings of Ernst-Ulrich PETERSMANN; see in particular, **Constitutional Functions and Constitutional Problems of International Economic Law**, Fribourg University Press, Fribourg (CH), 1991.

Trade Organization". Consequently, the Contracting Parties have been transformed into *members* of an organization vested with a distinct legal personality, acting through organs of its own: a Council and a Director-General at the head of an international Secretariat.

This process of "institutionalization" has been carried one step further in the field of dispute settlement by the creation of a distinct *Dispute Settlement Body* (DSB) composed of representatives of the members and capable of acting in accordance with its own rules of procedure. The general mission of the DSB is to "administer" the system of dispute settlement and to exercise some precise functions in this respect (Understanding, Article 1:1). The *panels* established for the purpose of dispute settlement, which were formerly a purely pragmatic device created *ad hoc*, have now received a statutory basis in the Understanding[3]. A procedure of appeals has been created above the panels in the form of a standing *Appellate Body* (AB), with its own secretariat. The AB has established its own Working Procedures, issued on February 15, 1996.

Thus, dispute settlement has been organized as a distinct function in the framework of the global structure of the organization. Hence it can be visualized as a genuine element of *separation of powers* in a formerly undifferentiated organism, in which political and jurisdictional functions had remained indistinctly confused. The procedure of dispute settlement, which basically still rests on *consensus* at the level of the DSB, has been organized in such a way that once proceedings have been introduced, the losing Party will be placed, at the end, before the inescapable alternative either to accept the determination of the first-level panel, or to appeal and accept, *ipso facto*, the final character of the AB decision. The procedural device by which this result has been achieved is the mechanism of *inverted consensus*. This is the main invention of the authors of the Understanding. Details can be seen from Article 17 of the same.

The important point, of an almost philosophical character, is that in any legal system the creation of *institutions* introduces new resources of autonomy, flexibility and dynamism into the normative structure. This dynamism appears quite spontaneously through the decisions taken in the performance of their task by the institutions, given the leeway those institutions enjoy in the perspective of the specific criteria of action assigned to each of them. To be more precise, in contrast to the political

---

[3] The word "panel", which in English is a trivial expression, has received an almost mystical significance in the other languages. Having been a member of a "panel" in GATT or WTO is worth being recorded in any *curriculum vitae* or Who's Who entry.

considerations which inspire the action of the other institutions of WTO, such as the Council in its different appearances, the basic criterion for the institutions competent for dispute settlement — i.e. the DSB, the panels and the AB — is not political expediency but *respect of the law*, to which only indirect references had been made in the General Agreement, notably through the terminology used in Article XXIII:1 of GATT. These references have become, to some degree, more express in the WTO language, especially in Article 17:6 of the Understanding in which, to describe the task of the AB, the authors could not help but refer to "issues of law" and to questions of "legal interpretation". We shall come back with some more detail to this matter in the second part.

3. The Unity of the System of DS

One of the fundamental purposes of the WTO construction is to reduce to a coherent system the rules of international trade at the political as well as at the legal level. In the field of DS, there was a problem in relation to the past and also a problem in relation to the future. Retrospectively, the problem was to recuperate into a reunified system of dispute settlement the provisions that had gone astray as an effect of a whole range of marginal agreements, most prominently the Tokyo "codes". Prospectively, the intention was to contain in the framework of a single system of dispute settlement the new fields opened to the influence of the organization, such as exchange of services and trade-aspects of intellectual property rights.

The problem was solved in principle by Article 1:1 of the Understanding, which conveys a broad meaning of the total scope of regular dispute settlement, applicable to all "covered agreements", extensively enumerated in Appendix I. Sure, there remain a number of well-identified specific provisions, but the general tendency is, gravitationally, towards unification.

Moreover, it must be underlined that the same provision of the Understanding introduces *an entirely new cause of action*, beyond the notion of "nullification or impairment of benefits", as defined by Article XXIII of the old GATT. It must be recalled that already the latter provision comprised, and still comprises, alongside with the classical "nullification or impairment" clause, the notion of impediments brought to the attainment of the General Agreement's *objectives* — a mention which has, so far, never been made explicit in practice, or in theory. The new feature of the WTO is that the second phrase of Article 1:1 of the Understanding extends still further the scope of dispute settlement by mentioning the case of disregard by members of their "obligations" under the agreement establishing the World Trade Organization and the Understanding itself, "taken in isolation or in combination with any other covered agreement." Thus, adding up elements old and new, we must visualize from now on the contentious system of the WTO in a *three-tier logic* comprising:

> (a) nullification and impairment of trade benefits;
> (b) frustration of the organization's objectives;
> (c) disregard of obligations flowing from the organization's constitutive instrument and from the rules governing dispute settlement.

Thus, a fundamental revision of the categories constituting the system of dispute settlement seems required since the entry into force of the new WTO provisions[4]. This will become even more evident when we consider the next point: opening of the system to general international law.

4. Influx of General International Law

Even in the days of the old GATT, an attentive observer could not overlook the links between the specific law of international trade and general international law, be it only to explain the binding character of the original protocol of provisional application and everything derived from it in the meantime. The link with general international law has now been made explicit both by the recourse to the solemn forms of international law for the conclusion of the Marrakesh Agreements and by the express recognition, in Article 3:2 of the Understanding, that dispute settlement serves to clarify the existing provisions of the various agreements "in accordance with customary rules of interpretation of public international law." It is not disputed that this provision refers essentially to the rules of interpretation as codified in the Vienna Convention on Treaty Law signed on May 23, 1969.

Since the Vienna Convention has already been referred to by several panels, including the AB, as we shall see[5], it is important to recall the

---

[4] This apparently has not yet been perceived by Judith HIPPLER BELLO in her article: *"The WTO Dispute Settlement Understanding: Less is More"*, published as an Editorial Comment in the **American Journal of International Law**, 1996, pp.416-418.

[5] See the precedents referred to under the keyword: "Vienna Convention on the Law of Treaties" in the Index of the **Handbook of WTO/GATT Dispute Settlement**, edited by myself together with William J. DAVEY & Andreas F. LOWENFELD, Ardsley-on-Hudson, N.Y., 1991, (hereafter quoted as **Handbook**).

relevant provisions of this convention, which go well beyond what has been explicitly mentioned so far in the determinations established by some panels and by the AB:

- international treaties are binding and must be implemented and interpreted in good faith (Articles 26 and 31);
- internal legislation is no excuse for failure to implement a treaty obligation (Article 27);
- treaty provisions are, in principle, non-retroactive (Article 28);
- treaty obligations coincide normally with the sphere of territorial jurisdiction of states (Article 29);
- treaties must be interpreted in good faith, in accordance with the ordinary meaning of their terms, in context and in the light of their object and purpose (Articles 31-32);
- linguistic difficulties, in case of multilingual treaties, are to resolved also by the object-and-purpose test (Article 33).

Attention must be paid not only to the articles just quoted, but also to the Preamble of the Vienna Convention, which contains two provisions directly relevant to this matter:

- Paragraph 3, which states *inter alia* that the principle of good faith and the *pacta sunt servanda* rule are universally recognized; and,
- Paragraph 8, at the end of the Preamble, which states as follows: "... the rules of customary international law will continue to govern questions not regulated by the provisions of the present Convention."

It is striking to see that the latter provision is fully coherent with the constant action of GATT, which relied heavily on *customary practice*, and with the reference to "customary rules of interpretation" in Article 3:2 of the Understanding. Quite obviously, we are standing here on common ground.

So far, as will appear more clearly in the third part of this report, only some of what may be called the "mechanical" rules of interpretation of the Vienna Convention have been referred to in practice. In my opinion, the major input of the Vienna Convention into the system of WTO is only to come. This input will be the *principle of good faith*, which so far has never been explicitly referred to and which in the future may reveal itself to be a potent stabilizing factor for the *perpetuum mobile* the old GATT was said to be. It may well happen that the introduction of the principle of good faith, *via* the Vienna Convention, will prove to be the major factor "providing security and predictability to the multilateral trading system" as has been stated in Article 3:2 of the Understanding.

5. A Multilateral System of Sanctions

It must be said, in contrast to current opinions, that the former GATT system, through the use of retaliation (mostly under the innocent cover names of "compensation" or "adjustment") was a comparatively well-sanctioned and therefore highly effective legal system. Realistically, we must recognize that this strength came from *unilateral* retaliation or, rather, from the menace of such retaliation. The effect of the new rules of the WTO, concentrated in Articles 22 and 23 of the Understanding, consists not in eliminating retaliation, far from it, but in organizing retaliation in a truly multilateral framework and in subordinating its application to the control of the organization. Thus, multilateralization combined with an effectively functioning system of dispute settlement is the factor that has deprived of any legitimacy the threat and the use of unilateral action. This again is a decisive progress.

6. Essential Procedural Features Preserved

The relatively satisfactory functioning of dispute settlement, even under the minimal rules of the old GATT, was due to some procedural devices which had developed gradually and which had been consolidated at the end, thanks in particular to the 1989 (Tokyo) Understanding on Dispute Settlement. Three essential achievements must be mentioned in this respect:

(a) The so-called *right to a panel*, which means that a Contracting Party which had gone regularly through the consultation process could not be refused the institution of a panel, if no satisfactory solution could be reached by consultation. The right to have a panel instituted upon unilateral request has been now clearly recognized by Articles 4:3 and 6:1 of the Understanding, with a remarkable shift from a still hesitant "may" in the first provision to an unequivocal "shall" in the second.

(b) The *composition of panels* will be, as formerly, proposed by the Secretariat. In case of objections, it is to be imposed in the last resort by the Director-General in consultation with the President of the DSB (Understanding, Article 8:6/7).

(c) The *terms of reference* of panels will normally be determined according to the standard terms indicated in Article 7:1 of the Understanding. The remarkable feature of this formula is that it defines the litigious "matter" by reference to the document introduced by the complainant Party, which makes clear that the definition of the terms of reference is unilateral and does not in any way depend on the defendant's agreement.

B. Problematical Aspects of the New Regime

After this description of the progress marked by the Marrakesh Agreements in relation to dispute settlement, it must be conceded that some fundamentals of the system still plunge into the shadow of legal uncertainty. As far as it is possible to penetrate into this margin of ambiguity maintained by the negotiators of the WTO Agreements, I shall try to make out the following features: (1) the system still remains hesitant as between conciliation and genuine adjudication; (2) dispute settlement is fundamentally bilateral, whereas multilateral aspects and, more generally, factors of objective legal determination remain secondary; (3) independent handling of cases by panels is hampered by systematic attempts at "teleguidance" by governments, especially through the medium of rules of evaluation superimposed on the normal criteria of legal appreciation; (4) the introduction into the Understanding of the artificial category of "non-violation complaints" constitutes an unnecessary weakening of the original concept of Article XXIII of GATT.

How can we explain these departures from a dispute settlement criterion based on the "rule-of-law" standard? In the author's opinion, the new provisions on DS are the work of government representatives who continue to reason basically in the categories not of the law, but of the defence of their national interest. Looking at matters from that one-sided perspective, they have no clear perception of the equality of the Parties in the judicial process and, even less so, of the independence of whoever has to decide contentious matters. I shall therefore discuss these problems not only with a merely descriptive purpose, but with the intention of indicating some ways and means which might permit, in a fundamentally ambiguous situation, the legal elements to prevail over the still lingering defence-of-interest mentality.

1. Conciliation *versus* Legal Adjudication

The authors of Article 3 of the Understanding, which comes under the title "General Provisions", manifestly had not made up their mind as between the perspective of conciliation and the perspective of legal adjudication. It must be remarked that the standard formula, providing for the settlement of disputes "on the basis of respect for law", as it is current in international life[6], has *not* been taken over into the WTO Understanding. This surely happened not by mere accident; it was the consequence of an inveterate state of mind. Indeed, we can easily distinguish two conflicting strains of thought in Article 3:

> A first range of provisions does, indeed, point in the direction of *conciliation*; the objective of the system is "the maintenance of a proper balance between the rights and obligations of the Members" (Article 3:3), to achieve in each case "a satisfactory settlement of the matter" (Article 3:4), to secure "a positive solution to a dispute", being understood that "a solution mutually acceptable to the Parties" is clearly to be preferred (Article 3:7). It must be said, by way of comment, that this language is of little comfort to all those who are defending themselves against the violation of the rules by other states, or seeking recognition of their legitimate rights, especially in conflicts opposing members of unequal economic and political strength. What those in need of legal protection are seeking is not some odd "balance" between right and wrong, but full recognition of their legal rights. The language of conciliation is good for economic giants, it is of no avail for the weaker members of the international community and it offers even lesser comfort for individual operators and consumers who are ultimately concerned by the "adjustments" reached at high level.

> Other provisions, mostly of a rather instrumental character, to be true, belong to the world of *legal adjudication*. So, when reference is made to "security and predictability" in the multilateral trading system and to clarification of the existing provisions in accordance with customary "rules of interpretation of public international law" (Article 3:2), or when it is said that the primary objective of dispute settlement is to secure the withdrawal of national measures found "inconsistent" with the provisions of one of the agreements (Article 3:7). The typically legal concept of

---

[6] A choice of pertinent clauses can be found in: Karin OELLERS-FRAHM & Norbert WÜHLER (eds), **Dispute Settlement in Public International Law**, Berlin, 1984. The first historic example in a multilateral context is Article 37 of the 1907 Hague Convention for the Pacific Settlement of International Disputes, from which I have taken the phrase quoted above. It is highly significant that none of these models has been taken over by the authors of the successive GATT and WTO texts. It may be remarked that the reference to "issues of law" crept into the AB's mission only by way of limitation, as explicitly indicated in Article 17:6 of the Understanding.

"infringement", which has been current in practice for a long time[7], has turned up now, together with the strong words "breach of the rules", in Article 3:8 of the Understanding. Article 3:10 provides as a rule that all members will engage in these procedures "in good faith" and in an effort to resolve the dispute. With this provision, the *bona fide* concept has entered for the first time into the thesaurus of the official GATT/WTO language.

In my opinion, it may indeed be this very idea of *good faith*, expressed already in some panel determinations of the past under the guise of "legitimate expectations"[8], will allow all those concerned to give to the provisions of the Understanding a spin away from the old "adjustment" ideology and toward the spirit of objective justice and respect for obligations assumed. That will be the true task of all those organs that will, from now on, take part in the successive steps of the process of dispute settlement.

2. Bilateralism in a Multilateral Shell

There is a startling contradiction at the heart of the system of dispute settlement of the WTO, inherited from the old GATT: though dispute settlement occurs in a multilateral context, though the rules to be applied and interpreted are essentially multilateral, the system of litigation remains fundamentally bilateral. This constitutes a constant menace of legal distortion by those few states who are the most frequent protagonists of litigation. As it appears from the record of cases[9], the system of dispute settlement is, at present, concentrated to a large extent inside a powerful triangle constituted by the dominating trading "blocks", i.e. the US, the EC and Japan. Unconscientiously but inescapably, the system has deviated to defend the trade interests of the partners who make part of that inner circle.

This influence is exerted through the selective use of two instruments: the terms of reference and the choice of arguments, essentially by keeping the process at the detail level and not allowing it to rise to the height

---

[7] See the numerous cases cited in the "Key Word Index" of the **Handbook**, under "Infringement" and "Impairment of benefits".

[8] See the cases recorded in the **Handbook**. The most conspicuous example is the *EC-Oilseeds* Case, where a tariff binding entered into in 1962 was recognized to have created a legitimate expectation which was still holding in 1990.

[9] See the "Index of Parties" in the **Handbook**, which shows in a striking way that the smaller states have only very exceptionally availed themselves of the dispute settlement possibilities. The well-known *Uruguayan Recourse* (Case 20) has remained an isolated example.

of matters of principle[10]. It is particularly significant in this respect that when the scope of possible actions was extended by Article 1:1 of the Understanding to disputes relating to the members' rights and obligations under the Agreements establishing the WTO, the sole disputes envisaged were those "between members". The organization as such has no stake and no part in these actions[11].

In my opinion, this tendency, which may result in a weakening of the legal rules in the hands of a minority of states capable of defending their interests by extra-legal means, could be counteracted and corrected to some extent if the following factors would be considered:

(a) The main multilateralizing factor in the system is *the Dispute Settlement Body*, in which all members of the organization are present. The main concern is therefore to give a specific legal profile to this organ, through: the election by the national delegations of representatives to the DSP, the personal action of the Chairman who concentrates important powers in his hands, and the medium of rules of procedure adapted to the performance of the DSB's specific duties. It is regrettable that the DSB has done no more, in this respect, than to take over the general Council's rules.

(b) A second multilateralizing factor is the awareness, on the side of *the panels and the AB*, of the fact that they are much more than umpires in bilateral disputes: far from it, their task is to act in the perspective of the general interest and to render objective justice. This is quite obvious for lawyers coming from the civil law tradition, imbued as they are by the principle *iura novit curia* (which means that a judge must apply *ex officio* the pertinent legal rules

---

[10] The panel report on the *US-Section 337 of the Tariff Act* Case (**Handbook** 74) provide an example of this way of handling an important issue. In Paragraph 5.21 of its report, the panel wondered whether all the detailed complaints of the EC against the procedure applied by the US International Trade Commission (USITC) in litigation relating to patent rights "could not be traced back to one common cause, this being the structure of the USITC which is fundamentally not a court but an administrative agency, and whether this structural difference could be said to entail in itself treatment incompatible with the requirements of Article III." To which the panel added: "The Panel however reached no conclusion in this respect, as this question had not been raised in such general terms by the Community." Here a question must be asked: Why did the EC not raise this problem? Was this due to an oversight, or to a lack of analysis? Or did the Community not wish, in its own interest, this question to be clarified?

[11] This marks a sharp contrast with the system of actions against Member States in the EC — but it should not be overlooked that the WTO, as a cooperative inter-state organization, has a fundamentally different structure from the EC.

to any factual situation brought before him), the sense of the general interest, or *ordre public,* and their innate rejection of denial of justice; an effort may be required in this respect from the lawyers belonging to the common law world, who are inclined to consider justice as being fundamentally a matter between litigating Parties and who seem much more easily accessible to a *non liquet* conclusion[12].

(c) Everything should be done to reinforce the rights of the *WTO Secretariat* and of the Director-General in the disput -settlement process. My suggestion would be to introduce some provisions into the rules of the DSB and of the AB which would allow a representative of the Director-General to give in each contentious case an independent statement on the requirements of the general interest.

(d) Finally, I would like to draw attention to the most useful contribution of the *intervention of third Parties*, in order to broaden the context of bilateral litigation. Third Parties are the genuine *amici curiae*. My personal experience shows that often the best information and the most convincing arguments came not from the main Parties, entangled as they were in the many strings of their argument, but from the more detached position of intervening third Parties.

3. The Long Arm of Governments Reaching into the Functioning of the DS System

Government influence is present, legitimately so, at all stages of the proceedings. The trouble is that this influence is not limited to the action typical for Parties in legal proceedings. There are consistent attempts at guiding the action of legal decision-makers by imposing *a priori* methods of evaluation that, in my opinion, rest on a fundamental miscomprehension of the legal process. Here again the situation is basically equivocal. On the one hand, as we have seen, Article 3:2 of the Understanding directs all the organs which take part in the DS process to act "in accordance with customary rules of interpretation of public international law." This provision is immediately counteracted by the addition of a *caveat:*

---

[12] I am taking my information from P. (Lord) DEVLIN's book, **The Judge**, Oxford, 1979. I am not aware of any writing that would show that this position has fundamentally changed. Further material on this problem, seen in a comparative perspective as between civil law and common law, has been assembled in my already quoted essay on interpretation, see note 2.

"Recommendations and rulings of the DSB cannot add to or diminish the rights and obligations provided in the covered agreements." Two specific provisions in the agreements must be singled out in this respect.

(a) The introduction of an *interim review stage* into the panel procedure by Article 15 of the Understanding. Under this provision a panel is bound to submit to the Parties an "interim report" including not only the descriptive section of its draft but also its findings and conclusions. This arrangement must be understood as a guarantee against unpredictable arguments — which admittedly are a real risk in a system where panels are pieced together *ad hoc* in each case as a consequence, interim review also becomes a precaution against unexpected rejection of reports at the level of the DSB. It is obvious that this procedure may lend itself to interventions by the Parties into the internal dealings of a panel, to premature disclosures and even to pressure exerted on panel members. We shall see in the third part of this report how the two first panels instituted since the entry into operation of the new rules have coped with this problem.

(b) A further question is the *standard of review problem* in a matter — international trade — which often entails evaluation of complex economic situations. It is obvious that a limit must be drawn somewhere between judicial control and political appreciation. A discussion on this matter has been aroused by Article 17:6 of the Anti-Dumping Agreement, on the evaluation by panels of the facts as established by national authorities:

(i) In the assessment of the facts of the matter, the panel shall determine whether the authorities' establishment of the facts was proper and whether their evaluation of those facts was unbiased and objective. If the establishment of the facts was proper and the evaluation was unbiased and objective, even though the panel might have reached a different conclusion, the evaluation shall not be overturned.

(ii) The panel shall interpret the relevant provisions of the agreement in accordance with customary rules of interpretation of public international law. Where the panel finds that a relevant provision of the agreement admits of more than one permissible interpretation, the panel shall find the authorities' measure to be in conformity with the agreement if it rests upon one of those permissible interpretations.

For the time being, this standard of review of national measures at the WTO level is limited to anti-dumping. Unfortunately, there is a Ministerial Decision recorded in the Final Act of the Marrakesh Conference which states the following:

> The standard of review in paragraph 6 of Article 17 of the Agreement on Implementation of Article VI of GATT 1994 shall be reviewed after a period of three years with a view to considering the question whether it is capable of general application.[13]

I would like to add the following comments on these provisions, which open a disquieting prospect for the WTO system of dispute settlement. *First*, Article 17:6 of the Anti-Dumping Agreement quite evidently begs the question, because it must be asked: what is a "proper" establishment of the facts and an "unbiased and objective" evaluation? *Second*, a panel, just as any judicial body, is there to establish and evaluate controverted facts, clear away doubts on interpretation, and not to maintain uncertainties for the benefit of one of the Parties. *Third*, the approach chosen by those who created Article 17:6 is incompatible both with the equality of the Parties in the judicial process and with the equality of states under international law. The relationship between the judiciary and the administration in a national framework is not a model for international relations.

4. A Word about "Non-Violation" Complaints

I am on record for having consistently, but without success, battled against this contradictory concept, the origin of which is to be found in

---

[13] These provisions have inspired a well informed and thoughtful comment of Steven P. CROLEY & John H. JACKSON, *"WTO Dispute Procedures, Standard of Review, and Deference to National Governments"*, in: **American Journal of International Law**, 1996, pp.193-213. According to this source, the quoted provisions are inspired from the so-called *Chevron Doctrine* of the US Supreme Court. The authors rightly think that, whatever the link of *Chevron* with Article 16:7 of the Anti-dumping Agreement, this doctrine, developed with a view to the problems raised by judicial control of the administration inside the US constitutional system, is not apt to be transposed to international law. In their conclusion, the authors say that anyhow WTO panels should be cautious about adopting "activist" postures and apply rather "judicial restraint" in the procedures. Thus, it would appear that the authors of Article 17:6 and the Ministerial Decision have fully reached their primary objective, which is to dissuade panels from exercizing their free appreciation of the facts and from seeking objective and just determinations. The well-known anti-activist and pro-restraint language, under the false appearance of moderation, tend in fact at favouring administrative discretion at the cost of legal control. I permit myself to refer to my contribution *"Jusqu'où le juge peut-il aller trop loin"*, in: **Festskrift til Ole Due**, Copenhagen, 1994, pp.299-338, where I have examined critically the concepts of French *Gouvernement des juges,* US *Activism* and German *Akzeptanz,* which are nothing more than three ways of minimizing the independence of the judicial power.

the reports of some panels coping with the allocation of the burden of proof[14]. To understand this curious construction we must go back to the wording of Article XXIII:1(b) of GATT, which opens a way of redress whenever interests of a Party have been prejudiced by "the application by another Contracting Party of *any* measure, *whether or not it conflicts* with the provisions of this Agreement..." (emphasis added).

The natural meaning of this provision, it would seem, is that compensation can be claimed *regardless* as to whether a measure causing nullification or impairment of benefits was or was not in conflict with the General Agreement. In other words, what counts is the damaging effect of *any* measure; the fact that this measure in a particular case was *not*, by itself, in conflict with the agreement constitutes no excuse from the duty of reparation. This has now been changed by Article 26:1(b) of the Understanding, which enjoys the same authority as Article XXIII of GATT. Under the new provisions of the Understanding it has become clear that the aggrieved Party may *not* claim the withdrawal of the damaging measure (this was not formerly excluded by Article XXIII); the allocation of compensation may still be suggested, but it cannot go beyond a "mutually acceptable adjustment", where of course "mutually" is the commanding element. As a consequence, there can be no sanction in the case of non-violation complaints. Thus, this theoretical construction has led to a weakening of legal protection. This shortfall will constitute, in turn, an incentive for members to shift, whenever possible, disputed cases from the "violation" to the "non-violation" compartment. But this will have to be reassessed in light of the *bona fide* requirement and the introduction of a new cause of action by Article 1:1 of the Understanding, as explained above; which shows that the resources of a system are definitely superior to an accumulation of inarticulate rules as was the case in the old GATT.

C. Comments on the First Elements of Practice under the New Rules

Two cases have come up since the entry into force of the new rules on dispute settlement: *US - Standards for Reformulated and Conventional Gasoline,* which has gone up to the Appellate Body, and *Japan - Taxes*

---

[14] See the cases referred to in the **Handbook**, under the words: "Impairment of benefits" and "Non-violation complaints".

on Alcoholic Beverages[15]. These determinations contain interesting elements on two points: (1) the handling, by the first level panels, of the issue of interim review; and, (2) the general approach of the Appellate Body to its task, especially on the issue of interpretation.

1. The Interim Review Stage Treated as an *Internal* Phase of Proceedings

At least two dangers were inherent in the introduction of the interim review stage: procedurally by causing a formal division of the proceedings into a pre-review and a post-review phase; substantially, by creating the temptation for the Parties to interfere with the internal process of panels. Both panels have shown their awareness of these problems. The most outspoken is the *Japan-alcoholic Beverages* Panel, which has taken an explicit position to defend the integrity of the deliberative process.

(a) The panel on the *US-Gasoline* Case devoted a short section (5.1-5.6) to interim review, at the end of the descriptive part of its report. In this section the panel recorded succinctly the objections of the US and the observations of the other Parties, indicating that in all respects the remarks received had been carefully considered. In two instances those remarks had led to drafting changes, and in two other instances to responses, embodied in the panel's arguments. No indications are given either of the first position of the panel, or on the bearing of the amendments induced by the Parties' observations. Thus, no comparative discussion can possibly arise as to the first and the final position of the panel.

(b) The panel on the *Japan-alcoholic Beverages* Case approached interim review on the same basis, as a purely internal matter. It was, however, much more explicit, by ruling first on a matter of principle relating to the interpretation of Article 15 of the Understanding. The purpose of this provision was not to allow the Parties to introduce new evidence or develop new arguments, nor "to enter into a debate with the Panel"; moreover, only points "sufficiently specific and detailed" could be considered at this stage (5.2). The panel also recorded that it was faced with press reports relating to its "interim report". As a reaction, the panel strongly underlined

---

[15] Doc. WT/DS2/AB/R, of 29 April 1996, containing both the AB opinion and the first level panel report in the *Gasoline* Case and WT/DS8/10-11, of July 11, 1996, on the *Alcoholic Beverages* Case. — See the Postscript to this report.

the importance of confidentiality "to preserve the credibility and integrity of the dispute settlement process" (5.3). The panel then passed review of a series of arguments, indicating that most had led to amendments, drafting changes or clarifications in the report, whereas some others had been discarded (5.4-5.15).

It would thus seem that the issue of interim review has been dedramatized and reduced to its true function from the beginning.

2. The First Opinion of the AB

The opinion rendered on April 22, 1996 in the *US-Gasoline* Case was a major event expected with great curiosity. This is not the place to recount the detail of this litigation. For the purpose of this report it will be sufficient to recall the following circumstances.

The content of the claim and the first-level panel determination. Venezuela and Brazil had complained of discriminatory treatment of their imports of gasoline into the US as a consequence of the differential standards of "cleanliness" imposed by the US Clean Air Act on imported gasoline, in comparison to domestic production. These standards, discussed under the name of "baseline establishment rules", had been defined in such a way that importers were subject to statutory baselines, whereas domestic refiners benefited from individually defined standards based on their previous performances, which admittedly were less demanding than the statutory standard. Already at that stage, the US had admitted that the preferential treatment reserved for its own producers served no other purpose than to exempt the US refineries from the burden of adapting their mostly outdated production facilities to the requirements of air preservation. The panel had therefore considered that the US legislation *was* incompatible with the national treatment rule of Article III:4 of the General Agreement. On the basis of the same considerations, the panel also rejected the plea of the US Government claiming for its legislation the exceptions of Article XX relating to the protection of the environment. In its final conclusions the panel found as follows:

> 8.1 In the light of the findings above, the panel concluded that the baseline establishment methods contained in Part 80 of Title 40 of the Code of Federal Regulations are not consistent with Article III:4 of the General Agreement, and cannot be justified under Paragraphs (b), (d) and (g) of Article XX of the General Agreement.

The appeal of the US and the AB Opinion. The determination of the panel was appealed by the US, but only on grounds of Article XX(g) relating to the "conservation of exhaustible natural resources". As a result, this was the sole issue submitted for review to the Appellate Body, which the AB examined in a relatively long-drawn reasoning in which, after having explored several avenues without reaching a clear conclusion, it finally, on the one hand, blamed the panel for not having gone more deeply into the details of Article XX, and, on the other hand, charged the US for having come short of the introductory terms of Article XX, by creating an unjustified discrimination and a disguised restriction on international trade. As a consequence, the AB declared that its own legal conclusions were meant to "modify" the conclusions of the panel.

This created a perplexing situation, which the DSB resolved at its session of May 20, 1996 by adopting *both* the AB Report, and the Panel Report "as modified by the AB", which leaves open the question as to what exactly **is** the content of the solution arrived at. The best explanation seems to be that the AB came to *the same conclusions* as the panel, but that this position was based *on pretendedly different grounds*. If this is so, we must try to make out what the difference **is** between both approaches. In my opinion, this difference has its origin in a series of misunderstandings bearing on the "matter" in dispute.

A misunderstanding at the base of the AB's determination. At the root of the AB's misgivings about the first-level panel report there seems to be a misconception of what the litigious *matter* was, in the sense of Article XXIII, in this particular case. For the panel, the matter to be considered was the "baseline establishment rules" and in its perception this matter was, quite evidently, *the same* for the purposes of Article III and Article XX. For the AB, the matter to be considered under Article III and Article XX apparently was *not* the same: for the purpose of Article III, it was the baselines; but for the purpose of Article XX, the whole of the Clean Air Act had to be considered.

To elucidate this question, one would have to consider what the panel's terms of reference had exactly been, but these terms are quoted nowhere, neither in the Panel Report (save a reference to a non-published document), nor in the AB Opinion, which did not care about this detail. Whatever it be, I permit myself to think that the matter in litigation cannot be different for the principle (Article III) and for the exception (Article XX). It was therefore excessive and unjust for the AB to say that by taking the baseline establishment rules to be the object of the dispute for the purposes of both provisions, the panel was "in error", and turning "Article XX on its head" (Part II, B, 5th paragraph) and that it "did not serve the cause of clarity" (Part III, A, concluding paragraph).

A further divergence between the AB and the panel flows from the preceding: the panel apparently thought that, since the discrimination against importers resulted not from the statutory standard, but from the preferential treatment reserved for domestic producers, the "baseline establishment rules" were not *"relating"* to the preservation of natural resources, quite to the contrary. There was, therefore, no need to further examine the conditions set by Article XX(g), which the Panel by no means ignored: were there corresponding restrictions on domestic production? (obviously there were none) and, was the application of differential "baselines" devised to create arbitrary or unjustifiable discrimination, or disguised restriction on international trade? Not in the AB's opinion: the latter condition, expressed in what it elegantly called the "chapeau" of Article XX, should have been examined, and the panel's principal "error in law" consisted precisely in not having taken that course.

Here the AB touched on a weak point in the determination of the first-level panel, whose reasoning, at Point 6.41 of its report, looks indeed like a short-cut. Had the panel carried its argument just one step further, it would have come across the requirement of "corresponding restrictions on domestic production" in Article XX(g) — which did not exist, as the US had admitted — and the matter would have ended there.

Critical observations — in general. In my humble opinion, the reasoning of the AB is not a contribution to enlightened jurisprudence. These are, in short, my objections, on form and on substance:

(a) As a whole, the AB's Opinion lacks an intelligible structure. It sets out on a lengthy description of the Clean Air Act, giving details that nowhere become relevant to the ensuing reasoning (Part I.B). In contrast, the grounds for appeal, which would have required a precise analysis in order to establish a coherent scheme for the AB's reasoning, have been passed over in a hurry (just six lines, in Part II.A). This lack of methodology on the part of the AB stands in the way of a rational analysis of the determination made and it denotes moreover a regrettable unawareness of the elementary canons of legal drafting[16].

---

[16] I permit myself to refer to Part V of my "Introduction" to the **Handbook**, on "Short-comings of Report Writing". I would like to stress in this respect that in the age of

(b) The AB's reasoning failed to address properly one fundamental problem, i.e., the relationship between Articles III and XX. Instead, it is overburdened with extraneous considerations, including an unnecessary excursion into the Vienna Convention on Treaty Law. Moreover, the arguments retained by the AB are not exempt from contradiction and almost all of them stop halfway, without a clear conclusion. On one point, the AB even went beyond its mandate when it singled out "omissions" by the US, to establish supplemental failures — not discussed by the Panel. I would like to add some comments, bearing on the more substantive points just raised.

The uncertain relationship between Articles III and XX. From the legal point of view, the fundamental point which called for clarification was a matter pertaining to the internal context of the General Agreement, more precisely, the relationship between the principle of Article III and the exceptions of Article XX. The principle embodied in Article III is national treatment to be accorded to imported goods in relation to any laws regulating e.g. the internal sale, distribution, or use of domestic goods. Article XX exceptions and safeguards could therefore enter into consideration only if it could be established that the fact of according *national treatment* to imported goods could possibly jeopardize the conservation ends as set out in Article XX. In relation to the national-treatment standard, the application of Article XX raises, indeed, a very specific problem which has no equivalent in other provisions of the General Agreement. To be sure, the AB seems to have perceived that problem, in Part IV of its opinion, but this track is abandoned further on when the AB says that there is no need to decide that issue or to make a ruling "at variance with the common understanding of the participants."[17]

The gist of the matter is that Article XX is in the nature of *a safeguard clause* which may enter into consideration only if some substantive rule of the General Agreement would demonstrably put in jeopardy the values or interests indicated in the various subsections of Article XX. As the first-level panel had rightly found, it was the standards applied to

---

electronics and data-bases adjudicators cannot go on writing their determinations with a goose quill.

[17] To justify that position, the AB, in its footnote 46, makes reference to the Panel Report on the *US - Imports of Certain Automotive Springs Assemblies* Case, which had been adopted in its time on the understanding that it would **not** constitute a precedent. This report was in fact overruled later on, in the *US - Section 337 of the Tariff Act* Case, just because it had improperly determined the relationship between Articles III and XX, as can be seen from the latter case.

domestic production that created a problem for the environment, and not the status of imported gasoline. In other words, the application of the Article XX safeguards creates a specific problem in relation to the application of Article III *only because Article III is based on the standard of national treatment*, the application of which renders largely superfluous the Article XX safeguards. There are many precedents relating to this type of problem under Article XI:2(c)(i) of the General Agreement, in the field of restrictions on agricultural production, to serve as a model, but apparently nobody was aware of their existence.

An Opinion mainly made of digressions. Under these circumstances, it would have been sufficient, for the AB, to supplement the panel's finding by a reference to the "in-conjunction-with-restrictions-on-domestic-production" test in Article XX(g), which it did under C of Part III — but unfortunately this part of the argument is not brought to a conclusion. Why? Apparently, the AB was so much attracted by the "chapeau" of Article XX that it did not want to conclude on the content of Article XX(g), because this conclusion would have blocked access to the introductory words.

This was not the sole useless digression of the AB. Was it necessary to make a lengthy excursion into the interpretation of the words "relating to" in the General Agreement, to finish with an interpretation which was admittedly *not* derived from the General Agreement, but from some previous Panel Report? To prove its point, the AB would have fared much better in leaving "relating to" as it stands in Article XX(g), thereby saving no less than five pages of pointless argument (see Part III, B). Just as pointless as the excursion into the intricacies of *anti-dumping* investigations and the finding of "omission" addressed in that context to the US. The US had argued rightly that gasoline is a fungible international commodity (see Panel Report, 3.42). Therefore, hypothetical investigations on the spot and arrangements with third producer countries were an illusory perspective.

A particular mention must be made in connection with the references made by the AB to the *Vienna Convention on the Law of Treaties*, introduced under the cover of a reproach addressed to the panel for having "overlooked a fundamental rule of treaty interpretation" (Part III, B, 7th paragraph). As is well known, Article 31 of this convention envisages a process of interpretation by progressive steps: "terms", "context", "object and purpose". The AB's example proves nothing because the criteria of the convention's methodology have been used by the AB in a totally disorderly fashion, starting at any level on the scale as it serves the argument of the moment (*cp.* Part III, B, para. 8seq.; *ibid.* C, para. 4; Part IV, para. 4, with a dubious "extrapolation")[18]. The AB even applies the Vienna Convention standards to the interpretation of a national statute (Part III, B, last paragraph).

Finally, attention must be drawn to the fact that the AB has left all of its major arguments *without any conclusion*: see the argument on "measures relating to", which concludes with the necessity to decide everything "on a case-to-case basis", which means strictly nothing (Part II, B); the argument on "made effective in conjunction with" (Part II, C), which potentially contained the solution of the case, but which was left, on purpose, without an answer, as said above, because such a conclusion would have barred access to the cherished "chapeau" of Article XX (see Part IV). The latter argument, at the end (see the last paragraph of the reasoning), is in its turn left in the twilight between an objective and a subjective determination — the latter raising a difficult problem of evidence, unresolved as all the rest.

Finally, there remained only one convincing argument, drawn from the admission by the US that the true reason for the contested measures was to the effect that application of the statutory baseline to domestic producers "would have been physically and financially impossible because of the magnitude of the changes in almost all of the US refineries." This was decisive indeed, but it must be said that these words were copied from the "erring" panel's report, as discreetly indicated in footnote 53 of the AB's own Opinion (see the latter part of Point 3.52 in the descriptive part of the panel report).

To sum up, it appears that this legal imbroglio came about, basically, because neither the first-level panel nor the AB had taken care to properly identify *the problem* to be resolved, before launching into the intricacies of legal argument. In the end, it would have been easy for the AB to clear up the situation and, in this perspective, to refute the grounds for appeal of the US, instead of seeking new grievances and charging the panel with "error in law" and a series of other equally undeserved reprimands.

---

[18] In Part III, at note 45, the AB says that "one of the corollaries of the general rule of interpretation in the Vienna Convention is that interpretation must give meaning and effect to all the terms of a treaty." This does not make sense here. Effect must be given to the terms of a treaty only insofar as they are *relevant* to the problem to be solved — and this applied in the instant case only to the words "in conjunction with restrictions on domestic production."

Postscript

On October 4, 1996 the AB issued its Opinion on the case of *Japan - Taxes on Alcoholic Beverages,* which had been appealed by both Parties[19]. The composition of the AB was completely different from the composition during the former case *(US - Gasoline).* The litigious matter in the *Alcoholic Beverages* Case was simple, not to say trivial. It must be recalled that this matter was no more than an epilogue to a 1987 Panel Report in which the Japanese taxation system relating to alcoholic beverages had been extensively examined. In spite of a precise analysis of the merits of this particular case, which was restricted to the preference reserved by Japan to *shotchu*, a common drink distilled from potatoes and cereals, Japan appealed the first-level panel's determination, whereas the US, supported by Canada and the EC, raised a counterclaim complaining about the fact that the panel had found only in favour of a series of named competing products and not of *all* distilled spirits. Apart from the substance, the US also contested the way in which the panel had tried to establish the authority of the 1987 precedent by equating it to "subsequent practice" in the sense of Article 31:3 of the Vienna Convention on Treaty Law.

In reaction to this, the AB launched an argument drawn from the Vienna Convention (see the first paragraph of Part H), enough to show that it is no less unfamiliar with the Convention's methods, as in fact it immediately plunges into a purely semantic interpretation of Article III, with no consideration of the underlying principles. Applying the context-object-and-purpose method of the convention correctly would have required from the AB quite different steps of reasoning. These steps might be reconstructed as follows.

To start with, the AB should have recognized the fact that Article III, in spite of its fundamental character in the GATT system, is a poorly drafted provision, and that clarity has not been served by the highly obscure footnote affixed to it. Therefore, an adequate understanding of the *terms* of this article could be reached only if its words had been visualized in the *context* of the General Agreement and in the light of its *object* and *purpose*. Considering these parameters, the AB should have said in the first place that the General Agreement by no means rules out protectionism as a matter of principle. In itself, protectionism is still allowed, but this end can be materialized under the GATT rules only through one single means, i.e. customs duties, which are submitted to

---

[19] Doc. WT/DSS 8, 10, 11/AB/R.

periodic negotiation and which, in the long run, tend to be stabilized in the form of customs bindings. Considering this, it must be said that the AB was badly mistaken when it criticized the panel for having made just that *rapprochement* (see last paragraph under letter E and footnote 39 of the AB's Opinion). This being advanced, it becomes clear that the particular purpose of Article III in the system of the General Agreement is to make sure that protectionism is not re-entered by the way of a discriminatory application of a range of national provisions relating to production, taxation and marketing of goods. The object of Article III is to achieve this result by one well-defined principle, i.e. *national treatment* (which is nowhere mentioned by the AB), in contradistinction to the principle of most-favoured-nation treatment enshrined in Article I of the General Agreement.

In the specific matter of taxation, the national-treatment standard is applied in two successive ranges of stringency by Article III:2:

-   as a *per se* rule in the case of "like products" (phrase 1); and,
-   under the condition of a more thorough factual investigation whenever products, without being "like" by their nature, are found to be, directly or indirectly, in a competitive relationship (phrase 2).

In both cases, the applicable standard is exactly the same — national-treatment. To introduce here a supplemental *de minimis* facility is an arbitrary addition to the provisions of Article III.

Moreover, it must be said that this distinction does not by any means, call for a restrictive interpretation of the notion of "like products", as the AB pretends, disregarding the words "moreover" and "otherwise" in phrase 2 (to which the first-level panel had duly drawn attention). Instead of a substantive argument, the AB uses here the magic image of an "accordion". The impression of arbitrariness conveyed by this paradigm is reinforced by the fact that the AB, once more, pretends that the Vienna Convention imposes a *case-to-case* approach (see Part H, 1(a) of the Opinion), which, as I have said already in my report, is not an argument, but a non-argument. By this whimsical interpretation, the AB has gravely damaged the effect of Article III, which is a key provision in the system of the General Agreement, not to speak of its own prestige.

Thus, it once more appears to be utterly unjustified for the AB to charge the first-level panel with having "erred in law", where it would have been sufficient to note that the panel had in fact not gone to the limits of its terms of reference, by not ruling on "all" spirits.

The only points of concurrence on my side are the considerations of the AB on the authority of precedents set in the framework of the GATT/WTO dispute-settlement system. Indeed, contrary to what the first-level Panel had expressed, this manifestly was no matter for "subsequent practice" in the sense of the Vienna Convention. It had to be resolved in light of the fundamental principles relating to the effect of case-law in any system of separation of powers. This incident shows, in a pointed way, what misunderstandings can result from the Vienna Convention when it falls into inexpert hands.

Text of the Oral Presentation by Professor Pierre **PESCATORE** of his Report on *"The New WTO Dispute Settlement Mechanism"*

No doubt, the Marrakesh Agreements brought about a considerable progress in the dispute settlement process — a genuine "leap forward" if it is permitted to use that expression. I shall try to sum up the content of my report under three headings: first, to take stock of the advances achieved, second, to recall that, in spite of that fundamental thrust, there still remain some points of weakness which call to be mended, third, to express my regret in face of the first determination of the new Appellate Body, which I consider to be a disaster for a start into the new dimension of dispute settlement.

Advances to Take Stock of

Apart from detail, I have drawn attention to three features of the new agreements, all of which belong to the "systemic" register.

First, in contrast to the old GATT, the conclusion of the Marrakesh Agreements took place according to the regular process of treaty making. Thus, WTO law found itself placed on a more solid legal basis at the level of international law and of national law. The Marrakesh "Agreements" are international treaties in the full sense of the word, duly negotiated, ratified and concluded according to international and constitutional requirements. This process has created a solid basis for the application of the rules of international trade law not only in interstate relations, but also in the sphere of domestic law, a point to which I shall have to revert in a moment.

Second, the Marrakesh Agreements have marked an advance in the direction of *a more coherent system of rules*, surpassing by this the old GATT, which represented no more than a conglomeration of individual rules without the cement of principles and general ideas. By the attraction of services and intellectual rights into the WTO galaxy the substantive content of the new organization found itself considerably enlarged. The WTO Agreement contains also the basic notions of any system when it speaks of the "scope" of the new organization (Article II), of its "functions" (Article III) and of its "structure" (Article IV). The impact of systemic thought is particularly remarkable in the field of dispute settlement. It gets apparent in the architecture of the Understanding, as expressed in the titles preceding the individual articles. Having recognized all this, we must however admit that at the level of substantive provisions the system will not be complete as long as the WTO will have no coherent rules on international competition. In this respect, as in some others, WTO has not yet attained the full extent of the systemic framework of the Havana Charter and an open task is therefore still lying ahead.

Third, and this is the most decisive advance; the WTO Agreement has created *an institutional framework*, well beyond the pragmatic arrangements of the old GATT. Article I of the WTO Agreement purports to establish an organization based on a diversified structure of organs. Those organs enjoy specific functions, at different levels. The General Council, the Secretariat and the Dispute Settlement Body with its sub-organs, namely the Panels and the Appellate Body, may indeed be considered as a first sketch of a tripartite *separation of powers*.

In other words, the new World Trade Organization commands the resources not only of a fairly articulated normative system, but also of the even larger potentialities of an institutional structure capable of responding to the necessities of adaptation and progress and of coping with unforeseeable events.

Points of Concern

In spite of these undeniable advances, there remain quite a number of points of concern, which I have tried to express in my report. The first relates to the restrictive attitudes taken by some members as to the legal effect of the agreements. The second to the confusion maintained as between conciliation and adjudication. The third to the unresolved conflict between bilateral and multilateral approaches. The fourth concern relates to the attempts of governments at interfering with independent fact-finding and interpretation by the panels.

First, we must note that at least two Members of the WTO have been at pains to *exclude a priori any direct effect* of the WTO Agreements in their domestic order. Their intention has been quite evidently to privilege their internal legislation over the WTO rules in case of conflict. I have given in my report the pertinent indications on the behaviour of the European Community in this respect. There is parallel legislation in the US, with which I am not familiar, and I hope that a competent person will explain the position in our discussion. I do not know whether other Members have taken parallel precautions in their implementing legislation. Whatever this be, such behaviour constitutes a serious danger for the existence of WTO as a legal entity and I would like therefore to make clear my position in this respect. These attitudes are incompatible with the most fundamental rules of international law. More precisely, they are irreconcilable with the principle of good faith and with the rule saying that a state may not pretend to alter the effect of an international treaty by its internal legislation. Not to speak of the offhandedness with which governments treat the rights of individual citizens in regimes otherwise based on democracy. May I recall in this respect that Article XVI:4 of the WTO Agreement provides that "each Member shall ensure the conformity of its laws, regulations and administrative procedures with its obligations as provided in the annexed agreements" and that Paragraph 5 of the same article excludes any reservations to the WTO Agreement.

Second, I have drawn attention to the confusion lingering in the Understanding (especially in Article 3) as between *conciliation and legal adjudication*. Conciliation rests on mutual concessions accepted by the Parties. Adjudication on a determination made according to the law by an independent authority. An effort at conciliation must precede recourse to adjudication, but a Party's rights may not be deteriorated by telescoping conciliation into the process of adjudication. It is important to note, under this angle, that the Marrakesh Agreements have considerably enlarged the reservoir of elements of legal determination. The Understanding, in particular, offers a number of entirely new legal clues in comparison to the old GATT (see Annexe).

This checklist must be complemented by the legal notions contained in the former Panel-determinations. We must not forget that the continuity clauses contained in the WTO Agreement and in the Understanding (Articles XVI:1 and 3:1, respectively) have carried on the effect of these options. This imports an even greater variety of normative concepts that combine easily with the terms of the Understanding.

Third, I have drawn attention to the paradox of a *bilateral pattern of dispute settlement functioning in the context of a multilateral system of law*. Taking account of the intensive consultations that must precede the contentious phase of dispute settlement, we cannot discount the danger of having the presentation of a dispute biased by the interests of the Parties, specially where litigation touches on fundamental questions. The problem therefore is to foster a general-interest approach at all stages of litigation and, more particularly, in the minds of the members of panels, of the AB and of the DSB. I have aligned in my report a whole series of practical devices that may favour that approach. The first thing to do *now*, in my opinion, would be, for the DSB to establish its own rules of procedure, as provided by Article IV:3 of the WTO Agreement, and to conceive these rules in such a way that the *general interest* of the organization can be expressed at all stages of litigation. The most efficient way of achieving this end would be to give the Director-General the possibility to make known his opinion in the course of each case. This practice has inspired the solution of thousands of cases in the EC, without any prejudice to the independence of the institutions or officers concerned.

Fourth, I have drawn attention to the disquieting attempts of member governments at *prejudging the objective play of the rules of evidence and the rules of interpretation*. These attempts are in my opinion irreconcilable with the equality of the Parties in the judicial process, because they invariably favour the defendant who is normally identical with the wrong-doer. They are irreconcilable also with the equality of states under international law, because they favour evidently the stronger members of the WTO community. They are irreconcilable with the very idea of international justice, conceived of as an objective process, administered by independent adjudicators. The best antidote against these tendencies is to make all those concerned aware of the fact that provisions such as Article 17:6 of the Anti-Dumping Agreement are based on a vicious circle. No worry: the adjudicators are perfectly capable of breaking up this circle in the light of the basic rules that govern their function. More precisely, they should act on the premise that an independent adjudicator has the inherent power to determine his own competence and to resolve the doubts which may arise in connection with the evaluation of the facts or with the interpretation of the law. In other words, it is the adjudicators' exclusive task to determine at the end what is the one and only "permissible" interpretation. With this, the artificial construction of Article 17:6 will collapse into the void from which it is originating.

An Unpromising Start of the AB

I need not elaborate further on my criticism of the first opinion of the Appellate Body. It is a pity that the AB has not managed to produce a more inspiring precedent as a first landmark on its way into the "new area" of dispute settlement. I would like just to sum up my attitude in three remarks.

The first one relates to *the extremely poor quality* of the Opinion, under the angle of legal craftsmanship. The way of redress defined by Article 17:6 of the Understanding, under the confusing name of "Appellate Review", is in fact what we are used to call *cassation* or *revision* in the world of the civil law system. There are standard techniques that allow to cope with the problems raised by remedies of this type. Manifestly the members of the AB have been unaware of this part of legal experience.

My second remark relates to the use made by the AB of the *Vienna Convention on Treaty Law*. With all respect for that convention, I must say that there was no matter of treaty interpretation involved in this case. There was only a matter of legal evaluation of the contested measures instituted by the US under the curious name of "baselines". Under these circumstances, the heavy insistence on the Vienna Convention served only to show the AB's incapacity of handling the categories of this fundamental text. In particular, I must take exception to the opinion that the Vienna convention suggests a "case-to-case" approach to interpretation. The Convention's intention is the exact contrary: to impose a well-considered logical and methodological process. The disorderly "case-to-case" approach has no place in the framework of the Vienna Convention.

In the third place, I would make known my regret on the way in which the AB has censured the work of the first level panel. The panel was reproached in grossly exaggerated terms with having blurred the problem (which is not true), with having ignored fundamental standards of interpretation (which the AB was itself incapable of properly handling) and with having "erred in law". The latter expression was taken over from the appellant's argumentation. This adds a touch of sadness to the AB's attitude, which evidently was to give a nominal satisfaction to the US, rather than frankly to uphold the first level panel's determination. To obtain a satisfactory resolution, a few explanatory words would have been sufficient in order to bridge the apparent short-cut in the panel's argument, to which I have drawn attention in my report. By using an aggressive argumentation against the panel, the AB may have thought to facilitate the acceptance of its Opinion by the US. This was at the price of a serious damage done to the system of dispute settlement.

Annex

- *Dispute settlement (1:1)*
- *Rights and obligations (1:1)*
- *Rules and procedures (1:2)*
- *Conflicts of rules (1:2)*
- *Administration of rules and procedures (2:1)*
- *Surveillance of implementation of rulings and recommendations (2:1)*
- *Principles for the management of disputes (3:1)*
- *Security and predictability (3:1)*
- *Preservation of the rights and obligations of Members (3:2)*
- *Rules of interpretation of public international law (3:2)*
- *Rights and obligations under the agreements (3:4)*
- *Attainment of the objectives of any of the agreements (3:5)*
- *Positive solution to a dispute (3:7)*
- *Withdrawal of inconsistent measures (3:7)*
- *Last resort consisting in suspension of concessions or obligations (3:7)*
- *Infringement considered* prima facie *as leading to nullification or impairment (3:8)*
- *Breach of the rules leading to reversal of the burden of proof (3:8)*
- *Good faith at basis of contentious procedures (3:10)*
- *No linkage of complaints and counter-complaints relating to distinct matters (3:10)*
- *Matter deferred to DSB (7:1)*
- *Relevant provisions to be addressed (7:2)*
- *Independence of Panel members (8:2, see also (8:9)*
- *Objective assessment of the matter, including facts, applicability of relevant provisions and conformity with the relevant provisions (11)*
- *Flexibility of procedures, to ensure high-quality panel reports (12:2)*
- *Panel reports to set out the findings of fact, the applicability of relevant provisions and the rationale of the solution (12:7)*
- *Action in cases of urgency (12:8)*
- *Right of Panels to seek information and technical advice (13:1)*
- *Confidential character of Panel deliberations (14)*
- *Demonstrated expertise in law required from AB members (17:3)*
- *Appeals to be limited to issues of law and legal interpretations (17:6)*

- *No ex parte communications with panels or AB (18:1)*
- *Inconsistent measures to be brought into conformity with relevant agreement (19)*
- *Prompt compliance with recommendations or rulings of DSB essential for effective resolution of disputes (21:1)*
- *Surveillance of implementation by DSB (21:6)*
- *Compensation and suspension of concessions or other obligations (22)*

COMMENTS

Celso LAFER

Ambassador,
Permanent Representative of Brazil in Geneva;
Chairman (1996), WTO Dispute Settlement Body;
Professor, Law School, University of São Paulo

- I -

I have the greatest admiration for Professor Pierre Pescatore's work. He is a most distinguished personality on international law, on the law of the European Community, on GATT/WTO dispute settlement, and on the general theory of law. I consider his activity as a judge of the European Court outstanding and creative. As the role of a commentator is to help stimulate debate, I will respectfully emphasize divergences instead of sharing consensus on his report.

- II -

(1) Going into specific issues raised by Professor Pescatore, I must firstly say that I have some doubts regarding the advantages, for the multilateral trading-system, of "direct application" — that is, to consider WTO law "municipal law", as suggested by Professor Pescatore. The reason is simple: the problem is the same as that which occurs with the "uniform law", internationally agreed and locally applied. National courts may have different interpretations of the same international obligations, such as, for example, the rules on nondiscrimination, just to mention a core obligation of the GATT/WTO system. Coherent interpretations of the covered agreements, to use the jargon of the Dispute Settlement Understanding (DSU), require a consensus which must be achieved in the

framework of the WTO. Besides, the WTO dispute settlement system is a system of international public economic law. *Locus standi* is restricted to Members. Private interests must be granted the diplomatic protection of a Member to reach the WTO and it is in the hands of each Member of the organization to decide which private interests are national interests.

(2) I certainly agree with the "institutional" dimension of the WTO and its importance regarding "rights and obligations" of the covered agreements. But I have doubts regarding the "constitutional" character of the WTO, as mentioned by Professor Pescatore.

(i) If we are to understand "constitutional" in terms of hierarchy of law ("higher law"), I believe that the only constitutional text of the international community is the UN Charter. It is true that the end of the Cold War has led to a more homogeneous international system (of shared values). There are fewer conflicts of conception regarding how to structure the world economy, such as those that prevailed in a world of defined polarities — East/West; North/South (for example, "managed trade" — Comecon, "new international economic order through global negotiations", the old UNCTAD). There is, thus, broad consensus regarding the management of interdependence in a globalized world economy. The WTO is an expression of the "GATT-plus" view. Yet the WTO is still not universal *ratione personae* (the problem of Russia and China's accession is not yet solved), and from a *ratione materiae* view, the logic of globalization that it enshrines has not yet been fully consolidated in the world scene to embody a "higher law" dimension. One has just to mention the ongoing debate regarding the relationship of conflict and cooperation between the WTO and the Multilateral Environment Agreements.

(ii) If we think of "constitutional" as "separation of powers" within the WTO, I believe we would be stretching the argument. The Dispute Settlement Body (DSB) is, as Professor Pescatore previously qualified it, a functional specialization of the General Council. This is important from the point of view of giving emphasis to the centrality of the dispute-settlement system of the WTO in providing security and predictability to the multilateral trading system. However, the DSB is a diplomatic and political body. It certainly operates in an atmosphere of a "thickening of legality", when compared with GATT. It is "rule-oriented" but it is not a judicial body. This leads me to discuss what Professor Pescatore considers the problematic aspects of the new regime.

(3) Professor Pescatore is concerned with what he considers as an inadequate combination of the "old" and the "new", that is, the simultaneity of "conciliation" and "legal adjudication" within the WTO dispute settlement system. He would rather have less "old"-adjustment-ideology and more objective justice spirit and respect for obligations assumed. In his view, this outlook should be guided by the idea of "good faith" as a positive influx of general international law within the WTO (Vienna Convention on the Law of the Treaties. Arts 31-32). He is also unhappy with the strength of the bilateralism litigation within a multilateral shell.

This combination, however, was a deliberate one. It was based on what the negotiators, as state practitioners, in the process of codification and progressive development of this part of the Uruguay Round thought was wise. That, I believe, has proven to be wise in the WTO practice.

In short, the Dispute Settlement Understanding (DSU) is **problem-oriented within a rule-oriented horizon**. It keeps open the possibility of a **conciliation of interests** even though the **"thickening of legality"** of the WTO, that creates a **legal** *iter* for dispute settlement, is always there and available.

The "thickening of legality" was a result of the Uruguay Round, examples of which are: the "inverted consensus rule", the automaticity that it entails, the rights that it provides (e.g. the right to the establishment of a panel, the right to the adoption of a panel report, the right to appeal a panel report, the right to the adoption of an Appellate Body report). These rights do not exclude the role of the DSB as a political-diplomatic instance of dispute settlement within the WTO. Much to the contrary. In fact, this is an important part of the function of the DSB, as a manager of the DSU.

The DSU evidences it when it recommends caution before bringing a case and gives explicit preference to negotiated solutions (DSU, Art.3.7). The DSU also recommends that interpretation of the WTO rules be strict and not constructively widened (DSU, Art.3.2). Finally, the DSU contains the obligation to consult, as a mandatory preliminary phase, before considering the establishment of a panel (DSU, Art.4).

I may also recall, in the same line, that Parties in a dispute have the alternative of requesting, by mutual agreement, good offices, conciliation or mediation. The Director-General may also, in an *ex officio* capacity, offer good offices, conciliation or mediation (DSU, Art.5). Another important feature of the system is the possibility given to Parties to suspend, at any moment, the work of a panel, in order to negotiate a solution.

It indicates the continuity of GATT's diplomatic jurisprudence tradition. In a recent case, the Parties requested the report of the panel — which was already known to them — not to be circulated to the rest of the membership. The reason was to allow for a negotiated solution in view of the conclusions of the panel. A mutually-agreed solution was communicated to the DSB at its meeting of July 5, 1996. This possibility also exists in the second instance (cf. Working Procedures for Appellate Review, Rule 30). That is why, in my view, the reports of panels and of the Appellate Body are not judgments, but opinions with a *vis directiva*. It results from a legal *iter* that may be interrupted at any moment, to allow for a diplomatically negotiated solution. These opinions *(consilia)* only become mandatory after their adoption by the DSB. It is this adoption that, through a political-diplomatic decision, — operates as an *exequatur* — transforms advice into a *prescription*, with a *vis congendi*.

The political and diplomatic dimension of the DSU in the settlement of disputes can also be demonstrated by the right of any member to express its view regarding the contents of the report of a panel or of the Appellate Body, at the time of adoption of such report (DSU, Arts 16.4; 17.4). A member of the WTO exercised this right during the session of the DSU that adopted the report of the Appellate Body in the *Gasoline* Case. On that occasion, the member in question — who was not involved in that dispute — reserved its rights regarding the interpretation of Article III:4 of GATT as contained in the panel report, which had not been modified, in this particular aspect, by the report of the Appellate Body. The exercise of this right represents a possibility of political control over the legal contents of a report, in the sense of surveillance. The aim of such right is, in my view, to safeguard other rights, making it clear that the findings in a given case only apply to the matter at hand and to the Parties involved in that particular case. In other words, the objective is to obstruct the concept of mandatory precedent — *stare decisis*.

A survey of the activities of the DSB, from the date of its establishment until today, shows that the body has been functioning in dealing with disputes both in the sense of encouraging negotiated settlements and in the promotion of solutions of a more legal nature. Eleven cases (distinct matters) were settled, in a negotiated manner, either in the period of consultations or after the panel was requested. Among these, the most famous is the Case *United States — Imposition of Import Duties on Automobiles from Japan under Sections 301 and 304 of the Trade Act of 1974* — complaint by Japan.

There are presently in the WTO six active panels, three pending panel requests, and twenty-two cases of pending consultations. The *Gasoline Case* — *United States* — *Standards for Reformulated and Conventional Gasoline* — complaints by Venezuela and Brazil — is the only one that has gone through all phases from Panel to Appellate Body and is now in the phase of implementation.

May I add that the DSB has been a venue for both negotiated conciliation of interests and dispute settlement of a more legal nature for developed-country members, for developing-country members, and developed and developing-country members, (complaints by developed-country members: twenty-two matters, twenty-nine requests; complaints by developing-country members: eleven matters, fourteen requests; complaints by both developed and developing-country members: four matters, ten requests).

(4) Professor Pescatore stresses that one of the new important dimensions of the WTO is the establishment of a true multilateral system of sanctions. That is of course very much the case. However, this does not mean we are in the realm of legal adjudication.

The DSU establishes a distinction between the process of findings and legal recommendations *(processo de conhecimento)* and the process of enforcement *(processo de execução)*. The first passes through the "due process" of panels and the Appellate Body. The second is rule-oriented to avoid unilateralism (Art.23 of the DSU). Yet these rules of surveillance of implementation (Art.21) and of compensation and suspension of concessions — trade sanctions — (Art.22), which are secondary rules of recognition of *quid sit juris* (to employ Hart's terminology) are a result of decisions of a political diplomatic body, the DSB. These rules leave room for what Prof. Pescatore qualifies as "old adjustment ideology" but set a legal *iter* in case there is no agreement.

(5) Professor Pescatore stresses that since "the system of litigation remains fundamentally bilateral" the WTO, via the DSU, cannot rise, easily, to the level of matters of principles. This, in short, means that dispute settlement in the WTO, basically tends towards a classical concept of international responsibility.

Litigation bilateralism, the GATT tradition, its focus on nullification and impairment of benefits and the "diplomatic jurisprudence" gravitation, tend to privilege the view of the present system as a legally strengthened case for a dispute settlement of reparation *(contencioso de reparação)* not for a dispute settlement of legality *(contencioso de legalidade)*. In other words, the protection of legality as a function of international responsibility, that is the concept that international responsibility goes beyond the Parties directly involved in a dispute, having a bearing on all members of the WTO, is not contemplated in the DSU.

Third Parties, as Professor Pescatore mentions, have implicitly raised this matter and have frequently acted as genuine *amici curiae*. What can we say about this matter, as it presently stands?

If the participation in the phase of consultations requires third Parties to have a "substantial trade interest" (DSU, Art.4.11), participation of third Parties in a panel or appellate proceeding requires a "substantial interest", without such qualification (DSU, Art.10.2; 17.4). The question is whether "substantial interest" can be understood as "systemic interest" that, in WTO jargon, may also be understood as an interest in the function of legality of international responsibility. In other words, the question is whether the panels and the Appellate Body, in dealing with the considerations of third Parties, must also pay attention — and how much attention — to these "systemic interests". There is no doubt that, in a dispute, only the nullification or impairment of benefits allows a third Party to become a full Party and have the right to start its own dispute-settlement procedure (DSU, Art.10.4). The same applies to appeal panel reports: only the Parties in dispute, and not the third Parties, have the right to appeal (DSU, Art.17.4). In other words, the indirect loss, originating from the systemic interest in the function of legality, does not provide a member with the right to exercise the role of public prosecution in the protection of a collective interest in the maintenance of the coherence of the WTO legal system. In this sense, I would say, using words of the International Court of Justice in 1966, in the *South West Africa and Namibia* Case, the system does not allow for an *actio popularis*, a right of each Member of the WTO to start a dispute settlement procedure aimed at the protection of the collective interest.

These problems of the larger or smaller scope of international responsibility, however, are still open, by force of certain third Party statements exercising the role of *amici curiae* that require reflection and decision. The answer to these questions will have to wait for the tendencies that will — or will not — be consolidated in the future "jurisprudence" of the WTO.

It also seems to me that WTO Members, who conceive the organization as being basically member-oriented, consider that time is not ripe to enlarge the rights of the Secretariat, enabling it to act as an *amicus curiae* in matters pertaining to the general interest, as suggested by Professor Pescatore. In other words, I believe there is no political will to insert, through the Secretariat, the function of legality in the concept of international responsibility within the WTO.

- III -

May I conclude with some less-lofty considerations on some procedural issues that, practice has shown, might be relevant to the future development and reinforcement of the WTO Dispute Settlement System. As far as the practice is concerned, I will try — as much as my present position of Chairperson of the DSB allows me — to draw some inferences from the almost two years of functioning of the body.

(1) One of the essential features of the GATT system that was preserved and developed in the WTO dispute settlement mechanism is the terms of reference of panels. Professor Pescatore has said that this formula "defines the litigious "matter" by reference to the document introduced by the complainant Party, which makes clear that the definition of the terms of reference is unilateral and does not in any way depend on the defendant's agreement."

In my view, although the provision of standard-terms-of-reference is certainly a remarkable formula for expediency and predictability in the system, the automaticity of the standard-terms-of-reference may also create imbalances in the system. The fact that only the matter referred to the DSB by the complaining Party will form part of the standard-terms-of-reference (Arts 6.2 and 7.1 of the DSU) — which define the jurisdiction of the dispute — confers an advantage to the complainant, which is not balanced by any other device on the side of the defendant. It is certainly true that the panel will have to look at arguments brought by all Parties, and that the standard-terms-of-reference mentions the covered agreement "cited by the **Parties** to dispute". But the matter under examination by the panel is defined exclusively by the complaining Party. If taken to extremes — and in conjunction with the automaticity, in practice, of the establishment of panels — absurd situations may result from the setting of standard-terms-of-reference. In theory, the provision relating to special-terms-of-reference (Art.7.3) does not seem to solve this imbalance, since the terms of reference drawn by the chairperson, under the authorization of the DSB, must be agreed to by the Parties. In practice, however, the problem of the definition of the matter under examination has been solved, one occasion where the issue of applicable law was at stake, by the setting of special-terms-of-reference, agreed by the Parties after the establishment of the panel.

(2) A further procedural aspect that merits our consideration has to do with the relationship between the conclusions of the panel and the examination of the matter by the Appellate Body. It is the tradition of the GATT system — and this tradition seems to have been kept in the WTO — that panels do not decide what need not be decided. Therefore, if a panel reaches its conclusions based on one of the claims and arguments, it will usually leave other claims and arguments aside and not address them following the principle of procedural economy. This practice poses an interesting question when the conclusions of the panel are examined by the Appellate Body and this body decides to amend the conclusions. The question is: What happens to those claims and arguments that were not addressed by the panel, because it considered that it need not tackle them, when the Appellate Body modifies or reverts the conclusions of the panel? Has the Appellate Body the authority to examine the evidence that was brought by the Parties on the other arguments not addressed by the panel or must the Appellate Body remand the issue to the original panel?

The issue is complicated because, on the one had, the DSU contains no provision on remand — that is, on a request, by the Appellate Body, that a panel re-examine a certain issue. On the other hand, according to Article 17.6 of the DSU, "the Appellate Body shall be limited to issues of law covered in the panel report and legal interpretations developed by the panel." This provision seems to indicate that the Appellate Body does not have the authority to examine issues of fact and evidence that were not tackled by the panel. In a situation where the Appellate Body modifies or reverses the findings and/or conclusions of the panel, a legal vacuum could be created, in case the panel had not addressed the totality of the claims and arguments brought by the Parties in dispute.

The answers to the questions above, therefore, have to be developed as the system evolves and, if no pragmatic solution is found, this issue will probably have to be faced when the Dispute Settlement rules and procedures are reviewed by the Ministerial Conference in 1998, according to the Decision on Application and Review of the Understanding on Rules and Procedures Governing the Settlement of Disputes, taken at Marrakesh in April 1994.

THE RECEPTION OF THE WTO AGREEMENT IN THE EUROPEAN UNION: THE LEGACY OF GATT

Inge GOVAERE

Lecturer, Law Department, College of Europe, Bruges

1. Introduction

A crucial issue arising from the conclusion of the WTO Agreement is how to ensure that the new agreements will also be properly enforced and applied in the domestic legal systems of the WTO Members. As the WTO Agreement remains silent on how it should be received in the domestic legal orders of the WTO Members it remains up to the latter to determine questions such as the direct effect or direct applicability of WTO provisions in their own legal systems[1].

In so far as the European Union is concerned the main question that needs to be addressed is to what extent the approach adopted towards the WTO Agreement will be influenced by the legacy of GATT (1947) (hereafter: GATT) and, in particular, the case law of the European Court of Justice (ECJ) on the effect of GATT in the Community legal order. The main purpose of this short contribution is not to give a detailed analysis of the issues thus arising but rather to highlight the main features of the EC approach towards GATT which will need to be re-evaluated in

---

[1] One can distinguish between "direct effect", which denotes the possibility for individuals to invoke a provision before national courts, and "direct applicability" which points towards the possibility for Member States and community institutions to invoke such provisions in order to challenge the validity of domestic legislation. See for instance CHEYNE, I., *"International Agreements and the European Community Legal System"*, in: **ELR**, 1994, pp.581-598. More often than not, however, these concepts are interchanged in practice.

the light of the fundamental changes brought about by the WTO Agreement[2].

2. Positioning the GATT/WTO in EC Law

It may be said that GATT has always occupied a special status in EC law when compared to other international agreements. In some respects its effect in EC law was greater than that of other international agreements whereas in other respects it was less. This mainly depends on whether GATT is compared to international agreements concluded by the Member States prior to the EC Treaty or to other international agreements concluded by the EC.

It should be recalled that GATT was concluded by the Member States at a time when the EC did not yet exist. Nonetheless, it was not so much Article 234 EC, concerning prior treaty obligations of the Member States, that determined the basis for the status of GATT in EC law. With respect to prior treaty obligations of the Member States the ECJ interprets Article 234 EC, in accordance with international law and in particular Article 30 of the Vienna Convention on International Treaties, to mean that the application of the EC Treaty does not affect the duty of Member States to respect the rights of third countries. In so far as the EC is concerned the ECJ has consistently held that, whereas its institutions may not impede the performance of prior treaty obligations by the Member States, the EC itself is not bound by those prior obligations as regards third countries[3]. Even though Article 234 EC is held to be of a general scope, applying to any international agreement irrespective of its subject-matter[4], the special nature of GATT led the ECJ to conclude in the *International Fruit Company* Case that the EC, and not only its Member States, was bound by GATT[5]. The ECJ pointed to *inter alia* the fact that the EC Treaty was largely modelled on GATT whereas the wish to observe the latter was expressed in the former; the exclusive competence of the EC in matters of commercial policy; and the practice whereby the GATT Contracting Parties recognized the transfer of competence from the Member States to the EC.

---

[2] For a detailed analysis, see the article by EECKHOUT, P., *"The Domestic Legal Status of the WTO Agreement - Interconnecting Legal Systems"*, in: **CMLRev.,** February 1997. Specifically with respect to GATT 1994, see LEE, P., KENNEDY, B., *"The Potential Direct Effect of GATT 1994 in European Community Law"*, in: **JWT**, 1996, pp.67-89.

[3] Case 812/79, *Burgoa*, **ECR** (1980) 2787, paras 8-9.

[4] Case 812/79, *op.cit.*, para.6.

[5] Joined Cases 21-24/72, **ECR** (1972) 1219, para.18.

Even though the EC was not formally a Contracting Party to GATT, in the hierarchy of norms GATT thus already occupied the same status as international agreements concluded by the EC. Such agreements take priority over secondary legislation whereas they may not be contrary to the EC Treaty[6]. The fact that the EC is now a signatory WTO Member, alongside the Member States, reflects better the status of the EC in the WTO but it does not fundamentally alter the ranking of the latter in the EC hierarchy of norms. The main question is therefore whether the WTO Agreement presents enough substantive modifications with respect to GATT in order to align its possible effect in EC law to the approach adopted by the ECJ with respect to other international agreements concluded by the EC.

3. Invocation of GATT/WTO before National Courts

In the same *International Fruit Company* Case the ECJ made clear that it is one matter to accept that the EC is bound by GATT but a totally different matter to attach specific conclusions to this in so far as the possible direct effect of GATT in the EC legal system is concerned. In particular, the ECJ drew the following distinction:

Before the incompatibility of a Community measure with a provision of international law can affect the validity of that measure, the Community must first of all be bound by that provision.

Before invalidity can be relied upon before a national court, that provision of international law must also be capable of conferring rights on citizens of the Community which they can invoke before the courts.[7]

Those conditions are not specific to GATT for they apply to all international agreements concluded by the EC. The specificity of the approach to GATT consists rather in the reasoning applied by the ECJ in order to deny the direct effect of GATT.

Instead of analysing whether the GATT **provision** invoked satisfied the conditions for conferring direct effect the ECJ considered the spirit, general scheme and the terms of GATT and found that GATT **as such** did not lend itself to conferring direct effect. The ECJ in particular underlined the following features of GATT:

This agreement which, according to its preamble, is based on the principle of negotiations undertaken on the basis of "reciprocal

---

[6] See Article 228(7) and 228(6) of the EC Treaty respectively.

[7] Joined Cases 21-24/72, *op.cit.*, paras 7-8.

and mutually advantageous arrangements" is characterized by the great flexibility of its provisions, in particular those conferring the possibility of derogation, the measures to be taken when confronted with exceptional difficulties and the settlement of conflicts between the Contracting Parties.[8]

On these grounds the ECJ did not consider whether or not specific provisions of GATT were sufficiently precise and clear in order to be able to be successfully invoked by individuals before national courts. Had the ECJ been willing to test individual provisions of GATT against the conditions of direct effect, it might have come to a different conclusion at least with respect to some provisions.

The reliance by the ECJ on the "reciprocity" argument and the "flexibility" argument as well as on the context and system of GATT in order to deny the direct effect of GATT as a whole was criticized in legal writings. Whereas the ECJ's appraisal of the functioning of the GATT system was sometimes contested[9], it was often pointed out that it seemed difficult to reconcile the reasoning applied by the ECJ to GATT with the reasoning adopted with regard to other international agreements concluded by the EC[10]. In particular, attention was drawn to the apparently contradictory statements in the *Kupferberg* Case[11]. In the latter, the ECJ held that the fact that provisions of a free trade agreement could not be directly invoked by individuals before the courts of the third country concerned did not constitute a lack of reciprocity which would, of itself, deprive the provisions of direct effect also in the EC legal system. Furthermore, the provisions of the free trade agreement concerning the possibility to take safeguard measures and on dispute settlement did not seem to carry much weight in the final outcome as to whether or not specific provisions of the agreement could be invoked by individuals before national courts[12].

---

[8] Joined Cases 21-24/72, *op.cit.*, para.21.

[9] See in particular PETERSMANN, *"Application of GATT by the Court of Justice of the European Communities"*, in: **CMLRev.**, 1983, pp.397-437, especially at pp.424-437, where he analyses each of these arguments also from a GATT perspective.

[10] See for instance BEBR, *"Agreements Concluded by the Community and their Possible Direct Effect: From International Fruit Company to Kupferberg"*, in: **CMLRev.**, 1983, pp.35-73, at pp.68-69.

[11] Case 104/81, *Kupferberg*, **ECR** (1982) 3641.

[12] See for instance KUYPER, P-J., *"The New WTO Dispute Settlement System: The Impact on the Community"*, in: BOURGEOIS, BERROD, GIPPINI FOURNIER (eds), **The Uruguay Round Results**, European Interuniversity Press, 1995, pp.87-114, at p.103; VAN DEN HENDE, L., *"Overzicht van Rechtspraak: Europees*

The reason for the denial of direct effect of GATT may, therefore, perhaps need to be sought not only in its structural weaknesses, as such, but in the fact that the latter are embedded in a multilateral treaty thereby reducing the possibility for the EC to react to non-performance of their obligations by other Contracting Parties[13]. If this is the case then the question emerges to what extent the ECJ will consider the structural reinforcement of the multilateral system as brought about by the WTO Agreement, and in particular the new Dispute Settlement Mechanism, to be sufficient to meet this concern[14]. If, on the other hand, it was the very multilateral nature of GATT that in effect formed the major obstacle to it having direct effect then it is plain that pointing out the fundamental structural changes brought about by the WTO Agreement will prove to be of no avail. It should, however, be pointed out that if the WTO Agreement, as a whole, may be found to have no direct effect this does not, of itself, preclude that the principle of state liability could perhaps be invoked by individuals in order to obtain redress in cases where Member States fail to comply with their obligations under the WTO Agreement, and in particular the TRIPS Agreement[15].

4. Invocation of GATT/WTO to Contest the Validity of EC Measures

A different question altogether concerned the possibility to invoke GATT to contest the validity of EC measures before the Community courts. As the ECJ had stated that the EC is bound by GATT it takes priority over secondary EC legislation[16]. This implies in principle that the latter needs to be in conformity with the former. In order for this to be so not only as a matter of principle but also in practice it would seem

---

Gemeenschapsrecht: Rechtsbescherming (1979-1994)", in: **Tijdschrift voor Privaatrecht**, 1995, pp.151-347, at pp.206-208.

[13] See NEUWAHL, N., *"Individuals and the GATT: Direct Effect and Indirect Effects of the General Agreement on Tariffs and Trade in Community Law"*, in: EMILIOU & O'KEEFFE (eds), **The European Union and World Trade Law after the GATT Uruguay Round**, John Wiley & Sons, 1996, pp.313-328, at p.320. She points to the following: "In the case of a multilateral treaty, a substantive non-performance by a Contracting Party may not always permit the suspension of (the internal enforcement of) the Community's obligations, and there may be no international authority capable of guaranteeing the enforcement of the agreement over the Contracting Parties."

[14] Several articles have already been devoted to this issue. See for instance LEE, P., KENNEDY, B., *op.cit.*, at pp.78-84; KUYPER, P-J., *op.cit.*; MENGOZZI, P., *"The Marrakesh DSU and its Implications on the International and European Level"*, in: BOURGEOIS, BERROD, GIPPINI FOURNIER (eds), *op.cit.*, pp.115-133.

[15] On this issue, see *infra*, at pt 5.

[16] See *supra*, at pt 3.

logical to subject the "GATT-consistency" of EC measures to scrutiny by the Community courts. Yet, contrary to other international agreements concluded by the EC, in so far as GATT is concerned the ECJ has qualified its approach to this matter.

It is not uncommon for the ECJ to interpret EC law in a "GATT-consistent" manner, thereby referring to GATT provisions in order to underscore the argument[17]. If in so doing a conflict between GATT and EC law may often be avoided there remain situations whereby this method is to no avail, in particular where the lawfulness of EC measures is challenged on the basis of GATT.

The reasons forwarded to deny direct effect of GATT in the *International Fruit Company* Case also lay at the basis of the reluctance of the ECJ to accept that EC measures may be challenged before it on grounds of incompatibility with GATT. This may seem surprising considering that the issue, in such cases, no longer is whether GATT confers rights upon citizens which they can invoke in litigation before national courts but rather whether the Community fully respects its international obligations under GATT. In spite of this crucial distinction, the ECJ has consistently held that the special features of GATT are such that it cannot be invoked to contest the validity of EC measures, be it by individuals or by a Member State[18]. It is, to say the least, surprising that the ECJ does not distinguish between the interests of Member States and individuals in so far as EC compliance with GATT is concerned.

The ECJ nonetheless leaves the door open, be it through a narrow gap, to a potential effect of GATT, and now of the WTO Agreement, in the Community legal order. For instance in the *Bananas* Case, the ECJ reiterated the following approach:

> The special features noted above show that the GATT rules are not unconditional and that an obligation to recognize them as rules of international law which are directly applicable in the domestic legal system of the Contracting Parties cannot be based on the spirit, general scheme or terms of GATT.

> In the absence of such an obligation following from GATT itself, it is only if the Community intended to implement a particular obligation entered into within the framework of GATT, or if the Community act expressly refers to specific provisions of GATT,

---

[17] For examples, see EECKHOUT, P., *op.cit.*, at pt 4; VAN DEN HENDE, L., *op.cit,* at p.213.

[18] Case C-280/93, *Germany v. Council (Bananas)*, Judgment of 5.10.1994, para.109.

that the Court can review the lawfulness of the Community act in question from the point of view of the GATT rules (see Case 70/87 *Fediol v. Commission* (1989) ECR 1781 and Case C-69/89 *Nakajima v. Council* (1991) ECR I-2069).[19]

It remains to be seen to what extent the fundamental structural reinforcements brought about by the WTO Agreement, and in particular on dispute settlement, will be considered to be sufficiently unconditional for the ECJ to infer that it is intended to be directly applicable in the domestic legal orders of the WTO Members[20]. The view has been advanced that, if uncertainty may prevail about the unconditional nature of certain WTO provisions, this will no longer be the case once WTO's dispute settlement decisions have been adopted which establish a violation of WTO rules by the EC, so that such decisions should be directly applicable in the EC[21]. It is clear that the ECJ would not be assuming the role of a "GATT or WTO-judge" in this instance but would rather be called upon to remedy an established violation of international obligations of the EC.

What is certain is that the WTO Agreement, similarly as GATT before, may be invoked before the ECJ to challenge the lawfulness of EC measures if the EC intended to implement a particular obligation entered into within the framework of the WTO Agreement, or if the Community act expressly refers to specific provisions of the WTO Agreement. This may prove to be of particular importance with respect to Agreements annexed to the WTO Agreement, such as the TRIPS Agreement. The latter expressly aims at conferring private rights to individuals, thus begging the question of the direct effect of its provisions[22]. The potential direct effect of TRIPS may be put into question by virtue of the obligation, resting on the WTO Members, to implement its provisions within a certain time-frame[23]. It is clear, however, that compliance with this

---

[19] Case C-280/93, *op.cit.*, at paras 110-111.

[20] For instance, divergences in view remain about the nature of the dispute settlement under the WTO Agreement, raising crucial questions such as whether it is concerned with conciliation or legal adjudication; whether the DSB is essentially a diplomatic and political body or a judicial body. Compare, for instance, the contributions to this book by P. PESCATORE & C. LAFER.

[21] EECKHOUT, P., *op.cit.*, at pt 5; CHEYNE, I., *op.cit.*, at p.595.

[22] See also EECKHOUT, P., *op.cit.*, at pt 3.3.

[23] See for instance Case 12/86, *Demirel*, **ECR** (1987) 3719, at para.14, where the ECJ held that for a provision in an agreement to be directly applicable it must contain a clear and precise obligation which is not subject, in its **implementation** or effects, to the adoption of any subsequent measure.

obligation should at least assure the direct applicability of TRIPS before the EC Courts in order to challenge the lawfulness of EC implementing measures.

5. Invocation of GATT/WTO to Contest the Validity of National Measures

It would at first sight seem to be logical that if Member States may not, in principle, invoke GATT to contest the lawfulness of EC measures then GATT may not be invoked either to challenge the lawfulness of national measures. In reality it is not that simple. The different application by the Member States, in their relations with third countries, of international agreements concluded by the EC could affect the unity of the EC market and lead to distortions of intra-Community trade. The ECJ has therefore consistently held that it is its task to ensure the uniform application of agreements concluded by the Community throughout its territory, also in so far as GATT is concerned[24]. This reasoning is not limited to settling the issue of direct effect of GATT throughout the Community but also applies to the issue of compliance by Member States with GATT obligations.

The ECJ recalled in the *International Dairy Arrangement (IDA)* Case that international agreements concluded by the EC are binding on both the EC and its Member States, pursuant to Article 228(7) of the EC Treaty, so that proceedings may be brought before it where a Member State has failed to fulfill its obligations under such an agreement[25]. In this particular case, the Commission essentially alleged that Germany had failed to comply with the IDA, which resulted from the GATT Tokyo Round negotiations. The ECJ did not consider whether or not the IDA as a whole, or the provisions invoked, could be directly applied. Instead, it proceeded directly to settle the dispute with respect to the proper interpretation of specific provisions of IDA through pointing out that:

> In order to interpret that provision, account must be taken of the purpose of the IDA, the context of Article 6 and the general rule

---

[24] See for instance Joined Cases 267 to 269/81, *SPI & Sami*, Judgment of 16.3.1983, **ECR** (1983) 801, paras 14-15. On this issue, see MARESCEAU, M., *"The GATT in the Case-law of the European Court of Justice"*, in: HILF, JACOBS, PETERSMAN (eds), **The European Community and GATT**, Kluwer, 1986, pp.107-126, at pp.110-113.

[25] Case C-61/94, *Commission v. Germany (IDA)*, Judgment of September 19, 1996, not yet reported, para.15.

of international law requiring the Parties to any agreement to show good faith in its performance.[26]

After interpreting the IDA provision according to these guidelines, the ECJ held that the contested German measure was indeed precluded by the IDA. In essence this means that GATT rules may be invoked before the ECJ to challenge the lawfulness of national measures but not, in principle, to challenge the validity of EC measures.

There would thus seem to be no reason why the compliance by the Member States with the WTO Agreement could not be challenged before the ECJ. This is certainly the case with respect to GATT 1994, which comes under the EC's exclusive competence under the common commercial policy heading. The issue gains even more in importance in so far as GATS and the TRIPS Agreement are concerned since the ECJ held in Opinion 1/94 that the EC and its Member States have shared competence for those matters[27]. Certain implementing measures may, therefore, be taken by the Member States rather than by the Community. It is not without importance that the ECJ clarified, with respect to TRIPS, that this does not imply that the Member States retain an exclusive competence for certain aspects of the agreement. Member States and the EC have a concurrent competence for TRIPS, except for counterfeit measures which belong to the exclusive competence of the EC under the Common Commercial Policy[28]. By virtue of the rationale underlying Article 228(7) of the EC Treaty it would seem to be logical that also national implementing measures, at least in so far as the EC has a concurrent competence in the matter, could be challenged upon their conformity with GATS and TRIPS before the ECJ[29]. It should be recalled that the ECJ has consistently held that Member States are not only under a duty to fulfill their obligations *vis-à-vis* third countries but also, and this is a weighty argument for the ECJ, *vis-à-vis* the Community[30]. It might suffice here to point out that it is clearly in the Community's

---

[26] Case C-61/94, *op.cit.*, para.30. There are other cases where the ECJ does not deal with the question of direct applicability of agreements but proceeds immediately with the interpretation of the contested provision, see for instance Case 270/80, *Polydor*, **ECR** (1982) 329.

[27] Opinion 1/94, WTO, **ECR** (1994) I-5267.

[28] See GOVAERE, I., *"Trade-related Aspects of Intellectual Property Rights: The EC Dichotomy Uncovered"*, in: **La place de l'Europe dans le commerce mondial**, Institut Universitaire International Luxembourg, Session de juillet 1994, pp.161-215, at pp.198-204.

[29] See also EECKHOUT, P., *op.cit.*, at pt 2, where he argues in favour of full jurisdiction of the ECJ with respect to the whole WTO Agreement.

[30] See for instance Case 104/81, *Kupferberg*, **ECR** (1982) 3659, para.13.

interest to ensure the conformity of the Member States to the WTO rules in order to avoid WTO panels proceedings[31].

It remains to be seen whether the ECJ would go so far as to extend the recent case law on state liability for manifest and grave breach of Community law by Member States to noncompliance by Member States with international agreements in breach of Community law[32]. State liability is an important new instrument to ensure respect for their Community obligations by Member States in particular as the ECJ has clearly stated that it is to be dissociated from the issue of direct effect[33]. The latter clarification would be of a crucial importance if state liability were ever to be invoked before the ECJ with respect to noncompliance of Member States with WTO rules. The ECJ has indeed held that the fulfilment of the following three conditions are necessary and sufficient for individuals to be able to obtain redress:

> the rule of law infringed must be intended to confer rights on individuals; the breach must be sufficiently serious: and there must be a direct causal link between the breach of the obligation resting on the state and the damage sustained by the injured Parties.[34]

It seems that a case could be made that these three conditions are fulfilled where a Member State fails to duly implement the TRIPS Agreement which is expressly intended to confer rights on individuals. If some uncertainty may exist with respect to the appreciation of whether, in so-doing, a Member State manifestly and gravely disregards the limits on its discretion[35], it is clear that this will no longer be the case if a Member State fails to duly implement such an agreement despite a judgment of the ECJ establishing an infringement[36].

Because of the different approach adopted by the ECJ, depending on whether GATT is invoked with respect to EC or national measures, a

---

[31] See KUYPER, P-J., *op.cit.* at p.111, where he points to the potential implications of Article XVI:4 of the WTO Agreement for the EC.

[32] Joined Cases C-46/93 and C-48/93, *Brasserie du Pêcheur and Factortame III*, Judgment of March 6, 1996, not yet reported.

[33] *Id.*, para.20.

[34] *Id.*, para.51, see also para.66.

[35] *Id.*, para.55. In para.56, the ECJ points to the following factors which may be taken into consideration: "the clarity and precision of the rule breached, the measure of discretion left by that rule to the national or Community authorities, whether the infringement and the damage caused was intentional or involuntary, whether any error of law was excusable or inexcusable, the fact that the position taken by a Community institution may have contributed towards the omission, and the adoption or retention of national measures or practices contrary to Community law."

[36] *Id.*, para.57.

specific problem arises when the national measures, which are challenged upon their conformity with GATT rules, conform with EC measures. This appeared to be the situation in the above-mentioned *IDA* Case. Advocate General Tesauro was of the opinion that there was a clear discrepancy between the IDA and EC measures, whereas the contested German measure was authorized by the latter. He therefore considered it unacceptable to assess the German measure with reference to the IDA alone, without taking into account the EC measures authorizing the national measure. In his view the case should have been dismissed on the following grounds:

> If the GATT rules cannot be relied on in order to challenge the validity of Community legislation and, as a consequence, the Council and the Commission are accorded a broad discretion as regards the content and effects of obligations entered into in that regard, such an approach cannot go so far as to entail that a Member State can be censured for having complied with the regulation and not the IDA.[37]

It is important to underline that in this particular case the national measure was alleged to be authorized, but not dictated, by EC measures. This made it ultimately possible for the ECJ, through applying the method of GATT-consistent interpretation, to hold that the EC measures concerned could not be construed in such a way as would be incompatible with the IDA[38]. Germany was thus held to have failed to fulfill its obligations under both the IDA and the EC measures concerned. For the time being, therefore, the problem remains unsolved as to what approach would be adopted when a national measure, which is challenged upon its conformity with WTO rules, is in fact in compliance with EC measures which are, themselves, contrary to WTO rules.

6. Conclusion

At present it is still unclear to what extent the legacy of GATT, on the one hand, and the fundamental reforms in the WTO Agreement, on the other hand, will weigh in the balance when the question will be posed to the ECJ of how the WTO Agreement should be applied in the Community

---

[37] Case C-61/94, *IDA*, Opinion delivered on May 7, 1996, not yet reported, para.24.

[38] Case C-61/94, *op.cit.*, paras 52-57. Advocate General Tesauro had implicitly rejected this solution on the basis of the principle of legal certainty, arguing that "the ambiguity and confusion generated by (**EC**) provisions which are manifestly irreconcilable (**with IDA**) exacerbate the difficulty faced by the state concerned in finding an internal (Community) solution to the problem", *op.cit.*, at para.25 (bold added).

legal order. Faced with this uncertainty, the Council inserted the following sentence in the preamble of its decision concerning the conclusion of the Uruguay Round:

> by its nature, the Agreement establishing the World Trade Organization, including the Annexes thereto, is not susceptible to being directly invoked in Community or Member State courts.[39]

An additional question thus arising is to what extent the ECJ will need to take this unilateral statement into account. It is traditionally thought that the EC takes a monist rather than a dualist approach to the reception of international agreement in its legal order so that, unless a provision concerning its application is inserted in the agreement itself, it is up to the ECJ to determine the status of the agreement in EC law[40]. This seems to be confirmed by the above-mentioned statement by the ECJ in the *Bananas* Case where it held that in the absence of an obligation concerning its direct applicability **following from GATT itself**, it could not be directly invoked in the EC[41]. It is, nonetheless, not altogether unlikely that the ECJ will pay due attention to the reasons underlying the insertion of this statement in the Council's decision. In particular the argument that if the WTO Agreement could be directly invoked before the ECJ then this would weaken the position of the EC institutions by reducing their margin of negotiation with the other WTO Members, especially if the latter do not recognize the direct effect of the WTO Agreement in their domestic legal orders, will need to be carefully considered. The image of EC negotiators arriving at the negotiating table with "their hands tied by the interpretation of their courts"[42], may well prove to be the crucial element which will dominate the whole picture.

---

[39] Council Decision of December 22, 1994 concerning the conclusion on behalf of the European Community, as regards matters within its competence, of the agreements reached in the Uruguay Round multilateral negotiations (1986-1994), **OJ** 1994 L 336/1.

[40] See in particular MENGOZZI, P., *op.cit.*, at p.132.

[41] See *supra*, at pt 4. This also seems to follow from statements made by the ECJ with respect to other international agreements, see BOURGEOIS, J., *"The Uruguay Round of GATT: Some General Comments from an EC Standpoint"*, in: EMILIOU & O'KEEFFE (eds), *op.cit.*, pp.81-90, at pp.89-90.

[42] KUYPER, P.-J., *op.cit.*, at p.105

DIRECT APPLICATION OF MULTILATERAL TRADE AGREEMENTS IN THE UNITED STATES

Richard H. STEINBERG

Acting Professor of Law,
University of California, Los Angeles

The impact on domestic law of direct application of international trade agreements and related international law has been far more limited in the United States than in Europe. To European lawyers, it is elementary that courts in EU Member States give direct effect to most provisions of the Treaty of Rome, some legislation enacted pursuant thereto, and decisions of the European Court of Justice[1]. Ceding that degree of sovereignty in an international agreement or to international organizations or tribunals would be extremely difficult in the United States for constitutional, political, and ideological reasons.

Part 1 describes briefly the law of international agreements and direct effects in the United States. Part 2 analyzes the extent to which the GATT 1947[2] was applied directly in US courts and explains why that direct application had limited impact on US law. Part 3 analyzes direct application of the Uruguay Round Agreements, including GATT 1994[3],

---

[1] See, e.g., Case 26/62, *Van Gend & Loos v. Nederlandse Administratie der Belastingen*, 1963 **ECR**, 1 **CMLR** 105 (1963); and Case 106/77, *Amministrazione delle Finanze dello Stato v. Simmenthal S.p.A.*, 1978 **ECR** 629.

[2] General Agreement on Tariffs and Trade, Oct. 30, 1947, TIAS No.1700, 55 **UNTS** 187.

[3] General Agreement on Tariffs and Trade, April 15, 1994, Agreement Establishing the World Trade Organization, Annex 1A, in Final Act Embodying the Results of the Uruguay Round of Multilateral Trade Negotiations, Marrakech, April 15, 1994 [hereinafter Final Act].

showing that the Uruguay Round implementing statute carefully circum-
scribes the impact that any direct application might have. Part 4 concludes, suggesting some reasons why the US system seems to resist a
broadly effective direct application of international law.

1. General Rules on Direct Application
of International Law in the United States

Under US law, the authority to negotiate and assume an international
obligation relating to international trade is shared between the executive
and legislative branches[4]. An international trade agreement may take one
of three forms under US law, each reflecting this shared authority[5].

First, an international trade agreement may be a "treaty". A treaty is
made by the President, "by and with the Advice and Consent of the Senate", and must be approved by a two-thirds vote of the Senate[6]. A ratified treaty becomes the "supreme Law of the Land"[7]. Therefore, if a
treaty is "self-executing" (i.e., if it "operates of itself" as opposed to
promising "to perform a particular act")[8], then it will be given direct
effect in US courts after ratification, and will prevail over prior inconsistent statutes, as well as inconsistent state laws[9]. However, if a treaty is
not self-executing, then it will not be directly applied in US courts; implementing legislation passed by a majority vote of both houses of Congress would be required to bring US law into conformity with international obligations contained in the treaty and the resulting statute would
be the significant source of law in US courts.

Second, an international trade agreement sometimes may be entered
into as an "executive agreement". Most international compacts (e.g.,

---

[4] For example, Congress has the power to "regulate Commerce with foreign Nations",
US Const, Art.I, §8, cl.3, while the President has the power to "make treaties", US
Const., Art.II, §2, cl.2. The President also has an implied constitutionally based
power to conduct foreign relations, which includes the negotiation of international
agreements. See *US v. Curtiss-Wright Export Corp.*, 299 US 304, 319 (1936).

[5] On these three types of agreements, see generally, Louis HENKIN, **Foreign Affairs
and the US Constitution**, (2d ed.), Clarendon Press, Oxford, 1996, especially
pp.171-230; and, Barry CARTER & Phillip R. TRIMBLE, **International Law**,
(2d ed.), Little, Brown, Boston, 1995.

[6] US Const., Art.II, §2, cl.2. A fourth, but minor form of international agreement in
US practice is an agreement contemplated or authorized by a prior treaty.

[7] US Constitution, Art.VI, cl.2.

[8] On the distinction between self-executing and non-self-executing treaties, see *Foster
v. Neilson*, 27 US (2 Pet.) 253, 314 (1829). See also HENKIN, **Foreign Affairs and
the US Constitution**, pp.198-204.

[9] *Missouri v. Holland*, 252 US 416, 40 S. Ct. 382, 64 L. Ed. 641 (1920).

exchanges of letters, bilateral agreements resolving certain disputes, etc.) do not engender a level of domestic political interest that demands their treatment as a "treaty" requiring the advice and consent of the Senate[10]. Moreover, while the executive branch is responsible for conducting the foreign affairs of the United States[11], the President's authority to negotiate and bind the United States internationally varies depending on the role or attitude of Congress and the specific foreign policy matter at hand[12]. When the President's Constitutional authority to act alone on an international matter is clear and the associated international agreement is self-executing, domestic political interest in the international agreement is not great, and the terms of the international agreement are not inconsistent with existing federal law, the President (or an agent vested with appropriate authority) may bind the United States internationally without any Congressional action. Executive agreements may have direct effect in US courts only to the extent that they are not inconsistent with any federal statutes, because they may not prevail over a prior inconsistent federal statute; executive agreements may, however, prevail over inconsistent state law[13].

Third, on matters for which Constitutional authority is shared between the executive and legislative branches, an international agreement may take the form of a "Congressional-Executive Agreement". In these cases, both houses of Congress delegate to the President clear authority to negotiate an international agreement according to specified parameters. This mechanism may be particularly sensible for non-self-executing international agreements, since such agreements would often require action by both houses of Congress anyway. For example, both houses of Congress by a simple majority vote may delegate to the President the authority to enter into international trade agreements that can be given

---

[10] See HENKIN, **Foreign Affairs and the US Constitution**, pp.215-30. See also *US v. Belmont*, 301 US 324, 330-31 (1937).

[11] John MARSHALL is often quoted for the proposition that "The President is the sole organ of the nation in its external relations, and its sole representative with foreign nations." See, e.g., *US v. Curtiss-Wright Export Corp.*, 299 US 304, 319.

[12] For example, the President has power as Commander in Chief over the Army and Navy. US Const., Art.II., §2, cl.1. But only Congress can declare war. US Const., Art.I, §8, cl.11. And the two branches may be seen as having concurrent power on various topics. See, e.g., *Youngstown Sheet & Tube Co. v. Sawyer*, 343 US 579, esp. 635-37 (1952) (JACKSON, J., concurring).

[13] *US v. Belmont*, 301 US 324; *US v. Pink* 315 US 203, 62 S. Ct. 552, 86 L. Ed. 796 (1942); and, *Clark v. Allen* 331 US 503, 67 S. Ct. 1431, 91 L. Ed. 1633 (1947). But see, *Dames & Moore v. Regan*, 453 US 654, 675-88 (President's "suspension" of claims pending in US courts held authorized by past Congressional acquiescence in similar situations and because it was a necessary incident to the resolution of a major foreign policy problem).

effect in US courts without further Congressional action, provided that the President's actions comply with the terms of the statutory delegation and the terms of such delegation meet various requirements established by the courts[14]. Although Congressional approval and implementation subsequent to signature of the international agreement is not required in these cases, the President may need to take implementing action, for example, in the form of a Presidential Proclamation or a Federal Regulation. Similarly, Congress may define the objectives of an international trade negotiation, and the process by which the Executive branch should undertake those negotiations and consult with Congress, in exchange for a commitment (technically adoption of rules of the House and the Senate) to consider approval and implementation of the agreement in an expedited process known as "fast-track"[15].

Finally, statutes enacted after an international agreement otherwise would have effect in US courts prevail over inconsistent terms in the international agreement; because a ratified treaty has the same Constitutional status as an act of Congress, that which is later in time controls[16]. Thus, a subsequent statute prevails domestically over an international obligation in a treaty, a Congressional-Executive Agreement, or Presidential proclamation of an executive agreement.

2. Direct Application of GATT 1947 in US Courts

The GATT 1947 had an unusually complicated status under US law. While the GATT 1947 was negotiated to be self-executing[17], Parts I-III of the GATT 1947[18] were applied by means of a non-self-executing Protocol of Provisional Application (PPA)[19]. Moreover, the PPA included a "grandfather clause", which stated that Part II of the GATT (i.e., Arts III through XXIII) shall be applied "to the fullest extent not inconsistent with existing legislation."[20] Nonetheless, subsequent to the signature of the

---

[14] *Star-Kist Foods, Inc. v. US*, 275 F.2d 472 (CCPA 1959).

[15] See e.g., Sections 1101-1106 of the *Omnibus Trade and Competitiveness Act of 1988*, 19 USC 2901 et seq. (1988).

[16] *Chinese Exclusion* Cases, 130 US 581 (1889) (sustaining legislation excluding the entry of Chinese even though such exclusion violated a treaty with China); *Whitney v. Robertson*, 124 US 190, 194 (1888).

[17] John H. JACKSON, **World Trade and the Law of GATT**, Michie Company, Charlottesville, Virginia, 1969, p.106.

[18] Part IV of GATT 1947 was added in the 1960s.

[19] Protocol of Provisional Application, Geneva, Oct. 30, 1947, 55 UNTS 194 [hereinafter PPA].

[20] PPA, para.1(b).

PPA, the GATT 1947 was proclaimed as domestic US law[21], in accordance with a Congressional delegation of power to the President[22], suggesting that the GATT 1947 had the status of a proclaimed Congressional-Executive agreement[23]. Congress never approved the GATT 1947 after it was signed[24]. This gave the GATT 1947 status as domestic US law that could be applied directly by US courts; but the effect of that direct application was quite constrained by US Constitutional doctrine on later-in-time statutes, the PPA's grandfather clause, and ambiguous language in the GATT 1947 on its application to sub-central government entities.

Operationally, this meant that if there were a direct conflict between a US statute and the GATT 1947, the federal statute would always control. The GATT 1947 could not be used by a US court to strike down a prior inconsistent federal statute, because the PPA grandfathered such statutes[25]. Moreover, regardless of its status, obligations in the GATT 1947 — like those in any international agreement — could never be used to strike down an inconsistent federal statute adopted later in time[26]. There was even considerable uncertainty as to whether the GATT 1947 could be used to construe the meaning of ambiguous terms in federal statutes, with some cases suggesting it should[27] and others suggesting it could not[28].

---

[21] Proclamation No.2761A, 12 Fed. Reg.8,863 (Dec. 30, 1947).

[22] Pursuant to authority under the *Reciprocal Trade Agreements Act*, as amended and extended, 59 Stat. 410 (1945).

[23] At least one commentator has argued that the terms of the GATT 1947 did not appear to exceed the authority of the relevant Congressional delegation of authority. John H. JACKSON, *"The General Agreement on Tariffs and Trade in United States Law"*, in: **Michigan Law Review** No.66, 1967, p.249.

[24] Indeed, in connection with extensions of the trade agreements authority, Congress declared on several occasions that its actions were neither expressions of approval nor disapproval of the GATT 1947. See e.g., 72 Stat. 673 (1958); 69 Stat. 162 (1955); 68 Stat. 360 (1954); and 67 Stat. 472 (1953). While Congress did begin appropriating funds in 1974 for the US contribution to the GATT budget, Congress added a provision to section 121 of the *Trade Act of 1974*, stating that authorization of such appropriations "does not imply approval or disapproval by the Congress of all articles of the GATT."

[25] *Footwear Distributors and Retailers v. US*, 852 F. Supp. 1078, 1090 (CIT 1994).

[26] Id. at 1088; *Mississippi Poultry Association, Inc. v. Madigan*, 992 F. 2d 1359, 1365-67 (5th Cir. 1993); and *Suramerica de Aleaciones Laminadas, C.A. v. US*, 996 F. 2d 660, 667-68 (Fed. Cir. 1992).

[27] *Footwear Distributors and Retailers v. US*, 852 F. Supp. 1078, 1090.

[28] *Mississippi Poultry Association, Inc. v. Madigan*, 992 F. 2d 1359, 1365-67.

Nonetheless, the direct effect of the GATT 1947 was meaningful in two respects. First, the tariff bindings embodied in the US Article II Schedule of Concessions to the GATT 1947 had direct effect through a Presidential Proclamation[29] to the extent they represented a reduction of preexisting tariff levels that did not exceed the reductions permitted in Congress's delegation of authority to the President in the 1945 Reciprocal Trade Agreements Act[30].

Second, obligations in the GATT 1947 were used to strike down some inconsistent state government statutes. As indicated above, US Supreme Court decisions hold that when an executive agreement, Congressional-Executive agreement, or a treaty conflict with a state statute, the international agreement prevails[31]. In the GATT 1947 context, the application of this doctrine to state law was presumably constrained by the PPA grandfather clause, which suggests that the GATT 1947 could be applied directly only to strike down state statutes enacted after the date of reference for the phrase "existing legislation"[32]. Moreover, there was considerable uncertainty about the extent to which the GATT 1947 Article XXIV:12 implies that sub-central government entities (e.g., the states in the United States; provinces in Canada; Lander in Germany) were bound to follow the terms of the GATT 1947[33]. These questions notwithstanding, in practice some US courts directly applied the GATT 1947 to strike down state statutes on the ground that they were inconsistent with US obligations under GATT 1947[34].

---

[29] Proclamation No.2761 A, 12 Fed. Reg. 8,863 (Dec. 30, 1947).

[30] See text accompanying notes 21 and 22.

[31] See discussion *supra*.

[32] The proper date of reference is October 30, 1947. *1984 Panel Report on "United States Manufacturing Clause,"* GATT Doc. L/5609, adopted on May 15, 1984, 31S/74, 88, para.35.

[33] GATT 1947 Art.XXIV:12 provides, "Each Contracting Party shall take such reasonable measures as may be available to it to ensure observance of the provisions of this Agreement by the regional and local governments and authorities within its territories." The Uruguay Round agreement on the subject offers little or no help in elaborating the meaning of this provision, which is verbatim identical in the GATT 1994. Understanding on the Interpretation of Article XXIV of the General Agreement on Tariffs and Trade 1994, April 15, 1994, Agreement Establishing the World Trade Organization, Annex 1A, in Final Act.

[34] *Baldwin-Lima-Hamilton Corp. v. Superior Court*, 208 Cal. App. 2d 803, 25 Cal. Rptr. 798 (1962) (part of California Buy American statute struck down as inconsistent with the national treatment requirement of GATT 1947 Art.III); *Hawaii v. Ho*, 41 Haw. 565 (1957) (Hawaii state law requiring special signs to accompany retail sale of foreign-produced eggs struck down as inconsistent with the national treatment requirement of GATT 1947, Art.III:4).

3. Direct Application of the Uruguay Round Agreements, including GATT 1994, in US Courts

In the absence of legal authority to the contrary, several members of Congress were concerned that the GATT 1994 might be applied directly in US courts so as to pose a serious challenge to various state and federal statutes. The international and domestic legal status of the GATT 1994 is clearer and simpler than that of the GATT 1947. The GATT 1994 was negotiated, approved, and implemented as a Congressional-Executive agreement, pursuant to a "fast-track" authority specified originally in the Omnibus Trade and Competitiveness Act of 1988[35]. Unlike the GATT 1947, the GATT 1994 has not been applied provisionally and prior US statutes are not grandfathered as they were in the 1947 PPA. WTO dispute settlement was seen as more likely than dispute settlement under the GATT 1947 system to yield final and legitimate panel decisions[36]. And several WTO Members, including the European Union, signalled their intention to attack the WTO-consistency of many US federal and state statutes[37]. Finally, awareness that direct application of the GATT 1947 had been used to strike down some state statutes heightened concern by many state Governors that the more substantively far-reaching Uruguay Round agreements might be used as a sword against state statutes.

In that context, the President and Congress agreed to include in the Uruguay Round implementing statute language that substantially limits the direct effects of the Uruguay Round agreements in US courts. Specifically, the Uruguay Round Agreements Act provides that US federal

---

[35] *Supra* at note 15.

[36] See Richard H. STEINBERG, *"The Uruguay Round: A Legal Analysis of the Final Act"*, in:, 6(2) **International Quarterly** 1, April 1994; and, Stephen P. CROLEY & John H. JACKSON, *"WTO Dispute Procedures, Standard of Review, and Defference to National Governments"*, in: **American Journal of International Law** No.90, 1996, p.193.

[37] See e.g., *Report on United States Trade and Investment Barriers 1993: Problems of Doing Business With the US* (Services of the Commission of the European Communities, Brussels, April 1993), especially pages 13-21 (attacking, *inter alia*, Section 301 of the *Trade Act of 1974*, as amended; US Export Administration Regulations, promulgated pursuant to the President's authority under the *International Emergency Economic Powers Act*; *The Cuban Democracy Act*; *The Marine Mammal Protection Act of 1972*, as amended). Subsequent annual reports by the European Commission on US barriers to trade and investment contain similar lists. See, e.g., most recently, Unit for Relations with the United States of America, Directorate-General for External Relations: Commercial Policy and Relations with North America, *Report on United States Trade and Investment Barriers 1996* (European Commission, Brussels, May 1996).

law prevails over a Uruguay Round agreement in the event of a conflict[38], but that Uruguay Round Agreements prevail over state and local law in any action brought by the federal government for the purpose of declaring such a law invalid[39]. However, notwithstanding Congressional approval of the Uruguay Round Agreements, the act also provides that: no person other than the United States has a cause of action or defense based on any provision of a Uruguay Round Agreement; no person other than the United States may challenge a federal, state, or local law or action based on its inconsistency with a Uruguay Round Agreement; and a private Party may not rely on the results of an action brought by the United States that was based on a holding of inconsistency with a Uruguay Round Agreement[40]. The statute thereby contemplates two situations in which the Uruguay Round Agreements could have direct application in US courts: (1) in an action against it, the federal government could attempt to rely on an obligation in a Uruguay Round Agreement as a defense; and (2) the federal government may file suit to strike down a state or local law or action on the ground that it is inconsistent with a commitment in a Uruguay Round Agreement.

In practice, federal government court challenges of state and local laws on the ground of WTO-inconsistency probably will be rare. In light of political considerations and concerns in the United States about states' rights and losing sovereignty to international organizations and tribunals, it is difficult to see the federal government initiating such a court action in the absence of a clear and final WTO dispute settlement decision holding that a state or local law is WTO-inconsistent. Even then, the President likely would be circumspect about authorizing legal action against a state or local government to bring its laws into compliance with WTO obligations. Federal policy-makers might be inclined instead to explain to state or local policy-makers the changes needed to bring the law in question into compliance with WTO obligations[41], and to predict that continued noncompliance would likely result in WTO-legal trade sanctions[42] aimed at products originating in that state or locality. The foreign

---

[38] *Uruguay Round Agreements Act*, §102(a)(1), 19 USC §3501 et. seq (1994).

[39] *Id.*, §102(b)(2).

[40] *Id.*, §102(c)

[41] Such consultations are clearly contemplated by the *Uruguay Round Agreements Act*, §102(b)(1).

[42] Trade sanctions under the authority of Article 22 of the Understanding on Rules and Procedures Governing the Settlement of Disputes, April 15, 1994, Agreement Establishing the World Trade Organization, Annex 2, in Final Act, and para.14 of the Understanding on the Interpretation of Article XXIV of the General Agreement on Tariffs and Trade 1994.

government that prevailed in WTO dispute settlement would likely echo that prediction. Thus, a political process would be used to yield compliance with WTO obligations — not the direct application of the Uruguay Round Agreements in US courts.

4. Conclusion: American Wariness of Direct Effects

The GATT 1947 and the Uruguay Round Agreements, including the GATT 1994, have had only limited direct effects in US law. As suggested by the analysis above, this may be explained by US Constitutional doctrines and acts of Congress. But more broadly, it is clear from the debates surrounding approval and implementation of the Uruguay Round Agreements that the contemporary US political climate is hostile to any action that would appear to diminish US sovereignty or control by Congress over the law applied in US courts[43]. This is not a new phenomenon: the United States has had a long tradition of policies that suggest non-involvement in foreign affairs or that resist a loss of formal authority to tribunals or sources outside the United States[44]. This outlook has been attributed to ideology[45] by some, and to sociological factors by others[46]. Some have even attributed it to historical-geopolitical factors[47]. In any event, it is clear that international trade agreements are less likely to have substantial direct effects in US law than in the law of most European countries.

---

[43] See, e.g., statements by Senator Bob Dole on the topic, reported in *"GATT: Sen. Dole Says He Is Still Undecided on Whether to Vote for GATT Trade Bill"*, in: 11(44) **International Trade Report** (BNA) 1715 (Nov. 9, 1994); and, *"Sen. Dole Says He Will Support GATT Bill If President Backs New Proposal on WTO"*, in: 11(45) **Intl. Trade Rep.** (BNA) 1742 (Nov. 16, 1994); and, Patrick J. BUCHANAN, *"A European Assault On Our Nationhood"*, in: **New York Times**, Feb. 27, 1997, at B6.

[44] George Washington's "farewell address" in 1796, warning against "permanent alliances", "inveterate antipathies against particular nations and passionate attachments for others", is one of the most enduring examples of that outlook. See Thomas A. BAILEY, **A Diplomatic History of the American People**, Appleton-Century-Crofts, New York, 1958, pp.90-91. On Congressional resistance to international adjudication, see Thomas FRANCK & Edward WIESBAND, **Foreign Policy by Congress**, Oxford Univ. Press, New York, 1979.

[45] Louis HARTZ, **The Liberal Tradition in America**, Harcourt, New York, Brace, 1955.

[46] Alexis DE TOCQUEVILLE, **Democracy in America**, Alfred Knopf, New York, 1945, especially Vol.I, Chaps IV, VIII, IX, and XIII.

[47] Stephen D. KRASNER, **Defending the National Interest**, Princeton Univ. Press, Princeton, 1978, especially pp.342-44 (arguing that the United States could afford isolationism during the nineteenth century because British naval power limited European incursions into the Western Hemisphere, and the Atlantic and Pacific oceans served as effective shields against foreign aggression or intervention that otherwise might have resulted from a failure to engage internationally, and during this century because of US hegemonic power).

THE MULTILATERAL RULES AND THE NEW DIMENSION OF REGIONAL INTEGRATION: WEAKNESSES, NEED AND SCOPE FOR MORE DISCIPLINES

Serge DEVOS

Consultant on International Trade Policy Issues;
Former Deputy Director, OECD, Paris

The regional integration issue which, for a long time, has centered on the European process and related developments, has acquired a new dimension with the proliferation of Regional Integration Agreements (RIAs). Reasons for the evolution of the regional integration phenomenon and its significance are briefly reviewed in Section I. It is noteworthy that there has been a change of attitude and of policy towards RIAs. They have taken a strategic and political importance following the end of the Cold War. The constant broadening of the field of trade policy and the growing number of significant players, together with the resulting complexity of multilateral negotiations, have also had a determinant role. The original GATT provisions were not meant to address the developments which have taken place in particular in the last ten years. Section II is devoted to the examination of the various relevant provisions. The assessment made (§§ 28-30) is that though GATT provisions were essential in allowing the issue to remain on the international agenda and to be discussed, they were unable to contain the regional integration phenomenon and to discipline RIAs. In Section III, the question is raised of whether there is scope for strengthening the provisions and how this could be achieved. The assessment (§§ 47-48), again negative, is based on technical and political reasons as well as on experience. It is doubtful that the political will exists now that most major partners are involved in

RIAs. The possibility of another approach is examined in Section IV. It rests on the assumption that the regional integration processes will continue and that, while on the whole and up to now RIAs have had a rather favorable impact on the Multilateral Trading System (MTS), it is nevertheless imperative to find ways and means to ensure a clearer and more positive relation between the regional and multilateral approaches to international trade issues. It is suggested that instead of concentrating on RIAs only, the new approach should aim at developing the synergy between the regional and multilateral systems. Two broad proposals (§§ 58-61) are offered which aim, on the one hand, at ensuring a more rapid adaptation of the MTS to the requirements of the market and, on the other hand, at promoting convergence of the regional and multilateral regulatory frameworks. The paper finishes with a brief overall conclusion.

I. THE GATT PROVISIONS AND THE EVOLVING REGIONAL INTEGRATION ISSUE

1. The original GATT already contained provisions for the creation of Customs Unions (CUs) and Free Trade Areas (FTAs), which had their origin in the Havana Charter. Its drafting was marked by some ambiguity about its purpose and reflected different views among the major partners on preferential regimes or arrangements. This was illustrated by a debate on the appropriateness or advisability of permitting FTAs in addition to CUs. Notwithstanding these differences, Article XXIV of GATT was not conceived to address the developments which have taken place since its drafting, and notably the proliferation of Regional Integration Agreements (RIAs). The original text has however survived, nearly unaltered, despite significant changes in the nature and dimension of the issue of regional integration in the multilateral context. The strengthening of the provisions or constrains on the formation and functioning of RIAs has come up against political, conceptual and technical difficulties. The Uruguay Round brought few explanations rather than changes to Article XXIV and similar provisions in the agreement on trade in services (GATS, Article V).

2. Also to be mentioned are the provisions which address the specific situations and needs of developing countries. They consist of Part IV of the GATT, adopted in 1965 and of the Enabling Clause, in 1979. In addition various articles, such as Article XXV on waivers, have either been used to set up preferential agreements or invoked to justify them. In all cases the result or intent was to escape the constraint of Article XXIV.

726

Indeed, some, if not most, of the major problems raised by the regional approach have their origin in the use of these provisions or in flagrant departures from the letter, spirit or fundamental aim of these provisions.

3. The creation of the European Common Market was the first significant case under Article XXIV. By its trade and economic size, the then European Economic Community (EEC) was bound to raise concerns for the effects of the preferential elements. It also exemplified the deficiencies of the GATT provisions on RIAs. In the context of the Cold War, however, the Western Countries, in particular the United States, supported the Common Market for its utmost political importance. The setting-up of a European Free Trade Association (EFTA) and later FTAs between the EEC and other Western European Countries also benefited to a certain extent from this not too hostile attitude of third countries. Two of the Multilateral Trade Negotiations (MTNs) were, however, initiated by the United States, and supported by other outsiders, to reduce the preferential or alternatively the discriminatory effects of the EEC: the Kennedy Round followed its creation and the Tokyo Round its first enlargement.

4. More serious concerns arose from preferential trade agreements concluded by the EEC and third countries, previous colonies of EEC Member States or Mediterranean Countries. The conformity with Article XXIV or other provisions were seen as even more arguable than those found in the Treaty of Rome. Objections bore both on the absence and on the existence of reverse or reciprocal preferences as well as on discrimination against imports of developed or developing countries not included in the trade arrangement in question. Some of the resulting problems are still on the agenda of international disputes, e.g. the import regimes of bananas into the European Market.

The New Dimension of the Regional Integration Issue

5. Following the EEC many regional agreements were concluded between developing countries in South America, Africa, the Middle East and Asia. But because of their objectives — economic development or political security — or because of their negligible impact on world trade, most of these did not attract much international attention. More significant developments, however, have taken place in recent years. They include a dramatic expansion of existing RIAs, particularly of the EU, and a multiplication of new ones, mainly FTAs. Of particular importance are the agreements between Canada and the United States (CUSFTA), the US, Canada and Mexico (NAFTA), Australia and New Zealand

727

(ANZCERTA), between the countries of ASEAN (AFTA), the Agreement between Brazil, Argentina, Uruguay and Paraguay, which became a customs union (Mercosur) and among the countries of the Pacific rim assembled in APEC.

6. There are still other important changes. The first is the **reversal of the US policy** towards the regional approach which has now become part of the US trade strategy at least as a complement to its previously exclusive support of the multilateral approach. The United States has taken initiatives for the achievement of free trade under APEC aiming in particular at the major Asian trading countries, as well as for a Free Trade of the Americas. Economic and political circumstances may slow or even provisionally halt the integration process involving the United States, but it may find its own dynamic, as testified by the various free trade agreements which have been signed or the "bilateral" FTAs which have been set up among Latin American countries. Since the United States has always played a leading role in the continuous strengthening of the MTS, this perceived new policy may indeed have broad consequences for other countries' policies.

7. In reality, RIAs have acquired a political and strategic importance and are playing a major role in the endeavours to secure a stable international order. But at the same time and as a possible consequence, a certain rivalry is emerging among actual or potential regional hegemonies. The EU has been reacting to the US initiatives by approaching Mercosur for a free trade agreement, as well as by establishing closer links with the group of Asian countries. Mercosur itself is starting to make itself the hub and leader of a regional integration process of Latin America, aiming at balancing what is seen as US domination. Asian countries are also pondering the ways to assert their independence as a group. A Transatlantic Free Trade Area (TAFTA) which has been talked of and was even made the subject of studies behind the scenes is also part of a global strategy. In the post Cold War area, trade policy has become a main instrument in international politics and this trend has enhanced the role of RIAs in international trade diplomacy and trade order.

8. Another apparently independent change has been the **broadening of the area of trade policy and of its instruments**. At the beginning of the process of regional integration, in the late 1950s, tariffs and quantitative restrictions were still perceived as the main trade instruments affecting the access to markets. It was through these instruments that preferential treatment was granted and that consequently, discrimination was perceived by outsiders of RIAs. These instruments were transparent and as their effects were relatively easy to measure, they lent themselves to — technically — easy negotiations. However, there has been a permanent and extensive expansion of the field of policies and their respective instruments to be covered in order to achieve true liberalization and "fair" trade. Obviously the need manifested itself first at regional level because notably of the greater reduction, already achieved, of the so-called traditional barriers to trade. The trade barriers of a new kind are often related to domestic policies and consist of national regulations which require another approach than the simple reduction or elimination. The methods can vary from one case to another, and include reconciliation, harmonization or, when national regulations have some basic principles in common, the method of mutual recognition which is used in the European Union (EU). These trade "barriers" may result in more subtle and even more effective discrimination in the access to the regional market in question. In fact, the regional integration phenomenon, which has a variety of causes, is enhanced by the need to deal with a wider range of policies than those that can reasonably and rapidly be addressed in the multilateral context. But it is also true that, with the globalization of markets, similar needs are felt at the multilateral level, so that the difference may be one of timing and scope of the solution. The reactions to the measures taken in the EU to achieve a single market and in particular the now largely bygone fear of a "Fortress Europe" illustrate this issue. The policy responses have been both regional and multilateral initiatives.

9. Globalization is another development that affects the regional integration trend in two opposite directions. On the one hand, the globalization trend seems likely to overtake the trend towards regionalization. On the other hand, increases in competition at the global level may induce firms to enlarge their "home" market as their springboard to competition in the world market.

II. SCOPE AND CONSTRAINING EFFECTS OF MTS RULES ON RIAS

10. Article XXIV deals with the formation of RIAs. It constitutes a major exception to the basic principle of the MTS which is the Most-Favoured-Nation (MFN) principle embodied in Article I. Article XXIV can be seen as the realistic recognition that RIAs cannot totally be banned but that permissible exceptions to the MFN principle have to be controlled and limited. The provisions as they appear in the article are nevertheless the result of a long debate and represent a weakening of the constraints put on the formation of RIAs as compared with an original US proposal. In the preamble of the GATT article, for instance, it is noted that RIAs can contribute to the desirable increase in liberalized trade. Also, and as already mentioned, FTAs were added to CUs as an acceptable form of RIA. Similarly, the possibility of interim agreements leading to CUs or FTAs has been included. Still other softening was introduced in the course of the drafting both of the Havana Charter and subsequently Article XXIV.

11. The exception to the MFN principle is tempered by the statement that the aim of RIAs should be to facilitate trade between Parties and not to raise barriers towards other countries. Expressed differently it also means that the aim is not to create preferences and that discrimination can only be an unavoidable consequence of the process of regional integration. This statement, however, does not provide an objective criterion and is not as such a real constraint to the formation of an RIA. The more operative provisions are examined hereafter.

Elimination of Restrictions to Mutual Trade

12. It is stipulated that an RIA should eliminate duties and other restrictions on "substantially all trade" among its members. This provision is a deterrent against mere preferential agreements and could even be an impediment to the multiplication of RIAs. But it is weakened to the extent that the requirement is limited to "substantially" all trade, which introduces a very subjective criteria. One major loophole is the possibility to exclude specific products or sectors for which free trade would not be acceptable to all the members of the RIA. That is what has happened for the agricultural sector in general in several instances but also for selected products of the industrial sector. Discussions in the GATT have indeed centered on this issue of whether "substantially all trade" was meant in quantitative or qualitative terms. The differences of interpretation in this regard have been one of the main causes of the absence of agreed conclusions on the conformity of regional agreements with GATT prescriptions.

13. Despite the endeavours made in the Uruguay Round (UR) on the basis of various proposals by participants, no improvement has been achieved on this point. Only in the Preamble of the UR Understanding is it recognized that the contribution of an RIA to the growth of world trade is increased if all the trade among the constituents is liberalized and is reduced if any major sector is excluded. But the UR has failed to come up with a stronger commitment.

14. Another issue under the same provision concerns the measures to be eliminated which are defined in broad terms as **duties and other restrictive measures**. Problems have arisen because of the lack of a precise definition of the measures covered. The only precision is that the provision does not affect those restrictions permitted under expressly mentioned GATT articles, such as measures taken for balance of payments, public morals, health, etc. It has given rise to the question of whether this list was exhaustive and meant that members of RIAs would lose their right under other GATT articles to apply restriction such as safeguards or anti-dumping duties on imports from their partners in the agreement. While reducing the constraint, the exclusion of certain types of measures, including contingency measures, it also reduces the scope of discrimination against countries outside the RIA. In practice, most RIAs allow the application of contingency measures on intra-trade even though sometimes countries enter a RIA with the hope of being exempted from such contingency measures. The reverse question, of whether members of RIAs can discriminate against outside countries in the application of contingency measures, seems more important and has in fact been seen so by third countries. In the EU, where a high level of integration is achieved, such internal restrictive measures are generally no longer permitted.

The "On the Whole not Higher nor no more Restrictive" Provision

15. Another major requirement for the formation and acceptability of an RIA concerns the duties and other trade regulations applied to nonmember countries. In the case of an FTA, they cannot be increased at the occasion of its formation; in other words the protection existing between each of the members and the ensuing preference from which they will benefit cannot be increased. For CUs, the common external duties and the other common regulations applicable to outsiders and instituted at the time of the formation of the union must not "on the whole be higher or more restrictive than the general incidence" of those duties and common regulations in the constituent countries of the union prior to its formation. This requirement raises the problem of the **methods of calculation** of the common external tariff (i.e. simple or weighted averages, lowest tariff) as well as that of the choice of duties used in the calculation (i.e. bound, unbounded or actually applied). Paragraph 5 of Article XXIV was silent on this. Depending on the choices, the effects on third countries may be significantly different. For instance the case arose for the EEC common external tariff, for which the Community had used the arithmetical average of applied duties.

16. The debate on this requirement focused on the concept of **"on the whole"** and of **"general incidence"**, which could mean according to the various views, either that it applies to third countries as a group and to total trade with the possible raising of barriers in certain sectors or for certain products compensated by a decrease in others; or, on the opposite side, that consideration had to be given to the effects on countries taken individually and on a sector by sector basis. It should be recalled that the words "general incidence" were introduced to replace the expression "average level", used in the original version, so as to allow greater flexibility.

17. The issues remained unresolved until the Uruguay Round where, concerning the method of calculation, it was agreed to use the weighted average tariff rates and the applied rates of duties. The other issue has not been solved but it seems that the computation made by the WTO Secretariat will result in the data being available on a country and sector basis.

18. A special problem arises when in the course of establishing the common external tariff, in the case of a CU, **bound duties** of any of the constituents are raised. Paragraph 6 of Article XXIV addresses this case and establishes that the normal GATT procedures which provide for the possibility of compensation, shall apply. The discussion has centered on three uncertainties in the provision: the timing of the negotiations, the nature of the compensation, and the items to be taken into account. On this latter point, the rule remains that due account must be taken of reduction of duties made for items on the same tariff line by other constituents. The UR Understanding opens the possibility for compensation on other items then those for which the negotiation is taking place, but only if it is so agreed by the third countries concerned. Moreover, it makes it clear that negotiations for compensation must start before the common external tariff is implemented.

Interim Arrangements and their Duration

19. Interim agreements entail the risk of leading to lasting selected preferences and discrimination. Two requirements aim at avoiding this occurrence: first, that the interim arrangements must include a plan and schedule for the formation of a CU or FTA; and second, that this formation should be achieved within a **"reasonable length of time"**. There

have been various proposals to fix a maximum duration but there has also been the view that some flexibility was necessary, in particular to take account of special situations and needs, such as those of developing countries. Finally, however, the UR Understanding fixed at ten years, as a general rule, the maximum duration of interim agreements, but left the door open for longer periods if fully justified.

Procedural Provisions

20. Most other provisions are of a procedural nature, but they are no less important. Procedures which guarantee transparency and examination of RIAs are an essential complement of the prescriptive provisions, the more so when those rules are vague and leave room for different interpretation. Article XXIV does not differ from other articles in requiring — **prompt** — **notification** of RIAs. The more advanced the notification, the greater the chances for other countries to comment and to try to alter the provisions of the RIA that affect their interests or, in their view, affect the functioning of the multilateral system. It had been implicitly agreed that notifications should be made immediately after the signature of the agreement. This practice has in fact deteriorated. Notifications have tended to be made after ratification or entry into force, making it nearly impossible for third countries to influence the regional integration agreement in question. It should, however, be acknowledged that it is difficult for countries to make notification when they are still in the process of negotiation or before the definite ratification. The problem is not specific to RIAs but is a general one. It may, however, be more acute in the case of RIAs. Negotiations for the conclusion of a regional agreement have to reconcile different interests and include delicate compromises. Participants do not wish to put them in danger by discussions in a wider body where the positions of a minority number of members of the RIA might well find support from similar positions of third countries.

21. Linked to notifications is the procedure which consists of an **examination**, by Contracting Parties as a group, of the notified measure or in this case, the regional agreement. Article XXIV of the GATT, however, did not impose such an examination which had to be decided on an individual basis. While it has been the normal practice, the systematic examination of all RIAs by a Working Party, has been made the rule by the understanding. Those Working Parties have to submit their reports to the Council of Trade in Goods. In view of the late notifications, the examination of agreements has tended to be made after their entry into force or their implementation. Moreover, as is well known, very few examinations have succeeded in concluding on the conformity of the RIA in question with the GATT provisions. In fact in only six instances of nearly a hundred cases has such a conclusion been reached. The problems raised by the lack of precision of the prescriptions of Article XXIV is one, but only one, of the reasons for that situation.

22. It is also normal GATT practice to follow up on first examination and to organize **regular review** of developments. The difficulty in agreeing upon the conformity of an agreement with GATT provisions makes this follow-up by Working Parties particularly important. The GATT Council was requested to fix a timetable for a review of RIAs every other year. But this decision has tended to become inoperative because, on the one hand, the need or obligation for such regular review has been contested by those RIAs which were fully implemented and in operation. The UR Understanding does not provide for regular reviews by Working Parties but RIAs are nevertheless requested to **report periodically to the Council on their operation**. Moreover, all important changes should be notified as they occur. This ensures a certain degree of transparency and gives the partners an opportunity to comment and to decide if any future action is necessary. The existence of such reporting may in itself induce the RIA to give greater attention to nonmembers' interests, and examination in the WTO Council may give the latter a greater chance of having their views taken into account. With regard to interim agreements, the understanding provides that, where no plan and schedule are included, the Working Party can make recommendations, the implementation of which shall be kept under review.

23. The UR Understanding makes it explicit that the **Dispute Settlement Procedure** (DSP), which is the enforcement mechanism, can also be invoked against preferences or discrimination resulting from an RIA if they are deemed not to be in conformity with Article XXIV. In view of the difficulty encountered in agreeing on the conformity of a regional agreement as a whole, the procedure might be an interesting substitute in cases where preferences or discriminations resulting from an RIA are harmful or debatable. However, there have been very few, in fact only three, requests for a DSP on such grounds. It remains to be seen whether the explicit understanding to that effect will encourage a greater recourse involving RIAs, to that procedure.

Applicability of other GATT Provisions to RIAs

24. In principle, all GATT provisions remain applicable to "external" trade policies of CUs and of countries which are members of FTAs. That is the case for instance with the provisions on anti-dumping. Here also the Consultation and Dispute Settlement Procedures are applicable to RIAs. The UR has resulted in a serious strengthening of the DSP and should result in greater efficacy, in particular since it is now impossible for a Party to the DSP to block the approval of the related report in the DS Body. Previously, a consensus was needed to adopt the report, since the UR the consensus is required for the report not to be adopted. It remains, however, that the effectiveness of the procedure depends on the existence or the strength of the GATT rule. But this is true not only for RIAs but also for any individual country. The difference is that the creation of an RIA leads to changes in a number of policies and measures affecting the trade within the RIA, as well as with outsiders. The divergence between the rule applying among members of the RIA and the rule applicable to outsiders will normally work in favour of trade among members. For instance, no allowance may exist within RIAs for anti-dumping measures or the conditions for their application may be harder than those which are applied to outsiders in conformity with GATT rules. The whole issue of regional integration is precisely whether the existence of different regional regulatory frameworks is to be strongly limited, avoided as much as possible, or whether it is tolerable or, alternatively, at the other extreme, whether it can even be profitable in the long run for the world community as a whole.

Specific Provisions Applicable to Developing Countries

25. Both Part IV of the GATT and the Enabling Clause are concerned with the special interests of developing countries and, in particular, the promotion of their trade and development. Neither are directly linked to Article XXIV or to regional integration in general, though they are evidently related. Part IV concerns measures taken by developed countries in favour of developing countries and, in particular, trade preferences. There have been, and still are, a number of bilateral agreements providing for trade preferences in favour of the developing Party. The debated question is whether these agreements could be considered under Article XXIV with, however, less stringent conditions as justified under Part IV. In practice all these agreements have lead to the request for a waiver under Article XXV. The **Enabling Clause** includes provisions for preferential trade agreements between developing countries, but it has been debated whether the clause was also meant to cover integration agreements between developing countries or whether they would be subject to Article XXIV. In reality, these agreements have mainly been blamed for the weakening of the GATT system and for infringements upon the MFN principle, whatever their justification or motivations. In particular when one developed country or one RIA is the centre of several such agreements with individual countries forming what has been called hub-and-spoke integration agreements. RIAs among developing countries also raise special problems because in most cases it is doubtful that the criteria of Article XXIV could be met both in regard to the scope of the agreements and to the length of time that can be expected for the achievement of free trade.

26. Indeed, the problem raised by RIAs among developing countries is that they are likely to include too many exceptions and to spread over too long a transition period. The definite move of developing countries towards more open economies based on market forces and export-lead growth represents a major change which may indeed alleviate the problem posed by the regional agreements among them. From one point of view such agreements may even have a positive impact if they accelerate the rhythm of the opening of markets in developing countries and increase further their support for a more open MTS. Moreover, the concept of preferences or of more favourable treatment for developing countries has lost most of its attraction even for the developing countries themselves. Though the UR did not modify the existing GATT provisions, they might, in practice, become progressively less relevant.

RIAs in the General Agreement on Trade in Services (GATS)

27. Article V of the GATS contains provisions which are close to those of Article XXIV of the GATT. Differences are generally due to the specificity of the services sector and the preexisting situation with many bilateral agreements. In particular the "not more restrictive" condition is more constraining since it applies to any country outside the RIA; sector or sub-sector wise. Moreover, foreign service-suppliers which already had substantive business operations in one of the member countries of the RIA are entitled to the treatment granted under the regional agreement. This provision does not apply to RIA among developing countries alone, which means that more favourable treatment may be granted to national suppliers in the RIA or, in other words, that discrimination can be applied against "established" foreign suppliers. On the procedural side, examination of the conformity of an RIA with GATS has to be decided in each specific case. So is it also for the periodic review of interim agreements.

736

Assessment

28. The GATT provisions on RIAs have not been able to formally exercise a real control over RIAs or to discipline them in their elaboration or functioning. If the question is whether RIAs have conformed to the rules and conditions set forth in Article XXIV, the response would have to be negative, though, as often the case with legal instruments, especially international ones, everything depends on the interpretation of those provisions. And not surprisingly, there have been wide differences of opinions between the Parties to the RIAs and those Parties remaining outside. The result has been that, of the hundred agreements or so examined by the GATT bodies, only six have been recognized as conforming to the relevant provisions. In all other cases, there was no unanimous conclusion in one direction or the other. The GATT practice of decisions by consensus only partly explains the situation. *Prima facie*, the latter results mainly from the vagueness of the provisions and, as a result, the room left for their interpretation. There is no strict criterion which would allow an "objective" judgement of the conformity. The UR has brought little improvement in this respect. It is true that it has established the method to assess the average duties and charges in the case of the formation of a CU. Also, while not a fixed rule, a period of ten years has been indicated as the "reasonable length of time" for an interim agreement. On the other hand, it has not succeeded in defining "substantially all trade" and the question of the quantitative or qualitative criteria to be used. In general, a similar situation is expected in the case of services and the role of Article V of GATS.

29. This is not to say that the GATT provisions have not had a useful role. They are definitely better than a complete vacuum. At least they have ensured a degree of transparency, even though it is far from perfect. They have allowed an examination and a discussion of specific measures, rules and regulations of regional integration agreements and of their effects on third Parties. The latter, through these examinations or consultations, may in certain instances have influenced the evolution of RIAs and their decisions. It has become clear for example that discussion in the UR on "the substantially all trade" criteria, while inconclusive, will have an impact, at least in some cases, when new RIAs are envisaged. There remains, however, a grey area which includes those policies or measures which are not specifically trade rules and for which the obligations or understanding may be arguable.

30. The GATT provisions have had no limiting effect on the expansion of RIAs. It can be argued that this was not the purpose of GATT, as long as RIAs conform to the relevant GATT provisions. This, however, is unfortunately not very helpful. In reality, and to date, the issue raised by RIAs — whether RIAs should be encouraged, tolerated or restrained — has not been discussed in political terms at the government or official level. Reality has gone faster than theory. In any case, it can probably be expected that a clear answer cannot be given to this question since more and more countries are members of a RIA of one sort or another. For the same reason, whether desirable or not, it may prove difficult to strengthen the multilateral provisions of RIAs. Some options are discussed in the next section.

III. SCOPE FOR STRENGTHENING OF THE MTS PROVISIONS ON RIAS

31. A number of proposals to strengthen the provisions have been made either during the UR or by experts. The options depend on the purpose of the strengthening of the rules and of the conditions for setting up RIAs as well as for their operation. For instance, is the purpose to reduce the effects on third countries and therefore the preferential elements or the size of the preferences? Is it to limit the number of RIAs that could be created if the strengthened provisions are complied with? Whatever the objective, to a large extent the result would be to make it more difficult to set up RIAs, if the WTO is made capable of ensuring enforcement of the stronger rules. These question-marks and reservations are left aside at this point although they are crucial. As noted earlier, nothing has stopped the proliferation of RIAs though their compatibility with the GATT provisions has almost never been agreed upon.

32. When examining the scope for a strengthening of the GATT provisions, both rules and procedures have to be considered. They are interrelated because if the rules are strong and can be enforced, follow-up procedures have a lesser role to play. But if the rules are too constraining and go against a strong political or natural trend, the rules will be disregarded. A better approach may then be to combine softer rules with stricter procedures to endeavour to achieve the same results while at the same time making it possible to take account of differences in circumstances that cannot be covered by the rules.

Strengthening the Rules

33. Most proposals have focused on the provisions as they now stand, i.e. in Article XXIV and in the UR Understanding. They concern, in particular, the scope of the RIAs or the **"substantially all trade"** concept. When not all trade is covered by the free trade agreement it is because specific sectors are excluded for protectionist motives, alternatively in this case the degree of liberalization may be lower. The solution here would lay in a combination of quantitative and qualitative criteria. This is needed because the exclusion of a very highly protected sector has no impact on the quantitative measurement of the share of trade. In fact, major countries seem to have accepted, in practice, the use of the two criteria. The "impossibility" of including agriculture has been mentioned as one of the reasons for not pursuing the idea of a Transatlantic Free Trade Area (TAFTA). Only special interim arrangements might be considered as acceptable under this approach.

34. Other proposals relate to the **"not on the whole, higher or more restrictive"** condition required for external trade barriers. This criteria raises several problems. It is based on the concept of balancing or compensating mechanisms, i.e. increases in certain cases are compensated by decreases in other cases. Individual countries have to negotiate compensation which may or may not bear on the sectors that are affected by the setting up of the RIA. In practice, outside countries are more concerned by the actual or potential effects on specific products than on the overall effect of newly adopted agreements. The definition of the method of calculation of the duties and other charges which has been agreed upon in the UR does not help much in meeting those third Parties' concerns, since the assessment is still based on averages. One simple way to overcome this problem would be to prescribe that the common external barriers should be aligned on the lowest among the barriers in place in members of the RIA prior to its formation. It is evident that such a provision would discourage the potential members with the highest protection to enter into a free trade agreement since they would be exposed to greater competition not only from inside the RIA but from the world.

35. Proposals have been made which aim at an *ex post* **assessment** on the basis of actual trade flows. These proposals are interesting because they correspond to reality, in practice outside countries will look at the effects of the RIA on their trade. However, it is doubtful that this criteria could be applicable, because observed changes in trade flows can be attributed to several arguable causes and not necessarily to the RIA. Nevertheless, the criteria may be of greater interest at the sector or product level for which the causes of changes in trade flows may be more easily identified. No doubt Parties to an RIA would be reluctant to accept it in view of the risks of disputes. More fundamentally, in economic policy terms, the sector approach, just as the bilateral approach, does not make much sense. It is different of course in political terms as to which governments are more sensitive.

36. The importance of duties and other charges cannot be totally neglected, in particular in the case of "developing" countries. However, in general their role has been significantly reduced in industrialized countries. Regulations — external or domestic — play a much greater role. Their comparative incidence cannot be measured *ex ante*. Whatever the difficulties, some evaluation could only be made *ex post* and trade flows could perhaps serve as a first indication of changes in access to the RIA market. Moreover, it is rare that during the initial stage RIAs include common regulations which could affect market-access.

37. On the **length of time** allowed to complete the RIA, not much could be added to the understanding that it should reasonably be limited to ten years: first, that time scale has generally been accepted for the implementation of negotiated tariff reduction; second, experience has shown that developing countries will continue to request somewhat longer periods.

38. One specific question is whether the agreements concluded among developing countries should continue to be considered as falling under the **Enabling Clause** or whether they should instead be examined under Article XXIV. It is no longer true or it will become less and less true that RIAs between developing countries are of little trade and political significance. It would therefore seem reasonable to bring them under the framework and provisions of Article XXIV, possibly with some greater flexibility in its application.

39. Some more drastic ideas have been advanced. For instance, it has been suggested that **only CUs should be authorized** and not FTAs. It can be argued that CUs are likely to evolve towards a fuller economic union and anyhow are bound, under present circumstances, to go well beyond elimination of internal duties and the establishment of a common external tariff. The trend towards harmonization of the legal framework leads to a broader and more unified market which also benefits third Parties. Also more constraining because of the common external trade policy and the greater intrusion in domestic policies, the creation of a CU supposes the existence of a strong political will and motivation. It has also been argued that it would be easier to obtain a reduction of overall protection from the creation of a CU rather than from a FTA. Authorising CUs only would very likely contain the creation of RIAs. FTAs are less intrusive and less constraining for the external and domestic policies of its members. Countries may, therefore, be more willing to conclude a FTA than to join a CU. Moreover, there are also greater possibilities of negotiating special tailor-made provisions for different products. FTAs are sometimes perceived as more of an infringement upon the MFN principle or more preferential in essence, while CUs or Economic Union look more like a sovereign state, with more or less decentralization of the regulatory process. This is probably the reason why FTAs were not originally included in the US proposal. FTAs were added in the Havana Charter which led to Article XXIV. An important point made about FTAs is that the differences in external tariffs and regulations require the adoption of rules of origin which often lead to dispute over their protectionist intention or effect.

40. The validity of these arguments is itself debatable. In listing the "pros and cons" account must be taken of the role that is seen for RIAs in the context of the MTS. In particular if RIAs are looked at as a stage on the road towards free trade at the multilateral level and if RIAs accelerate the process of liberalizing trade at that level, then FTAs may be considered a suitable, if not a better form of regional agreement. In fact FTAs are close to GATT in terms of basic philosophy and in methods of liberalizing trade. In certain aspects, the differences with CUs tend to be blurred. There is, for instance, a tendency for FTAs as well as GATT, to have coverage similar to that of CUs. Whatever the opinion on this comparison, it is certainly out of the question that FTAs would from now on be forbidden.

41. Other suggestions have been made. For instance, that the formation of an RIA should be accompanied by a lowering of the overall incidence of duties, or that the common external tariff should be made up, for each tariff line, of the lowest tariff applied by a member of the CU. In the case of an FTA, members could also be requested to reduce their external tariff by a certain percentage. Whatever the views on the possibility of adopting such a suggestion, it is to be noted that, in practice, the successive multilateral rounds of negotiation have achieved, be it with certain delays, the same results.

42. Another suggestion aims at opening the membership of RIAs to any country willing and capable of fulfilling the conditions and applying the rules of the RIA. While a provision of quasi-automatic accession to an RIA may contribute to the progressive passage from regional free trade to multilateral free trade, it is doubtful that it could be accepted as such. Entry of a new member into an FTA would, in any case, require negotiations when, as is often the case, the FTA does not provide for full liberalization across the board but also contains commitments which vary according to sector and country. In CU, there can be no negotiations: the candidate has to accept the common tariff and the common rules. Negotiations are limited to transitional or to certain financial measures. Membership in a CU is more constraining on external and domestic policies. A CU normally supposes greater similarities among its members. Moreover, there may be "constitutional" provisions limiting the membership to countries of the region for instance.

Strengthening the Procedures

43. As indicated above, there is still room after the UR to improve the provisions or practices that ensure transparency and the full and timely availability of information so that third Parties can assess their interests and take steps to defend them if they are at risk. Simple as it may seem, however, this raises practical and political problems. The basic question, which is traditionally on the agenda of GATT in other areas, is whether notification and examination should and could take place *ex ante* so that third Parties could still influence the final agreement through peer pressure. In theory this would be possible though the final say would remain with the national bodies in charge of ratification. The obstacle is rather that the negotiation of an RIA is a lengthy and difficult process. Members of the RIA would generally not jeopardize the compromises achieved by letting other countries discuss the agreement before it is finalized. This argument should, however, not be exaggerated: question and answer procedures have been successfully utilised, outside of the GATT forum, in advance of final adoption and outside a legal framework, notably in the OECD.

44. Nevertheless, it seems reasonable to put the emphasis on procedures of monitoring and surveillance. Except for the first examination, when an RIA is notified, or during interim agreements, no monitoring or surveillance procedure has been established even in the UR. Notification of changes are still required but there is no indication as to what should be notified in particular when the changes, including new measures, are in areas which are not at the time covered by GATT. Questions relating to the operation of the RIA are left to the DSP. It is true that the UR Understanding provides for consultation on a voluntary basis but again only for matters covered by GATT.

45. The Trade Policy Review Mechanism (TPRM) which is now in operation applies to sovereign states, including the European Union since it is a matter of common external policy. These reviews could be extended to other RIAs with a common external policy. It is less evident for FTAs but it is suggested that a formula should be devised that would also allow FTAs to be examined under the same procedure. Admittedly this would increase the burden on the WTO Secretariat and on the members of the RIA, but the review could be made for at least some of the important RIAs.

46. Many other formulae can be elaborated, as regards the improvement and installation of a monitoring procedure for RIAs. In order to make such monitoring beneficial, it should follow a pre-established pattern so that a general approach to RIAs could progressively emerge from the exercise. As a complement, and to address more specific issues or interests, members of RIAs should commit themselves to consultations on any issue in the WTO raised by other members, whether the subject matter falls within WTO competence or not. The setting up, in 1996, of a Committee on Regional Trading Agreements opens the way for an improved examination of these agreements, and of their implications for the MTS.

Assessment

47. In light of the experience it does not seem realistic to expect new improvements to the rules and provisions applicable to RIAs. There have been and no doubt will be technical difficulties in trying to elaborate more precise rules which at the same time take account of the complexities of the issue, the differences of circumstances and the differences in types of RIAs. It also has to be recognized that some of the theoretically possible ways to stiffen the provisions are two-sided. The larger the product coverage for instance, the greater scope for discrimination against outsiders and for trade effects. The same is true with the duration of the interim period: effects can only be greater or more serious if the RIAs are fully implemented in a short period.

48. However, the difficulties or the obstacles to a real improvement are more of a political nature. Members of RIAs are not willing to accept new multilateral constraints and nearly all major players are now members of one RIA or another. The drafting of comparable provisions in GATS may illustrate the present general attitude towards regional integration. It remains to be seen whether the proliferation of RIAs, which means that many countries have interests both as members of RIA as well as outsiders to other RIAs, may alter the reluctance towards stricter regulations. In fact such a development seems to be taking place. Regional Trading Agreements as such are again more frequently being criticized. The European Union itself is now concerned by the expansion of the phenomenon. These changes are leading to more substantive and significant work on Regional Trading Agreements in the WTO.

IV. ANOTHER APPROACH TO THE ISSUE OF RIAS IN THE CONTEXT OF AN MTS

49. Both GATT and GATS recognize the role that RIAs can play in the progress toward freedom of trade, but for several decades this has been more a statement of principle than the expression of a real conviction. Endeavours to strengthen GATT rules would indicate at best a lukewarm attitude toward RIAs, in particular from experts. Policy makers in countries not involved have had, in general and for a long time, a negative or a "yes, but" position. In recent years, the situation has changed. It has been stressed that the new US policy/strategy towards RIAs has modified the issue of the relation between RIAs and the MTS. For the US this amounts to putting the regional approach on par with the multilateral approach to trade liberalization. There are political motivations behind the US move, in addition to economic and trade objectives. The approach to RIAs is part of the search for a new world order after the end of the Cold War. The extension of the EU notably to Central European countries is part of this reorganization. The same is true for the Asia Pacific Economic Cooperation (APEC), the initiatives for a Free Trade Area of the Americas (FTAA), Mercosur as a new hub of free trade agreements, and many other developments. The tendency towards networks of regional agreements reflects the political, as much as the trade, stakes. In reality, political reasons, in a broad interpretation, are at the origin of almost all RIAs.

50. The debate about RIAs has focused, for more than two decades, on the European Common Market. Beyond the general issue, the focus has been on the Common Agricultural Policy (CAP) and on issues of access experienced for certain products, or raised by some kind of measures. While some problems were due to regional integration, others were not different from those arising from policies of individual states. It is, however, generally agreed that the EC (now the EU), has not stood in the way of further liberalization at the multilateral level. Even if sometimes initially hesitant or reluctant, the EU has responded positively to the launching of new rounds of multilateral negotiations aimed at further opening access to markets. And it can be seen that, as European integration progresses, and as a reaction to other developments on the international trade front, the EU demonstrates growing support for the MTS.

More generally, it has been found that RIAs help the MTS in different ways: for instance, they help the actors and the economies involved to accept and to face broader trade liberalization; they provide a learning experience and a laboratory for multilateral agreements; and they increase the awareness of interdependence, as well as of the need for regulations and for a system to enforce them.

51. There is, nevertheless, too rapid a tendency to extrapolate. No one would go as far as saying that RIAs are an alternative to the MTS, but one tends to consider the present trend towards more and more RIAs is favourable to the multilateral system in the long run. It is, however, not at all sure that the proliferation of RIAs will not damage the MTS. The risk is one of prolonged periods during which international trade would take place under very different regimes and regulatory frameworks with the implication of increased preferential or discriminatory conditions of access to the markets of the various RIAs. There is no reason to believe that multilateral liberalization of trade is no longer a valid objective. A multilateral system of rules and procedures is needed even more so when trade partners include important groupings of countries. To ensure a symbiosis between the regional and multilateral approach and the maintenance of a strong and ever improving MTS requires political will and initiative.

52. The issue is complex. In reality there are two forces at play: one working in the direction of regionalization and the other towards globalization. Both forces have their roots in the market and the behaviour of the market players. They both have effects on the regional and multilateral regulatory frameworks. Trade liberalization has become a much more complex task, since the main obstacles to trade or competition are nowadays due to domestic — and regional — regulations. The solution in those cases can often not consist of abolishing regulations but in some kind of approximation. This is more easily done among countries with a minimum of similarities in the need for regulation in various fields, in their economic and social objectives and possibly in the methods to achieve them. Such conditions are rarely found at the global or world level. Negotiations, if accepted at all, are therefore more difficult and lengthy; they are also susceptible to leading to the "second best" solution.

53. The concern that the multilateral approach may slow down progress among countries capable of going faster has for long been in the minds of the actors involved. The argument was one of those used in favour of the EC. It also inspired the "GATT Plus" suggestion and other similar proposals. It is even applied *de facto* in GATT for certain agreements.

The main question is that of the extent of discrimination allowed or the use of conditional MFN.

54. New ideas have emerged which found their origin in the EU. The **subsidiarity principle** is one example. Using a simple definition of this concept, it means that regulation should be kept at the lowest institutional level where it can be or managed at the lowest cost, while ensuring the full achievement of the relevant objectives. This principle can be applied in a sovereign state between the central and local authorities. The question to be considered here is that of the distribution of tasks between the RIAs and the MTS. The level, regional or multilateral, at which regulations should be elaborated can not be easily decided in the abstract. It requires a cost/benefit analysis to be made in each case. When decided, a decentralization of the regulatory process should probably be done on the basis of some agreed multilateral principles.

55. The trend towards regionalization goes hand-in-hand with the move towards globalization of the economy. The spread of global sourcing; the strategy of firms which goes well beyond the national or regional boundaries but which still rely on a strong "home" — national or regional — market; the customization of production as well as competition, which is now more between companies than countries, are factors which call for more global regulations. Economic actors are eager to pursue their international activities under similar regulations and they may press for home regulations which do not to put them at a disadvantage compared to their competitors in other countries or regional groupings. This should act as a strong support for the MTS and the continued extension to that level of the "liberalization" actions undertaken at the regional level. The continuous broadening of multilateral coverage, including the addition of the Agreement for Services and Intellectual Property, over the last three rounds of multilateral negotiations testifies to the synergy between regional and multilateral approaches.

56. Everything considered, the conclusion which may emerge is that instead of focusing attention only on disciplines concerning RIAs as such, another complementary approach should be used. The objective would be to ensure the greatest possible and lasting symbiosis between RIAs and the MTS. In practical terms, the purpose would be: on one hand, to avoid GATT, or more generally speaking the MTS, being left too far behind; and, on the other hand, to ensure that the multilateral regulatory framework evolves in line with developments in the regulatory frameworks of RIAs, in particular the major and more advanced ones. This in turn might help interim agreements or less elaborated RIAs, i.e. among developing countries, to move forward more easily.

57. One can take it for granted that the commitment to the MTS still stands and has even become stronger. The already extensive use made of the DSP in the WTO is perhaps one of the best testimonies of the political will to give strength and power to this new institution. The proliferation of RIAs or of regional integration initiatives may be one of the reasons. The simultaneous globalization process is another reason since firms prefer to operate with a maximum of certainty and under similar regulations.

Ensuring a more Rapid Adaptation of the MTS

58. It remains that there is a need to increase the capacity of the MTS to adapt to the changes in the world economy and to respond to the demands of the players in the market. The formula of global rounds of negotiations taking place every decade and lasting nearly as long, which has been the case up to now, does not allow for the rapid adaptation of the multilateral regulatory framework. The optimum solution would be to engage in selective negotiations on subjects for which the need is greatest or these which are ripe for an international agreement. It has been argued that the global approach is needed to allow for trade-offs among the various national interests. The results of the WTO meeting in Singapore, in December 1996, does not allow to conclude that this problem has now been surmounted, although progress were made in selected fields such as duties reduction on high tech products.

59. This leads to a second manner in which to address the issue of faster adaptation of the MTS. That is to allow for the conclusion of agreements on specific issues among those members of the WTO which have a direct interest and are prepared to take on new commitments where no rules presently exist, or to adopt stricter rules than those that presently exist. Practically, it has already been done in the past in various ways, either because certain members are exempted from immediate implementation of the agreement rules or because not every country participates in the agreement. Ideally, the first of the two formulae is preferable for the sake of the MTS. A greater effectiveness and dynamism of the MTS would probably slow down or halt the creation of RIAs which are motivated by the slowness or weakness of the system or because it is ill-adapted.

Promoting Convergence of Regulatory Frameworks

60. The following proposal is complementary to the previous one since its implementation would help to adapt the MTS faster while at the same time establishing a link between regional and multilateral integration processes. If various RIAs adopt regulations, on similar subjects, which are too far apart, the adoption of a multilateral rule on the same subjects will prove more difficult. RIAs may best contribute to a strong MTS and the achievement of its objectives if the regulations which they elaborate fit well into a multilateral pattern and correspond to similar objectives and some basic principles. To that end, ideally, RIAs should inform the WTO of their intention to develop or, as a second best, to introduce new rules or provisions. Such transparency would open the door to a common examination by trade partners of the kind of rules or provisions most appropriate not only for the RIA considered but also for other Parties and the MTS. It would also offer the possibility of agreement on trying to elaborate a multilateral rule which, at first, might be implemented in a RIA only. The multilateral effort might aim at simply establishing the basic and broad principles on which regulations on the specific subject should be modelled. Such an approach would lead to a certain degree of approximation of the rules adopted by various RIAs and leave the door open to further elaboration of a more precise multilateral rule.

61. That approach should evidently not be allowed to stop the regulatory process at the regional level. It may be felt that such a proposal does not have much of a chance of being accepted by policy makers. The regulatory process is difficult enough not to be further complicated by a parallel exercise at the multilateral level. But experience, e.g. with government procurement, has shown that the approach can be used in a mutually beneficial way. Moreover, in several instances, exploratory work on new issues, or rather on issues not yet subjected to multilateral trade related rules, has been undertaken in particular by the OECD, because of the need felt by all major partners, individual countries or RIAs, for multilateral rules. It would also be appropriate to examine the possibility of adapting at the multilateral level some of the techniques used at the regional level, e.g. the mutual recognition device.

V. CONCLUSION

62. The objective of trade liberalization or free trade at the multilateral level or at the regional level rests on the same philosophy of economic management and the same objective of achieving the greatest possible welfare. The logic of the theory is that free trade at the multilateral level is better than at the regional level. The question, however, is whether RIAs will stand in the way of continuous liberalization of trade at the multilateral level or, on the contrary, would encourage faster improvement of the MTS. Up to now, the experience has been rather positive. It cannot be guaranteed that this synergy will be maintained if there is continued expansion of RIAs. There will always be the risk that, at least temporarily, progress in the MTS might come to an halt. The favourable complementarity between the regional and multilateral approaches in the past has been largely due to political will. There is no reason that this will not hold true in the future since political will is, after all, largely based on economic and market realities. In particular, the forces pushing towards globalization can be expected to remain active.

63. At the same time, the regional phenomenon is likely to persist. RIAs are often politically motivated, and have become more and more part of a global strategy, so too will the need for a clearer relationship between RIAs and the MTS. This raises, first, the question of possible improvement in the disciplines concerning RIAs. It has been suggested on top of that, while the provisions under Article XXIV of GATT as well as those of Article V of GATS are rather weak, the scope for strengthening them seems limited. This is due to political as well as technical reasons. The conclusion to be drawn is that an improvement in the present situation should be looked for in two directions. First, in addition to the full use of the DSP, stronger disciplines should be obtained through procedures of examination and consultation entered into with a willingness on the part of RIAs, as well as of their partners to find solutions to the problems raised, be they problems of access to market or more general problems. Second, a closer link should be established between progress at the regional and at the multilateral level, in particular, through a greater and faster adaptation of the MTS to market needs, as well as through adequate ways and means of enhancing convergence between the RIAs and the MTS frameworks.

COMMENTS

William J. DAVEY

Director, Legal Affairs Division WTO, Geneva

The paper by Serge Devos on multilateral rules as a constraint on regional rules is an excellent summary of the content of the rules of the World Trade Organization (WTO) in respect to regional trade agreements and how they have been applied over the years by the WTO and its predecessor, the General Agreement on Tariffs and Trade (GATT). By and large, one must admit that some of the criteria in GATT Article XXIV that are used to judge the compatibility of free trade areas and customs unions with GATT are imprecise and have not been applied successfully. That is demonstrated most clearly by the fact that many free trade areas and customs unions have been examined by GATT Working Parties for consistency with Article XXIV over the years, but such Working Parties have seldom reached any concrete conclusion on the question of consistency. More recently, the GATT review process simply became unable to handle the large increase in regional trading arrangements that have been notified to GATT and now the WTO.

There have been, however, two recent significant developments in the WTO's approach to regional trading arrangements. These developments, which are not highlighted in Mr. Devos's paper, could potentially signal a more effective control of regional trading arrangements in the future in the WTO. The first development occurred in the Uruguay Round, where an understanding on GATT Article XXIV was adopted. The second development occurred earlier in 1996, when the WTO General Council created a Committee on Regional Trade Agreements. While it is too early to know exactly what impact these developments will have on the WTO's treatment of regional trading arrangements, they would each seem to be of great importance: the understanding for its impact on how the substantive provisions of Article XXIV will be interpreted; the new committee for its impact on the procedures under which the WTO examines regional trading arrangements and because of its potential as a vehicle for assessing on a systemic basis the overall impact of such arrangements on the multilateral trading system. I will comment on each of these developments in turn.

The Impact of the Uruguay Round Understanding on Article XXIV

Serge Devos has described in general how Article XXIV has not historically served as much of a limit on the creation of regional trading-arrangements. While there are some specific requirements that such arrangements are supposed to meet in order to benefit from the Article XXIV exception, there have been considerable differences over how they should be interpreted. For example, it is required in Article XXIV:8 that a qualifying regional trading arrangement should cover substantially all trade, but how to measure that requirement has never been clear — beyond the fact that "substantially" does mean a high percentage and that there is both a quantitative and qualitative aspect to the issue. A related issue is the extent to which non tariff restrictions on trade must be removed. The Uruguay Round Understanding does not address these issues. Similarly, there is the question of the period during which it is permissible to have interim arrangements leading to free trade areas and customs unions. Article XXIV:5(c) specifies that such interim arrangements are permitted only for a reasonable length of time. In respect to this question, the Uruguay Round Understanding specifies ten years as the normal maximum, but the understanding admits the possibility of exceptional cases. In addition, it has never been clear how the requirement in Article XXIV:5, that trade restrictions toward non Parties not be increased, should be interpreted. Here, the Uruguay Round Understanding provides some guidance as to how to measure this requirement in respect to customs unions. In addition, the understanding offers guidance on the interpretation of Article XXIV:6, which provides for compensation to be provided to adversely affected countries in certain cases where the formation of a customs union leads to an increase of a bound duty. However, Mr. Devos is certainly correct in saying that, overall, the Uruguay Round Understanding does not add very much precision to the terms of Article XXIV.

The Uruguay Round Understanding does, however, clarify one very important issue as to the interpretation of Article XXIV. Paragraph 12 of the understanding specifies:

> The provisions of Articles XXII and XXIII of GATT 1994 as elaborated and applied by the Dispute Settlement Understanding may be invoked with respect to any matters arising from the application of those provisions of Article XXIV relating to customs unions, free trade areas or interim agreements leading to the formation of a customs union or free trade area.

While one might have thought that this was obvious, it has been argued in the past that the GATT practice with respect to Article XXIV was to confide the examination of regional trading arrangements to Working Parties and that it was not appropriate for dispute settlement panels to consider the question of whether a regional trading arrangement was consistent with Article XXIV. A number of dispute settlement panel reports touching on this or related issues are ably described in Theofanis Christoforou's paper on *"Multilateral Rules as a Constraint on Regional Rules: A Regional Perspective"*. The reports he discusses, which did consider issues related to Article XXIV, were never adopted.

Prior to the implementation of the WTO Dispute Settlement Understanding, the question of considering regional trading issues in dispute settlement would not have been a practical way to interpret Article XXIV in any event. Under the GATT dispute settlement rules, any GATT Contracting Party could block the adoption of a dispute-settlement panel report. This meant that if a regional trading arrangement had been challenged before a panel as not consistent with the terms of Article XXIV and thus a violation of Article I and if a panel had agreed, it would have been possible for any member of the arrangement to prevent the panel's conclusions from ever having any effect.

Under the new WTO Dispute Settlement Understanding, which is discussed by Judge Pescatore in a paper presented in this book, if a WTO dispute settlement panel considers the consistency of a regional trading arrangement with Article XXIV (which the understanding specifically authorizes it to do), its results will be adopted automatically unless there is a consensus against the report or it is appealed. If appealed, the Appellate Body report would be automatically adopted, absent consensus against its report. Thus, it is clear that dispute panels may consider these issues and that their conclusions will be adopted.

The fact that dispute settlement panels may consider these issues does not mean, of course, that such cases will be brought frequently or at all. Nor does the fact that panels will consider these issues mean that the standards applicable for regional trading arrangements will be clarified in the short term or that a particular degree of strictness will be imposed. But the mechanism now exists for decisions to be made on these issues in a way that they never could be made when the examination consisted of discussions in a Working Party where all view points were represented.

In fact, it will probably be difficult for panels to interpret Article XXIV. As noted above and in Mr. Devos' paper, the standards are not clear and the myriad of inconclusive Working Party reports will not serve to provide much guidance. Nonetheless, the creation of a more automatic and binding dispute settlement system and the submission of Article XXIV issues to it, will ultimately lead to much greater precision in this area.

Committee on Regional Trade Agreements

The recently created WTO Committee on Regional Trade Agreements held its first meeting on May 21-22, 1996 and has met four times since (as of October 1996). The Committee has two principal functions. It is designed to centralize the examination in the WTO of regional trading arrangements and to provide a forum for the examination of the systemic implications of regional trading arrangements on the WTO and the multilateral trading system. This development, which was proposed and implemented within a very short time in 1996, should have a very significant impact on the way in which the WTO relates to regional trading arrangements.

Examination of Regional Trading Arrangements

As of the middle of 1996, the WTO Secretariat estimated that there were sixty agreements then in force that had been notified under Article XXIV, fourteen agreements that had been notified under the Enabling Clause and eleven regional and preference agreements covered by GATT/WTO waivers. (Of the latter, five will expire at the end of 1996). The GATT record in examining these various agreements was not all that satisfactory. Of the sixty agreements notified under Article XXIV, roughly one-half remained to be examined by a Working Party. It had become difficult to find chairmen for such Working Parties and to organize their work. Moreover, as Mr. Devos notes, almost all of those Working Party reports that were finished were inconclusive.

In addition to conducting an initial examination of regional trading arrangements, it was general GATT practice to require periodic reports on the operation of regional trading arrangements. It appears, however, that by the 1980s such reports were typically not made.

From the foregoing description, it is apparent that the GATT/WTO system of examining regional trading arrangements was hardly functional by the 1990s. It was falling desperately behind in producing Working Party reports and was not reviewing existing agreements at all on a systematic basis. Moreover, as noted above, when reports were produced, they were generally inconclusive.

The Committee on Regional Trade Agreements is designed to solve this problem. It will take over the task of examining regional trading arrangements, a task now performed by *ad hoc* Working Parties and to a limited degree by the Committee on Trade and Development. It will report, according to the type of regional trading arrangement to the Council for Trade in Goods, the Council for Trade in Services or the Committee on Trade and Development. It is obviously too early to tell whether the new committee will succeed, but it is off to a fast start. What the committee will do with respect to the review of new and existing regional agreements is to systematize the reporting obligations. It is hoped that the information that is relevant for the examination will be submitted more quickly and that the existence of a standing committee with no other functions will enable the reviews to be produced quickly (for example, in twelve to eighteen months of notification). While faster initial review and the resumption of regular periodic review does not necessarily imply reports with hard and fast conclusions, it will mean that there will be discussion and some oversight of regional trading arrangements where effectively none existed before.

Studies of Systematic Implications

The second function of the Committee on Regional Trade Agreements is to study the systemic implications of these agreements. As noted in Serge Devos' paper, it is somewhat controversial about whether these arrangements are desirable or not from the perspective of the multilateral trading system. There has been a long debate among economists over whether such arrangements tend to be trade creating or trade diverting, i.e. do they lead to more trade overall or do they basically just shift trading patterns so that those outside the region lose. There is also a debate over whether the existence of such arrangements eases the way for further multilateral trade liberalization or whether it slows that process.

One area where the new committee may be particularly useful is in preparing comparative studies that look across a wide range of regional trading arrangements. The tariff effects of regional arrangements are often studied, but in light of the expanded scope of the WTO agreements into such areas as technical barriers and sanitary/phytosanitary standards, it is also desirable to know what is done in respect of such non tariff issues in regional arrangements. Gathering and evaluating such information may provide new insights into the question of both the trade effects of regional arrangements and whether they promote or retard further multilateral liberalization. Such studies may suggest ways that the multilateral trading system may capitalize on developments in regional arrangements to implement similar changes multilaterally.

A second area where the new committee may be useful is in more broad-based studies on the economic effects of regional trading arrangements. It is not likely that the new committee will be able to resolve definitively the question of whether regional trading arrangements are generally desirable or compatible with the multilateral trading system. Indeed, given that so many WTO Members are participants in regional trading arrangements, members may be hesitant to permit too much in the way of free-ranging studies that might question some of their own arrangements. Nonetheless, the committee should be able to make an important contribution to systemic studies.

Conclusion

The GATT record in monitoring and studying regional trading arrangements was less than stellar. Potentially at least, the WTO may be far more effective in this regard as Article XXIV issues become a subject of dispute settlement and as the WTO Committee on Regional Trade Agreements rationalizes and systematizes the WTO monitoring and study of regional trading arrangements.

MULTILATERAL RULES AS A CONSTRAINT ON REGIONAL RULES: A REGIONAL PERSPECTIVE

Theofanis CHRISTOFOROU*

Legal Service, European Commission, Brussels

A. Introduction

There are several ways in which one may analyze the relationship and effects of multilateral trade rules on regional economic integration agreements. This paper will examine this relationship from the perspective of the most important regional integration agreement, viz. the European Community (EC).

First, a brief overview of the political, economic and legal considerations which have defined the EC's attitude towards the rules laid down in GATT 47 on regional integration agreements will be provided. The analysis will then focus on certain selected issues relating to the interpretation and application of Article XXIV GATT 47 which have been crucial in shaping the EC's policy on regional integration. The analysis will also discuss the potential constraints of the multilateral trade rules on the functioning of the EC itself, as a customs union, rather than on its capacity to conclude Article XXIV-type agreements with other countries. The paper will conclude with a few remarks on the future orientations of the EC in this area of trade policy, and in particular its new policy on regional integration after the entry into force of the WTO Agreement.

---

* All opinions are strictly personal.

B. *Political, Economic and Legal Considerations which Shaped the EC's Policy on Regional Economic Integration*

The history on the application of the GATT 47 rules to regional integration agreements is closely intertwined with the establishment of the European Community (or, more precisely, the European Economic Community, as it was then called).

The economic unification of Western European countries was viewed in the period after the Second World War predominantly as a political exercise. This view was held not only by the European countries which formed initially the ECSC and the EEC, but also by the other major trading power, the United States. For that reason, when the Rome Treaty of 1958 was examined under Article XXIV:7 GATT 47, a practical and realistic approach was taken to leave aside questions about its strict compatibility with the constraints of Article XXIV[1]. We will see that this event and the attitude of the GATT Contracting Parties on this issue are largely to blame for what followed as regards the application of Article XXIV GATT 47 to regional economic integration agreements.

The process of trade liberalization within the EC also lead to profound adjustments in its trade relations with other countries. The regulatory content and geographical expansion of Article XXIV-type agreements concluded by the EC led to the formation of a web of political, economic and legal provisions whose effects on the multilateral trading system are difficult to evaluate with precision.

The important point to make here is the following. The formation of regional trading groups (and in particular of customs unions) entails frequently the concentration of considerable trade (and the concomitant political) power in the institutions of the customs union. This potential power, which frequently drives the formation of customs unions in the first place, they tend somehow to exploit (through the conclusion of regional trade agreements with friendly or satellite countries), as such agreements are an important component of their external trade, economic and sometimes political policies.

It would seem that the drafters of Article XXIV GATT 47 only partly understood these trade and political implications of regional trade groupings. The subsequent application and implementation of Article XXIV

---

[1] See BISD 6 S/71.

GATT 47 also showed a complete lack of political will on the part of the Contracting Parties to contain effectively the problems associated with regional integration agreements.

Around the process of economic integration within the EC, there are now three other levels of regional integration involving the EC. First, the deepest level of integration is with the European countries which are members of the European Economic Area (EEA). Close to this level of integration are aspiring to become the customs union agreements concluded with Malta, Cyprus, Andorra and recently with Turkey. The second circle comprises the large number of FTA agreements concluded with a number of Eastern European countries and several Mediterranean countries. The third is the group of countries with which the EC has concluded an FTA or agreements leading to FTAs, but in which trade restrictions still remain or there are not yet reciprocal contractual commitments (essentially with the ACP countries).

Experience in the EC shows that the intention of the Community legislator, when concluding regional integration agreements, is not to raise trade barriers with countries outside the integrated space. If the degree of liberalization in these agreements is not as high as the EC would have wished (or sometimes Article XXIV GATT 47 would have required) this is almost always due to lack of political and economic potential of the regional partner to deliver (within a short or reasonable period of time) the required degree of trade liberalization. The examples are plenty, it suffices here to mention the Lome Conventions and the agreements concluded with some of the Mediterranean and North African countries.

It is also basically true that the protectionist forces have never gained control of the EC's trade policy-making process. As a result, the potential "fortress" effects of regional integration agreements have left virtually intact the trade liberalizing outlook of the European Community[2].

C. Past Experience and Future Developments in the EC's Trade Policy as regards Regional Economic Integration Agreements

In this part of the paper the turning points in the history of the EC's trade policy on regional integration will be highlighted, drawing from past experience. Actually, there is no need to go that far back into history,

---

[2] See WTO, *Regionalism and the World Trading System*, 1995.

as the potential power of the GATT 47 rules to put constraints on the type and scope of regional integration agreements concluded by the EC was felt seriously only very recently.

1. Article XXIV:7 GATT 47 and the Status of the EC

The working groups that have been established to examine the formation of the EC and its subsequent enlargements have failed to resolve basic methodological issues, such as a common understanding of the notions of "substantially all trade", "the general incidence of the duties and regulations of commerce", etc. As a result, the GATT Council and the Contracting Parties have failed to make recommendations which would have influenced, even *ex post facto*, the political will which has shaped the EC's trade policy. The same is also true as regards the formation and implementation of regional integration agreements concluded by the EC with other countries.

The EC was not unhappy with this legal situation, as it allowed it to enjoy the same status in GATT 47 as any other Contracting Party. In the meantime, the competence to formulate trade policy has been shifted from the constituent Member States to the Community institutions. This favoured a "power-oriented" approach, since in the international arena this maximized the trade and political benefits for the EC and its Member States.

a) The *Citrus Products* Panel Report (1985)

Despite the lack of a common understanding on the notions of "substantially all trade", "the general incidence of the duties and regulations of commerce applicable in the constituent territories", "shall not on the whole be higher or more restrictive", etc., the EC managed to satisfy all its trading partners in all the compensatory adjustment negotiations under Article XXIV:6 GATT 47 without any formal legal ruling on the conformity of its trade policy with GATT rules.

But not for too long, as the first shock came from the *Citrus Products* Panel Report[3]. This panel report found, *inter alia*, that:

> Given the lack of consensus among Contracting Parties, there had been no decision by the Contracting Parties on the conformity with Article XXIV of the agreements under which the EC grants tariff

---

[3] See L/577, 7.2.1985.

preferences to certain citrus products originating from certain Mediterranean countries, and therefore the legal status of the agreements remained open. [...]

The Panel had not been requested, nor would it be proper for it to pass judgement on the conformity of the EC Agreements as a whole with the provisions of Article XXIV.[4]

Thus, the EC saw for the first time written on paper something which it had always intimately feared but never wished to admit openly, namely that the GATT conformity of a number of its Article XXIV-type agreements with GATT "remained open". This finding was seen to be potentially disastrous, especially in political terms, as the EC **itself** has never received the formal approval under the procedures of Article XXIV:7 GATT 47.

The amazing capacity of the EC to absorb demands for offsetting or compensatory adjustments under Article XXIV:6 GATT, its "power-oriented" approach and, of course, the complicity of the GATT 47 rules themselves, which required **unanimity** for the adoption of panel reports, led the EC (and the US but for different reasons) to refuse the adoption of the *Citrus Products* Panel Report. In doing so, however, the EC has failed to seize a unique opportunity offered to it to save the legality of its regional integration agreements under Article XXIV GATT 47. Had that report been adopted, it might have established the principle that GATT panels can scrutinize the legality of **specific** measures only taken in implementation of Article XXIV-type agreements and not the conformity of the **entire** agreement with the requirements of Article XXIV GATT 47.

The findings of the *Citrus Products* Panel Report on this precise point is not, one may argue, legally unsound. In addition, it was consonant with the factual and legal situation and the generally held view at that time[5]. It is not unreasonable to suggest that had the *Citrus* Panel Report been adopted the legal fate of Article XXIV-type agreements might have been quite different today.

*b) The **Airbus** Panel Report (1992)*

Although the EC in the design of its regional integration policy never intended to subvert the GATT rules, it is nevertheless true that it preferred

---

[4] *Ibid.* at § 5.1; see also §§ 4.15-4.16.

[5] See J. JACKSON, **World Trade and the Law of GATT**, 1969.

to retain (like many other GATT members) a rather free hand in the pursuance of its broad policy objectives. The second shock to its capacity to manage its trade policy in a rather liberal way came from the unadopted *Airbus* Panel Report[6].

This panel report examined the exchange rate guarantee scheme operated by the German Government with respect to Deutsche Airbus, the German partner of the Airbus consortium. The report found that the scheme was an export subsidy covered by item (j) of the Illustrative List of subsidies and was prohibited by Article 9 of the 1979 Subsidies Agreement. The panel report contained certain passages in its reasoning (especially paras 5.5-5.7.) which, to put it bluntly, if adopted, could potentially destroy the degree of integration achieved **within** the EC. Clearly, the panel report not only touched upon the political foundations of the EC itself, but it was arguably also out of touch with the prevailing GATT 47 legal and political realities.

The panel report found that the "movement" of parts or components of Airbus models produced in Germany and transported to France constituted "exports" in the sense of Article XVI:4 GATT 47 and, hence, the 1979 Subsidies Agreement. This finding would have the potential of re-erecting on paper the "exports" and "export restrictions" **between** the Member States of the EC, something which the EC, **for the purposes of Article XXIV GATT 47**, had long before abolished.

The panel report also found that:

> The Member States of the EEC were today still GATT Contracting Parties, and GATT obligations, in particular that of Article XVI:4, still applied individually to them.

The reasoning of that passage is very formalistic and obviously more difficult to de-code, and, in the space available here, is best omitted. It suffices only to observe, that this reasoning did not conform with the legal status and actual treatment (albeit on an *ad hoc* basis) which the EC has been already receiving by the GATT 47 and the Contracting Parties in Geneva.

From a more broad perspective, as regards the anti-subsidies provisions of the GATT 47 and the 1979 Subsidies Code, the EC would have had no objection to be treated as one Contracting Party. In fact, only the EC had signed and ratified the 1979 Subsidies Code. To examine the

---

[6] See SCM/142, 28.4.1992.

exchange rate guarantee scheme operated by Germany in the wider context of the EC, as the only legally accountable Contracting Party, and review it in comparison with Airbus exports to other GATT members, would have probably posed no legal problems to the EC. The EC is known for applying one of the toughest policies on public subsidies amongst the GATT members.

I need only add that the *Airbus* Panel Report sent alarming signals to Brussels. For the first time it was clearly realized that there may be trade rules of a higher plane which can constrain severely the internal trade policy-making power of the EC and its Member States. But again the EC managed for, essentially, the same reasons as in the case of the *Citrus Products* Panel Report to put behind it another unpleasant incident in its ambivalent relationship with Article XXIV GATT 47[7].

c) The Two **Banana** Panel Reports (1993 and 1994)

The third and final blow to any hopes which the EC has nurtured as regards its capacity to shelter from legal scrutiny its Article XXIV-type agreements was dealt by the two panel reports on *Bananas*[8]. The unfortunate fact with these reports is that they both targeted an agreement to which the EC attached very high historical, political, economic and legal importance, i.e. the Lome Convention with the ACP countries.

The first Panel Report on *Bananas*, applying a slightly different test than the *Citrus* Panel Report, found that:

> ... the procedures of Article XXIV could reasonably be considered to prevail over those of Article XXIII only in those cases in which the agreement for which Article XXIV was invoked was *prima facie* the type of agreement covered by this provision, i.e. on the face of it capable of justification under it. (at para.367).

The panel report then went on to examine whether the Lome Convention was such a *prima facie* agreement. It concluded that it was not, because there was no reciprocity in the elimination of restrictive regulations of commerce on the part of the ACP countries. A broad reading of the report's reasoning seems to suggest that the panel did not rule on the relationship between Article XXIV:7 and Article XXIII GATT 47, in case

---

[7] The *Airbus* Panel Report also raised a more delicate question: Does Article XXIV:5 to :8 exonerate an economic integration agreement from all or only some of the provisions (i.e. essentially the MFN principle) of GATT 47?

[8] EEC-Member States' import regime for Bananas, DS 32/R, 3.6.1993, and EEC-Import regime for Bananas, DS 38/R, 11.2.1994, both unadopted.

a *prima facie* agreement of the type envisaged in Article XXIV was at stake (on which, as explained, the *Citrus Products* Panel Report had already taken a rather cautious and very pragmatic approach).

But any remaining hopes of the EC to protect from legal scrutiny the Lome Convention were completely dashed by the second panel report on *Bananas*. The arguments put to the panel by both Parties were very extensive and elaborated to an amazing degree of detail on the drafting history of Article XXIV, Part IV and Article XXXVI of GATT, as well as the structure, purpose and role of regional integration agreements[9]. The EC was now defending before the panel a developed and finely distinguished version of the finding on this issue by the *Citrus Products* Panel Report, namely that:

> ... a panel can on the basis of procedures of Article XXIII only examine the effects from the implementation of "specific measures", and not the "overall" consistency of Lome, because Article XXIV:7 provided for a special procedure for the examination of free trade areas. (at para.156).

It is important to note also that, by the time the case was argued before the panel, the Uruguay Round negotiations were already at their closing stages. Fearful of a panel finding as (or even more) negative as that of the first panel report on *Bananas* on this issue, the EC tried hard to catch up with treaty language. Thus, on December 12, 1993, it formally proposed to the Uruguay Round participants[10] to amend Paragraph 12 of the draft Understanding on the Interpretation of Article XXIV, as follows:

> 12. The dispute settlement provisions of the General Agreement may be invoked with respect to any **specific measures** arising from the **implementation** of those provisions of Article XXIV relating to customs unions, free trade areas or interim agreements leading to the formation of a customs union or free trade area. **Such recourse to the dispute settlement provisions, however, shall not be allowed to question the conformity with GATT of existing customs unions, free trade areas or interim agreements leading to customs unions or free trade areas which have been notified to the Contracting Parties, as long as the**

---

[9] In addition, the panel had put a large number of questions all centred around the interpretation of Article XXIV and Part IV GATT 47 and their relationship with the purpose and scope of dispute settlement procedures under Article XXIII GATT 47.

[10] See MTN.TNC/W/125, 13.12.1993.

Contracting Parties have not made a specific recommendation under Article XXIV:7 of the General Agreement." (emphasis in the original)[11]

That proposal arrived of course too late on the negotiation table to be taken into account, although the EC managed to gather written support by not less than thirty ACP countries by the time of its submission to the TNC group.

The second *Banana* Panel Report in essence upheld the finding of the first *Banana* Panel Report on this issue. It stated:

The Panel observed that, whatever the precise relationship between the procedures under Articles XXIII and XXIV, the provisions of Article XXIV:7 empower the Contracting Parties to make recommendations **only** on agreements establishing a customs union or free trade area, or interim agreements leading to such a union or area. These provisions thus do not apply to **any** agreement notified to the Contracting Parties but only to the four specified types of agreements. The Panel therefore concluded that, notwithstanding the issue of whether the procedures of Article XXIV:7 supersede those of Article XXIII:2, it would first have to examine whether the Lome Convention is an agreement of the type to which the procedures of Article XXIV:7 apply. The Panel could not accept that tariff preferences inconsistent with Article I:1 would, by notification of the preferential arrangement and invocation of Article XXIV against the objections of other Contracting Parties, escape any examination by a panel established under Article XXIII. If this view were endorsed, a mere communication of a Contracting Party invoking Article XXIV could deprive all other Contracting Parties of their procedural rights under Article XXIII:2, and therefore also of the effective protection of their substantive rights, in particular those under Article I:1. The Panel concluded therefore that a panel, faced with an invocation of

---

[11] A declaration accompanying the proposed amendment clarified further that: The MTO Members, signatories of the present declaration, do not agree that under Paragraph 12 of the Understanding on the interpretation of Article XXIV of the GATT panels could question the conformity of existing customs unions and free trade areas, as well as interim agreements leading up to customs unions or free trade areas **as such**, when such agreements have been notified to the Contracting Parties and the latter have not made specific recommendations with respect to such agreements. The signatories of this declaration propose that this matter be discussed in the Contracting Parties immediately after the conclusion of the negotiations in the Uruguay Round so as to reach a settlement acceptable to all.

Article XXIV, first had to examine whether or not this provision applied to the agreement in question. (at para.158) (emphasis in the original).

Although it may be argued that the panel report tried again to avoid taking a definitive position on the relationship between Article XXIV:7 and Article XXIII procedures, it is probably more realistic to suggest that its reasoning is based on the understanding that even a *prima facie* agreement of the type envisaged in Article XXIV:8 GATT 47 cannot escape legal scrutiny in dispute settlement proceedings brought under Article XXIII[12]. This interpretation came also two months after the EC proposal to amend Paragraph 12 of the Draft Understanding on the Interpretation of Article XXIV GATT 94, and appeared to provide an *ex post facto* legal recognition of the existing version of Paragraph 12 of the Draft Understanding. But, Paragraph 12 went through and approved unamended in Marrakesh[13], although the second panel report on *Bananas* itself was never adopted.

It would take much time and space to discuss here the internal discussions and power-politics in the EC and its constituent Member States that ensued the circulation of the second panel report on *Bananas*. As already pointed out, there were too many and very important historical, political, economic, legal and tactical considerations that played a role in the final decision of the EC to request a waiver for Lome IV under Article XXV GATT. What also played a vital role is that both these panel reports concerned a product (bananas) which has preoccupied the political and legal atmosphere in the EC since the inception of the 1958 Rome Treaty.

Be that as it may, the experience of the two panel reports on *Bananas* enable us to draw the following essential conclusion: for the first time,

---

[12] The panel's reasoning on this issue is arguably deficient in several respects, not so for its final conclusion as for the reasons on which its legal analysis was based (e.g. too formalistic on the legal basis on which Lome was notified to GATT; insufficient attention paid to the legal value of the reports of Working Parties established under Article XXIV:7 to examine notified agreement and the subsequent decisions of the GATT Council; circular reasoning as regards the hierarchy of norms between Article XXIV:7 and Article XXIII; application of a teleological method of interpretation ostensibly geared to cover up the lacuna in the procedural requirements of Article XXIV:7, etc.).

[13] Paragraph 12 of the Understanding, as it now stands, reads as follows:
The provisions of Articles XXII and XXIII of GATT 1994 as elaborated and applied by the Dispute Settlement Understanding may be invoked with respect to any matters arising from the application of those provisions of Article XXIV relating to customs unions, free trade areas or interim agreements leading to the formation of a customs union or free trade area.

as far as the EC is concerned, the GATT 47 dispute settlement procedures managed to produce a result which the procedures laid down in Article XXIV on regional integration agreements have so distinctly failed to achieve. This is the essential message that needs to be underlined here.

2. Article XXIV:6 GATT 47 Compensatory Adjustment Negotiations and the WTO Understanding on the Interpretation of Article XXIV GATT 94

Article XXIV:6 GATT 47 compensatory adjustment negotiations have been figuring prominently on the EC's trade policy agenda almost on a continuous basis for decades. This is mainly due to the successive enlargements of the EC, the large number of preferential agreements concluded by it and, of course, the vague and unhelpful language used in Article XXIV itself. Compensatory adjustment negotiations have almost always put the EC on the defensive *vis-à-vis* its principle trading partners and have frequently marred the trade relations of its constituent Member States.

It is submitted that although the vague wording of key concepts in Article XXIV GATT 47 provided a substantial margin of manoeuvre to the EC internationally, experience shows that the overall management of compensatory adjustment negotiations and of the preferential agreements themselves entails substantial costs which put constraints on the tendency to proliferate the conclusion of agreements of the type envisaged in Article XXIV.

The new Understanding on the Interpretation of Article XXIV GATT 94 is expected to improve the legal relationship between the two trading systems (multilateral and regional), despite the fact that several of its provisions (e.g. Paragraphs 2, 4 and 5 are still ambiguous in several respects). The EC has approved this understanding and is fully committed to faithfully and properly implement it.

3. The New WTO Committee on Regional Trade Agreements

Following the suggestion of the report on *Regionalism and the World Trading System*, published by the WTO in early 1995, as well as recommendations coming from other quarters, a new Committee on Regional Trade Agreements was established[14]. Its terms of reference, *inter alia*, include:

---

[14] See WT/L/127, 7.2.1996.

to consider the systemic implication of such (regional trade) agreements and regional initiatives for the multilateral trading system and the relationship between them, and make appropriate recommendations to the General Council.

A centralized system of examination of regional integration agreements is expected to improve transparency and efficiency and is likely to coordinate better the review process. It might also enable the WTO to act in advance, which is of great value in inducing compliance with GATT law.

The EC has actively supported the establishment of the Committee on Regional Trade Agreements and is fully committed to comply with its rules and procedures (see below).

4. The Crucial Role which the DSU is expected to Play

Both the Understanding on the Interpretation of Article XXIV and the new Committee on Regional Trade Agreements provide considerable hope for increasing pressure on WTO Members to comply with the requirement of Article XXIV GATT 94 during the formation and implementation of regional trade agreements.

Experience in the EC, however, shows that there is essentially only one source which can provide real hope for early and probably full compliance of regional integration agreements with the GATT rules. This source is the new and strengthened dispute settlement mechanism laid down in the Dispute Settlement Understanding (DSU), as the adoption of panel and appellate body reports can no longer be blocked by the loosing member and cross-retaliation is now permitted. In my view, these provisions constitute now the principle deterrence and are likely to induce compliance of regional agreements of the type envisaged in Article XXIV (as well as of regional agreements of the type envisaged in Article V GATS) with the philosophy, system and legal structure of the multilateral trading system set up by the WTO.

D. The New Orientations in the EC's Policy as regards Regional Economic Integration Agreements

The EC and its Member States have studied carefully the political, economic and legal implications of the existing (and future) regional trade agreements both before and, in particular, after the conclusion of the Uruguay Round. There are several elements which have influenced their analysis and have led them to adopt a new approach on regional trade agreements, such as:

- the new obligations resulting from the WTO Agreement;
- the new policy of the USA, as well as of other WTO Members, which shows an increasingly regionalist attitude;
- the basic and long-term interest of the EC to pursue sustained multilateral liberalization; and,
- the need to combat unilateralism in resolving trade disputes.

The European Commission has explained the motives behind this new approach as follows:

> The advent of the WTO brings with it new obligations, reinforces existing ones and strengthens procedural requirements. As such it has important implications for FTAs. This requires increased vigilance by the EC, with two key objectives in mind: to prevent Europe becoming exposed to action by our WTO partners, and to set a good example so that our partners, too, feel bound by the rules... The key question is whether on both the economic and political fronts, the benefits for the EC of duty-free access to deregulated third country markets are greater than the adjustment costs of the EC concessions needed to produce a WTO-compatible FTA.[15]

E. Conclusions

If one may venture a few conclusions, I would summarize as follows: the relationship between multilateral rules and regional trade agreements from the perspective of the European Community. The old GATT 47 structure had very few safety-valves build into the trading system, and even those that existed failed clearly to be applied correctly to regional integration agreements. As a result, GATT 47 failed to contain, from at least the legal point of view, the formation and proliferation of such regional agreements.

---

[15] See European Commission, IP/95/215 of 8.3.1995. This press release followed the European Commission's Communication to the Council on *Free Trade Areas: An Appraisal*, (SEC(95)322 final, 7.3.1995). The EC Commission's communication was approved by the Council of Ministers on June 22, 1995, where it was stated that:
... before taking any steps towards establishing a free trade area... (there is a need to assess) the compatibility of the planned agreement with WTO rules ... and the implications of such an agreement for the Union's common policies and for its relations with its main trading partners.

The new system put in place by the WTO Agreement is likely to increase control and monitoring of such regional trade agreements. However, the real hope of an early compliance of regional agreements with multilateral trade rules is expected to come, essentially, from the potential application of the reinforced rules on dispute settlement, as laid down in the Dispute Settlement Understanding of the WTO Agreement, to the entire regional integration arrangements.

THE COMPATIBILITY OF THE EURO-MEDITERRANEAN REGIONAL INTEGRATION WITH THE MULTILATERAL RULES

Erwan LANNON

Researcher,
European Institute, University of Ghent

Introduction

The establishment of the World Trade Organization as a common and multilateral institutional framework for the conduct of world trade relations, is of great importance for the creation of the future Euro-Mediterranean Economic Area (EMEA) that will include some 30-40 countries with 600-800 millions people[1] therefore constituting one of the largest regional integration in the world.

The Euro-Mediterranean project is clearly another expression of the so-called "new regionalism". However, the case of the Euro-Mediterranean region, considered as a "newly emerging geopolitical area"[2], is somewhat specific. The gap between the EC and third Mediterranean countries, in terms of economic and social development, is indeed

---

[1] *"Strengthening the Mediterranean Policy of the European Union: Establishing a Euro-Mediterranean Partnership"*, COM(94)427 final, 19/10/1994, p.10.

[2] See Eberhard RHEIN, *"Europe and the Mediterranean: A Newly Emerging Geopolitical Area?"*, in: **European Foreign Affairs Review** No.1, 1996, pp.79-86.

very important. In terms of nominal *per capita* GDP it may amount to 10:1[3]. At the same time the economic and social disparities among the Mediterranean Non-Member Countries (MNMCs), their low level of economic interdependence[4] and their differing competitive strengths are huge obstacles for regional integration in the zone. It is also important that the different political regimes be taken into account. The Euro-Mediterranean Economic Area will therefore constitute an "heterogeneous regional integration".

Another particularity comes from the kind and nature of legal relationships that will link the EU to the MNMCs. A network of twelve Euro-Mediterranean Agreements has to take place in 2010. This network will be composed of nine "Euro-Mediterranean Association Agreements" with a view to establishing a free trade area and three "association agreements" establishing Customs Unions (CUs) constituting the bilateral legal framework of the Euro-Mediterranean Partnership.

The second level of the partnership is the subregional cooperation. The promotion of this type of cooperation has been notably reinforced after the Oslo Israeli-Palestinian Agreements[5]. Two communications of the Commission have been issued on the future of the relationship between the Community and the Maghreb and the Middle East. The European Council of Lisbon (June 1992) has also defined a series of specific objectives for each zone. This subregional approach is part of a global strategy promoting regional integration among developing countries.

The foundations of "a lasting multilateral cooperation", one of the most important innovations of the Euro-Mediterranean partnership, were

---

[3] According to the World Bank: "the Middle East and North Africa (MENA) region achieved a modest upswing in growth of Gross Domestic Product (GDP) in 1995. Among the economies in which the Bank is active, Algeria, Egypt, Iran, Tunisia, and the West Bank and Gaza all achieved GDP growth ranging from 2.5 percent to 5 percent. Jordan and Lebanon both continued to do well, with growth in excess of 6 percent. Others fared less well. Morocco, hard hit by severe drought, suffered an estimated decline in GDP of over 6 percent. Yemen's GDP grew by just over 1 percent." *"Global Economic Prospects and the Developing Countries 1996 — Section 4: the Middle East and North Africa"*, World Bank, Washington, D.C, 1996.

[4] Trade among MNMCs is estimated at 4 to 5 percent of the total trade of these countries. See Isabelle BENSIDOUN & Agnès CHEVALLIER, **Europe-Mediterranée : Le pari de l'ouverture**, Collection CEPII, Economica, Paris, 1996, p.20. See also Henri REGHNAULT, *" Les intégrations économiques en Méditerranée : Etat des lieux et perspectives"*, in : Gilbert BENHAYOUN, Maurice CATIN & Henri REGHNAULT, **L'Europe et la Méditerranée : Intégration économique et libre échange**, Collection Emploi, Industrie et Territoire, L'Harmattan, Paris, 1997, p.93.

[5] See the two Communications of the Commission on the Maghreb: Doc. COM(92)401 final, April 30, 1992; and on the Middle East: Doc. COM(93)375, September 8, 1993.

laid down in the Barcelona Declaration[6] and the work program annexed to it, both adopted on November 27-28, 1995. This has given rise to important activity among the conference participants in various sectors. This process, known as the "Barcelona Process", is implemented and monitored by the Euro-Mediterranean Committee for the Barcelona Process, consisting of officials from the Troika (the current, previous and next presidencies of the EU) and from the twelve Mediterranean Partners. More than thirty meetings in various sectors, at both ministerial and senior official levels, were held in 1996[7].

Regarding the GATT rules, the question is whether this ambitious project will be compatible with the legal requirements of the multilateral system. Following the Barcelona Declaration, the foundation of the Mediterranean Partnership, the twenty-seven Partners[8] have agreed, in Malta, in the conclusions of the second Euro-Mediterranean conference, to "give a new impetus to the establishment of a Euro-Mediterranean free trade area with 2010 as a target date, with due observance of the obligations resulting from the WTO"[9]. One of the aims of the economic and financial Euro-Mediterranean Partnership, the second pillar of the overall Euro-Mediterranean Partnership, is to insert the MNMCs into the world economy progressively by the creation of a vast area of shared prosperity taking account of the different levels of development of the MNMCs. There is indeed a growing risk of a marginalization of these countries within the new multilateral trading system and consequently a direct threat to the stability of the Southern periphery of the EU.

---

[6] The three pillars of the overall Euro-Mediterranean Partnership are: 1) a political and security partnership aimed at creating a common area of peace and stability; 2) an economic and financial partnership establishing an area of shared prosperity notably by gradually introducing free trade; 3) a social, cultural and human partnership conceived in order to increase exchanges between the civil societies of the countries taking part, to develop human resources, and to promote understanding between cultures and exchanges between civil societies.

[7] See the list annexed to the Conclusions of the second Euro-Mediterranean Ministerial Conference of Malta.

[8] Fifteen Members States of the EU + Algeria, Cyprus, Egypt, Israel, Jordan, Lebanon, Malta, Morocco, Tunisia, Syria, Turkey and the West Bank and the Gaza Strip.

[9] See the conclusions of the second Euro-Mediterranean Conference Malta April 1997, published by *Agence Europe*. Seventeen months after Barcelona, the second Euro-Mediterranean Ministerial Conference held at Valletta, Malta, on April 15-16, 1997, reaffirmed the principles and objectives agreed at Barcelona in 1995 and set out a number of priorities for the future development of the partnership. The deep tensions within the Peace Process in the Middle East peace process have disturbed the Ministerial Conference. The project of a *"Charter for Peace and Stability in the Euro-Mediterranean Region"*, was, for example, deferred to a future ministerial meeting "when political circumstances allow".

The relationship between regionalism and a multilateral system based on the Most-Favoured-Nation (MFN) principle is indeed a complex one, and it's becoming more and more complex as the number of regional initiatives increase. In a communication sent to the Council of Ministers[10] the European Commission has concluded that the EU has a "strong interest in the development of clearer rules within the World Trade Organization, particularly where free trade areas are concerned". There is a concern that the WTO dispute settlement system might endanger the pyramid of preferences of the EU and the Common Agricultural Policy (CAP)[11].

Before examining the conformity of the Euro-Mediterranean Association Agreements with the multilateral rules on regional integration[12] it is necessary to define the nature and the reasons for such a process, to put back the Euro-Mediterranean Partnership in the overall new European trade strategy context (A), and to have a brief overview on the situation of the Mediterranean Non-Member Countries with regard to the World Trade Organization (B).

A. The Euro-Mediterranean Partnership in the New European Trade Strategy

1. The "Euro-Mediterranean Partnership": The First Conceptualization of the Mediterranean Policy of the European Union

a) The Reasons for the Creation of a Euro-Mediterranean Partnership

One can identify many reasons for the creation of a Euro-Mediterranean Partnership. A few of them are of interest to the present article and should be mentioned here:

---

[10] See *"Europe Presses for Clearer World Rules on Regional Blocs"*; Press. Information: PI/97/15, Brussels, January 16, 1997.

[11] See Catherine GOYBET, *"Les zones de libre échange : nouveau sujet de tension entre les Quinze ?"*, in : **Revue du Marché Commun et de l'Union européenne**, No.395, février 1996, p.77.

[12] As this legal analysis will focus on the FTA's to be implemented within the framework of the new Euro-Mediterranean Association Agreements one should therefore refer to the paper of Mr Kabaalioglu for an analysis of the EC-Turkey customs union. See also the paper of Mr Tovias for an economical appraisal of the Euro-Mediterranean Partnership and for the examination of the cumulation of rules of origin.

- First of all, it must be stressed that if, since the end of the Cold War, the Mediterranean has become less strategically significant within the new world (dis)order, at a regional level, the new (geo)political situation has allowed the EU to envisage the possibility of creating vast Pan Euro-Mediterranean Regional Economic Integration.

- The erosion of the traditional Euro-Mediterranean preferences[13], if not a recent trend, is another reason for the creation of a reinforced association with the MNMCs. From the impact of the accession of Spain and Portugal to the EEC in the late 1980s (which seems in fact to have had fewer effects than expected on the MNMCs[14]) to the (re)integration of Eastern and Central countries in the 1990s and, nowadays, the proliferation of Regional Integration, the significance of the "preferential regime" granted by the Community to the MNMCs has been considerably weakened.

- The potential effects of the GATT 94 on the Mediterranean Non-Member Countries[15] must also be taken into account. The increased world trade competition will affect sectors of importance for the MNMCs. Concerning the Maghreb, the eleventh report of the House of Lords Committee on the European Communities states that: "the relationships between the countries of North Africa and the EU has, however, been affected as a result of the GATT Uruguay round. The GATT settlement could lead to potential losses to North Africa of around $600 millions-worth of trade per year."[16]

---

[13] See Isabelle BENSIDOUN & Agnès CHEVALLIER, **Europe-Mediterranée : Le pari de l'ouverture**, Collection CEPII, Economica, Paris, 1996, pp.28-37.

[14] See Lionel FONTAGNÉ & Nicolas PÉRIDY, *"De la politique préférentielle de l'Union européenne-Maghreb au GATT 94 : évaluation et perspectives"*, in : **Le Maroc et l'Europe**, Ouest Éditions, University of Nantes, 1996, p.128.

[15] See Lionel FONTAGNÉ & Nicolas PÉRIDY, *"De la politique préférentielle de l'Union européenne-Maghreb au GATT 94 : évaluation et perspectives"*, in : **Le Maroc et l'Europe**, Ouest Éditions, University of Nantes, 1996.

[16] Select Committee on the European Communities, House of Lords: *"Relations between the EU and the Maghreb Countries"* (11th Report), Session 1994-95, May 1995, p.24. According to Lionel FONTAGNÉ & Nicolas PÉRIDY, the negative impact of the GATT 1994 will be concentrated on manufactured products. *"De la politique préférentielle de l'Union européenne-Maghreb au GATT 94 : évaluation et perspectives"*, p.132.

b) Reciprocity, Partnership, and Co-development: The Components of a New Type of Association Compatible with the Multilateral Rules?

Four "Euro-Mediterranean Association Agreements" have already been signed with Tunisia (17/07/1995[17]), Israel (20/11/1995[18]), Morocco (26/02/1996[19]), and the West Bank and Gaza Strip (24/02/1997[20]). The agreement with Jordan was initialled on April 15-16, 1997 (during the second Euro-Mediterranean Ministerial Conference of Malta) and nego-tiations are currently under way with Egypt, Lebanon and Algeria, while (shy) preliminary talks have begun with Syria. At the European Council held in Amsterdam on June 1997 the Member States have welcomed the progress made towards the creation of a Euro-Mediterranean Free Trade Area through the further extension of the network of Euro-Mediterranean Agreements considered as a "key element of the Partnership", and have stressed the importance of concluding the outstanding agreements as quickly as possible[21].

The associations between the Community and the Member States, on one hand, and their Mediterranean partners of the southern and eastern shores of the Mediterranean Basin, on the other hand, will be based on principles of "reciprocity, partnership and co-development" (see the sec-ond paragraph of the Preamble of the EC-Tunisia Agreement[22] for ex-ample). The insertion of three new concepts in the new generation of

---

[17] Proposal for a decision of the Council and the Commission on the conclusion of a "*Euro-Mediterranean Agreement establishing an Association between the European Communities and their Member States, of the one part and the Republic of Tunisia, of the other part*", COM(95)235 final 31/05/1995.

[18] Proposal for a decision of the Council and the Commission on the conclusion of a "*Euro-Mediterranean Agreement establishing an Association between the European Communities and their Member States, of the one part and the State of Israel, of the other part*", see the Interim Agreement on Trade: **OJ** L 71, 20/03/1996, p.1.

[19] Proposal for a decision of the Council and the Commission on the conclusion of a "*Euro-Mediterranean Agreement establishing an Association between the European Communities and their Member States, of the one part and the Kingdom of Morocco, of the other part*", COM(95)740 final 20/12/1995.

[20] Decision of the Council (97/430/EC-02/06/1997) of the conclusion of a "*Euro-Mediterranean Interim Association Agreement on Trade and Cooperation between the European Community and the Palestine Liberation Organization for the Benefit of the Palestinian Authority of the West Bank and Gaza Strip*", **OJ** L 187, 16/07/1997, p.1.

[21] Presidency conclusions on the Mediterranean - Amsterdam, June 16-17, 1997. See also Annex III: "*European Union call for peace in the Middle East*".

[22] Proposal for a decision of the Council and the Commission on the conclusion of a "*Euro-Mediterranean Agreement establishing an Association between the European Communities and their Member States, of the one part and the Republic of Tunisia, of the other part*", COM(95)235 final 31/05/1995.

Association Agreements and in the Barcelona Declaration reflects the will for a change in the nature of the Euro-Mediterranean relationships.

The European strategy aims to implement a more consistent, efficient and balanced policy towards its southern and eastern peripheries. A pyramid of preferences, within the privileged third countries benefiting from association with the EU, will be maintained between the declared and potential candidates and the non-eligible countries benefiting from an agreement establishing an FTA or a customs union.

i) Reciprocity

The passage from a non-reciprocal relationship (implemented in the framework of the current "Cooperation Agreements" signed with the Maghreb and Machrek countries in the 1970s) to a reciprocal one, is due to several factors but mainly to the reinforcement of the multilateral rules. According to the European Commission "decision to negotiate an FTA [...] has to be done in full awareness of the new WTO conditions (coverage, full reciprocity, transitional arrangements, the possibility of referral of such agreements to WTO dispute settlements...)"[23].

The insertion of a reference to the concept of reciprocity within the new EMAAs has, however, different meanings. The reference to reciprocity in the Preamble of the EMAAs seems to be an allusion to the GATT obligation[24] (see also Part C on reciprocity in the field of services). The concept of reciprocity also appears in a much more ambiguous[25] way in the chapter of the Euro-Mediterranean Association Agreements devoted to Agricultural and Fishery Products. Article 16 of the Tunisian Association Agreement states, for example, that "the Community and Tunisia shall gradually implement greater liberalization of their reciprocal trade in agricultural and fishery products."

---

[23] SEC(95)322 final 08/03/1995, p.2.

[24] The agreement signed with Tunisia states: "Considering that the Community its Member States and Tunisia wish to strengthen those links and to establish lasting relations based on reciprocity, partnership and co-development." The Preamble of the Marrakesh Agreement establishing the WTO states: "Being desirous of contributing to these objectives by entering into reciprocal and mutually advantageous arrangements directed to the substantial reduction of tariffs and other barriers to trade and to the elimination of discriminatory treatment in international trade relations." See Geert WILS, *"The Concept of Reciprocity in EEC Law: An Exploration into these Realms"*, in: **Common Market Law Review** No.28, 1991, pp.245-274.

[25] On the concept of reciprocity, see Piet EECKHOUT, **The European Internal Market and International Trade: A Legal Analysis**, Oxford European Community Law Series, 1994, pp.362-366.

One should also note that the introduction of reciprocity is a more orthodox form of association, as Article 238 provides that agreements establishing association involves "reciprocal rights and obligations"[26].

ii) Association and Partnership

The establishment of an "Association" based on Article 238 involves the creation of a very privileged relationship with the Community.

In the case of the Maghreb and Machrek countries, it is rather a reinforcement and an adaptation of the current preferential "Cooperation Agreements" already based on the Article above mentioned but for the State of Israel it is the first formal Association. The signature on November 20, 1995 of an association agreement between the EC and its Member States, on one hand, and the State of Israel, on the other hand, is indeed of great political significance for the latest. The previous agreement concluded with the State of Israel in 1975 and designed to establish an industrial free trade zone, was a preferential commercial agreement based on the Article 113 (common commercial policy) and not an "Association" or "Cooperation" agreement based on Article 238 (like all of the other agreements concluded within the framework of the overall Mediterranean policy). The new EC-Israel Agreement is a "Euro-Mediterranean Association Agreement" based on Article 238 and one should therefore underline the alignment of the latest on the agreements concluded and to be concluded with the Arab or non-Arab countries (Cyprus, Malta and Turkey). It must be also mentioned that it is the first Euro-Mediterranean Association Agreement signed with an Eastern Mediterranean country.

A "partnership association" with the Community and its Member States implies the implementation of a regular political dialogue in every field of reciprocal interest and an overall economic and financial cooperation sustained by regular dialogue. The observance of human rights, democratic principles and economic freedom is considered as the "very basis of the association" (see the Preamble of the Tunisian Agreement) while the importance of social and cultural cooperation differs substantially from one country to another (see for example the differences between the agreements concluded with Morocco, Jordan and Israel in the field of cooperation in social domain and more particularly the provisions on workers). One should also mention the fact that the Euro-

---

[26] See Jean RAUX, *"Les compétences expresses de caractère général (Art.238)"*, **Jurisclasseur**, fascicule 2200, Editions Techniques, Paris, 1/90, pp.1-10.

Mediterranean Association Agreements (with the exception of the Interim Agreement concluded between the EC and the PLO), as they are covering domains going beyond the Community's competencies[27], are mixed agreements. Therefore, they need to be ratified by the fifteen Member States in order to be implemented.

If the establishment of a "Partnership" relation seems to be another degree in the EU pyramid of preferences implemented via association, the need to rationalize the nature and types of preferential agreements has however been highlighted in several articles[28]. The question is whether partnership can really be a new form of association[29] or just an adaptation of the "traditional associations" concluded in the 1970s. The "spirit of partnership" that conducted the Community to fully associate the MNMCs in the writing of the Barcelona Declaration should also be mentioned.

iii) "Development Cooperation" and "Co-development" Strategy

The twelve Mediterranean Partners of the EU, apart from the Palestinian Territories[30], are not directly apprehended within the framework of the "development cooperation" policy of the Community (Art.130U to 130Y; Title XVII of the Treaty establishing the European Community) but one should note that, as Article 130V states that: "The Community and the Member States shall take account of the objectives referred to in Article 130U in the policies that it implements which are likely to affect developing countries", this policy should therefore be taken into account regarding the Euro-Mediterranean relationships. The provision on the need to foster "the smooth and gradual integration of the developing countries into the world economy" (Art.130U(1)) should, for example, be mentioned.

---

[27] Such as the political dialogue.

[28] See *"Associations, Inner Circle and Outer Circle"*, Editorial, **European Law Review**, No.6, December 1995, p.537.

[29] Michael SUTTON, *"Euro-Maghreb Partnership: A New Form of Association?"*, in: **EUI European Trends** No.3, 1992.

[30] The new Euro-Palestinian Interim Agreement is based on Articles 113 and 130Y with a reference to the objectives of Article 130U. See Erwan LANNON, *"L'accord d'association intérimaire Communauté européenne-OLP : l'institutionnalisation progressive des relations euro-palestiniennes"*, in : **Revue des Affaires Européennes** No.2, 1997, p.169. It must be noticed that some autonomous regulations such as the regulation on "ECIP" ("European Community Investment Partners"), a program assisting the creation of Euro-Mediterranean joint-ventures, are based on provisions of the development cooperation policy (in this particular case the Article 130W).

The Mediterranean Partners will benefit, within the EMEA, from a "co-development" strategy reflecting the evolution of the approach of the EU towards its eastern and southern peripheries. Such a strategy is implemented mainly because of the proximity factor and the level of economic dependence and interdependence between the twenty-seven partners. This concept must also be put in parallel with the will to reach a "sustainable economic and social development" (see Art.42 of the EC-Tunisia Agreement). In other words, it reflects the choice of a long-term strategy based on mutual interests.

2. The Importance Granted to the Mediterranean in the Framework of EU's Trade Policy

After the publication, in March 1995, of a first communication from the European Commission on the issue of free trade areas, the Florence European Council (June 1996) gave the Commission a mandate to report on the evolution of the EU's trade policies and Preferential Agreements and requested the Commission to produce studies on the WTO conformity of new proposed Preferential Agreements involving the EU. Several communications[31] have been issued on this fundamental aspect of the external relations of the Union. In order to understand the importance of the Mediterranean Preferential Agreements within the global European strategy it is therefore essential to examine the place given to the Mediterranean Basin (and the Middle East to some extent) in comparison with other Preferential Agreements.

a) European Union's Preferential Trade Agreements with Third Countries and the WTO

Several points concerning the Euro-Mediterranean relationships are contained in the Communication entitled *"WTO Aspects of EU Preferential Trade Agreements with Third Countries"*. In mentioning the Preferential Agreements concluded with Greece, Turkey, Malta, Cyprus as well as the EFTA countries "and the so-called "first generation" of agreements with countries of North Africa and the Middle East" the Commission insists on the fact that "as well as serving [...] transitional and

---

[31] Communication from the Commission *"Free Trade Areas: An Appraisal"*; 08/03/1995; SEC(95)322 final. Communication from the Commission: *"The Global Challenges of International Trade: A Market Access Strategy for the European Union"*, 15/02/1996. Communication from the Commission *"WTO Aspects of EU Preferential Trade Agreements with Third Countries"* SEC(96)2168 16/01/1997, p.5. Published in: **Agence Europe, Europe documents**, No.2025, February 27, 1997.

developmental goals [...] the EU's Preferential Agreements do serve to open the market by pushing forward a pattern of tariff disarmament in partner countries, helping them to prepare for further multilateral liberalization. This feature of EU's agreements has become more significant in recent years, as the EU has concluded or is negotiating in the context of its new Mediterranean policy new Association Agreement with Mediterranean partners, which include the establishment of free trade areas on a reciprocal basis. The EU has also been encouraging partners to join the WTO if they have not done so."

These are clearly arguments that could be used in a dispute on the compatibility of a EMAA with the multilateral rules. For the Commission, within a clarified Article XXIV framework *(see infra)* the needs of developing countries should be reflected in a "properly focused, flexible framework to allow the smooth and gradual integration of developing countries into the multilateral trading system through regional trade agreements among themselves or with developed partners. But this flexibility, of course, would need to be properly graduated according to the level of development so as not to jeopardize the legitimate trade interests of third Parties."

b) The EU's "Market Access Strategy" and the Challenges of International Trade

The "Market Access Strategy", launched on November 12, 1996, in order to open foreign markets more aggressively for European exports, treats WTO action as one of the main policy options when a dispute arises. Regarding the provisions on the "Multilateral Agenda" the Communication states that "the first means to strengthen the multilateral trade system will consist in ensuring the accession to the WTO of major trading partners which are still not members as well as in encouraging less developed countries to integrate further. The Union can also work with other WTO countries, and in particular those with which it has bilateral agreements, in order to obtain their support for its WTO objectives."[32] The political support of other WTO countries could be very useful indeed for the EU.

In the paragraph devoted to the "Regional integration" the Commission indicates that the market access strategy aims to take account of the increasing moves towards regional integration "in America and Asia"

---

[32] *"The Global Challenge of International Trade: A Market Access Strategy for the European Union"*, COM(96)53 final, 14/02/1996, Point 38.

where "the Community has every interest in strict application of the rules ensuring that greater geographical intensity of trade relations is compatible with the principles of multilateralism (i.e. with our own right of access to the markets of other regional groupings). The Community must therefore play an active role in the WTO's work in this area."[33] As the Mediterranean countries are not mentioned, while they constitute the largest of the EC's trade surplus zone, means clearly that they are fully part of a "Pan-Euro-Mediterranean" strategy that will lead, in 2010, to the creation of a regional economic integration capable of challenging other RI located in Asia and on the American continent.

c) EC Support for Regional Economic Integration Efforts among Developing Countries

The third communication of the Commission that needs to be briefly examined deals with "European Community support for regional economic integration efforts among developing countries"[34]. It reflects the aim of the EU to promote open regionalism as "the European Union is a "natural" supporter of regional initiatives"[35]. Regional integration is considered as not being an "end in itself" but "part of a strategy to coordinate economic policies and to improve the prospect for sustainable development". The compatibility between the new multilateral rules and "outward oriented regional integration" is also reaffirmed.

Regarding the Euro-Mediterranean relationships in particular, it is useful to examine the Appendix A of the Communication referring to an "overview of EC support for regional integration among developing countries" as the second point (b) is devoted to the "Mediterranean Basin (including the Middle East)". The first thing that needs to be remarked upon is the association of the Middle East and the Mediterranean. Within a global approach the five members[36] of the Gulf Cooperation Council (GCC), the twelve MNMCs, and even "non-Arab Muslim states in Western/Central Asia" are apprehended via a single framework. Three regional organizations are mentioned:

---

[33] *"The Global Challenge of International Trade: A Market Access Strategy for the European Union"*, COM(96)53 final, 14/02/1996, Point 39.

[34] *"Communication from the Commission "European Community Support for Regional Economic Integration Efforts among Developing Countries"*, COM(95)219 final, 16/06/1995.

[35] COM(95)219 final, p.6.

[36] Saudi Arabia, Bahrain, Kuwait, Qatar, United Arab Emirates.

- The Economic Cooperation Organization (ECO)[37]
- The Arab Maghreb Union (AMU)[38]
- The Gulf Cooperation Council (GCC)[39]

One should stress that the conformity of such regional intra-Mediterranean trade arrangements with WTO substantive rules will be essential.

After the examination of the approach of the Community with regard to the preferential agreements, one should now describe the present status and situation of the Mediterranean Non-Member Countries with regard to the World Trade Organization.

B. The Mediterranean Non-Member Countries and the World Trade Organization

Two points must be highlighted: the issue of the status of the Mediterranean Non-Member Countries in the new multilateral trade system and the question of the different levels of development of the MNMCs.

1. The Status of the Mediterranean Non-Member Countries in the New Multilateral Trade System

Concerning membership and accession of the MNMCs to the WTO it must be noticed that, on one hand, Cyprus, Egypt, Israel, Malta, Morocco, Tunisia and Turkey are part of the 131 Members of the WTO (April 1997) and that Algeria and Jordan have begun preliminary talks within the working groups dealing with the accessions. On the other hand, Syria and the Palestinian Territories are not Members of the WTO and, as far as we know, have not yet submitted their applications.

The countries requesting their application to the WTO will present a Communication to the Director-General of the WTO which will be distributed to all WTO Members. The WTO General Council will then analyse this communication and decide whether a working group needs to be established.

---

[37] Afghanistan, Azerbaijan, Islamic Republic of Iran, Kazakhastan, Kyrgystan, Pakistan, Tajikistan, Turkmenistan, Turkey, Uzbekistan.

[38] See Mohamed BEN EL HASSAN EL ALAOUI, **La coopération entre l'Union européenne et les pays du Maghreb**, Nathan, Paris, 1994, 237 p.

[39] See *"The Middle-East and Europe: An Integrated Communities Approach"*, edited by Gerd NONNEMAN, Federal Trust for Education and Research, London, February 1992.

Mr Bakhti Belaib, the Algerian Minister for Trade, remarked at the Singapore Conference that "paradoxically, the rapid and encouraging success of the Organization [the WTO], its indisputable attraction and the great importance of the issues it addresses, now seem to be complicating the task of new applicants for membership. Consequently, consideration should be given to simplifying the accession procedures for all applicants, mainly developing countries, so that their integration into world trade does not interfere with their efforts to solve their domestic economic problems."[40]

2. The Question of the Different Levels of Development of the MNMCs: The Need of a Gradual and Differentiated Approach

One could ask which category — developing countries, least developed countries, developed countries… — the MNMCs belongs to. The problem is that the present status of developing countries is decided on the basis of "self-selection"[41]. In fact all of the above-mentioned "categories" are applying to the MNMCs. The West Bank and the Gaza Strip should belong to the "least developed countries"[42], most of the Arab countries and Turkey seem to belong to the "developing countries" category, while Israel is generally considered as a developed country by the EC but perceived as a developing country in some spheres covered by the GATT such as in the Public Procurement Code[43]. It should be noticed that Egypt, Morocco and Tunisia are also included on the WTO list of net food importing developing countries[44].

The question of the level of development of the MNMCs is of importance regarding the GATT/WTO rules as they are conferring differential and more favourable treatment for (least) developed countries. In the Declaration adopted at the first Ministerial Conference of the WTO (held

---

[40] World Trade WT/MIN(96)/ST/131, December 12, 1996, Organization (96-5302) Ministerial Conference, Singapore, December 9-13, 1996, Algeria Statement Mr. Bakhti BELAIB, Minister for Trade.

[41] See Communication from the Commission SEC(96)2168, 16/01/1997, p.5.

[42] West Bank and Gaza are not included in the UN list of least developed countries. See COM(97)156 final *"Improving Market Access for Least Developed Countries"*, 16/04/1997.

[43] See Moshe HIRSCH, Eyal INBAR & Tal SADEH, **The Future Relations between Israel and the European Communities: some Alternatives**, Bursi, Tel Aviv, 1996, p.46.

[44] World Trade G/AG/5/Rev.2; March 17, 1997 Organization (97-1099).

in Singapore on December 9-13, 1996) the WTO Members have reaffirmed that "The integration of developing countries in the multilateral trading system is important for their economic development and for global trade expansion." In this connection, they recall "that the WTO Agreement embodies provisions conferring differential and more favourable treatment for developing countries, including special attention to the particular situation of least-developed countries. [...]" and agreed "to recommendations relative to the decision [they] took at Marrakesh concerning the possible negative effects of the agricultural reform programme on least-developed and net food-importing developing countries."[45]

At the same conference, the Egyptian Minister of Trade and Supply drew the attention of the participants to the fact that, after the signature of the Final Act embodying the Agreements of the Uruguay Round, "most of the developing countries including Egypt were exerting utmost effort to implement all their obligations derived from those agreements. In the process of implementation, Egypt as well as other developing countries encountered difficulties [...]." Taking the example of the Ministerial Decision on measures concerning the possible negative effects of the reform programme on least developed countries and net food-importing developing countries, the Egyptian Minister declared: "we spent two years debating and deliberating on how to implement the provisions of the said Ministerial Decision with limited success, in addition to the obstacles that were put ahead to prove the real reason behind the increase in the prices of imported food."[46]

C. The Conformity of the Euro-Mediterranean Association Agreements with the Multilateral Rules on Regional Integration

The Community must ensure that the Euro-Mediterranean Agreements are **fully consistent** with GATT/WTO rules. This is emphasised by the

---

[45] Point 13 of the Declaration of Singapore.

[46] World Trade WT/MIN(96)/ST/73, December 11, 1996, Organization (96-5248) - Ministerial Conference Singapore, December 9-13, 1996 - Egypt - Statement by H.E. Dr. Ahmed GOUELI, Minister of Trade and Supply.

new provisions on dispute settlement of the WTO[47], especially the fact that the adoption of a panel report can no longer be blocked by a veto, and by the recent developments concerning the well known *Banana*[48] and *Hormone*[49] Panels. One should therefore insist on the fact that the issue of the conformity of the provisions of the new generation of agreements with the GATT/WTO is not a theoretical issue.

Very often Parties to the WTO have succeeded in resolving disputes at the consultation stage rather than engaging the full weight of the panel and appeal processes but the later stages of the procedure have first to be tested in order to appreciate the degree of constraint in the new WTO.

An overview of the state-of-play of WTO Disputes was prepared by the WTO Secretariat in July 1997. Eighty-eight Consultation Requests, sixty-three Distinct Matters, twelve Active Cases, five Completed Cases and seventeen Settled or Inactive Cases have been identified. Regarding

---

[47] Point 12 of the Understanding on the interpretation of Article XXI of the GATT 1994: "The provisions of Articles XXII and XXIII of the GATT 1994 as elaborated and applied by the Understanding on Rules and Procedures Governing the Settlement of Disputes may be invoked with respect to **any matters arising from the application of those provisions of Article XXIV relating to customs unions, free trade areas or interim agreements leading to the formation of a customs union or free trade area**."

[48] European Communities - Regime for the Importation, Sale and Distribution of Bananas, complaints by Ecuador, Guatemala, Honduras, Mexico and the United States (WT/DS27). The complainants in this case other than Ecuador had requested consultations with the EC on the same issue on September 28, 1995 (WT/DS16). After Ecuador's accession to the WTO, the current complainants again requested consultations with the EC on February 5, 1996. The complainants allege that the EC's regime for importation, sale and distribution of bananas is inconsistent with GATT Articles I, II, III, X, XI and XIII as well as provisions of the Import Licensing Agreement, the Agreement on Agriculture, the TRIMs Agreement and the GATS. A panel was established at the DSB meeting on May 8, 1996. The Panel Report is being circulated as an unrestricted document from May 22, 1997 pursuant to the Procedures for the Circulation of WTO Documents (WT/L/160/Rev.1). On June 11, 1997, the European Communities notified its intention to appeal certain issues of law and legal interpretations developed by the panel.

[49] Brussels 1/07/1997 European Communities - Measures Affecting Livestock and Meat (Hormones), complaint by Canada (WT/DS48). On June 28, 1996, Canada requested consultations with the European Communities regarding the importation of livestock and meat from livestock that have been treated with certain substances having a hormonal action under GATT Article XXII and the corresponding provisions in the SPS, TBT and Agriculture Agreements. Violations SPS Articles 2, 3 and 5; GATT Articles III or XI; TBT Article 2; and Agriculture Article 4 are alleged. The Canadian claim is essentially the same as the US claim (WT/DS26), for which a panel was established earlier. The DSB established a panel on October 16, 1996. The panel found that the EU ban of such imports was not in conformity with a number of provisions of the Agreement on Sanitary and Phytosanitary Measures. See *"Commission wants to appeal against WTO Hormone Panel Conclusions"*, IP/97/590.

the MNMCs it must be noticed that Turkey appears in one active panel[50] and in three pending consultations[51].

The WTO Members have reaffirmed in Singapore "the primacy of the multilateral trading system, which includes a framework for the development of regional trade agreements", and renewed their "commitment to ensure that regional trade agreements are complementary to it and consistent with its rules." In this regard, they have also welcomed the "establishment and endorse the work of the new Committee on Regional Trade Agreements."[52] (see *infra*).

All of the Euro-Mediterranean Agreements contain (or will contain) a clause assuring their consistency with the legal requirements of the multilateral system. Article 6 of the EC-Tunisian and EC-Moroccan Agreement state that: "The Community and Tunisia [or Morocco] shall gradually establish a free trade area over a transitional period lasting a maximum of twelve years starting from the entry into force of this agreement in accordance with the provisions of this agreement and in conformity with those of the General Agreement on Tariffs and Trade 1994 and the other multilateral agreements on trade in goods annexed to the

---

[50] Turkey - Taxation of Foreign Film Revenues, complaint by the United States (WT/DS43). This request for consultations, dated June 12, 1996, concerns Turkey's taxation of revenues generated from the showing of foreign films. Violation of GATT Article III is alleged. On January 9, 1997, the United States requested the establishment of a panel. At its meeting on February 25, 1997, the DSB established a panel. Canada reserved its third Party rights to the dispute.

[51] 1) Turkey - Restrictions on Imports of Textile and Clothing Products, complaint by Hong Kong (WT/DS29). This request, dated February 12, 1996, claims that Turkey's quantitative restrictions on imports of textile and clothing products are in violation of GATT Articles XI and XIII. The background to this dispute is a recently concluded customs union agreement between Turkey and the European Communities. Hong Kong claims that GATT Article XXIV does not entitle Turkey to impose new quantitative restrictions in the present case. 2) Turkey - Restrictions on Imports of Textile and Clothing Products, complaint by India (WT/DS34). This request, dated March 21, 1996, claims that Turkey's imposition of quantitative restrictions on imports of a broad range of textile and clothing products is inconsistent with GATT Articles XI and XIII, as well as ATC Article 2. Earlier, India had requested to be joined in the consultations between Hong Kong and Turkey on the same subject matter (WT/DS29). See above and below. 3) Turkey - Restrictions on Imports of Textile and Clothing Products, complaint by Thailand (WT/DS47). This request for consultations, dated June 20, 1996, concerns Turkey's imposition of quantitative restrictions on imports of textile and clothing products from Thailand. Violations of GATT Articles I, II, XI and XIII as well as Article 2 of the Textiles Agreement are alleged. Earlier, Hong Kong (WT/DS29) and India (WT/DS34) separately requested consultations with Turkey on the same measure.

[52] Singapore Declaration: *"Regional Agreements"*, point 7.

Agreement establishing the WTO."[53] The inclusion of such a provision[54] is now required by the legal principle implying that: "Each Member shall ensure the conformity of its laws, regulations and administrative procedures with its obligations as provided in the annexed agreements."[55]

In order to examine the issue of the conformity of the Euro-Mediterranean Association Agreements (EMAAs) with the GATT one should ask at least the following questions:

1. Are other WTO Members notified of the details of the new agreements?

2. Do the EMAAs raise trade barriers to the trade of other WTO Members?

3. Do the EMAAs cover "substantially all trade" between partners?

4. Do the EMAAs include a plan and schedule for the formation of the free trade area and will the integration be completed within a "reasonable length of time"?

5. Do the EMAAs cover services and are these provisions consistent with Article V of the GATS Agreement?

It should be stressed that a lot of uncertainties remain concerning the reinforced dispute settlement procedure and regarding the interpretation of the different provisions of the GATT concerning regional integration.

The second point that needs to be mentioned is that none of the Euro-Mediterranean Association Agreements already signed (Tunisia, Israel, Morocco) have been yet ratified (see *infra* the specific case of the agreement concluded with the PLO) and that five of them must be concluded (Algeria, Egypt, Jordan, Lebanon, Syria).

In order to try to answer the above questions, one should refer to the provisions of the understandings on rules and procedures governing the settlement of disputes and on the interpretation of Article XXIV. We will not describe in details the different procedures one should therefore refer

---

[53] Note that in the preamble of EC-Tunisia, for example, it is said: "Considering the commitment of both the Community and Tunisia to free trade, in compliance with the rights and obligations arising out of the General Agreement on Tariffs and Trade (GATT)."

[54] In must be noted that the inclusion of such a provision was requested by the European Community during negotiations of the Uruguay Round.

[55] Article XVI:4 of the Marrakesh Agreement establishing the World Trade Organization.

to the detailed analyses of the paper of Theophanis Christofourou, Serge Devos, and Pierre Pescatore.

1. The Notification and Examination of the Euro-Mediterranean Association Agreements (EMAA)

Free Trade Agreements constitute an exception to the MFN but they are permitted under certain conditions. First of all, they must be notified to other WTO Members and then be examined by the Committee on Regional Trade Agreements.

a) The Notification of the Euro-Mediterranean Association Agreements

According to Article XXIV:7(a) of the GATT: "Any Contracting Party deciding to enter into a customs union or free trade area, or an interim agreement leading to the formation of such a union or area, shall promptly notify the Contracting Parties and shall make available to them such information regarding the proposed union or area as will enable them to make such reports and recommendations to Contracting Parties as they may deem appropriate."

However it does not define precisely when such a notification should intervene. In practice, notification has generally occurred after the agreements have entered into force. According to the "Brittan Memorandum" (published in February 1997[56]), the EU "will be notifying the new-generation Mediterranean agreements shortly". It is however obvious that negotiations, or even preliminary discussions, are still underway with Algeria, Egypt, Lebanon and Syria and that the GATT notification procedure is time-consuming. WTO Members have already regretted that compliance with notification requirements has not been fully satisfactory and have suggested that those members which have not submitted notifications in a timely manner, or whose notifications are not complete, should renew their efforts[57].

It must be noticed that the Commission has informed the Members of the WTO that "the European Community has concluded the Euro-Mediterranean Interim Association Agreement on Trade and Cooperation between the European Community and the Palestine Liberation Organization for the benefit of the Palestinian Authority of the West Bank and Gaza Strip" forming "a free trade area between the two Parties within

---

[56] **Agence Europe/Documents** No.2025, 27/02/1997.

[57] Singapore Declaration: Notifications and Legislation, point 11.

the sense of Article XXIV of GATT 1994."[58] This interim agreement entered into force on July 1st, 1997[59].

It is the first notification of an agreement concluded under the framework of the Euro-Mediterranean Partnership. The case of the Euro-Palestinian Accord, even if the Palestinians are fully integrated into the overall partnership, however differs from the new generation of association agreements as it is not a mixed agreement (the political dialogue is, for example, implemented on the basis of a separate declaration) and therefore does not require ratification of the fifteen Member States.

b) The Examination of the EMAA by the Committee on Regional Trade Agreements (CRTA)

After the notification and according to the provisions on *"Review of Customs Unions and Free Trade Areas"* included in the understanding on the interpretation of Article XXIV of the GATT 1994, "all notifications made under Article XXIV:7(a) shall be examined by a Working Party in the light of the relevant provisions of the GATT 1994 and of Paragraph 1 of this Understanding. The Working Party shall submit a report to the Council for Trade in Goods on its findings in this regard. The Council for Trade in Goods may make such recommendations to Members as it deems appropriate."

This task has been given to the "Committee on Regional Trade Agreements" (CRTA), from January 1996. The CRTA replaces the system of *ad hoc* GATT Working Parties which have hitherto conducted such examinations. The examination process is aimed at considering the extent to which the notified agreement is in conformity with WTO rules, and to make recommendations aimed at improving that conformity. The examination deals essentially with the coverage requirement *(*see *infra)* and it must be stressed that such an examination is different than the much more constraining dispute settlement procedure.

In the examination process, the main objective of the EU and its Mediterranean Partners will be to acquire political support from other WTO Members to obtain a positive judgement in order to avoid a panel.

---

[58] See World Trade Organization, WT/REG43/N/1, June 30, 1997, (97-2665). Committee on Regional Trade Agreements.

[59] See the Decision of the Council (97/430/EC, 02/07/1997) on the conclusion of the *"Euro Mediterranean Interim Association Agreement on Trade and Cooperation between the European Community and the Palestine Liberation Organization for the Benefit of the Palestinian Authority of the West Bank and Gaza Strip"*, **OJ** L 187, 16/07/1997, p.136.

2. The "Not-on-the-whole-higher-or-more-restrictive"[60] Requirement

It is expected that the MNMCs will not only dismantle tariffs for products originating from the EU but will, to a certain extent, reduce the level of tariffs applicable to other third countries in order to avoid excessive distortions and/or because of political pressure. There is however no guarantee of such a trade-creating effect. Furthermore, it will be quite difficult to evaluate precisely the impact of new "regulations of commerce" (technical standards, rules of origins...) adopted within the framework of the new generation of Euro-Mediterranean Agreements.

It is however obvious that, if the objectives of the Euro-Mediterranean Agreements and those of the Barcelona Declaration are reached (especially the subregional integration of the zone via the cumulation of rules of origin[61]), the creation of a vast Euro-Mediterranean Economic Area (EMEA) will have an important impact on the whole area and on third countries and especially on countries already benefiting from bilateral or regional agreements with the twenty-seven founding members of the Euro-Mediterranean Partnership. The question is whether, in the medium term, this EMEA will be more "trade-creating" than "trade-diverting".

3. The Coverage (or "Substantially All Trade"[62]) Requirement: How to Conciliate the Objectives of the Common Agricultural Policy with the GATT/WTO Rules

As underlined by the European Commission "within GATT Working Parties on FTA's various quantitative thresholds have been mentioned

---

[60] According to Article XXIV:5(b) of the GATT "with respect to a free trade area, or an interim agreement leading to the formation of a free trade area, the duties and other regulations of commerce maintained in each of the constituent territories and applicable at the formation of such free trade area or the adoption of such interim agreement to the trade of Contracting Parties not included in such area or not Parties to such agreement shall not be higher or more restrictive than the corresponding duties and other regulations of commerce existing in the same constituent territories prior to the formation of the free trade area, or interim agreement, as the case may be."

[61] See the paper by Alfred Tovias.

[62] Article XXIV:8(b): "A free trade area shall be understood to mean a group of two or more customs territories in which the duties and other restrictive regulations of commerce (except, where necessary, those permitted under Articles XI, XII, XIII, XIV, XV and XX) are eliminated on substantially all the trade between the constituent territories in products originating in such territories."

ranging from 80 to 90 percent[63] of trade between the partners, but the qualitative aspect of the notion has also been stressed; the exclusion of a whole sector, such as agriculture, has been deplored."[64] The results of the Uruguay Round have furthermore reduced the freedom of action of the Community with regard to the coverage of a preferential agreement. The most important issue that has delayed the signature of the first Euro-Mediterranean Association Agreements (Tunisia, Israel, Morocco) was the negotiation of provisions on the achievement of a greater liberalization of trade in agricultural products.

At a more general level the question should be: are the objectives of the CAP (and more particularly their impact on the external relations of the Community) compatible with the GATT rules on regional integration? The examination of the European Agreements (that will be notified and examined before the EMAAs[65]) will be a good test in order to evaluate this compatibility as the agricultural sector remains of great importance in the relationships of the EU with the Central and Eastern European Countries[66].

The situation is however different for the Euro-Mediterranean Agreements concluded, or to be concluded, with the MNMCs of the eastern and southern shores of the Mediterranean Basin as there is no accession perspective for them, contrary to the East European countries. According to the Communication of the European Commission on *"Strengthening the Mediterranean Policy of the European Union: establishing a Euro-Mediterranean Partnership"*, the Euro-Mediterranean Free trade Area will provide for:

- "reciprocal **free trade in all manufactured goods** between the enlarging Union and most Mediterranean countries;
- **preferential and reciprocal access for agricultural goods of interest to both Parties;**

---

[63] The report of the sub-group of the Committee on the "European Economic Community" which examined the consistency of the ECC Treaty provisions with the Article XXIV for the association of overseas countries stated: "a free trade area should be considered has having been achieved for substantially all the trade when the volume of liberalized trade reached 80 percent of total trade." L/778, adopted on November 29, 1957, 6S/70, 99. Para.30. See also the report of the Working Party on "the European Free Trade Area" where the percentage of the trade covered was not considered to be the only factor to be taken into account. L/1235, adopted on June 4, 1960, 9S/70, 83-85, paras 48-49, 51, 54.

[64] *"Free Trade Areas: An Appraisal"*; 08/03/1995; SEC(95)322 final, Annex 1, p.11.

[65] Communication from the Commission *"WTO Aspects of EU Preferential Trade Agreements with Third Countries"* SEC(96)2168, 16/01/1997, p.5. Published in **Agence Europe, Europe Documents**, No.2025, February 27, 1997.

[66] See the paper of Marc Maresceau in this book.

- and free trade among Mediterranean countries themselves."[67]

A brief, and non-exhaustive, examination (see the table below) shows that the agreements already signed are implementing a variable geometry approach depending on the third Mediterranean country situation (level of development, trade structure...), the degree of sensibility of particular products...

"Euro-Mediterranean Agreement establishing an Association between the European Communities and their Member States, of the one part, and the Republic of Tunisia, of the other part"
i) The Community and Tunisia shall gradually establish a FTA over a transitional period lasting a maximum of twelve years (Art.6).
- With regard to import arrangements into Tunisia, it is laid down that customs duties and charges having equivalent effect will be abolished in the case of 60% of imports of Community industrial products over a 5-year period. For the other products, the process of elimination will be completed over a transitional period lasting not more than twelve years.
- Remaining restrictions on certain **textile products** are the subject of a separate Regulation outside the terms of the Agreement.
ii) Regarding **agricultural products**, the preferential arrangements currently applied by the Community are confirmed and will be further improved. The Agreement contains liberalization measures to be applied over an initial 5-year stage on Tunisian exports to the Community. In the case of **olive oil**, the existing arrangements whereby the customs duty is reduced within the limits of a quota of 46,000 t per marketing year have been extended. It was also agreed that the Parties would review the situation during the second half of 1999.
- The Agreement contains a clause under which the Parties undertake to examine the agricultural trade situation from January 1st, 2000 to establish new reciprocal concessions. (Art.18).
iii) With regard to **services**, the parties have confirmed the obligation entered into under the GATS and have agreed to negotiate longer term preferential arrangements.
iv) Other provisions of interest:
- **Right of establishment**: the Agreement provides for national treatment to be granted under certain conditions to companies of either party with a commercial presence in the territory of the other. This right applies in principle to all sectors, unless stated to the contrary or in special provisions.
- The gradual mutual and extensive opening-up of the **services market** is also advocated and a revision clause is included to make provision for any amendment of these provisions, in the light, particularly, of the conclusions of the Uruguay Round negotiations.

---

[67] COM(94)427 final, 19/10/1994, p.10.

> **"Euro-Mediterranean Agreement establishing an Association between the European Communities and their Member States, of the one part, and the State of Israel, on the other part"**

i) The **Free trade area** between the Community and Israel shall be reinforced according to the modalities set out in this agreement and in conformity with the General Agreement on Tariffs and Trade (Art.6)

ii) Concerning **agricultural products**, preferential treatment is extended and concessions have been made by the Community on cut flowers and citrus fruits. The Community's agricultural exports to Israel will benefit from a series of concessions designed to maintain existing patterns of trade. The goal is progressively to achieve a "greater liberalization" of trade in agricultural products. In the case of processed agricultural products, Israel will apply trade arrangements similar to those applied by the Community.

iii) With regard to **services**, the Parties have confirmed the obligation entered into under the GATS and have agreed to negotiate longer term arrangements.

iv) Other provisions of interest:

- **public procurement**: the Parties have agreed to begin negotiations with a view to achieving the greatest possible degree of effective reciprocal liberalisation.

- with regard to **competition and public aid**, the substance of the 1975 Agreement has been maintained, and extended to cover services.

v) **Interim Agreement**

The Commission has adopted (on 29/11/1995) a proposal for a Council decision on the conclusion by the European Community of an Interim Agreement on trade-related matters between the European Community and the European Coal and Steel Community on the one part and the State of Israel on the other part. (See IP/95/1302).

> **"Euro-Mediterranean Interim Association Agreement on Trade and
> Cooperation between the European Community and the Palestine Liberation
> Organization for the Benefit of the Palestine Authority of the West Bank
> and Gaza Strip"**

i) The Community and the Palestinian Authority shall establish progressively a **free trade area** over a transitional period, not extending beyond December 31st, 2001, "according to the modalities set out in this Title and in conformity with the provisions of the General Agreement on Tariffs and Trade of 1994 and of the other multilateral agreements on trade in goods annexed to the agreement establishing the World Trade Organization (WTO)." (Article 3).

ii) That liberalisation will supplement and formalise the existing trade arrangements in the form of autonomous concessions in the agricultural and industrial sectors granted by the Community in the past. The Parties to the Agreement will begin a review of the preferential arrangements for agricultural products in two years, starting on January 1st, 1999 (Article 14).

iii) Other provisions of interest

- **Movement of capital**:

    "1. With regard to transactions on the capital account of balance of payments, the Parties undertake to impose no restrictions on the movement of capital relating to direct investments in the West Bank and the Gaza Strip in companies formed in accordance with current laws, nor on the liquidation and repatriation of the yield from such investments, or any profit stemming there from.

    2. The Parties shall consult each other with a view to facilitating the movement of capital between the Community and the West Bank and the Gaza Strip". (Article 28)

- **Competition**

    "1. The following are incompatible with the proper functioning of this Agreement, insofar as they may affect trade between the Community and the Palestinian Authority:

(i) all agreements between undertakings, decisions by associations of undertakings and concerted practices between undertakings which have as their object or effect the prevention, restriction or distortion of competition;

(ii) abuse by one or more undertakings of a dominant position in the territories of the Community or the West Bank and the Gaza Strip as a whole or in a substantial part thereof;

(iii) any public aid which distorts or threatens to distort competition by favouring certain undertakings or the production of certain goods." (Article 30)

- **Public procurement**:

    "The Parties agree on the objective of reciprocal and gradual liberalization of public procurement contracts." (Article 34)

iv) A separate Joint Statement by the European Union and the Palestine Liberation Organisation has been issued on **Political Dialogue.**

Agricultural products are clearly, at least until the year 2000 (see *infra*), excluded from the benefit of total free trade and subjected to a "reciprocal" and "gradual" liberalization on a case-by-case analysis. The non-tariff discrimination instruments of the CAP (tariffs calendars, references quantities...) will continue to play their role (see for example the Annexes 1, 2 and 3 of the EC-Tunisia Agreement). There is indeed an ambiguity: on one hand there is no explicit commitment to complete full liberalization of agricultural trade within the twelve years transitional period and, on the other hand, the objective of establishing a FTA is not **formally** limited to industrial products. It must be also noticed that regarding processed agricultural goods, which are submitted to specific provisions, each Party may retain custom duties on agricultural components (see Art.10 of EC-Tunisia Agreement).

The issue of the compatibility of the Euro-Mediterranean Free Trade Area(s) with the GATT/WTO rules, and more particularly the temporary exclusion of agricultural products from the benefit of free trade, has been mentioned by the French National Assembly in a report published in 1996[68]. The report stresses that there is a danger that, one day, a third country might raise the issue of the compatibility of the preferential Association Agreements concluded with the East European and third Mediterranean countries with the WTO rules. Regarding the above mentioned countries, the report also notes the need for a consistent policy towards those two areas[69].

4. Do the Agreements Include a "Plan and Schedule" for the Formation of the Free Trade Area within a "Reasonable Length of Time"?

Article XXIV of GATT requires that a customs union or a free trade area eliminate substantially all duties and other restrictive regulations of commerce within reasonable time. According to the Understanding on the Interpretation of Article XXIV of the GATT 1994 "the "reasonable length of time" referred to in Article XXIV:5(c) should exceed ten years

---

[68] See *"L'OMC : une entreprise encore inachevée"*, Rapport de l'Assemblée Nationale No.2948, 1996, Rapporteur P. HOGUET, p.63.

[69] See *"L'OMC : une entreprise encore inachevée"*, Rapport de l'Assemblée Nationale No.2948, 1996, Rapporteur P. HOGUET, p.135. The report also cite a document submitted by the Italian Presidency on May 1996 to the Agricultural Council (Informal meeting devoted to "the question of FTA's and their effects on Community agriculture" - May 5-7, 1996 - Otranto) declaring that "Free Trade Area's a Real Threat for the European Agriculture".

only in exceptional cases. In cases where members believe that ten years would be insufficient they shall provide a full explanation to the Council for Trade in Goods of the need for a longer period." As the EMAAs concluded with Morocco and Tunisia "shall gradually establish a free trade area over a transitional period lasting a maximum of twelve years" (Art.6 of the EC-Tunisia Agreement) they might need a derogation and Parties should therefore provide a full explanation. But, as with many areas of the Article XXIV, there is as yet however no clear guidance on how and on what basis the "full explanation" should be provided.

It must be stressed that this general provision ("a transitional period lasting a maximum of twelve years") must be appreciated with regard to the type of products concerned. As already mentioned, the MNMCs of the southern and eastern shores of the Mediterranean Basin (with the exception of Israel and the Palestinian entity[70]) will gradually eliminate trade barriers affecting the Community's **industrial** exports over a period lasting no more than twelve years (and as MNMCs already benefit from a free market access to the Community for their industrial products it will therefore be a **unilateral** trade barriers dismantling).

Regarding the provisions on **agricultural products** the situation is somewhat different. The agreement concluded with Tunisia states that:

1. After January 1st, 2000 the Community and Tunisia shall assess the situation with a view to adopting the liberalization measures to be applied by the Community and Tunisia with effect from January 2001 in accordance with the objective set out in Article 16[71].
2. Notwithstanding the provisions of the preceding paragraph and taking account of the volume of trade in agricultural products between the two Parties and the particular sensitivity of such products, the Community and Tunisia shall examine, product by product on a reciprocal basis, the possibilities of granting each other further concessions.

The schedule and the extent of the dismantling of trade barriers for agricultural products after 2000 remains undefined and the provision is indeed very vague.

---

[70] Paradoxically, the agreement signed with the PLO schedules an industrial free trade zone for the year 2001. It would be the second industrial FTA (after the EEC-Israel industrial FTA) to be completed with a country of the southern and eastern shores of the Mediterranean Basin.

[71] Article 16: "The Community and Tunisia shall gradually implement greater liberalization of their reciprocal trade in agricultural and fishery products."

If the status of Morocco and Tunisia (developing countries) and the objectives of the agreements (such as the full integration of the MNMCs economies in the world economy in compliance with the GATT rules) give the Parties pertinent arguments for a full explanation of the reasons for the implementation of a transitional period exceeding ten years for industrial products, the uncertainties of the "plan and schedule" for the dismantling of trade barriers for agricultural products may generate many more problems.

5. Do the Agreements Cover Services and are these Provisions Consistent with Article V of the GATS Agreement?

As the Euro-Mediterranean Agreements are covering services they must comply with Article V of the GATS Agreement. Article 31 of the provisions on "right of establishment and services" of the EC-Tunisian Agreement states that:

> 1. The Parties agree to widen the scope of the agreement to cover the right of establishment of one Party's firms on the territory of the other and liberalization of the provisions of services by one Party's firm to consumers of services in the other.
> 2. The Association Council will make recommendations for achieving the objective described in Paragraph 1. In making such recommendations, the Association Council will take account of past experience of implementation of reciprocal most-favoured-nation treatment and of obligations of each Party under the General Agreement on trade in services annexed to the Agreement establishing the WTO, hereinafter to as the "GATS", particularly Article V of the latest.

First of all it must be noticed that the right of establishment is limited to "firms" and not extended to workers. The will of a compliance with multilateral rules is clearly affirmed but, again, the provisions are still quite vague. Article 32 of the EC-Tunisian Agreement also states that:

> 1. At the outset, each of the Parties shall reaffirm its obligation under the GATS, particularly the obligation to grant reciprocal most-favoured-nation treatment in services sectors covered by that obligation.
> 2. In accordance with the GATS, such treatment shall not apply to:
> (a) advantages granted by either Party under the terms of an agreement of the type defined in Article V of the GATS or to measures taken on the basis of such an agreement;

(b) other advantages granted in accordance with the list of exemptions from most-favoured-nation treatment annexed by either Party to the GATS.

The essential aim of the insertion of provisions on services in the EMAAs seems to have been essentially the necessity to put this area on the agenda for further negotiations within the framework of the new generation of accords and to guarantee the conformity of the coming liberalization with GATS rules.

Conclusion

Is the Euro-Mediterranean Economic Area a form of "open regionalism" compatible with the multilateral rules? There are in fact two different approaches. The first is based on the assumption that the Euro-Mediterranean FTA will be consistent with the legal requirements of the multilateral system. The fact that most MNMCs are developing countries, that the Euro-Mediterranean Association Agreements are implementing a gradual liberalization in respect of most economic sectors on the basis of the market economy and are including a conformity clause to GATT/WTO rules, points towards the gradual convergence of regional groupings on the basis of the principles agreed in the multilateral framework of the GATT/WTO. The security and political goals of the regional integration will, for sure, be taken into account given the strategic importance of the region.

The second approach is based on a strict interpretation of GATT/WTO rules. One could stress that there is no guaranty that the gradual (and incomplete) elimination of internal barriers to trade scheduled within the future Euro-Mediterranean Free Trade Zone will be, at the same time, implemented with a lowering of barriers towards nonmembers. Furthermore, the temporary exclusion of agricultural products from free trade and the uncertainties remaining concerning the "gradual implementation of a greater liberalization of reciprocal trade in agricultural and fishery products"[72] might be highlighted by other WTO Members.

As stated in the Communication of the Commission on the *"European Union's preferential trade agreements with third countries and the WTO"*: "the EU [...] has an interest in further reinforcing the position of its own agreements in the WTO. There is an unwelcome level of

---

[72] Article 16 of the EC-Tunisia Agreement.

uncertainty in GATT rules which do not mesh well with the binding nature of the Dispute Settlement System. Therefore, while we need to be aware of the need to avoid putting at risk our own free trade agreements, clearer GATT rules would help both the EU's market access interests and its interest in greater certainty for its own agreements." The search for a conciliation process will undoubtedly be the best solution for the twenty-seven Euro-Mediterranean Partners. There is however no guaranty of such an "happy end" of the examination of the new generation of Association Agreements.

The 1985 Panel Report on *"EC-Tariff-Treatment on Imports of citrus products for certain countries in the Mediterranean Region"*, which has not been adopted, has already demonstrated that the compatibility of the preferential agricultural regime implemented within the framework of the Mediterranean policy with the multilateral rules is not certain. Indeed, during discussions in the Council concerning the establishment of the Panel one delegation noted that in the reports of the Working Parties some members have held the view that, concerning the Agreements with Algeria, Cyprus, Israel, Malta, Morocco and Tunisia, "it was doubtful that these agreements were entirely compatible with the requirements of the general agreement."[73] Moreover, the *Citrus* Panel Report noted "that at the time of the examination of the agreements entered into by the Community with certain Mediterranean countries, there was no consensus among Contracting Parties as to the conformity of the agreements with Article XXIV:5..."[74] The Panel "considered that, in effect, the Contracting Parties has withheld the judgement at that time as to the conformity of the agreements with the requirements of Article XXIV. The agreements had not been disapproved, nor had they been approved. The Panel found therefore that the question of the conformity of the agreements with the requirement of Article XXIV and their legal status[75] remained open."[76]

Regarding the new generation of Euro-Mediterranean Agreements it is clear that their conformity to the new obligations undertaken by the Community in the GATT/WTO could be contested by other WTO Members in the present context of increasing world competition. It is important to remember that the WTO process is political as well as rule-based.

---

[73] C/M/162, 15, See *Guide to GATT Law and Practice*, (6th ed.), Geneva, 1994, p.761.
[74] L5776/ (unadopted, dated February 7, 1985), § 4.6.
[75] MNMCs were not Contracting Parties to the GATT.
[76] L5776/ (unadopted, dated February 7, 1985), § 4.10.

Therefore, the Community and its twelve Mediterranean Partners should define a consistent strategy aiming to prepare arguments and political alliances that could be used in the case of a new Panel Report that, after the Uruguay Round, could in theory no longer be blocked.

Bibliography

Gilbert BENHAYOUN, Maurice CATIN & Henri REGHNAULT, **L'Europe et la Méditerranée : Intégration économique et libre échange**, Collection Emploi, Industrie et Territoire, L'Harmattan, Paris, 1997.

Isabelle BENSIDOUN & Agnès CHEVALLIER, **Europe-Mediter-ranée : Le pari de l'ouverture**, Collection CEPII, Economica, Paris, 1996.

Robert BISTOLFI (ed.), **Euro-Méditerranée : une région à construire**, Publisud, 1995.

Fadi S. HAKURA, *"The Euro-Mediterranean Policy: The Implications of the Barcelona Declaration"*, in: **Common Market Law Review**, No.34, 1997, pp.337-366.

Guide to GATT Law and Practice, (6th ed.), Geneva, 1994.

Louise FAWCETT & Andrew HURELL, **Regionalism in World Politics**, Oxford University Press, 1995.

FLORY T. (ed.), **La Communauté européenne et le GATT : évaluation des cycles de l'Uruguay Round**, Editions Apogée, Rennes, 1995.

Erwan LANNON, *"La Conférence interministérielle de Barcelone, acte fondateur du partenariat euro-méditerranéen"*, in : **Revue du Marché commun et de l'Union européenne** No.398, mai 1996.

Erwan LANNON, *"L'accord d'association intérimaire Communauté européenne-OLP : l'institutionnalisation progressive des relations euro-palestiniennes"*, in: **Revue des Affaires Européennes** No.2, 1997, p.169.

Erwan LANNON & Jean RAUX, *"La coopération financière et technique bilatérale avec les Pays de la Méditerranée Sud et Est"*, **Jurisclasseur-Europe**, "Relations extérieures", Fascicule 2233, Editions Techniques, Paris, mai 1995; *"La coopération financière multilatérale et régionale intéressant l'ensemble des pays tiers méditerranéens"*, **Jurisclasseur-Europe**, "Relations extérieures", Fascicule 2234, Editions Techniques, Paris, mai 1995.

Moshe HIRSCH, Eyal INBAR & Tal SADEH, **The Future Relations between Israel and the European Communities: Some Alternatives**, Bursi, Tel Aviv, 1996.

Eberhard RHEIN, *"Europe and the Mediterranean: A Newly Emerging Geopolitical Area?"*, in: **European Foreign Affairs Review** No.1, 1996, pp.79-86.

Nancy SCOTT, *"Compatibility of EU Regional Trade Agreements with WTO Rules in the Post-Uruguay-Round"*, in: **International Trade Law Review**, 1996, p.219.

Michael SUTTON, *"Euro-Maghreb Partnership: A New Form of Association"*, in: **EIU-European Trends** No.3, 1992.

Peter XUEREB & Roderick PACE (eds), **The European Union, The IGC and the Mediterranean**, Malta, 1996.

"L'OMC : une entreprise encore inachevée", Rapport de l'Assemblée Nationale No.2948, 1996, Rapporteur P. HOGUET.

"Regionalism and the World Trading System", Study of the WTO Secretariat, Geneva, 1995.

BY WAY OF CONCLUSION

The Reciprocal Influence of Multilateral and Regional Trade Rules: A Framework of Analysis

Paul DEMARET

Director, Institut d'Etudes Juridiques Européennes,
University of Liège;
Director of Legal Studies, College of Europe, Bruges

SUMMARY

Relying on the previous papers, this paper attempts to weave together various strands of the relationship between multilateral and regional trade rules. It does not in any way pretend to give a definite answer to the many questions raised by this complex relationship, but merely to provide a framework of analysis.

The first section briefly compares the multilateral trade system and regional integration agreements from the standpoint of their respective objectives and coverage. The second section stresses certain implications for the multilateral trade system which result from the existence and the development of regional integration agreements build on the customs union model as opposed to the free trade area model. The third section identifies different types of influence exerted by the multilateral trade system and multilateral rules on regional integration agreements and regional rules, whereas the fourth examines different types of influence exerted by the latter on the former.

I. THE MULTILATERAL TRADE SYSTEM AND REGIONAL INTEGRATION AGREEMENTS: RESPECTIVE GOALS AND COVERAGE

A. *Goals*

The multilateral trade system and regional integration agreements share at least a common goal: trade liberalization. But trade liberalization is neither the only nor always the main objective which states pursue through regional integration agreements.

1. Trade Liberalization: A Common Goal

It is obvious that both the multilateral trade system and regional integration agreements aim at liberalizing trade between their members, but sometimes through different methods. However, the methods used respectively at the multilateral level and at the regional level seem now more convergent than in the past. This can be illustrated in two respects.

Today, no regional integration agreement aims at increasing intra-regional trade through a deliberate policy of import substitution as the *Grupo Andino* did in the past[1], at least outside the agricultural sector.

In order to free trade between their members, the most far-reaching regional integration agreements provide not only for the removal of protectionist measures, i.e. trade barriers in the traditional sense, but also for the establishment of a level-playing field through the harmonization of standards and regulations in various sectors. The European Community[2] and the European Economic Area[3] are the best examples in this regard. Until the Uruguay Round, the multilateral system, for its part, was mainly concerned with the elimination of measures discriminating formally or materially against foreign trade. As a result of the Uruguay Round, it has gone a step further. In the field of intellectual property, WTO Members have been required to subscribe to minimum (and rather high) standards of protection and to adapt their domestic laws as a result. The TRIPs Agreement reveals that, in certain circumstances and

---

[1] See A. FAIRLIE REINOSO, *"The Andean Community Case"*, *supra* in this volume.

[2] See G. SACERDOTI, *"Standards of Treatment, Harmonization and Mutual Recognition: A Comparison between Regional Areas and the Global Trading System"*, *supra* in this volume.

[3] See R. SCHWOK & Ch. BONTE, *"EEA and Switzerland-EU Bilateral Agreements in Comparative Perspective: What Lessons?"*; and, J. MYHRE, *"Comments"* on the Schwok & Bonte's contribution, *supra* in this volume.

under the lead of the United States and the European Union[4], the multilateral system is capable of reaching results which one would have
thought only the most advanced form of regional integration agreements
could achieve.

2. Political Factors Underlying
   Regional Integration Agreements

The birth and the development of regional integration agreements
cannot be solely explained by the desire to liberalize trade at the regional
level. Political reasons explain to a large degree most regional economic
groupings[5].

This is quite plain in the case of European economic integration. The
main purpose of the Coal and Steel Treaty and the subsequent EEC Treaty
was to secure peace in Europe. Non-economic considerations played a
significant role in the adhesion of Greece, Spain and Portugal to the
EEC[6]. They largely explain why Central and Eastern European countries
have applied to join the European Union[7]. The enlargement of the European Union to the East is seen as one the best means to anchor democracy
in formerly communist-led countries. Political motives are central in the
decision taken by the European Union to launch the Euro-Southern
Mediterranean partnership: it is meant to ensure peace and stability on
the Southern flank of the European Union[8]. The very manner specific
trade provisions are designed may serve a political objective, as shown
by the role which the cumulation of origin could play in the promotion
of regional integration and industrial cooperation in the Middle East[9].

---

[4] See I. GOVAERE, *"Convergence, Divergence and Interaction of Regional Trade
    Agreements and the Agreement on Trade-Related Aspects of Intellectual Property
    Rights (TRIPs)"*; and, H. ULLRICH, *"Comments"* on the Govaere's contribution,
    supra in this volume. See also R. STEINBERG, *"Transatlanticism in Support of
    Multilateralism? Prospects for Great Power Management of the World Trading
    System"*, *supra* in this volume.

[5] See S. DEVOS, *"The Multilateral Rules and the New Dimension of Regional Inte-
    gration: Weaknesses, Need ans Scope for more Disciplines"*, *supra* in this volume.

[6] Admittedly, political factors played a lesser role in the establishment of the Euro-
    pean Economic Area and in the subsequent adhesion of Austria, Finland and
    Sweden to the European Union. These developments were, however, facilitated by
    the new political context created by the end of the cold war, see R. SCHWOK &
    Ch. BONTE, *supra*.

[7] See M. MARESCEAU, *"The European Union and Central and Eastern Europe"*,
    supra in this volume.

[8] See E. LANNON, *"The Compatibility of the Euro-Mediterranean Regional Inte-
    gration with the Multilateral Rules"*, *supra* in this volume.

[9] See A. TOVIAS, *"The EU and Mediterranean Countries"*, *supra* in this volume.

To a lesser degree, similar observations can be made concerning NAFTA, Mercosur and ASEAN. From the standpoint of the United States, NAFTA may be seen as serving the same purpose with respect to Mexico as the Euro-Southern Mediterranean partnership does from the standpoint of the European Union with respect to its Southern Mediterranean neighbours. Mercosur helps not only to lock in open market policies in the Southern Cone, but also to strengthen democracy[10], as illustrated by a recent event in Paraguay. If Vietnam recently decided to join ASEAN, this can be ascribed at least in part to its sometimes tense relations with China[11].

The multilateral trade system is certainly not completely insulated from world politics. It may even be seen as a piece in the development of a new world order after the end of the cold war[12]. Nevertheless, the objectives pursued by the multilateral trade system are first and foremost of a trade nature. The criteria on the basis of which the consistency of regional integration agreements with multilateral rules is to be assessed are defined from a purely trade perspective. As a result, problems may arise when, for political reasons, regional agreements are concluded, which do not fully conform to multilateral rules. Some regional agreements which the European Community concluded in the past or which it is negotiating now may provide examples[13].

B. Coverage

As a result of the Uruguay Round, the multilateral trade system has undergone both a widening and a deepening, to borrow words from the European Community language.

The EC Treaty still has a much broader scope and deeper reach than the multilateral system headed by the WTO. It deals not only with trade in goods and services, but also with movement of natural persons, the right of establishment, the circulation of capital and restrictive trade practices[14]. So does the European Economic Area.

---

[10] See F. PEÑA, *"Some Lessons from the Mercosur Initial Experience"*, *supra* in this volume.

[11] See J. PELKMANS, *"ASEAN and APEC: A Triumph of the 'Asian Way'?"*, *supra* in this volume.

[12] See S. DEVOS, *supra*.

[13] See E. LANNON, *supra*; and, Th. CHRISTOFOROU, *"Multilateral Rules as a Constraint on Regional Rules: A Regional Perspective"*, *supra* in this volume.

[14] Concerning regional integration agreements and the control of restrictive trade practices, see J.F. BELLIS, *"The Treatment of Dumping, Subsidies and Anti-Competitive Practices in Regional Trade Agreements"*, *supra* in this volume.

The multilateral trade system covers fewer fields than NAFTA, which deals explicitly with investments and the enforcement of environmental[15] and labour standards[16]. NAFTA provides for the movement of business people[17], but not of salaried workers.

Actually, with the exception of the EC Treaty, the European Economic Area and the ANZCERTA[18], regional integration agreements either do not provide for, or have not effectively implemented[19], the free circulation of workers. Workers are permitted to circulate freely only where the regional context makes important migratory movements unlikely[20]. In this respect, the situation is more or less the same under GATS, NAFTA and the Europe Agreements. NAFTA, the Europe Agreements and the Euro-Southern Mediterranean Partnership are meant to develop trade with, and improve economic conditions in, the poorer participating members so as to prevent or reduce the influx of immigrants.

In terms of coverage and reach, the multilateral trade system does not rival the most developed integration agreements. However, it now compares favourably with other regional integration agreements, whose effective scope is limited to trade in goods and the elimination of customs duties and quantitative restrictions. With respect to subsidies, technical standards, not to mention services, intellectual property rights and the dispute settlement mechanism, the multilateral rules are often more detailed than those found in regional agreements notably in Latin America and South-East Asia.

---

[15] See D. ESTY & D. GERADIN, *"Environmental Protection in Regional Trade Agreements: The European Community and NAFTA"*; and, TH. DOUMA & M. JACOBS, *"Towards an Equitable Relation between Trade and Environment: The EC, NAFTA and WTO Compared"*, *supra* in this volume.

[16] See A. CANELA-CACHO, *"'The Social Dimensions of the Liberalization of World Trade' and 'Trade and Labour Standards: Can Common Rules be Agreed?' The View from ILO - A Commentary and a Rejoinder"*, *supra* in this volume.

[17] See P. SAUVE, *"Regional versus Multilateral Approaches to Services and Investment Liberalization: Anything to Worry About?"*, *supra* in this volume.

[18] See P. SAUVE, *supra.*

[19] See H. KABAALIOGLU, *"The Turkish Model of Association: Customs Union before Accession"*, *supra* in this volume.

[20] Concerning the issue in the relations between the European Union and Switzerland, see R. SCHWOK & Ch. BONTE, *supra.*

II. REGIONAL INTEGRATION AGREEMENTS IN THE MULTILATERAL TRADE SYSTEM: THE FREE TRADE AREA AND THE CUSTOMS UNION MODELS

There are different kinds of regional integration agreements depending on the degree of economic integration achieved or aimed at, the institutional apparatus, the nature and the size of the national economics involved, the culture(s) shared by the participating countries. But what most directly affect the relationship between the multilateral trade system and regional integration agreements relates to the distinction between customs unions and free trade areas.

The most important regional integration agreements are, of course, no longer confined to trade in goods. They extend their coverage to services, investments, intellectual property rights and beyond. This applies to regional integration agreements whether they are build on the model of customs unions or on the model of free trade areas, as NAFTA illustrates. Actually, NAFTA has a more extensive coverage and, in several respects, provides for more detailed rules and mechanisms than the present Mercosur, which is in the process of establishing a customs union and which has the ambition of becoming a common market[21]. Nevertheless, the distinction between regional integration agreements according to whether they are of the customs union or the free trade area type has significant implications.

First, regional integration agreements of the customs union type are supposed to behave as single entities within the multilateral trade framework. This is not the case when they are of the free trade area type. Canada, a member of NAFTA, may negotiate its own free trade agreement with Chile[22], whereas a member of the European Community or a member of Mercosur may not do so. Trade agreements with third countries must by necessity concern the entire customs union[23].

Second, the fact that regional integration agreements build on the model of a customs union implement a single external trade policy gives them leverage *vis-à-vis* third countries and within the multilateral trade system. The power of a state or group of states to set the rules of

---

[21] See F. PEÑA, *supra.*

[22] See D. MACKAY, *"The North American Free Trade Agreement: Its Possible Extension to South American Countries"*, *supra* in this volume.

[23] If they do not so, this means that the regional agreement does not yet constitute a customs union; see concerning the Andean Group, A. FAIRLIE REINOSO, *supra.*

international trade is, of course, commensurate to its market size[24]. In this respect, the establishment of the European Common Market, its enlargements, its gradual transformation into an "internal market", may be seen as the means for Western European countries to increase their trade (and also political) leverage on the world scene. Mercosur could serve the same purpose for South American countries.

Third, the relationship between the multilateral system and regional agreements of the customs union type changes when the latter achieve a high level of economic integration and external coherence. As long as national markets remain clearly distinct, regional agreements are viewed as exceptions to the MFNC in the sense of Article XXIV of GATT or Article V of GATS. However, if a regional agreement eventually reaches the stage of an "internal market" and, relying on common institutions, effectively behaves as a single entity *vis-à-vis* third countries in all matters affecting its "internal market", it may no longer be seen and treated as an exception to the MFNC. The adequate reference becomes then the US federal common market[25].

With the completion of the Internal Market — coupled with the probable creation of a common currency — the European Union is entering this stage where the perspective shifts. But, outside the field of goods and cross-border services, the European Union experiences difficulty in truly behaving as a single and coherent entity *vis-à-vis* third countries[26]. In addition, it is not certain that the European Community and its Member States are ready to fully accept the logical implications flowing from the concept of an "internal market". Let us assume that the Community truly constitutes a single market, as is largely the case with respect to trade in goods. The reference for the implementation by the Community of the national treatment principle, which various multilateral rules mandate, should then become the intra-Community trade regime, even when the latter differs from the regime prescribed under the domestic law of each Member State. This means that Member States, would no longer be allowed to treat trade between themselves better than trade with third countries, except with respect to customs duties and legitimate safeguard measures. The famous *Cassis de Dijon* Case law may be used as an example.

---

[24] See R. STEINBERG, *"Transatlantism in Support of Multilateralism? Prospects for Great Power Management of the World Trading System"*, *supra* in this volume.

[25] See D. PALMETER, *"Rules of Origin in Regional Trade Agreements"*, *supra* in this volume.

[26] See the *"Introduction"* of this volume.

That case law provides that, in the absence of specific Community legislation, Member States may not as a rule impose their domestic standards on goods imported from other Member States. Save where mandatory reason apply, they must recognize the standards in force in the Member State of exportation. If the Community is a single market and is to be treated as such within the multilateral system, the argument can be made that, as the *Cassis de Dijon* Case law is an essential element of the intra-Community trade regime, it ought to be extended to the EC external trade, i.e. to goods directly imported from third countries entitled to national treatment. This would be but the logical result of applying the national treatment principle to the European Community itself[27].

III. THE INFLUENCE OF
THE MULTILATERAL TRADE SYSTEM
ON REGIONAL INTEGRATION AGREEMENTS

This section is divided into three parts. The first part examines whether the multilateral trade system does not indirectly stimulate the growth of regionalism. The second part deals with the influence which multilateral rules, understood as legal obligations, may exert on the shape of regional integration agreements and on specific regional rules. The third part identifies the harmonizing influence which multilateral rules may have on regional rules beyond specific legal obligations.

A. *The Multilateral Trade System as a Stimulus to Regionalism?*

From its birth in 1947, the multilateral trade system allowed the creation of regional integration agreements. Article XXIV of GATT, as a derogation to the MFNC, is usually explained by political considerations: the United States was favourable to some form of economic integration in Western Europe and the Benelux experience was about to start. The state of the economic thinking at the time may also have played a part: it is only in 1950, with Viner, that the theory of customs union took shape.

The mere fact that the multilateral trade system does allow the establishment of customs unions and free trade areas does not mean that it has been as such responsible for the emergence of regional integration agreements. However, the multilateral system in some indirect ways stimulates the growth of regionalism.

---

[27] Concerning the case law *Cassis de Dijon* and trade with Switzerland, see R. SCHWOK & CH. BONTE, *supra*.

First, the less than precise wording of Article XXIV and the unprincipled manner in which Article XXIV was enforced under the GATT of 1947 may have been perceived as an encouragement for the establishment of regional integration agreements[28].

Second, as already mentioned, the influence which states have in and on the multilateral system is in direct proportion of the size of their market. This applies to the negotiations of trade concessions, to the design of new multilateral rules and also to the settlement of disputes[29]. As a result, there is an incentive for members of the multilateral system to create regional groupings in order to speak with a stronger voice and to emulate in some ways what Western European countries have achieved through the European Community. In this regard, how Mercosur evolves in the future will deserve attention.

The very development of the multilateral trade system may increase the incentive to create and strengthen regional groupings. There are indeed administrative reasons for this, in addition and beyond the motivation to gain more power. The multilateral system covers an increasing variety of subject-matters and its rules are getting more complex. For small and poor countries, with meagre administrative resources, it is becoming difficult first to play a role in the drafting of multilateral rules, second to effectively implement these rules at the domestic level — the TRIPs Agreement for instance — and perhaps also to defend successfully their case in the framework of the dispute settlement mechanism. Regional cooperation may be the only way to overcome these handicaps[30].

B. Multilateral Rules as Binding Rules on Regional Integration Agreements

Three questions are examined hereafter. The first, and most obvious, relates to the constraining effect of those multilateral rules which specifically deal with regional integration agreements. This is the traditional Article XXIV problematic. The second is whether multilateral rules, other than Article XXIV, apply to trade between members of regional

---

[28] On this issue see S. DEVOS, *supra*; and, W. DAVEY, *"Comments"* on the Devos' contribution, *supra* in this volume; Th. CHRISTOFOROU, *supra*; and, K. FALKENBERG, *"Comments"* on P. Sauvé's contribution, *supra* in this volume.

[29] The impact of retaliatory measures is proportional to the size of the complainant's market.

[30] See with respect to Central America, D. MACKAY, *supra*.

integration agreements. The third concerns the effect of multilateral rules on the external trade regime of regional integration agreements. This last question is relevant only in the case of regional groupings of the customs union type.

1. The Formal Consistency of Regional Integration Agreements with the Multilateral Trade System

From an economic point of view, one may argue that only those regional integration agreements which are net creators of trade, i.e. whose trade creating effect more than cancels out their unavoidable trade diverting effect[31], are consistent with the multilateral trade system. However, in practice there is no sure way to identify the overall positive or negative effect on trade which can be ascribed to a regional integration agreement, not to say to make predictions. Thus, the economic test cannot be used to pass judgement on the compatibility of regional integration agreements with the multilateral trade system, at least beforehand[32]. Only their formal consistency with the conditions set out in Article XXIV of GATT and now in Article V of GATS can be assessed.

a) Before the Uruguay Round: Article XXIV of GATT

i) The Absence of Effective and Meaningful Control

Up until 1995, regional integration agreements had to conform with conditions set at the multilateral level only to the extent that they covered trade in goods. For various reasons, the creation of customs unions and free trade areas has not been subject to a truly effective control by GATT[33].

Many regional agreements raised serious questions because either they excluded agricultural products, or were asymmetrical or did not provide for a definite and reasonable timetable for the establishment of a full free trade zone or customs union. Before NAFTA, the EEC was probably the regional agreement which best complied with the letter of Article XXIV[34].

---

[31] Concerning the trade diverting effect of specific rules of origin under free trade agreements, see D. PALMETER, *supra*; and, A. TOVIAS, *supra*.

[32] See P. DEVOS, *supra*.

[33] See footnote 28.

[34] See K. FALKENBERG, *supra*.

In the definition of customs unions and free trade areas, there is an element which sometimes is overlooked. Article XXIV § 8 requires that not only customs duties, but also all "other restrictive regulations of commerce" be removed between members of regional agreements. On the external side, in the case of customs unions, Article XXIV § 8(a) prescribes that substantially the same regulations of commerce should apply *vis-à-vis* third countries. If these words were given their full meaning, the European Community itself became a customs union in full conformity with Article XXIV § 8(a) only in the 1990s. For instance, it is only in 1994 that all goods imported in the EC became subject to a common regime as a result of the removal of the last remaining national import quotas. Even today, all non-tariff trade barriers have not been harmonized at the EC level.

ii) The Influence of Article XXIV on the EEC Treaty

The fact that Article XXIV was not effectively or meaningfully enforced, does not mean that it did not exert any influence on the shape or behaviour of regional integration agreements. First, one does not know what these agreements would have looked like if Article XXIV had not existed. Second, during this conference, it was indicated that this provision had a rather significant influence on the shape of the EEC. Apparently, the six founding members of the EEC decided that the free movement and a common commercial policy would apply to all categories of goods only because they needed to comply with Article XXIV § 8(a) of GATT. The comprehensive and uniform character of the internal and external trade regime of the European Community can thus be ascribed in part to GATT. Third, Article XXIV yielded some concrete consequence when the European Community enlarged in 1986 and 1995. Relying on Article XXIV, the United States obtained in the first case the establishment of a quota to keep the Spanish market open to certain US agricultural products[35]. In the second case, the United States was granted some trade concessions to compensate for the fact that access to the Swedish and Austrian market had become more difficult for certain US products as a result of the extension of the EC external trade regime to Sweden and Austria. Of course, the exact role played by Article XXIV in these cases is not easy to evaluate. The United States might have extracted concessions from the European Community even in the absence of Article XXIV.

---

[35] See Th. CHRISTOFOROU, *supra.*

b) After the Uruguay Round

i) Article XXIV of the GATT of 1994

In the GATT of 1994, Article XXIV has remained unchanged, but, in some respects, its meaning has been made more precise as a result of the understanding concerning its interpretation. The understanding also makes it clear that compliance with Article XXIV is an issue to which the WTO dispute settlement mechanism applies. Whether this will lead to a much stricter control of customs unions and free trade areas than under the GATT of 1947 has been debated. Some of the conditions imposed by Article XXIV continue to lend themselves to different interpretations or may seem too rigid. The suggestion has been made to relax somewhat the substantive criteria[36] or to interpret them in a more reasonable way than in the past[37] and to strengthen the review procedure[38]. The establishment of a Committee on Regional Trade Agreements may be a step in that direction[39].

Overall, it seems that WTO Members will enjoy a lesser margin of freedom than the contracting parties to the GATT 1947 when negotiating the establishment of customs unions or free trade areas at the regional level or at the inter-regional level. A free trade agreement between the EC and Mercosur that would exclude agricultural products would probably be challenged before the WTO as it would not cover "substantially all trade..." as required under Article XXIV. The conclusion of a free trade agreement between the EC and Mercosur is still a few years away. In the more immediate future, the compatibility with Article XXIV of the free trade agreements which the European Community is negotiating with Southern Mediterranean countries will have to be assessed. They do not cover agricultural products during an initial phase[40] and do not provide a precise timetable for the termination of this phase[41]. The very caution shown by the European Community regarding this issue demonstrates in a sense that, under the GATT of 1994, Article XXIV is taken more seriously than under the GATT of 1947.

---

[36] See P. DEVOS, *supra.*
[37] See K. FALKENBERG, *supra.*
[38] See P. DEVOS, *supra.*
[39] See W. DAVEY, *supra.*
[40] See the criticism made by A. TOVIAS, *supra.*
[41] See E. LANNON, *supra.*

ii) Article V and V*bis* of GATS

As a result of GATS, the multilateral trade system does now, for the first time, deal with regional integration agreements extending beyond trade in goods and covering the supply of services (and, indirectly, foreign direct investments and movement of workers). One should recall that the free supply of services, the right of establishment and the free movement of salaried workers were already contemplated by the EEC Treaty of 1957. NAFTA was also concluded before the adoption of GATS, even though it was influenced in some regards by the GATS negotiations[42].

With respect to services and movement of workers, there seems little doubt that the EC Treaty, as implemented today, and, for that matter, the European Economic Area are fully consistent with Article V and V*bis* of GATS. As one could expect, these provisions confirm the international legitimacy of the European Common or Internal Market. As was pointed out[43], for legal persons supplying services, the connecting factor (incorporation and substantive business operations) provided under Article V of GATS parallels the connecting factor which the European Community requires in order for a legal person to benefit from the freedom to supply services or the freedom of establishment across the Common Market.

The Australia-New Zealand Closer Economic Relations Trade Agreements also complies with Article V and V*bis* of GATS.

Whether other regional integration agreements covering services are in all respects consistent with the letter and spirit of Article V of GATS might, however, be discussed. Article V requires that regional agreements do have "substantial coverage" in terms of number of sectors, volume of trade affected and modes of supply. With respect to the latter, Article V indicates that agreements should not provide for the *a priori* exclusion of any mode of supply. However, as already mentioned, under the Europe Agreements concluded by the European countries as well as under NAFTA, firms established in the territory of a Contracting Party are not allowed to use their entire workforce for the supply of services in the territory of another Contracting Party. They are only permitted to send key personnel. Such a restriction amounts almost to the exclusion of a particular mode of supply, particularly for countries and firms which rely

---

[42] See P. SAUVE, *supra.*

[43] See K. FALKENBERG, *supra.*

on a low-skilled workforce. In the near future, the effectiveness of Article V of GATS could be tested as a result of the sectoral agreements which the European Community and Switzerland are negotiating and which would cover only a limited number of services[44].

iii) Article XXIV of GATT and Article V of GATS

Since, as a result of the Uruguay Round, the multilateral system now extends its coverage to both goods and services, one may wonder why the conformity with the multilateral system of a regional integration agreement extending to both goods and services, should not be examined as a whole, on the basis of Article XXIV of GATT and Article V of GATS combined[45].

Another related question is whether in the future trade in goods and trade in services should not be lumped together in order to determine whether a regional agreement satisfies the "substantially all trade ..." test. If this was the case, regional agreements would have to cover substantially all trade in goods **and** services within a certain time-frame in order to be compatible with the multilateral system. This would be in keeping with the single package approach which underlies the WTO itself and with the increasing importance of services in modern economies. If there is a rationale behind the idea that preferential agreements should not be seen as conforming to the multilateral system when they exclude an important volume of trade in goods, the same rationale ought to apply when they exclude trade in services.

In the same vein, one might also consider that for a regional agreement to satisfy the "substantially all trade" requirement under Article XXIV of GATT or under Article V of GATS, the agreement should explicitly contemplate the opening up of public procurement[46].

Of course, if these ideas were implemented, the margin of preference and the amount of trade diversion entailed by regional agreements would at the same time increase. That brings back to the paradox underlying Article XXIV of GATT and Article V of GATS[47], which stems from the fact that the logic of the MFNC and the logic of regional agreements do

---

[44] Concerning these agreements, see R. SCHWOK & Ch. BONTE, *supra.*

[45] See P. MAVROIDIS, *"Comments"* on J.F. Bellis' contribution, *supra* in this volume.

[46] See P. DELSAUX, *"Government Procurement in a Multilateral Context"*; and, N. MICHEL, *"Comments"* on P. Delsaux's contribution, *supra* in this volume.

[47] See S. DEVOS, *supra.*

not square. Only when a regional integration agreement evolves into a fully-fledged internal market and behaves in all respects as a single entity *vis-à-vis* third countries does the paradox go away, because then the regional agreement is no longer being perceived as a preferential agreement.

iv) The TRIPs Agreement

The TRIPs Agreement does not specifically refer to regional integration agreements, except with respect to border controls in relation to trade in counterfeited goods. This can be explained by the fact that the rationale of the TRIPs agreement is not trade liberalization in the traditional sense. When trade liberalization is the focus, exceptions have to be provided for regional integration agreements as they free trade between their members more than *vis-à-vis* third countries. The TRIPs rationale is the protection of intellectual property owners and the creation of a level-playing field, at least to the extent that all WTO Members are required to grant a (high) minimum level of protection to various types of intellectual property[48]. This, in turn, is expected to have a favourable effect on the export of goods and services protected by intellectual property rights, on technology transfers and on investments. In the same way as other members of the WTO, regional integration agreements may provide for a level of protection higher than the one imposed by the TRIPs Agreement.

However, in a rather oblique way, the TRIPs Agreement actually allows members of a regional integration agreement to liberalize trade (in the usual sense) in goods protected by intellectual property rights more between themselves than *vis-à-vis* third countries. This concerns parallel imports. The TRIPs Agreement leaves the exhaustion of rights question open, subject to the MFNC and the national treatment principle. NAFTA, for instance, does not provide for the exhaustion of intellectual property rights in trade between its members, whereas the law of the European Community does. But the European Community remains free not to apply the exhaustion doctrine in its external trade[49], because under the

---

[48] See I. GOVAERE, *"Convergence, Divergence and Interaction of Regional Trade Agreements and the Agreement on Trade-Related Aspects of Intellectual Property Rights (TRIPs)"*; and, H. ULLRICH, *supra*.

[49] Under the European Economic Area, the exhaustion of rights applies as under EC "domestic" law. But the former free trade agreements concluded by the EC and EFTA countries were not construed as implying the exhaustion of intellectual property rights. The same interpretation would probably be given to Europe Agreements, see S. SOLTYSINSKI, *"The Proliferation of the European Union Rules on Free Trade in Central and Eastern Europe: Towards a Pan-European Integrated Market"*, *supra* in this volume.

TRIPs Agreement it is the owners of intellectual property rights, and not the parallel importers or the imported goods, which serve as the point of reference for the MFNC or the national treatment. Although this may sound arcane, this in fact encapsulates the TRIPs basic rationale. Owners of intellectual property rights get the possibility to export their goods or to invest abroad, but they may remain protected in their home market and in their other markets against parallel imports. In other words, under the TRIPs Agreement, they are allowed to practice international price discrimination.

2. Multilateral Trade Rules and Trade between Members of Regional Integration Agreements

The question is whether WTO rules, other than Article XXIV of GATT and Article V of GATS, bind members of a regional integration agreement in their mutual trade. There is no simple answer.

First, let us assume that WTO rules have wider coverage than the regional integration agreement, a not infrequent situation following the Uruguay Round. To that extent, multilateral rules remain applicable to trade between members of the regional agreement. For example, the GATS applies to trade in services between countries which are member of a customs union or a free trade area whose coverage is limited to goods. In order to supplement regional rules, regional integration agreements increasingly refer to multilateral rules. Recent regional agreements between Latin American countries provide examples.

Second, let us assume that the regional rules have coverage similar as, or greater than, the WTO rules. Assuming that only the mutual trade interests of the members of the regional agreement are at stake, regional rules may then prevail over multilateral rules[50]. Whether they do or not prevail basically depends on the degree of integration the members of the regional agreement are ready to accept when they negotiate the

---

[50] To the extent that trade interests of third countries would be affected, these third countries ought to remain entitled to invoke their rights under the multilateral system, except if they have accepted to treat the regional integration agreement as a single entity within the multilateral system. One should, however, mention here the position taken by a GATT panel in 1992 in the *Airbus* dispute opposing the United States to the European Community (March 4, 1992, SCM/142, not adopted). The panel was of the opinion that the Tokyo Code on subsidies applied to intra-Community trade, the reason being that, at the time, the European Community could not be considered to form a true internal market yet. Whatever the merits of this panel ruling, today at least with respect to trade in goods, the European Community should be treated as a single market. See on this point, Th. CHRISTOFOROU, *supra.*

agreement. The European Community and NAFTA are worth comparing in this respect.

In the framework of the EC Treaty, Member States may not directly rely on WTO substantive rules in a trade dispute which would arise with another Member State. Neither may a Member State resort to the GATT/WTO dispute settlement mechanism for the same purpose. Intra-Community trade is exclusively governed by EC law, under the control of EC institutions[51]. This is in keeping with the will of the EC Member States to constitute a single entity equipped with its own comprehensive institutional machinery.

Under NAFTA, Parties do not renounce the rights to which they are entitled under the multilateral system, but they have agreed that in case of inconsistency between multilateral and NAFTA rules, the latter prevail[52]. In addition, when NAFTA and the WTO Agreements (or GATT in the past) share the same substantive rules, Parties to NAFTA are allowed to choose between the regional and the multilateral mechanism to solve disputes[53]. Canada did use that possibility. When regional integration agreements do not completely exclude the application of multilateral rules in their mutual trade, this reflects and ensures a measure of convergence between multilateral and regional rules[54].

3. Multilateral Trade Rules and the External Trade Relations of Regional Integration Agreements or Members thereof

In their trade relations with third countries, regional integration agreements, if they behave as a single entity, or otherwise their members are, of course, bound by the multilateral rules to which they have subscribed, in the same way as other members of the multilateral system. There are, nevertheless, two points worth making in relation to the influence of multilateral rules on the external trade regime of regional integration agreements build on the model of customs unions. The first is the fact

---

[51] The Community system to adjudicate disputes rests upon the European Court of Justice. Member States themselves almost never bring before the Court violations of Community law committed by other Member States. Infringements of Community law by Member States are brought before the Court either directly by the Commission or, indirectly, by private individuals acting through domestic courts.

[52] See S. LOPEZ-AYLLON, *"Comments"* on D. Mackay's contribution, *supra* in this volume.

[53] Except with respect to environmental, health or safety matters, see Th. DOUMA & M. JACOBS, *supra*.

[54] Concerning the absence of DSM under AFTA and the complaint brought by Singapour against Malaysia before the WTO, see J. PELKMANS, *supra*.

that multilateral rules at times help regional integration agreements to acquire an external dimension. The second concerns the weight multilateral rules are given in the legal order of a regional integration agreement. The case of the European Community will be used to illustrate both points. At the present time, the second point probably has practical significance only in the case of the European Community.

a) Multilateral Rules as a Means to Complete the External Trade Regime of Regional Integration Agreements

Regional integration agreements whose objective is to establish a customs union and, beyond, a common or an internal market are supposed to acquire an external dimension. However, in some instances, the harmonization or the uniformization of the external trade regime of the members of a regional agreement results not from autonomous action taken at the regional level, but from a multilateral initiative. This occurs even in the case of the European Community, the most developed integration system to date.

Until now, the European Community has not devised on its own a common regime for export subsidies in general and for export credits and export guarantees in particular, even though this ought to have been achieved by 1970 according to the EEC Treaty of 1957. In fact, it took an OECD arrangement to define the conditions under which EC Member States could grant export credits and a GATT code, now succeeded by a WTO multilateral trade agreement, to regulate in some detail the granting of subsidies affecting the export trade of the European Community. This can be explained in part because the Member States could not readily agree on these matters and in part because it made sense to tackle them at the multilateral level.

A somewhat similar observation can be made with respect to GATS. This multilateral agreement had no direct influence on the liberalization of intra-Community trade in services, which had been under way for many years through methods (enforcement of prohibitions, extensive mutual recognition, legislative harmonization) which go beyond the methods contemplated under GATS. Rather, the importance of GATS and related agreements (such as the provisional agreement on trade in financial services) lies in the fact that these multilateral agreements, which bind the European Community and its Member States, constitute important pieces of the external trade regime of the European Union[55].

---

[55] The picture which emerges after the conclusion of GATS and related agreements by the European Community and its Member States is, however, rather complex. The

The TRIPs Agreement had also some influence on the external trade regime of the European Union. Border measures relating to counterfeited goods imported from third countries were strenghtened as a result and former reciprocity provisions had to be deleted.

Regarding foreign direct investments, there is, up to now, no uniform external Community regime. Except where the Community has adopted specific legislation relating to foreign direct investments or concluded specific agreements with third countries[56], Member States remain competent to regulate foreign direct investments in their territory. They also remain competent to conclude agreements with third countries to protect foreign direct investments abroad. Here again, the development of the European Union external regime and agreements negotiated at the multilateral level by the European Community and its Member States cannot be separated. As already indicated, the GATS in part deals with foreign direct investments to the extent that commercial presence is being allowed for the purpose of supplying services. In addition, negotiations concerning the conclusion of a Multilateral Agreements on Investments (MAI) are taking place within the framework of the OECD[57].

---

extent to which the EC has granted access to its market to foreign suppliers of services can be measured only after examining the extent to which access has been granted to the national market of each Member State. The EC external regime applicable to trade in services with third countries is thus less uniform than in the case of trade in goods. This, of course, is due to the fact that the traditional obstacles to trade in goods are in the nature of customs duties and quantitative restrictions, whose external regime had to be unified in order to ensure the free movement of goods, including goods originating in third countries, between Member States. Trade in services is not restricted through the imposition of customs duties, nor usually through the imposition of ceilings on the volume of imports, but through limitations on market access or the denial of national treatment. Under EC law, Member States had to remove obstacles of this nature insofar as intra-Community trade and suppliers established in the Community were concerned. But national measures restricting trade in services with third countries were not merged to form a uniform external regime as in the case of goods. There was indeed no explicit provision to that effect in the EC Treaty. Whether or not to liberalize trade in services with third countries was thus largely an issue for each Member State to decide, at least until the Uruguay Round. On that occasion, the Court of Justice decided that trade in services with third countries was an element of the common commercial policy, which as such fell within the exclusive competence of the Community provided it did not involve movement of natural or legal persons. Trade in services with third countries involving movement of persons, on the other hand, has remained within the competence of the Member States at least insofar and as long as such trade is not covered by specific Community legislation.

[56] The agreement establishing a European Economic Area and, to a lesser extent, the Europe Agreements cover not only the supply of services, but also direct investments.

[57] A still debated question is whether the future OECD Agreement should include a provision allowing regional integration agreements to free intra-regional investments more than investments originating outside the region.

What precedes is not to deny that the European Union played or is playing a major role in the negotiation of the multilateral rules just mentioned.

b) The Weight Given to Multilateral Rules in the Legal Order of a Regional Integration Agreement and the Issue of Coordination

As indicated, the point concerns regional integration agreement which have build their own specific legal order, distinct form the domestic legal system of their members. Obviously, the greater the weight given to multilateral rules by the regional integration agreement, the greater the convergence between regional and multilateral rules. The issue is of practical importance in the external trade relations of the European Community.

There is no doubt that multilateral trade rules become more effective when they are given direct effect or at least when they may be invoked before a court by private individuals against allegedly inconsistent regional rules[58].

However, this is not the end of the matter. Assuming that direct effect or invokability is admitted, the question then is how the multilateral trade rules are going to be construed by the "regional" court and whether the regional rules run the risk of being found inconsistent with the former. For instance, in several cases brought before the European Court of Justice, it was alleged that a conflict existed between GATT rules and EC trade measures. But the Court of Justice never ruled against EC law, even in those cases where it had allowed a party to invoke GATT rules. The point made here is best understood if one imagines the situation where identical or similarly worded provisions are found at both the multilateral level and at the intra-regional level. The first bind the regional entity when it trades with third countries, whereas the second govern trade between its members. Provisions prohibiting respectively taxes with the same effect as customs duties, internal discriminatory taxes, or restrictive commercial regulations provide examples. The case law of the Court of Justice clearly reveals that provisions prohibiting trade barriers tend

---

[58] On the issue of direct effect, see the debate between P. PESCATORE, *"The New WTO Dispute Settlement Mechanism"*; and, C. LAFER, *"Comment"* on P. Pescatore's contribution, *supra* in this volume. Concerning the effect of GATT/WTO rules in the legal order of the EC, see I. GOVAERE, *"The Reception of the WTO Agreement in the European Union: The Legacy of GATT"*, *supra* in this volume; and of the US, see R. STEINBERG, *"Direct Application of Multilateral Trade Agreements in the United States"*, *supra* in this volume.

to be construed in a more trade-friendly manner when they apply to intra-Community trade than when they apply to its external trade.

To achieve full convergence between similarly worded multilateral and regional rules, one might think, for the sake of the argument, to prescribe that the multilateral rule not only be treated as having direct effect, but also that it be interpreted in the same manner as the intra-regional rule. Such proposal is, of course, quite unrealistic. It would be met by at least three objections.

First, in the case of the European Community, the Court of Justice is not even ready to extend its most trade liberalizing case law to regional agreements concluded by the Community, except perhaps to the EEA.

Second, it would be necessary, for obvious reasons, that the interpretation of the same provisions at the WTO level (in the framework of the DSM) be as broad and as trade-friendly as the regional interpretation.

There is also a policy objection, which relates to the free rider issue and to traditional reciprocity considerations (based on domestic producers' interests). To make multilateral rules truly binding at the level of a regional integration agreement and to interpret them with a free trade bias cannot be accepted as long as the most important WTO Members, such as the United States, Japan, India or, in the future, China, are not ready to give a similar degree of effectiveness to multilateral rules in their domestic legal system. That objection would, however, lose strength if the WTO Appellate Body were to operate as a truly independent and impartial adjudicator on the basis of the rule of law[59] and were at the same time able to get its rulings accepted and implemented by the most powerful WTO Members.

What will appear as pure legal science fiction is another idea, directly inspired by the EC experience. To ensure a measure of uniformity in the interpretation of multilateral rules both at the WTO level and at the regional or national level, one might think of giving the possibility to (or imposing the obligation on) the highest regional or national courts to ask the WTO Appellate Body for its interpretation of multilateral rules. Today, such an idea, may seem a bit far-fetched. Nevertheless, it shows what needs to be done if true and effective convergence between multilateral rules and regional rules is to be achieved, or more generally between multilateral rules and the domestic law of the WTO Members.

---

[59] See P. PESCATORE, *supra*.

C. Multilateral Trade Rules as a Harmonizing Influence on Regional Integration Agreements?

It is now worth examining whether multilateral rules, independently of whether they are binding or not, exert an harmonizing influence on regional rules. Are regional integration agreements more or less patterned after the multilateral trade system? Do they borrow rules from the multilateral system? Or do they distinguish themselves from the latter in important respects? These questions have been treated in detail in several papers reproduced in this volume. Here they are addressed in broad and (unavoidably) sweeping terms. It will not come as a surprise that regional integration in Europe (and its vicinity) and regional integration outside Europe need again to be distinguished. The characteristics of European regional integration agreements justify the question mark in the sub-title.

1. Regional Integration Agreements in Europe and its Vicinity

The main vehicle for European economic integration is the EC Treaty. But European economic integration also proceeds on the basis of the regional agreements which the European Community (together with its Member States) has concluded or is about to conclude with its neighbours. Some of these agreements span the Mediterranean Basin.

a) The EC Treaty

Multilateral rules have much less influenced the EEC Treaty of 1957 and its subsequent development than most regional integration agreements outside Europe. The reasons are well known. Even though the GATT existed at the time the Coal and Steel Community and, later, the European Economic Community, were established, the objectives pursued by the founding fathers of European integration were much broader than the objectives assigned to GATT and this translated into agreements with a much broader coverage than GATT. The EEC Treaty provided not only for the creation of a customs union, but for the liberation of factor movement and for competition rules, some designed to curb restrictive business practices, other to control the grant of state aids, and this not only for the sake of preserving competition, but also to foster market integration. Except with respect to trade in goods, the internal and external development of the common market took place in the absence of any comprehensive multilateral framework, at least until 1994.

The institutional means used by the Community to achieve economic integration were also in large measure foreign to GATT, whether one refers to the (permanent) capacity of EC institutions to legislate in relation to the Common Market or to the mechanisms used to enforce and to interpret uniformly EC law. With respect to both enforcement and interpretation of Community law, the importance of the cooperation between domestic courts and the European Court of Justice needs to be stressed. It is an essential feature of the Community legal system and the source of its effectiveness. The existence of a strong and, on the whole, well-accepted adjucatory system of a pre-federal nature has played and continues to play a major role in the implementation of the basic economic freedoms and the competition rules, on which the Common Market or Internal Market is based.

At a structural level, the multilateral system has had little influence on the European Community, except with respect to the shape of its customs union (see *supra*). Nevertheless, multilateral rules have in some instances directly influenced the content of EC rules. In addition to cases already mentioned in relation to the completion of the EC external trade regime, the TRIPs Agreements should be cited because it resulted in the modification of certain provisions of EC law, but also because it contributed in some degree to the harmonization of the domestic laws of the EC Member States in the area of intellectual property[60].

One should also recall that, at the origin, certain GATT provisions did influence the wording of provisions of the EEC Treaty. Article 95 of the present EC Treaty, which forbids discriminatory taxes in trade between Member States, and Articles 30 and 36, which respectively deal with quantitative restrictions and restrictive commercial regulations, bear the imprint of respectively Article III § 2 and Articles XX and XXI of GATT[61]. However, thanks to the elaborated institutional machinery set up by the EC Treaty, these EC provisions have acquired a broader scope and achieved a greater effectiveness than similar GATT provisions. The "EC" interpretation might now, in some respects at least, gradually inspire the GATT/WTO interpretation.

---

[60] See I. GOVAERE, *"Convergence, Divergence and Interaction of Regional Trade Agreements and the Agreement on Trade-Related Aspects of Intellectual Property Rights (TRIPs)"*, *supra*.

[61] There are also a few cases where the European Court of Justice refers to GATT law to construe the meaning of provisions of EC law, see *Werner* Case C-70/94, **ECR** (1995) I-3189; *Leifer* Case C-83/94, ECR (1995) I-3231; *IDA* Case C-61/94, **ECR** (1996) I-3989.

Rules governing intra-Community trade have at times to be modified because new multilateral rules applies to the EC external trade. This happens when multilateral rules are in some ways more liberal than EC internal rules, something which, if left uncorrected, would result in foreign competitors being better treated on the Community Market than Community firms. Adjustments of this kind were made after the Uruguay Round in the field of public procurement and research.

*b) The Regional Agreements between
the European Community and its Neighbours*

i) Agreements with European Countries

Throughout Northern, Central and Southern Europe, regionalism progresses along lines largely dictated by the European Community. The content of regional integration agreements concluded by the European Community with its European neighbours (the European Economic Area, the Europe Agreements, the Association Agreements with Southern European countries, including the customs union with Turkey) reflects directly, with various degrees of coverage and depth, the EC model and EC law at least insofar as substantive provisions are concerned. Only the sectoral agreements being negotiated with Switzerland stand somewhat part[62].

Multilateral rules have not had much influence on the detailed content of all these agreements. There was a reference to Article VI of GATT in the old free trade agreements of 1973[63]. There is a reference to the multilateral agreement on subsidies in the Europe Agreements, but which is of a transient nature[64], as indeed the Europe Agreements themselves. Basically, trade between European countries is now largely outside the direct influence of multilateral rules as they apply to trade relations at the world level[65]. Where the multilateral system may still have an impact

---

[62] But this observation should be qualified by the fact that Switzerland to a significant degree proceeds on its own to harmonize its laws with EC law, see R. SCHWOK & Ch. BONTE, *supra*.

[63] One may also mention the fact that the European Court of Justice explicitly referred to Article XXIV § 8(b) of GATT when it had to determine the scope of the prohibition of taxes with an equivalent effect to customs duties under the 1973 free trade agreement between the EC and Sweden, see the *Legros* Case C 163/90, **ECR** (1992) I-4265.

[64] See J.F. BELLIS, *supra*.

[65] The EC model is extending its influence beyond the Europe agreements linking the European Union and its neighbours, see concerning CEFTA, P. BALÁZS, *"Subregional Cooperation in Central and Eastern Europe - The Visegrad Declaration and the Central European Free Trade Agreement"*, *supra* in this volume; and concerning agreements within the former Soviet Union, see S. SOLTYSINSKI, *supra*.

is when the consistency of the agreements negotiated by the European Community and its neighbours with Article XXIV of GATT and Article V of GATS is assessed.

If the substantive content of the regional agreements is more or less a replica of provisions found in the EC Treaty, the situation is quite different on the institutional side. Only full members of the European Community may share in its institutional system. As a result, the regional partners of the European Community are either legally or *de facto* obliged to adapt their regulations to EC regulations in the drafting of which they have played no part[66]. In addition, they have no access to anything similar to the elaborated EC judicial mechanisms.

Free trade, cooperation or association agreements which the European Community has concluded with its neighbours do not contain dispute settlement mechanisms that would be inspired by the GATT or the WTO system. In that regard, regional agreements under the direct influence of the European Community are different form regional agreements such as NAFTA or Mercosur. Preferential agreements linking the European Community and its neighbours usually provide for *ad hoc* compulsory arbitration as a possible means to settle disputes which might arise between the Parties. However, the scope of compulsory arbitration is subject to various restrictions. In addition, there have been very few cases of arbitration proceedings being started and no case at all of arbitration proceedings running their full course[67]. Trade disputes between the Community and its neighbours are resolved through political means rather than legal proceedings. This is in stark contrast with the way disputes are settled within the framework of the European Community system itself, which relies on the rule of law, but also with the way disputes are now being settled within the WTO multilateral framework, where the rule of law plays an increasing role. The overall impression which emerges is that basically the European Community does not want to relinquish too much of its trade sovereignty and institutional autonomy to independent arbitral organs. The European partners of the Community

---

[66] EFTA countries, member of the European Economic Area, had to establish institutions and enforcement mechanisms patterned after the EC system, but were not allowed to play a significant role within the latter, see R. SCHWOK & Ch. BONTE, *supra*.

[67] See M.A. GAUDISSART, J.V. LOUIS & L. VAN DEN HENDE, *Les clauses de règlement des différends dans les accords internationaux conclus par les Communautés européennes*, in : **L'Arbitrage et le droit européen**, Bruylant, Bruxelles, 1997, pp.143-181.

seem to accept that as a fact, either because they are in a weaker position or because they hope to join the EC system in the future.

ii) Agreements with Southern Mediterranean Countries

The observations just made concerning the regional agreements between the European Community and its European neighbours also apply in the main to the agreements which the European Community has concluded or is about to conclude with Southern Mediterranean countries. These agreements, however, have less coverage than the agreements with European countries. They refer explicitly to the GATS. They also raise more questions under Article XXIV of GATT and Article V of GATS since they are not meant to prepare the entry of these Southern Mediterranean (and non European) countries into the European Union[68].

2. Regional Integration Agreements outside Europe

In general terms, multilateral rules have exerted and continue to exert a greater influence on regional integration agreements outside Europe than regional integration agreements in Europe. There are two main reasons for this. The most important regional integration agreements outside Europe are of rather recent origin. None does, at this time at least, aim at achieving the same degree of political integration as the European Union and the regional agreements surrounding it.

The role left to multilateral rules in the trade relations between NAFTA Parties, most notably with respect to trade disputes, has already been mentioned[69]. Equally important is the fact that NAFTA rules are much closer to multilateral rules in terms of coverage, methods and dispute settlement mechanism (at least if one does not refer to the sectoral dispute settlement mechanisms)[70] than EC rules. The multilateral negotiations which led to the GATS influenced to some degree the services aspects of NAFTA[71], whereas NAFTA provisions regarding intellectual property rights were to a large extent directly borrowed from the TRIPs

---

[68] See on these points, E. LANNON, *supra*.

[69] See *supra*.

[70] Concerning the sectoral dispute settlement mechanisms, see J.F. BELLIS, *supra*; and, Th. DOUMA & M. JACOBS, *supra*.

[71] See P. SAUVE, *supra*.

Agreement when the latter was still in draft form[72]. Other fields where the content or structure of multilateral or plurilateral rules and NAFTA rules bear a resemblance are technical standards[73] and public procurement[74].

The preceding remarks can be extended to NAFTA-like agreements such as, for instance, the free trade agreement between Canada and Chile which is patterned after NAFTA, but also refer directly to WTO obligations in some sectors[75].

Although Mercosur stated goal is to establish a common market like the European Common Market, the method it uses at the customs union stage of its development is not the same as the method used by the European Community. It basically relies on intergovernmental cooperation evolving in a pragmatic fashion[76]. This is not altogether different from the method used to free trade at the multilateral level. The dispute settlement mechanism offers some analogy with the panel system of the GATT of 1947 and is thus less developed than the new WTO dispute settlement mechanism. At present, Mercosur is a regional agreement whose coverage does not exceed that of the multilateral system. This leaves the possibility for the latter to influence the future development of the former.

The draft free trade agreement between the Andean Community and Mercosur refers explicitly to multilateral agreements to supplement the regional rules in different sectors.

In the case of AFTA-ASEAN, regional economic integration has progressed in ways which were neither GATT like, nor EC-like since the Western legal method does not play there a prominent role. However, things are now changing. Greater emphasis is now put on the legal aspects of the regional integration process. For its future development, AFTA-ASEAN relies on the WTO model and on what has been achieved at the multilateral level in the field of services, intellectual property rights and dispute settlement[77].

---

[72] See I. GOVAERE, *"Convergence, Divergence and Interaction of Regional Trade Agreements and the Agreement on Trade-Related Aspects of Intellectual Property Rights (TRIPs)"*, *supra*.

[73] See G. GARCIA JIMENEZ & M. GARDENES SANTIAGO, *"Technical Standards in a Context of Regional Integration Agreements"*, *supra* in this volume.

[74] See P. DELSAUX, *supra*.

[75] See D. MACKAY, *supra*; and, S. LOPEZ-AYLLON, *supra*.

[76] See F. PEÑA, *supra*.

[77] See J. PELKMANS, *supra*.

IV. THE INFLUENCE OF REGIONAL INTEGRATION AGREEMENTS ON THE MULTILATERAL TRADE SYSTEM

Regional integration agreements influence the multilateral trade system in two main ways. First, the very growth of regionalism at times stimulates progress at the multilateral level. Second, regional integration agreements may serve as models or laboratories not only for other regional agreements, but also for the multilateral trade system itself.

A. *Regionalism as a Stimulus to the Multilateral Trade System*

In the 1960s, the completion of the EEC common customs tariff explained in part the US proposal to open the Kennedy Round, which brought about a worldwide reduction of customs duties. The Tokyo Round followed the 1973 enlargement of the European Community[78]. More recently, the initiative taken by the European Community to transform its Common Market into an "internal market" by 1993, together with the widening of the Community to the North and to the East, were factors in the conversion of the Unites States to regionalism, the revival of regionalism in South America and even in the launching of APEC[79].

Initially fuelled by the fear of the emergence of a "Fortress Europe", the development of regionalism in North America at the end of the 1980s and in the early 1990s in turn had significant effects on the multilateral trade system. First, the Canada-US Free Trade Agreement (CUSFTA) and then the negotiating of NAFTA indicated that the United States was now ready to move away from multilateralism. Second, the scope of the CUSFTA and NAFTA, even though not as broad as that of the EC Treaty, went much beyond the scope of the GATT of 1947. This was a warning that, unless the GATT was revised, the organization of world trade would then more and more depend on the balance of power between large regional blocks, plus Japan and, in the future, China. The successful completion of the Uruguay Round, which significantly broadens the coverage of the multilateral trade system and which should increase the role played by the rule of law in the conduct of world trade, must be seen against that background.

---

[78] See S. DEVOS, *supra*.

[79] See J. PELKMANS, *supra*.

B. Regional Integration Agreements as "Laboratories" for the Multilateral Trade System

Whether regional experiences in trade liberalization like the European Community or NAFTA have served in the past or could serve in the future the multilateral trade system is a question that can be examined from a general and from a sectoral perspective.

1. General Perspective

The European experience in a sense is not entirely relevant, because the EC Treaty aims at the creation of a fully integrated market through supranational institutions. NAFTA seems more relevant as it constitutes the most developed regional integration agreement build on the model of a free trade area and on the basis of intergovernmental cooperation. However, NAFTA is not totally relevant either, as one of its three members, the United States, dwarfs the other two. The European Community constitutes a more balanced group, where bargains have to be made between less unequal partners and where majorities have to be build. The NAFTA institutional framework is not a perfect model either since NAFTA in its present shape could not accommodate many new members[80].

Although not an entirely relevant model for the multilateral system with regard to the methods used, European economic integration may nevertheless serve as a reference or a kind of yardstick. As was pointed out, the European experience shows vividly the links which exist between the free movement of goods, services, capital, natural and legal persons and the parallel enforcement of competition rules[81]. It also indicates the importance of a strong judge (to which private Parties have access) in order to effectively implement provisions prohibiting public and private obstacles to trade, as well as the importance of an active legislator in order to promote legislative harmonization and mutual recognition[82].

In this respect, it will be most interesting to see in the future whether or not Mercosur members, and most particularly, the most powerful member, Brazil, will feel the need to add a measure of supranationality as they move further down the road of economic integration[83]. Regional

---

[80] See D. MACKAY, *supra*.

[81] See P. SAUVE, *supra*.

[82] See G. SACERDOTI, *supra*.

[83] In the case of the European Community, the adoption of supranational institutions in the 1950s can be explained by the fact that the respective weight of France and

economic integration may achieve considerable progress without supranational institutions, at least if it is build on the model of a free trade
area. The creation of supranational institutions from the start is also no
guarantee that an experiment in regional integration will succeed if the
economic and political context is not right. The Andean Group, which
started in part on the basis of the EC model, but with less than open
economies and in a rather unstable political context, is an example. Intergovernmental cooperation at the highest level is now emphasized in order to relaunch the Andean integration process.

Nevertheless, the EC experience tends to demonstrate that, at a certain point, supranational institutions and mechanisms are needed in order to fully implement the free movement of goods, services and persons down to the level of the private individual and the business operator.
If this is correct, this would mean that the multilateral system would
never be able to emulate the most developed form of regional economic
integration except if, in order to make its rules truly effective, it could
rely on the cooperation of the domestic legal orders of it members in the
same way as the European Community does.

Where the European experience could become relevant to the WTO
is with respect to "differentiation". Differentiation today is a prominent
feature of regionalism in Europe as a whole and to a lesser degree, of the
European Union. Actually, the draft Treaty of Amsterdam provides for
the development of "variable geometry" within the Treaty on European Union. Most cases of differentiation, but not all (see the case of
Switzerland or Turkey), are intended to be or will in fact be of a transitional nature. For the WTO, which already allows some differentiation
and may have to allow more differentiation in the future, the most interesting cases are those which have been or will be allowed inside the EC
itself, because they may reveal the extent to which differentiation can be
accommodated within a single institutional framework. For the long term
survival of the WTO, it may seem important that cases of differentiation
and conditional MFN remain under its umbrella, and that "slower" WTO
Members do not feel completely ignored by faster members.

2. Sectoral Perspective

The merits of the NAFTA and ANZCERTA approach with respect to
services and investments compared to the GATS approach have been

---

Germany, the main actors, was more or less equal and by the special situation of
Germany after the Second World War.

stressed and it has been suggested that future work at the multilateral level should follow that kind of approach, as is already the case at the OECD level[84]. The manner in which NAFTA emphasizes the effective enforcement of existing norms in the environmental and labour fields could also serve as an example for the WTO in the future.

NAFTA (and US law) influenced the WTO standard of review applicable to anti-dumping cases[85].

The method of reducing customs duties across the board, which the EEC adopted, served as an example for the Kennedy Round. Provisions of several agreements concluded as part of the Uruguay Round also reflect, at least in their wording, the influence of the EC experience in regional integration[86]. This is the case of certain provisions of the Agreement on Technical Standards[87], the Agreement on Subsidies, the Agreement on Government Procurement[88], and the GATS[89]. As mentioned earlier, the EC was also quite influential in the drafting of the TRIPs Agreement

But again, the fact that WTO provisions and EC provisions may have the same wording does not mean that their effectiveness will be the same. The political, economic and institutional contexts are quite different. As an illustration, the effectiveness of the notification requirement imposed by the WTO Agreement on Technical Standards (already present in the Tokyo Round Code) can hardly match that of the notification requirement imposed by the so called *EC Information Directive* of 1983. The latter, which deals with technical regulations and technical standards applicable to goods (and in the future, information services), has become one of the most potent instruments in the preservation and development of the Internal Market as a result of the combined action of the Commission, the Court of Justice and national courts[90].

---

[84] See P. SAUVE, *supra*.

[85] See J.F. BELLIS, *supra*.

[86] About the role played by the European Community in the Uruguay Round, see H. PAEMEN & A. BENSCH, **From the GATT to the WTO. The European Community in the Uruguay Round**, Leuven University Press, 1995.

[87] See G. GARCIA JIMENEZ & M. GARDENES SANTIAGO, *supra*.

[88] See P. DELSAUX, *supra*.

[89] See P. SAUVE, *supra*.

[90] Not only official, but also private, national standardization bodies have to notify new technical regulations and new technical standards before they can be put into force or applied at the national level. The Commission, after being notified, may impose a period of standstill in order to examine whether the national technical regulation or standard whose adoption is being contemplated does not unduly restrict intra-Community trade or whether a common technical regulation or standard

CONCLUSION:
DIVERGENCE, CONVERGENCE, INTERACTION

The growth of regionalism during the Uruguay Round had, as indicated, a positive effect on the multilateral trade system. But regional agreements beside creating trade between their members, also divert trade from third Parties. To the extent they end up diverting more trade then they create, something difficult to know precisely, they diverge from the central objective of the multilateral system, if not from the letter of Article XXIV of GATT or Article V of GATS. This is the factor of divergence between the multilateral system and regional agreements which free traders always stress. In addition, the creation of large regional trade groupings produces a snowballing effect. Some of their trade partners are keen to enter into preferential agreements with them or with some of their members in order to reduce the potential trade diverting effect of the first regional agreement. The European Union, for instance, is negotiating a free trade agreement with Mexico as a reaction to NAFTA and has entered into cooperation agreements with Mercosur and Chile, which could pave the way for future free trade agreements[91]. Depending on the circumstances, the new free trade areas could either create[92] or divert trade.

To reduce divergence and increase convergence between regional integration agreements and the multilateral system various suggestions have been made. To practice open regionalism has been one. However, if open regionalism truly means to free trade unilaterally[93], it is unlikely that it would be accepted by many. Reciprocity underlies most trade liberalization projects whether at the regional level or at the multilateral level. The best that can be hoped — and this is achieved at both the regional and the multilateral level — is that reciprocity be not required on a sectoral basis. If open regionalism means that regional integration

---

ought not to be adopted at the Community level. The effectiveness of the notification requirement has been considerably increased as a result of a recent ruling of the Court of Justice. Questioned by a Belgian court, the Court of Justice decided that private economic operators are not bound by technical regulations which Member States have put into force without notifying them beforehand to the Commission.

[91] See G. GARCIA JIMENEZ, *"The New Commercial Strategy of the European Union towards Latin America: In Search of Market Access through a Regional and Specific Approach"*, *supra* in this volume.

[92] Some members of the European Union oppose the idea of a free trade agreement as it would erode the Community preference regarding agricultural products.

[93] Concerning, open regionalism in that sense, see J. PELKMANS, *supra*.

agreements should always be open for accession to third countries[94], this does not seem to be an entirely realistic idea either at least if one thinks that many regional integration agreements, customs unions in particular, pursue political objectives. The European Union, for example, admits only European countries with a democratic system of government. But, there are other ways to limit the potential discriminating effect of regional integration agreements[95].

With respect to customs duties, quantitative restrictions and other market access restrictions, the best way is, of course, the lowering of the same trade barriers at the world level through multilateral negotiations. More is to be done in the case of free trade areas, particularly when they overlap and when external trade barriers remain high. Multilateral rules of origin should be negotiated so as to reduce the cost of complying with regional rules of origin and more particularly the insidious protectionist effect arising from the manner in which some are designed[96]. This today applies essentially to trade in goods, but could also in the future concern services[97]. Compared to free trade areas, customs unions seem, in this regard, somewhat more in tune with the multilateral system. The completion of their external trade regime goes beyond the establishment of a common customs tariff and may produce certain positive effects for third countries, which have to be balanced against any possible trade diverting effect. As part of the establishment of the EC Internal Market, import rules had to be fully uniformized at the EC level. This was not always easy to achieve and may have had on some occasions the consequence that import barriers increased at least with respect to some parts of the EC. The *Banana* Case is an example. However, on the other hand, the completion of the external dimension of the Internal Market has often made the external trade regime of the EC more transparent and more predictable for third country firms than when it consisted of many different national regimes not always easy to identify. This facilitates trade and is in keeping with the spirit of the Uruguay Round Agreements, which stresses the need for transparency and the importance of the rule of law. A similar observation can be made when national regulations are being harmonized or replaced by uniform rules, again under the proviso that they are not systematically aligned on the most restrictive national

---

[94] Concerning, open regionalism in that sense, see P. SAUVE, *supra*.

[95] See in particular S. DEVOS, *supra*.

[96] See D. PALMETER, *supra*.

[97] See E. NAVARRO VARONA, *"Comments"* on D. Palmeter's contribution, *supra* in this volume.

rules or are not fraught with ambiguity like the TV without frontiers directive.

For other types of trade barriers, such as commercial and technical regulations, institutional convergence has been offered as probably the best means to minimize trade diversion resulting from regional trade liberalization[98]. As already pointed out, the most significant case of institutional convergence is to be found in the intellectual property field as a result of the TRIPs Agreement. Other examples of convergence have been mentioned above, which result from the growing interaction between regional agreements and multilateral rules and *vice-versa*. In this respect, as the reach of the multilateral system gets deeper, the European experience becomes more meaningful. But there is little doubt that for many years to come the distance between what has been achieved under the EC Treaty, the EEA or even NAFTA and what could be achieved at the WTO level will remain considerable, particularly with respect to the enforcement of rules at the level of the business operator.

To close in part this gap, there are different ways which could be travelled in parallel. The first is for the United States and the European Union, to take the initiative within the WTO and to propose to the other members to both deepen and widen the scope of the WTO[99] with a particular emphasis on the effective enforcement of WTO and domestic rules. This would require that the United States and the European Community, which are the two main actors on the multilateral stage and also the main regional actors, no longer act as rival in promoting of competitive regionalism either in Latin America or in Asia. The second would be for the WTO Members and their regional or national courts to give greater weight to WTO rules in their legal order. The third would be for the WTO adjucatory system to gradually interpret WTO rules as judges would and use as inspiration the interpretation by the European Court of Justice of the "free movement" provisions of the EC Treaty.

---

[98] See P. SAUVE, *supra*. See also S. DEVOS, *supra*.

[99] See on that point, the proposals made by R. STEINBERG, *"Transatlanticism in Support of Multilateralism? Prospects for Great Power Management of the World Trading System"*, *supra*.

COMMENTS

Christoph BAIL

*L.L.M., Head of Unit for Global Environment,
Directorate-General for Environment,
Nuclear Safety and Civil Protection,
European Commission, Brussels*

The following comments contain personal views based upon my own experience, not those of the institution for which I work. They are an attempt to provide tentative answers to the following four questions which have arisen in the context of the debate about the interaction between regional and multilateral rules:

1) Have multilateral rules influenced regional integration agreements?
2) Should they have a stronger influence on regional rules in the future?
3) Have regional rules influenced multilateral rules?
4) Should they have a stronger influence in the future?

1. Have Multilateral Rules Influenced Regional Integration Agreements?

Historically multilateral rules, in particular Article XXIV of GATT, have certainly had a strong influence in shaping regional free trade and customs union agreements, including the Treaty of Rome establishing the European Economic Community. However, it is also my impression that multilateral rules have only had a limited influence on the evolution of regional rules under existing regional integration agreements, in particular those of the European Internal Market. I would go even a step further by arguing that we should not be overly concerned about the declining influence multilateral rules have on the evolution of Community law, because if multilateral rules had had a stronger influence that might have retarded or even prevented beneficial regional developments.

The GATT approach to regional integration agreements is basically this: they are essentially bad, but we accept them for political reasons when they succeed. Article XXIV GATT has of course to some extent shaped the negotiation of Free Trade Areas (FTAs) and Custom Unions (CUs) between states or between the European Community and neighbouring states. However, the language of Article XXIV has (in my view fortunately) been vague and flexible enough to allow politically desirable and commercially beneficial deviations, such as European Free Trade Area (EFTA) or the agreements between the European Community and EFTA countries. Whether from a trade perspective the same can be said with respect to the agreements between the European Community and Mediterranean Countries may be more doubtful, but there were certainly strong political, as well as policy, arguments in favour of these agreements, while their potentially trade distortive elements can hardly be said to have had a very significant impact.

It remains, however, true that the GATT has had a beneficial dissuasive effect in preventing purely defensive or predominantly protectionist regional initiatives. Moreover, the language of Article XXIV provides a strong basis for exercising pressure to ensure that the net result of the formation or extension of a customs union has a positive or at least neutral trade effect for third countries. This has allowed some countries, in particular the United States, to press for additional trade concessions on the basis of a very extensive, as well as legally questionable interpretation of Article XXIV:6, as demonstrated in the *Sorghum* Case after the Spanish and Portuguese accession to the European Community.

2. Should Multilateral Rules have a Stronger Influence on Regional Rules in the Future?

My answer would be: generally speaking, "no", at least as far as the development of customs unions or internal markets is concerned, because multilateral rules applying globally tend to lack the sophistication of rules established within a regional more closely knit and more communitarian context. The "fortress Europe" debate of a few years ago was for instance an example of an attempt of some governments (in particular the US and Japan) using GATT-inspired nondiscrimination arguments out of context in order to achieve a better deal regarding the right of establishment within the Internal Market without offering any reciprocity for the benefits they were trying to gain. The debate in reality did not have much, if any, influence on the Internal Market rules of the European Community.

I would, however, tend to answer the second question with "yes" at least in one respect, namely the monitoring of "strategic" regional integration initiatives. I am referring here to initiatives which do not really have as their objective the integration of neighbouring economies and the definition of common rules for managing the interdependencies of proximity. Initiatives such as APEC, AFTA, TAFTA or EU/Mercosur would in my personal view tend to fall into this category.

Incidentally, TAFTA was promoted primarily by people who were looking for a new glue for the Transatlantic Alliance which they perceived to be crumbling because NATO had lost the thread which had held it together. However, few persuasive arguments were made to demonstrate that TAFTA would make sense economically while many experts saw a risk that a free trade area among the two big trading blocks would undermine the multilateral trading system. There is of course a lot to do bilaterally in the transatlantic context to take account of interdependences, find common solutions to common problems and avoid silly conflicts. A particularly promising area is cooperation towards regulatory convergence. However, the main new transatlantic challenge is in my view how to deal jointly with the increasing number of global challenges and provide leadership on such issues as the further development of the WTO, the threats to the global environment, population growth, migration, drugs trafficking, terrorism and other forms of international crime.

3. Have Regional Rules Influenced Multilateral Rules?

As with respect to the first question my tentative answer would be: a little, but not very much. A little, in particular because the European Union is an important player in trade and other multilateral policies and because, when the EU formulates its position on new issues — e.g. on how to deal with subsidies, how to liberalize trade beyond national treatment, how to harmonize intellectual property rights or how to set international environmental standards — it naturally looks first at its own internal experience.

In some areas, the experience of the development of regional rules have indeed had a decisive influence on the definition of multilateral rules because the regional evolution often naturally previews what is to come at a later stage multilaterally by identifying solutions which bridge the differences of interests between more and less developed economies or between different legal systems.

The development of multilateral rules, such as through GATT negotiations, has, however, tended to follow its own logic driven by the different interests of the major players. They have only looked to a limited extent at existing regional experiences, norms and mechanisms developed in relation to problems similar to those faced at the global level.

4. Should Regional Rules have a Stronger Influence on Multilateral Rules in the Future?

Given my own professional background, it may not come as a surprise that I would tend to answer this question with yes. The basic reason for this is that the multilateral system is, at least in my view, seriously imbalanced and does not provide an adequate framework for dealing with the interdependencies of the globalized economy.

Regional Integration Agreements, on the other hand, are "laboratories" for the exploration of ways countries can manage jointly common problems while respecting their differences, i.e. in line with the principle of subsidiarity which should govern the interaction between different levels of government.

The WTO, in particular, needs to learn more from the successes and failures of regional endeavours because, despite the success of the Uruguay Round, it is still largely inadequate in setting the rules for competition within a globalized economy. It has so far failed to address in a coherent manner such crucial issues as the definition of international standards and rules for the internalization of environmental externalities, and for restrictive business practices such as cartels and abuses of dominant positions of market powers. It has also failed to clarify the interaction between WTO rules and the fundamental labor standards embodied in the core conventions of the ILO. Only in the area of intellectual property has the WTO so far, under pressure from big industry, moved beyond trade liberalization and established worldwide standards.

The multilateral system is even further behind in other areas, such as immigration, movement of labor and transnational criminal activities. Regional initiatives and regional rules in these areas, beyond being necessary because of the regional dimension of the issues, can and should play the role of pacemakers for the evolution of more coherent multilateral rules and for the development of a coherent system of global governance in line with the *de facto* existing interdependencies of activities, challenges and legal solutions

SELECTED BIBLIOGRAPHY*

THE WORLDWIDE TREND
TOWARDS INCREASED REGIONALISM

A. The New European Trade System

- The EU and Non-EU Western European Countries

BLANCHET Th. & WESTMAN-CLEMENT M., *La Cour AELE - Un Premier Bilan (2ème partie)*, in : **Revue du Marché commun et de l'Union européenne**, No.399, 1996.

BLANCHET Th., PIIPONEN R. & WESTMAN-CLEMENT M., **The Agreement on the European Economic Area (EEA): A Guide to the Free Movement of Goods and Competition Rules**, Clarendon Press, Oxford, 1994.

BOULOUIS J., *Les Avis de la Cour de Justice des Communautés sur la compatibilité avec le Traité CEE du projet d'accord créant l'Espace Economique Européen*, in : **Revue Trimestrielle de Droit Européen**, 1992.

CHARLTON H., *EC Competition Law: The New Regime under the EEA Agreement*, in: **European Common Law Review**, No.2, 1994.

CREMONA M., *The Dynamic and Homogeneous EEA: Byzantine Structures and Variable Geometry*, in: **European Law Review**, 1994.

DUTHEIL DE LA ROCHERE J., *L'EEE sous le regard des juges de la Cour de Justice des Communautés européennes*, in : **Revue du Marché commun et de l'Union européenne**, No.360, Editions Techniques et Economiques, Paris, 1992.

EFTA SURVEILLANCE AUTHORITY, *Annual Report '95*, EFTA, Brussels, 1995.

FELDER D., *Structure institutionnelle et procédure décisionnelle de l'EEE (Articles 89-114 AEEE)*, in: Olivier JACOT-GUILLARMOD (ed.), **Accord EEE : commentaires et réflexions**, Schulthess Polygraphischer Verlag, Zürich, 1992.

FRISCH J.-G. & MEYER A.-C., *Le Traité sur l'Espace économique européen : cadre juridique d'une Europe du deuxième cercle*, in : **Revue du Marché commun et de l'Union européenne**, No.360, Editions Techniques et Economiques, Paris, 1992.

---

* Provided by P. DEMARET, X. DENOËL, G. GARCÍA JIMÉNEZ and the authors.

JACOT-GUILLARMOD O. (ed.), **Accord EEE : commentaires et réflexions**, Schulthess Polygraphischer Verlag, Zürich, 1992.

LIPENS DE CERF P. & ARACHTINGI Th., *Présentation générale de l'Accord sur l'Espace Economique Européen*, in : **Revue des Affaires européennes**, No.4, L.G.D.J., 1992.

NELL P.G., *Liechtenstein Strategy for joining the European Economic Area while Remaining Part of the Swiss Monetary Union*, in: **Aussenwirtschaft**, Heft I, Zürich, Verlag Rüegger, 1996.

NELL P.G., *Rules of Origin: Problems and Solutions to the Swiss Non-Participation in the European Economic Area*, in: **Journal of World Trade**, Vol.XXVIII, No.6, 1994.

NORBERG S., HOKBORG K., JOHANSSON M., ELIASSON D. & DEDICHEN L., *EEA Law: A Commentary on the EEA Agreement*, Kluwer and Taxation Publishers and CE Fritzes AB, Stockholm, 1993.

PEDERSEN Th., **European Union and the EFTA Countries. Enlargement and Integration**, Pinter, London, 1994.

PERSSON J., *Norway and the EEA*, in: Emil EMS (ed.), **Thirty-five Years of Free Trade in Europe. Messages for the Future**, European Free Trade Association, Geneva, 1995.

ROUAM C., *Remarques générales sur les règles de concurrence dans l'EEE and Aides d'Etat*, in: Olivier JACOT-GUILLARMOD (ed.), **Accord EEE - Commentaires et réflexions**, 1992.

SCHWOK R., *Switzerland: The European Union's Self-appointed Pariah*, in: John REDMOND (ed.), **Prospective Europeans: New Members for the European Union**, Harvester Wheatsheaf, New York/London, 1994.

SCHOWK R., **Switzerland and the European Common Market**, Praeger, New York, 1991.

SCHWOK R., **Horizon 1992 : la Suisse et le grand marché européen**, Institut universitaire d'études européennes, Geneva, 1989.

STUYCK J. & LOOIJESTIJN-CLEARIE A. (eds), **The European Economic Area EC-EFTA. Institutional Aspects and Financial Services**, Kluwer Law and Taxation Publishers, Deventer/Boston, 1994.

WIJKMAN, Per M., *The Winding Voyage to and beyond the EEA,* in: Emil EMS (ed.), **Thirty-five Years of Free Trade in Europe. Messages for the Future**, European Free Trade Association, Geneva, 1995.

- The EU and Central and Eastern European Countries

BRADA J.C., *Regional Integration versus Integration into the World Economy: the Choices for Central and Eastern Europe*, in: **The World**

Economy, Vol.17, No.4, July 1994.

LEQUESNE & RUPNIK (eds), **L'Union européenne : ouverture à l'Est ?**, PUF, 1994.

MARESCEAU M. (ed.), **Enlarging the European Union. Relations between the EU and Central and Eastern Europe**, Longman, London, 1997.

MARESCEAU M. & MONTAGUTI E., *The Relations between the European Union and Central and Eastern Europe: A Legal Appraisal*, in: **Common Market Law Review**, Vol.32, 1995.

MARESCEAU M., *A Legal Analysis of the Community's Association Agreements with Central and Eastern European Countries: General Framework, Accession Objectives and Trade Liberalization*, in: KONSTADINIDIS (ed.), **The Legal Regulation of the European Community's External Relations after the Completion of the Internal Market**, Dartmouth, 1996.

MARESCEAU M., *Europe Agreements: A New Form of Cooperation Between the European Community and Central and Eastern Europe, East Central European States and the European Communities: Legal Adaptation to the Market Economy*, in: MÜLLER-GRAFF (ed.), Nomos, 1993.

NYSSEN L., *L'Ostpolitik de l'Union européenne à la lueur de l'Accord d'association avec la République tchèque*, in : **Revue d'études comparatives Est-Ouest**, 1996.

PIONTEK M.E., *European Union and Countries of Central and Eastern Europe: New Structures of Relations and Trade Prospects, La place de l'Europe dans le commerce mondial*, **I.U.I.L.**, July 1994.

SHEMIATENKOV V., *The Relations between Russia and the EU*, in : **Revue des Affaires européennes**, 1997.

- The EU and Mediterranean Countries

BENSIDOUN I. & CHEVALLIER A., **Europe-Mediterranée : Le pari de l'ouverture**, Collection CEPII, Economica, Paris, 1996.

FONTAGNE L. & PERIDY N., *De la politique préférentielle de l'Union européenne-Maghreb au GATT 94: évaluation et perspectives*, in : **Le Maroc et l'Europe**, Ouest Editions, University of Nantes, 1996.

GALAL A. & HOEKMAN B. (eds), **Regional Partners in Global Markets: Limits and Possibilities of the Euro-Med Agreements**, ECES/CEPR, 1997.

HIRSCH M., INBAR E. & SADEH T., **The Future Relations between Israel and the European Communities, some Alternatives**, Bursi, Tel Aviv, 1996.

HOEKMAN B., *The WTO, the EU and the Arab World: Trade Policy Priorities and Pitfalls*, **Discussion Paper Series**, No.1226, CEPR, August 1995.

HOEKMAN B. & DJANKOV S., *Catching Up with Eastern Europe? The European Union's Mediterranean Free Trade Initiative*, **Discussion Paper Series**, No.1300, CEPR, November 1995.

LANNON E., *L'accord d'association intérimaire Communauté européenne-OLP : l'institutionnalisation progressive des relations euro-palestiniennes*, in : **Revue des Affaires Européennes**, No.3, 1997.

LUDLOW P. (ed.), **Europe and the Mediterranean**, Brassey's, London, 1994.

MEZDOUR S., *Opportunité théorique d'une zone de libre-échange Maghreb-UE*, in : **Revue du Marché commun et de l'Union européenne**, No.399, June 1996.

REGHNAULT H., *Les intégrations économiques en Méditerranée : Etat des lieux et perspectives*, in : BENHAYOUN G., CATIN M. & REGHNAULT H., **L'Europe et la Méditerranée : Intégration économique et libre échange**, Collection Emploi, Industrie et Territoire, L'Harmattan, Paris, 1997.

RHEIN E., *Europe and the Mediterranean: A Newly Emerging Geopolitical Area?*, in: **European Foreign Affairs Review**, No.1, 1996.

SCOTT N., *Compatibility of EU Regional Trade Agreements with WTO Rules in the Post-Uruguay-Round*, in: **International Trade Law Review**, 1996.

STEVENS C., *The Impact of Europe 1992 on the Maghreb and Sub-Saharan Africa*, in: **Journal of Common Market Studies**, Vol.29, No.2, December 1990.

TOVIAS A., *Options for Mashrek-Israeli Regionalism in the Context of the Euro-Mediterranean Partnership*, **CEPS Paper**, No.67, Center for European Policy Studies, Brussels, 1997.

TOVIAS A., *The EU's Mediterranean Policies under Pressure*, in: **Mediterranean Politics**, Vol.2, 1996.

XUEREB P. & PACE R. (eds), **The European Union, the IGC and the Mediterranean**, Malta, 1996.

B. *Regionalism outside Europe*

- NAFTA and its Possible Extension to Southern American Countries

ABEYRATNE R., *The Legal and Economic Effects of NAFTA on Canada, Mexico and the United States*, in: **World Competition**, Vol.18, No.2, December 1994.

ABBOTT F., **Law and Policy of Regional Integration: The NAFTA and Western Hemispheric Integration in the World Trade Organization System**, Martinus Nijhoff Publishers, 1995.

ALAN GLICK L. (ed.), **Understanding the North American Free Trade Agreement. Legal and Business Consequences of NAFTA**, Kluwer Law and Taxation Publishers, 1994.

BERNAL R., *From NAFTA to Hemispheric Free Trade*, in: **The Columbia Journal of World Business**, Vol.39, No.3, 1994.

BRYAN A.T., *Más allá del Tratado de Libre Comercio de América del Norte: el dilema de CARICOM*, in: **Integración latinoamericana**, July 1994.

DESCHAMPS I., *L'accord de libre-échange Nord-Américain : une nouvelle voie pour l'Amérique*, in : **R.I.D.E.**, No.3, 1993.

ENDSLEY H. B., *Dispute Settlement under the CUFTA and NAFTA: From Eleven-Hour Innovation to Accepted Institution*, in: **Hasting International and Comparative Law Review**, Vol.18, No.4, 1995.

FATEMI K. & SALVATORE D., **The North American Free Trade Agreement**, Pergamon, 1997.

GUDIÑO P., **Norteamérica y su proceso de integración**, Editorial Fundación UNA, Costa Rica, 1994.

HUFBAUER G.C. & SCHOTT J., **NAFTA: An Assessment**, Institute for International Economics, 1993.

JOHNSON J., **The North American Free Trade Agreement: A Comprehensive Guide**, Canada Book Inc., 1994.

KRUGMAN P., *Le véritable impact de l'ALENA*, in : **Problèmes économiques et sociaux**, No.2383, July 1994.

LUDWISZESKI R.B. & SELEY P.E., *'Green' Language in the NAFTA: Reconciling Free Trade and Environmental Protection*, in: BELLO, HOLMER & NORTON (eds), **The North American Free Trade Agreement: A New Frontier in International Trade and Investment in the Americas**.

MURRAY S., *The North American Free Trade Agreement: Global Impacts, Regional Integration and the Global Trading System*, in: ANDERSON & BLACKHURST (eds), Harvester Wheatsheaf, 1993.

PASTOR R.A., **US Foreign Policy toward Latin America and the Caribbean**, Princenton University Press, 1992.

SPIELMAN S, *America's Plan for Regional Trade: Where will it lead?*, in: **European Business Journal**, Vol.7, No.2, 1995.

STERN P. & PARETZKY R., *Engineering Regional Trade Pacts to keep*

Trade and US Prosperity on a Fast Track, in: **The Washington Quarterly**, Vol.19, No.1, 1996.

U.N. ECONOMIC COMMISSION FOR EUROPE, *The Free Trade Agreement between Canada and the United States, Economic Integration in Europe and North America*, in: **Economic Studies**, No.5, 1995.

WHALLEY J., *CUSTA and NAFTA: Can WHFTA be far behind?*, in: **Journal of Common Market Studies**, Vol.30, No.2, June 1992.

THE WORLD BANK, *How does the North American Free Trade Agreement Affect Central America?*, **Policy Research Working Paper**, No.1464, May 1995.

- Mercosur and Other Regional Trade Agreements in Latin America

AROCENA M., *Common Market of the Southern Cone: Mercosur, Inter-American Development Bank*, **Working Papers Series** No.204, September 1995.

BATALLER F., *Sombras y luces de ayer y hoy en la integración latinoamericana*, in: **La integración regional en America Latina**, No.24, December 1995.

BATALLER F., *Regional Integration Initiatives among Developing Countries: their Nature Past Performance and Current Challenges*, in: **European Economy**, No.52, 1993.

ECLAC (Economic Commission for Latin America and the Caribbean), *Open Regionalism in Latin America and the Caribbean: Economic Integration as a Contribution to Changing Production Patterns with Social Equity*, United Nations, 1994.

GUERRA BORGES A., *Regionalización y bloques económicos. Tendencias mundiales desde una perspectiva latinoamericana*, in: **Integración Latinoamericana**, May 1994.

GUDIÑO P., *Le processus d'intégration dans le continent américain*, in : **Revue d'intégration européenne**, Vol.18, Nos 2-3, 1995.

IRELA (Institute for European-Latin American Relations), *Las relaciones entre el GRAN y el MERCOSUR: Hacia un espacio integrado en América del Sur?*, **Informe Conferencia** No.3, Madrid, 1995.

IRELA, *Comunidad Europea - Pacto Andino: hacia la profundización de las relaciones birregionales*, Madrid, 1994.

GRANDI G., *Le Mercosur en période de transition : évaluation et perspectives*, in : **Problèmes d'Amérique Latine**, No.17, April-June 1995.

NOGUES J. & QUINTANILLA R, *Latin America's Integration and the Multilateral Trading System*, World Bank and CEPR Conference on New Dimensions in Regional Integration, April 1992.

OAS (Organization of American States), *Trade and Integration Arrangements in the Americas: An Analytical Compendium*, Trade Unit, Washington D.C., September 1996.

PEÑA F., *New Approaches to Economic Integration in the Southern Cone*, in: **The Washington Quarterly**, Vol.19, No.1, Summer 1995.

PEÑA F., *The Mercosur and its Prospects: an Option for Competitive Insertion in the World Economy, Prospects for the Process of Sub-Regional Integration in Central and South America*, IRELA, 1992.

PIZARRO R., *Renovación y dinamismo de la integración latinoamericana en los años noventa*, in: **Estudios internacionales**, Vol.XXVIII-110, 1995.

UNITED NATIONS (ECLAC), *Open Regionalism in Latin America and the Carribean*, Santiago, 1994.

- ASEAN and APEC

ARIFF M., *The Prospects for an ASEAN Free Trade Area,* in: **The World Economy** (special issue on Global Trade Policy), Vol.18, 1995.

DE DIOS E., *The APEC Dividend: Assessing the Results of Concerted Unilateral Liberalisation*, paper for the conference 'APEC and Europe', European Institute for Asian Studies, Brussels, Oct. 11, 1996 (conference volume forthcoming).

DRYSDALE P. & GARNAUT R., *The Pacific: A General Theory of Economic Integration, Pacific Dynamism and the International Economic System*, in: BERGSTEN & NOLAND (eds), Institute for International Economics, Washington D.C., 1993.

FUKASAKU K., *Macroeconomic Framework for Sustaining ASEAN's Outward-oriented Growth,* Paper for the ASEAN Round Table, ISEAS & OECD Development Centre, Singapore, Sept. 16/17, 1996 (conference volume forthcoming).

FUKASAKU K. & PELKMANS J. (eds), **Evolving Trade Links between Europe and Asia: Towards Open Continentalism?**, 1995.

KIRPATRIK C., *Regionalisation, Regionalism and East Asian Economic Cooperation*, in: **The World Economy**, Vol.17, No.2, March 1994.

KWAN C.H., **Economic Interdependence in the Asia-Pacific Region**, Routledge, 1994.

MORRISON CH., *Regime Building in Asia Pacific and the Dangers of Regulatory Rift in US-European Relations*, Paper for the workshop "Towards rival regionalism?" (July 4-6, 1996), Ebenhausen (Stiftung Wissenschaft und Politik) (conference volume forthcoming).

MURRAY G.S., **Economic Integration in the Asia Pacific Region: Is Open Regionalism an Oxymoron?, Reshaping the Transatlantic Partnership: An Agenda for the Next 10 years**, College of Europe, Bruges, March 1996.

OTANI Y., *Les défis de la région d'Asie-pacifique vers le XXIème siècle : l'APEC après la conférence au sommet d'Osaka*, in : **Revue du Marché commun et de l'Union européenne**, No.395, February 1996.

PANAGARIYA A., *East Asia and the New Regionalism in World Trade*, in: **The World Economy**, Vol.17/6, November 1994.

PELKMANS J., *European Integration, Methods and Economic Analysis*, Longman - Addison Wesley, London, 1997 (forthcoming).

PELKMANS J. & CARZANIGA A., *The Trade Policy Review of the EU*, in: **The World Economy** (special issue on Global Trade Policy), Vol.19, 1996.

PELKMANS J. & SHINKAI H., *APEC and its Meaning for Europe*, Paper for the Conference 'APEC and Europe', European Institute for Asian Studies, Brussels, Oct. 11, 1996 (conference volume forthcoming).

PELKMANS J. & FUKASAKU K., *Evolving Trade Links between Europe and Asia: Towards Open Continentalism?*, in: K. FUKASAKU, **Regional Cooperation and Integration in Asia**, OECD, Paris, 1995.

PELKMANS J., *Institutional Requirements of ASEAN, with Special Reference to AFTA*, in: P. IMADA & S. NAYA (eds), **AFTA, The Way Ahead**, ISEAS, Singapore 1992.

SINGH B., *The Fourth ASEAN Summit - A New Milestone in Political Will*, in: L.T. LEE & A. WEHRHOERNER (eds), **ASEAN and the EC in the 1990s**, SIIA & FES, Singapore, 1993.

SMITH M., *Economic Integration in the Asia Pacific Region: Is Open Regionalism an Oxymoron?*, in: **Reshaping the Transatlantic Partnership: An Agenda for the Next 10 years**, College of Europe, Bruges, March 1996.

YAMAZAWA I., *Market Opening in East Asia: Implementation of the Uruguay Round, APEC Commitments and Trade Policy Reform*, Paper for the Conference "Asian-European Trade Cooperation in a WTO Context", European Institute for Asian Studies, Brussels, Nov.1996.

YOUNG S., *East Asia as a Force for Globalism, Regional Integration and The Global Trading System*, in: ANDERSON & BLACKHURST (eds), Harvester Whaetsheaf, 1993.

C. Inter-Regional Trade Agreements

ALDECOA F., *El acuerdo entre la Unión Europea y el Mercosur en el marco de la intensificación de relaciones entre Europa y América Latina*, in: **Revista de Instituciones Europeas**, Vol.22, No.3, September, 1995

ARNAUD, V.G. (ed.), **Mercosur, Unión Europea, NAFTA y los procesos de integración regional**, Abeledo Perrot, Buenos Aires, 1996.

DUESTERBERG T.J., *Prospects for an EU-NAFTA Free Trade Agreement*, in: **The Washington Quarterly**, Vol.19, No.1, Winter 1996.

IRELA, *The European Union and Mercosur: Towards a New Economic Relationship?*, June 1996.

IRELA, *El acuerdo interregional entre la UE y el MERCOSUR: Una nueva estrategia de la UE en América Latina?*, September 14, 1995.

KAHLER Miles, **Regional Futures and Transatlantic Economic Relations**, Council on Foreign Relations Press, New York, 1995.

KRENZLER H.G. & SCHOMAKER A., *A New Transatlantic Agenda*, in: **European Foreign Affairs Review**, Vol.1 No.1, pp.9-28.

PRESTOWITZ C., Jr., CHIMERINE L., & SZAMOSSZEGI A. Z., *The Case for a Transatlantic Free Trade Area*, in: Bruce STOKES (ed.). **Open For Business: Creating a Transatlantic Marketplace**, Council on Foreign Relations, New York, 1996.

STEINBERG R., *Transatlantic Management of the Global Trading System*, in: Bruce STOKES (ed.). **Open For Business: Creating a Transatlantic Marketplace**, Council on Foreign Relations, New York, 1996.

WOOLCOCK S., *Strengthening EU-US Commercial Relations?*, in: **Reshaping the Transatlantic Partnership: An Agenda for the Next 10 years**, College of Europe, Bruges, March 1996.

REGIONALISM AND MULTILATERALISM: IN GENERAL

ANDERSON K. & BLACKHURST R. (eds), **Regional Integration and the Global Trading System**, Harvester Wheatsheaf, Geneva, 1993.

ALADI, SECRETERÍA GENERAL, *Apreciación general de los resultados de la Ronda Uruguay y su impacto en la integración regional*, in: **Integración Latinoamericana**, June 1994.

BLACKHURST R. & HENDERSON D., *Regional Integration Agreements*, in: ANDERSON & BLACKHURST (eds), **World Integration and the**

GATT, Regional Integration and The Global Trading System, Harvester Wheatsheaf, 1993.

BOURGEOIS, BERROD & GIPPINI FOURNIER (eds)., **The Uruguay Round Results: A European Lawyers' Perspective**, College of Europe, European Interuniversity Press, Brussels, 1995.

CARNEGIE ENDOWMENT FOR INTERNATIONAL PEACE, *Reflections on Regionalism: Report of the Study Group on International Trade*, Brooking Institution Press, 1997.

CROOME J., **Reshaping the World Trading System (A History of the Uruguay Round)**, WTO, 1995.

DE LA TORRE A. & KELLY M.R., *Regional Trade Arrangements*, **Occasional Paper**, No.93, International Monetary Fund, 1992.

DEMARET P., *The Metamorphoses of the GATT: From the Havana Charter to the World Trade Organization*, in: **Columbia Journal of Transnational Law**, Vol.34, No.1, 1995.

DEMARET P., *Le régime des échanges internes et externes de la Communauté à la lumière des notions d'union douanière et de zone de libre-échange*, **Du droit international au droit de l'intégration**, Liber Amicorum Pescatore, 1987.

DE MELO J. & PANAGARIYA A. (eds), **New Dimensions in Regional Integration**, Cambridge University Press, 1993.

EMILIOU N. & O'KEEFFE D. (eds), **The European Union and World Trade Law after the Uruguay Round**.

HART M., *Doing the Right Thing: Regional Integration and the Multilateral Trade Regime*, **Occasional Paper**, No.39, Centre for Trade Policy and Law, University of Ottawa, 1996.

HUDEC R.E., *GATT's Influence on Regional Trade Agreements: A Comment*, in: DE MELO & PANAGARIYA (eds), **New Dimensions in Regional Integration**, Cambridge University Press, 1993.

JACKSON J., **The World Trading System. Law and Policy of International Economic Relations**, The MIT Press, 1991.

MARCEAU G., *Transition from GATT to WTO: A Most Pragmatic Operation*, in: **Journal of World Trade**, Vol.29, No.4, August 1995.

OECD, *Regionalism and its Place in the Multilateral Trading System*, Paris, 1996.

OECD, *Regional Integration and the Multilateral Trading System. Synergy and Divergences*, Trade Directorate, Paris, 1995.

OECD, *Globalization and Regionalization: The Challenge for Developing Countries*, Development Centre Studies, Paris, 1994.

PAEMEN H. & BENSCH A. (eds), **From the GATT to the WTO: The European Community in the Uruguay Round**, Leuven University Press, 1995.

PETERSMANN E.U., *Why do Governments need the Uruguay Round Agreements, NAFTA and the EEA?*, in: **Aussenwirtschaft**, Vol.49, No.1, January 1994.

PREEG E.H., **Traders in a Brave New World (The Uruguay Round and the Future of the International Trading System)**, University of Chicago Press, 1995.

ROESSLER F., *The Relationship between Regional Integration Agreements and the Multilateral Trade Order*, in: ANDERSON & BLACKHURST (eds), **Regional Integration and the Global Trading System**, Harvester Wheatsheaf, 1993.

SAMPSON G., *Compatibility of Regional and Multilateral Trading Agreements: Reforming the WTO Process*, in: **Amercican Economic Review**, 1996.

STERN R.M. (ed.), **The Multilateral Trading System. Analysis and Options for Change**, Harvester Wheatsheaf, 1993.

VAN DIJCK P. & FABER G. (eds), **Challenges to the New World Trade Organization**, Kluwer Law International, 1996.

WOOLCOCK S., *The European Acquis and Multilateral Trade Rules: Are they compatible?*, in: **Journal of Common Market Studies**, Vol.31, No.4, December 1993

WTO SECRETARIAT, *Regionalism and the World Trading System*, April 1995.

REGIONAL AND MULTILATERAL TRADE RULES: SELECTED ISSUES

- Rules of Origin

NAVARRO VARONA E., **Reglas de origen para las mercancías y los servicios en el GATT, la CE y EEUU**, Ed. Civitas, 1995.

NAVARRO VARONA E., *Rules of Origin in the GATT*, in: E. VERMULST, P. WAER & J. BOURGEOIS (eds), **Rules of Origin in International Trade**, 1993.

PALMETER N.D., *Rules of Origin in Customs Unions and Free Trade Areas*, in: ANDERSON & BLACKHURST (eds), **Regional Integration and the Global Trading System**, Harvester Wheatsheaf, 1993.

PALMETER N.D., *The US Rules of Origin Proposal to GATT: Monotheism or Polytheism?*, in: **Journal of World Trade**, Vol.24, No.2, 1990.

SIMPSON J.P., *North American Free Trade Agreement. Rules of Origin*, in: **Journal of World Trade**, Vol.28, No.1, 1994.

STEPHENSON S.M. & JAMES W.E., *Rules of Origin in the Asia-Pacific Economic Cooperation*, in: **Journal of World Trade**, Vol.29, No.2, April 1995.

VERMULST E., *Rules of Origin in the Future: Selected Issues*, in: BOURGEOIS, BERROD & GIPPINI FOURNIER (eds), **The Uruguay Round Results. A European Lawyers' Perspective**, European Interuniversity Press, 1995.

VERMULST E., WAER P. & BOURGEOIS J.H.J (eds), **Rules of Origin in International Trade: A Comparative Study**, University of Michigan Press, Ann Arbor, 1994.

- Dumping, Subsidies and Anti-Competitive Practices

GASTLE C. M. & CASTEL J-G., *Should the NAFTA Dispute Settlement Mechanism in Antidumping and Countervailing Duty Cases be Reformed in the Light of Softwood Lumber III?*, in: **Law & Policy International Business**, No.26, 1995.

HORLICK G.N. & SHEA E.C., *The World Trade Organization Antidumping Code*, in: **Journal of World Trade**, Vol.29, No.1, February 1995.

MARCEAU G., **Anti-dumping and Anti-Trust Issues in Free Trade Areas**, Clarendon Press, Oxford, 1994.

MAVROIDIS P. & HOEKMAN B., *Anti-trust Based Remedies and Dumping in International Trade*, **Policy Research Working Paper**, The World Bank, August 1994.

MAVROIDIS P. & HOEKMAN B., *Competition, Competition Policy and the GATT*, in: **The World Economy**, Vol.17, No.2, March 1994.

MESSERLIN P.A., *Should Antidumping Rules be Replaced by National or International Competition Rules?*, in: **World Competition**, Vol.18, No.3, March 1995.

PALMETER N.D., *United States Implementation of the Uruguay Round Antidumping Code*, in: **Journal of World Trade**, Vol.29, No.3, June 1995.

PALMETER N.D., *A Commentary on the WTO Anti-dumping Code*, in: **Journal of World Trade**, Vol.30, No.4, August 1996.

VAN BAEL & BELLIS (eds), *Anti-dumping and other Trade Protection Laws of the EEC*, CCH, (3rd ed.), 1996.

VERMULST E. & WAER. P., *The Post Uruguay Round EC Antidumping Regulation: After a Pit Stop, Back in the Race,* in: **Journal of World Trade**, Vol.29, No.2, April 1995.

- Government Procurement

BROWN A. & POUNCEY C., *Expanding the International Market for Public Procurement: The WTO's Agreement on Public Procurement*, in: **International Trade Law and Regulation**, No.3, 1996.

DE GRAFF G. & KING M., *Towards a More Global Procurement Market: The Expansion of the GATT Government Procurement Agreement in the Context of the Uruguay Round*, in: **International Lawyer**, Vol.29, No.2, 1995.

FERNANDEZ MARTIN J.M., **The EC Public Procurement Rules: A Critical Analysis**, Clarendon Press, Oxford, 1996.

FOOTER M., *Remedies under the New GATT Agreement on Government Procurement*, in: **Public Procurement Law Review**, No.4, 1995.

HOEKMAN B. & MAVROIDIS P. (eds), **Law and Policy in Public Purchasing: The WTO Government Procurement Agreement**, University of Michigan Press, Ann Arbor, (forthcoming).

PRIES H-J., *Public Procurement Law in the European Union: The New GATT Agreement on Government Procurement*, in: **International Trade Law and Regulation**, No.2, 1996.

WALLACE D. Jr., *The Changing World of National Procurement Systems: Global Reformation*, in: **Public Procurement Law Review**, No.4, 1995.

WALLACE D. Jr. & LINARELLI J, **International Procurement: Law and Policy**, Kluwer, (forthcoming).

- Services and Investment

BELLO J., HOLMER A. & NORTON J. (eds), **The North American Free Trade Agreement: A New Frontier in International Trade and Investment in the Americas**, American Bar Association, 1994.

GESTRIN M. & RUGMAN A., *The NAFTA Investment Provisions: Better Rules but New Problems*, **The NAFTA Papers: C.D. Howe Commentary**, No.42, C.D. Howe Institute, Toronto, 1993.

HOEKMAN B., *Assessing the General Agreement on Trade in Services*, in: MARTIN W. & WINTERS L.A. (eds), **The Uruguay Round and the Developing Economies**, The World Bank Discussion Paper, No.307, 1995.

HOEKMAN B. & SAUVÉ P., *Liberalizing Trade in Services*, **The World Bank Discussion Paper**, No.243, 1994.

HOEKMAN B. & SAUVÉ P., *Regional and Multilateral Liberalization of Service Markets: Complements or Substitutes?*, in: **Journal of Common Market Studies**, Vol.32, No.3, September 1994.

MENGOZZI P., *L'Europe et le commerce des services, La place de l'Europe dans le commerce mondial*, **I.U.I.L.**, 1994.

SAUVÉ P., *Assessing the General Agreement on Trade in Services: Half-Full or Half-Empty?*, in: **Journal of World Trade**, Vol.29, No.4, August 1995.

SAUVÉ P. & BEGLIVIA A., **Market Access after the Uruguay Round. Investment, Competition and Technology Perspectives**, Trade Directorate, OECD, 1996.

SAUVÉ P. & SCHWANEN D., **Investment Rules for the Global Economy**, C.D. Howe Institute, Toronto, 1996.

WIMMER, A. M., *The Impact of the General Agreement on Trade in Services on the OECD Multilateral Agreement on Investment*, in: **World Competition**, Vol.19, No.4, June 1996.

- Intellectual Property Rights

EVANS G.E., *Intellectual Property as a Trade Issue: the Making of the Agreement on TRIPS*, in: **World Competition**, Vol.18, No.2, December 1994.

FOX, *Trade, Competition, and Intellectual Property-TRIPs and its Antitrust Counterparts*, in: **Vanderbilt Journal Transnational Law**, No.29, 1996.

GONZALEZ G.Y., *An Analysis of the Legal Implications of the Intellectual Property Provisions of the North American Free Trade Agreement*, in: **Harvard International Law Journal**, Vol.34, No.2, Spring 1993.

GOVAERE I., *Trade-related Aspects of Intellectual Property Rights: the EC Dichotomy Uncovered*, **La place de l'Europe dans le commerce mondial**, **I.U.I.L.**, 1994.

McGRATH, *The Patent Provisions in TRIPS: Protecting Reasonable Remuneration for Services Rendered - or the Latest Development in Western Colonialism?*, in: **European Intellectual Property Review**, 1996.

O'REGAN, *The Protection of Intellectual Property, International Trade and the European Community: The Impact of the TRIPs-Agreement of the Uruguay Rand of Multilateral Trade Negotiations*, in: **Legal Issue of European Integration**, No.1, 1995.

REICHMAN, *Compliance with the TRIPs-Agreements- Introduction to a Scholarly Debate*, in: **Vanderbilt Journal Transnational Law**, No.29, 1996.

SOLTYSINSKI S., *International Exhaustion of Intellectual Property Rights under the TRIPs, the EC Law and the Europe Agreements*, in: **GRUR Int**, 1996.

ULLRICH H., *TRIPs: Adequate Protection, Inadequate Trade, Adequate Competition Policy*, in: **Pacific Rim Law & Policy Journal**, 1995.

- Social Protection and Social Clause

CHARNOVITZ S., *Environmental and Labour Standards in Trade*, in: **The World Economy**, Vol.15, No.3, May 1992.

HANSENNE M., *Trade and Labor Standards: Can Common Rules be Agreed?*, 46th Wilton Park Conference on Liberalizing World Trade and Prospects for the Singapore Ministerial Meeting, West Sussex, March 1996.

KELLEHER J.P., *The Child Labor Deterrence Act: American Unilateralism and the GATT*, in: **Minnesota Journal of Global Trade**, Vol.3, Spring 1994.

LEVINSON J., *NAFTA's Labor Side Agreement: Lessons From the First Three Years*, Institute for Policy Studies & International Labor Rights Fund, Washington D.C., 1996.

MAUPIN F., *La protection internationale des travailleurs et la libéralisation du commerce mondial : un lien ou un frein?*, in : **Revue Générale de Droit International Public**, Vol.1, 1996.

MOREAU M., STAELENS P. & TRUDEAU G., *ALENA, CEE, EEE : nouveaux espaces économiques et distorsions sociales*, in : **Problèmes économiques**, No.2831, June 1994.

ROBINSON I., *How will the North American Free Trade Agreement Affect Worker Rights in North America?*, in: COOK & KATZ (eds), **Regional Integration and Industrial Relations in North America**, ILR Press, Ithaca NY, 1994.

WORLD DEVELOPMENT REPORT, *Workers in an Integrating World*, published for the World Bank, Oxford University Press, 1995.

- Environmental Standards

BAKER FOX A., *Environment and Trade: The NAFTA Case*, in: **Political Science Quarterly** , Vol.110, No.1, 1995.

CAMERON, DEMARET & GERADIN (eds), **Trade and Environment: The Search for Balance**, Cameron & May, 1994.

CHARNOVITZ S., *The North American Free Trade Agreement: Green Law or Green Spin?*, in: **Law and Policy in International Business**, Vol.25, No.1, 1994.

ESTY D., **Greening the GATT. Trade, Environment and the Future**, Institute for International Economics, July 1994.

GERADIN D., *Trade and Environmental Protection in an Integrated Market: A Survey of the Case Law of the United States Supreme Court and the Euro-*

pean Court of Justice, in: **Florida University Journal of Transnational Law and Policy**, No.2, 1993.

HESSION M. & MACRORY R., *Balancing Trade Freedom with the Requirements of Sustainable Development*, in: Nicolas EMILIOU & David O'KEEFFE (eds), **The European Union and World Trade Law. After the GATT Uruguay Round**, John Wiley & Sons Ltd., Chisester/New York/Brisbane/Toronto/Singapore, 1996.

JANS J.H., **European Environmental Law**, Kluwer Law International, The Hague/London/Boston, 1995.

KENNEDY, *Reformulating US Trade Policy to Protect the Global Environment: A Multilateral Approach*, in: **Harvard Environmental Law Review**, Vol.18, 1994.

KRAMER L., **EC Treaty and Environmental Law**, (2nd ed.), Sweet & Maxwell, London, 1995.

PETERSMANN E.-U., **International and European Trade and Environmental Law after the Uruguay Round**, Kluwer Law International, London/The Hague/Boston, 1995

SAUNDERS J.O., *Trade and the Environment: the Fine Line between Environmental Protection and Environmental Protectionism*, in: **International Journal**, Vol.2, No.47, 1991.

STEINBERG R. H., *Trade-Environment Negotiations in the EU, NAFTA, and WTO: Regional Trajectories of Rule Development*, in: **American Journal of International Law**, No.91, 1997.

STEWART R., *Environmental Regulation and International Competitiveness*, in: **Yale Law Journal**, No.102, 1993.

THOMAS C. & TREPOSKY G.A., *The NAFTA and the Side-Agreement on Environmental Cooperation*, in: **Journal of World Trade**, Vol.27, No.6, December 1993.

- Technical Standards

IAMARINO C.J., *Technical Barriers to Trade under the NAFTA System: A Call for Legitimate Protection*, in: **Journal of Legislation**, No.21, 1995.

SYKES A.O., **Product Standards for Internationally Integrated Goods Markets**, The Brookings Institution, Washington D.C., 1995.

VÖLKER E., *The Agreement on Technical Barriers to Trade,* in: BOURGEOIS, BERROD & GIPPINI FOURNIER (eds), **The Uruguay Round Results. A European Lawyer's Perspective**, College of Europe, European Interuniversity Press, Brussels, 1995.

VÖLKER E., *Technical Regulations and Standards and Commercial Policy*, in: MARESCEAU (ed.), **The European Community's Commercial Policy after 1992: The Legal Dimension**, Martinus Nijhoff Publishers, 1993.

WILSON, J.S., **Standards and APEC: An Action Agenda to 2020**, Institute for International Economics, Washington D.C., 1995.

- ## National Treatment, Mutual Recognition and Legislative Harmonization

BHAGWATI J. & HUDEC R.E., **Fair Trade and Harmonization: Prerequisites for Free Trade?**, The MIT Press, 1996.

BHAGWATI J., *Fair Trade, Reciprocity and Harmonization: The New Challenge to the Theory and Policy of Free Trade*, in: DEARDOFF A. & STERN R. (eds), **Analytical and Negotiating Issues in the Global Trading System**, University of Michigan Press, Ann Arbor, 1993.

CURZON-PRICE V. & CURZON G., *Non-Discrimination and Reciprocity in the GATT: Two Principles on a Collision Course?*, in: DEMARET, BOURGEOIS & VAN BAEL (eds), **Trade Laws of the European Community and the United States in a Comparative Perspective**, Story Scientia-College of Europe, 1990.

JOLIVET CH., *Traitement national : pilier de la réglementation du commerce des services dans l'Accord canado-américain de libre-échange*, in : **Canada-US Business Law Review**, No.3, 1995.

ROESSLER F., *Diverging Domestic Policy and Multilateral Trade Integration, Fair Trade and Harmonization*, in: BHAGWATI & HUDEC (eds), 1996.

WANG Y., *Most-Favoured-Nation Treatment under the GATS*, in: **Journal of World Trade**, Vol.30, No.1, 1996

- ## Dispute Settlement Mechanism

CANELA-CACHO J.A., *NAFTA Dispute Settlement Mechanism*, Proceedings of the 1993 Meetings of the American Society of International Law, 1994.

CROLEY S. P. & JACKSON J.H., *WTO Dispute Procedures, Standard of Review, and Deference to National Governments*, in: **American Journal of International Law**, No.90, 1996.

DAVEY W., PESCATORE P. & LOWENFELD A.F. (eds), **Handbook of WTO/GATT Dispute Settlement**, Kluwer, New York, 1993.

ENDERS A., *Dispute Settlement in Regional and Multilateral Trade Agreements*, in: ANDERSON & BLACKHURST (eds), **Regional Integration and The Global Trading System**, Harvester Wheatsheaf, 1993.

GARRÉ B., *Solución de controversias en el Mercado Común del Sur*, **Estudios Multidisciplinarios sobre el Mercosur**, Fundación de Cultura Universitaria, Uruguay, 1995.

HIPPLER BELLO J., *The WTO Dispute Settlement Understanding: Less is More*, in: **American Journal of International Law**, 1996.

HORLICK G., *Dispute Resolution Mechanism: will the United States play by the Rules?*, in: **Journal of World Trade**, Vol.29, No.2, April 1995.

KOMURO N., *The WTO Dispute Settlement Mechanism - Coverage and Procedures of the WTO Understanding*, in: **Journal of World Trade**, Vol.29, No.4, August 1995.

KUYPER P-J., *The New WTO Dispute Settlement System: the Impact on the Community*, in: BOURGEOIS, BERROD, GIPPINI FOURNIER (eds), **The Uruguay Round Results**, European Interuniversity Press, Brussels, 1995.

MOYER H. E., Jr., *Chapter 19 of the NAFTA: Binational Panels as the Trade Courts of Last Resort*, in: **International Lawyer**, No.27, 1993.

PETERSMANN E.U. (Ed), *International Trade Law and the GATT/WTO Dispute Settlement System*, **Studies in Transnational Economic Law**, Kluwer, 1996.

REISMAN M. & WIEDMAN M., *Contextual Imperatives of Dispute Resolution Mechanisms: some Hypotheses and their Applications in the Uruguay Round and NAFTA*, in: **Journal of World Trade**, Vol.29, No.3, June 1995.

THOMAS J.C. & LOPEZ-AYLLÓN S., *NAFTA's Extension of Specialized Dispute Settlement to Mexico: Challenges in Treaty Interpretation and Reconciling Common Law and Civil Law Systems in a Free Trade Area*, **The Canadian Yearbook of International Law**, 1996.

INTERNET ADDRESSES

I. Selected International Organizations

Asia Pacific Economic Cooperation Forum (APEC) - Canberra -
http://www.apecsec.org.sg

Association of South-East Asian Nations (ASEAN) - Jakarta -
http://www.asean.or.id/

**United Nations Economic Commission for Latin America
and the Caribbean (ECLAC) - Santiago -**
http://www.eclac.cl/iindex.html

European Union (EU) - Brussels -
http://www.chemie.fu-berlin.de/adressen/eu.html
http://europa.eu.int/index-fr.htm

Food and Agriculture Organization (FAO) - Roma -
http://www.fao.org/

Free Trade Area of the Americas (FTAA) *(In process)*
http://www.ftaa-alca.org/

International Labour Organization (ILO) - Geneva -
http://www.unicc.org/ilo/

International Standardization Organization (ISO) - Geneva -
http://www.iso.ch/welcome.html

Latin American Integration Association (LAIA) - Montevideo -
http://www.aladi.org/

Southern Common Market (Mercosur) - Buenos Aires -
http://www.mercosur.org/
http://www.demon.co.uk/Itamaraty/msul.html
http://www.eurosur.org/eurosur/

North American Free Trade Agreement (NAFTA) - Washington -
http://law.wuacc.edu/scall/nafta.html

**Organization for Economic Cooperation and Development (OECD) -
Paris -**
http://www.oecd.org/

**United Nations Commission on International Trade Law
(UNCITRAL) - Vienna and New York -**
http://www.un.or.at/uncitral/
http://itl.irv.uit.no/trade_law/nav/uncitral.html

United Nations Conference on Trade and Development (UNCTAD) - Geneva -
http://www.unicc.org/unctad/

World Intellectual Property Organization (WIPO) - Geneva -
http://www.uspto.gov/wipo.html

World Trade Organization (WTO) - Geneva -
http://www.unicc.org/wto/

II. Selected International Agreements

Latin American Integration Association (LAIA)
http://www.sice.oas.org/tradee.stm

Andean Community
http://www.sice.oas.org/tradee.stm

Caribbean Community (Caricom)
http://www.sice.oas.org/tradee.stm

European Union (EU)
http://europa.eu.int/abc/obj/treaties/en/entoc.htm
http://ue.eu.int/Amsterdam/en/treaty/treaty.htm

Southern Common Market (Mercosur)
http://www.sice.oas.org/tradee.stm

North American Free Trade Agreement (NAFTA)
http://www.sice.oas.org/tradee.stm

World Trade Organization (WTO)
http://www.sice.oas.org/tradee.stm

III. Other Links Related to International Trade

Organization of American States (OAS) - Trade Unit
http://www.sice.oas.org/

Federation of International Trade Organizations in the United States
http://www.webhead.com/FITA/home.html

InfoManage - International Trade
http://infomanage.com/International/Trade/

International Trade Center (ITC)
http://www.intracen.org/

International Trade Information System
http://www.lanic.utexas.edu/project/itis/

The New Transatlantic Agenda (US Information Agency)
http://www.usia.gov:80/topics/atlinit/agenda.html

European Policy
La Cité europenne

EUROPEAN INTERUNIVERSITY PRESS - EIP

PRESSES INTERUNIVERSITAIRES EUROPÉENNES - PIE

No.1 - Henri BRUGMANS, **La Cité européenne**,1985, 176 p.

No.2 - René MILAS, **Au nom de l'Europe. La sanction dans l'ordre juridique communautaire**, 1988, 324 p.

No.3 - Marc HALEVY, **Les métamorphoses de l'homme papillon. Quelques pistes à la recherche de la grande mutation de notre civilisation**, 1989, 220 p.

No.4 - Harald MÜLLER (ed.), **European Non-Proliferation Policy 1988-1992**, 1993, 259 p.

No.5 - Jacques VANDAMME & Jean-Denis MOUTON (eds), **L'avenir de l'Union européenne : élargir et approfondir**, 1995, 223 p.

No.6 - Harald MÜLLER (ed.), **Nuclear Export Controls in Europe**, 1995, 275 p.

No.7 - Jacques TOINT, **Un monde d'hommes libres**, 1995, 190 p.

No.8 - SCEPS-EPM, **Quadrillage du futur. 2005, les questions**, 1996, 117 p.

No.9 - Jean-Victor LOUIS, **L'Union européenne et l'avenir de ses institutions**, 1996, 192 p.

No.10 - Harald MÜLLER, **European Non-Proliferation Policy 1993-1995**, 1996, 315 p.

No.11 - Paul VAN DEN BEMPT & Greet THEELEN, **From Europe Agreements to Accession. The Integration of the Central and Eastern European Countries into the European Union**, 1996, 168 p.

No.12 - Paul DEMARET, Jena-François BELLIS & Gonzalo GARCÍA JIMÉNEZ, **Regionalism and Multilateralism after the Uruguay Round. Convergence, Divergence and Interaction**, 1997, 862 p.

Achevé d'imprimer sur les presses de l'imprimerie Artigraph,
à Bruxelles, en novembre 1997